# The Sociology
## of
# Race Relations

# The Sociology
## of
# Race Relations

## Reflection and Reform

EDITED BY

**Thomas F. Pettigrew**

THE FREE PRESS
*A Division of Macmillan Publishing Co., Inc.*

NEW YORK
Collier Macmillan Publishers
LONDON

The Free Press
A Division of Macmillan Publishing Co., Inc.
866 Third Avenue, New York, N.Y. 10022

Collier Macmillan Canada, Ltd.

Library of Congress Catalog Card Number: 79-54666

Printed in the United States of America

printing number

1 2 3 4 5 6 7 8 9 10

Library of Congress Cataloging in Publication Data
 Main entry under title:

The Sociology of race relations.

   Includes bibliographical references and index.
   1.  Race relations--History--20th century--Addresses,
essays, lectures.  2.  United States--Race relations--
Addresses, essays, lectures.  I.  Pettigrew, Thomas F.
HT1521.S546     301.45'1'04209     79-54666
ISBN 0-02-925110-9

**Dedicated to
My Wife, Ann, and
My Son, Mark**

# Contents

Preface      xi

Introduction      xiii

**Part I:   The Nadir: 1895–1915**      1

1. William I. Thomas, *The Psychology of Race-Prejudice*      7
2. William I. Thomas, *The Mind of Woman and the Lower Races*      10
3. Alfred Holt Stone, *Is Race Friction Between Blacks and Whites in the United States Growing and Inevitable?*      15
4. W. E. B. DuBois, *A Reply to Stone*      28
5. Robert E. Park, *Racial Assimilation in Secondary Groups with Particular Reference to the Negro*      33

**Part II:   The Beginnings of Change: 1916–1929**      45

6. Ellsworth Faris, *The Mental Capacity of Savages*      50
7. Monroe N. Work, *The Race Problem in Cross Section: The Negro in 1923*      54
8. Ira De A. Reid, *Mirrors of Harlem: Investigations and Problems of America's Largest Colored Community*      63
9. Guy B. Johnson, *A Sociological Interpretation of the New Ku Klux Movement*      90
10. Guy B. Johnson, *The Negro Migration and Its Consequences*      76
11. Herbert J. Seligmann, *Twenty Years' Pioneering in Race Relations*      82

**Part III:   Surviving the Great Depression: 1930–1940**      87

12. John P. Murchison, *Some Major Aspects of the Economic Status of the Negro*      94
13. E. Franklin Frazier, *The Changing Status of the Negro Family*      99
14. Melville J. Herskovits, *On the Provenience of New World Negroes*      109

15. Emory S. Bogardus, *A Race-Relations Cycle*    113
16. Richard T. LaPiere, *Attitudes vs. Actions*    117
17. W. Lloyd Warner, *American Caste and Class*    122

**Part IV:   Change Quickens: 1941–1950**    **127**

18. Oliver C. Cox, *The Modern Caste School of Race Relations*    134
19. Charles S. Johnson, *The Present Status of Race Relations
    in the South*    143
20. E. Franklin Frazier, *Sociological Theory and Race Relations*    151
21. E. Franklin Frazier, *Review of Myrdal's An American
    Dilemma*    159
22. Leonard Bloom, *Familial Adjustments of Japanese-Americans
    to Relocation: First Phase*    163
23. Bruno Bettelheim and Morris Janowitz, *Ethnic Tolerance:
    A Function of Social and Personal Control*    168

**Part V:   The Great Promise: 1951–1960**    **179**

24. Guy B. Johnson, *A Sociologist Looks at Racial Desegregation
    in the South*    186
25. Roy Wilkins, *The Role of the National Association for the
    Advancement of Colored People in the Desegregation
    Process*    196
26. Ernest Q. Campbell and Thomas F. Pettigrew, *Racial and
    Moral Crisis: The Role of Little Rock Ministers*    200
27. Arnald M. Rose, *Intergroup Relations vs. Prejudice: Pertinent
    Theory for the Study of Social Change*    210
28. Lewis M. Killian, *The Adjustment of Southern White
    Migrants to Northern Urban Norms*    214
29. Frank R. Westie and Margaret L. Westie, *The Social-Distance
    Pyramid: Relationships Between Caste and Class*    220
30. Pierre L. van den Berghe, *The Dynamics of Racial Prejudice:
    An Ideal-Type Dichotomy*    227
31. R. A. Schermerhorn, *Power as a Primary Concept in the
    Study of Minorities*    233

**Part VI:   The Civil Rights Movement: 1961–1970**    **237**

32. Joseph S. Himes, *The Functions of Racial Conflict*    245
33. Joan W. Moore, *Colonialism: The Case of the Mexican
    Americans*    256
34. H. M. Blalock, Jr., *Occupational Discrimination: Some
    Theoretical Propositions*    265

35. Johnnie Daniel, *Negro Political Behavior and Community
    Political and Socioeconomic Structural Factors*                    273
36. Karl Taeuber, *Negro Residential Segregation: Trends and
    Measurement*                                                       280
37. Robert L. Crain, *School Integration and Occupational
    Achievement of Negroes*                                            287
38. H. Edward Ransford, *Isolation, Powerlessness, and Violence:
    A Study of Attitudes and Participation in the Watts Riot*          302

**Part VII:   Consolidation and Retrenchment: 1971–1980**             **313**

39. Seymour Spilerman, *Structural Characteristics of Cities and
    the Severity of Racial Disorders*                                  320
40. Edna Bonacich, *Advanced Capitalism and Black/White Race
    Relations in the United States: A Split Labor Market
    Interpretation*                                                    341
41. Wayne J. Villemez and Alan R. Rowe, *Black Economic Gains in
    the Sixties: A Methodological Critique and Reassessment*           363
42. Reynolds Farley, *Trends in Racial Inequalities: Have the Gains
    of the 1960s Disappeared in the 1970s?*                            376
43. David F. Sly and Louis G. Pol, *The Demographic Context of
    School Segregation and Desegregation*                              397
44. Cardell K. Jacobson, *Desegregation Rulings and Public
    Attitude Changes: White Resistance or Resignation?*                408
45. Ernest A. T. Barth and Donald L. Noel, *Conceptual Frameworks
    for the Analysis of Race Relations: An Evaluation*                 416

Index                                                                  439

# Preface

"[T]he problem of the Twentieth Century," wrote W. E. B. DuBois prophetically in 1903, "is the problem of the color-line."

This volume traces "the problem of the color-line" in the United States since 1895 through the medium of sociological journal articles. The book offers a time capsule with which to view both American race relations and American sociology. We shall see how the sociological understanding of race relations developed by reading chronologically nearly four dozen influential papers that appeared in four of the discipline's leading journals: the *American Journal of Sociology* (initiated in 1895), *Social Forces* (1922), the *American Sociological Review* (1936), and *Social Problems* (1954). The story of American race relations over the last four generations unfolds as seen and analyzed by sociologists who studied and wrote about the phenomena at the time. The articles chronicle the nation's failures and triumphs; they provide for each period contemporary rationalizations for the *status quo* as well as farsighted calls for change. In short, these selected articles show how sociological analyses have reflected each of the racial eras of this century while simultaneously serving as an advance force for reform.

Thus, *The Sociology of Race Relations: Reflection and Reform* is designed to meet two complementary purposes. First, it provides an overtime view of American race relations in the twentieth century. Second, it is also designed as a portable source book for a sociology-of-knowledge treatment of race relations theory and research in the United States.

If relevancy is defined as discussions of black, Native, Asian, or Hispanic Americans, there are more than a thousand relevant papers in these four journals (see Table 2 in the Introduction.) My reading of these articles, together constituting what is euphemistically termed "the literature," was an engrossing and stimulating experience. I hope the selection of articles made here can convey to readers some of the interest and excitement I have experienced. Many of the articles I had never read. But, more important, I had never before read the race relations "literature" in chronological sequence. To be sure, there are numerous dubious analyses and cul-de-sacs along the way. Yet when this longitudinal perspective is adopted, the genuinely cumulative nature of the discipline in both theory and method becomes vividly apparent. I believe readers will agree once they have proceeded through the book's seven time periods in turn.

Because of the variety of sources and the diversity of authors, the pieces in this book show, naturally, variety and diversity of writing and editorial styles. Beyond basic typographics, no attempt has been made to impose an artificial consistency of style on this collection.

I wish to express my deep appreciation to the many authors of the papers reproduced here for granting permission for reprinting and to the editors of the four journals surveyed for their kind cooperation: Professor Edward O. Laumann of the University of Chicago, editor of the *American Journal of Sociology;* Professor Rita J. Simon of the University of Illinois at Urbana, editor of the *American Sociological Review;* Professor Richard Colvard of Southern Oregon State College, editor of *Social Problems;* and Professor Everett K. Wilson of the University of North Carolina at Chapel Hill, editor of *Social Forces.* I especially want to thank the staff of *Social Forces* for their invaluable help. Indeed, the very idea for such a volume originated with Ev Wilson; I was honored to have been asked by the *Social Forces* staff to edit this first book in a projected series of similar books. Particularly important aid was also rendered by Priscilla McFarland and Professor M. Richard Cramer of the University of North Carolina and Donald Cunnigen of Harvard University.

I only hope that this rather unusual reader meets the expectations of the *Social Forces* staff that conceived it, and that it serves the same valuable functions for its readers that its preparation served for me.

THOMAS F. PETTIGREW
Cambridge, Massachusetts

# Introduction

In 1905 a small group of young black intellectuals, led by the ubiquitous W. E. B. DuBois, gathered near Niagara Falls. Reservations had been made for them at a Buffalo hotel, yet when they arrived they were refused accommodations because of their color. Ironically, these militant young men were convening to demand their full rights as American citizens, but they were forced to leave their native land and cross over to Canada in order to hold their Niagara Conference. The denial of service to DuBois and the other Niagara conferees symbolizes the legacy of racism and discrimination with which the twentieth century began. Likewise, the Niagara Conference itself, meeting to map strategy for racial change, symbolizes what was to unfold throughout the century.

The turn of the century, from roughly 1890 to the start of World War I, is the beginning of our story, for that period witnessed the simultaneous birth in the United States of both modern race relations and modern sociology. Both were institutionalized in those ostensibly tranquil years, but their futures appeared anything but promising. Black, Native, Asian, and Hispanic Americans were out of the majority's view, their fortunes at an especially low ebb, their varying hopes for the future dimmed by repeated reverses. Likewise, sociology was out of academic view, generally regarded as not belonging in the halls of ivy, its hopes for acceptance as a new, all-embracing social science dimmed by repeated rejection. Here the analogy ends. With few exceptions, such as DuBois himself, sociologists were white "Anglo" males, comfortably ensconced in the nation's dominant group. Yet the two fields were to influence each other profoundly; the nature and underlying tensions of this mutual influence is the focus of this volume.

## Race Relations at the Turn of the Century

The low ebb that the nation's four principal minority groups had reached by the start of the century is difficult to appreciate from our perspective, more than three quarters of a century later. The starkest symbol of racial oppression, the lynching of blacks in the South, reached its highest recorded levels during the 1890s. Formal disenfranchisement of the black citizens of Mississippi came in 1890. This act was followed by a raft of voting requirements enacted over the

South—property holding, regular employment, the poll tax, nebulous tests of literacy, "understanding," "good character," and the infamous "grandfather clause," which restricted the franchise to just those citizens who had voted immediately after the Civil War and their descendants. The U.S. Supreme Court sanctioned the "separate-but-equal" doctrine in Plessy v. Ferguson in 1896, a doctrine that did not fall until the High Court's school desegregation rulings in 1954. This acceptance of supposed "separate-but-equal" tempted the white South to establish the vast system of racially separate facilities that only recently has been dismantled. Racial segregation became in these years the legally supported "Southern way of life," pervading almost every realm and corner of society. Between 1890 and 1915 the whole complex of "Jim Crow" law was enacted—separate railroad cars, separate lunch counters, separate doorways, and separate waiting rooms. No detail was too minute. Oklahoma required separate telephone booths, and many courts began to use separate Bibles for swearing in witnesses.

Native Americans were faring no better. Matching the violence of Southern lynching, the era began with a massacre of Sioux at Pine Ridge. In December 1890 the Indian agent called for soldiers when a large encampment gathered for tradition-reviving Ghost Dance ceremonies. Misinterpreting Indian actions, the Army killed the entire encampment of 300 men, women, and children and left their bodies to freeze for three days at Wounded Knee, South Dakota. The era also began with the passage in 1887 of the General Allotment Act (or the Dawes Act), a legislative action analogous to the Southern disfranchisement and segregation legislation against blacks. This law in effect completed the long-term expropriation of Indian land. It provided Indian families with 160 acres each, with titles to those allotments to be held in trust for twenty-five years by the government and "surplus" Indian land to be sold to the government. The act violated the communal conception of landholding of most tribes, provided no reserve lands for future Indian generations, and ultimately led during the next forty-five years to the loss of 90 million out of 135 million Indian-owned acres.

What few rights Indians still retained, such as the principle of tribal consent and self-government for the "Five Civilized Tribes" (the Creeks, Cherokees, Choctaws, Chickasaws, and Seminoles), were abrogated. The same policy was now to be employed for all tribes, regardless of the vast differences between them. The U.S. Supreme Court repeatedly sanctioned the right of Congress "to abrogate the provisions of an Indian treaty"; and in Lone Wolf v. Hitchcock (1902) it held that Indians "were in substantial effect the wards of the government." "The position of the United States was now unmistakable," writes Edward Spicer. "It had embarked on a program of forcing the Indians into the cultural mould of what was then the dominant set of values in the United States."[1]

This same "spirit of the times" similarly affected Asian Americans. Mob violence against Chinese workers was common in the late nineteenth century,

[1] Edward H. Spicer, *A Short History of the Indians of the United States* (New York: D. Van Nostrand, 1969), p. 98.

especially in the mining regions. And with the completion of the transcontinental railroad and the rise of "yellow peril" imagery, legislation to end Chinese entry began. The first Chinese Exclusion Act was passed in 1882, renewed in 1892, and made permanent in 1904. By the turn of the century, Chinese-American workers were concentrated in urban domestic service and rarely found in mining and railroading. The establishment of a solid middleman minority status in commercial trades and services, with a flourishing subeconomy, was only beginning to be institutionalized in those years.

The major immigration of the Japanese to the mainland followed that of the Chinese, often after earlier immigration to Hawaii. Though less violence was directed toward the Japanese, agitation for the restriction of their entry began early in the century. In 1907–8 Japan and the United States signed a "gentleman's agreement" that stipulated that Japan would issue passports for the American mainland only to those who either were once residents of the United States or were parents, wives, or children of U.S. residents. Though often circumvented, this restriction slowed immigration and the sweepingly restrictive Immigration Act of 1924 virtually halted it altogether. These formative years of Japanese-American development began with a willingness to accept the lowest-paid work; but the landowning and entrepreneurial values of these immigrants soon led to the purchase of their own farms and the initiation of middleman status in urban retail sales and personal services.

Though Chinese- and Japanese-Americans are the largest Asian groups in the United States, they together constitute today only about half of the nation's population of Asian origin (the total Asian population was roughly 2.1 million in 1970). Filipino-Americans, Hawaiian-Americans, Korean-Americans, and most recently Vietnamese-Americans also boast sizable communities. But we shall find that sociology has concentrated its attention upon black Americans, with only brief looks at the two largest Asian groups and virtual neglect of the smaller Asian groups. Three examples of these brief looks are presented. In Selection 15, Emory Bogardus advances a seven-stage "race-relations cycle" that emphasizes the similarities in the American reception of Chinese, Japanese, Filipino, and Mexican immigrants. In Selection 16, Richard LaPiere demonstrates for motel establishments throughout the country in the 1930s the ambivalence toward accepting Chinese guests. And, finally, Leonard Bloom describes in Selection 22 the initial effects upon Japanese-American families of forced internment by the federal government during World War II.

Similarly neglected have been the Hispanic Americans, though they constitute the second largest minority group in the country. Mexican Americans comprise by far the largest Hispanic group, numbering in 1977 about 6.5 million out of a total Hispanic population of 11.3 million.[2] Mainland Puerto Ricans are the next

[2] There are definitional problems involved in calculating the size of Hispanic groups; parents' birthplace, mother tongue, Spanish surname, and self-identification all produce different figures. These estimates are based on self-identification and drawn from U.S. Bureau of the Census, *Persons of Spanish Origin in the United States: March 1977,* Advance Report, Current Population Report Series, P-20, No. 317 (Washington, D.C.: U.S. Government Printing Office, 1977).

largest (1.7 million), followed by Cubans (0.7 million). Though there are strong elements of Indian ancestry among Mexican Americans and Negro ancestry among Puerto Ricans, Hispanic Americans are recorded officially by the U.S. Bureau of the Census as Caucasian. Thus, they do not technically qualify as being involved in *race* relations. Moreover, the issues they raise for American society are primarily cultural. Yet they are included in this volume because their treatment and history in America, while containing vividly distinctive components, also bear important similarities with that of the nations's racial minorities. Some of these similarities were specified as early as 1931 by Bogardus, reprinted here as Selection 15.

The 1890–1915 period of U.S. history was also a critical period for Hispanic Americans. When Spain in 1898 ceded Guam, the Philippines, and Puerto Rico to the United States in the Treaty of Paris following the four-month Spanish–American War, the nation entered upon its brief and inglorious imperialistic phase. Indeed, this turn-of-the-century era in America reflected a general unity of thought in the Western world about the right of powerful nations to dominate others, a unity of thought also reflected in the nation's dealings with its domestic minorities. Puerto Ricans, then, entered American society as a colonized people. They were not to receive citizenship until the Jones Act of 1917; Puerto Rico itself was not to receive its special commonwealth status (*Estado Libre Asociado*, or Associated Free State) until 1948. Mass Puerto Rico migration to the mainland did not begin until World War II.

The colonized model also fits Mexican Americans, as Joan Moore persuasively argues in Selection 33. A significant minority of today's Mexican Americans are descendants of Hispanics who became Americans through conquest. The Treaty of Guadalupe Hidalgo, signed in 1848 following the Mexican–American War, annexed Texas and ceded California and most of Arizona and New Mexico to the United States. It also provided American citizenship for those Hispanics who remained in the acquired territories after one year. But modern Chicano–Anglo relationships were importantly shaped by events during the fateful years at the turn of the century. First, border "troubles," a recurrent event after 1848, heightened during these years and culminated in the ill-fated chase of 1916 into Mexico itself by General John Pershing's U.S. Army troops after Pancho Villa and his raiders. Second, Anglo migration to the Southwest and California was so extensive in the closing years of the nineteenth century that they became a majority by 1900 in every state save New Mexico, where Spanish Americans remained a majority until 1950. Third, land expropriation from Mexican Americans, not unlike that from Indians in the same period, was completed during these years. Finally, and most important of all, the Mexican Revolution that erupted in 1909 meant the end of near-chattel peonage for hundreds of thousands of Mexicans, who thereafter would seek employment. At the same time, rapid expansion of agriculture was occurring in the U.S. border states, and a large labor force was needed. Thus was triggered massive Mexican immigration into the Southwest. While recorded Mexican immigration for the first decade of this century was less than 25,000, it swelled to 174,000 between 1910 and 1919 and to almost half a million in the 1920s. It declined sharply during the Great Depression and the 1940s, began to rise in the early 1950s, and has averaged about 40,000 a year ever since. These data reflect the harsh fact that when labor is in demand in the United States, Mexican immigration has been encouraged (Los Braceros Program), and when there is a labor surplus, Mexican immigration has been discouraged (repatriation efforts and Operation Wetback). This twentieth-century pattern, then, also established itself during this pre-World War I period, a fateful period for minority relations in general in America.

Table 1 places this period in historical context for black-white relations. Drawn from Turner and Singleton's interesting analysis,[3] this table outlines the chief racial structures of each phase of U.S. history together with the dominant and "progressive" beliefs of whites that supported or challenged the prevailing structures. The low ebb of 1890–1915, it will be noted, arose from a centuries-long tradition that was warped largely by slavery.[4] In addition to being influenced by the worldwide rationalizations of the time for colonial domination by Western powers, the period was also a reaction to the idealism of the post–Civil War Reconstruction era. It is in this sense that the present period of retreat and resistance in American race relations can be described as "a second post-Reconstruction," a reaction to the idealism of the Civil Rights Movement of the 1960s.

Table 1 also traces for us the racial structures and beliefs that have evolved from World War I to the present. It is these years that we shall focus upon in this volume, following them through the analyses that sociologists provided at the time. It is in this manner that we shall learn how both race relations and sociology underwent sharp qualitative changes in this century.

## Sociology at the Turn of the Century

Modern American sociology came into existence during these same critical years. Robert Nisbett has called the 1830–1900 period in Europe "a golden age in sociology."[5] He stresses the seminal contributions of Tocqueville, Comte, Le Play, Marx, and later Tönnies, Durkheim, Weber, and Simmel during the European confrontation of the dying *Gemeinschaft* social order and the emerging *Gesellschaft* order. American sociology arose later, at the close of the nineteenth century; it borrowed heavily from the European tradition but planted

[3] J. H. Turner and R. Singleton, Jr., "A theory of ethnic oppression: Toward a reintegration of cultural and structural concepts in ethnic relations theory," *Social Forces 56* (1978): 1001–1018.

[4] The best one-volume history of black Americans, highly recommended for those who are not familiar with the background outlined in Table 1, is John Hope Franklin, *From Slavery to Freedom: A History of American Negros,* 2d ed. (New York: Knopf, 1961).

[5] Robert A. Nisbet, *The Sociological Tradition* (New York: Basic Books, 1966), p. 315.

**TABLE 1. A Summary of the Structure of Racial Oppression and Racial Beliefs in American History**

| PERIOD[a] | STRUCTURE OF OPPRESSION | DOMINANT BELIEFS | "PROGRESSIVE" BELIEFS |
|---|---|---|---|
| *English Heritage* –1650 | 1. Colonial expansion 2. Indentured servant system | 1. Blacks are uncivilized heathens 2. Blackness is evil—a curse of God 3. Blacks are bestial by nature | |
| *Colonial America* 1650–1760 | 1. Slave trade 2. Institutionalization of slavery | 1. Black bestiality, especially their sexual aggressiveness, requires control | |
| *Revolutionary Era* 1760–1820 | 1. Abolition of slave trade 2. Confinement of slavery to South | 1. Slavery is a "necessary evil" 2. Blacks are ill-suited or unprepared for freedom | 1. Slavery is inconsistent with Revolutionary ideology 2. While culturally deprived and debased by slavery, blacks are capable of betterment |
| *Ante-Bellum* 1820–1860 | 1. Further institutionalization of slavery in face of ideological challenges and North–South economic and political competition 2. Spread of Northern Jim Crow practices | 1. Slavery is a "positive good" that protects the interests of masters and slaves alike 2. Slavery harnesses the savage nature of blacks, civilizing them as far as possible 3. The childlike dependency of blacks requires white protection 4. Northern stereotype defines blacks as ignorant, lazy, and immoral | 1. There are "racial" differences 2. Blacks' "childlike simplicity" reveals a basic Christian nature 3. Slavery is morally wrong—it corrupts and takes advantage of a naturally submissive people |
| *Civil War and Reconstruction (1861–1877)* | | | |
| *Post-Reconstruction to WWI* 1877–1914 | 1. Dismantling of Radical Reconstruction 2. Growing legalized segregation in all institutional spheres 3. Relegation of blacks to menial | 1. Black corruption in Reconstruction confirms their inherent inferiority 2. Blacks have failed to take advantage of "equal" opportunities | 1. The Negro race is less advanced than the white because it has not progressed as far on the scale of evolution |

| | | | |
|---|---|---|---|
| | farm-factory occupations<br>4. Enforcement of segregation and relegation through white violence<br>5. Legalized and de facto disenfranchisement | and, in accordance with social Darwinism, should be left to find their social niche<br>3. Without the supervision and compulsion of slavery, blacks have degenerated to their natural state, where they are lazy, prone to crime, and lust for white women<br>4. The traits of blacks which make them different from and inferior to whites require separation of the races | 2. Blacks are potentially useful citizens—their natural docility and kindness can be channeled through education, industrial training, and white guidance<br>3. Racial purity and the instinct of race prejudice necessitate racial segregation |
| *WWI to WWII 1914–1941* | 1. Northern migration of Southern blacks and their confinement to ghettos<br>2. Last hired and first fired policy<br>3. Union exclusion and confinement to low-scale occupations<br>4. Segregation and disenfranchisement backed by violence, formal law, and de facto practices | 1. Black inferiority is an indisputable scientific fact backed by evolutionary theory and intelligence testing<br>2. Segregationist doctrine continues to be affirmed: racial segregation is natural and instinctive, for the good of and desired by both races; blacks are permanently inferior beings necessitating segregation to control their criminality and lust and to guard against amalgamation | 1. All apparent social, cultural and intellectual differences between the races are the result of the environment<br>2. Blacks are the victims of an oppressive environment that creates discontent, frustration, and fatalistic sense of powerlessness |
| *WWII (1941–1948)*<br><br>*2nd Reconstruction 1948–1968* | 1. Efforts to increase opportunity without alterations of basic institutional and community patterns<br>2. Efforts to keep domestic tranquility through control by welfare system | 1. Rejection of legal segregation<br>2. Blacks have been discriminated against in the past<br>3. Blacks are not inherently inferior to whites and are capable of change<br>4. Change is best accomplished by | 1. Black appearances of inferiority reflect cultural deprivation and the impact of undesirable environments<br>2. Complete social integration is the only viable means to racial harmony |

**TABLE 1.** Continued

| PERIOD[a] | STRUCTURE OF OPPRESSION | DOMINANT BELIEFS | "PROGRESSIVE" BELIEFS |
|---|---|---|---|
| | 3. Community and economic resistance to integration<br>4. Sporadic and inconsistent government pressure to decrease segregation and exclusion | improving substandard schools, providing more vocational schools, and renovating black ghettos, in other words, by providing "equal opportunities" | 3. Forced integration of schools is essential to any program of change |
| *1968–present* | 1. Continued de facto residential segregation<br>2. White violence and protest of educational integration<br>3. Decreased political and legal efforts to enforce civil rights legislation, even in face of "affirmative action" policies | 1. Blacks' inferior status is largely attributable to blacks themselves, especially their lack of motivation<br>2. The pace of change in race relations has been too fast<br>3. Enough has been done—reverse discrimination and forced integration measures such as open housing laws and busing are wrong | 1. Racism is generic to the social structure of American society<br>2. The "equal opportunities" doctrine has failed—there is need to redress for past wrongs<br>3. Immediate integration is not possible—community control and group power are more practicable |

[a]Dates correspond to the following historical events:

1650: roughly marks the beginning of the distinction, soon recognized in law, between indentured servitude for whites and lifetime servitude for blacks

1760: first serious antislavery crusade gets into full swing (see Jordan, ch. 7)

1820: height of debates leading to the Missouri Compromise; reemergence of strong antislavery sentiment

1860: election of Lincoln; beginning of Southern secession

1877: election of Hayes; withdrawal of federal troops from the South

1914: World War I

1941: World War II

1948: Truman establishes Commission on Civil Rights, issues executive order desegregating armed forces

1968: Assassination of Martin Luther King; publication of the Kerner Report; election of Nixon

Source: Reprinted from *Social Forces 56* (June 1978): 1001–1018. "A Theory of ethnic oppression: Toward a reintegration of cultural and structural concepts in ethnic relations theory," by J. H. Turner and R. Singleton, Jr. Copyright (ⓒ) The University of North Carolina Press.

the new discipline in sharply different soil. With no medieval background as a model but with vast dislocations from extremely rapid urbanization and industrialization, sociology on New World shores was shaped from the start by a moral response to immediate national social problems—racial and cultural concerns prominent among them.

Yale University's William Graham Sumner is credited with presenting the first sociology course in the United States in 1875. But the second such course was not introduced until 1890 by Albion Small at Colby College in Maine. Though Sumner is highly regarded to this day as a theorist, it was the energetic and single-minded Small who led the push toward institutionalization of the new discipline at the turn of the century. He went in 1892 to the University of Chicago .to occupy the first American chair in sociology, founded there the nation's first department of sociology, and was its effective chairman until his retirement in 1925. With George Vincent, he wrote the field's first textbook, published in 1894. The following year, Small founded the field's first journal, the *American Journal of Sociology,* and rigorously edited it for the next three decades. In 1905 he joined with other sociologists who were dissatisfied with their lowly place in existing social science associations to establish the American Sociological Society (now the American Sociological Association). Small served as president of the young society from 1912 to 1913 and tirelessly edited and published the *Annual Proceedings* of its meetings. He was also president of the Institut International de Sociologie in 1922. Other early American sociologists may have made greater theoretical contributions to the field—Sumner, Franklin Giddings, Lester Ward, Charles Cooley, and Edward Ross—but it is the indefatigable Small who must receive the major credit for institutionalizing the profession and thereby shaping its initial thrust and direction.

Right from its beginning, American sociology showed signs of its unique dilemma as a social science. On the one hand, a vital mission of the field is to be a critic of society, to judge skeptically the conventional wisdom of its time and place, to "debunk" the popular myths. Yet, on the other hand, sociology of necessity is a part of its society and depends on it for support and acceptance. This tension between being both critic and supplicant, between being both outside and inside society, has advantages and disadvantages for sociology. It can be a creative force for the sociological imagination. But it can lead to a desire to avoid the practical, to remain deceptively "neutral"—in short, to retreat from the role of critic altogether and, at times, even to pander uncritically to society's most conspicuous current fallacies and prejudices. We shall review examples of both of these tendencies throughout this volume.

This tension between the roles of critic and supplicant of society is elegantly illustrated in Albion Small's distinguished career. As Ernest Becker describes sympathetically in his *The Lost Science of Man,*[6] Small had a vision for a science of man that was whittled away in the process of attaining academic acceptance

---

[6]Ernest Becker, *The Lost Science of Man* (New York: George Braziller, 1971).

for sociology. Like so many of the country's early sociologists (e.g., Giddings and Thomas were sons of ministers, and Sumner and Vincent had been ministers themselves), Small was the son of a Protestant minister and had spent three years himself studying theology at a seminary. He wanted sociology to supply useful answers to "the social problem," needed reforms to correct the ravages of un- bridled laissez-faire capitalism, and pointed critiques of what was wrong with contemporary society. His own interest in the field, his hopes for what it could be, and his constant professional pleas in the *American Journal of Sociology* in its first years all pointed toward this view of sociology as a policy-oriented, applied science.

But Small sought another goal—the establishment of sociology as a recognized social science. We have just noted how immensely successful he was in this en- deavor, though at the expense of his initial hopes for the discipline. As Becker observes tartly, "a society which is willing to apply social science in the active process of changing its own vested-interest institutions has never yet been seen on the face of this planet."[7] Small had to compromise continually to win ap- proval from the established social disciplines of political science, history, and especially economics, from which sociology usually had to differentiate itself on most college campuses. A rigorous image of "science" had to be projected, an image that allowed little place for the policy-oriented vision of a field that would address the central societal problems of its day. In his famous 1929 presidential speech to the American Sociological Society just three years after Small's death, William Ogburn advanced the new radical positivism in blunt terms: "Sociology as a science is not interested in making the world a better place in which to live, in encouraging beliefs, in spreading information, in dispensing news, in setting forth impressions of life, in leading the multitudes, or in guiding the ship of state. Science is interested directly in one thing only, to wit, discovering new knowledge."

One can agree with Becker's lament that "social science has been unable to face frankly the fact that its authentic posture is the posture of social criticism"[8] without accepting fully his dour judgment that "sociology has degenerated into . . . an uncritical but sophisticated scientific technique in the service of the ongoing ideology, which stresses plenty of jobs, plenty of market, plenty of movement and ferment."[9] True, the joining of the social science disciplines in order to achieve a broad view of mankind's condition seems more distant than ever, save for occasional broad-scale application efforts.[10] True, professional

---

[7] *Ibid.*, p. 70.

[8] *Ibid.*, pp. 54–55.

[9] *Ibid.*, p. 41.

[10] Thus, interdisciplinary applied research during World War II led for a while to a marked increase in such work. It also led to the formation of such academic structures as the University of Michigan's Social Psychology Program, which spanned both the Sociology and the Psychology departments, and Harvard University's Social Relations Department, which combined sociology with social psychology, social anthropology, and clinical psychology. But in the late 1960s and early 1970s these interdisciplinary efforts were dissolved in favor of traditional disciplinary structures.

concerns of jobs, grants, and recognition dominate the attention of the American Sociological Association, as reflected in the pages of its *Footnotes* publication. But it is not an either-or situation. Small's vision did not die with Ogburn's address. The creative potential is maximized when a delicate balance is struck between values and rigor, between the Enlightenment Dream of human betterment and that of strict science. And this dynamic balance to be struck shifts with time and place. The two parts are not mutually exclusive. Nor does one without the other promise a meaningful sociology: Criticism without method would not offer the discipline a special role, and method without a critical focus all too easily becomes what Becker fears, "technique in the service of the ongoing ideology."

The dilemma of sociology as critic and supplicant, as a discipline that challenges the very society in which it must subsist, can be seen to operate as an underlying tension throughout this century. More than any other science, sociology *is* critical of American society—indeed, critical of *all* societies. Even Ogburn's empirical positivism has often been put to uses that would have intrigued Albion Small. For example, Samuel Stouffer, an Ogburn student and one of sociology's greatest empiricists, applied his survey genius continuously to a range of America's problems throughout his life—from the Depression, U.S. Army morale and adjustment in World War II, and McCarthyism, to world population problems.[11] Selections 36, 37, 39, 41, and 42, among others, offer further examples of this coming together of the dilemma's two horns. To be sure, sociology has not attained the high aspirations held for it by Small and Becker, but neither is it simply an uncritical servant of "the highest cash bidder."[12]

## Values and Race Relations Research

The creative potential, as well as the attendant failures, attributable to this dilemma is well illustrated in the explosive issue of race relations. As one of the most critical and persistent domestic issues throughout American history, the issue occasions both the discipline's harshest critiques of society and the greatest resistance to these critiques by the society. Not surprisingly, then, the forty-five papers republished here demonstrate sharply the operation of this tension in sociology's response to the unfolding events of American race relations in the twentieth century. The critical role of sociology can be judged directly from W. I. Thomas's reasoned attacks in 1904 and 1907 upon the prejudices and racism of the time (Selections 1 and 2) to the pointed analyses of the Ku Klux Klan in the 1920s (Selection 9), Japanese-American internment in the 1940s (Selection 22), and race riots of the 1960s (Selections 38 and 39).

Black sociologists in particular have shared Small's vision of the field.

[11] S. A. Stouffer, *Social Research to Test Ideas: Selected Writings of Samuel A. Stouffer* (New York: Free Press, 1962).
[12] Becker, *Lost Science of Man,* p. 41.

Throughout the history of American sociology, they have seen in the discipline, writes Morris Janowitz, "the intellectual tools for the redefinition of race relations, and, in turn, a positive element for social change."[13] We shall note the truth of this statement in the many contributions by black writers contained in these pages—DuBois (Selection 4), Monroe Work (7), Ira Reid (8), John Murchison (12), E. Franklin Frazier (13, 20, and 21), Oliver Cox (18), Charles S. Johnson (19), Roy Wilkins (25), Joseph Himes (32), and Johnnie Daniel (35). Different as their varied approaches are, the common thread among them is their emphasis upon positive *structural change* in American race relations.

Another spokesman for the Small position is Gunnar Myrdal, whose massive *An American Dilemma* in 1944 serves as a classic landmark of sociology's contribution to the nation's understanding of race relations. We shall look at this major contribution by contrasting Frazier's enthusiastic review with a more guarded and defensive review of the two-volume work (Selection 21). But it should be noted here that the Swedish social economist Myrdal advanced the earlier critical perspective of sociology by advocating the explicit exposure of the investigator's value position. American sociology was established by men from rural, small-town, often Protestant ministerial backgrounds, men fired by Populist, Social Gospel, and Progressive perspectives to correct the nation's social ills with the tools of their new science. They made no split between fact and value; indeed, they expected new values to emerge from sociology's uncovering of "the natural law." Myrdal, writing a third of a century later after such positivists as Ogburn had split fact from value and even believed that they had dispensed with values as hindrances to true "science," maintained that explicit value premises are actually necessary for social research. They lead us to new insights even if they also blind us to others. But they are hardly substitutes for humility and an open mind. Writing with characteristic vigor, Myrdal argued: "A 'disinterested social science' is . . . pure nonsense. It never existed and it will never exist. We can make our thinking strictly rational in spite of this, but only by facing the valuations, not by evading them."[14]

The uneasy merging of the evaluative, problem-centered approach with a less radical empiricism favored by Myrdal raised the eyebrows of sociologists in the 1940s. But applied social research in wartime combined with a large new post–World War II cohort of young sociologists led to a gradual acceptance of such a merger in most quarters of the discipline. Noteworthy in this regard is the position of Robin Williams of Cornell University, a product of this era and a distinguished contributor to many branches of sociology including race relations.[15] Williams maintains that sociology makes its contribution to American life in part by sensitizing the society to unnoticed relationships and by debunking

---

[13] James E. Blackwell and Morris Janowitz (eds.), *Black Sociologists: Historical and Contemporary Perspectives* (Chicago: University of Chicago Press, 1974), p. xiv.

[14] Gunnar Myrdal, *An American Dilemma* (New York: Harper & Row, 1944), p. 1064.

[15] Robin M. Williams, Jr., "Sociology in America: The experience of two centuries," *Social Science Quarterly 57* (1976): 77–111, and *idem,* "A neglected form of symbolic interactionism in sociological work: Book talks back to author," *American Sociologist 11* (1976): 93–103.

simplistic assumptions and beliefs. And the unnoticed relationships and simplistic assumptions to be addressed change with time. Sociology, therefore, plays its same valuable role by emphasizing different aspects of social reality at different points in history. To quote Williams:

> In the 1940s and 1950s, a responsible sociological analysis needed to say sharply that "prejudice" (or "attitudes" or "personality") could *not* account for systematic segregation and discrimination. . . . In the 1950s and 1960s, it was a useful contribution to analyze the means by which judicial and legislative actions could reduce racial discrimination and segregation. By the late 1960s, it was equally necessary to reappraise the consequences of collective violence and to cast a skeptical eye upon the effectiveness of a rhetoric of total threat when used by weak movements against very powerful adversaries. On the other hand, by the mid-1960s, it had become important to repudiate the conception of protest movements and rebellions as anomic outbursts from disoriented and uprooted elements of the population. . . . But the pendulum swung too far, and we need to remind ourselves that both the expressive and the instrumental images are partial truths. The basic lesson is that the most general polar conceptions are too general to be usefully defended or attacked.[16]

In this view, sociology serves its critical function by limiting the excesses of popular thought with hard-headed analysis. Sociology is at its most useful when it fights the fashions, counters the dominant ideology, and employs its theoretical and empirical tools to rein in the contemporary passions. Albion Small and Gunnar Myrdal would agree. And a chronological look at American sociology's varied analyses of race relations over the years reveals that by this standard the field has carried through its debunking function somewhat better than its critics, from Myrdal to Marxists, have allowed.

To be sure, the critical work is in the minority throughout. Analyses that *reflect* the limitations of their time—and thereby legitimate these limitations with the imprimatur of social science—dominate the journals. Selection 3 by Alfred Stone, politely answered by DuBois in Selection 4, is a case in point. Moreover, the critical papers are overwhelmingly liberal and reformist in cast, not radical and revolutionary. Most of them, such as Guy Johnson's blunt analysis of the Ku Klux Klan in its heyday (Selection 9) and Charles Johnson's insistence that interracial conflict during World War II was actually a symptom of positive change (Selection 19), look pallid, even timid, to modern eyes. But the force of the volume will escape readers if they judge the older articles by today's standards alone. One need only compare Guy Johnson's Klan article

---

[16]Williams, "A neglected form," 97–98. To the extent that sociology plays this role, it is often seen by elites as more critical and politically radical than it is in fact. Howard Becker advances an interesting speculation for why this occurs. In what he calls "the hierarchy of credibility," Becker notes that information tends to flow up, and thus provides elites with a more complete view and greater capability. By often not following this trend, by not giving "equal time" to official authority, sociology, therefore, looks especially biased to the left in the eyes of elites. Howard S. Becker, "Whose side are we on?" *Social Problems 14* (1967): 239–247.

with the then-current apologia, or Charles Johnson's conflict piece with the then-current outcries, to realize that these papers were in fact the needed critiques of their time. As Williams makes clear, sociology's critical function is served by emphasizing different points at different times. And we shall see how each of the seven periods covered in this book required a special critique.

The sociological literature on race relations, therefore, both *reflects* American society and attempts to *reform* it—hence the subtitle of this volume. It is in this fashion that it uneasily resolves the discipline's dilemma of being both supplicant and critic of society. We shall review examples of reflection and of reform in each time period, though the selection of articles is biased toward articles that epitomize the critical function of sociology. There are three reasons for this bias. First, the critical work has often been more influential in shaping later work in the field. Second, we wish to demonstrate to the skeptics that at least a minor chord of protest and reform has in fact characterized the sociology of race relations over the past eight decades. Finally, the critical articles expose their times more clearly and thus better serve the volume's aim of providing readers with a historical sequence of twentieth-century racial phenomena.

The main bias of the book's selection of articles is that they come exclusively from four major sociological journals. Book material is not covered, save as it appears in journal form (as with Bettelheim and Janowitz's paper, Selection 23), is reviewed (as with Frazier's review of *An American Dilemma,* Selection 21), or is discussed in the editorial commentary. Nor is material from other sociological journals covered, though this is not a serious bias until recent years when the number of journals burgeoned. But in spite of these biases, the dominant characteristics and tone of the most influential literature, that which is written technically by sociologists largely for other sociologists, are undoubtedly captured in these four major journals.

## Characteristics of the Sociological Journal Literature on Race Relations

Table 2 shows the counts by journal and time period of articles that are concerned in a significant way with black, Native, Asian, or Hispanic Americans. The figures in parentheses indicate the number of papers reprinted in this book from each journal and time combination. These figures disclose that in proportional terms the book's selections necessarily favor the thinly published early periods and the two older journals at the expense of the later time periods and the two newer journals.

### VARYING ATTENTION TO RACE RELATIONS

Table 2 shows the rapid increase during the first half of the century in the volume of papers devoted to race relations, from only 23 in the 1895–1915 period to 174 in the 1941–1950 period. This growth reflects accurately the

**TABLE 2.** The Sociological Race Relations Literature in Four Leading Journals by Time Period[a]

| | 1895–1915 | 1916–1929 | 1930–1940 | 1941–1950 | 1951–1960 | 1961–1970 | 1971–1978[c] | TOTALS | PERCENTAGES |
|---|---|---|---|---|---|---|---|---|---|
| *American Journal of Sociology* (1895– ) | 23 (5)[b] | 22 (1) | 50 (2) | 44 (2) | 40 (2) | 49 (2) | 54 (1) | 282 (15) | 26.8 (33.3) |
| *Social Forces* (1922– ) | — | 50 (5) | 62 (4) | 80 (2) | 65 (4) | 97 (2) | 59 (3) | 413 (20) | 39.2 (44.4) |
| *American Sociological Review* (1936– ) | — | — | 11 (0) | 50 (2) | 47 (0) | 33 (0) | 58 (3) | 199 (5) | 18.9 (11.1) |
| *Social Problems* (1954– ) | — | — | — | — | 34 (2) | 62 (3) | 63 (0) | 159 (5) | 15.1 (11.1) |
| Totals | 23 (5) | 72 (6) | 123 (6) | 174 (6) | 186 (8) | 241 (7) | 234 (7) | 1,053 (45) | |
| Percentages | 2.2 (11.1) | 6.8 (13.3) | 11.7 (13.3) | 16.5 (13.3) | 17.7 (17.8) | 22.9 (15.6) | 22.2 (15.6) | | 100.0 (100.0) |

[a]The inclusion of an article as part of the race relations literature is governed by whether it is judged to be concerned in a "significant" way with black, Native, Asian, or Hispanic Americans or any combination of these groups. These counts are somewhat larger than those reported previously by other reviewers because of the broader definitions both of "race relations" groups and of "significance" employed here. In particular, articles that focused on other topical areas but utilized minority data in an informative manner are included here but have been generally omitted previously. These changes, however, do not appear to alter the trends reported previously and discussed in the text.

[b]Numbers in parentheses indicate the number of articles reprinted in this volume.

[c]Note that this period is two years shorter in duration than the three earlier periods surveyed.

general expansion in sociological publication over these years. Table 2 also demonstrates that much of the increase was a function of the entry upon the scene of new journals—*Social Forces* in 1922, the *American Sociological Review* in 1936, and *Social Problems* in 1954.

A notable exception to the upward trend occurs in the 1950s. All three established journals show their first drop, the difference being made up by the entry of *Social Problems*. This official publication of the newly formed Society for the Study of Social Problems (SSSP) was begun precisely because many sociologists felt that the discipline was not paying enough attention to a wide range of social concerns, of which race relations was only one. Nonetheless, the general decline of sociological attention to race relations is attested to by other indicators; Richard Simpson found for 1955-1959 that "race and ethnic relations" not only recorded fewer publications in the *American Sociological Review,* but fewer papers delivered at the meetings of the American Sociological Association and a decreasing number of sociologists who listed the area as a specialty in the Association's directory.[17] Interestingly, the only exception to the trend that Simpson uncovered was a modest relative increase in the number of college courses offered on the subject.

This phenomenon is curious when one considers that this was the decade of Brown *v.* Board of Education, the historic Supreme Court ruling that declared racially separate public schools to be inherently unequal and therefore unconstitutional. It was these years that spawned the hope and idealism that created the Civil Rights Movement of the 1960s. And some observers cite this declining sociological interest in race relations in the 1950s as one reason for sociology's having failed to foresee more clearly the coming Movement and protest. At any rate, the reasons for the falling sociological interest are undoubtedly complex, but two can be specified. First, resources were minimal while they were beginning to increase for other specialties. Both private foundations and the federal government refused to support work in the area.[18] As a graduate student in the 1950s, the editor recalls being advised by well-meaning peers not to specialize in race relations because of the lack of research support and jobs.

A second cause was more abstract. There was widespread sentiment in sociology of the 1950s that the old race relations models—Park's race cycle, caste and class, etc.—were not sufficient and that social psychological explanations in terms of prejudiced attitudes and authoritarian personalities were too simple. New structural models were needed, models that emphasized power and conflict and ignored psychological factors. In Parts V and VI, we shall read the results of this theoretical ferment. For the present, it suffices to record that this dissatisfaction with the dominant race relations theories contributed to the declining interest in the field.

[17] Richard L. Simpson, "Expanding and declining fields in American sociology," *American Sociological Review 26* (1961): 458–466.

[18] S. W. Cook, "Desegregation: A psychological analysis," *American Psychologist 12* (1957): 1–13, and T. F. Pettigrew and K. W. Back, "Sociology in the desegregation process: Its use and disuse," in P. F. Lazarsfeld, W. H. Sewell, and H. L. Wilensky (eds.), *The Uses of Sociology* (New York: Basic Books, 1976), pp. 692–722.

The growth trend returns in the last two periods. This conclusion emerges despite the fact that the totals for the 1960s and 1970s shown in Table 2 represent sharp underestimates of the actual awakened interest. Books on race relations multiplied, and new journals began in these years. And the last period in Table 2, 1971–78, contains two fewer years than the three previous periods and will surely reach a considerably higher figure for the complete decade.

The increment in the sociological attention paid to race relations is hardly surprising in the 1960s, the time of change, protest, and riots. But the continued growth in the 1970s seems more problematical; like the inattention of the promising 1950s, the attention of the retrenching 1970s is counterintuitive. Some of the early 1970s work represents a carryover of research from the exciting 1960s; but this is hardly a sufficient explanation, because publications in race relations continue unabated in the late 1970s as well. Has sociology been playing the debunking role during these years of retreat, as Small and Williams envisioned? We shall look closely at this phenomenon in Section VII.

## THE FOCUS UPON BLACK AMERICANS

Another characteristic of the race relations literature in sociology is its concentration upon black Americans and the relative neglect of Native, Asian, and Hispanic Americans. Lavender and Forsyth reviewed the *American Journal of Sociology, Social Forces,* and the *American Sociological Review* for 1900–1974 and classified all articles dealing directly with racial and ethnic minorities.[19] They found that 71 percent of these articles focused upon blacks compared to only 5 percent upon Native Americans, 7 percent upon Asian Americans, 4 percent upon Hispanic Americans, and the remaining 13 percent upon other white ethnic groups.

The present review replicates this finding, despite a slightly longer time period covered, the addition of *Social Problems,* and different inclusion rules for groups and articles. Of the 1,053 papers reviewed for this work and recorded in Table 2, black Americans and black-white relations were the topics in 75 percent, as compared to Native Americans in 4 percent, Asian Americans in 6 percent, Hispanic Americans in 4 percent, other groups in 3 percent, and general racial discussions in 8 percent. This volume reflects this characteristic of the literature on race relations. Black Americans and black-white relations are the focus in 71 percent of the selections, other racial and minority groups in 9 percent, and general racial discussions in 19 percent.

## BACKGROUNDS OF THE RESEARCHERS

Black-white relations are intertwined with American history, and especially with the history of the South. Not surprisingly, then, *Social Forces,* based at the University of North Carolina at Chapel Hill and long associated with the

[19] A. D. Lavender and J. M. Forsyth, "The sociological study of minority groups as reflected by leading sociological journals," *Ethnicity 3* (1976): 388–398.

Southern Sociological Society, has published a disproportionately large number of articles dealing with black Americans. Table 2 reveals that about two out of every five race relations articles in these four journals have been printed in *Social Forces;* and that journal led the others in number of papers on race relations in five of the six time periods in which it has been published.[20] Black-authored articles have particularly appeared in its pages;[21] eight of the twelve such pieces reprinted in this volume, for instance, appeared first in *Social Forces.*

These data suggest that Southern sociologists, black and white, may have disproportionately contributed to the race relations literature. And this possibility has been verified for the four leading journals, 1895–1970, by Gaston and Sherohman.[22] They show that for white authors birth in the South is the regional characteristic that most disposes a sociologist to study race relations. Obtaining one's first college degree in the South and currently holding a Southern institutional affiliation slightly predispose sociologists to work in the area, but completing one's highest degree in the South acts as a deterrent. Black authors of race relations papers overwhelmingly "(1) were born in the South, (2) took their first degree in the South, (3) took their highest degree in the North, (4) were affiliated with southern institutions, and (5) rarely published on any other topic than on black Americans."[23] Altogether, Gaston and Sherohman show that Southern-born authors account for about one-fifth of all articles but more than two-fifths of articles on blacks in these journals. These results fit closely with the articles in this book, 42 percent of which are written by native black and white Southerners.

This preponderance of Southerners helps to explain a number of other characteristics of the race relations literature. Thus, the liberal political tone and assumptions that dominate the literature and have increasingly been challenged in recent years from both the right and left are at least in part a result of Southern writers. There has long been a Southern liberal ideology, widely shared by the region's black and white intellectuals. Like other ideologies, its content addresses the chief strains of its society: necessarily, then, Southern liberal ideology revolves primarily around racial concerns. Though most non-Southerners are hardly aware of its existence much less its content, strong traces of this evolving ideology undergird many of the papers in this volume, from Thomas (Selections 1 and 2) to the Johnsons (9, 10, 19, 24), Campbell and Pettigrew (26), Killian (28), Himes (32), Daniel (35), and Crain (37). This assertion in no way detracts from the sociological value of these works. *All* social science work,

---

[20] This statement is valid for the absolute number of articles published. But if the index were the proportion of a journal's total number of papers devoted to race relations, the smaller and more specialized *Social Problems* would outrank *Social Forces.* See Jerry Gaston and James Sherohman, "Origins of researchers on black Americans," *American Sociologist 9* (1974): 75–82, Table 3.

[21] Butler Jones, "The tradition of sociology teaching in black colleges: The unheralded professionals," in Blackwell and Janowitz (eds.), *Black Sociologists,* p. 134.

[22] Gaston and Sherohman, "Origins of researchers."

[23] *Ibid.,* p. 80.

particularly that involved with issues of great controversy and social significance, is rooted implicitly or explicitly in an ideological base. The point is simply that the critics of the liberal underpinnings of this literature raise a valid point when they question the wisdom of one particular ideology having such widespread influence.

## THREE PRIMARY THEMES

The heavy representation of black and white Southerners also helps to account for the concentration of the black–white relations literature around three basic themes that have special force in the South. Vander Zanden summarizes these themes as: "(1) a description and documentation of Black disadvantage within American life; (2) an attack upon racist notions of black biological inferiority; and (3) an interpretation of Black disadvantages as derived from White prejudice and discrimination."[24]

The first two selections of the book by W. I. Thomas were among the opening salvos of sociology's efforts on theme 2, the attack on claims of genetic inferiority. This theme received considerable attention throughout the first half of the century. Theme 1, the documentation of black disadvantage, became a central concern in the 1920s (note Selections 7 and 8 by Work and Reid); and it remains a central concern today (note Selections 41 by Villemez and Rowe and 42 by Farley). The third theme, relating black disadvantage to white oppression, can be traced also through the years and remains a major theme of contemporary sociological writing on the subject (for examples, see Selections 10 by Guy Johnson and 40 by Bonacich).

## THREE ANALYTICAL BIASES

Concentration on these three themes has contributed to three analytical biases of race relations work that have also recently come under heated attack. In documenting black and other minority disadvantages, sociological work has emphasized *static* description far more than dynamic process; and it has stressed the reactive and *pathological* features of black life more than its proactive, healthy features. Moreover, in attacking white racist notions and demonstrating white culpability, the literature has often focused on the *individual* level and such phenomena as prejudiced personalities at the expense of the institutional and societal levels and such critical phenomena as group discrimination.

These biases are not nearly as descriptive of newer work as they were of older work, for research that views race relations as a dynamic social process is now common (see, for instance, Selections 36, 38, 39, and 41). But the prevalence of these biases during the first six decades was widespread. Back analyzed 255 research papers on intergroup relations published in twenty sociological journals

[24]James W. Vander Zanden, "Sociological studies of American blacks," *Sociological Quarterly 14* (1973): 32.

from 1900 to 1958.[25] He found that 71 percent of them studied only static features; 48 percent remained exclusively on the individual level. These biases led, Back argued, to greater sociological attention during these years to racial segregation (58 percent of the papers) than to racial integration (30 percent of the papers).

Employing current standards to judge past work, recent critics of the race relations literature have stressed proactive models in reaction to the past over-emphasis on the pathological views of black Americans as merely reactive victims of oppression.[26] These critical attacks of the late 1960s and early 1970s corresponded to radical and black challenges to the profession as a whole that we shall discuss later; and they served a valuable corrective function for the literature. But, to quote Williams again, "the pendulum swung too far. . . . The basic lesson is that the most general polar conceptions are too general to be usefully defended or attacked."[27] In stressing the healthy, proud aspects of minority life, these critiques came close to denying that racial oppression damages human beings. Soon these critiques provoked counter-criticism, from which a more balanced synthesis might be hoped for.[28] At any rate, we should keep these analytical biases of sociology's race relations literature in mind as we review it chronologically in this volume.

## Outline of the Book

Our story begins in 1895, when Albion Small began the *American Journal of Sociology*. The first of the seven eras covered in the book extends to 1915, a watershed year in American race relations, for it marked the initiation of the great black migration out of the rural South. The second part continues our review for the fourteen years from 1916 to 1929. These were exciting years, marked by the changes wrought by war, migration, and the cultural Harlem Renaissance of the 1920s. But they also witnessed the inevitable reaction to change in the form of the reappearance of the Ku Klux Klan and the passage of the exclusionistic Immigration Act of 1924—both threat-induced, nativistic attempts to return to a simpler day of uncontested white Protestant control.

The Great Depression completely dominates the next era, 1930–1940. Sur-

---

[25] Kurt W. Back, "Sociology encounters the protest movement for desegregation," *Phylon* 24 (1963): 232–239; also contained in Pettigrew and Back, "Sociology in desegregation process," pp. 714–717.

[26] For example, see J. D. McCarthy and William L. Yancy, "Uncle Tom and Mr. Charlie: Metaphysical pathos in the study of racism and personal disorganization," *American Journal of Sociology 76* (1971): 648–672.

[27] Williams, "A neglected form" (note 15 *supra*), p. 98.

[28] Barry D. Adam, "Inferiorization and 'self-esteem,'" *Social Psychology 41* (1978): 47–53; Roberta G. Simmons, "Blacks and self-esteem: A puzzle," *Social Psychology 41* (1978): 54–57; and T. F. Pettigrew, "Placing Adam's argument in a broader perspective: Comment on the Adam paper," *Social Psychology 41* (1978): 58–61.

vival, the rise of unionization, and the unfair distribution of governmental relief were the principal racial issues. Likewise, World War II and postwar adjustment dominate the 1940s. The pace of racial change quickened once more. But the war also occasioned one of the lowest points in American racial history— the forced federal internment of Japanese-Americans. Part IV also includes an insightful interpretation of the relationship between sociology and race relations up to that point (Selection 20). E. Franklin Frazier's influential paper, published in 1947, supplies a candid view of how the discipline's founding fathers had shaped the study of race relations in the first half of the century.

Part V of the book covers the years from 1951 through 1960. Though in retrospect those years seem to be uneventful, quiet times under a popular and unassertive President, Dwight Eisenhower, that decade did witness the U.S. Supreme Court's momentous public school desegregation ruling in 1954 and the first violent resistance to the decision in Little Rock, Arkansas, in 1957. Articles in this section analyze these events and illustrate how sociology reacted to them by reshaping the dominant theories of the time.

Major theoretical shifts continue into the book's sixth section, which spans 1961 through 1970. Sociological advances in research method become apparent here in the detailed analyses of the dynamics of racial discrimination in occupations, politics, housing, and schools. As the momentum of the Civil Rights Movement of the 1960s cooled, race riots erupted in cities throughout the United States. Sociologists studied this phenomenon intensely; two papers from this effort are reprinted. H. Edward Ransford (Selection 38) provides a social psychological profile of the supporters and participants of the Watts riot in Los Angeles in 1968. And Seymour Spilerman (Selection 39) opens Part VII, 1971–1980, with a structural model of riot severity across cities. This last section of the book includes papers that check carefully on what actually changed for black Americans during the 1960s and how these changes were maintained during the 1970s. Part VII also looks at the school desegregation problems of the period in terms of population trends (Selection 43) and public acceptance (Selection 44). And it reprints two examples of theoretical advances. Edna Bonacich (Selection 40) applies her interesting split labor market ideas to a historical explanation of black employment problems throughout the twentieth century. And in the final article of the volume, Ernest Barth and Donald Noel (Selection 45) draw together the various theoretical threads of the sociology of race relations in a balanced and creative manner that fittingly closes the book by providing coherence to the many ideas and arguments that have evolved in this literature.

# Part I

# The Nadir: 1895-1915

## Introduction

Albion Small made clear his aspirations for sociology and its first journal. In the pages of the first volume of his new publication, he promised that "the editors will attempt to make the *American Journal of Sociology* a factor of restraint upon premature sociological opinion, a means of promoting the development of a just and adequate social philosophy, and an element of strength and support in every wise endeavor to insure the good of men."[1] Toward that end, he wanted sociologists to free themselves of the "do-nothing traditions." "I would have American scholars, especially in the social sciences . . . repeal the law of custom which bars marriage of thought with action."[2]

Yet there are no articles directly concerned with American race relations in the first five volumes of the *Journal.* This fact becomes more curious—or perhaps is explained—in light of the low ebb to which America's treatment of its racial minorities had fallen, as described in the Introduction. Rayford Logan has aptly termed this period the *nadir* of black American history since Emancipation;[3] his description, as we have seen, just as aptly fits the fortunes of other racial minorities. Apparently, black, Indian, Asian, and Hispanic Americans were just as much out of the view of sociologists as they were of white Americans generally.

One important reason for this early neglect was the hold that biological thinking, and evolution in particular, had on social thought at the time. Small complained that "scholars of this generation" were "so dazzled by the play of evolution" in the past that they did not see its operation in the present. "It is

[1] Albion Small, "The era of sociology," *American Journal of Sociology 1* (1895):15.

[2] Albion Small, "Scholarship and social agitation," *American Journal of Sociology 1* (1896): 564.

[3] Rayford W. Logan, *The Negro in the United States: A Brief History* (Princeton, N.J.: Van Nostrand, 1957).

2

neither consistent nor intelligent," he wrote, "to act as though evolution terminates in us."[4] Looking back fifty years later, Small's student, E. B. Reuter,
regarded the gradual replacement of this biological perspective with a cultural
one to have been one of the half-century's major steps forward.[5]

Not surprisingly, then, the first articles on racial questions involved racist
theories of European nationalities. Following the Aryan theories of the Frenchman Georges Lapouge, Carlos Clossen provided "the hierarchy of European
races" in the *Journal's* third volume.[6] Using social status and wealth criteria
as well as geographical mobility and physical differences, "Homo Europoeus"
(or Aryans) ranked highest, "Homo Alpinus" ranked in between, and the
Mediterraneans ranked lowest. Two volumes later Clossen translated a Lapouge
article defining Aryans.[7] These notions were not only a fundamental part of
Nazi ideology three decades later[8] but also central to the later agitation in the
United States that resulted in the restrictive Immigration Acts of 1921 and
1924.

Equally biological, though less blatantly racist, papers appeared in the *Journal*
throughout this period. Francis Galton, the famous British scientist, published
two lengthy defenses of eugenics in the *Journal* at the close of his long life.[9]
James Collier, an Australian, argued for the sociological merits of the "natural
selection" concept by holding that it is *racial* strength and force that determine
history.[10] And Ulysses Weatherly, later elected president of the American Sociological Society in 1923, inveighed against both social and biological assimilation
in two articles.[11] There was, Weatherly maintained, a natural organic aversion to
biological assimilation so that "stimulating and beneficent" traits and capacities
could be retained; similarly, social assimilation works well only between socially
similar races. Consistent with such thinking, a 1914 paper that provided the
outline of a "reasonable department of sociology" advocated that a course on
race be given as part of a *bio*-social section.[12] Consistent, too, are an argument

---

[4] Small, "Scholarship and social agitation," p. 564.

[5] E. B. Reuter, "Racial theory," *American Journal of Sociology 50* (1945): 452–461.

[6] Carlos C. Closson, "The hierarchy of European races," *American Journal of Sociology 3*
(1897): 314–327.

[7] Georges V. de Lapouge, "Old and new aspects of the Aryan question," *American Journal
of Sociology 5* (1899): 329–346.

[8] Heinz Maus, *A Short History of Sociology* (London: Routledge & Kegan Paul, 1962),
pp. 39–40. Lapouge feared "a Jewish-led Russian domination of Europe."

[9] Francis Galton, "Eugenics: Its definition, scope, and aims," *American Journal of Sociology 10* (1904): 1–25, and *idem*, "Studies in eugenics," *American Journal of Sociology 11*
(1905): 11–25, 277–296.

[10] James Collier, "Natural selection in sociology," *American Journal of Sociology 14* (1909):
352–370.

[11] Ulysses G. Weatherly, "Race and marriage," *American Journal of Sociology 15* (1910):
433–453, and *idem*, "The racial element is social assimilation," *American Journal of Sociology 16* (1911): 593–612.

[12] Frank W. Blackman, "Reasonable department of sociology for colleges and universities,"
*American Journal of Sociology 20* (1914): 261–263.

in the *Journal's* pages that the racial capabilities of blacks were best served by slavery[13] and another that advocates *compulsory* work relief for all black men, women, and children, complete with uniforms, in model mills, farms, and shops "without the strain of personal initiative and responsibility."[14]

But articles in the *American Journal of Sociology* did not just reflect the racial nadir of post-slavery America; they also rose above the times and countered current thinking. One argued that there "can be no 'yellow peril,'" described the modernization of Japan, and held that the Japanese were fully the equals of Caucasians.[15] Another raised the question of the forgotten Fourteenth Amendment just five years after the "separate-but-equal" doctrine of *Plessy* had been established, and noted that blacks were still second-class citizens in 1900 in both voting and quality of education.[16] Still another attacked Herbert Spencer's thesis that the determinant of social organization is the instinct for race preservation.[17] And Monroe Work, then at the University of Chicago, the first black author published in the *Journal,* reported on a study of black crime in Chicago.[18] Work related black criminality to personal variables and concluded that the social milieu "accounts for a large part" of any excess of black crime.

Small, then, opened up his pages to all sides on the question, though he made his personal position nakedly clear in a blistering review of a racist book.[19] He also encouraged his student and colleague, W. I. Thomas, to publish a series of lengthy and pointed articles on the subject, excerpts from two of which are printed here. In Selection 1, Thomas counters the prevailing notion of "racial antipathy as a fixed and irreducible element."[20] While employing some of the popular concepts of the times, such as "instinct," the Tennessee-born social psychologist suggests that racial prejudice freed of caste-feeling is, perhaps, no more stable than fashions. And he ends on the optimistic note that the day will come when individual abilities will count for more than skin color. Selection 2 carries this argument further. Although the title may well seem patronizing to modern sensibilities, Thomas states the modern environmentalistic position in

---

[13] H. E. A. Belin, "A Southern view of slavery," *American Journal of Sociology 13* (1908): 513–522.

[14] Charlotte P. Gilman, "Suggestion on the Negro problem," *American Journal of Sociology 14* (1908): 78–85.

[15] Edmund Buckley, "The Japanese as peers of Western peoples," *American Journal of Sociology 11* (1906): 326–335.

[16] Max West, "The fourteenth amendment and the Negro question," *American Journal of Sociology 6* (1901): 248–254.

[17] Antonio Llano, "The race-preservation dogma," *American Journal of Sociology 5* (1900): 488–505.

[18] Monroe N. Work, "Crime among the Negroes of Chicago: A social study," *American Journal of Sociology 6* (1901): 204–223.

[19] *American Journal of Sociology 6* (1901): 849–852.

[20] The popularity of this belief at the time is shown in John M. Mecklin, "The philosophy of the color line," *American Journal of Sociology 19* (1914): 357.

direct terms: "The world of modern intellectual life is in reality a white man's world. Few women and perhaps no blacks have ever entered this world in the fullest sense." His comparison of the oppression of blacks with that of women antedated Myrdal's similar argument by four decades;[21] only Thomas's fellow social psychologist at the University of Michigan, Charles Horton Cooley, made such a sociological assault on the racist thinking of their time.[22]

Full appreciation of how advanced Thomas's contentions were is gained by reading Selection 3. Alfred Stone came from Washington, D.C., to give his paper on "race friction" to the newly organized American Sociological Society meeting in December 1907 at the University of Wisconsin in Madison. He presents the "progressive," intellectual viewpoint of the time on the subject (see Table I-1 in the Introduction). And in Selection 4, W. E. B. DuBois politely challenges many of Stone's basic assumptions. This is the early DuBois, still believing that America was capable of overcoming its racism and that sociology could contribute importantly to this effort. And this is the already intellectually confident DuBois, a product of the best schools, a correspondent with William James,[23] and a middle-aged, published author of such sociological classics as *The Philadelphia Negro* (1899) and *The Souls of Black Folk* (1903).

The last article of Part I is by one of the most famous and influential of all early American sociologists, Robert E. Park, a former newspaperman and a secretary to Booker T. Washington at Tuskegee Institute in Alabama. C. U. Smith and Lewis Killian note the irony that Washington, the long-time antagonist of DuBois, may have influenced the sociology of race relations indirectly through Park more than DuBois managed to do directly.[24] At any rate, Parks shaped the field more than anyone else during the first third of the century, and his debt to Washington was considerable. DuBois never won the recognition he deserved from sociology,[25] and he left academia for his more famous role as editor of the NAACP's magazine *Crisis* in 1910.

Selection 5 is one of Park's most influential papers on race relations, written just after arriving at the University of Chicago from Tuskegee. His Southern experience in a black community, as well as his European travels and his close friendship with Thomas, are evident in these pages. And though his theory of

---

[21] Gunnar Myrdal, *An American Dilemma* (New York: Harper & Row, 1944), Appendix 5, pp. 1073–1078.

[22] Charles H. Cooley, "Genius, fame and the comparison of races," *Annals of the American Academy of Political and Social Sciences 9* (1897): 1–4.

[23] The closeness of this connection, lasting from DuBois's student days to James's death, 1888–1910, has recently been revealed in a study of the DuBois–James letters. Eugene Taylor, "Transcending the veil: William James and W. E. B. DuBois, 1888–1910," unpublished paper, Harvard Divinity School, 1979.

[24] Charles U. Smith and Lewis Killian, "Black sociologists and social protest," in James E. Blackwell and Morris Janowitz (eds.), *Black Sociologists* (Chicago: University of Chicago Press, 1974), pp. 199–200.

[25] *Ibid.*

the race cycle, to be discussed in Selection 45, was not formulated until later, the theory's emphasis upon assimilation is foretold in this article. Indeed, sociology's emphasis on group assimilation was already obvious in the pages of the *Journal.*[26] The same volume in which Park's piece appeared contained another on "the assimilation of the American Indian."[27]

[26]Sarah E. Simons, "Social assimilation," *American Journal of Sociology 6* (1901): 790–822, and 7 (1902): 53–79, 234–248, 386–404, 539–556.

[27]Fayette A. McKenzie, "The assimilation of the American Indian," *American Journal of Sociology 19* (1914): 761–772.

# 1

# The Psychology of Race-Prejudice

*WILLIAM I. THOMAS*

[R]ace-prejudice is in one sense a superficial matter. It is called out primarily by the physical aspect of an unfamiliar people—their color, form and feature, and dress—and by their activities and habits in only a secondary way. The general organic attitude, growing out of experience (though reflex rather than deliberative experience), is that the outside world is antagonistic and subject to depredation, and this attitude seems to be localized in a prejudice felt for the characteristic appearance of others, this being most apprehensible by the senses. This prejudice is intense and immediate, sharing in this respect the character of the instinctive reactions in general. It cannot be reasoned with, because, like the other instincts, it originated before deliberative brain centers were developed, and is not to any great extent under their control. Like the other instincts also, it has a persistence and a certain automatism appropriate to a type of reaction valuable in the organic scheme, but not under the control of the deliberative centers. But for all its intensity, race-prejudice, like the other instinctive movements, is easily dissipated or converted into its opposite by association, or a slight modification of stimulus. There is no stronger contrast among the races than that between the black and white, but travelers relate that after long residence with African blacks they look on the white skin with something akin to prejudice:

> One feels ashamed of the white skin; it seems unnatural, like blanched celery —or white mice.[1]

[1] Livingstone, *The Zambesi and Its Tributaries*, p. 379.

Abridged from *American Journal of Sociology* 9 (1904): 593–611. Used by permission of The University of Chicago Press.

. . . The negro, for his part, not only loses race-prejudice in the presence of the white man, but repudiates black standards. In America the papers printed for black readers contain advertisements of pomades for making kinky hair straight and of washes to change the Ethiopian's skin; and the slaves returned to Sierra Leone in 1820 assumed the role of whites, even referred to themselves white, and called the natives "bush niggers."

Then Chinese are today regarded by many, particularly by the southern whites, as the most repulsive of races in physical appearance—more shocking to the sensibilities than the negro even. The Japanese, on the other hand, are also a yellow race and have all the physical marks of aliens, but contact with them has revealed a surprising fund both of charm and ability, and it is an interesting fact that they have many enthusiastic white admirers, and that the sympathy of a large part of the white world is with them in their war against a white group. It is, indeed, probable that in the event of a successful struggle with Russia little will remain in the way of prejudice against this smallish, yellow people, or of impediment to social and matrimonial, as well as political and commercial, association with it. It would not, in fact, be a matter of surprise if the checks to this were found rather on the side of the oriental race—small and yellow, but able, ancient, and traditionally set against occidental intrusion.

When not complicated with caste-feeling, race-prejudice is, after all, very impermanent, of no more stability, perhaps, than fashions. The very fact of difference, indeed, and of new appeals to the attention, may act as a stimulus, a charm, as is shown by the fact that the widespread practice of exogamy has its root in the interest of men in unfamiliar women. The experiences of each group have created a body of traditions and standards bound up with emotional accompaniments, and these may be so opposed as to stand in the way of association, but it is particularly in cases where one of the groups has risen to a higher level of culture that contempt for the lower group is persistent. In this case antipathy of the group for an alien group is reinforced by the contempt of the higher caste for the lower. Psychologically speaking, race-prejudice and caste-feeling are at bottom the same thing, both being phases of the instinct of hate, but a status of caste is reached as the result of competitive activities. The lower caste has either been conquered and captured, or gradually outstripped on account of the mental and economic inferiority. Under these conditions, it is psychologically important to the higher caste to maintain the feeling and show of superiority, on account of the suggestive effect of this on both the inferior caste and on itself; and signs of superiority and inferiority, being thus aids to the manipulation of one class by another, acquire a new significance and become more ineradicable. Of the relation of black to white in this country it is perhaps true that the antipathy of the southerner for the negro is rather caste-feeling than race-prejudice, while the feeling of the northerner is race-prejudice proper. In the North, where there has been no contact with the negro and no activity connections, there is no caste-feeling, but there exists a sort of *skin*-prejudice— a horror of the external aspect of the negro—and many northerners report that they have a feeling against eating from a dish handled by a negro. The association of master and slave in the South was, however, close, even if not intimate, and much of the feeling of physical repulsion for a black skin disappeared. This was particularly true of the house servants. White girls and boys kissed their black mammies with real affection, and after marriage returned from other states to the funeral of an old slave. But while color was not here repulsive, it was so ineradicably associated with inferiority that it was impossible for a southern white to think the negro into his own class. . . .

Race-prejudice is an instinct originating in the tribal stage of society, when solidarity in feeling and action were essential to the preservation of the group. It, or some analogue of it, will probably never disappear completely, since an identity of standards, traditions, and physical appearance in all geographical zones is neither possible nor aesthetically desirable. It is, too, an affair which can neither be reasoned with nor legislated about very effectively, because it is connected with the affective, rather than the cognitive, processes. But it tends to become more insignificant as increased communication brings interests and standards in common, and as similar systems of education and equal access to knowledge bring about a greater mental and social parity between groups, and remove the grounds for "invidious distinction." It is, indeed, probable that a position will be reached on the race question similar to the condition now reached among the specialized occupations, particularly among the scientific callings, and also in business, where the individual's ability to get results gives him an interest and a status independent of, and, in point of fact, quite overshadowing, the superficial marks of personality.

# 2

# The Mind of Woman and the Lower Races

*WILLIAM I. THOMAS*

. . . We have been accustomed to think that there is a great gulf between our-selves and other races; and this persists in an undefinable way after scores of Japanese have taken high rank in our schools, and after Hindus have repeatedly been among the wranglers in mathematics at Cambridge. . . .

The instinct to belittle outsiders is perhaps at the bottom of our delusion that the white race has one order of mind and the black and yellow races have another. But, while a prejudice—a matter of instinct and emotion—may well be at the beginning of an error of this kind, it could not sustain itself in the face of our logical habits unless reinforced by an error of judgment. And this error is found in the fact that in a näive way we assume that our steps in progress from time to time are due to our mental superiority as a race over the other races, and to the mental superiority of one generation of ourselves over the preceding.

In this we are confusing advance in culture with brain improvement. If we should assume a certain grade of intelligence, fixed and invariable in all individ-uals, races, and times—an unwarranted assumption, of course—progress would still be possible, provided we assumed a characteristically human grade of intelli-gence to begin with. With associative memory, abstraction, and speech men are able to compare the present with the past, to deliberate and discuss, to invent, to abandon old processes for new, to focus attention on special problems, to encourage specialization, and to transmit to the younger generation a more intelligent standpoint and a more advanced starting-point. Culture is the accumu-lation of the results of activity, and culture could go on improving for a certain

Abridged from *American Journal of Sociology 12* (1907): 435–469. Used by permission of The University of Chicago Press. © 1907 by The University of Chicago. All rights reserved.

time even if there were a retrogression in intelligence. If all the chemists in class A should stop work tomorrow, the chemists in class B would still make discoveries. These would influence manufacture, and progress would result. If a worker in any specialty acquaints himself with the results of his predecessors and contemporaries and *works,* he will add some results to the sum of knowledge in his line. And if a race preserves by record or tradition the memory of what past generations have done, and adds a little, progress is secured whether the brain improves or stands still. In the same way, the fact that one race has advanced farther in culture than another does not necessarily imply a different order of brain, but may be due to the fact that in the one case social arrangements have not taken the shape affording the most favorable conditions for the operation of the mind.

If, then, we make due allowance for our instinctive tendency as a white group to disparage outsiders, and, on the other hand, for our tendency to confuse progress in culture and general intelligence with biological modification of the brain, we shall have to reduce very much our usual estimate of the difference in mental capacity between ourselves and the lower races, if we do not eliminate it altogether; and we shall perhaps have to abandon altogether the view that there has been an increase in the mental capacity of the white race since prehistoric times.

The first question arising in this connection is whether any of the characteristic faculties of the human mind—perception, memory, inhibition, abstraction— are absent or noticeably weak in the lower races. If this is found to be true, we have reason to attribute the superiority of the white race to biological causes; otherwise we shall have to seek an explanation of white superiority in causes lying outside the brain.

In examining this question we need not dwell on the acuteness of the sense-perceptions, because these are not distinctively human. As a matter of fact, they are usually better developed in animals and in the lower races than in the civilized, because the lower mental life is more perceptive than ratiocinative. The memory of the lower races is also apparently quite as good as that of the higher. The memory of the Australian native or the Eskimo is quite as good as that of our "oldest inhabitant;" and probably no one would claim that the modern scientist has a better memory than the bard of the Homeric period.

There is, however, a prevalent view, for the popularization of which Herbert Spencer is largely responsible, that primitive man has feeble powers of inhibition. Like the equally erroneous view that early man is a free and unfettered creature, it arises from our habit of assuming that, because his inhibitions and unfreedom do not correspond with our own restraints, they do not exist. Sir John Lubbock pointed out long ago that the savage is hedged about by conventions so minute and so mandatory that he is actually the least free person in the world. But, in spite of this, Spencer and others have insisted that he is incapable of self-restraint, is carried away like a child by the impulse of the moment, and is incapable of rejecting an immediate gratification for a greater future one. Cases like the one mentioned by Darwin of the Fuegian who struck and killed his little son when the latter dropped a basket of fish into the water are cited without regard to the fact that cases of sudden domestic violence and quick repentance are common in any city today; and the failure of the Australian blacks to throw back the small fry when seining is referred to without pausing to consider that our practice of exterminating game and denuding our forests shows an amazing lack of individual self-restraint.

The truth is that the restraints exercised in a group depend largely on the traditions, views, and teachings of the group, and if we have this in mind, the savage cannot be called deficient on the side of inhibition. It is doubtful if modern society affords anything more striking in the way of inhibition than is found in connection with taboo, fetish, totemism, and ceremonial among the lower races. In the great majority of the American Indian and Australian tribes a man is strictly forbidden to kill or eat the animals whose name his clan bears as a totem. The central Australian may not, in addition, eat the flesh of any animal killed or even touched by persons standing in certain relations of kinship to him. At certain times also he is forbidden to eat the flesh of a number of animals, and at all times he must share all food secured with the tribal elders and some others. . . .

Altogether too much has been made of inhibition, anyway, as a sign of mentality, for it is not even characteristic of the human species. The well-trained dog inhibits in the presence of the most enticing stimulations of the kitchen. And it is also true that one race, at least—the American Indian—makes inhibition the most conspicuous feature in its system of education. From the time the ice is broken to give him a cold plunge and begin the toughening process on the day of his birth, until he dies without a groan under torture, the Indian is schooled in the restraint of his impulses. He does not, indeed, practice our identical restraints, because his traditions and the run of his attention are different; but he has a capacity for controlling impulses equal to our own.

Another serious charge against the intelligence of the lower races is lack of the power of abstraction. They certainly do not deal largely in abstraction, and their languages are poor in abstract terms. But there is a great difference between the habit of thinking in abstract terms and the ability to do so.

The degree to which abstraction is employed in the activities of a group depends on the complexity of the activities and on the complexity of consciousness in the group. When science, philosophy, and logic, and systems of reckoning time, space, and number, are taught in the schools; when the attention is not so much engaged in perceptual as in deliberate acts; and when thought is a profession, then abstract modes of thought are forced on the mind. This does not argue absence of the power of abstraction in the lower races, or even a low grade of ability, but lack of practice. To one skilled in any line an unpracticed person seems very stupid; and this is apparently the reason why travelers report that the black and yellow races have feeble powers of abstraction. It is generally admitted, however, that the use of speech involves the power of abstraction, so that all races have the power in some degree. When we come further to examine the degree in which they possess it, we find that they compare favorably with ourselves in any test which involves a fair comparison.

The proverb is a form of abstraction practiced by all races, and is perhaps the best test of the natural bent of the mind in this direction, because, like ballad poetry and slang, proverbial sayings do not originate with the educated class, but are of popular origin. . . .

If we assume, then, that the popular mind—let us say the peasant mind—in the white race is as capable of abstraction as the mind of the higher classes, but not so specialized in this direction—and no one can doubt this in view of the academic record of country-bred boys—the following comparison of our proverbs with those of the Africans of the Guinea coast . . . is significant:

*African.* Stone in the water-hole does not feel the cold.
*English.* Habit is second nature.
*A.* One tree does not make a forest.
*E.* One swallow does not make a summer.
*A.* "I nearly killed the bird." No one can eat nearly in a stew.
*E.* First catch your hare.
*A.* Full-belly child says to hungry-belly child, "Keep good cheer."
*E.* We can all endure the misfortunes of others.
*A.* Distant firewood is good firewood.
*E.* Distance lends enchantment to the view.
*A.* Ashes fly back in the face of him who throws them.
*E.* Curses come home to roost.
*A.* If the boy says he wants to tie the water with a string, ask him whether he means the water in the pot or the water in the lagoon.
*E.* Answer a fool according to his folly. . . .


# II

The mind and the personality are largely built up by suggestion from the outside, and if the suggestions are limited and particular, so will be the mind. The world of modern intellectual life is in reality a white man's world. Few women and perhaps no blacks have ever entered this world in the fullest sense. To enter it in the fullest sense would be to be in it at every moment from the time of birth to the time of death, and to absorb it unconsciously and consciously, as the child absorbs language. When something like this happens, we shall be in a position to judge of the mental efficiency of woman and the lower races. At present we seem justified in inferring that the differences in mental expression are no greater than they should be in view of the existing differences in opportunity.

Whether the characteristic mental life of women and the lower races will prove to be identical with those of the white man or different in quality is a different question, and problematical. It is certain, at any rate, that our civilization is not of the highest type possible. In all of our relations there is too much of primitive man's fighting instinct and technique; and it is not impossible that the participation of woman and the lower races will contribute new elements, change the stress of attention, disturb the equilibrium, and force a crisis which will result in the reconstruction of our habits on more sympathetic and equitable principles. Certain it is that no civilization can remain the highest if another civilization adds to the intelligence of its men the intelligence of its women.

# 3

# Is Race Friction Between Blacks and Whites in the United States Growing and Inevitable?

*ALFRED HOLT STONE*

On the evening of December 17, 1855, there assembled a gathering of the colored citizens of the city of Boston to do honor to a member of their race. The man was William C. Nell, a name familiar to students of negro history. The occasion was the presentation to him of a testimonial of appreciation of his labors in behalf of the removal of the color line from the public schools of Boston. . . . It marked the close of a quarter-century of patient and unremitting struggle with established law and custom. The meeting was made memorable by the presence of such men as Wendell Phillips and William Lloyd Garrison, who rejoiced with their colored brethren that "the prejudice against color was dying out." This was the keynote of all the addresses made—the faith that the final surrender of this long-stormed citadel marked the passing of the prejudice of race.

Fifty-two years later in November of the present year, a great concourse of Boston's colored citizens assembled in Faneuil Hall to protest against the steady and wide increase of race prejudice in America. The meeting was addressed by

Abridged from *American Journal of Sociology 13* (1908): 676–697. Used by permission of The University of Chicago Press. © 1908 by The University of Chicago. All rights reserved.

the gray-haired son of the great abolitionist, in tones which were far from sound-ing an echo of the hopeful, long-forgotten words of his father.

And after this more than half-century of American advance in moral and intellectual and material things, we too have come together . . . to consider cooly and dispassionately the causes which really lay behind these two meetings in Boston—farther apart in spirit and in purpose than in time. We have come to inquire whether friction between the white and negro races in Amerca is grow-ing and inevitable.

In the first place, what is race friction? To answer this elementary question it is necessary to define the abstract mental quality upon which race friction finally rests. This is racial "antipathy," popularly spoken of as "race prejudice." Whereas prejudice means a mere predilection, either for or against, antipathy means "natural contrariety," "incompatibility," or "repugnance of qualities." . . . I would define racial antipathy, then, as a natural contrariety, repugnancy of qualities, or incompatibility between individuals or groups which are suffi-ciently differentiated to constitute what . . . we call races. What is most impor-tant is that it involves an instinctive feeling of dislike, distaste, or repugnance, for which sometimes no good reason can be given. Friction is defined primarily as a "lack of harmony," or a "mutual irritation." In the case of races it is accen-tuated by antipathy. We do not have to depend on race riots or other acts of violence as a measure of the growth of race friction. Its existence may be mani-fested by a look or a gesture as well as by a word or an act. . . .

When we speak of "race problems" or "racial antipathies," what do we mean by "race?" Clearly nothing scientifically definite, since ethnologists themselves are not agreed upon any classification of the human family along racial lines. Nor would this so-called race prejudice have the slightest regard for such classifi-cation if one were agreed upon. It is something which is not bounded by the confines of a philological or ethnological definition. The British scientist may tell the British soldier in India that the native is in reality his brother, and that it is wholly absurd and illogical and unscientific for such a thing as "race preju-dice" to exist between them. Tommy Atkins simply replies with a shrug that to him and his messmates the native is a "nigger," and in so far as their attitude is concerned that is the end of the matter. . . . We have wasted an infinite amount of time in interminable controversies over the relative superiority and inferiority of different races. Such discussions have a certain value when conducted by scientific men in a purely scientific spirit. But for the purpose of explaining or establishing any fixed principle of race relations they are little better than worthless. The Japanese is doubtless quite well satisfied of the superiority of his people over the mushroom growths of western civilization. . . . The Chinese do not waste their time in idle chatter over the relative status of their race, as compared with the white barbarians who have intruded themselves upon them with their grotesque customs, their heathenish ideas, and their childishly new religion. . . . Only the white man writes volumes to establish on paper the fact of a superiority which is either self-evident and not in need of demonstration, on the one hand, or is not a fact and is not demonstrable, on the other. The really important matter is one about which there need be little dispute—the fact of racial differences. It is the practical question of differences—the fundamental differences of physical appearance, of mental habit and thought, of social customs and religious beliefs. . . .—these are the things which at once create and find expression in what we call race problems and race prejudices, for want of better terms. In just so far as these differences are fixed and permanently associated characteristics of two groups of people will the antipathies and problems between the two be permanent. We speak loosely of the race problems which are the result of European immigration. These are really not race problems at all. They are purely temporary problems, based upon temporary antipathies between different groups of the same race, which invariably disappear in one or two generations, and which form only a temporary barrier to physical assimilation by intermarriage with native stocks.

Probably the closest approach we shall ever make to a satisfactory classification of races, as a basis of antipathy, will be that of grouping men according to color, along certain broad lines, the color being accompanied by various and often widely different, but always fairly persistent differentiating physical and mental characteristics. This would give us substantially the white—not Caucasian, the yellow—not Chinese or Japanese, and the dark—not negro—races. The antipathies between these general groups and between certain of their subdivisions will be found to be essentially fundamental, but they will also be found to present almost endless differences of degrees of actual and potential acuteness. Here elementary psychology also plays its part. One of the subdivisions of the negro race is composed of persons of mixed blood. In many instances these are more white than black, yet the association of ideas has through several generations identified them with the negro—and in this country friction between this class and white people is on some lines even greater than between whites and blacks.

Race conflicts are merely the more pronounced concrete expressions of such friction. They are the visible phenomena of the abstract quality of racial antipathy—the tangible evidence of the existence of racial problems. The form of such expressions of antipathy varies with the nature of the racial contact in each instance. Their different and widely varying aspects are the confusing and often contradictory phenomena of race relations. They are dependent upon diverse conditions, and are no more susceptible of rigid and permanent classification than are the whims and moods of human nature. It is more than a truism to say that a condition precedent to race friction or race conflict is contact between sufficient numbers of two diverse racial groups. There is a definite and positive difference between contact between individuals and contact between masses. The association between two isolated individual members of two races may be wholly different from contact between masses of the same race groups. The factor of numbers embraces indeed the very crux of the problems arising from contact between different races.

A primary cause of race friction is the vague, rather intangible, but wholly real feeling of "pressure" which comes to the white man almost instinctively in the presence of a mass of people of a different race. In a certain important sense all racial problems are distinctly problems of racial distribution. Certainly the definite action of the controlling race, particularly as expressed in laws, is determined by the factor of the numerical difference between its population and that of the inferior group. This fact stands out prominently in the history of our colonial legislation for the control of negro slaves. These laws increased in severity up to a certain point as the slave population increased in numbers. The same condition is disclosed in the history of the *ante-bellum* legislation of the southern, eastern, New England, and middlewestern states for the control of the free negro population. So today, no state in the Union would have separate car laws where the negro constituted only 10 or 15 per cent of its total population. No state would burden itself with the maintenance of two separate school systems with a negro element of less than 10 per cent. Means of local separation might be found, but there would be no expression of law on the subject.

Just as a heavy increase of negro population makes for an increase of friction, direct legislation, the protection of drastic social customs, and a general feeling of unrest or uneasiness on the part of the white population, so a decrease of such population, or a relatively small increase as compared with the whites, makes for less friction, greater racial tolerance, and a lessening of the feeling of necessity for severely discriminating laws or customs. And this, quite aside from the fact of a difference or increase or decrease of actual points of contact, varying with differences of numbers. The statement will scarcely be questioned that the general attitude of the white race, as a whole, toward the negro would become much less uncompromising if we were to discover that through two census periods the race had shown a positive decrease in numbers. Racial antipathy would not decrease, but the conditions which provoke its outward expression would undergo a change for the better. There is a direct relation between the mollified attitude of the people of the Pacific Coast toward the Chinese population and the fact that the Chinese population decreased between 1890 and 1900. . . . There is the same immediate relation between the tolerant attitude of whites toward the natives in the Hawaiian Islands and the feeling that the native is a decadent and dying race. Aside from the influence of the Indian's warlike qualities and of his refusal to submit to slavery, the attitude and disposition of the white race toward him have been influenced by considerations similar to those which today operate in Hawaii. . . .

The character and violence of race friction or conflict will depend upon the immediately provoking cause but will be influenced by a variety of accompanying considerations. Open manifestations of antipathy will be aggravated if each group feels its superiority over the other. They will be fewer and milder when one race accepts the position of inferiority outwardly, or really feels the superiority of the other. In all cases the element of individual or racial self-assertiveness plays an important part. The white man on the Pacific Coast may insist that he does not feel anything like the race prejudice toward the Chinaman that he does toward the Japanese. In truth the antipathy is equal in either case, but the Chinaman accepts the position and imputation of inferiority—no matter what or how he may really feel beneath his passive exterior. On the other hand the Japanese neither accepts the position nor plays the role of an inferior, and when attacked he does not run. Aside from all question of the relative commendable traits of the two races, it is easy to see that the characteristics of one group are much more likely than those of the other to provoke outbreaks of antipathy when brought into contact with the white race. . . .

It is a common remark that the relations between the white and negro races in this country are not "as good," as the expression runs, as they were before the [Civil] War. The fundamental cause of most race friction is in the operation of racial antipathy which leads to the denial by one race of the racial equality of another, coupled with the assertion of equality by the other party to the contract. *Post-bellum* racial difficulties are largely the manifestation of friction growing out of the novel claim to equality made by the negro after emancipation, either by specific declaration and assertion, or by conduct which was equivalent to an open claim, with the refusal of the white man to recognize the claim. The commonest mistake of race-problem discussions is that of treating such problems as a heritage from slavery. Slavery was responsible only in so far as it was responsible for bringing the races into contact. The institution, *per se,* was not only not the cause of the problem, but, on the other hand, it actually furnished a basis of contact which as long as it existed minimized the problems which result from racial contact upon a plane of theoretical equality. We may obtain a conception of an American race problem without the background of antecedent slavery relations, if we can imagine the situation which would be created by the precipitation upon the population of the Pacific Coast of a million Japanese. The late Professor Shaler, of Harvard, summed up with absolute accuracy the function of slavery in making possible relations of mutual amity between the white and negro races in this country when he declared that, "the one condition in which very diverse races may be brought into close social relations without much danger of hatred, destructive of social order, is when an inferior race is enslaved by a superior." . . . He declared his utter detestation of the institution, but said it should be recognized that "it was effective in the prevention of race hatreds." . . .

But Professor Shaler recognized the innate potential force of antipathy of race and he observed that "it remains to be seen whether the race hatred, which was essentially lost during the period of slavery, will return in the condition of freedom." Twenty-one years have elapsed since Professor Shaler wrote, and it is in the light of these two decades of additional experience that we are today attempting to answer his query. . . .

In the first place, I lay down as a fundamental law of racial contact the proposition that the terms and conditions of racial association will be dictated by the stronger of the two parties to such association, actuated by motives of self-interest, or by instincts of self-preservation. In the second place, the resulting relations will be least conducive to friction when the terms insisted upon by the stronger race are accepted without protest by the weaker. The converse of this follows as a corollary, that the relations which are most conducive to friction are those under which the conditions laid down by the stronger party are not accepted by the weaker. The friction which racial contact engenders under such conditions will be in proportion to the degree of the insistence of one party upon its terms of association, and of the resistance to such conditions offered by the other.

The absence of *ante-bellum* racial friction was due to the general acceptance by the negro of the status assigned him by the white race. The farther removed the two races are from this basis of association . . . the greater the probability that friction will follow contact between them. The whole matter resolves itself into very simple terms. The simpler the relations between diverse races, the less friction there will be; the more complex the relations, the greater the friction. The simplest relations possible are those in which the relative status of superior and inferior is mutually accepted as the historical, essential, and matter-of-fact basis of relationship between the two. The most complex relation possible between any two racial groups is that of a theoretical equality which one race denies and the other insists upon. The accepted relation of superior and inferior may exist not only without bitterness on one side, or harsh feelings upon the other, but it may be characterized by a sentiment and affection wholly impossible between the same groups under conditions demanding a recognition of so-called equality. We should try to gain a clear idea of the importance of this mutual recognition of a different racial status in minimizing racial friction, and of the significance of the converse condition in increasing it.

The northern white man often remarks upon the inconsistent position of the southern white man. The former objects more than the latter to personal contact and association with the negro, but theoretically, he is willing to grant to the negro the full exercise of all the legal rights and privileges which he himself enjoys. The southern white man, on the other hand, does not object to personal association with the negro—provided it be upon terms which contain no suggestion of equality of personal status—but he is not willing to grant the privileges which his northern brother concedes to the race in the mass. The truth is that the difference between their respective attitudes is largely a matter of fiction. It is more apparent than real. The attitude of the northern man toward the matter of personal association is really the natural attitude of the white man. It is the unconscious expression or feeling of instinctive racial antipathy in its elementary form. The attitude of the southern man toward the same association is in reality the wholly artificial product of the relations made possible by slavery. The northern man prides himself on not "looking down on the negro," as the expression goes. He regards him unconsciously as theoretically, potentially, his racial equal. His unconscious mental attitude does not immediately upon personal contact establish between himself and the negro the relation of superior and inferior. He is conscious only of strangeness, difference. But in the presence of this difference his mind reacts normally, and a sufficient degree of latent antipathy is aroused to create a natural barrier, which he merely "feels" and does not attempt to explain. On the other hand, through the influence of generations of association under the purely artificial relations of slavery, the mind of the southern white man instinctively responds to accustomed contact upon inherited lines with the unconscious concept of an inequality of racial status which neutralizes or prevents the operation of racial antipathy. In other words, . . . the long-continued association has destroyed the normal operation of elementary racial antipathy. In its primary form, it is simply not provoked by an association to which it has long become accustomed. It may be asked at once, if such association has been sufficient thus to impair what is claimed to be an instinctive mental impulse, and not only to do this, but to establish in lieu of such a feeling, relations and sentiments of genuine and unquestioned affection, why it is not able to destroy all racial antipathy and thereby in time enable the races to live together in absolute concord? Where is the ground for even the possibility of increased racial friction? The answer is not difficult. The potential results of long-continued racial contact and association may be fully granted, for the sake of discussion. But the question is the primary one of accomplishing the association. Our original proposition is that racial harmony is greater under an association determined by one party and accepted by the other. This was precisely what made for such relations under slavery. But slavery is dead, and with the passing of the generation of whose life it was an accepted part, both black and white, the relations which it slowly evolved are passing also. A new basis of contact is presented—that of unconditional equality. It is a basis which the white race is not willing to concede in practice, whatever the white man may do in theory, and hence we have the essential elements of racial friction—a demand for and a denial of racial equality.

Whether or not race friction in the United States is increasing and inevitable depends upon the attitude of the two parties to the racial contact. Does the American negro demand racial equality, and does the American white man deny it? The latter branch of the question we shall attempt to answer first. Racial antipathy . . . is practically universal on the part of the white race toward the negro, and is beyond question stronger in the so-called Anglo-Saxon stocks than in any other. If it is less apparent in one place than in another, the difference is a mere incident to differences of local condition. It is protean in its manifestations—and subject to such a variety of provoking causes as to defy classification. It is exhibited here in the individual, and there in the mass, and elsewhere in both. One man may draw the line against association in a public conveyance, another at the relations of domestic service. One may draw it in the public dining-room of a hotel, another at his private table. . . . Here and there we find a man who realizes no feeling at such contact, and he imagines himself to be "free from race prejudice." But even for him there exists the point of racial recoil, though it may be reached only at the altar or the grave. It is, after all, merely a difference of degree. Racial antipathy is a present, latent force in us all. As to this we need not deceive ourselves.

At no time in the history of the English-speaking people, and at no place, of which we have any record, where large numbers of them have been brought into contact with an approximately equal number of negroes, have the former granted to the latter absolute equality, either political, social, or economic. With the exception of five New England states, with a total negro population of only 16,084 in 1860, every state in the Union discriminated against the negro politically before the Civil War. The white people continued to do so—North as well as South—as long as they retained control of the suffrage regulations of their states. The determination to do so renders one whole section of the country practically a political unit to this day. In South Africa we see the same determination of the white man to rule, regardless of the numerical superiority of the black. . . . The proposition is too elementary for discussion, that the white man when confronted with a sufficient number of negroes to create in his mind a sense of political unrest or danger, either alters his form of government in order to be rid of the incubus, or destroys the political strength of the negro by force, by evasion, or by direct action.

If we survey the field of economic contact we find but one considerable area in which the white man permits the negro to share his occupancy practically upon equal terms. That field is the southern part of the United States. The unusual conditions there are the direct and immediate product of relations established, or made possible by slavery, coupled with the maintenance of a rigid color line, which minimizes, if it does not prevent racial friction. This condition, like the other purely artificial products of slavery favorable to amicable race relations, is changing, and will disappear with the increased tendency toward general uniformity of labor conditions and demands throughout the country. Such measure of freedom of economic opportunity as the negro has is not due to any superior virtue on the part of southern people, any more than is the larger political tolerance of the north due to any peculiar virtue of that section. Each situation is a mere incident of general racial conditions. Outside the South, whether in New York, Philadelphia, Chicago, the Middle West, or New England, the absence of economic racial friction is due to the economic segregation of the negro. The race outside the South is in the main confined to humbler occupations, where the absence of white competition makes for racial peace. I am speaking of the many, not of the exceptional few who here and there are not discriminated against. What is true of the North is true of South Africa. Economically, every country apparently is either a "white man's country" or a "black man's country." It does not exist half one and half the other—always excepting the South. . . .

But it is in the sphere of relations which the world calls social that the white man's attitude toward the negro becomes most uncompromising—at least the attitude of the English-speaking white man. This too is universal. This social prejudice is no respecter of geographical lines. Its intensity varies of course with local influences—primarily with differences of numerical distribution. But that is a mere superficial consideration. This form of "race prejudice" . . . is probably more fundamental and far reaching than any other.

This fact is clearly recognized by Professor Kelly Miller, of Howard University, who says:

> Where two races of widely different corporal peculiarities and cultivated qualities are brought into contact, serious frictional problems inevitably arise. . . . . The American negro may speak the same language, conform to the same institutions, and adopt the same mode of religious worship as the rest of his fellow men, but it avails him nothing in the scale of social eligibility, which is the one determinative test of all true equality. . . . . Without social equality, which the Teuton is sworn to withhold from the darker races, no other form of equality is possible.[1]

. . . In spite of all our protestations of democracy, the people of this country are not superior in their racial charity to the people of other parts of the world. I question if we are even as liberal in that regard as the average of Caucasian mankind. I sometimes feel that the very democracy among American white men of which we boast so much develops a concomitant intolerance toward men of another race or color. Without other fixed or established distinctions in our social order, we seem instinctively to take refuge in that of color, as an enduring line of separation between ourselves and another class. Now and then, as the southern part of our country comes to be more dispassionately studied, an occasional observer finds himself puzzled by the conclusion that among its white population the South, taken as a whole, is the most democratic part of America. In the presence of the negro, and by contrast and comparison, all white men are equal. A horizontal racial line is drawn between the two sections of the population. All on one side of the line are conceded certain privileges and a certain status, based not upon merit but solely upon the accident of color. To the whole group on the other side of the line a certain status is assigned solely because of identity with another racial class. In each case what should be controlling differences within each group, along certain fairly tangible lines, are wholly ignored. In steadily increasing degree, it seems to me, certain privileges and a certain place in the larger life of the country are coming to be regarded as the peculiar and particular asset of Caucasian racial affiliation.

We have seen the fulfiling of DeTocqueville's prophecy that emancipation would be but the beginning of America's racial problems. . . . We have no excuse if we wilfully blind ourselves to the stubbornest facts in human experience, and persist in regarding racial antipathy, or "race prejudice," as a mere passing relic of slavery, peculiar to one part of the country. We can make no progress even in the comprehension of our problem if we circumscribe our vision by any such narrow view. It was Jefferson's opinion that the emancipation of the American negroes was one of the inevitable events of the future. It was also his conviction that the two races could never live together as equals on American soil. His solution was colonization, but the time for that had probably passed when he wrote. . . .

[1] *Southern Workman,* November, 1900, pp. 601, 602.

To me the problems of racial contact, of which friction is but one, seem as inevitable as apparently they did to De Tocqueville and Jefferson and Lincoln. But I have no solution, because of my conviction that in a larger, final sense there is no solution of such problems, except the separation of the races or the absorption of one by the other. And in no proper conception is either of these a "solution." We do not solve a problem in geometry by wiping from the blackboard the symbols which are the visible expression of its terms. The question which the American people must first be prepared to answer, if they demand a solution of their problem, is whether, within a period which may practically be considered, they will grant to another race, darker, physically different, and permanently distinguished from themselves, all and singular the rights, titles, and privileges which they themselves enjoy, with full and complete measure of equality in all things, absolutely as well as theoretically. If they can do this, they will reverse the whole history of their own people, and until they do it, not only will there be race friction here, but it will increase as the weaker race increases its demands for the equality which it is denied.

Thus we return to the first branch of our inquiry—the attitude of the negro as one of the determining factors in the increase or decrease of race friction. It is more difficult to answer for him than for the white man. The latter has a history in the matter of his relations with other races, perfectly well defined to anyone who will study it candidly. He has either ruled or ruined, to express it in a few words, and pretty often he has done both. It has been frequently said that the negro is the only one of the inferior, or weaker, or backward, or undeveloped races (the terms are largely interchangeable and not at all important), which has ever looked the white man in the face and lived. But for all the significance the statement holds, we have only to go to Aesop's fable of the tree which would, and the tree which would not bend before the storm. I know of no race in all history which possesses in equal degree the marvelous power of adaptability to conditions which the negro has exhibited through many centuries and in many places. His undeveloped mental state has made it possible for him to accept conditions, and to increase and be content under them, which a more highly organized and sensitive race would have thrown off, or destroyed itself in the effort to do so. This ability to accept the status of slavery and to win the affection and regard of the master race, and gradually but steadily to bring about an amelioration of the conditions of the slave status made possible the anomalous and really not yet understood race relations of the *ante-bellum* South. The plain English of the situation was that the negro did not chafe or fret and harass himself to death, where the Indian would have done so, or massacred the white man as an alternative. In many respects the negro is a model prisoner—the best in this country. He accepts the situation, generally speaking; bears no malice; cherishes no ill will or resentment, and is cheerful under conditions to which the white man refuses to reconcile himself.

This adaptability of the negro has an immediate bearing on the question before us. It explains why the negro masses in the southern states are content with their situation, or at least not disturbing themselves sufficiently over it to attempt to upset the existing order. In the main, the millions in the South live at peace with their white neighbors. The masses, just one generation out of slavery and thousands of them still largely controlled by its influences, accept the superiority of the white race, as a race, whatever may be their private opinion of some of its members. And, furthermore, they accept this relation of superior and inferior, as a mere matter of course—as part of their lives—as something neither to be questioned, wondered at, or worried over. Despite apparent impressions to the contrary, the average southern white man gives no more thought to the matter than does the negro. As I tried to make clear at the outset, the status of superior and inferior is simply an inherited part of his instinctive mental equipment—a concept which he does not have to reason out. The respective attitudes are complementary, and under the mutual acceptance and understanding there still exist unnumbered thousands of instances of kindly and affectionate relations—relations of which the outside world knows nothing and understands nothing. . . . In the mass, the southern negro has not bothered himself about the ballot for more than twenty years, not since his so-called political leaders let him alone; he is not disturbed over the matter of separate schools and cars, and he neither knows nor cares anything about "social equality."

I believe there may develop in process of time and evolution a group of contented people . . . satisfied in the enjoyment of life, liberty, and the pursuit of happiness, and afforded the full protection of the law. I believe it is possible for each of the various groups of the two races which find themselves in natural juxtaposition to arrive at some basis of common occupancy of their respective territories which shall be mutually satisfactory, even if not wholly free from friction. I express a belief that this is possible, but to its accomplishment there is one absolute condition precedent; they must be let alone and they must be given time. It must be realized and accepted, whether we like it or not, that there is no cut-and-dried solution of such problems, and that they cannot be solved by resolutions or laws. The process must be gradual and it must be normal, which means that the final basis of adjustment must be worked out by the immediate parties in interest. It may be one thing in one place and another thing in another place, just as the problem itself differs with differences of local conditions and environment. We must realize that San Francisco is not Boston, that New Orleans is not New York. Thus much for the possibilities as to rank and file.

But what of the other class? The "masses" is at best an unsatisfactory and indefinite term. It is very far from embracing even the southern negro, and we need not forget that seven years ago there were 900,000 members of the race living outside of the South. What of the class, mainly urban and large in number, who have lost the typical habit and attitude of the negro of the mass, and who, more and more, are becoming restless, and chafing under existing conditions? There is an intimate and very natural relation between the social and intellectual advance of the so-called negro and the matter of friction along social lines. It is in fact only as we touch the higher groups that we can appreciate the potential results of contact upon a different plane from that common to the masses in the South. There is a large and steadily increasing group of men, more or less related to the negro by blood and wholly identified with him by American social usage, who refuse to accept quietly the white man's attitude toward the race. I appreciate the mistake of laying too great stress upon the utterances of any one man or group of men, but the mistakes in this case lies [sic] the other way. The American white man knows little or nothing about the thought and opinion of the colored men and women who today largely mold and direct negro public opinion in this country. Even the white man who considers himself a student of "the race question" rarely exhibits anything more than profound ignorance of the negro's side of the problem. He does not know what the other man is thinking and saying on the subject. This composite type which we poetically call "black," but which in reality is every shade from black to white, is slowly developing a consciousness of its own racial solidarity. It is finding its own distinctive voice, and through its own books and papers and magazines, and through its own social organizations, is at once giving utterance to its discontent and making known its demands.

And with this dawning consciousness of race there is likewise coming an appreciation of the limitations and restrictions which hem in its unfolding and development. One of the best indices to the possibilities of increased racial friction is the negro's own recognition of the universaility of the white man's racial antipathy toward him. This is the one clear note above the storm of protest against the things that are, that in his highest aspirations everywhere the white man's "prejudice" blocks the colored man's path. And the white man may with possible profit pause long enough to ask the deeper significance of the negro's finding of himself. May it not be only part of a general awakening of the darker races of the earth? . . . [E]ven before the Japanese-Russian conflict, "Ethiopianism" and the cry of "Africa for the Africans" had begun to disturb the English in South Africa. . . . There can be no doubt in the mind of any man who carefully reads American negro journals that their rejoicing over the Japanese victory sounded a very different note from that of the White American. It was far from being a mere expression of sympathy with a people fighting for national existence against a power which had made itself odious to the civilized world by its treatment of its subjects. It was, instead a quite clear cry of exultation over the defeat of a white race by a dark one. The white man is no wiser than the ostrich if he refuses to see the truth that in the possibilities of race friction the negro's increasing consciousness of race is to play a part scarcely less important than the white man's racial antipathies. . . .

In its final analysis the sum and substance of the ultimate demand of those Americans of African descent whose mental attainments and social equipment identify them much more closely with the Anglo-Saxon than with the negro masses, is definitely and clearly stated in the words of Dr. Dubois:

There is left the last alternative—the raising of the negro in America to full rights and citizenship. And I mean by this, no half-way measures; I mean full and fair equity. That is, the chance to obtain work, regardless of color, to aspire to position and preferment on the basis of desert alone, to have the right to use public conveniences, to enter public places of amusement on the same terms as other people, and to be received socially by such persons as might wish to receive them. These are not extravagant demands, and yet their granting means the abolition of the color line. The question is; Can American negroes hope to attain this result?[2]

With equal clearness and precision, and with full comprehension of its larger meaning and significance and ultimate possibilities, the American white man answers the question in the language of another eminent American sociologist, Professor Edward A. Ross, in contrasting the attitudes of Anglo-Saxons and Latins toward other races on this continent, says:

The superiority of a race cannot be preserved without pride of blood and an uncompromising attitude toward the lower races. . . . Whatever may be thought of the (latter) policy, the net result is that North America from the Behring Sea to the Rio Grande is dedicated to the highest type of civilization; while for centuries the rest of our hemisphere will drag the ball and chain of hybridism.[3]

And thus the issue is joined. And thus also perhaps we find an answer to our own question, whether racial friction in this country is increasing and inevitable.

[2] *The East and the West,* January, 1904, p. 16.
[3] *The Foundation of Sociology* (1905), p. 379.

# 4

# A Reply to Stone

*W. E. B. DUBOIS*

[*American Journal of Sociology* editorial note:] Dr. DuBois was unable to attend the meeting and sent the following paper; but it did not reach Madison in time to be read at the meeting devoted to the discussion of Mr. Stone's paper. It is, however, with the consent of Mr. Stone, and because Dr. DuBois presents the views of a distinguished Negro educator, inserted at this place.

I think we may all of us agree in the main with Mr. Stone's very careful presentation of the real significance of racial distinctions today, and also his explanation of the differing attitude of white men toward Negroes North and South and the role of slavery in making race contact practicable. There remain, then, three pressing questions: First, Is the old status of acknowledged superiority and inferiority between the white and black races in America longer possible? Secondly, Are the race differences in this case irreconcilable? And thirdly, Is racial separation practicable?

Taking up the first question as to the possibility of a continuance of the old status of acknowledged superiority and inferiority between white and black races, it is certain that physical slavery was a failure, not because it mistook altogether the relative endowment of most of the men who were enslavers and most of those who were the enslaved, but because it denied growth or exception on the part of the enslaved and kept up that denial by physical force.

Emancipation was simply the abolition of the grosser forms of that physical force. The Negro freedman, just as the freedman of Rome or Germany, stepped out of a world of physical restraint into a spiritual world. In this thought-world there is still slavery of ideas and customs; and given men as they are, this is probably fortunate. Yet we all hope for gradual emancipation in thought and custom, and it is peculiarly dangerous for a people of today, who expect to keep up with modern civilization, to base their hope of peace and prosperity on the ignorance of their fellows or the lack of aspiration among working-men—on the survival of such virtues for instance as we expect and cultivate in dogs but not in men. Moreover, even if a people like those in the South do hope that the Negro is not going to aspire and not going to demand equal rights and fair treatment, then they are bound to disappointment. There is today in the South growing protest from the mass of negroes, protest to which whites are yielding today and must yield. These matters are not yet, to be sure, the greater matters of voting and freedom of travel, but they are the more pressing matters of wages and personal treatment, of housing and property-holding. Protest is not confined to a few leaders, it is not confined to the North; it is not confined to mulattoes. Daily and yearly it is growing. And it is that growing which makes the Negro problem today; without it there would be no race problem.

Mr. Stone refers to the meetings in Boston, the Nell meeting and the last Protest, and notes their similarity. He might, however, have noted very distinct differences. The Nell meeting represented four million people, over nine-tenths of whom were physically owned by the whites, and the rest of whom were largely ignorant and without property; while the meeting this year represented ten millions of people whose property runs into the hundreds of millions, most of whom can read and write and some of whom are well educated (indeed, the leader in the last meeting was a *magna cum laude* bachelor of Harvard, and member of the Phi Beta Kappa). In the Nell meeting the leading moving force was after all the white friends of the Negro; in this meeting the Negro was leading himself and the whites assisted. The attitude of men toward Nell was that of tolerant contempt or amusement or irritation; the attitude toward his descendants is that of consternation and perplexity and more or less veiled dislike. Such a change in fifty years is not only significant. It is tremendous, and only those unacquainted with the deeds of time can discount it.

Have we then today the old case of the irresistible force and the immovable body? If we assume the white South as planted immovably on the proposition that most human beings are to be kept in absolute and unchangeable serfdom and inferiority to the Teutonic world; and if we assume that not only the Negroes of America but those of Africa and the West Indies—not only Negroes, but Indians, Malays, Chinese, and Japanese, not to mention the Mediterranean lands—are determined to contest this absurd stand to the death, then the world has got some brisk days ahead, and race friction will inevitably grow not only in the United States but the world over. But if, as seems more reasonable, we have in the South the beginning of a set of honest reasonable people, beset with hard social questions, but determined to think them through with reason and not with rope, and if we have a set of aspiring and rising serfs determined to be free, but willing to be patient, then race friction need not grow and meantime the nation can calmly scrutinize and answer the second of our queries:

How great is this incompatibility and repugnancy of qualities between white and black Americans? And here we find ourselves facing a field of science rather than opinion. As I have often said before, it is a matter of serious disgrace to American science that with the tremendous opportunity that it has had before it for the study of race differences and race development, race intermingling and contact among the most diverse of human kinds right here at its doors, almost nothing has been done.

When we at Atlanta University say that we are the only institution in the United States that is making any serious study of the race problems in the United States, we make no great boast because it is not that we are doing so much, but rather that the rest of the nation is doing nothing, and that we can get from the rest of the nation very little encouragement, co-operation, or help in this work. It has been my dream for many years that we could in the United States begin at a small Negro college a movement for the scientific study of race differences and likenesses which should in time revolutionize the knowledge of the world. If for instance the dictum of Professor Boaz of Columbia University be true, namely, "that an unbiased estimate of the anthropological evidence so far brought forward does not permit us to countenance the belief in a racial inferiority, which would unfit an individual of the Negro race to take his part in modern civilization. We do not know of any demand made on the human body or mind in modern life that anatomical or ethnological evidence would prove to be beyond the powers of the Negro"—if this dictum be true (and there is certainly strong scientific backing for it), then how different an aspect this would put upon race differences in the United States than would be the case if it were proven that really black men and white men were of such differing powers and possibilities that they could not be treated as belonging to the same great branch of humanity. As I have said, this is primarily a scientific question, a matter of scientific measurement and observation; and yet the data upon which the mass of men, and even intelligent men, are basing their conclusions today, the basis which they are putting back of their treatment of the Negro, is a most ludicrous and harmful conglomeration of myth, falsehood, and desire. It would certainly be a most commendable thing if this and other learned societies would put themselves on record as favoring a most thorough and unbiased scientific study of the race problem in America. Meantime, in the absence of such scientific basis for our conclusions, there are certain antecedent probabilities in the case which we have a right to take into account: we remember for instance that not many generations ago the very same arguments that are brought to prove the impossibility of white men and Negroes living together, except as inferior and superior, were also brought to prove that white men of differing rank and birth could not possibly exist in the same physical environment without similar subordination. And in still nearer time it was proved to the absolute satisfaction of certain economic philosophers, that the conflict between capitalists and laborers was an inevitable conflict which must lead to poverty and social murder of the masses. Today what seems to many of us an exactly similar fight is being made on the subject of race. Not only is it assumed without proof that here, as in the matter of birth and work, substantial equality of treatment is impossible, but it is also assumed that the physical conditions of life and social contact are today practically what they were in former ages. But this is not so today; a physical living together of differing groups and kinds of individuals is possible today to a degree which was unthinkable one, two, and three centuries ago. Indeed when the bars between aristocrat and peasant were broken down, it did not mean that the aristocrats disappeared or that the peasants all became dukes; it simply meant that men lived and mingled together and rose and fell freely according to their individual desert, without artificial prop or bars. A spiritual world took the place of the strait walls and ghettos of their former physical environment. So in the race problem in America, we may ask with regard to this question of incompatibility of whites and blacks: Just what degree of social compatibility is absolutely essential to group contact today? And in answering this question we must realize that not only does the modern world spell increased and increasing contact of groups and nations and races, but that indeed race or group segregation is impossible.

This brings us to our third question, Is race separation practicable? People say very often with regard to the Negro that the Pilgrims of England found a place for liberty when they could not get it at home; why then does not the Negro do the same of his own motion and will? And then they explain it by a shrug and a reminder that one set of people were English and the others are Negroes. Flattering as this is to the sayers, yet this does not explain all. Today we have in the world growing race contact. The world is shrinking together; it is finding itself neighbor to itself in strange, almost magic degree. No one has done more for increasing this contact of the nations than we here in America. We not only brought Negroes here in defiance of law, right, and religion, but we have pounded masterfully, almost impudently, at the gates of China and Japan. Europe has insisted upon the opening of Africa. Now when the world suddenly appears open, with chance of access for all to all parts, we find ourselves standing amazed before a curious exemplification of the old adage, "What's sauce for the goose is sauce for the gander"! If the world can enter Asia, why cannot Asiatics enter the world? We could of course in case of a helpless nation like China chivalrously refuse to answer the question and bar out Chinese. But when it comes to a question of Japan and Japanese guns, the dilemma before the modern world is somewhat startling. Just so with the Philippines. Here is a group of colored folks half a world away, yet the United States is not content until it goes, annexes them, and rules them according to its own ideas. Now if these things are so, what chance is there for a new nation to establish itself, especially if it be a colored nation, on any spot in the world worth having? And is it going to be possible in the future for races to remain segregated or to escape contact or domination simply by retiring to themselves? Certainly it is not. Race segregation in the future is going to be impossible primarily because these races are needed more and more in the world's economy. Mr. Stone has often expressed the cheerful hope that the Negro would be supplanted by the white man as worker in the South. But the thing does not happen. On the contrary there are today more Negroes working steadily and efficiently than ever before in the world's history. The world is beginning to work for the world. This work is necessary. A new standard of national efficiency is coming. And that efficiency is marked by the way in which a great modern advanced nation can be neighborly to the rest of the world. It is the counterpart to the sort of rivalry for the world-empire that went on when France and England made a hundred years' struggle for empire in America and India. And while we in America may sneer at neighbors, who are neither as rich or impudent or lucky as we, we can also, if we will, remark that the English again are learning certain things in advance of the rest of the world. They are learning how to get on in peace and amity with colored races; how to treat them as men and gain their friendship and gain the results of their work and skill and brain. And if the United States expects to take her place among the new nations beside England and France, the nations which first are going to solve this problem of race contact, then certainly she has got right here in her own land to find out how to live in peace and prosperity with her own black citizens. If she does that, she will gain an advantage over the rest of the world in the development of the earth which will be simply inestimable in the new commerce and in the new humanity. If she does not, she will always have in her contact with the rest of the world not only the absolute dislike and distrust of the darker two thirds, but a tremendous moral handicap such as she met when she asked Russia to stop her atrocities and it was answered with perfect truth that they did not compare with the barbarities committed right here in the land of the free. We may therefore justly conclude, first, that the Negro is not going to submit any longer than he must to the present serfdom and the disgraceful and humiliating discrimination; secondly, that while we do not know as much of race differences as we may know if we study this problem as we ought, we certainly do know that the chances are that most men in this world can be civilized, and that the world of races just as the world of individuals does not consist of a few aristocrats and chosen people and a mass of dark serfs and slaves. And that thirdly, any dream of separating the races in America or of separating the races of the world is at present not only impracticable but is against the whole trend of the age, and that what we ought to do in America is to seek to bind the races together rather than to accentuate differences. No part of the world could play a greater role in the future moral development of the world than the South, if it would. And while today there are few signs that the South realizes this, yet may we not hope that this will be the case before another generation passes? Finally, rhetoric like that quoted by Mr. Stone is not in itself of particular importance, except when it encourages those Philistines who really believe that Anglo-Saxons owe their pre-eminence in some lines to lynching, lying, and slavery, and the studied insult of their helpless neighbors.

God save us from such social philosophy!

5

# Racial Assimilation in Secondary Groups with Particular Reference to the Negro

*ROBERT E. PARK*

## I

The race problem has sometimes been described as a problem in assimilation. It is not always clear, however, what assimilation means. Historically the word has had two distinct significations. According to earlier usage it meant "to compare" or "to make like." According to later usage it signifies "to take up and incorporate."

There is a process that goes on in society by which individuals spontaneously acquire one another's language, characteristic attitudes, habits, and modes of behavior. There is also a process by which individuals and groups of individuals are taken over and incorporated into larger groups. Both processes have been concerned in the formation of modern nationalities. The modern Italian, Frenchman, and German is a composite of the broken fragments of several different racial groups. Interbreeding has broken up the ancient stocks, and interaction

---

[1] The distinction between primary and secondary groups used in this paper is that made by Charles H. Cooley.

Abridged from *American Journal of Sociology 19* (1914): 606–623. Used by permission of The University of Chicago Press. © 1914 by The University of Chicago. All rights reserved.

and imitation have created new national types which exhibit definite uniformities in language, manners, and formal behavior.

It has sometimes been assumed that the creation of a national type is the specific function of assimilation and that national solidarity is based upon national homogeneity and "like-mindedness." The extent and importance of the kind of homogeneity that individuals of the same nationality exhibit have been greatly exaggerated. Neither interbreeding nor interaction has created, in what the French term "nationals," a more than superficial likeness or like-mindedness. Racial differences have, to be sure, disappeared or been obscured, but individual differences remain. Individual differences, again, have been intensified by education, personal competition, and the division of labor, until individual members of cosmopolitan groups probably represent greater variations in disposition, temperament, and mental capacity than those which distinguished the more homogenous races and peoples of an earlier civilization.[2]

What then, precisely, is the nature of the homogeneity which characterizes cosmopolitan groups?

The growth of modern states exhibits the progressive merging of smaller, mutually exclusive, into larger and more inclusive social groups. This result has been achieved in various ways, but it has usually been followed, or accompanied, by a more or less complete adoption, by the members of the smaller groups, of the language, technique, and mores of the larger and more inclusive ones. The immigrant readily takes over the language, manners, the social ritual, and outward forms of his adopted country. In America it has become proverbial that a Pole, Lithuanian, or Norwegian cannot be distinguished, in the second generation, from an American born of native parents.

There is no reason to assume that this assimilation of alien groups to native standards has modified to any great extent fundamental racial characteristics. It has, however, erased the external signs which formerly distinguished the members of one race from those of another.

On the other hand, the breaking-up of the isolation of smaller groups has had the effect of emancipating the individual man, giving him room and freedom for the expansion and development of his individual aptitudes.

What one actually finds in cosmopolitan groups, then, is a superficial uniformity, a homogeneity in manners and fashion associated with relatively profound differences in individual opinions, sentiments, and beliefs. This is just the reverse of what one meets among primitive peoples, where diversity in external forms, as between different groups, is accompanied with a monotonous sameness in the mental attitudes of individuals. . . .

What, then, is the rôle of homogeneity and like-mindedness, such as we find them to be, in cosmopolitan states?

So far as it makes each individual look like every other—no matter how dif-

[2] F. Boas, *Journal of American Folk-Lore*, quoted by W. I. Thomas, in *Source Book for Social Origins*, p. 155.

ferent under the skin—homogeneity mobilizes the individual man. It removes the social taboo, permits the individual to move into strange groups, and thus facilitates new and adventurous contacts. In obliterating the external signs, which in secondary groups seem to be the sole basis of caste and class distinctions, it realizes, for the individual, the principle of *laissez-faire, laissez-aller.* Its ultimate economic effect is to substitute personal for racial competition, and to give free play to forces that tend to relegate every individual, irrespective of race or status, to the position he or she is best fitted to fill.

As a matter of fact, the ease and rapidity with which aliens, under existing conditions in the United States, have been able to assimilate themselves to the customs and manners of American life have enabled this country to swallow and digest every sort of normal human difference, except the purely external ones, like the color of the skin.

It is probably true, also, that like-mindedness of the kind that expresses itself in national types, contributes, indirectly, by facilitating the intermingling of the different elements of the population, to the national solidarity. This is due to the fact solidarity of modern states depends less on the homogeneity of population than, as James Bryce has suggested, upon the thoroughgoing mixture of heterogeneous elements. Like-mindedness, so far as that term signifies a standard grade of intelligence, contributes little or nothing to national solidarity. Likeness is, after all, a purely formal concept which of itself cannot hold anything together.

In the last analysis social solidarity is based on sentiment and habit. It is the sentiment of loyalty and the habit of what Sumner calls "concurrent action," that gives substance and insures unity to the state, as to every other type of social group. This sentiment of loyalty has its basis in a *modus vivendi,* a working relation and mutual understanding, of the members of the group. Social institutions are not founded in similarities any more than they are founded in differences, but in relations, and in the mutual interdependence of parts. When these relations have the sanction of custom and are fixed in individual habit, so that the activities of the group are running smoothly, personal attitudes and sentiments, which are the only forms in which individual minds collide and clash with one another, easily accommodate themselves to the existing situation. . . .

It is this practical working arrangement, into which individuals with widely different mental capacities enter as co-ordinate parts, that gives the corporate character to social groups and insures their solidarity.

It is the process of assimilation by which groups of individuals, originally indifferent or perhaps hostile, achieve this corporate character, rather than the process by which they acquire a formal like-mindedness, with which this paper is mainly concerned.

The difficulty with the conception of assimilation which one ordinarily meets in discussions of the race problem, is that it is based on observations confined to individualistic groups where the characteristic relations are indirect and secondary. It takes no account of the kind of assimilation that takes place in primary groups where relations are direct and personal—in the tribe, for example, and in the family.

Thus Charles Francis Adams, referring to the race problem in an address at Richmond, Va., in November, 1908, said:

> The American system, as we know, was founded on the assumed basis of a common humanity, that is, absence of absolutely fundamental racial characteristics was accepted as an established truth. Those of all races were welcomed to our shores. They came, aliens; they and their descendants would become citizens first, natives afterward. It was a process first of assimilation and then of absorption. On this all depended. There could be no permanent divisional lines. That theory is now plainly broken down. We are confronted by the obvious fact, as undeniable as it is hard, that the African will only partially assimilate and that he cannot be absorbed. He remains an alien element in the body politic. A foreign substance, he can neither be assimilated nor thrown out.

More recently an editorial in the *Outlook,* discussing the Japanese situation in California, made this statement:

> The hundred millions of people now inhabiting the United States must be a united people, not merely a collection of groups of different peoples, different in racial cultures and ideals, agreeing to live together in peace and amity. These hundred millions must have common ideals, common aims, a common custom, a common culture, a common language, and common characteristics if the nation is to endure.

All this is quite true and interesting, but it does not clearly recognize the fact that the chief obstacle to the assimilation of the Negro and Oriental are not mental but physical traits. It is not because the Negro and the Japanese are so differently constituted that they do not assimilate. If they were given an opportunity the Japanese are quite as capable as the Italians, the Armenians, or the Slavs of acquiring our culture, and sharing our national ideals. The trouble is not with the Japanese mind but with the Japanese skin. The Jap is not the right color.

The fact that the Japanese bears in his features a distinctive racial hallmark, that he wears, so to speak, a racial uniform, classifies him. He cannot become a mere individual, indistinguishable in the cosmopolitan mass of the population, as is true, for example, of the Irish and, to a lesser extent, of some of the other immigrant races. The Japanese, like the Negro, is comdemend to remain among us an abstraction, a symbol, and a symbol not merely of his own race, but of the Orient and of that vague, ill-defined menace we sometimes refer to as the "yellow peril." This not only determines, to a very large extent, the attitude of the white world toward the yellow man, but it determines the attitude of the yellow man to the white. It puts between the races the invisible but very real gulf of self-consciousness.

There is another consideration. Peoples we know intimately we respect and esteem. In our casual contact with aliens, however, it is the offensive rather than the pleasing traits that impress us. These impressions accumulate and reinforce natural prejudices. Where races are distinguished by certain external marks these furnish a permanent physical substratum upon which and around which the irritations and animosities, incidental to all human intercourse, tend to accumulate and so gain strength and volume.

## II

 . . . At the outset it may be said, then, that assimilation rarely becomes a problem except in secondary groups. Admission to the primary group, that is to say, the group in which relationships are direct and personal, as, for example, in the family and in the tribe, makes assimilation comparatively easy and almost inevitable.

The most striking illustration of this is the fact of domestic slavery. Slavery has been, historically, the usual method by which peoples have been incorporated into alien groups. When a member of an alien race is adopted into the family as a servant, or as a slave, and particularly when that status is made hereditary, as it was in the case of the Negro after his importation to America, assimilation followed rapidly and as a matter of course.

It is difficult to conceive two races farther removed from each other in temperament and tradition than the Anglo-Saxon and the Negro, and yet the Negro in the southern states, particularly where he was adopted into the household as a family servant, learned in a comparatively short time the manners and customs of his master's family. He very soon possessed himself of so much of the language, religion, and the technique of the civilization of his master as, in his station, he was fitted or permitted to acquire. Eventually, also, Negro slaves transferred their allegiance to the state, of which they were only indirectly members, or at least to their masters' families, with whom they felt themselves in most things one in sentiment and interest.

The assimilation of the Negro field hand, where the contact of the slave with his master and his master's family was less intimate, was naturally less complete. On the large plantations, where an overseer stood between the master and the majority of his slaves . . . this distance between master and slave was greatly increased. The consequence is that the Negroes in these regions are less touched today by the white man's influence and civilization than elsewhere in the southern states. The size of the plantation, the density of the slave population, and the extent and character of the isolation in which the master and his slave lived are factors to be reckoned with in estimating the influence which the plantation exerted on the Negro. In Virginia the average slave population on the plantation has been estimated at about ten. On the Sea Islands and farther south it was thirty. . . .

As might be expected there were class distinctions among the slaves as among the whites, and these class distinctions were more rigidly enforced on the large plantations than on the smaller ones. . . . In Virginia and the border states, and in what was known as the Back Country, where the plantations were smaller and the relation of the races more intimate, slaves gained relatively more of the white man's civilization. . . . The differences in the Negro population which existed before the Civil War are still clearly marked today. They are so clearly marked, in fact, that an outline of the areas in which the different types of plantation existed before the War would furnish the basis for a map showing distinct cultural levels in the Negro population in the South today.

The first Negroes were imported into the United States in 1619. At the beginning of the nineteenth century there were 900,000 slaves in the United States. By 1860 that number had increased to nearly 4,000,000. At that time, it is safe to say, the great mass of the Negroes were no longer, in any true sense, an alien people. They were, of course, not citizens. They lived in the smaller world of the particular plantation to which they belonged. It might, perhaps, be more correct to say that they were less assimilated than domesticated.

In this respect, however, the situation of the Negro was not different from that of the Russian peasant, at least as late as 1860. . . .

A right understanding of conditions in the South before the War will make clear that the southern plantation was founded in the different temperaments, habits, and sentiments of the white man and the black. The discipline of the plantation put its own impress upon, and largely formed the character of, both races. In the life of the plantation white and black were different but complementary, the one bred to the rôle of a slave and the other to that of master. This, of couse, takes no account of the poor white man who was also formed by slavery, but rather as a by-product.

Where the conditions of slavery brought the two races, as it frequently did, into close and intimate contact, there grew up a mutual sympathy and understanding which frequently withstood not only the shock of the Civil War, but the political agitation and chicane which followed it in the southern states.

Speaking of the difference between the North and the South in its attitude toward the Negro, Booker T. Washington says: "It is the individual touch which holds the races together in the South, and it is this individual touch which is lacking to a large degree in the North."

No doubt kindly relations between individual members of the two races do exist in the South to an extent not known in the North. As a rule, it will be found that these kindly relations had their origin in slavery. The men who have given the [raucus] tone to political discussion in southern states in recent years are men who did not own slaves. . . .

# III

The Civil War weakened but did not fully destroy the *modus vivendi* which slavery had established between the slave and his master. With emancipation the authority which had formerly been exercised by the master was transferred to the state, and Washington, D.C., began to assume in the mind of the freedman the position that formerly had been occupied by the "big house" on the plantation. The masses of the Negro people still maintained their habit of dependence, however, and after the first confusion of the change had passed, life went on, for most of them, much as it had before the War. As one old farmer explained, the only difference he could see was that in slavery he "was working for old Marster and now he was working for himself."

There was one difference between slavery and freedom, nevertheless, which was very real to the freedman. And this was the liberty to move. To move from one plantation to another in case he was discontented was one of the ways in which a freedman was able to realize his freedom and to make sure that he possessed it. This liberty to move meant a good deal more to the plantation Negro than one not acquainted with the situation in ths South is likely to understand.

If there had been an abundance of labor in the South; if the situation had been such that the Negro laborer was seeking the opportunity to work, or such that the Negro tenant farmers were competing for the opportunity to get a place on the land, as is so frequently the case in Europe, the situation would have been fundamentally different from what it actually was. But . . . there is more land in the South than there is labor to till it. Land owners are driven to competing for laborers and tenants to work their plantations.

Owing to his ignorance of business matters and to a long-established habit of submission the Negro after emancipation was placed at a great disadvantage in his dealings with the white man. His right to move from one plantation to another became, therefore, the Negro tenant's method of enforcing consideration from the planter. He might not dispute the planter's accounts, because he was not capable of doing so, and it was unprofitable to attempt it, but if he felt aggreived he could move.

This was the significance of the exodus in some of the southern states which took place about 1879, when 40,000 people left the plantations in the Black Belts of Louisiana and Mississippi and went to Kansas. The masses of the colored people were dissatisfied with the treatment they were receiving from the planters and made up their minds to move to "a free country," as they described it. At the same time it was the attempt of the planter to bind the Negro tenant who was in debt to him, it his place on the plantation, that gave rise to the system of peonage that still exists in a mitigated form in the South today.

When the Negro moved off the plantation upon which he was reared he severed the personal relations which bound him to his master's people. It was just at this point that the two races began to lose touch with each other. From this time on the relations of the black man and white, which in slavery had been direct and personal, became every year, as the old associations were broken, more and more indirect and secondary. There lingers still the disposition on the part of the white man to treat every Negro familiarly, and the disposition on the part of every Negro to treat every white man respectfully. But these are habits which are gradually disappearing. The breaking-down of the instincts and habits of servitude, and the acquisition, by the masses of the Negro people, of the instincts and habits of freedom have proceeded slowly but steadily. The reason the change seems to have gone on more rapidly in some cases than others is explained by the fact that at the time of emancipation 10 per cent of the Negores in the United States were already free, and others, those who had worked in trades, many of whom had hired their own time from their masters, had become more or less adapted to the competitive conditions of free society.

One of the effects of the mobilization of the Negro has been to bring him into closer and more intimate contact with his own people. Common interests have drawn the blacks together, and caste sentiment has kept the black and white apart. The segregation of the races, which began as a spontaneous movement on the part of both, has been fostered by the policy of the dominant race. The agitation of the Reconstruction Period made the division between the races in politics absolute. Segregation and separation in other matters have gone on steadily ever since. The Negro at the present time has separate churches, schools, libraries, hospitals, Y.M.C.A. associations, and even separate towns. There are, perhaps, a half-dozen communities in the United States, every inhabitant of which is a Negro. . . .

It is hard to estimate the ultimate effect of this isolation of the black man. One of the most important effects has been to establish a common interest among all the different colors and classes of the race. This sense of solidarity has grown up gradually with the organization of the Negro people. It is stronger in the South, where segregation is more complete, than it is in the North where, twenty years ago, it would have been safe to say it did not exist. Gradually, imperceptibly, within the larger world of the white man, a smaller world, the world of the black man, is silently taking form and shape.

Every advance in education and intelligence puts the Negro in possession of the technique of communication and organization of the white man, and so contributes to the extension and consolidation of the Negro world within the white.

The motive for this increasing solidarity is furnished by the . . . increasing sensibility of Negroes to the pressure and the prejudice without. The sentiment of racial loyalty, which is a comparatively recent manifestation of the growing self-consciousness of the race, must be regarded as a response and "accommodation" to changing internal and external relations of the race. The sentiment which Negroes are beginning to call "race pride" does not exist to the same extent in the North as in the South but an increasing disposition to enforce racial distinctions in the North, as in the South, is bringing it into existence.

One or two incidents in this connection are significant. A few years ago a man who is the head of the largest Negro publishing business in this country sent to Germany and had a number of Negro dolls manufactured according to specifications of his own. At the time this company was started Negro children were in the habit of playing with white dolls. There were already Negro dolls on the market, but they were for white children and represented the white man's conception of the Negro and not the Negro's ideal of himself. The new Negro doll was a mulatto with regular features slightly modified in favor of the conventional Negro type. It was a neat, prim, well-dressed, well-behaved, self-respecting doll. Later on, as I understand, there were other dolls, equally tidy and respectable in appearance, but in darker shades with Negro features a little more pronounced. . . .

This substitution of the Negro model for the white is a very interesting and a very significant fact. It means that the Negro has begun to fashion his own ideals and in his own image rather than in that of the white man. It is also interesting to know that the Negro doll company has been a success and that these dolls are now widely sold in every part of the United States. Nothing exhibits more clearly the extent to which the Negro had become assimilated in slavery or the extent to which he has broken with the past in recent years than this episode of the Negro doll.

The incident is typical. It is an indication of the nature of tendencies and of forces that are stirring in the background of the Negro's mind, although they have not succeeded in forcing themselves, except in special instances, into clear consciousness.

In this same category must be reckoned the poetry of Paul Lawrence Dunbar. . . . Before Paul Lawrence Dunbar, Negro literature had been either apologetic or self-assertive, but Dunbar "studied the Negro objectively." He represented him as he found him, not only without apology, but with an affectionate understanding and sympathy which one can have only for what is one's own. In Dunbar, Negro literature attained an ethnocentric point of view. Through the medium of his verses the ordinary shapes and forms of the Negro's life have taken on the color of his affections and sentiments and we see the black man, not as he looks, but as he feels and is.

It is a significant fact that a certain number of educated—or rather the so-called educated—Negroes were not at first disposed to accept at their full value either Dunbar's dialect verse or the familiar pictures of Negro life which are the symbols in which his poetry usually found expression. The explanation sometimes offered for the dialect poems was that "they were made to please white folk." The assumption seems to have been that if they had been written for Negroes it would have been impossible in his poetry to distinguish black people from white. This was a sentiment which was never shared by the masses of the people, who, upon the occasions when Dunbar recited to them, were fairly bowled over with amusement and delight because of the authenticity of the portraits he offered them. At the present time Dunbar is so far accepted as to have hundreds of imitators.

Literature and art have played a similar and perhaps more important role in the racial struggles of Europe than of America. One reason seems to be that racial conflicts, as they occur in secondary groups, are primarily sentimental and secondarily economic. Literature and art, when they are employed to give expression to racial sentiment and form to racial ideals, serve, along with other agencies, to mobilize the group and put the masses *en rapport* with their leaders and with each other. In such case art and literature are like silent drummers which summon into action the latent instincts and energies of the race.

These struggles, I might add, in which a submerged people seek to rise and make for themselves a place in a world occupied by superior and privileged races, are not less vital or less important because they are bloodless. They serve to stimulate ambitions and inspire ideals which years, perhaps, of subjection and subordination have suppressed. In fact, it seems as if it were through conflicts of this kind, rather than through war, that the minor peoples were destined to gain the moral concentration and discipline that fit them to share, on anything like equal terms, in the conscious life of the civilized world.

## IV

The process of race adjustment in the southern states since the emancipation has, on the whole, run parallel with the nationalist movement in Europe. The so-called "nationalities" are, for the most part, Slavic peoples, fragments of the great Slavic race, that have attained national self-consciousness as a result of their struggle for freedom and air against their German conquerors. It is a significant fact that the nationalist movement, as well as the "nationalities" that it has brought into existence, had its rise in that twilight zone, upon the eastern border of Germany and the western border of Russia, and is part of the century-long conflict, partly racial, partly cultural, of which this meeting-place of the East and West has been the scene.

Until the beginning of the last century the European peasant, like the Negro slave, bound as he was to the soil, lived in the little world of direct and personal relations, under what we may call a domestic régime. It was military necessity that first turned the attention of statesmen like Frederick the Great of Prussia to the welfare of the peasant. It was the overthrow of Prussia by Napolean in 1807 that brought about his final emancipation in that country. In recent years it has been the international struggle for economic efficiency which has contributed most to mobilize the peasant and laboring classes in Europe.

As the peasant slowly emerged from serfdom he found himself a member of a depressed class, without education, political privileges, or capital. It was the struggle of this class for wider opportunity and better conditions of life that made most of the history of the previous century. . . .

This sketch of the racial situation in Europe is, of course, the barest abstraction and should not be accepted realistically. It is intended merely as an indication of similarities, in the broader outlines, of the motives that have produced nationalities in Europe and are making the Negro in America, as Booker Washington says, "a nation within a nation."

It may be said that there is one profound difference between the Negro and the European nationalities, namely, that the Negro has had his separateness and consequent race consciousness thrust upon him, because of his exclusion and forcible isolation from white society. The Slavic nationalities, on the contrary, have segregated themselves in order to escape assimilation and escape racial extinction in the larger cosmopolitan states.

The difference is, however, not so great as it seems. With the exception of the Poles, nationalistic sentiment may be said hardly to have existed fifty years ago. Forty years ago when German was the language of the educated classes, educated Bohemians were a little ashamed to speak their own language in public. Now nationalist sentiment is so strong that, where the Czech nationality has gained control, it has sought to wipe out every vestige of the German language. It has changed the names of streets, buildings, and public places. . . .

The fact is that nationalist sentiment among the Slavs, like racial sentiment among the Negroes, has sprung up as the result of a struggle against privilege and discrimination based upon racial distinctions. The movement is not so far advanced among Negroes; sentiment is not so intense, and for several reasons probably never will be. One reason is that Negroes, in their struggle for equal opportunities, have the democratic sentiment of the country on their side.

From what has been said it seems fair to draw once conclusion namely: under conditions of secondary contact, that is to say, conditions of individual liberty and individual competition, characteristic of modern civilization, depressed racial groups tend to assume the form of nationalities. A nationality, in the narrower sense, may be defined as the racial group which has attained self-consciousness, no matter whether it has at the same time gained political independence or not.

In societies organized along horizontal lines the disposition of individuals in the lower strata is to seek their models in the strata above them. Loyalty attaches to individuals, particularly to the upper classes, who furnish, in their persons and in their lives, the models for the masses of the people below them. Long after the nobility has lost every other social function connected with its vocation the ideals of the nobility have survived in our conception of the gentleman, genteel manners and bearing—gentility.

The sentiment of the Negro slave was, in a certain sense, not merely loyalty to his master, but to the white race. Negroes of the older generations speak very frequently, with a sense of proprietorship, of "our white folks." This sentiment was not always confined to the ignorant masses. An educated colored man once explained to me "that we colored people always want our white folks to be superior." He was shocked when I showed no particular enthusiasm for that form of sentiment.

The fundamental significance of the nationalist movement must be sought in the effort of subject races, sometimes consciously, sometimes unconsciously to substitute, for those supplied them by aliens, models based on their own racial individuality and embodying sentiments and ideals which spring naturally out of their own lives.

After a race has achieved in this way its moral independence, assimilation, in the sense of copying, will still continue. Nations and races borrow from those whom they fear as well as from those whom they admire. Materials taken over in this way, however, are inevitably stamped with the individuality of the nationaties that appropriate them. These materials will contribute to the dignity, to the prestige, and to the solidarity of the nationality which borrows them, but they will no longer inspire loyalty to the race from which they are borrowed. A race which has attained the character of a nationality may still retain its loyalty to the state of which it is a part, but only in so far as that state incorporates, as an integral part of its organization, the practical interests, the aspirations and ideals of that nationality.

The aim of the contending nationalities in Austria-Hungary at the present time seems to be a federation, like that of Switzerland, based upon the autonomy of the different races composing the empire. In the South, similarly, the races seem to be tending in the direction of a bi-racial organization of society, in which the Negro is gradually gaining a limited autonomy. What the ultimate outcome of this movement may be it is not safe to predict.

# Part II

# The Beginnings of Change: 1916-1929

## Introduction

World War I abruptly ended the turn-of-the century era. Beginning in August 1914, the "war to end all wars" soon began to reshape American race relations. It ended European immigration and simultaneously led to new war orders. Industry turned to the South with its large labor surplus and began to recruit furiously among poor blacks and whites alike. A train ticket combined with a guaranteed job at what looked to Southern eyes like big wages represented a powerful temptation to leave the region. And millions did for the next half-century. This massive long-distance migration of blacks from farm to city and from South to North made race relations not just a provincial regional concern but for the first time a major urban and national concern.

The pages of the *American Journal of Sociology* did not reflect this fundamental alteration during the war years. The older discussions continued. For example, two future presidents of the American Sociological Society wrote on the alleged "superiority of the mulatto"[1] and the cost to the South of racial prejudice and discrimination.[2] The most remarkable paper, however, was published by Howard Woolston, a respected product of Giddings at Columbia.[3] In one of the earliest "statistical studies" in the sociological literature, Woolston asked twenty-five "experts" to rate ten personal traits of white and black Americans and of eight European immigrant groups. Though only ten returned his questionnaire, Woolston confidently published his results; those results

[1] E. B. Reuter, "The superiority of the mulatto," *American Journal of Sociology 23* (1917): 83–106.

[2] George E. Howard, "The social cost of southern race prejudice," *American Journal of Sociology 22* (1917): 577–593.

[3] Howard B. Woolston, "Rating the nations: A study in the statistics of opinion," *American Journal of Sociology 22* (1917): 381–390.

record for us the stereotypes of the day that led seven years later to the Immigration Act of 1924. As might be guessed, white Americans who were native to the country were assigned the most favorable image, black Americans the least favorable. Blacks were granted a favorable ranking on only one trait, "sympathy," indicating that the loyal "Old Black Joe" image still dominated "expert" opinion. German and English immigrants ranked high; their alleged "self-control" and "moral integrity"were particularly admired. At the bottom of the immigrant rankings were the "South Italians" and "Austrian Slavs," whose "physical vigor" and "intellectual ability" were severely questioned. Group stereotypes did not become an object of study until the following decades; in 1917 they entered the literature as expert ratings.

*Laissez-faire* paternalism of conservative writers versus the assimilationist beliefs of liberal writers differentiate the articles of this second era. The differentiation is especially evident in the writings on Native Americans. One of the more extreme examples of paternalism is provided by Louis Sears in his historical treatment of "the Puritan and his Indian ward":

> [F]ate had sealed the destiny of the Red Man and his works, both good and evil. The New World was reserved not for the Indian and his uplift, but as the testing-ground for a new political and social order.
>
> Toward upbuilding this, the Indian played a negative part. Though some of his contributions have been incorporated into American culture, and though his memory has inspired a great literature, first in the gruesome narratives of his foemen, later in the romantic afterglow of the sunset on his camp-fires, yet his chief distinction is to have been the human element in a wilderness of difficulties. It was in his conquest over primitive man and nature that the Puritan girded his loins for that later combat with the problems of our democracy, in which he has ever stood for progress. As for the vanquished, the vast concerns of the universe pause not to lament his fate. The future ever lies with the victor, and as we look backward through the years to the childhood of New England, we know that it was best that she unfold her destinies as a homogeneous people.[4]

Historical and comparative materials were heavily relied upon by race relations authors in the nineteenth and early twentieth centuries, for empirical research as we know it today was only beginning to be established. And for this purpose, Hawaii, as a multiracial area under the American flag, served as a favorite comparison for mainland racial norms. Indeed, Hawaii still serves this function for American social scientists. All told, thirty papers on race relations in the four journals under review pertain to Hawaii, constituting 3 percent of the entire literature and spread out over each decade of this century. Critics of America's racial norms particularly employed Hawaiian comparisons. They used them to demonstrate repeatedly two points relevant to the mainland debate:

[4] Louis M. Sears, "The Puritan and his Indian ward," *American Journal of Sociology 22* (1916): 80–93.

(1) the widespread and successful racial intermarriage and miscegenation of the islands,[5] and (2) the extensive degree of successful assimilation of all races to an Hawaiian core culture.[6] The importance of this interracial outpost of America is underscored by the fact that Robert Park's studies in Hawaii led directly to his important race cycle framework positing an evolving pattern between racial groups of "contact, competition, accommodation, and eventual assimilation."[7]

If reformers favored Hawaiian comparisons, those who reflected their times favored African comparisons. Or, more precisely, the reflectors employed comparisons with an Africa they usually knew about only from anecdotes and travel books of non-social scientists who had been to "the dark continent." Following the use of such materials by Herbert Spencer, these defenders of the status quo especially used this comparison to bolster stereotyped arguments about the limited mental abilities of nonwhite peoples everywhere. It is within this context that the importance of Selection 6 by Ellsworth Faris is to be understood. Like W. I. Thomas, Faris was a native of Tennessee, a social psychologist, and later a president of the American Sociological Society. In 1919 he replaced Thomas at the University of Chicago; and in the mid-1920s he assumed Small's duties as department chairman and editor of the *American Journal of Sociology*. Like many of the early sociologists, Faris had been active in Protestant church work, and had spent a number of years as a missionary in Africa. It was this missionary experience together with the discipline's growing empirical sophistication that enabled him to write this hard-headed attack upon the chief "evidence" of Spencer and his followers.

Race relations work received an important boost when *Social Forces* made its debut in 1922. The very first issue made it clear that this Southern-based publication was going to focus on racial concerns. The editor, Howard Odum, another future president of the American Sociological Society, noted that racial problems "are becoming each year more and more a national problem"; and he pledged that *Social Forces* would "face frankly this most difficult of problems" by offering "contributions from both races wherever they may be found available and adequate."[8] The first issue also began a section headed "inter-racial cooperation," and its initial articles tell much about the times. One by Will Alexander, an activist Southern liberal, describes the activities of the Commission on Inter-Racial Cooperation (later called the Southern Regional Council, which still operates out of Atlanta).[9] The other, by an Atlanta minister, the Reverend M. Ashby Jones, allowed that "the races should be separated by such social barriers as are necessary to preserve the purity of the blood of the

[5] For example: Ernest J. Reece, "Race mingling in Hawaii," *American Journal of Sociology 20* (1914): 104–116.

[6] For example: William C. Smith, "Changing personality traits of second generation Orientals in America," *American Journal of Sociology 33* (1928): 922–929.

[7] Robert E. Park, *Race and Culture* (New York: Free Press, 1950), p. 150.

[8] Howard W. Odum, "Editorial notes," *Social Forces 1* (1922): 59.

[9] Will Alexander, "A useable piece of machinery," *Social Forces 1* (1922): 41–42.

two peoples" but urged on moral grounds that "no other barriers or discriminations are justified."[10]

*Social Forces* soon made good on its editor's promise. Selections 7 through
11, all drawn from its pages, reveal a more direct and data-oriented, less abstract
approach than the philosophical outlook of many of the earlier sociological
papers. For example, Selections 7 and 8 attempt to present factual descriptions
of black life in much the same way DuBois had presented it in his earlier books.
Monroe Work of the Tuskegee Institute, editor for many years of the highly regarded *Negro Yearbook,* provides an overview of the status of black Americans
in 1923. He first considers in turn trends in demography, migration, health,
wealth, education, and occupations before making his policy arguments. Note
that, like white liberals of the period, Work saw the task as one of "making the
Negro a more assimilable group." In the next article, Ira Reid, who went on to
become a well-known sociologist, takes a detailed look at fast-growing Harlem.
Writing while associated with the Urban League in New York City, he correctly
sees Harlem's development as the wave of black America's future and deserving
of far more sociological attention than it was receiving. Editor of *Phylon* after
DuBois, a vice-president of the American Sociological Society, and long associated first with Atlanta University and then with Haverford College, Reid was
best known as the author of *In a Minor Key, The Negro Immigrant,* and (with
Arthur Raper) *Sharecroppers All.* In 1978 Reid was posthumously given the
DuBois–Johnson–Frazier award of the American Sociological Association.

Selections 9 and 10 extend the analysis of the 1920s further by interpreting
the significance of organized white resistance to change, as revealed by the
return of the Ku Klux Klan, and of black migration out of the South. Guy Johnson, a native Texan who has spent his entire sociological career at the University
of North Carolina at Chapel Hill, analyzes the Klan with the unpretentious
directness that characterizes all of his work. Such a blunt view was rare at the
time, as demonstrated by another interpretation of the Klan that appeared two
years later in the *American Journal of Sociology* as a near-apology for the
organization.[11] In his discussion of the critical significance of black migration,
Johnson demonstrates the sociological imagination at its best. Thoroughly
grounded in his subject matter, he is able to predict accurately the future rise
in black nationalism from the demographic data of the present. Johnson's
special gifts for prediction will be shown again in Selection 25.

The final paper of Part II describes the work of the National Association for
the Advancement of Colored People. The "victories" recorded by Seligmann
may seem minor today—limiting laws for residential segregation, peonage,
and white primary elections. But looking back now we know that this was
the persistent NAACP legal strategy that twenty-five years after Seligmann's
article appeared was rewarded by Brown *v.* Board of Education in 1954.

[10]M. Ashby Jones, "The approach to the South's race question," *Social Forces 1* (1922):
40–41.
[11]Frank Bohn, "The Ku Klux Klan interpreted," *American Journal of Sociology 30* (1925):
385–407.

# 6

# The Mental Capacity of Savages

*ELLSWORTH FARIS*

The conception of the mind of "primitive man" held by Herbert Spencer[1] had the advantage of aesthetic symmetry and proportion. If animals can be arranged in seried ranks, and if the highest of these is infinitely below the civilized man, there ought surely to be, not only a missing link, but also grades or ranks of men varying in their capacities and possibilities. If this assumption be made, and if the isolated sentences quoted from travelers and residents among savages be duly cited, it is possible to make out a good case, as the classical statement of Spencer shows. The criticism of this point of view by J. R. Angell, F. Boas, John Dewey, W. I. Thomas, and others has grown in volume in recent years.[2] It is possible now to declare one thing confidently, namely, that should it finally be demonstrated that the savage is inferior to civilized man it will have to be proved on other grounds than those formerly held sufficient. The old arguments are discredited and the old facts questioned. The inquiry may be now prosecuted with methods of scientific precision impossible to an earlier generation, and the next chapter of the investigation should be written with the help of our recently acquired technique of modern experimental psychology. . . .

[T]here are half a dozen sources of error which are sufficiently noteworthy to be set down here as explaining in part how such a mistaken view could have been formed, assuming that it is a mistaken view. Let us consider these:

[1] H. Spencer, *Principles of Sociology.*

[2] J. R. Angell, *Chapters in Modern Psychology;* F. Boas, *The Mind of Primitive Man;* John Dewey, *Psychological Review,* Vol. IX; W. I. Thomas, *Sex and Society.*

Abridged from *American Journal of Sociology 23* (1918): 603–619. Used by permission of The University of Chicago Press.

1. The most obvious force operating to tip the scales of sober judgment is *race prejudice,* the assumption that other people are inferior to us in so far as they are different. We are coming to realize that the Hindu, Chinese, and Japanese are not convinced of their inferiority, but rather are certain of our inferiority to them. . . . The same is true eminently of the Congo native. In a good-natured debate one day I was giving arguments for the superiority of the white man over the black, and instanced the fact that in a territory containing twenty million natives the absolute authority was exercised by the Belgians, who numbered less than a thousand. The reply was immediate.

"Give us breech-loading guns and ammunition, and within a month there will not be one of the thousand left alive here."

"But," says the white man, "that is the point. The white men invented and made their guns and ammunition."

"Sir, do you know how to make a gun and ammunition?"

"Well, no, not yet, but I could learn to make them in a factory."

"Certainly you could, if they would teach you, but so could we."

Many of those who observed and recorded their experiences and whose record became the source of the older views were men whose perceptions were colored by the conviction of a measureless superiority—and judicial fairness in such circumstances is not always easy.

2. *Unwarranted generalization* is the commonest danger in scientific research, against which the carefully trained scientist is likely to be sufficiently on his guard. But most of the observers whose words are quoted in the books were not careful scientists, and their unwarranted but explicable leaps of inference are set down as unprejudiced and dependable fact. For example, a native finds his way back home unaided when the white man in the party is hopelessly lost, whereupon it is set down in imperishable record, to be copied with an uncritical credulity, that primitive people have a mysterious instinct of direction and carry compasses in their heads. Or one of them is very stupid in handling a new tool and makes a laughable blunder in trying to use a saw, and forthwith it is demonstrated that his whole race has no power of logical thought!

It is fair to say that some of the most careful of writers have at times been guilty of using isolated anecdotes from travelers, and have thus fallen into this type of error. It is like the foreign traveler who saw a street fight from the window of a Pullman car, and, having inquired the name of the state, wrote in his notes, "The inhabitants of Illinois are a very warlike race." Primitive man has been treated that way many times.

3. Another source of error might, by a slight stretch of terms, be called *the psychologist's fallacy*. It is the assumption that we are viewing the matter exactly as the person under observation does, which assumption is uniformly untrue. . . . We have assumed that any human being could observe the facts of social life. No one would accept the observations of an uneducated sailor to determine the facts of botany or geology, but ability to report on social facts is equally dependent on training.

The Western observer thinks of religion in terms of doctrines and theologies and is able to report the beliefs and doctrines of the native in a way that is very complete and systematic and misleading. In fact, a safe rule would be to trust implicitly the account of an actual happening reported by a reputable traveler or explorer or missionary, but to be very slow to accept his explanation of the event.

For example, the natives are supposed to have a belief in spirits which extends to everything they see in their world. The trees have a spirit, there is a spirit of the river, a spirit in the stones, and in every object in their world.

Now the very great difficulty that I found in getting a satisfactory word that would answer to the concept of "spirit" leads me to question this statement. And I can imagine a psychologically inclined Eskimo coming among us and reporting in a paper before the Polaris Scientific Institute that white people believe every chair to be inhabited by a spirit, proving his point by declaring that he has seen many a white man curse a chair after it had maliciously got in his way and caused him to stumble over it. White people believe that spirits inhabit golf balls and billiard balls, and are frequently seen to offer short prayers to them in order to induce them to roll where they are wanted. They also imprecate them if they do not obey. . . . The interpreter of the savage mind must beware of the psychologist's fallacy.

4. A fourth source of error may be called *the mythopeic error,* the tendency of a native to invent an explanation rather than confess ignorance. Most of their customs are due to the unthinking adherence to the ways of the former generations, and they are not conscious of why they do them. If they are asked a reason they will often invent one, but this is not necessarily the true reason. Few of us could give offhand the explanation of why we remove our hats in saluting a lady acquaintance. In fact, it does seem almost unreasonable "to make the meeting of a female friend the occasion for taking off part of your clothes to wave in the air." Any explanation that the man in the street might give of the custom would be a guess, and this is doubly true of the uncultured peoples in their attempt to explain—and yet the traveler can tease out an explanation if he tries. . . .

5. Two more sources of error remain to be noticed, the first of which is due to *ignorance of language.* It is very easy to fall into the error of supposing that because a word has not been found, none exists. The character of the languages of different peoples is so different that it is next to impossible to make any valid argument on the absence of a word.

6. Finally a sixth sort of error may be said to be the error due to *knowledge of language.* An illustration may be found in the argument of a recent writer made from the manner of designating relationships by blood. There is in many primitive languages a lack of any word to distinguish brother from cousin, and this failure to distinguish brother from cousin, and son from grandson, means that the primitive man has such a vague idea of personality that he has not been able to make the fine distinctions. We, on the other hand, distinguish brother

from cousin, and stepson from blood kin, etc., therefore we have a much more highly developed sense of personality.

In order to appreciate the native point of view it is necessary to call in our primitive psychologist once more. I recall a time in the Congo when I had occasion to refer to the tail of a chicken, and used the word that was in my notes as meaning "tail." I had pointed out the caudal appendage of a dog, and had been told that it was called *bongongo.* This word proved quite intelligible when I applied it to designate the tail of a sheep or a buffalo, but when I said something about the *bongongo* of a chicken, the whole company burst out into loud laughter. A chicken is not a dog, of course not, and did I not see that a chicken had just feathers sticking out behind and it was not a *bongongo* at all? They called that *mpete,* of course. Was it really true that white people called the feathers of a chicken by the same name that they called the real tail of a dog? Later on I found that the word for tail of a fish is a very different word from either of the other two.

Now the Eskimo psychologist might, on the basis of these facts, write that English-speaking people have such vague, undefined notions of tailhood and of spinality that they cannot distinguish the difference between the feathers of a chicken and the tail of the dog and call both these by the same name as the steering gear of a fish. It is true that Western people distinguish the snout of the pig from the lip of a man, and these two from the beak of a bird, and all three from the muzzle of a horse, and are therefore in a state of evolution which will probably lead them to a stage where they can develop a notion of distinction in tails in the process of time. I submit that the analogy is fair.

The sources of error being so many, what methods are to be relied upon for dependable results? The answer is that careful, painstaking, scientific experiment and inquiry will alone give dependable findings. Most of those we now have are not to be depended upon. . . .

The hypothesis that has been forming, therefore, in recent years concerning the mind of so-called primitive man, meaning the uncivilized races of the present day, is that in native endowment the savage child is, on the average, about the same in capacity as the child of civilized races. Instead of the concept of different stages or degrees of mentality, we find it easier to think of the human mind as being, in its capacity, about the same everywhere, the difference in culture to be explained in terms of the physical geography, or the stimuli from other groups, or the unaccountable occurrence of great men. But this is only a hypothesis. It has not been proved. It may well be that differences in anatomical structure can be correlated with differences in mental capacity. One would suppose that the size or weight of the brain could be so correlated. The difficulty is in finding a crucial test. To measure the achievements of the tribes in their own habitat is inconclusive, and to import youths into our schools is to fail to isolate the years of childhood which recent psychology considers the most potent in their influence on the after-life. . . .

# 7

# The Race Problem in Cross Section: The Negro in 1923

*MONROE N. WORK*

## Statement of Facts

Some of the important facts about the negroes of the nation in 1923 are: they are increasing numerically, they are a forward looking group and are making rapid progress. On the other hand there is still a great deal of ignorance, inefficiency, poverty and general backwardness to be found among them. As a group the negroes of the country are optimistic, their confidence in themselves is increasing, they are trying to do the same things, make the same achievements which the white people have made. This is not a slavish imitation of the white man but is a most serious effort to master modern civilization and to make it his own.

The 1920 census reported the negro propulation of the nation to be 10,463,131, or 9.9 per cent of the total population. The proportion of negroes in the total population is steadily decreasing mainly because of the rapid increase of the white population through immigration. . . .

### NORTHERN MIGRATION

The movement of negroes to the North is not to this section as a whole but rather to a few industrial centers. It is found that 1,139,505 or 73.4 per cent of

Reprinted, abridged, from *Social Forces* 2 (January 1924): 245–252. Copyright © The University of North Carolina Press.

the negro population of the North is living in ten industrial districts, as follows:

| | |
|---|---:|
| Indianapolis district............................... | 47,550 |
| Detroit-Toledo district............................. | 55,918 |
| Cleveland district.................................. | 58,850 |
| Kansas City district................................ | 65,393 |
| Pittsburgh district................................. | 88,273 |
| Columbus-Cincinnati district....................... | 89,651 |
| St. Louis district................................... | 102,607 |
| Chicago district.................................... | 131,580 |
| Philadelphia district............................... | 242,343 |
| New York district.................................. | 251,340 |
| Total .......................................... | 1,139,505 |

The so-called migration to the North is a part of the movement of negroes to cities, both North and South. The increase of negro urban population in the South, 1910–1920, was 396,444, or 66,000 more than the increase for the same period in the number of negroes in the North from the South, 330,260. . . .

**Number and Per Cent of Negroes in United States Living in Urban and Rural Communities, 1890–1920**

| | *Number* | | *Per Cent* | |
|---|---|---|---|---|
| YEAR | URBAN | RURAL | URBAN | RURAL |
| 1920....... | 3,559,473 | 6,903,658 | 34.0 | 66.0 |
| 1910....... | 2,689,229 | 7,138,534 | 27.4 | 72.6 |
| 1900....... | 2,005,972 | 6,828,022 | 22.7 | 77.3 |
| 1890....... | 1,481,142 | 6,007,534 | 19.4 | 80.6 |

It would appear that the tendency for the concentration of negroes in the black sections of the South is decreasing. The census reports show that those sections of the South in which there is a more rapid increase of negroes does (*sic*) not correspond with the area of maximum density of negro population. . . . The population of the counties having half or more of their population negroes was in 1880, 3,392,235: in 1890, 3,555,970; in 1900, 4,057,619; in 1910, 3,932,484 and in 1920, 3,330,294.

The white population of the South is increasing at a more rapid rate than the negro population with a result that the proportion of negroes in the population of the South is decreasing. In 1900 the percentage of negroes in the South's population was 32.3; in 1910, 29.8, and in 1920, 27.0. There are now no cities of importance in the United States in which 50 per cent or more of their population are negroes. It is very probable that the 1930 census will show that South Carolina and Mississippi will have a majority of whites. In 1920 negroes constituted 50.4 per cent of the population of South Carolina and 52.2 per cent of the population of Mississippi.

## HEALTH

The most recent available information indicates that the health of negroes is improving. The death rates for negroes are considerably higher than those for whites. Mortality statistics indicate that the death rates for both races are decreasing.

**Death Rate Per 1,000 for the Registration Area**

|  | 1910 | 1911 | 1912 | 1916 | 1920 | 1921 |
|---|---|---|---|---|---|---|
| White . . . . . | 14.5 | 13.7 | 13.5 | 13.5 | 12.8 | 11.4 |
| Colored . . . . | 24.2 | 23.6 | 22.9 | 20.5 | 18.4 | 15.9 |

It appears that there is a greater decrease in the death rates for negroes in recent years than that for whites. The decline of the rate for whites in the registration area in the period 1910–1921 was 21.4 per cent; that for negroes, 34.3 per cent. The death rate for negroes now is about what it was for whites twenty years ago. The rate for whites in 1900 was 17.1 per cent; that for negroes in 1921 was 15.9 per cent. It further appears that at any one time the death rate among negroes compares favorably with that of whites in many foreign countries; as for example, in 1910 the death rate was for Hungary, 23.6 per cent; Roumania, 24.8 per cent; Spain, 23.3 per cent, Austria, 21.3 per cent; negroes of the United States, 24.2 per cent.

Life insurance tables show that there is a broadening of the lifespan of insured negroes. The Metropolitan Life Insurance Company recently stated that in the two years, 1911–1912, the expected lifespan of the colored male policyholders at age ten was 41.32 years. In 1922, the expectation was 46.74 years, an increase of about 5½ years of 13.1 per cent. . . This indicates that better economic conditions and better living conditions and changes in life and labor which have recently come to the negro is tending to increase his lifespan.

## WEALTH

When compared with the wealth of the nation the wealth of negroes is small. Since their emancipation, however, the property accumulation of negroes has rapidly increased from some $20,000,000 in 1866 to over 1,500,000,000 in 1923. Through purchases and increases in value, their property holdings are increasing in value, their property holdings are increasing at the rate of about $50,000,000 per year. The lands which they now own amount to more than 22,000,000 acres or over 34,000 square miles, an area greater than that of the five New England States, New Hampshire, Vermont, Massachusetts, Connecticut and Rhode Island. Home owning is an important phase of property accumulation. It is estimated that negroes now own over six hundred thousand homes; that is, one home out of every four which they have established is owned. This is a remarkable showing and has great significance for the future of the race. It is safe to say that any people, starting with a handicap of poverty and ignorance, who can in fifty years become owners of one-fourth of all the homes which they occupy, are making progress along those lines which make for a high degree of citizenship.

## EDUCATION

With respect to the education of the negro it is found that there is much improvement. The illiteracy of the group has decreased from 70.0 per cent in 1880 to 22.9 per cent in 1920. . . . . Although during the past fifty years there has been great progress in negro education the equipment and facilities in negro schools today are on the whole far below those in white schools. A large part of the rural schools in the South are still without school buildings and the average length of the terms of many of these schools is still from three to five months. Although the negroes constitute about [10] per cent of the total population of the country, only a little more than 2 per cent of the $1,300,000,000 expended annually for education is spent upon them.

## OCCUPATION

The negroes as a group are rising in the scale of occupations and now have a better economic footing than at any time since their emancipation. The negroes in 1923 are found in many and varied occupations; in fact, there are very few, if any, occupations or grades of occupations in which there are not some negroes. The distribution of negroes, ten years and over, with reference to occupations as reported in the 1920 census is shown in the following table:

| OCCUPATIONS | NUMBER | PER CENT DISTRIBUTION |
|---|---|---|
| Agriculture. . . . . . . . . . . . . . . . . . | 2,178,888 | 45.2 |
| Domestic and personal service . . . . . . . | 1,064,590 | 22.1 |
| Manufacturing and mechanical industries . . . . . . . . . . . . . . . . . | 886,810 | 18.4 |
| Trade and transportation . . . . . . . . . . | 452,888 | 9.4 |
| Professional work . . . . . . . . . . . . . . . | 80,183 | 1.7 |
| Mining industries. . . . . . . . . . . . . . . | 73,229 | 1.5 |
| Public service, municipal, state and federal. . . . . . . . . . . . . | 50,552 | 1.0 |
| Clerical occupations. . . . . . . . . . . . . . | 37,011 | 0.8 |

## THE NEGRO AND CIVIL RIGHTS

The status of the negro with respect to civil rights in 1923 is that he must look to the several states for whatever civil rights he wishes to secure under the guarantee of the Constitution through the 14th Amendment. After the United States Supreme Court in 1883 declared the Civil Rights Bill of 1875 unconstitutional, the burden of securing for the negroes equality and accommodation in public places was placed upon the states. Since that time seventeen states outside of the South have adopted civil rights bills which practically copied the Civil Rights Bill of 1875. . . . Laws for the separation of races in public conveyances are now in force in Tennessee, Florida, Mississippi, Texas, Louisiana, Alabama, Kentucky, Arkansas, Georgia, South Carolina, North Carolina, Florida, Virginia, Maryland and Oklahoma. Separate school laws with respect to races are now found in force in Alabama, Arkansas, Delaware, Florida, Georgia, Maryland, Mississippi, Missouri, North Carolina, Oklahoma, South Carolina, Tennessee, Texas, Virginia and West Virginia. Laws restricting the suffrage with special application to the negro are now in force in Mississippi, South Carolina, Louisiana, North Carolina, Alabama, Virginia, Georgia and Oklahoma.

The laws restricting suffrage, however, appear to operate to disfranchise both whites and negroes. An indication of this is shown by a comparison of the votes cast in Southern states in the 1920 presidential election with the number of males, white and negro, of voting age in these states. It appears that from one-half to four-fifths of the males of voting age are not voting, 83 per cent in South Carolina and 58 per cent in Alabama. Because of the growing intelligence of negroes in the South and the progress which they are making along all lines, suggestions are being made with respect to their admission to a greater extent to the exercise of the franchise. Some of the prominent white newspapers of the South have stated that it would be a good thing to increase the number of negro voters and "it would not endanger white supremacy and it could not lead to negro supremacy.'" In spite of disabilities negroes are taking more and more interest both North and South in politics. The negro newspapers of the South are urging negroes to qualify for voting. As over against national politics the tendency appears to be to take more and more interest in local politics. The reason for this is that negroes are appreciating to a larger extent those civic advantages which come largely through politics; such as, better educational facilities, better police protection, better sanitary conditions, etc.

## A GROWING RACE CONSCIOUSNESS

The racial struggle of the years has gradually resulted in the negro thinking largely in terms of his race, and as a result of this there has evolved a racial consciousness. This group or group consciousness of the negro is growing. This growth is manifesting itself in various ways important among which are an increasing interest in race literature, more faith in race leadership, a demand for patronage of negro business, a tendency to boycott white firms which do not treat the negro with courtesy and a tendency to move away from communities in which lynchings have occurred.

Organization is an indication of the growth of racial consciousness. This means not only organizations through the church, through secret societies, but also organizations for the betterment of conditions, for better educational facilities, for civic improvement, for economic development and for greater participation in politics. There are among negroes national organizations as follows: professional, (including education, law and medicine); business; labor, for political and civic advancement, and organizations in interest of women.

Another phase of the growth of race consciousness is that the negro is developing a literature of his own. Through his numerous newspapers, periodicals, books and articles he is becoming more and more able to set forth his own needs, to state his own case and to champion his own cause.

## RACE RELATIONS

Since the negro and the white man live as two separate groups the relations of these groups present a situation that has become a matter of vital importance to both races. The main facts about race relations are that prejudice and discriminations continue. There are lynchings and occasional riots. There is an apparent growth and spread of both tolerance and intolerance. This is a result of a wider and a more continued contact which the negro group is establishing with the white group. The friendly relations of the two groups are being furthered by the inter-racial coöperation movement which is bringing representatives of the two groups into working relations with each other. The spirit of inter-racial cooperation appears to be growing. There is more and more of a disposition for the white people of the South to aid in efforts for the betterment of conditions among negroes. Another phase of race relations is that the negro group is tending to share to a larger degree in the community life. Its importance as a part of the community is being more and more recognized and community activities are being extended to this group. This group is also being asked to participate in the community activities; and as a result, the negro group is tending to take a more active part in community life.

## THE NEGRO IS AN ASSET OF THE NATION

The negro is one of the most valuable assets of the nation's population elements. The conditions brought about by the World War gave the negro opportunity to demonstrate in a striking way his importance as an economic asset to the nation. The crisis which developed in the nation by reason of the World War disclosed the fact that many elements of the population were a weakness to the nation and in some instances a hindrance and a danger. It was found that the negro along with the native American element was one of the strongest assets which the nation had and that in every instance he remained loyal to the nation in spite of German propaganda. When called upon to contribute of his wealth for the prosecution of the war he made a proportionately larger contribution than did any other group. Over $225,000,000 was contributed which is more than $20 for each man, woman and child of the race. The negroes offered themselves freely for service in the World War and furnished a larger percentage for their group than did the whites for their group. 70.41 per cent of the whites and 74.60 per cent of the negroes were accepted for service and 26.84 per cent of the whites and 31.74 per cent of the negroes were accepted for full military service. As combat troops, as pioneer and working battalions and in whatever service the negro was placed he acquitted himself with credit and honor. They were the first soldiers of the American expeditionary forces to get into action and the first soldiers of the American army to be decorated for bravery.

## Analysis and Interpretation

. . . In the Ante-Bellum Period the problem of racial adjustment was primarily that of accommodation; that is, of adjusting the slave group to the interests and needs of the master group without any change in status of the slave group and without any special effort to better the social and moral conditions of the group. The basis of adjustment in the Post-Bellum Period and since has been primarily that of assimilation; that is, to take this group of freedmen and by giving them the opportunity for economic, educational, moral and religious development to make them a real part of the nation. The two phases of adjustment, accommodation and assimilation, while in a sense complementary to each other, have continued to the present time in more or less opposition to each other. The accommodation phase of adjustment has been largely expressed in the efforts to continue to keep the negro in the same relations to the white group as obtained during the period of slavery. This has been crystallized in the expression, "Keep the negro in his place." It is well to point out here that by assimilation is not meant either miscegenation or amalgamation. . . .

### METHODS OF DEALING WITH THE RACE PROBLEM

. . . During the Reconstruction Period and for some considerable time after the major portion of the discussion of the race problem was largely in northern periodicals by means of articles written by northern writers, by negroes and by southern writers. . . . The present tendency with reference to discussing the race problem in the South by residents of that section appears to be that when an individual, white or black, wishes to express himself on the race problem he more often publishes his views in a southern paper than in a northern paper, thus more effectively molding opinion in the section in which he lives.

The next step resulting from this moulding of opinion is the coming together of whites and negroes in conferences with reference to outlining a basis of adjustment. We have as a result and as an outgrowth of these conferences what is known as the Inter-Racial Coöperation Movement, which is primarily an effort of southern whites and negroes to get together on a basis of coöperation.

The inter-racial conference method of handling the race problem has universal application. The general advantage is that representatives of the interested groups may meet face to face and outline a policy that is of mutual benefit to both groups. Another aspect of the universality of this method is that it is very closely related to and embodies the idea of working with and not for a group. Under assimilation, (the interracial method) things are done for the best interest of the two groups and for the general good. But under the accommodation method things are done by one group for the other. . . .

## THE RACE PROBLEM NO LONGER SECTIONAL BUT NATIONAL

The race problem in the United States is no longer sectional. It has always been national in that it concerned the whole nation; but so long as there were comparatively few negroes in the North and the problem in its acuteness was in the South, it was thought of as being sectional. It was on this ground that the statement was often made that the South should be permitted to handle the problem in its own way. The recent migration of the negro has made the problem in its acuteness a national one. It should be considered, not as a problem of the negro in the South or the negro in the North, but as a problem of the nation.

## WORLD CONTACTS

The negro groups of the world by means of the World War came into strikingly influencing contact with each other. This contact has been strengthened and continued through the perfecting of world methods of communication and the general diffusion of knowledge concerning what is going on in every part of the world. The negroes by means of the literature which they have developed in America, in Africa, in the West Indies and through the general literature of the world have continued this contact. The negroes in America know what the negroes in Africa and in the West Indies are thinking. The Pan-African Movement and the so-called Garvey Movement are the direct results of this contact through communication which the negroes in different parts of the world have established. It is probable, however, that it will be very difficult for the problem of the negro in America, the problem of the negro in the West Indies and the problem of the negro in Africa to be handled as one universal problem of the negro. These groups, however, may be able to give moral and other support to each other.

## PROGRESS AND THE RACE PROBLEM

It is sometimes stated that the progress of the negro will be a solution of the race problem. The facts, however, indicate that progress, instead of being a solution of the problem, may sometimes intensify, complicate and make it more difficult. The negro by reason of his making progress along all lines is coming into contact with the white group in many and varied ways. This contact has two tendencies; one favorable, one unfavorable. One tends to increase friction, the other to promote more friendly relations. An important part of the adjusting of the race problem is to reduce friction and to bring about more friendly relations, more inter-racial coöperation.

## PROGRESS IS MAKING THE NEGRO A MORE ASSIMILABLE GROUP

It has sometimes been stated that through custom and law the negro to a large degree is excluded from participating freely in the higher expressions of culture as exemplified in schools, churches, theaters, desirable residential neighborhoods, social contact with cultured people and all that is elevating in modern life. It is sometimes further stated that by reason of this exclusion the negro will never be able to enter fully into and acquire the culture of the white group. It is very probable that this has never been true in so literal a sense as the statement would imply for the negro group has never been as much out of contact with the best culture of the white group as is sometimes claimed. During the days of slavery through the house servant and mechanic, the free negro class and in other ways the negro group was in contact with the best culture of the South. Since emancipation through northern education the negro, as a group, has been in touch with the best culture and traditions of the North. From this standpoint it was a distinct advantage that negro education was for so long a period of time and to such a large degree in the hands of northern people. The ideals and aspirations of the race were greatly influenced by this contact with the culture of the South and the culture of the North. Through the progress which the negro is now making and the many and varied contacts resulting from his progress he is tending to break down this isolation, this exclusion from the higher expressions of modern culture. The negroes of America, as a group, have no traditions binding them to another country or another culture. They have no heritages in the sense that the foreign elements of the country have. No part of the negro group is advocating that the group should not acquire the culture of the nation, on the other hand, the whole effort of the group is to foster the ideals of America and to make progress not only as negroes but as Americans.

# Mirrors of Harlem: Investigations and Problems of America's Largest Colored Community

*IRA DE A. REID*

Within the past decade the attention of people everywhere has been at some time centered on Harlem. Never before has this particular section of New York received such notice despite the fact that the connotation of the word itself has changed from Dutch to Irish to Jewish to Negro. One may reasonably expect that it will remain Negro unless there is an industrial encroachment.

It is quite hard to define Harlem in the light of social organizations. A visitor sees that it is neither slum nor ghetto, resort nor colony, and after such a variance of ideas regarding the organization of a community I feel certain that Harlem is not a community. Unfortunately Harlem is almost a social nonentity save for the many distorted and half-truth pictures given by the press. . . . On the other hand, it is cajoled with the expression "The Mecca of the New Negro." It appears however, that Harlem is The Maker of the New Negro when one considers the several definite phases of its growth and activity.

Reprinted, abridged, from *Social Forces* 5 (June 1927): 628–634. Copyright © The University of North Carolina Press.

## The Growth of Harlem

In the middle days of the last century the Negro population of New York was scattered in little groups to the south, east and west of Washington Square which was at that time the center of New York aristocracy. These Negroes were the servants of the upper class families and found their habitat close to the places where they worked. In the late eighties, the Negro population had increased and moved about five blocks north. In the Nineties, they had shifted to the lower twenties and thirties west of Sixth Avenue, and by 1900 another northward shift had been made to west 53rd Street. . . . Singularly, each district in which the Negro has lived has been an improvement over the other. About 1900 the move to Harlem began. Inadequate transportation and empty houses in this section gave colored residents their opportunity. A unique story has been weaved around this development. The first residents on 134th Street east of Lenox Avenue—the gradual filling of blocks east of Lenox Avenue—the spread westward—the efforts of the whites to check the movement and evict colored tenants—the violent objection of the Property Owners Improvement Association—the counter attack of the Afro-American Realty Company—and the beginning of Harlem. It will be interesting to note at this time the economic arguments advanced by the Property Owners Improvement Association regarding this racial encroachment. On December 30, 1913, they issued a circular which included the following statements: "The assessed value of property in this section for the year 1913 was $260,000,000 the estimated value of this property is about $4,000,000." (2) "Is it good business to place property estimated at more than $4,000,000 at the disposal of the Negro population who have neither the certainty of number nor the financial strength to absorb even 1 per cent, who are not able to maintain a market value and cause depreciation in the value of property in the entire district?" (3) "There are about 35,000 Negroes here at the present and more expected, most of whom are unable to pay rents necessary to maintain values." (4) "General business in Harlem has been seriously injured due to the changed character of the population." (5) "The Negro population is spreading southward very fast. Each year shows a further increase, and more blocks occupied by them." (6) "This movement of the Property Owners Improvement Association includes a plan to place at the disposal of the Negroes, buildings arranged for their special use so that they may be able to pay the rents and will not find it necessary to overspread the district."

Such a movement was futile. Today the Negro population is sprinkled in the districts from 112th Street to 116th Street in this area; checks itself; endeavors again to substantiate itself from 117th Street to 124th Street; in a sudden impact it rushes from 126th Street to 150th Street and again scatters itself as far as 155th Street. In 1913 there were 35,000 Negroes here. Today there are more than 175,000, and we find ourselves in a very acceptable district. The natural boundary of the Harlem River checks movement down the east though there are one or two small Negro districts across the river. On the south the northern end of Central Park seems to be the objective and the population has moved within two blocks of the park frontage. To the immediate west stands the New York Teachers Training School and City College of New York. Harlem is most conveniently located, and is easily reached by elevated, surface, and bus lines. Harlem merchants have not lost money—they admit that business has never been better. They have altered their stock to meet the needs and profited thereby. Instead of property depreciating, it has doubled in value. Reliable real estate men claimed that Harlem real estate was unsalable before the rapid influx. By 1923 it was at a premium. In 1925 it was estimated that Negroes owned $60,000,000 of Harlem's realty. Though the district has run down physically, there has been an increase in its property values, a natural accompaniment of the change in the racial character of the population. Yet, it continues to be the outstanding Negro quarters of America.

## Population Elements

. . . [T]he problems of Harlem are infinitely greater than those of any other Negro section. Here are several different groups of darker peoples with different experiences in their primary group affiliations, different governmental attitudes, all classed as Negroes by public opinion if not by the interpretation of the law. Among these groups are the British West Indian, the Danish West Indian, the Porto (*sic*) Rican, the African, the South American, and the American Negro of the North and South. These groups are expected to adjust themselves to one particular classification when such is possible. Thirty thousands of Harlem's colored population are reported by the Federal census as having been born in foreign countries, chiefly the West Indies. . . .

## The Problem of Employment

One of the outstanding difficulties in effecting social adjustment for the Negro in Harlem is his job. . . . The bulk of the male population finds its employment as elevator operators, porters, messengers, and longshoremen. Skilled mechanics are few. The census for 1920 gave the number as 462. There has been a very slight increase in the skilled trades. One would think that the opportunities to join the various trade union bodies would mean much toward improving such a situation. We find that in the majority of cases however, there has been a very small increase in the number of Negro members. This may be due to one of three things: (1) the barrier set up by the union; (2) restriction of work opportunities after joining the union; (3) lack of knowledge on the part of the Negro regarding the specific trade. In the Longshoremen's Union, where Negroes are present in large numbers, we find the old difficulty arises in that the wage scale is much higher, working conditions better, but that there are approximately two men for every job. For the women, another acute problem exists. The cost of living demands that they leave home to work. Their specific occupations are chiefly public laundry work, domestic service, and the unskilled branches of the needle trade. Employment in public laundries is a new development. Within the last five years the laundry industry has been moving from Central Manhattan to North Harlem bringing with it the opportunity for approximately 20,000 Negro women to be employed in this particular trade. More than 3,000 are employed in the needle trades, a very few of whom are doing skilled work. Domestic service continues to be the one hope for their economic existence. It is singular to note in this connection that the proportionate ratio of Negro mothers who work as compared with white and immigrant mothers is three to one. In New York City 90.3 per cent of all Negro men and 57.9 per cent of all Negro women 10 years of age and over are at work.

The particular problem that looms in the face of any social adjustment is the mal-adjustment of Negro workers. West Indians who come to this country with exhaustive experience along clerical lines and bookkeeping and also skilled in trades find the Negro population unable to absorb their services in this connection and find numerous rebuffs from white employers. The same is true of the American Negro. In effecting an adjustment these persons take jobs as elevator operators, porters, and longshoremen and probably remain there as long as they are in New York. The employment problem, however, is not entirely one of the everyday worker, but it also affects the high school student. Teachers in the New York high schools find it very difficult to place their Negro graduates. Efforts are made to have this group cared for by its own people, but with very little success. A few women find an opportunity through Civil Service to work in clerical offices in the city, while the men seek employment in the post office. The boy or girl graduating from a trade school however, is often forced to forget his training and take up unskilled work. The question naturally arises "What shall we teach the colored children to prepare them for living in this community?" All in all this is the vital problem. The population is governed by a low wage scale for which it is not entirely to blame. This makes it necessary for all persons in the family to work, and while the population is endeavoring to live up to the false standards of living set around them, many different problems arise.

In an effort to improve the industrial and economic conditions among Negroes, the Urban League has been particularly interested in finding opportunities for those persons who are prepared to do certain types of work. . . . Quite recently at its initiation, an employment campaign for Negro workers was conducted in Harlem. A survey was made of 258 stores employing 160 Negroes chiefly as porters—and places that had a very large Negro patronage—asking that they permit opportunities for colored workers along with white in other occupations. Despite the fact that many persistent efforts were made, it was only possible to place 4 stenographers with one concern. The general attitude seemed to be either that Negroes were not capable of doing the work and employers were not willing to give them a trial, or that they were totally undesirable. Many of them of course were willing to employ them as porters and maids but nothing more. It appeared that Harlem business enterprises are indifferent toward the employment of colored help and will remain so until there is competition on the part of the Negro business which will force them to offer some inducements.

## Real Estate, Politics and Churches

. . . [T]here are no Negro banks in Harlem or elsewhere in New York. The most outstanding business development is that of real estate which increased from 98 to 247 during the period from 1910 through 1920. Since 1920 there have been an increase and a decrease in this number. The rapid rise in real estate values in Harlem gave many men their opportunity for financial success—others failed. True enough, the main businesses in this community are carried on not by Negroes, but by Jews and Caucasians [*sic*]. The development of Negro business has been confined—apart from real estate—to undertakers, venders, cigar stores, and insurance. One may note with satisfaction however, the rise of an investment company with $50,000 capital. This company is handled by a colored man who has had both academic and practical training having served as sales manager, and department trader for a Finance and Trust company. It is now listed in the 1926 Polk's Encyclopedia of Bankers and Brokers of the World. This is the first of its kind ever run by colored and its success has been phenomenal.

In politics Harlem is not solidly Republican. Both Democrat and Republican social clubs find seat in this section of New York. A Negro Democrat is Municipal Commissioner of Civil Service. The Republicans still strive for supremacy and at each election have colored candidates for various offices from this district. . . . With a population of almost 200,000 only 22,000 Negroes registered for the last gubernatorial election and only 10,000 of this number voted.

The increase in the population of Harlem naturally brought an increase of churches. In June 1926 there were more than 150 churches between 125th Street and 150th Street. Some of this number moved from the 53rd Street district of New York following their membership. Others are now institutions resultant of the migration from the South, while others are new approaches to the religious problems of the people. Despite the fact that the number is so large, recent figures . . . show that 60,000 of 175,000 of the Negro population in New York belong to churches. A meager few of them have community activities or attempt social approach to the problems of their members. Efforts at unification and improvement have been few and with little success. Fraternal societies, lodges, beneficiary leagues, and similar institutions continue to hold sway. The migration gave rise to such institutions as the Sons and Daughters of Virginia, the United Sons and Daughters of Georgia, and several other clubs representative of the states from which they came. These institutions have as their particular aim the adjustment of migration from that section of the country.

## Health and Housing

The problem of Health is outstanding. Statistics for a period of 25 years show some improvement as well as some losses in the battle for health. In view of the fact that at one time it was believed that the Negro peoples in America were doomed to extinction because of the diseases to which they appeared to be particularly susceptible and against which they had seemed to have little resistance, the health problem of the Negro during the last quarter of a century is particularly interesting. There has been a substantial decrease in the rates for tuberculosis, pneumonia, Bright's disease, and nephritis. For this period there has been a 30 per cent decrease in the death rates from tuberculosis, 25 per cent decrease from pneumonia, and 55.2 per cent in death rates from Bright's disease and nephritis. However, in common with the whites, the Negro has suffered an increase in his mortality rates in cancer and heart disease. During this period there has been a 120 per cent increase in death rates in cancer and heart disease. The rate of death from violence has increased 60 per cent since 1900, during the same period the white population's rate decreased 15.2 per cent. Phenomenal is the increase in the cancer rate of the Negro, the per cent increase from 1900–1925 being 120.5 per cent contrasted with 62.7 per cent for the white population. How much of this cancer is due to more exact diagnosis, better reporting, and to the increased length of the life of the Negro is an interesting and complex problem.

For the year 1924 it is interesting to note the death rate of the Negro population in Harlem. Comparing three sanitary areas comprising Harlem with the total rate for the borough of Manhattan we find that in one district the infant mortality rate is more than twice as high as the infant mortality rate for the borough. District 200 which comprises one of the older sections of Harlem has an infant mortality rate of 160 per 1,000 births as compared with 76 for the borough. The average yearly death rate for the Negro in Harlem is 22 per 1,000 while that for the borough is 12 per 1,000. . . .

Closely allied with the problem of health is that of housing. In the district where the health figures are most disappointing, the housing conditions are most undesirable in natural sequence. The basic housing situation in Harlem is not comparable with that of the lower East Side, but the social results are much more disappointing. Negro Harlem inherited the homes and tenements of people more economically secure than they. However, with its large increase in population, congestion and accompanying standards of living of the district became the particular problem. When the social and natural boundaries restricted them to certain territory, they found it necessary to live within a prescribed area. With the high increase in rents and inability to secure more space, the taking in of lodgers became an essential. A few houses have been erected in this area for the colored. In 1924–1925 approximately three new tenements were erected. John D. Rockefeller, Jr. has recently purchased a city block in Harlem on which are being erected modern tenements for the use of Negro residents of this district. This is the first big step toward improving the situation. The housing problem in Harlem also gave rise to one of the unique phases of Harlem, that is the rent parties. For many years these parties have been conducted for the specific purpose of raising funds to meet living expenses. An examination of several of their unique invitations show that they are held chiefly around the first and the 15th of the month, and that there is always good music and refreshments.

## Need of Study

. . . [Harlem] is a social laboratory in which racial and economic theories are being proved, disproved, and formulated. It has given birth to a new conception of American life. Its people are restless, socially, politically, and economically. To those interested in social research, it offers a virgin field. But what has been done? Aside from a few journalistic efforts our spasmodic investigations into various phases of its activity by a few students, no concerted efforts have been made to analyze the forces and factors at work in this section. It is not a fixed community, but constantly shifts its social processes. It does not know its resources, but gropingly seeks to find them. Here is a great need for a systematic, exhaustive study of Harlem, not into its single problems, as housing, recreation, health, justice, etc., but an integrated study of it in all its phases—which will emphasize diagnosis and treatment for its many problems.

# 9

# A Sociological Interpretation of the New Ku Klux Movement

*GUY B. JOHNSON*

While much has been said both for and against the K. K. K., very little has been written in the way of unprejudiced analysis and explanation of this movement which has aroused so much public discussion in the past few years. The present investigation was prompted by the desire to determine the salient sociological factors behind the origin and growth of the new Ku Klux Klan and to estimate the significance of those factors....

... [T]he chief articles of faith in the Ku Klux creed might be reduced to: (1) White Race Supremacy; (2) Pure Americanism; (3) The Preservation of Protestant Christianity; (4) The Protection of Womanhood and Morality. The noticeable thing in the whole program is the defensive characteristic: the Klan aims to *preserve,* to *protect,* to *prevent,* to *suppress.* In fact, the Ku Klux philosophy might be expressed briefly as interference with anything that conflicts with the established order of American society.

What really caused the new Ku Klux movement? This is one of the pertinent questions confronting the sociologist and social psychologist. As we have already

Reprinted, abridged, from *Social Forces 1* (May 1923): 440–445. Copyright © The University of North Carolina Press.

stated, it is useless to attempt to trace the movement back to any single cause. Rather it is an expression of certain attitudes, sentiments, antipathies, and fears, which have been produced by social forces and which have found release in the form of the Ku Klux movement.

1. In the first place the movement is very plainly a *post-war phenomenon.* In this the Klan is not an exception. Crises, especially wars, throughout history have been followed by various secret societies, such as the Assassins, the Knights Templars, the Fehm-Gerichte, the Fascisti, and the original Ku Klux Klan.

The end of war always means the breaking up of old habits and the facing of new crises. A war may be thought of as a long continued act of a group—an act which involves strain and tension and which, when it is finally brought to an end, releases the actors from their strain, but not from the effects of it. Thus it happens that the aftermath of war is often worse than the war itself. Confederates know that their most trying days came during the Reconstruction and not during the actual fighting of the Civil War. The analogy between the appearance of the original Ku Klux movement and the appearance of the new movement is striking. Both sprang up in the year following the close of a war; both were defensive secret societies, and both originated in the South.

The exact sociological effects of the late war have not yet been determined, but certain tendencies developed under, and accentuated by, the war strain are too plain to elude observation. Chief among these is the tendency toward nationalism: The America First philosophy. In Liberty Loan campaigns and in other patriotic work, the "one hundred per cent patriotic" cry became popular, while open hostility to aliens became a part of the patriotic duty of every American. German was thrown out of the schools; Germans were mistreated and mistrusted; wild stories of the underhand scheming of the enemy with Mexico, Brazil, and Japan were deliberately circulated to keep up the morale of the nation. And when the struggle was over, there was left a residue of the alarmist attitude which has not yet spent its force. It has continued to act in the capacity of protector of pure Americanism. If defeated the League of Nations program of Wilson, it put the bars on immigration, it deported aliens wholesale, it discouraged disarmament, and now it can be plainly seen in the new Ku Klux movement. The Ku Klux motto of "One hundred per cent pure Americanism" is but the echo of war experiences.

The war doubtless led also to an intensification of race feeling: the whites are more suspicious of the growing power of the negroes, while the negroes are less patient in their endurance of discriminatory treatment. The experience of service men in Europe served to accentuate race antipathies rather than to reduce them. Not only the South, but the nation as a whole, added fuel to its race fires as a result of the increased racial consciousness which the negro derived from his participation in the war, and this has been no small factor in precipitating the Ku Klux movement.

One reason why the aftermath of war is often worse than the struggle itself is the fact that economic conditions usually go through a period of depression following a war. The recent depression has had pronounced effects upon the amount of crime, poverty, unemployment, and general misery in the nation. But the worst part of the panic has been psychological rather than economic. A decade from now the so-called wave of crime, moral laxity, and general social deterioration of the post-war period may appear as a mere ripple on the surface; but in the hysteria of the post-war stage they have been magnified many times and have caused an amount of alarm wholly out of proportion to their real significance. The Ku Klux movement is, in great measure, the crystallization of the fears that have prevailed since the World War.

In brief, the World War necessitated the making of quick and radical adjustments to new conditions. Some have adjusted, but there remains a great body of Americans who have not only failed to adapt themselves to the currents of recent times, but have formed the new Ku Klux movement in the hope of retaining those doctrines, customs, and traditions which they consider to be essential for the security and well-being of the nation.

2. *A Reaction to "Modernism."* How much allowance should be made for the effects of the war cannot be said, but there were other currents contributing to the rise of the new Ku Klux movement independent of war influences, chief among which are: the loss of control by the church, especially over the young; the breakdown of strict parental control; the shifting of moral standards to a more individualistic basis; and an increasing liberalism in thought and speech, especially in academic circles. These tendencies are all interwoven and practically inseparable, but they may be noted separately for discussion.

The loss of control by the church has been the cause of much misgiving among orthodox religious people. Many of the functions which were once completely in the hands of the church have, in the last two decades, disappeared or passed over to some other institution. The complexity of modern life has decreased the time allowance which one might devote to things religious, while the greater attractiveness of amusement and recreation facilities has lessened the inclination toward religious conformity. The rather sudden rise of the movie, the automobile, and the modern dance has left the church on the defensive in regard to its control over the younger generation. . . .

Closely allied with the religious control problem is the disappearance of strict parental discipline. The Puritanic home of yesterday, with its unspared rod, its altar, and its taboos, is now a mere joke. As in the case of the church, in recent years the movie, the dance hall, the social club, and recreational agencies have taken from the home some of its traditional features. There are those who regard this as a natural step in the process of evolution, or as a healthful sign for the future methods of parental control; but there are also those who view it as the beginning of Bolshevism and the complete destruction of family ties. Their reaction has manifested itself in various ways, and one of the crystallizations of it is the new Ku Klux movement.

The tendencies toward individualism and liberalism go hand in hand. The degree of economic and political independence to which woman has attained is one indication of the extent of individualism. The failure of strict religious codes to adjust to modern conditions marked the advent of a more individualistic type of morality. Moral codes in general have been undergoing a period of unsettlement. Things that were once strictly taboo have become incorporated into daily life. Every habit, custom, and tradition have been subjected to critical inspection, and many, not being able to show any ready *raison d'etre,* have been treated with contempt or relegated to the dead past. The freedom in social relations between the sexes, the frankness in discussion of questions once tabooed, the extremes in women's clothes, the fad for jazz music and extreme forms of dancing—these and similar characteristics of the past few years have caused conservative people to hold grave doubts and fears for the future if "modernism" continues to lead the younger generation from the beaten paths.

In political circles there has arisen a host of socialistic and communistic doctrines which were either tolerated or ignored prior to the war. But the reactions of Americans in the war period has carried over until the nation as a whole has come to fear the alien and the radical as dangerous enemies to the national welfare.

In those academic circles where freedom of speech is complete, liberalism has become the order of the day. Especially has liberalism been manifested in matters pertaining to religion and theology. Orthodox Christians have looked in amazement at the seeming destruction of the foundations of their faith and hope. The stand of William J. Bryan on "modernism," evolution, etc., is typical of the reaction of the strictly orthodox Christians. Mr. Bryan is probably not a member of the Ku Klux Klan, but his attitude is synonymous with the attitudes of the great majority of Klansmen.

"Modernism," then, may be said to include all those forces which have been pulling away at the foundations of the established order of American society. We do not mean to say that all those Americans who have reacted negatively to the "modernistic" tendencies are participators in the new Ku Klux movement, but it is true that it is from such Americans that the new Ku Klux movement has emanated. The Imperial Wizard probably spoke with more truth than he realized when he said:

"The Ku Klux spirit . . . has never questioned the right of any man of any race to live his life and conduct his own affairs as he sees fit as long as such conduct does not conflict with the established order of societies." (The K. K. K. Forever, p. 12.)

3. *As a Special Southern Phenomenon.* While all that has been said in the two preceding sections is true, to some extent, of the whole nation, it is all doubly true of the South. There we find the stronghold of orthodox Protestantism, the practical application of the doctrine of white superiority, the adherence to a solid political doctrine which is intolerant of innovations in race relations, and an attachment to tradition and custom which places a premium on conformity to the established order. The tragedy of slavery and Reconstruction decreed

that southern politics and religion should be forever interwoven with the race question, so that healthful division on political, economic, and social questions has not been tolerated since the Civil War.

The New South is not. It is in the making. Until there is healthful division of political issues and tolerance of a greater degree of non-conformity, the New South cannot be said to have replaced the old. But those who are familiar with southern history and present conditions know that there are forces at work to dissolve the foundations of the Old South. The struggle between the New and the Old is sometimes open and bitter, sometimes unseen, but it goes on nevertheless.

In the first place, there is a very visible struggle between religious orthodoxy and liberalism. The South takes its religion much more seriously than does any other section of the country. Unorthodoxy in those matters controlled by the church—and these are surprisingly numerous—is a sin that has never been erased from the list of unpardonables. Every year sees its crop of academic men deserting their scientific work in southern religious schools because of their inability to adhere strictly to the accepted theology. Every year marks the desertion from the ministry of hundreds of young men who find it impossible to conform. Every year marks a clearer line of division between the "believers" and the "atheists." The new Ku Klux movement is one way by which the "believers" express their condemnation of the rising tide of "modernism" in religion and essay to preserve the old beliefs in all their purity.

In the second place, the rising consciousness of the negro race is slowly surpassing the capacity of present racial adjustments. The negro has asserted with increasing strength that his "place" is going to be a better place or he is not going to stay in it. The southern Klansman looks with misgivings as he watches the color line gradually grow dimmer to the negro. He realizes that if the modern radical negro has his way, the race problem of today is nothing compared to the race problem that will come. Anyone reared in the South can testify to the intricate maze of thought which greets the southerner when he tries to contemplate the future of the Southland with the negro possessing a degree of social and political equality which would give him a voice in the control of his own legal status. One might as well ask him, "What was before God?" as to ask the typical southerner to contemplate the negro on a plane of social equality. The thinking, forward-looking sourtherner can see some ray of hope, some way out of the problem, as he has shown in his attempts at inter-racial coöperation; but the masses are yet blindly afraid of "social equality," and the new Ku Klux movement is merely a more frank way of expressing what they have begun to feel so strongly in the past two decades.

As an historical fact, the Ku Klux method of treatment for obnoxious negroes has never disappeared from the South since it was popularized by the original Ku Klux Klan. The revival of the Klan has been proposed at various times since the old Klan disbanded. For example, during the Atlanta riot of 1906, newspapers in Georgia and South Carolina advocated the revival of the

Klan. It is not surprising, then, that the practice of extra-legal regulation has been revived during the times of stress and unsettlement following the World War. In point of the number of recorded cases of extra-legal regulation since the new Klan began operations, over ninety percent of them have occurred in the former slave states.

The "Solid South" has been no mere philosophical concept—it has been reality. And it is the conservative element of the Old South which now points with alarm to innovation and the breakdown of the old order. The new Ku Klux movement has spread to all sections of the nation and has significance as a national phenomenon, but primarily the reaction of the Old South to the advent of the New, accentuated of course by the aftermath of the Great War, is what has produced the new Ku Klux movement. The movement is, of course, a national phenomenon, but it is only in the South that social attitudes and sentiments are in such close concord with the general spirit of the movement that the Ku Klux philosophy has had free play in all of its forms.

To summarize, then, the analysis of the Ku Klux movement reveals the fact that it is a *security movement*. The Klansman is afraid of something, to put it plainly. Sometimes he is aware of his fears and admits that he fears; sometimes it is his subconscious mental conflict which causes him to subscribe to the Ku Klux creed, from an avowedly unselfish motive. He fears that Catholics and Jews or foreigners and negroes—or all of these—are making advances which undermine the institutions, beliefs, and attitudes which he holds to be final and everlasting. His defense reaction is in every way natural. The conflict between opposing social attitudes is a real and painful thing. The few people who think through their conflicts on a rational basis and make new adjustments to new situations do not resort to defensive measures. The Klansman does not adjust, he defends: that is why he is a Klansman. . . .

# 10

# The Negro Migration and Its Consequences

*GUY B. JOHNSON*

The northward movement of the negro attracts attention, not because it is a migration, but because it is a *negro* migration. What is there about the shifting of a mere half-million negroes from the South to the North to cause the nation more anxiety than did the arrival annually of one million foreign-born in the pre-war days? Why should it be considered more serious than the great urban migration which has in the last forty years transformed us from a rural to an urban nation? Such a phenomenon indeed calls for intelligent explanation.

The various explanations which have been propounded are more partisan than scientific. At one extreme there is the belief that the migration is primarily a flight from persecution. . . .

At the other extreme is the attitude taken by so many southern writers who see nothing but ingratitude in the negro's repudiation of the Southland; for, think they, the South is the natural home of the negro, and no one in all the world understands him like the southern white man. Still others believe that the migration is artificial and cannot proceed much further.

Between these extremes the truth is somewhere to be found. . . . Is the negro migration motivated primarily by economic forces or by social forces? This question has monopolized much of the discussion on the problem. And indeed it deserves a great part of our attention, for the final significance of the negro migration in American history shall depend upon whether it is a temporary response to unusual economic conditions, or a permanent phenomenon representing fundamental changes in our agricultural and industrial organization.

Reprinted, abridged, from *Social Forces* 2 (March 1924): 404–408. Copyright © The University of North Carolina Press.

## Analysis of the Migration

Obviously no single factor can explain the migration. One always comes nearer the truth by assuming a multiplicity of factors in explaining the causation of a social movement.

1. *A process of urbanization*—First of all, the negro migration must be regarded as a part of the great process of urbanization. Ever since the Civil War there has been a steadily increasing drift of negroes to the cities of both the North and the South. Emancipation alone was a force making for greater mobility of the once subject race, and the subsequent direction of southern agriculture made it inevitable that the negro should have to seek his fortune more and more in the urban world.

Some northward migration there has always been, but it did not become remarkable until after the World War began. Does the fact that the main current of negro migration turned to northern cities make it any less an urbanization process? Many writers become confused at this point, preferring to interpret the migration across the Mason-Dixon line as a flight from persecution. But there is no more than a negligible difference between the attitudes and motives of the negro who moves from southern farm to southern city and the negro who moves from southern farm to northern city.

Now the result of this changed direction of the negro urban trend is a different matter. Life in the North for the negro is going to have far-reaching effects upon him—effects which he perhaps does not now remotely perceive. If this were not true, the migration would have very little national significance....

2. *An economic phenomenon*—Urbanization is itself a phase of the great industrial revolution. Therefore we must suppose economic motives to a greater or lesser degree to be behind the negro migration. To begin with, the curve for the northward migration shows two high points: one during the industrial high-tide of the war, and the other in 1923 after the recovery from business depression. The latter suggests another factor: restriction of immigration. Statistics show that while the Three Per Cent Law admits some 300,000 or more Europeans annually, the net gain in unskilled laborers is slightly over 60,000. Certainly the negro is filling a part of the vacancy occasioned by the shortage of foreign labor.

Industrial expansion during the war and the restriction of immigration, then, may be called the economic "pull" of the North. On the other side there has been a corresponding "push" from the South.[1] Short cotton crops have contributed their share to the negro's dissatisfaction with the southern farm. Furthermore, a tendency toward the concentration of land ownership in many of the Southern states is halting the negro in his acquisition of agricultural lands....

3. *An expression of social unrest*—That the northward migration also repre-

---

[1] The "pull" is, psychologically speaking, what makes the "push" felt, for dissatisfaction with one environment often depends upon the knowledge that a better situation is a possibility.

sents a growing restlessness of the American negro cannot be denied. The relative importance of this element of unrest cannot yet be determined because of the complexity of factors, but there is evidence to show that it is operating. Too often this spirit of unrest has been regarded as a fiercely rebellious attitude which the southern negro has developed in the past few years, from which it is reasoned that the migration is a reaction from unfair conditions and persecutions.[2] But those who are thoroughly acquainted with negroes in the South are well aware that the illiterate, indifferent, dependent negro is still typical. Race consciousness and racial aspirations mean practically nothing to him, and the spirit of unrest is very little more than the mere realization that he could move if conditions became unbearable.

There is a small minority of southern negroes, however, who, having advantages above the average of their race in education, culture, and living conditions, are keenly aware of their problems, are race conscious, and resent sharply their position as an inferior caste. Doubtless this class is adding more and more to the stream of migrants; but for the great mass of negroes in the south unrest is yet a somewhat unsubstantial feeling—not a primary motive for migration, but occasionally strong enough to turn the scales in favor of a northward move.

Social unrest will doubtless in time become characteristic of negro life. It is inevitable that as the process of education widens and the circle of race consciousness expands, the negro shall be less and less inclined to accept his present status. The real test of strength of this factor in the present migration will come later when the economic motives mentioned above have receded in importance.

To repeat, the final significance of the negro migration depends upon whether it is a temporary adjustment to abnormal industrial conditions or a permanent reaction representing fundamental changes in the economic and social fabric of the nation. If southern agriculture sees the passing of King Cotton and the wholesale adoption of scientific methods, the day of the negro on the southern farm is over, and well might he seek home and fortune in the more promising North and West. After all, only a half-million negroes have deserted the South during the present migration—not enough to justify much anxiety yet—and the movement must go on until it has deprived the South of several millions of its colored population before its national consequences can be remarkable. That southern agriculture is changing, however, cannot be doubted, so that at least one cause of the migration may be regarded as permanent. Then, too, the presence of a negro labor supply in the North has already done much to quiet the cry for immigration, so that the restriction of immigration also bids fair to become a permanent feature. It would do no harm, at any rate, for the nation to regard the migration as a force which shall in the end achieve a complete redistri-

---

[2] The following statistics are significant here: Between 1888 and 1918, Montgomery County, Georgia, had five lynchings. The negro population decreased from 7,310 to 4,348; the white population from 12,328 to 4,768. If lynching caused migration from this county, it affected the whites more than the blacks. In Harrison County, Texas, in spite of 16 lynchings between 1900 and 1920, the negro population increased from 13,544 to 15,639.

bution of negro population and to prepare accordingly to meet the strain on existing racial adjustments.

## Consequences of the Migration

Assuming, then, that the migration is to go far beyond its present proportions, what are the consequences? . . . The more *immediate results* of the migration need little elaboration. Let us outline them briefly.

1. *Agricultural*—Southern agriculture has few regrets over the loss of the negro, for the southern white land-owner is waking to the fact that the exodus of the negro is a result and not a cause of the agricultural crisis and that his elimination is a healthful sign. . . .

2. *Industrial*—The negro as a laborer in the north is already creating new problems. On the one hand, they are the same problems as appear with respect to an influx of cheap foreign labor; on the other hand, they are problems of race. The East St. Louis and Chicago race riots are evidence of the inevitable race conflict which must precede the mutual adjustment of the negro and northern industry.

3. *Political*—The negro vote has already become the pawn of politicians in northern cities, notably Chicago, and it is not improbable that the negro may become such a power in municipal politics that the philosophy and practice of the North in regard to his political status may be at variance. Of course, the extent to which the negro in the North will use the ballot toward improving his racial status cannot be foreseen but we may point out the fact that a wide range of problems may arise from that direction.

4. *An intensified struggle for existence* is not least among the consequences of the migration—not only of negro versus negro and versus white labor, but of the negro with the northern winters, low wages, poor housing, social discrimination, and a host of other conditions. . . .

Now let us take the broad look and attempt to detect the more *ultimate consequences* of the redistribution of negro population.

1. *The race problem cannot remain sectional*—that is certain. Once it could be ignored or disposed of philosophically by the North and West. Gradually, however, as the entire nation comes into daily contact with the negro at an increasing number of points, problems of race relations shall begin to have a national tone. Sections which have never known the meaning of the negro question are destined to become intensely interested in their new "race problems." Between the discriminating practices of the South and the abstract equality of the North opinion shall vacillate in these new negro sections until black-white relations are re-defined.

2. *New racial adjustments*—Old racial adjustments are rapidly weakening. The rise of the Ku Klux Klan is largely attributable to a reaction to the liberal tendency in race relations. Certainly the redistribution of the negro population is to

strain present racial adjustments still more. The North is going to learn more about the negro in the next ten years than it has learned since the Civil War; and however much we would like to believe otherwise, the attitude of the North cannot help but become a shade less tolerant than it has been. Thousands of negroes who find economic salvation in the North are to be disappointed socially. That inevitable color line will intrude, and the negro will be forced back into his own race, will be thrown more and more upon the organizations and institutions of his own race for his salvation.

We must not think of the negro in the North as being permanently a mere industrial factor. Sooner or later he will enter commercial, business, and professional pursuits and shall live in the smaller cities and towns of the North as well as in the industrial centers. It is then—when the negro is distributed fairly evenly throughout the North—that the real test of present racial attitudes shall come. . . .

What passes for tolerance in the North is often only a passive intolerance, and there is danger that the North may react too far from its traditional belief in equality.

Truly, racial adjustments are going to be tested in every way. However much we would like to believe that the spirit of coöperation in race relations is going to become supreme as a result of the North's new interest in the problem, we must admit that human nature and history point the other way, namely, that the attitude of the masses of the whites is more likely to become less tolerant.

In the South, too, the agricultural exodus is leaving an urban-dwelling negro race more and more at the mercy of the white man. While the movement toward inter-racial coöperation will doubtless continue to grow, it cannot counteract the tendency toward a more rigid southern caste system.

Both in the North and in the South, then, the opportunity to put race relations on an intelligent and coöperative basis shall challenge us; but our emotional and impulsive reactions are likely to triumph, with the net result that the negro shall be forced to depend upon himself to an increasing extent. How difficult to dare test democracy in race relations, to practice equality, to permit open competition; and how easy to put the whole thing out of the realm of conflict by entrenching behind the barriers of caste.

3. *Birth of negro nationalism*—Any attempt to solve the race problem by a caste arrangement merely postpones the day when the white man must face the issue squarely and settle it, not according to his own convenience, but by making concessions to the powerful and race-conscious blacks. The progress of the negro since emancipation should be warning enough against the caste method.

The city has ever been the birthplace of intense racial consciousness and of nationalism. The case of the negro is not far different from that of the Central European racial groups which developed the spirit of nationalism during the nineteenth century. The concentration of negro population in American cities points toward the rise of a class of negroes dependent upon industrial labor and limited business pursuits—the negro middle class. And it is only a matter of time until this class manifests that consciousness which has so often been the mother of nationalism.

Is the rise of negro nationalism too improbable, impossible? No. Does not every intolerant move of the white man beget stronger consciousness in the negro race? And does not every inter-racial coöperative effort teach the negro the way to self-development and power? Negro leaders are even now grasping the idea of a racial mission, of a divinely ordained plan behind the negro's bondage and his struggle with the white race, of the negro's right to a national existence, and soon the disciples of the new nationalism shall carry the message to all their race.

It is not that the negro is at present fully aware of any nationalistic movement on his part. His motives for migration are a different matter from the remote effects which that migration is going to have upon him. But history teaches us that the subordinate race, having tasted half-freedom and having sipped of the higher culture of the "superior" race, but finding the barriers set up against complete equality, turns to nationalism as a means of achieving its aspirations; and the broad look through the present shifting of negro population leads to the conviction that one of its greatest consequences shall be a movement toward negro nationalism.

# 11

# Twenty Years' Pioneering in Race Relations

*HERBERT J. SELIGMANN*

Perhaps the best measure of the social change which has taken place since the founding of the National Association for the Advancement of Colored People, in 1909, is the wide acceptance and endorsement of a program which had then few protagonists or defenders.

A race riot, late in 1908, in Springfield, Illinois, erstwhile home of Lincoln, crystallized the thinking and brought together the people that were to form the N.A.A.C. P. A Southerner, William English Walling, in Chicago when the riot occurred, went promptly to the scene. He saw sights that horrified and shocked him. His investigations and studies of the conditions that had produced this breakdown of civilization took form in public lectures, and in articles.

One of his articles attracted the attention of a northern woman, Miss Mary White Ovington, who had been studying the Negro's adjustment to conditions in New York. Others were communicated with, Charles Edward Russell, Bishop Alexander Walters, Miss Lillian D. Wald, Mrs. Florence Kelley, Oswald Garrison Villard, then editor of the New York *Evening Post;* and Henry Moskowitz, later an officer in the administration of Mayor Mitchell.

This group of people augmented by others were agreed in feeling that there was "pressing need for an organization to combat the tide of race prejudice that was then rising throughout the nation."

Reprinted, abridged, from *Social Forces 8* (September 1929): 105–108. Copyright © The University of North Carolina Press.

To the white and colored people who first held meetings was added a colored leader of national prominence, Dr. W. E. B. Du Bois, at that time professor in Atlanta University and leader of a group of Negroes known as the Niagara movement seeking justice for their race.

In writing of the foundation of the National Association for the Advancement of Colored People in 1909, Mr. Walling has "dated" it from the time Mr. Bois came inasmuch as "we all felt that the organization itself had to give an example of successful coöperation of the races and that it must be founded upon the American principle of self-government and self-development."

From its inception the Association concerned with the fundamental citizenship status of the American Negro, studied the most flagrant violation of his rights through lynchings by which mobs deprived him of court trial and of his life. A statistical study was made, derived from the Chicago Tribune's records and other available sources, and published as "Thirty Years of Lynching." In addition, investigators were sent to the scene of mob murders to study the individual instance and the conditions producing it.

The result of this work was to disprove the current assumption that rape was a determining cause of most lynchings: this charge being made in the case of less than one in five of mob victims, and an accusation stimulating mob action being far from proof of guilt.

The struggle against lynching took the form of publications, a press campaign, lectures and mass meetings, and even of legislative action. It was gradually made clear that lawlessness was no cure for crime, and that the barbarities of lynching were a national concern. The repeated introduction in the House of Representatives of a federal anti-lynching bill—passed there in 1922 by a vote of 230 to 119, though blocked in the Senate—fostered the sentiment which helped to lessen the number of lynchings in 1928 to their lowest record, eleven.

Its defense of the Negro's citizenship rights necessarily made legal action an outstanding part of the Association's work. By good fortune, its President, Moorfield Storey, one of the most distinguished lawyers of the country, a former President of the American Bar Association, was able actively to prosecute a number of its more important actions; and was the only representative of any private organization to file a brief in the celebrated case in which, in 1915, the United States Supreme Court held Grandfather Clauses to be unconstitutional.

Five victories in all have been won by the Association before the United States Supreme Court, each of them arising out of a question that affected not alone the Negro, but all minority racial groups in the country. Thus, in 1917, in the celebrated Louisville Segregation case (Buchanan vs. Warley), it was established that state laws or city ordinances ordaining separate residential districts for white and colored people were unconstitutional, a decision reinforced by the Supreme Court's opinion of 1927 in the Louisiana Segregation case, also fought by the Association.

The Association's investigation of the peonage conditions which produced the Arkansas riots of 1919, eventuated not only the liberation of colored farmers unjustly sentenced to death and long prison terms; but, again through the United States Supreme Court, established a vital principle, namely, that trials held in an atmosphere of mob domination did not constitute due process of law.

The fifth of the Association's victories before the Supreme Court, in the so-called Texas White Primary Case, 1927, attacked the bulwark of Negro disfranchisement in the South. The law enacted in 1924 by the Texas legislature, excluding Negroes from Democratic party primaries in that state, and therefore from any real voice in elections, was held unconstitutional. The attack thus begun against disfranchisement of properly qualified Negro citizens, is being carried forward through the courts in cases challenging the right of state political committees to exclude Negroes from primaries by passing upon the qualifications of party members and requiring that only party members so accepted may vote.

The victories won before the Supreme Court and state courts of last resort, are only part of a comprehensive scheme which has included the framing of New York's model civil rights act and the contest of innumerable civil and criminal cases. Altogether, the legal and legislative work of the N. A. A. C. P. has been aimed at equal public status and equal administration of the law for all citizens, irrespective of race. One of the most significant effects of this work has been the increasing number of appeals from white men in the South, who recognize the impartial nature of the program of the N. A. A. C. P., and wish its help in obtaining justice where colored people personally known to them are the victims of discrimination or brutality.

Two kinds of courts are essential to more enlightened contact between the races, the courts of justice and the court of public opinion. Recognizing this fact, the N. A. A. C. P. has consistently worked with leaders of public opinion in the South toward the common end. Representatives of the Commission on Interracial Coöperation have spoken at N. A. A. C. P. meetings, and communication has been frequent with this body and with outstanding editors of Southern dailies.

The positive contribution of the Negro has had a prominent part in the Association's educational campaign. Before the present era, in which Negro authors, singers, musicians, actors, playwrights take such a prominent part, the N. A. A. C. P. had begun to award annually the Spingarn Medal; utilizing the occasion to call public attention to outstanding achievements by Negroes in music and literature, in science, business, and in the fields of government and public service. The award of the Spingarn Medal came to be recognized as an event of national and even international significance. To its staff the Association attracted those men who were able to voice its program and, in the form of essays, social studies, poetry interpreting the Negro, the Association's staff have published some twenty-odd books of general circulation leaving out of consideration numerous contributions to leading magazines and newspapers. . . .

The social and political affiliations of the N. A. A. C. P. are no less varied than its racial constituents. It has mattered nothing whether a man or woman were of the shade of opinion labeled radical or conservative, so long as the Association's general program furnished a point of focus. In this way it has been able to bring into contact varied talents toward peaceful progress in the adjustment of the interracial relations that threatened more than once to degenerate into violent and brutal dislocation. . . .

# Part III

# Surviving the Great Depression: 1930-1940

## Introduction

For those who have known only the prosperous years since World War II, it is difficult to imagine the fear and despair that swept America during the 1930s. The stock market crash of 1929 was followed by a full decade of extremely lean and difficult times. A proud, confident, optimistic nation was disoriented; high aspirations for the future gave way to hopes of just getting by. Survival became the basic concern.

Such times are not conducive to improved race relations. The promise of positive change engendered during the 1920s gave way, too, to issues of survival. Black, Native, and Hispanic Americans were overwhelmingly poor even before the Great Depression struck; Asian-Americans were only beginning to advance economically. So racial minorities were particularly vulnerable to the full force of the economic collapse. Necessarily, then, the chief race relations issues centered upon attainment of equal access to jobs and relief benefits. The sociological literature responded rapidly to this altered racial scene.

In Selection 12, John Murchison, a black economist working for the federal government in Washington, D.C., analyzes black economic difficulties. He presents extensive relief data, answers the then current rationalizations justifying lower minimum wages for black workers, and emphasizes the intense racial discrimination of craft unions. A host of other pointed papers considered these same issues. One study presented evidence to support the "suspicion" that blacks were systematically underrepresented on the relief rolls in farm areas throughout the country.[1] Another made a close inspection of conditions in seven North Carolina counties and unearthed some surprising results; while illegitimate births and prison commitments had both risen, so had better bal-

---

[1] O. L. Harvey, "Negro representation on relief," *Social Forces 14* (1936): 582–584.

anced diets and black solidarity.[2] Other papers detailed how the South's system of agricultural credit kept black farmers down,[3] and how the U.S. Communist Party attempted to organize a sharecropper's union in Alabama in the early 1930s.[4] Charles Johnson, the Chicago-trained black sociologist who was now at Fisk and establishing his position as a major commentator on the Southern scene, documented in two papers how the Depression inflicted its most severe effects upon blacks and how racism influenced industrial employment and worker solidarity.[5] Finally, a series of *Social Forces* articles viewed the black worker in the 1930s, and held out hope that the newly formed Congress of Industrial Organizations (CIO) would at long last allow black workers to join unions on an equal basis.[6] A longer-term view of this vital issue will be supplied later by Bonacich (Selection 40).

One of the lasting debates of the sociology of race relations began in the 1930s, even though it had little immediate relevance to the problem of survival. The basic question was: How much of black life can be attributed to slavery, segregation, and other salient conditions of the New World experience? And how much can be attributed to African survivals? The next two selections, which helped to open the debate, were authored by its two principal participants, E. Franklin Frazier and Melville Herskovits. Frazier, later elected the first black president of the American Sociological Society, was firm in his conviction that slavery was the chief determinant. In Selection 13, he states flatly that "our present knowledge of the conditions under which slavery was established in America leads us to believe that *the Negro was completely stripped of his social heritage* in the process." (Italics added.)

By contrast, Herskovits, the famous anthropologist long at Northwestern University,[7] maintains with equal firmness that a full understanding of black American life is impossible without "knowing the cultural base-line from which the New World Negroes were launched into their adventures in the New World." Furthermore, Herskovits attempts to demonstrate the principal regions of West

[2] Guy B. Johnson, "The Negro and the depression in North Carolina," *Social Forces 12* (1933): 103–115.

[3] Roland B. Eutsler, "Agricultural credit and the Negro farmer," *Social Forces 8* (1930): 565–573.

[4] John Beecher, "The share croppers' union in Alabama," *Social Forces 13* (1934): 124–132.

[5] Charles S. Johnson, "Incidence upon the Negroes," *American Journal of Sociology 40* (1935): 737–745, and *idem,* "The conflict of caste and class in an American industry," *American Journal of Sociology 42* (1936): 55–65.

[6] Robert C. Francis, "The Negro in industrial unionism," *Social Forces 15* (1936): 272–275; Seaton Manning, "Negro trade unionists in Boston," *Social Forces 17* (1938): 256–266; and Arthur M. Ross, "The Negro worker in the Depression," *Social Forces 18* (1940): 550–559.

[7] Three of Part III's articles were written by anthropologists (Herskovits and Warner) and an economist (Murchison). The two anthropologists are widely known in sociology, and their work on American topics was always of great interest to sociologists. But their publishing in sociological journals also reflects the fact that the social sciences in the 1930s were far less differentiated than they are now. Thus, sociology separated from economics at Harvard only in 1931; and anthropology from sociology at Chicago in the 1930s, at North Carolina in the 1960s, and not at all to this day at Oberlin College and many other smaller campuses.

Africa from which the slaves were acquired and some of the fascinating cultural links that may exist between these areas and black life in the New World (though, of course, behavioral parallels do not prove common origin).

Like many heated debates within social science, the Frazier-Herskovits dispute extended over many years,[8] exaggerated the actual differences between the two positions, carried within it significant political implications, but ultimately involved arguments that did not directly address the same issues. In large measure, the two adversaries talk past each other in Selections 13 and 14 by using totally different contexts. Frazier, a student of Park's and a sociologist who believed causal origins derive from social structure, was primarily interested in the black American family.[9] His doctoral dissertation at the University of Chicago was published in 1931 as *The Negro Family in Chicago;* the major work of his distinguished carrer, *The Negro Family in the United States,* appeared in 1939 and received the Ainsfield Award as the most important race relations book of the year.[10] These prolific and persuasive writings, as well as a growing tendency within sociology at this point to ascribe black and white differences of all types to racial discrimination, caused Frazier's thesis to win wide acceptance among both black and white sociologists.[11]

The sweeping degree of Frazier's influence can be indicated quantitatively through cross-citations, the number of times his works are cited by other specialists in race relations. A 1971 study of the citations of racial and minority relations papers published between 1944 and 1968 showed that Frazier was

[8] Thus, both Frazier and Herskovits battled on into the 1940s. M. Herskovits, *The Myth of the Negro Past* (New York: Harper & Row, 1941); E. F. Frazier's rejoinder to Herskovits, *American Sociological Review 8* (1943): 402–404; and E. F. Frazier, *The Negro in the United States.* (New York: Macmillan, 1949), pp. 3–21.

[9] For an informed assessment of Frazier's life and work, see: G. Franklin Edwards (ed.), *E. Franklin Frazier on Race Relations* (Chicago: University of Chicago Press, 1968), and G. Franklin Edwards, "E. Franklin Frazier, " in J. Blackwell and M. Janowitz (eds.), *Black Sociologists* (Chicago: University of Chicago Press, 1974), pp. 85–117.

[10] In addition, Frazer published numerous articles on the black family and his slavery-causation thesis during the 1930s: "Certain aspects of conflict in the Negro family," *Social Forces 10* (1931): 76–84; "An analysis of statistics on Negro illigitimacy in the United States," *Social Forces 11* (1932): 249–257; "Children in black and mulatto families," *American Journal of Sociology 39* (1933): 12–29; and "The impact of urban civilization upon Negro family life," *American Sociological Review 2* (1937): 609–618.

[11] For example, though citing Frazier only once in another context, Charles Johnson advanced the same thesis a few years later ("The present status and trends of the Negro Family," *Social Forces 16* [1937]: 247–257). And even papers of this period concerned with black nationalism do not counter Frazier's dominant position. Thus, T. G. Standing, "The possibility of a distinctive culture contribution from the American Negro," *Social Forces 17* (1938): 99–106, in arguing that a distinctive black culture was forming in America, still maintained that it would not be very different from the dominant white culture. And a sympathetic account of the early days of "the Black Muslims" made it clear that this movement was a consequence of white racism and not African survivals. E. D. Beynon, "The voodoo cult among Negro migrants in Detroit," *American Journal of Sociology 43* (1938): 894–907.

the single most cited author of this period, followed closely by Robert Park and Gunnar Myrdal.[12]

Herskovits, as an anthropologist, emphasized the causal power of culture. In selection 14, the reader will note that Herskovits is interested in the cross-Atlantic transmission of place-names, superstitions, dance steps, singing forms, speech patterns, and religious folk customs. These are all cultural items of more limited scope than the broad structural features of black families that intrigued Frazier. And just as detailed case studies of black American families had profoundly influenced Frazier's thinking, an extended field trip to Surinam as well as his lifelong interest in Africa profoundly shaped Herskovits's thinking. Later he broadened his contentions into book form, *The Myth of the Negro Past* (1941). His arguments were received cooly at the time by sociologists and black intellectuals alike. Observe Herskovits's initial attack on DuBois for holding a position similar to that of Frazier. But the African survival position gained followers in the 1960s. Some of these followers were, not surprisingly, anthropologists, armed with extensive data on Africa and in opposition to the then current notion of a "culture of poverty."[13] Many were black intellectuals, for the political implications of the debate had shifted over the three decades. While DuBois and Frazier sought to establish white culpability for black social disorganization, many black thinkers by the late 1960s sought recognition for a distinctive black American culture. This shift substantiates Robin William's point cited in the Introduction. Rarely does the complexity of social life allow simple absolutes. Both Frazier and Herskovits were correct in uncovering part of the puzzle; a synthesis of their arguments is now taking shape in the sociological understanding of American race relations.

The 1930s also marked the beginning of attention to Mexican Americans. Study of the large-scale migration of Mexicans to the United States from 1910 on was suddenly reported on in four papers in two successive volumes of the *American Journal of Sociology*. First, Robert Redfield, the Chicago anthropologist, and Max Handman, of the University of Texas, each discussed factors that led Mexicans to immigrate.[14] Then Emory Bogardus, the University of Southern California sociologist, sympathetically described how discrimination, and segregation in particular, retarded the assimilation of Mexican immigrants.[15] Paul Taylor demonstrated three rather distinct streams of Mexican migration:

[12] H. E. Bahr, T. J. Johnson, and M. R. Seitz, "Influential scholars and works in the sociology of race and minority relations, 1944–1968," *American Sociologist 6* (1971): 296–298.

[13] Charles A. Valentine, *Culture and Poverty: Critique and Counter-Proposals* (Chicago: University of Chicago Press, 1968).

[14] Robert Redfield, "The antecedents of Mexican immigration to the United States," *American Journal of Sociology 35* (1930): 433–438, and Max S. Handman, "Economic reasons for the coming of the Mexican immigrant," *American Journal of Sociology 35* (1930): 601–611.

[15] Emory S. Bogardus, "The Mexican immigrant and segregation," *American Journal of Sociology 36* (1930): 74–80.

one from northeastern Mexico to south Texas; another from the central plateau of Mexico to Chicago; and the third from the west coast of Mexico to California's Imperial Valley.[16]

Interest in Asian Americans also increased in the journals under review. Nine of the twelve articles, however, involved Hawaii. The three exceptions described the evolution of Chinese tongs, Chinese family life in America, and the Japanese Americans of Puget Sound, Washington.[17] The Hawaiian articles still stressed assimilation but began now to present a less idealized view of the islands. Social distance preferences between groups and stereotypes of Hawaiians as dumb and slow-moving are revealed for the first time.[18]

Selection 15 draws these new trends together with an interesting cycle theory. Bogardus, like Frazier, is one of the most cited authors in the race relations literature;[19] he is particularly well known for his measurement of social distance between social groups. Here Bogardus applies a seven-stage model to the American reception of Mexican, Filipino, Chinese, and Japanese immigrants. A somewhat modified and elaborated version of Park's famous cyclical theory of contact, competition, accommodation, and assimilation (see Selection 45), this model shares with Park's such problems as an unjustified assumption of a unilinear progression. Nonetheless, Selection 15 usefully emphasizes the similarities in the American experience of these otherwise diverse groups.

Sociological work during the 1930s is also characterized by marked improvement in both quantification and research design. A recent analysis of the establishment of the *American Sociological Review* in 1935 as the official journal of the American Sociological Society, replacing the Society's sponsorship of the *American Journal of Sociology,* suggests that resistance to this quantification trend was involved in this heated internal struggle within the discipline.[20] At any rate, the trend toward empirical rigor is unmistakable and soon affects the race relations literature. To be sure, the older biological framework was still, if now scantily, represented. One article authored by a Swedish scientist, repeats Galton's eugenics arguments; another actually holds that the "Chinese represent the eastern wing of the Alpine race."[21] But the new empirical look now pre-

---

[16] Paul S. Taylor, "Note on streams of Mexican migration," *American Journal of Sociology 36* (1931): 287–288.

[17] C. N. Reynolds, "The Chinese tongs," *American Journal of Sociology 40* (1935): 612–623; Norman S. Hayner and Charles N. Reynolds, "Chinese family life in America," *American Sociological Review 2* (1937): 630–637; and John A. Rademaker, "The Japanese in the social organization of the Pudget Sound region," *American Journal of Sociology 40* (1935): 338–343.

[18] Jitsuichi Masuoka, "Race preference in Hawaii," *American Journal of Sociology 41* (1936): 635–641, and Margaret M. Lam, "Racial myth and family tradition-worship among part-Hawaiians," *Social Forces 14* (1936): 405–409.

[19] Bogardus ranked a close fourth behind Frazier in the number of 1944–1968 cross-references to his work in the race relations literature. Bahr, Johnson, and Seitz, "Influential Scholars."

[20] Patricia M. Lengermann, "The founding of the *American Sociological Review*," *American Sociological Review 44* (1979): 185–198.

[21] Herman Lundborg, "Race biology perspectives," *Social Forces 9* (1931): 397–401, and

dominates. A content analysis of daily newspapers shows disproportionately heavy reporting of "anti-social" news about blacks;[22] an analysis of jail sentences suggests racial discrimination in the administration of justice;[23] and another study demonstrates that different social class neighborhoods in the Durham, North Carolina, black district had crime rates that varied by more than a factor of five.[24]

Perhaps, the most remembered and still-cited empirical article of the 1930s is Selection 16. Richard LaPiere, a Stanford sociologist, conducted a simple field experiment on the acceptance of Chinese travelers at hotels and restaurants around the country. His results show a sharp discrepancy between denial of service requested through the mails and general acceptance in face-to-face situations. The interpretation of these findings is one of the longer-running debates in the social psychological literature; it becomes involved in the theoretical ferment of the 1950s we shall discuss shortly. Many have believed that this famous investigation demonstrated that attitudes do not predict behavior. But recent discussion points out that this research design does not allow such a sweeping interpretation.[25] Notice carefully that the respondents to LaPiere's questionnaire were not necessarily the same individuals whose behavior was observed. More important, LaPiere's instructive study shows the distinction between words and deeds, between "two behavioral responses in two very different structured situations" that place "the person into two very different roles"—not the distinction between "attitudes and behavior" as such.[26] Nevertheless, LaPiere's investigation rates as one of the most theoretically significant empirical studies of this period.

The dominant theoretical model for black–white relations in the South at this time is described by its originator in Selection 17. W. Lloyd Warner, another distinguished anthropologist from the University of Chicago, advanced his caste and class model in 1937. It was a needed formalization of ideas that had been informally accepted for some time in sociology: namely, that both race and class must be considered to achieve a balanced picture. This model guided the work of Warner's associates—Allison Davis, Burleigh Gardner, and Mary Gardner —that led to the classic report of a southern town, *Deep South*.

---

Griffin Taylor, "The Nordic and Alpine races and their kin: A study of ethnological trends," *American Journal of Sociology 37* (1932): 67–81.

[22] Noel P. Gist, "The Negro in the daily press," *Social Forces 10* (1932): 405–411.

[23] Thorsten Sellin, "Race prejudice in the administration of justice," *American Journal of Sociology 41* (1935): 212–217.

[24] Hugh Brinton, "Negroes who run afoul of the law," *Social Forces 11* (1932): 96–101.

[25] Howard Schuman and Michael P. Johnson, "Attitudes and behavior," in Alex Inkeles (ed.), *Annual Review of Sociology* (Palo Alto, Cal.: Annual Reviews, 1976), pp. 161–207; Ronald C. Dillehay, "On the irrelevance of the classical negative evidence concerning the effects of attitudes on behavior," *American Psychologist 28* (1973): 887–891; and Herbert C. Kelman, "Attitude and behavior: A social-psychological problem," in J. M. Yinger and S. J. Cutler (eds.), *Major Social Issues* (New York: Free Press, 1978), pp. 412–420.

[26] Kelman, "Attitude and Behavior," p. 415.

# 12

# Some Major Aspects of the Economic Status of the Negro

*JOHN P. MURCHISON*

Since the major concern of this paper is not "whence" or "what," but "whither" the Negro economically, the general picture of the present economic status of the Negro has been surveyed under four main divisions: (1) the gainful Negro workers in the United States classified into socio-economic groups in 1930; (2) for purposes of comparison, Negro workers in the relief population classified into socio-economic groups as of May, 1934; (3) the more insistent economic problems confronting the Negro in the recovery program and; (4) that the solution of the Negro's economic plight is not to be found in any kind of tie-up with organized craft unionism in the United States. . . .

Of the 5,503,535 Negroes gainfully employed in the United States in 1930, 36.1 per cent were engaged in agriculture, and 63.9 per cent in industrial or other urban occupations. Of those employed in urban occupations, 18.6 per cent were employed in manufacturing and mechanical industries, 28.6 per cent in domestic and personal services, and 7.2 per cent in transportation and communication. Of all the Negroes gainfully occupied in 1930, 81 per cent were employees and 19 per cent were proprietors, managers, and professional persons; 15.9 per cent of the proprietor class were farmers.

Of all the Negroes gainfully occupied in 1930, 3.2 per cent were skilled workers and foremen, 9.4 per cent were semi-skilled workers and 66.9 per cent

Reprinted, abridged, from *Social Forces 14* (October 1935): 114–119. Copyright © The University of North Carolina Press.

were unskilled laborers and servants; 20.2 per cent of these unskilled workers were farm laborers. Any policy and plan, therefore, that may result in the greatest good for the greatest number of Negroes must be concerned primarily with semi-skilled and unskilled laborers and servants.

In October, 1933, there were approximately 13,600,000 persons or 3,450,000 cases[1] on relief, of which 81.3 per cent were white and 16.7 per cent were Negroes. Negroes on relief constituted about 17.8 per cent of the entire Negro population, while whites on relief constituted 9.5 per cent of the entire white population. Thus, the percentage of Negroes receiving relief was almost twice that of whites. Those on relief were highly concentrated in certain sections of the country; 96 per cent of the Negroes on relief in October, 1933, were found in 24 states, 17 of which were southern states. The range of percentages of Negroes on relief was from 4.3 per cent in Virginia to 38 per cent in Ohio, while the range of percentages of whites on relief was from 2.2 per cent in Virginia to 22.6 per cent in West Virginia. In only four states, Mississippi, Arkansas, Kentucky, and West Virginia, the percentages of whites on relief exceeded the percentages of Negroes on relief. In all cities with appreciable Negro population the percentages of Negroes on relief exceeded those of whites.

In October, 1934, there were approximately 18,000,000 persons, or 4,700,000 cases on relief. While an analysis of such data as have been collected subsequent to the 1933 census does not enable one to give a precise estimate on the number of Negroes now on relief, the Research Statistics and Finance Section of the Federal Emergency Relief Administration estimated that there were 857,000 Negro cases on relief rolls in May, 1934. This estimate and other evidence available give very little reason to believe that the proportion of the relief load which is Negroid has shifted markedly since October, 1933.

A preliminary estimate of the occupational distribution of gainful workers on urban relief rolls in 1934 indicates that, in May, 65.5 per cent of the Negroes on the relief rolls were unskilled workers, 18 per cent were semi-skilled, 8.3 per cent were skilled workers and foremen, 1.9 per cent were clerical workers, 0.7 per cent were proprietary workers and 0.8 per cent were professional workers. There were a total of 29,600 white-collar workers, embracing professional, proprietary, and clerical groups, who constituted 3.4 per cent of the total number of Negroes on the urban relief rolls. Of the gainful Negro workers in the United States in 1930, 19.5 percent were classified as white-collar workers. Of the 561,600 unskilled Negro workers on relief in 1934, 386,000 or 45.1 per cent were of the servant classes. Of the gainful Negro workers in the United States in 1930, 25.1 per cent were classified as servant classes. Of the 154,200 semi-skilled Negro workers on relief in 1934, 97,900 or 11.4 per cent were of the manufacturing classes. Of the gainful Negro workers in the United States in 1930, 3.3 per cent were classified as semi-skilled workers in

---

[1] A case is considered a group of related or unrelated persons living together at one address, the head of which has been resident in the state for at least a year.

manufacturing. Of the Negores on relief in 1934, 70,700, or 8.3 per cent, were skilled workers and foremen. Of the gainful Negro workers in the United States in 1930, 3.2 per cent were classified as skilled workers and foremen.

The above comparison shows that the white-collar classes among Negroes have either fared best of all classes during the depression or they have had the most pride. The significant fact is that the semi-skilled manufacturing worker has fared worst of all classes. There are more than three times as many semi-skilled workers on relief as are proportionately warranted by the figures on gainful workers in 1930. Next in line are the skilled workers, of which class almost three times as many are on relief as are proportionately warranted. Next in line are the servant classes, of which almost twice as many are on relief as are proportionately warranted.

Moreover, the fact that the percentage of Negroes receiving relief was almost twice that of whites indicates that the Negro's economic status is much more precarious than that of the white population; and it may be safely said that on the whole their economic status has been, and still is, submarginal. Whether the economic status be judged by property holdings, by bank savings, by incomes or expenditures, or by relief rolls, the findings will converge upon the one conclusion that the Negro generally is on "the narrow ridge of economic survival." In the broad programs for economic security for the masses, moreover, the Negro in actuality still remains outside of the total picture. Economic security is contingent upon the distribution of purchasing power to the masses in order relatively to equate demand with supply; but there can never be a relative equilibrium of demand and supply until the Negro is permitted to produce and to enjoy the fruits of production in a much wider sense than he has ever before. While so large a part of our man power is exploited and wasted, there can be little hope of the acquisitive system being saved in America. The New Deal must not use the deck that has been stacked economically against the Negro.

A brief survey of the more insistent economic problems confronting the Negro in the recovery program, i.e., wage differentials for the Negro and the attitudes of trade unions toward the Negro, will make the picture more concrete. When the codes of fair competition were initiated there resulted considerable agitation, especially in the South, for lower minimum wages for the Negro. The justification for the racial differential was based on the allegation that (1) the Negro's standard of living was lower than that of the white workers; (2) the Negro was not as efficient as white workers; and (3) the Negro traditionally received lower wages than white workers and it is desirable not to break the crust of tradition.

It must be admitted that the Negro workers' standard generally is lower than that of white workers; but this admission calls forth again the old "egg and the hen" controversy—which is responsible for the other(?) From my point of view, however, very little digging into the problem is necessary to prove that the lower cost of living among Negroes is due to their lower incomes. Negroes live on less because they have less to spend, and, in our price-system society, even the development of appropriate folkways is impossible without adequate income.

As to the Negro's being less efficient, there is considerable doubt that this contention is generally true. Certainly under present conditions it is impossible to prove or disprove this contention. Until a "test-tube" experiment can be performed which will involve the same occupations and the same plant and working conditions, no precise comparisons can be made. Certainly, also, under present conditions where Negroes are selected for the most casual and most killing jobs and at the same time are offered much less inducement, comparison is odious.

As to breaking the crust of tradition, that in many instances is the purpose of the whole recovery program. The custom of paying Negroes lower wages is a social lag which must be corrected if the Negro market is to possess appropriate buyers, if goods and services are to be fairly exchanged, if supply and demand are ever to arrive at relative equilibrium, and if the "New Deal" is to accomplish its purpose. Certainly in the present program, the needs must not be colored too greatly by the ways of the past.

The application of the codes of fair competition has involved some displacement of Negroes, which fact has caused some Negro leaders to favor a racial wage differential. There was, however, due primarily to the depression, considerable displacement of Negroes before the application of the codes; and much of the recent displacement could not, even if it were expedient, have been prevented by a racial wage differential. Certainly a racial wage differential would be inexpedient, because it would label Negroes industrially inferior and perhaps make them the victims of a caste system in which it would become increasingly difficult for them to obtain the same pay for the same work. The loss of relatively a few jobs is better by far than this.

Labor union practice is the other problem that I am concerned with here. The Norris-LaGuardia Anti-Injunction Law gives wage earners the right to organize, to self-representation and other concerted actions for purposes of collective bargaining. Moreover, section seven of Title I of the NIRA and its recent substitute, the Wagner-Connery Law provide for the enforcement of the terms of collective bargaining upon all employers; and such important recognition has been given the unions by the present administration that a quasi-partnership between the aristocrats of labor and government has developed. Yet, even with the Negro constituting approximately eleven per cent of the gainfully occupied, labor unions generally have consistently discriminated against Negro workers. Many of them openly restrict their membership to white workers. Even in some cases where Negroes have been admitted to unions, they are discriminated against as to job opportunities. Consequently, Negro workers believe that labor unions generally oppose the economic interests of Negroes. Another effect of such labor union practice has been the discouragement and the prevention of the development of skilled Negro workers. If the present administration continues to recognize unions which engage in such practice, Negro workers will be excluded from all desirable jobs in most of those localities where labor unions exist. The present administration, consequently, should require labor unions to abolish their practice of racial discrimination by also recognizing officially organizations of Negroes or only those including Negroes.

Finally, conditions which forbid the solution of the Negro's economic plight by any kind of tie-up with organized craft unionism in the United States cannot be omitted. In the first place, operating on the basis of economic scarcity, craft unionism represents, and will continue to represent, an aristocracy of labor. It has little intention of organizing all labor in the United States, because in our acquisitive set-up various types of labor, like other commodities, are dear only when they are scarce. We find it opposed, consequently, to the government codification of labor standards—minimum wage and maximum hours. It contends that organized labor is hurt by the standards set, because standards set for the unorganized tend to become the normal standards for all. If craft unionism were interested in American labor as a whole, it would not be interested in removing standards that protect the unorganized, even if in only a small way, but in improving these standards in order that they may become unquestionably the normal standards for all. It would not want a "cultural wage" for organized labor only, but for all labor. Cutting wages below the figure where the producer can be a consumer of his own product is no less harmful to the unorganized producer than to the organized producer.

Moreover, craft unionism offers no solution for the general problems of unemployment. It contends that industry by economic planning can absorb the 11,000,000 unemployed. This it would do by shortening the working week without cutting wages, which can be nothing other than a mere gesture in our profit seeking economy. This gesture makes it obvious that such strength as craft unionism seems still to possess is much more apparent than real. Numbering only about one-seventh of the number of those gainfully occupied, it is an organized minority posing as the champion of labor.

The Negro's economic pauperism is due primarily to the inequitable employment opportunities offered him. His economic problem is predominantly a labor problem. The solution of his problem, because the position of Negro labor is bound up with the fate of American labor generally, is contingent to a large degree upon a united and concerted attack. Such an attack, however, will not be engineered by white labor. The Negro, therefore, must accomplish his own deliverance. This, perhaps, can best be done through the organizing of Negro labor into the council-type union. This type consists of a council of representatives of local unions who plan concerted action for the industry as a whole. In some instances to break down the opposition of labor unions, the Negro even may find it profitable to organize company unions. Then, finally, with the Federal Government's work-relief program in the offing, government unions, organized and operated on much the same principle as the Federation of Federal Government Employees might serve as the beginning of a labor movement in the United States that would include Negro labor on an equitable footing.

# 13

# The Changing Status of the Negro Family

## E. FRANKLIN FRAZIER

Attempts to explain the character and problems of the Negro family by seeking their origins in African traditions and customs have ended in barren speculations. These speculations have been based upon two assumptions: first, that premarital sex experience among African Negroes indicated the absence of social control; and secondly, that there was an unbroken tradition from Africa to America. Concerning the first assumption it is only necessary to remark that this misconception is only a part of the general body of false opinion concerning 'primitive' peoples. Although a survival of African family life was once reported in Alabama,[1] out present knowledge of the conditions under which slavery was established in America leads us to believe that the Negro was completely stripped of his social heritage in the process.[2] The complete effacement of tribal life in America left the lingering memories of Africa to be borne only by isolated individuals in a world where these memories ceased to have any meaning.

Therefore, for the roots of the Negro family one must go to the slave family as it developed on the plantation and under the system of domestic slavery; and to the free Negro family which developed outside of the slave system. Our information concerning the character of the slave family has been furnished chiefly by apologists for slavery, who have given us a picture of idyllic happiness under benevolent patriarchs; and by abolitionists whose literature abounded in stereo-

---

[1] W. E. B. DuBois. *The Negro American Family*. Atlanta, 1908. p. 21.

[2] Robert E. Park. The Conflict and Fusion of Cultures. *Journal of Negro History,* IV, 117.

Reprinted, abridged, from *Social Forces 9* (March 1931): 386–393. Copyright © The University of North Carolina Press.

typed scenes of slave families being torn asunder by soulless masters. The absence of legal marriage, legal family, and legal control over children which DuBois regards as the essential features of the slave family characterize the family negatively. The real social relations between the masters and slaves and between the slaves themselves can neither be deduced from legal definitions nor inferred from the romantic tradition in which antebellum life in the South has been enshrined. While to some extent the Negro slave family was subject to the individual judgment and caprice of the masters, it represented on the whole an accommodation to the slave system as it varied from section to section.

The chief question of sociological interest is, to what extent did the slave family constitute a real social group capable of exercising control and of passing on a tradition? It is impossible to answer this question statistically. One limitation upon the functioning of the slave family as an autonomous group was the control of the master which began often with the choice of a mate. This control varied from friendly, patriarchal oversight under domestic slavery to pure animal breeding where the slave was regarded as a utility for trade. Within the family group itself the status of the father was always subject to limitations which could be imposed by the masters. The mother who represented the more stable element in the slave family probably occupied a more important position than in a free family. Under the most favorable conditions of slavery, especially among the house slaves and skilled artisans who were allowed to hire their time, the father's position was dominant and family discipline was good. The extent to which family consciousness was developed in some slave families is shown in the life of J. W. C. Pennington. When Pennington's father was given a whipping, he said, "This act created an open rupture with our family—each member felt the deep insult that had been inflicted upon our head; the spirit of the whole family was roused; we talked of it in our nightly gatherings, and showed it in our daily melancholy aspect."[3]

The organization and solidarity of the slave family was not only affected by the character of the institution of slavery in different sections but also by the varying fortunes of masters which caused the disruption of families under the most favorable conditions. On the other hand, where families of slaves were retained in the same family for generations we can note the beginnings of traditions as, for example, in the case of those slaves who succeeded their fathers as preachers and in positions of trust under slavery.

However much the slave family served as an accommodation of the personal wishes and family interests of the slaves to the institution of slavery, a crisis was precipitated by emancipation. During this crisis the social bonds of the slaves were dissolved in the general breakup of the social organization that had sustained them. In order to realize his new status the slave began to move about and

[3]W. C. Pennington. *The Fugitive Blacksmith; or Events in the History of James C. Pennington.* London, 1850. p. 7.

in many cases changed his identity by acquiring a new name.[4] Thus the Negro family became subject to all the fluctuations of vagrant impulses and individual wishes. The subsequent history of the Negro family in the South has been the establishment of new accommodations to the rural South. Increase in farm ownership up to 1910 has been an index to the stabilization of Negro life. Descendants of slaves have acquired farms which have been parcelled out from the larger plantations. In the towns of the South a few families have achieved some degree of economic independence and culture that has set them apart from the mass of laborers and domestic servants. In many cases these families are descended from slaves having the advantage of contacts with the master class as house slaves. In the larger cities, especially the educational centers, there has grown up a class of educated Negroes with middle class standards and outlook on life. Within this group family traditions have been built up and from this class many of the leaders in the northern cities have come.

Of great significance for the family life of the Negro have been the free Negroes who were scattered for the most part in the cities along the Atlantic seaboard. The usual picture of the free Negro has represented them as a group of social outcasts living in ignorance and poverty. Yet in Charleston, South Carolina, after the abortive attempt at insurrection by Denmark Vesey, it was argued in a memorial to the Senate and House of Representatives that the free Negroes through their monopoly of the mechanical arts were preventing the settlement of immigrants in that city. In New Orleans the property owned by free Negroes amounted to fifteen million dollars in 1860. It was through the guilds of caterers that the more energetic Negroes in Philadelphia were able to meet the competition of foreign labor before the Civil War.[5] There were settlements of free Negroes in Baltimore, New York, Washington, D.C., in the Northwest Territory, and in the Tidewater Region of Virginia in which families were founded with a tradition of achievement coming down to the present. Consciousness of the distinction which free birth gave caused even the poorer elements of the free Negroes to look down on the new "ishy"—recently emancipated from slavery. The free Negro class furnished many of the leaders of the emancipated slaves, and their descendants are still playing an important role in the Negro group.

# I

The northward migration of Negroes during and since the World War tended to dramatize the process of urbanization of the Negro population. Between 1900 and 1910 the urban Negro population increased 34.1 per cent for the entire country. During this period southern cities showed a larger percentage increase

[4] Booker T. Washington. *Up From Slavery.* New York, 1902.
[5] W. E. B. DuBois. *The Philadelphia Negro.* Philadelphia, 1899. pp. 32–39.

than northern cities. This aspect of the urbanization of the Negro has often been overlooked. Although during the decade from 1910 to 1920 the increase in Negro urban population was 32.6 per cent for the whole country, the increase in southern cities was 21.4 per cent and nearly 60 per cent for northern cities. The migrating Negro population has gone chiefly to northern cities of 100,000 and over, which showed an increase in the Negro population of 98.4 per cent. The movement of the Negro to northern industrial centers has been regarded as the second emancipation of the race. The effects of the migrations on the social life of the Negro have been similar to those resulting from the Civil War. The old accommodations to life in the South were destroyed and the disorganization of Negro life in northern cities has been registered in social agencies and courts. In Chicago, for example, the Negro cases constituted a fifth of the major service cases handled by the United Charities in 1928. The extent of family disorganization among Negroes is indicated by the large number of cases of family desertion and non-support, illegitimacy, and juvenile delinquency. The disorganizing effect of urban life on the Negro has caused forebodings concerning his ability to withstand the rigorous competition of the North.

**TABLE 1.** Birthplace and Place of Residence of 314 Persons Listed in Who's Who in Colored America

| PLACE OF BIRTH | Place of Residence | | | | |
|---|---|---|---|---|---|
| | NORTH | BORDER | SOUTH | WEST | TOTAL |
| North . . . . . . . . . . . . | 40 | 4 | 2 | 0 | 46 |
| Border. . . . . . . . . . . | 24 | 21 | 3 | 1 | 49 |
| South . . . . . . . . . . . | 98 | 23 | 83 | 6 | 210 |
| West . . . . . . . . . . . . | 4 | 1 | 1 | 3 | 9 |
| Total . . . . . . . . . . | 166 | 49 | 89 | 10 | 314 |

**TABLE 2.** Birthplace and Place of Residence of 125 Graduates of a Negro College

| PLACE OF BIRTH | Place of Residence | | | | |
|---|---|---|---|---|---|
| | NORTH | BORDER | SOUTH | WEST | TOTAL |
| North . . . . . . . . . . . | 11 | 2 | 3 | 1 | 17 |
| Border. . . . . . . . . . . | 8 · | 12 | 2 | 0 | 22 |
| South . . . . . . . . . . . | 32 | 10 | 40 | 3 | 85 |
| West . . . . . . . . . . . | 0 | 0 | 0 | 1 | 1 |
| Total . . . . . . . . . . | 51 | 24 | 45 | 5 | 125 |

An important but often neglected aspect of the migration of the Negro has been the movement of the more intelligent and energetic members of the race. The rise of large Negro communities in northern cities has opened a field for enterprise and service. A study of the birthplace and residence of 314 persons listed in *Who's Who in Colored America* and 125 graduates of a Negro college indicates the northward movement of educated Negroes.

In the *Who's Who in Colored America* group we find that only about 40 per cent of those born in the South have remained there. The college group in Table 2 shows a slightly smaller migration northward. This group was composed to a large extent of teachers who were compelled to find employment chiefly in the South.

These two groups give some indication of the changing status of the Negro family when we study the occupations of the fathers of those engaged in business and the professions. In both groups about 25 per cent of the professional men and women have come from families whose heads were in the professions. This group represents the second generation of the Negroes in fields where their fathers were pioneers. On the other hand, the rise in occupational status for the majority of the group represents a tremendous change in social status in the Negro group. This change in status carries with it new conceptions of life which affect the stability and the organization of the Negro family.

Between the Negro peasant from the South with his fatalistic resignation to the place given him by the white man and the educated Negro, sometimes representing several generations of culture, both seeking their fortunes in the northern city, there is a disparity in cultural development that only the nascent race consciousness, engendered in part by race conflict, tends to bridge. The peasant in the new environment seeks fulfillment of his awakened ambitions and hopes for a new status.[6] The consequent social disorganization is not merely a pathological phenomenon for the care of social agencies but also represents a step towards a reorganization of life on a more intelligent basis. . . .

# II

The city of Chicago has offered a laboratory in which to study the changes taking place in Negro life. The expansion of the Negro community in this city has followed the growth of the city. Studies of city growth have shown that the process of expansion can be measured in rates of change in home ownership, poverty, and other variable conditions for unit areas along the main thoroughfares radiating from the center of the city.[7] The growing Negro community was

[6] Charles S. Johnson. "The New Negro in a New World" in *The New Negro,* edited by Alain Locke. New York, 1927. pp. 285–288.

[7] Ernest W. Burgess. "The Determination of Gradients in the Growth of the City." *Publication of the American Sociological Society,* XXVI (1927), pp. 178–184.

**TABLE 3.** Occupations of the Fathers of Selected Groups of Negroes in the Professions and Business

| OCCUPATION OF PERSON | Occupation of Father | | | | | | | | |
|---|---|---|---|---|---|---|---|---|---|
| | AGRICULTURE | COMMON LABOR | DOMESTIC AND PERSONAL SERVICE | SKILLED OCCUPATIONS | CLERICAL | BUSINESS | PROFESSIONAL SERVICE | PUBLIC OFFICE | TOTAL |
| *Who's Who in Colored America* | | | | | | | | | |
| Professional . . . | 62 | 36 | 23 | 46 | 12 | 20 | 70 | 3 | 272 |
| Business. . . . . | 10 | 4 | 3 | 5 | 1 | 4 | 6 | 0 | 33 |
| Total . . . . . . | 72 | 40 | 26 | 51 | 13 | 24 | 76 | 3 | 305 |
| *Graduates of a Negro college* | | | | | | | | | |
| Professional . . . | 21 | 16 | 7 | 24 | 6 | 13 | 30 | 0 | 117 |
| Business. . . . . | 2 | 1 | 0 | 1 | 1 | 0 | 1 | 0 | 6 |
| Total . . . . . . | 23 | 17 | 7 | 25 | 7 | 13 | 31 | 0 | 123 |

**TABLE 4.**

*Rate per Hundred Population 10 Years of Age and Over*

| | ZONE I | ZONE II | ZONE III | ZONE IV | ZONE V | ZONE VI | ZONE VII |
|---|---|---|---|---|---|---|---|
| Professional and Public Service, Trades and Clerical: | | | | | | | |
| Male | 5.8 | 5.5 | 10.7 | 11.2 | 12.5 | 13.4 | 34.2 |
| Female | 3.0 | 6.5 | 13.3 | 13.3 | 14.8 | 15.2 | 33.3 |
| Skilled: | | | | | | | |
| Male | 6.2 | 10.8 | 12.3 | 13.6 | 11.1 | 14.4 | 13.0 |
| Female | 3.9 | 3.9 | 7.5 | 7.7 | 7.8 | 7.4 | 16.6 |
| Railroad Porters | 1.4 | 3.9 | 6.7 | 6.5 | 7.5 | 7.7 | 10.7 |
| Semi-skilled, Domestic Service, and Laborers: | | | | | | | |
| Male | 86.1 | 78.8 | 68.9 | 67.9 | 68.6 | 63.6 | 41.6 |
| Female | 92.9 | 88.3 | 78.4 | 78.1 | 76.1 | 76.8 | 46.9 |
| Women Employed | 46.1 | 48.1 | 42.3 | 45.2 | 39.7 | 36.6 | 34.5 |
| Home Ownership | 0 | 1.2 | 6.2 | 7.2 | 8.3 | 11.4 | 29.8 |

**TABLE 5.**

*Rate per Hundred*

| | ZONE I | ZONE II | ZONE III | ZONE IV | ZONE V | ZONE VI | ZONE VII |
|---|---|---|---|---|---|---|---|
| Charity cases: 1927 | 8.0 | 8.2 | 5.3 | 2.8 | 1.9 | 1.0 | 1.1 |
| Family desertions: January 1, 1926, to June 30, 1928 | 2.5 | 2.6 | 2.1 | 1.5 | 1.1 | 0.4 | 0.2 |
| Delinquent boys: 1926 | 42.8 | 31.4 | 30.0 | 28.8 | 15.7 | 9.6 | 1.4 |

an opportunity to study statistically the social selection and segregation of different elements of the Negro population.

The majority of the 110,000 Negroes in Chicago in 1920 constituted the Negro community which extended from the outer boundary of the business center or the Loop—twelfth Street—southward along one of the main arteries, State Street, for a distance of over seven miles. The area occupied by this community of Negroes, who comprised as much as about ninety per cent of the total population in some sections in it, was about a mile and a quarter wide except where it was bounded by Lake Michigan. By dividing this whole area into seven unit areas bounded by streets running east and west at intervals of about one mile each, it has been possible to study small enough units of the Negro population in order that the changes taking place in the social life of the Negro could be measured. The differences in the character of the Negro population in these zones together with the varying rates of home ownership, poverty, and family disorganization become indices of the social processes which we seek to measure.

The process of selection and segregation of economic classes in the Negro community is reflected in the distribution of occupational classes in these seven unit areas.[8] In the first area near the Loop where marked deterioration, high land values, and low rental presage the expansion of the business center, Negro laborers and servants, most of whom were born in the South, are able to get a foothold in the city. The second area showed the same characteristics as the first but gave some indication of the character of the third area where the higher occupational classes were more largely represented. The proportion of the higher occupational classes in the Negro population increased for the succeeding three areas. It was especially in the seventh area that the higher classes were concentrated. The steady decline in the proportion of females employed was also an index to higher culture in the succeeding areas. The rate of home ownership among Negro families in these areas was an indication of family stability. Among the poorer migrant families of the first area, there was no homeownership and the 1.2 per cent for the second area was due to the presence of a small group of Negroes of a higher cultural status. The gradual increase for the succeeding areas followed the increase in the proportion of the higher occupational classes in the population. In the seventh area where a third of the men and women employed were in professional services, about thirty per cent of the families owned their homes. The variation in proportion of the different occupational groups living in these areas and in the rate of homeownership indicated the differences in cultural levels and organization of the Negro community.

When the statistics on the breakdown of Negro family life were related to the culture and organization of the Negro community instead of being taken as a description of average conditions in the entire population, the significance of these statistics as indices to the processes of disorganization and reorganization

[8]E. Franklin Frazier. "Occupational Classes Among Negroes in Cities." *American Journal of Sociology*, XXXV, 718–738.

becomes apparent. In the first and second areas in which, as we have seen, were located the propertyless migrants of the lower occupational classes, the rate of dependency measured by charity cases was about eight per cent. The rates of family desertion were also high for these areas. The high rates of juvenile delinquency—42.8 per cent and 31.4 per cent—were also indicative of the breakdown of family discipline and social organization in a large northern city. The extent of family disorganization reflected in these three indexes declined gradually from the third to the seventh area. The decline in the rate of dependency, desertion, and juvenile delinquency followed the rise in the rate of home ownership and the increase in the proportion of the higher occupational classes in the population.

The significance of these changes in the rates of family disorganization is due to the fact that they reflect the processes of selection and segregation in the Negro community. In Chicago, as in most northern cities, there was a small group of families, many of them mulattoes with free ancestry, who had achieved an economic and cultural status that separated them from the masses. Some of these families which had acquired a place in the community represented the successful struggles of earlier migrants. These people regarded the migration of the ignorant black masses from the South as a menace to their own position. Before the flood of ignorance, crudeness and poverty from the South, they moved to areas where they could maintain their own standards of behavior. The migrant families who posessed some wealth and culture acquired in the South sought a congenial environment in these same areas.

In the keen competition to serve the newly created desires and wants of the Negro community a new leadership has come to the top with a new conception of life. Among high and low alike, life has come to have a different meaning from that in the South or that of a small Negro community accommodated to a large city. These changes mean disorganization and reorganization of life on another basis. The family is the social group which bears the burden of these cultural changes. In the third area where social disorganization is greatest in the Negro community, family life tends to disappear. In the area near the "Loop" the poorer migrant families struggle against the anonymity and mobility of urban life, while at the other end of the community both those who have been successful in the struggle and those who had the advantage of family traditions and cultural contacts seek to secure these advantages for coming generations.

## Summary

In this brief account of the changing status of the Negro family it has been necessary to give some account of the twofold background from which it had developed. On the one hand, the Negro family developed under the institution of slavery as an accommodation of the sex and family interests of the slaves to the various forms of slavery. On the other hand, there grew up alongside of slavery a class of free Negroes, among whom some achieved wealth and culture which became the basis of a tradition extending down to the present day. The slave family failed to withstand the crisis produced by the Civil War which swept away the only social organization sustaining the slave family. Since the Civil War the Negro family has been making new accommodations to the South. Increase in farm and home ownership has been an indication of the growing stabilization. The general urbanization, which has been signalized by the northern migrations during and since the World War, has produced another crisis in the Negro family. The disorganization and reorganization of Negro life in the northern city offers a laboratory for the study of these changes. Some of the results of a quantitative study of these changes in the city of Chicago, where the indices of family disorganization could be related to cultural differences and the processes of community growth, indicate the civilizational process in Negro life.

# 14

# On the Provenience of New World Negroes

## MELVILLE J. HERSKOVITS

A knowledge of the provenience of the Negroes in the New World is basic to the study of New World Negro cultures, since to comprehend the cultural equipment with which these people entered upon their lives in the western hemisphere is essential in any successful attempt to utilize the materials gained from investigations of their present-day life for an analysis of the processes of cultural change and of the results of culture-contact. In the United States it has long been held useless to attempt to do more than refer African origins to such vague geographical regions as the Guinea Coast, the Congo, the Gambia, and the "interior," since it is felt that documents contemporary to the period of the slavetrade have recorded place and tribal names so poorly that accurate identification of the peoples brought to the western world is impossible. This view has been strengthened by the belief that the diverse cultures represented by these Africans, and the multiplicity of mutually unintelligible languages spoken by them, promptly gave way before the impact of European civilizations, so that whatever African survivals exist are so few and so extraneous to the basic life of the Negro in the New World that they may be looked upon as cultural curiosities.[1]

The frequent restatement of these hypotheses has led to such definite stereotypes regarding Negro origins that most students fail to recognize the desirability of investigating anew the problem of Negro provenience. Two approaches may be utilized in such an investigation. One is historical, the other ethnological,

[1] *Cf.* for example, W. E. B. Dubois, *The Negro,* (New York and London, 1915), pp. 148-149, or E. R. Embree, *Brown America,* (New York, 1931), pp. 10-11.

Reprinted, abridged, from *Social Forces 12* (December 1934): 247-262. Copyright © The University of North Carolina Press.

and the two are not only related, but, in the study of this particular problem, depend definitely on one another. For, if African cultural traits are to be discerned in the beliefs and behavior of New World Negroes, and if these traits, when traced to their African counterparts, are found to derive from the regions mentioned in the historical documents as the principal sources of the Negro slaves brought to the western hemisphere, then there should be reasonable grounds for deducing that these regions do in fact represent the areas from which the greatest supplies of slaves originated,–those areas, at least, which during the first century and a half of slaving furnished the cultural base for Africanisms in the New World.

. . . Africanisms in the Negro cultures of South America and the islands of the Caribbean, not only point to specific regions in Africa, but . . . the evidence supports the hypothesis of provenience based on an analysis of historical documents. Yet it is to be observed that . . . Yoruban, Dahomean, and Gold Coast tribal designations predominate in identifying place-names, names of gods, and details of religious belief and practice. What of the other peoples who, from Loango to the Gambia, also supplied the slave traffic? Unquestionably, insufficient data are responsible for the comparative absence of survivals from these regions of Africa. But it may be that, because of larger numbers and priority of arrival, slaves belonging to the tribal groups from the Gold-Coast-Dahomean-Nigerian region imposed their customs on the Negroes from other portions of the slave-belt. It must not be assumed, however, that everything from other than this central region was lost, though such survivals may prove more difficult to identify and segregate. Nevertheless, an hypothesis which involves postulating the cultural unity of West Africa, and which might account for the dominance of the cultures from the Gold Coast, from Dahomey and from Nigeria in the New World may be tentatively advanced. This unity, I believe, has not been recognized, though in such matters of basic structure as the inner organization of social life, and in types and functions of deities (though not their names), there is great similarity from people to people in the forest belt of the west coast, and in the country immediately to the north of the forested region. . . .

That West African customs manifest an important degree of fundamental similarity does account for the unity in New World Negro culture. The shifting about of the slaves, and the policy of separating those of the same tribe, has operated to cause the retention of Africanisms in implications and inner structure rather than externals. That is why, when we search for intimations of definite sources of origin in the United States, we find a generalized expression of West African behavior, modified by or welded to customs derived from the European civilization of the masters. That there is much of this generalized African character in Negro behavior in the United States cannot be gainsaid, for many studies of "superstitions" and folk-customs of Negroes of the United States have shown that Africanisms abound in their daily life.[2]

[2] Cf. such a work as N. N. Puckett, *Folk Beliefs of the Southern Negro* (Chapel Hill, 1926). Puckett, in spite of the fact that his thesis is to indicate how much the Negro slaves ob-

Although Negroes in the United States are Christians, yet it is possible to see expressions of religious ritual that would not be out of place in West African tribal villages. One witnesses spirit possession, though by the "Holy Ghost," dancing with the identical steps and the same motor behavior that characterizes the worship of aboriginal African gods; singing that derives, in manner if not in actual form, directly from Africa. I have myself been present at a Negro communion service where the concept underlying the taking of the sacrament, as it was expressed,—"If you take this Body and Blood, and you're not pure of heart, you'll get sick, it'll put you in bed! I'll see to it!," the warning of the preacher,— was that of the maker of charms on the West Coast, in Suriname, or in the West Indian Islands. Negroes are Christians, yet their dead must "cross the river Jordan" in a manner that exactly parallels that in which the West African dead must cross their rivers before they may reach the spirit world. The importance of wakes for the dead is African, as is the entire complex of ritual surrounding death, even to the "burying shallow" until arrangements can be made for a proper funeral, the passing of small children over the coffin, and the inclusion of food and money in the coffins. The souls of young children are called to accompany their elders on a projected journey just as is done in Suriname, in Dahomey, and elsewhere in West Africa. The behavior of those preparing for baptism, and the ceremony of baptism itself, follows that of cult initiation in Africa; the fear of "cussing" is allied to the seriousness of oaths; the improvisations of songs of ridicule are as known in the United States as they are on the West Coast of Africa, in Suriname or in the West Indies.

Finally, we may cite the speech of the Negroes of southern United States. A study of idiom of the Negro-English spoken in Suriname, as compared with that occurring in British Guiana, Jamaica, and the United States shows that the expressions which distinguish Negro-English from "proper" English recur in all these regions, as they recur in the pidgin of West Africa itself, while further analysis shows that there are exact parallels in several West African languages for these idioms. Any good grammar of a West African tongue, indeed, explains the oddities of speech which it has become customary to ascribe to the influence of Elizabethan English, or to the grammatical perversions of a child-like folk.

Yet to point to a Senegambian name, an Ashanti deity, a Congo belief among Negroes of the United States, recognizable as such, is almost impossible.[3] We know from contemporary documents that the Gambia River, Gold Coast, Sierra Leone, Masse-Congo, Whidah, Fantee, Coro mantine, Bassa, Bance Island, Angola, the Bight (of Benin?), Calabar, and Eboe (Ibo) were mentioned in the Charlestown slave-market during the days of the slave-trade, and that in South

---

tained from the culture of their masters, actually gives an encyclopaedic amount of data which shows how much of African custom has been retained in this country!

[3] Despite the truth of this statement, a reading of the data contained in the paper by Zora Hurston, "Hoodoo in America," *Jour. of Amer. Folk-Lore*, XLIV (1931), 317–417, should convince the most skeptical that the Africanisms in American Negro worship are anything but negligible.

Carolina, "The favorite negroes were those from Gambia and the Gold Coast. . . ." That the slaves who were brought to the continent were of the same stocks as those who were sent to the islands is not only confirmed from statements such as this but also from the instructions to masters of slave-ships, telling them where to proceed in the event of lack of success in selling the cargoes— ". . . Antigua . . . Newis (Nevis) . . . So. Carolina"—and other documents concerning the transportation of slaves. We can assume that Gold Coast Negroes were present in Virginia in the middle of the eighteenth century, from the form of the drum which, collected at that time from the Negroes of Virginia, now reposes in the British Museum, and we can further assume the presence of Gold Coast Negroes from the survival of some of their day-names, such as Codjo, Cuffy and Quashie, in the United States, and from the fact that the cognate names of "Thursday" or "Saturday," are found among the Negroes of the South-eastern states. Or we may consider the "Place Congo" in New Orleans where the voodoo rites, transported from Haiti, were held up to a relatively short time ago. But these are only hints, and do not constitute sufficient evidence. Generalized West African types of behavior are present among the Negroes of the United States, it is true, but on the basis of available data they are not of such a character as to localize provenience in the same way as can be done for Brazil, for Haiti, for Cuba, for Jamaica, for Suriname.

However, both from historically documented fact, and from the ethnology of the Negro peoples of the New World, it is evident that ample data are available to indicate the principal regions from which the slaves were acquitted. To ascertain the details of the native cultures of these regions is merely a question of field research; with the results of such research in hand, the problem of knowing the cultural base-line from which the New World Negroes were launched into their adventures in the New World will be solved.

# 15

# A Race-Relations Cycle

*EMORY S. BOGARDUS*

. . . The history of treatment by Americans of races conspicuously different from themselves in one or more particulars reveals several recurring stages. By conspicuously different races is meant those made distinctive by color, religion, political and economic doctrines, or by other physical and cultural factors. . . . The natural history of American responses to the Chinese, Japanese, and now to Filipino and Mexican immigrants reveals sufficient recurrences in each case, as well as similarities in the behavior recurrences, to justify the label of a race-relations cycle.

1. *Curiosity.*—The first comers of these culturally strange races have been uniformly viewed with curiosity. Sympathetic responses have been widely generated by the lone stranger far away from his home base. His strangeness coupled with his original fewness of numbers make him appear helpless. Defense mechanisms and mores were not aroused against him. With a certain supposedly secret air of superiority, Americans have met and greeted him, curious as to who and why he is. His strange culture traits have invited passing comments, while he, seeing the culture traits of Americans, has responded cautiously at first but with rising hopes.

2. *Economic welcome.*—The strange newcomers have put in an appearance sometimes because of a spirit of adventure, sometimes because of a luring halo attached to the United States, but more often because of high wages. To make "big money," to save as much as possible, to return wealthy is often the plan which has led on occasion to long hours of labor in this country and to a willingness to work for less than American standards permit.

Abridged from *American Journal of Sociology* 36 (1931): 612–617. Used by permission of The University of Chicago Press. © 1931 by the University of Chicago. All rights reserved.

Employers of labor, therefore, have been quick to employ, and at least indirectly to encourage these immigrants to send for relatives and friends. American wages have seemed unusually high, and the immigrants have sent the good news home. Relatives and friends have responded with alacrity. Increasing numbers of kinsfolk have come. There has been great rejoicing because of the golden opportunities offered by the economic welcome in the United States.

3. *Industrial and social antagonism.*—Suddenly and perplexingly to these immigrant peoples, reactions have broken out against them. They have hardly been prepared for the vicious propaganda that has been spread against them, especially in this land of the free, where brotherhood of man, a square deal, and a high degree of enlightenment are boasted. First, sporadic outbursts of prejudice against them have occurred, and then organized movements have gained a tremendous momentum, reaching to the farthermost corners of the nation. At the time these immigrants seemed to be getting a footing and to be reaching a degree of economic independence for which Americans are noted, they have heard the roar of an oncoming storm. Organized labor has usually been the leader in protesting against the conspicuously different immigrants, on grounds of protecting labor against unfair competition and the pulling down of standards built up at great sacrifice by American workers. Organized labor has had the prompt co-operation of patriotic societies of one kind or another, who usually are the watch dogs of the national mores. Silver-tongued politicians and crowd-exciting chauvinists have stood forth in this hue-and-cry phase of the race-relations cycle.

The organized opposition to conspicuous immigrants acquires momentum because the immigrants have come in such increasing volume. There has seemed to be uncounted millions on the way. It is easy for the imagination of natives to picture this country being overrun and overwhelmed by literal millions of these foreigners. It is natural for the latter to immigrate faster than they can be assimilated. Because of wide differences in culture traits, assimilation must necessarily take place slowly.

The high birth-rate of both Orientals and Mexicans is disturbing to many Americans. All these numerous children, it is asserted, will soon grow up, will be citizens, will outvote the natives, and will take control of political affairs. Seen in a teeming perspective, these strange peoples arouse every conceivable type of defense mechanism of the natives. Their very conspicuousness seems to multiply their numbers manifold. Sheer numbers of immigrants plus high birth-rates constitute a tremendous threat against the established order.

The fact that the assimilation of these immigrants is hindered if not prevented by natives is not considered. The related fact that the acculturation of the children of these immigrants is in the hands of natives is also but vaguely conceived. Natives do not appreciate how they may bring about the assimilation and acculturation of both the first-and second-generation immigrants, and thus avoid foreign usurpation.

A special type of antagonistic expression is found in the reactions of a neighborhood invaded by the conspicuous foreigner. Like other immigrants, the Chinese, Japanese, Filipinos, and Mexicans all tend on arrival to live together in groups or immigrant settlements. After a time, however, some of the more progressive, catching the progressive spirit of natives, seek a higher status for themselves and better homes for their families. They acquire the worthy idea of moving out of the despised (by Americans) foreign quarters, and of moving into a "respectable" American neighborhood. At once adverse opinions are heard. Signs go up: "Japs are not wanted," or "Japs get out." Danger to property values looms up. Realtors who have taken a part in the selling or leasing of property to these conspicuously different people are threatened by the irate neighbors.

The native considers that his status, or the status of his neighborhood, is lowered by "race invasions." His friends raise invidious questions when they visit him. A few strange neighbors may soon lead to an "influx," and an influx may mean ultimately a complete change of population. Old and well-established sentiments are aroused; crowd psychology and even mob psychology may become rampant. Neighborhood antagonism joins with patriotic or chauvinistic antagonism.

4. *Legislative antagonism.*—The next phase of the race-relations cycle logically follows. Bills are introduced into legislatures and into Congress. A fullfledged campaign is organized against the "undesirable" immigrants. The latter are openly, publicly, and sometimes viciously denounced. Only one side of the case is presented to the general public. Politicians attempt to make their legislative berths secure by campaigning in behalf of the public, the state, and the nation—against the invaders. These tirades are inexpensive, for Orientals are ineligible to vote, and Mexicans are unnaturalized to any extent and hence cannot vote. The legislative phase gains momentum until its objective is reached or until the threatened danger is past.

5. *Fair-play tendencies.*—Belatedly but invariably a "fair-play" movement develops. Broadminded Americans initiate a countermovement, not only because of friendship for the immigrants but because the latter are being attacked unjustly. This counterphase operates under serious handicaps. It is usually not well organized, is lacking in financial support, is not steadily aggressive, is hampered by the zealots and dreamers among its numbers who bring it into disrepute. It is, however, a source of comfort and understanding to many of the immigrants in question. It helps them to retain confidence in American life and principles. It holds somewhat in check the antirace reactions and prevents the race antagonists from going to ultimate extremes. It serves as a balance wheel to an otherwise one-sided mechanism. It maintains the idealistic reputation of the nation in the eyes of the world.

6. *Quiescence.*—After the sought-for restrictive or prohibitive legislation was passed, in both the Chinese and Japanese race cycles, there was a sudden slowing up of the antagnoistic activities. Assured that the impending danger is safely thwarted, the antagonistic organizations modify their attitudes. After the Japa-

nese were excluded in 1924, the anti-Japanese groups announced a friendly but guarded attitude toward the Japanese in the state and nation.

If the antirace movement goes to the extreme of complete exclusion, as it did in dealing with both Chinese and Japanese immigration, then the protagonist groups express sympathy for the unjustly treated immigrants and silently vow to secure justice for the latter some day. If needed restriction, but not exclusion had been adopted in both the Chinese and Japanese race-relation cycles, it is probable that the protagonistic phase would have passed away entirely.

7. *Second-generation difficulties.* . . . The children of the Japanese and Mexicans have been undergoing assimilation in the schools and through many other contacts. They have been losing contact with the home-country culture, and have been partially ostracized. But because of their conspicuous nature (color or culture heritage), they have been only partially accepted in the land of their birth and citizenship.

This statement of a race-relations cycle has developed naturally out of a study of Chinese-immigrant and Japanese-immigrant experiences in the United States. It is significant as a measuring stick for considering the developing Mexican and Filipino situations in this country. At first (1) Mexican immigrants were viewed with some curiosity and with pity; (2) they were, and are, being sought as laborers by large-scale employers; (3) reactions against them have developed, and are still in process. Bills have been introduced (4) in Congress against them; (5) and a fair-play movement in their behalf is in operation. There are strong indications that the sixth and seventh phases are materializing. The Filipinos likewise have experienced the first five phases of the race-relations cycle. They will doubtless experience the sixth, but will escape the seventh, for their numbers are so largely male.

# 16

# Attitudes vs. Actions

*RICHARD T. LAPIERE*

. . . Beginning in 1930 and continuing for two years thereafter, I had the good fortune to travel rather extensively with a young Chinese student and his wife. Both were personable, charming, and quick to win the admiration and respect of those they had the opportunity to become intimate with. But they were foreign-born Chinese, a fact that could not be disguised. Knowing the general "attitude" of Americans towards the Chinese as indicated by the "social distance" studies which have been made, it was with considerable trepidation that I first approached a hotel clerk in their company. Perhaps that clerk's eyebrows lifted slightly, but he accommodated us without a show of hesitation. And this in the "best" hotel in a small town noted for its narrow and bigoted "attitude" towards Orientals. Two months later I passed that way again, phoned the hotel and asked if they would accommodate "an important Chinese gentleman." The reply was an unequivocal "No." That aroused my curiosity and led to this study.

In something like ten thousand miles of motor travel, twice across the United States, up and down the Pacific Coast, we met definite rejection from those asked to serve us just once. We were received at 66 hotels, auto camps, and "Tourist Homes," refused at one. We were served in 184 restaurants and cafes scattered throughout the country and treated with what I judged to be more than ordinary consideration in 72 of them. Accurate and detailed records were kept of all these instances. An effort, necessarily subjective, was made to evaluate the overt response of hotel clerks, bell boys, elevator operators, and waitresses to the presence of my Chinese friends. The factors entering into the situations were varied as far and as of often as possible. Control was not, of course, as exacting as that required by laboratory experimentation. But it was as rigid as is humanly possible in human situations. For example, I did not take

Reprinted, abridged, from *Social Forces 13* (December 1934): 230–237. Copyright © The University of North Carolina Press.

the "test" subjects into my confidence fearing that their behavior might become self-conscious and thus abnormally affect the response of others towards them. Whenever possible I let my Chinese friend negotiate for accommodations (while I concerned myself with the car or luggage) or sent them into a restaurant ahead of me. In this way I attempted to "factor" myself out. We sometimes patronized high-class establishments after a hard and dusty day on the road and stopped at inferior auto camps when in our most presentable condition.

In the end I was forced to conclude that those factors which most influenced the behavior of others towards the Chinese had nothing at all to do with race. Quality and condition of clothing, appearance of baggage (by which, it seems, hotel clerks are prone to base their quick evaluations), cleanliness and neatness were far more significant for person to person reaction in the situations I was studying than skin pigmentation, straight black hair, slanting eyes, and flat noses. And yet an air of self-confidence might entirely offset the "unfavorable" impression made by dusty clothes and the usual disorder to appearance consequent upon some hundred miles of motor travel. . . . My Chinese friends were skillful smilers, which may account, in part, for the fact that we received but one rebuff in all our experience. Finally, I was impressed with the fact that even where some tension developed due to the strangeness of the Chinese it would evaporate immediately when they spoke in unaccented English.

The one instance in which we were refused accommodations is worth recording here. The place was a small California town, a rather inferior auto-camp into which we drove in a very dilapidated car piled with camp equipment. It was early evening, the light so dim that the proprietor found it somewhat difficult to decide the genus *voyageur* to which we belonged. I left the car and spoke to him. He hesitated, wavered, said he was not sure that he had two cabins, meanwhile edging towards our car. The realization that the two occupants were Orientals turned the balance or, more likely, gave him the excuse he was looking for. "No," he said, "I don't take Japs!" In a more pretentious establishment we secured accommodations, and with an extra flourish of hospitality.

To offset this one flat refusal were the many instances in which the physical peculiarities of the Chinese served to heighten curiosity. With few exceptions this curiosity was considerately hidden behind an exceptional interest in serving us. Of course, outside of the Pacific Coast region, New York, and Chicago, the Chinese physiognomy attracts attention. It is different, hence noticeable. But the principal effect this curiosity has upon the behavior of those who cater to the traveler's needs is to make them more attentive, more responsive, more reliable. A Chinese companion is to be recommended to the white traveling in his native land. . . .

What I am trying to say is that in only one out of 251 instances in which we purchased goods or services necessitating intimate human relationships did the fact that my companions were Chinese adversely affect us. Factors entirely unassociated with race were, in the main, the determinant of significant variations in our reception. It would appear reasonable to conclude that the "attitude" of the American people, as reflected in the behavior of those who are for pecuniary reasons presumably most sensitive to the antipathies of their white clientele, is anything but negative towards the Chinese. In terms of "social distance" we might conclude that native Caucasians are not averse to residing in the same hotels, auto-camps, and "Tourist Homes" as Chinese and will with complacency accept the presence of Chinese at an adjoining table in restaurant or cafe. It does not follow that there is revealed a distinctly "positive" attitude towards the Chinese, that whites prefer the Chinese to other whites. But the facts as gathered certainly preclude the conclusion that there is an intense prejudice towards the Chinese.

Yet the existence of this prejudice, very intense, is proven by a conventional "attitude" study. To provide a comparison of symbolic reaction to symbolic social situations with actual reaction to real social situations, I "questionnaired" the establishments which we patronized during the two year period. Six months were permitted to lapse between the time I obtained the overt reaction and the symbolic. It was hoped that the effects of the actual experience with Chinese guests, adverse or otherwise, would have faded during the intervening time. To the hotel or restaurant a questionnaire was mailed with an accompanying letter purporting to be a special and personal plea for response. The questionnaires all asked the same question, "Will you accept members of the Chinese race as guests in your establishment?" Two types of questionnaire were used. In one this question was inserted among similar queries concerning Germans, French, Japanese, Russians, Armenians, Jews, Negroes, Italians, and Indians. In the other the pertinent question was unencumbered. With persistence, completed replies were obtained from 128 of the establishments we had visited; 81 restaurants and cafes and 47 hotels, auto-camps, and "Tourist Homes." In response to the relevant question 92 per cent of the former and 91 per cent of the latter replied "No." The remainder replied "Uncertain; depend upon circumstances." From the woman proprietor of a small auto-camp I received the only "Yes," accompanied by a chatty letter describing the nice visit she had had with a Chinese gentleman and his sweet wife during the previous summer.

A rather unflattering interpretation might be put upon the fact that those establishments who had provided for our needs so graciously were, some months later, verbally antagonistic towards hypothetical Chinese. To factor this experience out responses were secured from 32 hotels and 96 restaurants located in approximately the same regions, but uninfluenced by this particular experience with Oriental clients. In this, as in the former case, both types of questionnaires were used. The results indicate that neither the type of questionnaire nor the fact of previous experience had important bearing upon the symbolic response to symbolic social situations. . . .

The questionnaire is cheap, easy, and mechanical. The study of human behavior is time consuming, intellecturally fatiguing, and depends for its success upon the ability of the investigator. The former method gives quantitative results, the latter mainly qualitative. Quantitative measurements are quantitatively

**TABLE 1.  Distribution of Results from Questionnaire Study of Establishment "Policy" Regarding Acceptance of Chinese as Guests**

Replies are to the question: "Will you accept members of the Chinese race as guests in your establishment?"

| | HOTELS, ETC., VISITED | | HOTELS, ETC., NOT VISITED | | RESTAURANTS, ETC., VISITED | | RESTAURANTS, ETC., NOT VISITED | |
|---|---|---|---|---|---|---|---|---|
| Total............... | 47 | | 32 | | 81 | | 96 | |
| | 1* | 2* | 1 | 2 | 1 | 2 | 1 | 2 |
| Number replying........ | 22 | 25 | 20 | 12 | 43 | 38 | 51 | 45 |
| No.................... | 20 | 23 | 19 | 11 | 40 | 35 | 37 | 41 |
| Undecided: depends upon circumstances............ | 1 | 2 | 1 | 1 | 3 | 3 | 4 | 3 |
| Yes.................. | 1 | 0 | 0 | 0 | 0 | 0 | 0 | 1 |

*Column (1) indicates in each case those responses to questionnaires which concerned Chinese only. The figures in columns (2) are from the questionnaires in which the above was inserted among questions regarding Germans, French, Japanese, etc.

accurate; qualitative evaluations are always subject to the errors of human judgment. Yet it would seem far more worth while to make a shrewd guess regarding that which is essential than to accurately measure that which is likely to prove quite irrelevant.

# 17

# American Caste and Class

## W. LLOYD WARNER

The social organization of the Deep South consists of two different kinds of social stratification. There is not only a caste system, but there is also a class structure. Ordinarily the social scientist thinks of these two different kinds of vertical structure as antithetical to each other. It is rare that the comparative sociologist finds a class structure being maintained together with a caste structure.

Caste as used here describes a theoretical arrangement of the people of the given group in an order in which the privileges, duties, obligations, opportunities, etc., are unequally distributed between the groups which are considered to be higher and lower. There are social sanctions which tend to maintain this unequal distribution. Such a definition also describes class. A caste organization, however, can be further defined as one where marriage between two or more groups is not sanctioned and where there is no opportunity for members of the lower groups to rise into the upper groups or of the members of the upper to fall into the lower ones. In class, on the other hand, there is a certain proportion of interclass marriage between lower and higher groups, and there are, in the very nature of the class organization, mechanisms established by which people move up and down the vertical extensions of the society. Obviously, two such structures are antithetical to each other, the one inflexibly prohibiting movement between the two groups and intergroup marriage, and the other sanctioning intergroup movement and at least certain kinds of marriage between higher and lower classes. Nevertheless, they have accommodated themselves to each other in the southern community we examined.

Reprinted from *American Journal of Sociology 42* (1937): 234–237. Used by permission of The University of Chicago Press. © 1937 by The University of Chicago. All rights reserved.

Perhaps the best way to present the configurations of the two kinds of vertical structure is by means of Figure 1. The diagonal lines separate the lower Negro caste (*N*) from the upper white caste (*W*), and the two broken lines in each segment separate the three general classes (upper, middle, and lower) in each caste from each other. The two double-headed vertical arrows indicate that movement up and down the class ladders in each caste can and does take place and is socially sanctioned, but that there is no movement or marriage between the two segments. The diagonal arrangement of the parallel lines which separate the two castes expresses the essential skewness created by the conflict of caste and class in the South. The gradual elaboration of the economic, educational, and general social activities of the Negro caste since slavery (and to some extent even before) has created new groups which have been vertically arranged by the society until certain fairly well-marked class groups have developed within the Negro caste. As the vertical distance of the Negro group has been extended during the years, the top Negro layer has been pushed higher and higher. This has swung the caste line on its axis (*c*), so that the top Negro group is higher in class than the lower white groups and is so recognized. (This recognition is expressed in circumlocutions and by unconscious actions, but is at times also consciously and openly stated by the members of both the white and the Negro groups.) If this process continues, as it seems to be doing at the present time, it is possible, and indeed probable, that the lines *AB* might move on the axis *c*

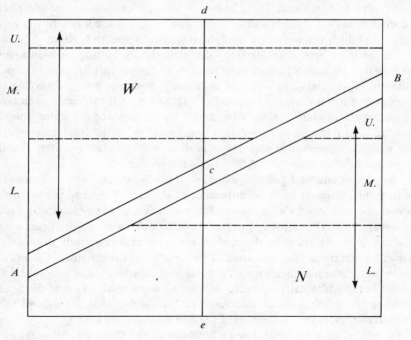

**FIGURE 1**

until they approximate the hypothetical line *de*. (Theoretically, of course, this process could go farther, but it seems unlikely.) This tendency to bring the two groups out of vertical opposition and organization into a horizontal arrangement is being reflected at the present time in such movements as "parallelism," as expounded by Dr. DuBois. Such terms as "parellelism" are kinds of collective representations which have come into existence and approximately express the social facts of the changing social structure; at the same time, of course, allowing the sentiments of some of the people who live in the structure also to find expression. Should the line *AB* reach the position *ed*, the class situation in either group would not be fundamentally disturbed, except that the top Negro group would be equivalent with the top white, while the lower classes in each of the parallel groups would also be equivalent. Even the present approximation of this gives the top Negro group certain advantages over his lower-class fellows which he is anxious to maintain.

On the other hand, the social skewness created by the present class-caste conflict which results in the process of changing the social location of the caste line has placed the upper-class Negro in a decidedly difficult situation. The Negro who has moved or been born into the uppermost group (see the chart) of his caste is superior to the lower whites in class, but inferior in caste. In his own personality he feels the conflict of the two opposing structures, and in the thinking and feeling of the members of both groups there is to be found this same conflict about his position. He is known to be superior to the "poor white" (he is a doctor, say), but he is still a "nigger" or "Negro," according to the social context in which the words are used. Metaphorically speaking, although he is at the top of the Negro class hierarchy, he is constantly butting his head against the caste line. He knows himself to be superior to the poor white, yet to the poor white the upper-class Negro is still a "nigger," which is a way of saying the Negro is in a lower caste than himself. Furthermore, if it ever came to an issue, the supraordinate white class would maintain the solidarity of the white group by repudiating any claims by any Negro of superiority to the lower-class whites. This would be true even though the admission might be made privately that the Negro was superior to certain of the lower-class whites.

The present and past political behavior of the South has to be understood, it seems to me, in terms of the maintenance of the caste lines, and as an effort to prevent the continued elaboration and segmentation of the class groups within the lower caste. The unequal distribution of school funds and privileges are an excellent example of how the system tends to maintain itself through the changing generations. The operation of the courts and the activities of the police also reflect the same conscious or unconscious maintenance of control by the supraordinate white caste. For that matter, all social institutions in the South, including the family, school, association, clique, and church, are formed to fit the dominant caste social situation of the dominant social caste.

An interesting hypothesis may be built out of the skewed social position of the upper-class Negro. It seems possible that the instability of many of the individuals in this group (as compared, let us say, with the Negroes of the lower positions) may be due to the instability and skewness of the social situation in which they live. They are always "off balance" and are constantly attempting to achieve an equilibrium which their society, except under extraordinary circumstances, does not provide for them.

# Part IV

# Change Quickens: 1941-1950

# Introduction

World War II was the most massive global conflict to date. The extent of the changes wrought by this international conflagration were so profound as to influence virtually all societal institutions of the principal combatants. Race relations and sociology were no exceptions. Change quickened as the United States shook off the last vestiges of the Depression. Black sociologists were among the first to sense that these alterations had far-reaching implications for future American race relations.

Black contributions to the leading sociological journals, especially during this critical period, are not generally appreciated.[1] Landmark books in race relations by black authors are well known—from *The Philadelphia Negro* (Du-Bois) to *Black Metropolis* (St. Clair Drake and Horace Cayton), *Caste, Class, and Race* (Oliver Cox), and *The Negro in the United States* (Frazier). Yet, despite two recent volumes about black sociologists,[2] many observers of both races do not realize the many influential black journal contributions of this period. Our first four selections offer evidence of these contributions from three sharply contrasting figures—Oliver Cromwell Cox, Charles S. Johnson, and Frazier. But there were an array of additional publications by black authors during these years in the journals under review. Cox published two additional papers,[3] Johnson and Frazier about a half-dozen each.[4] Mozell Hill, at Langston University, had six

---

[1] Butler Jones, "The tradition of sociology teaching in black colleges: The unheralded professionals," in J. Blackwell and M. Janowitz (eds.), *Black Sociologists* (Chicago: University of Chicago Press, 1974), p. 134.

[2] *Ibid.,* and John Bracey, August Meier, and Elliott Rudwick, *The Black Sociologists: The First Half-Century* (Belmont, Cal.: Wadsworth, 1971).

[3] *E.g.,* Oliver Cox, "Race prejudice and intolerance: A distinction," *Social Forces* 24 (1945): 216–219.

[4] *E.g.,* Charles S. Johnson, "The Negro," *American Journal of Sociology* 47 (1942): 854–

papers focusing on social stratification among black people and the all-black community of Boley, Oklahoma;[5] Charles Gomillion, the activist Tuskegee sociologist, predicted in 1942 a future rise in black militancy based on "a changing conception of self."[6] Many of these papers looked closely at black community institutions—secret societies,[7] the family,[8] and particularly the church.[9]

As the next four selections illustrate, there is also a pronounced concern for structural change running through these journal publications. Selection 18 by Cox is an unrelenting attack upon the dominant racial model of sociology at that point—the caste and class position put forth by Warner in the previous selection. The full significance of this interesting piece can be grasped only by placing it in its social context. Cox, a proud native of Trinidad, spent all but the close of his long career at small black colleges cut off from the principal sociological centers of professional ferment. He was as "invisible" and little known as Johnson and Frazier were celebrated. More interested in social theory than other black sociologists of the time, his lonely battle against the application of India's caste system model to American race relations theory ultimately led to his masterpiece in 1948, *Caste, Class, and Race.* Though granted little attention at the time of its appearance, this fascinating book deserves careful reading today as one of the few thoroughgoing Marxist interpretations of American race relations.

Selection 18 details a number of Cos's objections to the Warner formulation. Here and elsewhere he raised three fundamental criticisms. "Caste" was used in many different, loose, often conflicting ways. And while caste restrictions were accepted as "right" and religiously ordained in India, black Americans did not accept them. Moreover, the concept implies a static, one-dimensional, permanent structure instead of the dynamic, complex, ever changing process preferred by Cox. On the first of these objections, there can be little argument. The term, "caste," had been (and still is occasionally) imprecisely employed throughout the literature, as a brief scanning by the reader of previous selections will readily reveal. On his second criticism, Cox was often taken to task.[10] Numerous writers, including an Indian specialist,[11] held that many low-caste Indians no more

864, and E. Franklin Frazier, "Race contacts and the social structure," *American Sociological Review 14* (1949): 1–11 (Frazier's Presidential Address to the American Sociological Society).

[5] *E.g.,* Mozell C. Hill, "A comparative analysis of the social organization of the all-Negro society in Oklahoma," *Social Forces 25* (1946): 70–77.

[6] Charles C. Gomillion, "The influence of the Negro on the culture of the South," *Social Forces 20* (1942): 386–390.

[7] Edward N. Palmer, "Negro secret societies," *Social Forces 23* (1944): 207–212.

[8] Charles E. King, "The Negro maternal family: A product of an economy and a culture system," *Social Forces 24* (1945): 100–104.

[9] V. E. Daniel, "Ritual and stratification in Chicago Negro churches," *American Sociological Review 7* (1942): 352–361, and Harry W. Roberts, "The rural Negro minister: His personal and social characteristics," *Social Forces 27* (1949): 291–300.

[10] M. F. Ashley Montagu, "The nature of race relations," *Social Forces 25* (1947): 336–342.

[11] Gerald D. Berreman, "Caste in India and the United States," *American Journal of Sociology 66* (1960): 120–127.

accepted the correctness of the caste system than did many black Americans. The third criticism soon won support from non-Marxist black sociologists who also objected to the status quo implications of permanency in the caste concept.[12] Fortunately, Cox lived long enough to see his critique of the caste analogy generally accepted by the discipline and to receive belatedly in 1971 the DuBois-Johnson-Frazier Award of the American Sociological Association.

But the very name of the Association's award tells in what different circumstances both Johnson and Frazier found themselves. Johnson, like Frazier, was trained by Park and others at the University of Chicago, though he never completed his doctoral work. His first sociological contribution was work on a 1922 report of a Chicago commission formed in the wake of race riots, *The Negro in Chicago*. At the height of the Harlem Renaissance from 1923 to 1928, he acquired national recognition as the effective editor of *Opportunity*, the official publication of the National Urban League in New York City. In 1928 Johnson went to Fisk University, where he developed a strong social science department dedicated to research on Southern race relations. He became president of Fisk in 1947 but remained a productive scholar until his sudden death in 1956 in a railroad station on his way to yet another speech. His most lasting books include the moving *Shadow of the Plantation* (1934) and the insightful *Growing Up in the Black Belt* (1941).

Johnson and Frazier are sometimes accused today by black and white critics alike of being too accommodationist, of not rebelling from current formulations in the manner of Cox. Yet a careful reading of both of them shows that virtually all of their work rendered a broad-scale indictment of the racism of their time. With Johnson in particular, his formal, polite style, in contrast to Cox's thunder from the sidelines, adds to this critical view. But Selection 19 reveals this style together with an anything but accepted thesis of rapid change. While rising domestic racial conflict during World War II was widely being deplored by many white observers, Johnson calmly and with characteristic understatement and formality presents precisely the opposite thesis. The new "troubles" were symptomatic, he argues perceptively, of the coming of needed and fundamental racial change in the South.

Selections 20 and 21 show a similar pointedness in Frazier's writings. First, he presents a scholarly but candid analysis of the racial assumptions of the founding fathers of American sociology, an especially valuable article for this reader. Next he reviews Gunnar Myrdal's *An American Dilemma* in glowing—and again candid—terms. Myrdal's tome appeared in 1944 and is without challenge the single most cited book in the sociology of race relations.[13] Myrdal's work did not di-

---

[12]*E.g.*, Maxwell R. Brooks, "American class and caste: An appriasal," *Social Forces 25* (1946): 207-211.

[13]H. M. Bahr, T. J. Johnson, and M. R. Seitz, "Influential scholars and works in the sociology of race and minority relations, 1944-1968," *American Sociologist 6* (1971): 296-298.

rectly generate much new research,[14] nor has its basically psychological thesis of a dilemma between the consciences and practices of white Americans gone without severe sociological criticism. But its ambitious and successful attempt to describe systematically the entire front of American race relations in the late 1930s was an unquestioned success. Thus, *An American Dilemma* serves today as an important time capsule for comparing today's racial patterns and conditions with those of the past. And consequently, all 1,000 pages should be required reading for those young observers who never experienced American race relations prior to the 1960s and who mistakenly believe that "nothing has changed."

Frazier's immediate recognition of Myrdal's encyclopedic work as a classic is made more interesting when it is compared with the lukewarm reviews it received from leading white sociologists. Kimball Young especially, in his critique in the *American Sociological Review*,[15] conceded that the "book is a real contribution to social science" but took sharp exception to Myrdal's blunt criticism of white American sociologists for not having been more active in their opposition to racial oppression. Young answered in *ad hominem* fashion, noting that Myrdal's Swedish homeland possessed a "relatively homogeneous and small society" without so many problems. "It is my own feeling," he wrote tartly, "that we have here a certain friendly projection of views from one reared in a more stable society upon our society wherein the dynamic forces are really far more varied and complex than he realizes."[16]

Myrdal's book and Johnson's article on wartime changes could look forward to positive changes in black–white relations. But for Japanese Americans, these same war years wrenched their lives and communities and raised basic questions as to whether they could ever hope to gain equal rights and win acceptance in the United States. Within six months of Japan's destructive attack upon Pearl Harbor on December 7, 1941, more than 100,000 persons of Japanese ancestry had been removed from the West Coast and placed in "relocation centers" for "security" reasons. Figure 1 shows the placement of both the initial assembly centers and the relocation centers. This fear reaction of a startled and scared nation occurred despite *not one* verified instance of Japanese American sabotage. Furthermore, the effort was confined to the West Coast and did not occur in the far more militarily sensitive Hawaiian Islands, where, after all, the surprise attack had occurred and the proportion of residents of Japanese ancestry was much higher. Even California's then Governor Earl Warren, the great civil libertarian Chief Justice of the United States in the next two decades, was involved in the

---

[14] An early exception sampled 200 black residents of Columbus, Ohio, and largely validated Myrdal's rank order of sensitivity to discrimination by black Americans. W. S. M. Banks, II, "The rank order of sensitivity to discrimination of Negroes in Columbus, Ohio," *American Sociological Review 15* (1950): 529–534.

[15] Kimball Young, "Review of *An American Dilemma*," *American Sociological Review 9* (1944): 326–330.

[16] *Ibid.*, p. 330.

### FIGURE 1   World War II Assembly and Relocation Centers

decision. In retrospect, it was a grave national injustice with harsh racial implications, for no Caucasian citizens with ancestry tracing to foreign enemies have ever been similarly treated in any American war.

The leading sociological student of this tragic phenomenon was Leonard Bloom of the University of California at Los Angeles. He published Selection 22 as his first contribution toward understanding the devastating effects of the relocation upon the basic Japanese American institution of the family. He followed this up with a later article in 1947,[17] as well as a biting reply to a 1946 article that attempted to put the phenomenon in the best possible light of "building new communities."[18] To the charge that the "whimsical character of social science research" had prevented it from being of much help to the organizers of the relocation centers, Bloom questioned if anyone "had a right to expect American social scientists to have investigated the concentration camp."[19]

[17]Leonard Bloom, "Transitional adjustments of Japanese-Americans to relocation," *American Sociological Review 12* (1947): 201–209.  Bloom is best known today as Broom.

[18]John H. Provinse and Solon T. Kimball, "Building new communities during war time," *American Sociological Review 11* (1946): 396–409, and L. Bloom, "Discussion," *American Sociological Review 11* (1946): 409–410.

[19]*Ibid.,* p. 410.

The postwar years were characterized by the dominance of psychological analyses of race relations with emphasis upon "prejudice." Indeed, over the 1944-1968 period, two completely psychological volumes—T. W. Adorno, *et al.'s The Authoritarian Personality* and Goraon W. Allport's *The Nature of Prejudice*—were among the most cited books in sociological articles on race relations.[20] While Allport provided some discussion of societal factors, *The Authoritarian Personality* study virtually ignored structural considerations. When the prisoners in San Quentin prison filled out their questionnaires in highly authoritarian manners, the Berkeley authors took this as an accurate reading of prisoners' personalities without seriously considering the fact that these respondents could have been influenced by the remarkably authoritarian structure under which they lived.

This psychological trend of the 1940s is represented in Selection 23 on prejudice by Bruno Bettelheim, a psychiatrist, and Morris Janowitz, then a new sociologist, both of the University of Chicago. But this influential study, later produced in book form as *The Dynamics of Prejudice* (1950), is exceptional for this period in that it carefully places the individual phenomena into the context of social mobility.

This concentration on psychological factors in the 1940s faithfully reflects the reluctance to tackle controversial structural problems of race relations. The object lesson of Hitler's Germany in World War II gave bigotry "a bad name"; yet the difficult structural issues were assiduously avoided. "Prejudiced people" caused the problem, went the logic. So remedies envisioned "curing" prejudice as an individual, not a societal, disease, without facing issues of direct group conflict. The sociological literature, surprisingly, reflects this all too simple reasoning during these years almost as much as the psychological literature. Three examples from *Social Forces* illustrate the point. One paper describes only "educational" approaches for the South's Commission on Interracial Cooperation;[21] another discusses "the control of ethnic conflict" (not the control of intergroup injustice), and argues against legal methods because they "may lead to increased hostility."[22] Finally, George Haynes, the distinguished black sociologist and longtime head of the Department of Race Relations of the Federal Council of Churches, advocates presenting awards to strategic people as a means of altering interracial attitudes and practices.[23] Indeed, Brotherhood Week, complete with Brotherhood Awards, began in these years. But sociology was soon to turn sharply from this psychological reductionism, as we shall see in Parts V and VI.

---

[20] Bahr, Johnson, and Seitz, "Influential Scholars."

[21] William E. Cole, "The role of the Commission on Interracial Cooperation in war and peace," *Social Forces 21* (1943): 456–463.

[22] Simon Marcson, "The control of ethnic conflict," *Social Forces 24* (1945): 161–165.

[23] George E. Haynes, "Public approbation as a means of changing interracial attitudes and customs," *Social Forces 24* (1945): 105–110.

# 18

# The Modern Caste School of Race Relations

*OLIVER C. COX*

During the last decade a prolific school of writers on race relations in the United States, led mainly by social anthropologists, have relied religiously upon an ingenious, if not original, caste hypothesis. Professor W. Lloyd Warner is the admitted leader of the movement, and his followers include scholars of considerable distinction. We propose here to examine critically the position of this school.

## The Hypothesis

Strictly speaking, the school has no hypothesis. . . . In the South, they maintain, Negroes form one caste and whites another, with an imaginary rotating caste line between them. "The white caste is in a superordinate position and the Negro caste in a subordinate social position." . . .

A class system and a caste system "are antithetical to each other. . . . Nevertheless they have accommodated themselves in the southern community. . . ."[1] The caste line is represented as running asymmetrically diagonally between the two class systems of Negroes and whites. . . .

It is assumed that during slavery the caste line . . . was practically horizontal,

[1]W. Lloyd Warner, *American Journal of Sociology*, XLII, 234. (Selection 17 in this volume.)

Reprinted, abridged, from *Social Forces 21* (December 1942): 218–226. Copyright © The University of North Carolina Press.

but that since then with the cultural progress of Negroes it has rotated upward. . . . It is thought further that the social disparity between Negro classes and white classes is particularly disconcerting to upper-class Negroes. . . .

It is believed that in many countries of the world besides India there are developed caste systems, but the school has never found it convenient to demonstrate this proposition. "Caste," Warner and Davis assert without proof, "is found in most of the major areas of the world; this is particularly true of Africa, Asia, and America. The Indians of the southeastern United States and those of British Columbia have well-developed, if not castes, then castelike structures. We cannot take time to examine those American systems, but we shall briefly summarize the material on East Indian caste. . . ."[2] Thus the caste system in India has been taken as the criterion; nowhere has the school relied upon any other system.

On the crucial question of marriage among castes Warner and Davis give Émile Senart credit for the belief that castes "isolate themselves to prevent intermarriage"; while they regard hypergamy as an example of "variations from the caste ideal." Kingsley Davis, however, thinks that hypergamy distinguishes two major types of caste systems. In India hypergamy is possible because the Indian caste system is a "non-racial caste system"; in the United States and South Africa, on the other hand, hypergamy is impossible because there are in these situations "racial caste systems."[3] Warner and Davis depend further upon Senart and Bouglé for their significant conclusion that *"no one occupation has but one caste assigned to it."*

Considerable emphasis is put upon the fact that a Negro or white person, who was born Negro or white, could never hope to be anything but Negro or white: "Children and grandchildren of Negroes will continue to be born into, live in, and only die out of the Negro 'caste.'" Further, this biological fact of inheriting racial marks strikes Kingsley Davis as providing an ideal foundation for a caste system:

> The reason that race serves as an excellent basis of caste is that one gets one's racial traits by birth from parents having those traits, and one cannot change these traits during the rest of one's life.

## Estimate of Basic Principles

. . . Although the school has relied completely upon references to the caste system in India for its authority, it has nowhere made anything approaching a careful study of the caste system. Yet, even so, it has been difficult to determine

[2] "A Comparative Study of American Caste," in *Race Relations and the Race Problem,* Edgar T. Thompson (ed.).

[3] "Intermarriage in Caste Societies," *American Anthropologist, 43* (July–September, 1941), 376–395.

which of their selected "essences" of the caste system will be controlling in given situations. For example, after one tentative discussion of caste in India, the conclusion was reached that:

> There has been no attempt in these last few paragraphs to demonstrate that our caste structure and Indian caste structure are exactly the same, but rather we have attempted to show that they are the same kind of social phenomena . . .[4]

At this point the question may easily devolve upon the meaning of the expression *same kind*. We have had considerable difficulty also in finding clear-cut statements of principle. Usually some such phrase as "for our purpose," "as here used," or "generally" limits statements that are forthwith given universal applicability. Of course one could hardly question such a contrivance; it may be likened to the researcher who says: "This animal before us is not a horse, but *for our purpose* it is convenient to call it a horse; if you examine it closely you will discover that it is a water-buffalo. That does not matter, for we are not going to use it in the water-buffalo sense. Of course, you cannot say this animal is not a horse; after all, it has four legs; and what does it matter in any event whether we say horse or water-buffalo?"

At points where clarity is most needed the school invariably becomes impressionistic and circuitous. It has been accepted that the form of social organization in Brahmanic India constitutes a caste system. This system has certain distinguishing characteristics; hence we shall consider these the norm.

Definitions of a society are difficult to formulate; they are usually insufficient. For example A. L. Kroeber wrote an article on caste[5] and came to the conclusion that a caste system is not possible in western society; notwithstanding, Warner adopted his definition of "a caste" and reached the opposite position that: "The social system of Old City (in the South) fits this definition of Kroeber's and of most of the ethnologists and social anthropologists."[6] The play with definitions usually results in debate rather than constructive interest in the social problem. At any rate, Warner's own definition of caste considers two factors as determining: (a) that intermarriage between groups is not sanctioned, and (b) that there is no opportunity for members of lower groups to rise into upper groups nor for those of the upper groups to fall into the lower groups.

It should be emphasized that a definition of "a caste" does not describe "the caste-system." . . . [U]pper caste men in India have always been able to marry women of lower castes without disturbing the caste system, a procedure which could not be sanctioned in the South. Endogamy may be an isolator of social

---

[4] Edgar T. Thompson, *op. cit.,* p. 232.
[5] *Encyclopaedia of the Social Sciences,* III, "Caste" by A. L. Kroeber, pp. 254–256.
[6] W. Allison Davis, Burleigh B. Gardner, Mary R. Gardner, and W. Lloyd Warner, *Deep South* (Chicago, 1941), p. 9.

classes, castes, tribes, sects, or any other social groups which think they have something to protect; hence, the final test of caste is not endogamy but the social values which endogamy secures. . . .

Probably the most insidious analogy between race and caste relations rests in the idea of life membership in each group. The identity of the phenomena, however, is only apparent. It must be obvious that a man born in a certain race cannot have the choice of leaving it and going into another race. This biological affiliation has not been the position of one caste man with respect to another in India. In fact, this very distinction should raise the suspicion that different social forces are operating in the caste system from those in situations of racial adjustment. But what really do we mean by saying that a white man cannot fall into the Negro group? To the extent that he can have sex relations with Negro women he can "fall" biologically. The mixed blood children that are born are, in the long run, the most potent equilibrator of the races; and the law makers of the South are by no means unmindful of this fact. The Negro may "rise" biologically if he is able to pass.

From too much preoccupation with the unchangeableness of physical inheritance, the conclusion is reached that the social status of Negroes and whites in the South may become identical, yet they will continue to constitute two castes. In explaining his diagram, Professor Warner holds that there is a theoretical possibility of Negroes' advancing to the point where they may become the dominant caste. And this makes his theory particularly illogical and sterile. So far as its logic is concerned, it asserts that Negroes may become equal to whites, evidently in wealth, in learning, in opportunity to control the government of the state—in short, culturally equal. Yet Negroes and whites will still be unequal; unequal, obviously, in color. For a person born white could never have the privilege of becoming black. Clearly it must be on the grounds of this latter disability that his caste system will still be maintained. And since, so far as we know, time will not alter the possibility of a man's changing his racial marks, we must expect the white caste and the black caste to remain indefinitely intact—an ideal leopard-and-spots theory of race relations.

The theory goes happily past the meaning of the racial dichotomy in the South. It makes it appear that the white man is protecting his color and that the Negro is equally interested in protecting his; so that with the ballot in the hands of Negroes and with the opportunity for cultural participation open to him as a normal citizen, the black code which keeps the races segregated will still be the law of the South. . . .[H]owever, . . . the greater the relative cultural advancement of Negroes, the less will be the need of the white man's protecting his color. The theory sees a caste system set up in the South in the interest of the white man's color and, for that matter, the Negro's also. None the less it may be shown that the white man has no such obsession about his color. He will protect it only so long as it helps him to reserve a calculable cultural advantage.

The caste interpretation of race relations in the South does not see that the intermarriage restriction laws are a social affront to Negroes; it cannot perceive that Negroes are smarting under the Jim Crow laws; it may not recognize the overwhelming aspiration among Negroes for equality of social opportunity; it could never realize that the superiority of the white race is due principally to the fact that it has developed the necessary devices for maintaining incontestable control over the shooting iron; and it will not know that "race hatred" may be reckoned in terms of the white man's interest. Hence it is possible for the school to imagine the anomaly of Negroes fully assimilated culturally and yet living symbiotically apart from whites on the basis of some unexplained understanding that their colors should never be mixed. In other words, the races will, as Warner and Davis believe: "isolate themselves to prevent intermarriage!"

In order that the authors might come to terms with the disturbing question of the relationship of occupation and caste, it is concluded that even in India there is no identification of every occupation with a caste. It is argued, in other words, that since many castes have the same occupation, occupation is no significant factor in the system. The point to remember here, however, is that every caste has a traditional occupation, and not that every occupation has a caste.

Considerable importance is given to interracial etiquette in the South as a factor supporting the caste hypothesis. . . .

However, in the South, there is also an etiquette intended to keep poor whites at a proper distance from upper class whites, and it is probably more severely non-reciprocating there than in other parts of the country. To upper class Negroes, also, lower class Negroes are unusually respectful. Indeed, a system of social etiquette which distinguishes superior persons or classes is no exclusive trait of the caste system. It is found in armies, churches, among social classes, as well as among peoples and races who live in relationship of subordination and superordination.

## Personality of Upper Class Negroes

It is a common belief, not peculiar to the caste school, that upper class Negroes are especially maladjusted. The bi-racial system in the United States, it must be admitted, is a pathological situation, and insofar as this is so, it affects adversely the personalities of both whites and blacks. But sensitivity to social wrongs need not imply derangement or an "off balance" personality. We may mention at this point that although this assertion calls for explanation, the caste theorists evidently do not realize that it is most damaging to their hypothesis. A person belonging to a lower caste is not "constantly butting his head against the caste line." In fact, the absence of such a phenomenon is so vital to the persistence of a caste order that it would hardly be inaccurate to maintain that it is definitely incompatible with a caste system. Caste barriers in the caste system are never challenged; they are sacred to caste and caste alike. The personalities developed in the caste system are normal for that society.

Negroes are moving away from a condition of extreme white domination and subjection to one of normal citizenship. The determinant of unrest or social dysphoria among a people is not so much their *state* of subjugation or seeming oppression; it is rather the process of changing from some accommodated stage of well-being to one of subservience. Since the Civil War the situation among Negroes in the South has been opposite to this. . . . [I] t is not difference in class so much as difference in age which determines the attitude of Negroes toward whites. . . . Older Negroes were reared in an earlier school of racial beliefs; and, indeed, the younger are not infrequently very impatient with their compromising attitudes toward whites. Among Negroes in the South the "Uncle Toms" are distributed through all the social classes.

Of course militance in the interest of racial progress should not be mistaken for personality imbalance. In fact, dissatisfaction with the *status quo* is the common preoccupation of all Negro leaders. There is, furthermore, some compensation to upper class Negroes. Frequently they meet whites under flattering conditions, mostly in business relations. They have considerable prestige among their own people, sometimes even more than that which whites of similar attainments can hope for within their own group. This windfall may not only compensate for loss of respect from low class whites, but it may even result in a sort of grandiose importance inconsistent with reality. The "big Negro," a recognized personality type, is usually indelicate and grossly lacking in humility; yet, he is not pathological.

Upper class Negroes do not envy poor whites in the South because the latter are beyond the purview of the black code. One might as well argue that some human beings suffer severe personality traumas because the dogs and cats of the rich have certain advantages that they do not have. The resentment of upper class Negroes is rather against the ruling class, the guardians of the *status quo*. Enlightened Negroes recognize clearly the cultural inferiority of the poor whites. As a youth, W. E. B. DuBois says of himself: "I cordially despised the poor Irish and South Germans, who slaved in the mills, and annexed the rich and well-to-do as my natural companions."[7] Thus, bitter as it is, the real conflict is usually between Negroes and their cultural equals or superiors. Sometimes it may seem to end in despair, as when Countee Cullen exclaimed:

> Yet do I marvel at this curious thing:
> To make a poet black, and bid him sing!

Ordinarily, however, it is a persistent challenge to Negroes, an integrating force in a cause which must be served. . . .

## The Social Organization of Negroes

. . . [W] e may think of the larger American society as fundamentally antipathetic to the non-Christian, non-democratic, bi-racial system in the South; hence it is continuously "feeling its way" to something else. To put such a situa-

---

[7] *Darkwater* (New York, 1921), p. 10.

tion easily into a typology of societies which includes the caste system in India, indeed, to identify it with the caste system, must be misleading to say the least. The caste system of India is a minutely segmented, assimilated social structure; it is highly stable and capable of perpetuating itself indefinitely.

When two racial or nationality groups become more or less isolated from each other because of some continuing conflict situation or basic repugnance, we do not refer to them as forming a social status hierarchy even though their relationship is one of superordination and subordination or of conqueror and conquered. As an illustration, Adolf Hitler in his *My Battle* says: "It must be held in greater honour to be a citizen of this Reich, even if only a crossing-sweeper, than to be a king in a foreign state."[8] Suppose now that this philosophy be made a reality in future German-Polish relationships; all Poles will then be considered inferior to the least of Germans; and an etiquette will be developed to implement the attitude. But there will be here no social status hierarchy; neither would Hitler there and then have enacted a caste system. The Poles will seek a *modus vivendi* in some sort of society of their own; and the intergroup relationship will most likely be one of antagonism, a latent power group relationship.

So, too, Negroes and whites in the Deep South do not constitute an assimilated society. There are rather two societies. Thus we may conceive of Negroes as constituting a quasi or tentative society developed to meet certain needs resulting from their retarded assimilation. Unlike the permanence of a caste, it is a temporary society intended to continue only so long as whites are able to maintain the barriers against their assimilation. It provides the matrix for a universe of discourse in which members of the group give expression to their common sympathies, opinions, and sentiments; and in which their primary social institutions function. The political and economic structure is controlled by another and larger society to which the whites are assimilated and toward which all Negroes are oriented.

The "public" of the white society includes Negroes only in the broadest sense; and when Negroes in their institutional functions declare that "everybody is invited," white people who turn up must assume the role of strangers. The "we feeling" of the white and of the Negro society tends to be mutually exclusive. Says Robert E. Park: "Gradually, imperceptibly, within the larger world of the white man, a smaller world, the world of the black man, is silently taking form and shape."[9] . . .

One device for retarding Negro assimilation, which does not have to be resorted to in the caste system, is the policy of guarding against any development of an overt expression of indispensability of Negroes within the social organization. Whatever their *de facto* importance, they must never appear as an integral part of the society. Instead, they pay little taxes; hence little or none of certain public expenditures should be diverted to their benefit. The theory of taxation

[8] E. T. S. Dugdale, trans. (Cambridge, 1933), 182.
[9] "Racial assimilation of secondary groups." Selection 3 of this volume.

according to ability to pay and expenditure according to need does not include them. Crime, sickness, death, and poverty almost characterize Negroes; hence they are a drag on "society" and may be ostensibly sloughed off to advantage. Whites are generally protected from contact with cultured Negroes. The successful practice of this contrivance tends to give the Negro a sense of worthlessness and unwantedness, which contributes finally to the retardation of his assimilation. In Brahmanic India, however, where the population is assimilated to the caste culture, it is openly admitted that low-caste men are indispensable to the system, and this admission does not conduce to any advancement in the latter's social status.

By using the caste hypothesis, then, the school seeks to explain a "normal society" in the South. In short, it has made peace for the hybrid society that has not made peace with itself; and insofar as this is true its work is fictitious.

## Contribution of the School

A remarkable characteristic of this caste school of race relations is its tendency to conceive of itself as being original. It believes that it has made a discovery. It is difficult, however, to determine wherein rests the originality. We do not know who made the first analogy between race relations and the caste system of India, but it is certain that the idea was quite popular during the middle of the last century. One of the most detailed and extended discussions of this hypothesis is that of the Hon. Charles Sumner published in 1869.[10] Since then, many textbooks have accepted the idea. Some students, like Sir Herbert Risley have used the hypothesis as the basis of extensive research. Many wirters such as E. B. Reuter and Charles S. Johnson have applied the term casually to the racial situation in the Unites States. . . .

It is difficult to see what the modern caste school has added to this, other than perhaps publicity. . . .

With respect to the scientific precision of the word "caste" the school argues that: "by all the physical tests the anthropologists might apply, some social Negroes are *biologically* white," hence the word race cannot have meaning when applied to Negroes.[11] We should remember here, however, that the racial situation in the South never depended upon "physical tests of anthropologists." It developed long before anthropometry became of age. The sociologist is interested, not in what the anthropometrists set up as their criteria of race, but in what peoples in interaction come to accept as a race. It is this latter belief which controls their behavior and not what the anthropometrist thinks. But in reality the term caste does not economize thinking on this subject. It is always necessary first to say what kind of people belong to the Negro caste before we can

---

[10] *The Question of Caste,* Wright and Potter (Boston, 1869).

[11] *Deep South,* pp. 7–8.

know what the Negro caste means. Therefore in the process of defining Negro caste we have defined Negro race, and the final accomplishment is a substitution of words only. One may test this fact by substituting in the writings of this school the words *Negroes* or *white people* wherever the words *Negro caste* or *white caste* are used; and observe that the sense of the statement does not change.

For this reason the burden of the productions of this school tends to be old wine in new bottles. In other words, much that has come to us by earlier studies has taken on the glamour of caste; and the school seldom refers to the contributions of out-group students. One could hardly help recalling as an analogous situation the popularity which William McDougall gave to the instinct hypothesis. Without making any reference to William James, Lloyd Morgan, and others who had handled the concept with great care, McDougall set out with pioneering zeal to bend all social behavior to his instinct theory. It was not long, however, before reaction came. And so too, until comparatively recently, the race-caste idea had a desultory career. It has now been made fashionable; yet, already, students who had once used the term caste begin to shrink from it. But we should hasten to add that this school has none of the anti-color complexes of the instinct school. Its leadership merely lacks, as Robert E. Park might say, a sociological tradition.

# 19

# The Present Status of Race Relations in the South

*CHARLES S. JOHNSON*

There is fairly widespread agreement that race relations in the South have de-
teriorated in character since the beginning of the war. This, of course, is popular
agreement based upon the assumption that quiescence and absence of racial
tensions are a major, if not exclusive, index to the most wholesome race relations. The thesis of this paper is that the emotional disturbances of the present
period, involving racial issues, are symptoms of accelerated social changes, and
that these changes are wholesome, even if their temporary racial effects are bad.

Where there is preoccupation with race and relative racial positions in the
social system of the region, it is inevitable that many factors which are essentially non-racial in character will be invested with dangerous racial implications,
and it is equally likely that many underlying elements responsible for the new
stress on race will be overlooked.

Total war is a cataclysmic national event that shakes and loosens many traditions form their deep moorings, whether these traditions are economic, religious,
racial or romantic. The impersonal and direct imperatives of sudden war cannot
trace a careful path around the embedded orthodoxies of race any more than
can a flood or earthquake. When these racial traditions have been disturbed,
when the comfortable patterns of living have been broken or warped, a sense of
insecurity is inevitable. New guides to behavior must be worked out, new situa-

Reprinted, abridged, from *Social Forces 23* (October 1944): 27–32. Copyright ©The University of North Carolina Press.

tions must be met and solved by reference to new or at least altered values. The race problem in such situations becomes more personal, and in becoming more personal it becomes more emotional.

Several major crises induced by the war should be noted here as a background for understanding what is happening to race relations. There was, as is everywhere evident, a prompt necessity for accelerating mechanical production in the South, as in the rest of the Nation. Although the South is primarily agricultural it shared richly in the appropriations for cantonments, shipyards, munitions plants, and these were located in or near the cities. A result was the uprooting and migration of hundreds of thousands of workers to the industrial production centers. They carried their personal backgrounds with them and sought, as would be natural, to find a new basis of community, without risking the personal security incident to losing the values of these backgrounds. This alone was a personal and an industrial revolution of great significance crowded into a brief period. The major training camps for the ten million or more troops are in the South, and there is more current mobility than this country has ever before experienced. The demands for manpower have pressed hard again the old established racial occupational cleavages; the high wages, together with the national minimum wage legislation, have disturbed another traditional racial differential. New occupations have been created without racial definition. The familiar Negro domestic, unprotected by employment legislation, and long underpaid according to national standards, has disappeared into the new war industries, leaving a trail of dismay and bitter resentment among housewives. New economic and military hierarchies have intruded into the social system. There has been an inescapable penetration of more and more national regulation into the region in the form of soldiers' family allowances, civilian defense measures, army regulations.

These objective changes have been moving hand in hand with changes in southern agriculture. The country has yielded millions of its population to the city and, at the same time increased its production with fewer hands, thereby closing the door to the return of many of the emigres. More important still, these changes have been accompanied by a necessary emphasis upon the American creed of democracy as the idological support of the total war effort.

This campaign for democracy and the rights of the common man the world over has had unique effects in the southern region where the principle has encountered historical difficulties when applied inferentially to the Negro population. It has, however, been taken hopefully, if not seriously, by the Negroes. The harbingers of danger to the traditional racial patterns have appeared in the form of: (a) extensions of various types of New Deal legislation into the South; (b) national campaigns for the abolition of the poll tax; (c) campaigns for the broadening of the social security laws which would affect most directly the southern region in the agricultural and domestic service fields, and the Negro worker; (d) court decisions virtually compelling the equalization of educational expenditures for whites and Negroes; (e) persistent attempts to attach antidiscrimination riders on Federal bills; and (f) the President's Fair Employment Practice Committee, and similar measures.

These measures have appeared to the South to force racial adjustments on a new level ahead of public readiness for such changes, and a result has been resistance to this pressure from the outside, impatience with outside interference, re-assertion of the regional policy of racial segregation, and a determination to handle the regional racial problem under conditions imposed by the region itself.

Over recent months we have been observing points of racial tension in the southern region. Between March 1st and December 31st we noted 111 racial incidents in the South of sufficient importance to be given attention in the national press. In order of numerical importance they were as follows: (1) incidents growing out of new racial contacts in industrial employment; (2) incidents associated with congestion in various modes of public transportation; (3) incidents associated with crimes committed or suspected, and the police handling of these situations; (4) incidents involving conflicts between Negro service men and civilian or military police, or other civilians; (5) incidents involving Negro status, with respect to civil rights, the racial etiquette; (6) other incidents, including attempts of Negroes to vote, migrate, move into a non-Negro area; challenge of white status, and lynching.

The most serious of the employment incidents was . . . the Mobile affair, in which an attempt to introduce essential Negro workers on new shipbuilding jobs met resistance from white workers. Attitudes regarding labor are less tolerant in the southern region than in some other sections of the country, and the issues of race and labor constitute in themselves a complex of new problems seeking redefinition. The highest temperatures have been registered in the areas of greatest labor demand. The demands of production schedules, under the stress of the war emergency, have tended to overcome popular resistance to the altering of caste lines in general occupational fields, and there has been recently increased racial accommodation in the war plants. In most instances the principle of segregation, actual or token, has been preserved, both with respect to physical contact on the jobs and higher and lower grades of work.

The point of most frequent physical contact between whites and Negroes is in transportation, and more minor clashes have occurred in these relationships than in any other. The new conditions of population congestion, shortage of carriers, the use of raw personnel replacements for the more experienced drivers and conductors, and the flexible and frequently undeterminable limits of racial segregation on public carriers tend to reduce the *customary* patterns of segregation to highly volatile issues of *personal* status in racial situations. . . .

Where there is at the same time inadequacy of carrier space and a racial etiquette that demands first service for white passengers, it is inevitable that there should be numerous and various challenges by Negroes of the etiquette, if they are to travel at all. Moreover, the minor patterns of the etiquette vary widely among cities, and mistakes are easy to make and may be interpreted as deliberate flaunting of the principle of segregation and of the dictum of proper racial respect. This has frequently been the issue in racial conflict situations involving Negro soldiers from the North who have been sent to the South for military training. The arming or deputizing of bus drivers in these situations seems to have proved an inadequate solution of the difficulty.

Crimes and the police handling of such situations as appear to have racial significance have very often reflected fears on the part of the police that unruly Negroes would get out of the racial as well as legal controls. This is not a new problem but an old one greatly accentuated by war conditions. Ordinary crimes of Negroes against Negroes, normally high, have not held any important or new implications for race relations. It has been observed, however, in a growing number of southern cities—twenty-one, according to our records—that the use of Negro police has salutary effects.

The presence of northern Negro service men in the small southern towns near their camps has been fairly generally resented by the white population, and there have been numerous unsuccessful efforts to influence the Army to train these Negroes in the North. It is understandable how problems would arise with the sudden pressure of Negro soldiers on leave against the narrow recreational limits of the Negro quarter of a small southern town. The community fears of violence on the part of Negroes, in resentment of unfamiliar practices, have been justified in several cases, and the Negro violence has been all too often anticipated by a demonstration of white violence.

Other examples of recent racial clashes in the South have followed fairly familiar patterns. Of importance to underlying racial sentiment and tensions, although not directly always responsible for overt conflict, is the widespread experience of white middle-class households with their Negro domestic servants. The inconvenience of being without the familiar Negro domestics has proved to be one of the most intimate effects of the war in many households. Some of these domestics have gone temporarily to better paying war jobs, some have been able, as a result of family allowances from soldiers, to stay at home and care for their own households, and some have just quit work. Although this is a contingency to be expected in war time, it has become one of the most serious barriers to interracial tolerance and good will. This basically economic movement has been invested with the deepest private and political fears and disaffections of the southern white middle-class, and has been the occasion of a vast array of unwholesome rumors.

The problem of race is definitely and acutely in the focus of attention throughout the South, and in such a way as to give emphasis to the greatest range of disaffections, fears, resentments, and gloomy future prospects. It is reflected in the articulateness of the racial fundamentalists in Congress whose reaction to the "New Deal" government, to the President and his wife are associated emotionally with their concern for preserving the racial *status quo*. It is further reflected in the gratuitous but emphatic resolutions of the South Carolina Legislature regarding the manifest destiny of the white race. . . .

While the Negro in the South has made many types of adjustment to the southern cultural pattern, there seems to be general agreement, and a great deal of objective evidence that his attitude is increasingly becoming one of protest. A recent poll by the Denver Opinion Research Center, as well as the Negro press itself, bears this out. This is a natural result of his increasing contacts with the outside world, especially through the schools, but also through modern means of communication, notably the press and the radio. Much has been made of the fact that the southern cultural pattern is actually a caste system, and with respect to the mental attitude of southern whites, and the historical adjustment of the majority of Negroes it has been substantially a caste. A true caste system, however, is based on the acceptance of each individual of his place in the system, which is rigid and cannot be changed. This caste theory is ruled out in the American South by the basic democratic philosophy of the American system of government, and the American creed, to which the section also adheres in principle. This philosophy has power enough in the South to make it impossible to exclude the Negro altogether from opportunities for education and self-advancement. As long as this is so, the perpetuation of a caste system becomes impossible, and the gradual extension of the feeling of protest against discrimination and segregation becomes inevitable.

This protest, of course, is expressed in a variety of ways, depending upon the educational background, economic position, and character of the individual. Negro leaders in the South have sometimes accepted segregation while calling for equality of opportunity and an end to discrimination. There is some evidence, however, that this point of view is fundamentally a matter of expediency rather than conviction. . . .

There can be little doubt that the development of this Negro protest reaction has been stimulated by the war and situations arising out of the war, but there seems little question that, even without the war, education, increasing means of communication, and social and economic changes would have produced the same results in the long run.

The mass of southern Negroes naturally do not express their protest in any such conscious terms, although race consciousness is increasing. Protest may be expressed in a variety of forms, ranging from withdrawal and self-segregation to inefficiency on the job, or aggressive manners. In the more isolated areas where education and social and economic change have had least effect there may be very little feeling of protest on the part of the Negro, and this gives a semblance of justification to the conviction that the old patterns were harmonious and thus more acceptable. This situation, however, is probably a function of mental and physical isolation which cannot long be maintained in a dynamic society. It should be noted that migration itself, which often occurs from just such areas as these, is a form of protest.

We have, then, in the South, on the one hand, a situation in which the great majority of southern Negroes: are becoming increasingly dissatisfied with the present pattern of race relations and want a change, and, on the other hand, the great majority of southern whites, while certainly not altogether satisfied with things as they are, seem unable to contemplate the possibility of change in any fundamental sense. Working on the side of fundamental change are the basic tenets of the American creed, together with the forces of a society which is still dynamic. . . . On the side of the *status quo* stand custom and habit—the folkways, as well as local and regional laws—the stateways; police authority, and most important, the mental attitude of the white South.

There is another factor in the southern racial situation . . . —the attitude of northern whites and northern Negroes. There can be no doubt that northern liberals, spurred by the racial implications raised by the Second World War, are taking an increasing interest in the problem of race relations, and in the South as the source of many of the racial attitudes and established patterns of adjustment. Criticism from an outside source is never palatable and is deeply resented. It is entirely possible that the South will do more to raise the standards of race relations on its own authority than under the prodding of northern liberals. However, it seems doubtful whether, as some assert, it is entirely the North that is driving the South into an intransigent attitude. Given the basic local interpretation of the South's position, it appears that northern criticism affects not so much the attitude itself as the violence of its expression.

The real doubt is that the region believes its own racial postulates as deeply as it believes in the fundamental implications of the American creed. It is, in fact, no longer intellectually respectable to hold on to the postulates that originally determined the present patterns of racial behavior.

Similarly, it is felt that the statements and activities of northern whites and northern Negroes are responsible for the protest attitude of southern Negroes. There can be little doubt that these are accelerating factors. But the interpretation already given of the increasing dissatisfaction of southern Negroes points to the conclusion that this would be an inevitable development even without outside influence. The articulate northern Negro is not a member of a distinct race; typically either he was born in the South or his parents were born there. He is a southern Negro, with enough experience to know that a different pattern is possible, and is living in an environment where he can express extreme opinions with some degree of safety. His influence is therefore not so much an outside influence as an extension of the personality of the southern Negro.

It has been suggested in this paper that the racial climate is at present bad, but that the overall trend is wholesome and promising. There are indications of forces other than disruption at work in the total situation:

(a) In spite of the tensions, threats, abuses, and limitation of the racial system, large scale racial violence has seldom occurred and gives no indication of occurring, although the frictions and antagonisms threaten to continue indefinitely. Lynchings have almost entirely disappeared, in large part through the efforts of the South itself, and particularly the southern women.

(b) The pressure of population over the long period is being relaxed by the migration of both whites and Negroes to the North and West.

(c) Constant improvements in education are changing the character of race relations by gradually removing one of the sources of personal insecurity.

(d) The increased industrialization and unionization of the region has been, in a vital if unexpected way, increasing the number and character of racial contacts between whites and Negroes in the most numerous population class. The necessities for labor and class solidarity in a common interest are bringing about, as an incident of the association, the first large scale erosion of many racial customs and traditions. . . .

There are at least 500,000 Negroes in unions in the South and many of these unions are considering for the first time the value of effective co-relations as a basis for workers' security in the region and in the Nation. Church groups over the South are giving new and increasing study to the problem, and in local situations are acting to modify the harsher angles of racial incompatibility.

White youth in the colleges and churches, where there is any desire to break the bonds of their provincialism and get into the larger intellectual currents of the Nation, seem less disposed than their elders to devote their lives and energies to fighting against currents of enlightened change. Some colleges of the region are finding a new prestige value in a socially liberal view of the region's economic and human resources.

One of the most significant developments of recent years is the organization of the Southern Regional Council composed of representative white and Negro leadership of the region, which is focusing its attention upon the broader issues of social and regional economy in which the question of race has had a place along with the lagging attitudes in agriculture, labor, and political statesmanship.

It is increasingly evident that the relation of the southern region to the rest of the world will be influenced and affected by the region's ability to handle satisfactorily its own problem of a racial minority, in a new conception of world democracy in which small peoples are promised security in their basic human rights.

What is most important in all of these considerations is the underlying, even if disturbing, conviction that is growing, and that is being documented by responsible scholars of the region, that the soundest development of the region is in the direction of its total development, and the welfare of all its people.

As for the Negro in this situation, despite a considerable handicap in education, economic stability, and cultural level, there is the conviction that, in an ultimate sense, his cause is consistent with the overall trend of the national philosophy and the economic future of the Nation.

Many white Southerners, perhaps the majority, are concerned about race relations, and anxious to do something about them if it does not involve changing the fundamental pattern. This has resulted in a great deal of sincere effort which has borne fruit in better education for the Negro, better facilities, and increased understanding. However, it should be pointed out that activities such as these may tend in the long run to increase rather than decrease tension. For, as improved opportunities raise the cultural level of the Negro, increase his awareness of himself and his relation to society, he will become less, rather than more, satisfied with the inferior position involved in enforced segregation and the discrimination which is invariably associated with segregation.

There are indications of a disposition to improve social and economic conditions in the direction of "separate but equal" facilities, within certain limits. It is felt, however, that this will involve a long period of time, even though some of these adjustments, as, for example, equalization of teachers' salaries are being accomplished within a shorter period than was anticipated. But as differentials are removed there is left less zest for segregation in all aspects of civic life. Further, as the educational and economic status of Negroes improves there is, paradoxically, more apparent racial solidarity among them, which tends to encourage self-segregation.

What conclusions, we might ask, can be drawn from these currents of change? Is it that opportunities for Negroes should be further restricted so that they will not develop self-respect and awareness of their own rights as American citizens? Thinking Southerners do not advocate this, and it is doubtful whether such a policy, even if systematically attempted, could be successfully put into effect. General ameliorative programs designed to develop the economy and social organization of the South as a whole are certainly desirable, and would mitigate many sources of friction. But these again would have the effect of raising the status of the Negro along with that of the southern populations as a whole, and of placing him in conflict with the traditional conceptions of caste. It would seem, therefore, that the most fruitful avenue of inquiry, as far as the future of race relations is concerned, is to seek some acceptable methods of revising the racial attitudes and beliefs of the white South, and overcoming the educational and cultural lag in both the Negro groups and certain elements of the white population.

We shall probably have in the South for some time yet what Dr. Robert E. Park described as a process which involves the "accommodation of a moving equilibrium of diverse groups." The objective will be that of attaining the most satisfactory and useful ends that are consistent with the interests of the groups in conflict, and with the total welfare of the region and the Nation.

# 20

# Sociological Theory and Race Relations

## E. FRANKLIN FRAZIER

The first sociological treatises to be published in the United States were concerned with race relations. In 1854 there appeared Henry Hughes' *Treatise on Sociology, Theoretical and Practical* which undertook to demonstrate that the slave system was "morally and civilly good" and that "its great and well-known essentials" should "be unchanged and perpetual."[1] During the same year there appeared George Fitzhugh's *Sociology for the South: or the Failure of Free Society,* which possessed more significance because of the political philosophy upon which it was based.[2] As indicated in the title, this book was not only a justification of Negro slavery, but was opposed to the democratic theory of social organization. . . . Only in a society built upon slavery and Christianity as the South was built, could morality and discipline be maintained. . . .

Although their sociological theories cannot be ignored in the history of sociological theories of race relations in the United States, they have scarcely any relation to the later development of sociological thought in this field. Therefore, we shall turn to the so-called fathers of sociology—Ward, Sumner, Giddings, Cooley, Small and Ross—who established sociology as an academic discipline.

Although Lester Ward did not make any specific contribution to the theory of race relations in the United States, his sociological theories contain implications concerning the racial problem. Ward accepted the position of Gumplowicz and Ratzenhofer that the state and other phases of social organization such as

[1] Henry Hughes, *Treatise on Sociology, Theoretical and Practical* (Philadelphia, 1854).

[2] George Fitzhugh, *Sociology for the South: or the Failure of the Society.* (Richmond, 1854).

Abridged from *American Sociological Review 12* (1947): 265–271. Used by permission.

caste and class had grown out of group conflict, especially the struggle of races.[3] But in accepting the theory of race struggle Ward did not accept the theory of fundamental racial differences. He rejected the theories of Galton concerning superior races and superior classes. In fact, he took the position that the dominant position of the superior races in the world was due to "the longest uninterrupted inheritance and transmission of human achievement."[4] Through what he termed "sociocracy" or the scientific control of the social forces by the collective mind, equal opportunities for all races and classes would remove the differences in achievement in civilization. Finally, he looked forward to the "period in which the races of men shall have all become assimilated, and when there shall be but one race—the human race."[5]

Sumner's sociological theories have had an influence upon the study of race relations that is still reflected in studies of race relations at the present time. I refer especially to his concept of the mores. First, it should be pointed out that Sumner took the position that "modern scholars have made the mistake of attributing to race much which belongs to the ethos" of a people.[6] Therefore, the most important factor that separated the various races were their mores. In the South, before the Civil War the two races had learned to live together and mores had developed regulating their relations. The Civil War had destroyed the legal basis of race relations and the resulting conflict and confusion had prevented the emergence of new mores. However, new mores were developing along lines different from those advocated by reformers and legislators who could exercise no influence on the character of the developing racial patterns. Myrdal in his *An American Dilemma* has pointed out the fatalism contained in this conception of the problem of race relations and in fact the inapplicability of the concept of mores to a modern urban industrial society.[7]

Giddings did not offer any broad and systematic theory of race relations although he thought his concept of the "consciousness of kind" explained racial exclusiveness. In regard to the racial mixture, he accepted current notions concerning the instability of mixed races.[8] He was of the opinion, however, that the mental plasticity of mixed races was an important contribution to the development of nations. The social disabilities suffered by the Negro and Indian were an indication of the extent to which the social constitution had not become differentiated from the social composition of the nation.

Cooley's position in regard to the native endowment of different races is set forth in a criticism of Galton's theories in an essay which appeared in *The Annals* in 1897. In that essay, he pointed out that even Galton admitted that Negroes

[3] Lester F. Ward, *Pure Sociology* (New York, 1921), pp. 203–20.

[4] *Ibid.,* p. 238.

[5] *Ibid.,* p. 220.

[6] William G. Sumner, *Folkways* (New York, 1906), p. 74.

[7] Gunnar Myrdal, *An American Dilemma* (New York, 1944), Vol. 2, pp. 1031–32.

[8] Franklin H. Giddings, *The Principles of Sociology* (New York, 1908), pp. 324–35.

and whites could not be compared because they do not mingle and compete in the same social order under the same conditions.[9] However, Cooley's sociological theory regarding race relations was set forth in his *Social Organization*. He stated: "Two races of different temperament and capacity, distinct to the eye and living side by side in the same community, tended strongly to become castes, no matter how equal the social system may otherwise be."[10] In a chapter devoted to caste, Cooley presented a clear analysis of the caste character of race relations in the South. In his *Social Process* which was published nine years later in 1919, he continued his analysis of Negro-white relations in a chapter on "Class and Race." In this chapter he pointed out the lack of positive knowledge of racial differences but felt it reasonable to assume that during the process of biological differentiation of races, mental differences had developed.[11] His conclusion was that race should not be dealt with as a separate factor. He recognized that caste and democracy could not be reconciled and hoped for some form of cooperation and good-will between the races. He concluded, however, that Orientals should be excluded from the United States and whites from Oriental countries in order not to create racial problems.

The remaining two "fathers" of American Sociology, Small and Ross, did not make any contributions to sociological theory in regard to race relations. Ross was of the opinion that there was a "Celtic temperament" and that there was no doubt that races differed in regard to intellectual ability.[12] Moreover, he felt that the more intelligent white race had an obligation to civilization to prevent Negroes from overwhelming it by mere numbers. He did not believe, however, that the superior race should exploit or mal-treat the inferior race.

In discussing the development of sociological theory and race relations, one cannot overlook a book by one of Giddings' students which had considerable influence on thinking in regard to the Negro. In 1910 Odum published his *Social and Mental Traits of the Negro*, which became for many students a source of information on the mental and social condition of the Negro. When one views today the opinions expressed in the book, it is clear that they reflect not only outmoded conceptions concerning primitive people but all the current popular prejudices concerning the Negro.

The point of view of Odum's book was that the Negro was primarily a social problem and would remain a social problem because he could not be assimilated. It is not strange, therefore, that in the treatment of the Negro as a social problem there is an implicit sociological theory concerning race relations. We might

---

[9] Charles H. Cooley, "Genius, Fame and Comparison of Races," *Annals of the American Academy of Political and Social Science*, IX (May, 1897), pp. 1–42, in Charles H. Cooley, *Sociological Theory and Social Research* (New York, 1930), pp. 121–59.

[10] Charles H. Cooley, *Social Organization* (New York, 1923), p. 218.

[11] Charles H. Cooley, *Social Process* (New York, 1925), pp. 274 ff.

[12] Edward A. Ross, *Principles of Sociology* (New York, 1921), pp. 59 ff. In his autobiography *Seventy Years of It* (New York, 1936), pp. 276 ff., Ross repudiated his former notions concerning racial differences.

take as typical of the first two decades of the present century two books. In his *Sociology and Modern Problems,* first published in 1910, Ellwood devoted a chapter to the Negro problem. In this chapter it is assumed that the Negro has a "racial" temperament and that his "shiftlessness and sensuality" are partly due to heredity and that he is inferior in his adaptiveness to a complex civilization. The infiltration of white blood is responsible for ambition and superiority on the one hand and vice and immorality on the other. It is not strange that since "industrial education" was one of the shiboleths at the time, industrial training is regarded as one of the means of solving the problem. . . .

The second book on social problems, first published in 1920, by Dow, not only regards the Negro as an unassimilable element in the population but proposes his gradual segregation in a single area or state.[13] Dow accepts as true many of the stereotypes concerning the racial traits of the Negro but states that he believes selection and environment are stronger. While Ellwood thinks that more white teachers should be employed to help the inferior Negro race, Dow thinks that white teachers should not be employed because of the possible tendency toward social equality. White teachers from the North did more harm than good, and the Fifteenth Amendment to the Constitution was the worst political blunder in the history of the American people. Northern people do not understand Negro nature. Mulattoes are addicted to crime because, as Dow states, they have the degenerate blood of good white families. Industrial education is a partial solution and caste is the solution for the present though ultimate segregation is necessary.

In considering these books, one should not overlook an article by Weatherly which appeared in the *Journal* in 1910 on "Race and Marriage." The author took the position that there was a natural aversion to intermarriage which was designed to preserve race purity as a necessary condition for social development. Another article along similar lines, entitled "The Philosophy of the Color Line" by Mecklin appeared in the *Journal* in 1913.[14] This writer found justification for "white supremacy" in the necessity to preserve purity.

The sociological theory in regard to race relations which was current during the first two decades of the present century was doubtless not unrelated to public opinion and the dominant racial attitudes of the American people. The racial conflict in the South had subsided and the North had accepted the thesis that the South should solve the racial problem. The southern solution had been the disfranchisement of the Negro and the establishment of a quasi-caste system in which the Negro was segregated and received only a pittance of public funds for education and social services. The famous formula of Booker T. Washington, invovling the social separation of the races and industrial education, had become the accepted guide to future race relations. The sociological theories which were

---

[13] Grove S. Dow, *Society and Its Problems* (New York, 1920), pp. 157 ff.

[14] Ulysses G. Weatherly, "Race and Marriage," *American Journal of Sociology,* Vol. 15 (1910), pp. 433-53. John M. Mecklin, "The Philosophy of the Color-Line," *American Journal of Sociology,* Vo. 19 (1913), pp. 343-57.

implicit in the writings on the Negro problem were merely rationalizations of the existing racial situation.

During this period there began to emerge a sociological theory of race relations that was formulated independent of existing public opinion and current attitudes. As early as 1904, W. I. Thomas presented in an article entitled "The Psychology of Race Prejudice," in the *Journal,* a systematic theory of race relations.[15] Thomas undertook first to determine the biological basis for the phenomenon of race prejudice. He thought that he discovered this in certain reflex and instinctive reactions of the lower animals to strange elements in their environment. But in the case of human beings, he held that the development of sympathetic relations was the important factor. Sympathetic relations were most highly developed within the family group and only gradually included larger social groupings. Although race prejudice had an organic basis and could not be reasoned with, it could be dissipated through human association. Thus Thomas assumed that race prejudice could be destroyed and he did not assume that people of divergent racial stocks must inevitably remain apart or could only live together in the community where a caste system existed. . . .

Thus as early as 1904 Thomas had shown the caste character of race relations in the South and had shown how race relations there differed from race relations in the North. Moreover, Thomas in another article had undertaken to show how social and mental isolation had been responsible for the failure of the Negro to make outstanding achievements in civilization.[16]

The sociological theories of Park in regard to race relations were developed originally in close association with Thomas. Park, who was observing race relations in the South, was in constant communication with Thomas. Park's theories which represent the most comprehensive and systematic sociological theories of race relations developed by American sociologists and have had the greatest influence on American sociology began to appear at a time when the Negro problem was assuming a new character in American life. The migration of Negroes to the metropolitan areas of the North had destroyed the accommodation that had been achieved to some extent following the racial conflict during and following Reconstruction. The publication of *Introduction to the Science of Sociology* by Park and Burgess coincided with the study of the race riot in Chicago in 1919. The new impact of the Negro problem on American life undoubtedly helped Park as much as his experience in the South in the formulation of a sociological theory.

For Park the phenomenon of race relations is to be studied within his general sociological frame of reference—competition, conflict, accommodation, and assimilation. "Nowhere do social contacts so readily provoke conflicts as in the

[15] William I. Thomas, "The Psychology of Race Prejudice," *American Journal of Sociology,* Vol. 9, pp. 593–611. [Selection 1 in this volume].

[16] W. I. Thomas, "Race Psychology: Standpoint and Questionnaire," *The American Journal of Sociology,* Vol. 17, pp. 745, ff.

relations between the races, particularly when racial differences are re-enforced; not merely by differences of culture, but of color. . . ."[17]

Although Park held that there was an instinctive element in race prejudice, he nevertheless stated that the conflict of culture was a more positive factor in race prejudice. The central fact in the conflict of culture was, he wrote, "the unwillingness of one race to enter into personal competition with a race of a different or inferior culture." In a later article he made the factor of status the most important element in race prejudices. In making status the most important factor in race prejudice, Park took the position that race prejudice was based upon essentially the same attitudes as those at the basis of class and caste. A prejudiced reaction to members of another race is the normal tendency of the mind to react to individuals as members of categories. The categories into which people are placed generally involve status. Since the Negro is constantly rising in America, he arouses prejudices and animosities. Race prejudice is "merely an elementary expression of conservatism."[18]

Up to about 1930, Park's sociological theory in regard to race relations in the United States did not go beyond the theory of a biracial organization in which vertical social distance between the two races would become a matter of horizontal social distance. A biracial organization would preserve race distinctions but it would change its content in that there would be a change in attitudes. The races would no longer look up and down but across. The development of the biracial organization marked a fundamental change in status since the Negro was acquiring the status of a racial or cultural minority. In an article published in 1939, Park presented the case of the American Negro in the general frame of reference which he had developed for the study of race relations in the modern world.[19] In that article he showed how the migration of the Negro to northern cities had changed the character of race relations and he pointed out that caste was being undermined and that the social distance between the races at the different class levels was being undermined. Moreover, he regarded race relations in the United States as part of a world process in which culture and occupation were coming to play a more important role than inheritance and race. Thus for Park, the "racial frontiers" that were developing in various parts of the world were the seed-beds of new cultures.

In Park's development of a sociological theory in regard to race relations, there are several important features which are significant for the future of sociological theory in this field. The original emphasis of his theory was upon the social psychological aspects of race contacts. It was concerned primarily with providing an explanation of behavior in terms of attitudes. This was not only

---

[17] Robert E. Park, *Introduction to the Science of Sociology* (Chicago, 1924), p. 578.

[18] Robert E. Park, "The Basis of Race Prejudice," *The American Negro. The Annals,* Vol. 140 (1928), pp. 11–20.

[19] Robert E. Park, "The Nature of Race Relations," in Edgar T. Thompson (Ed.), *Race Relations and the Race Problem* (Durham, N.C., 1939).

peculiar to Park's theory but it was characteristic of the theories of other scholars. . . . In the social psychological approach there was a tendency to ignore or pay little attention to the structural and organizational aspects of race relations on the one hand and the dynamic aspects of the problem on the other. The so-called "caste and class" school of students of race relations who have challenged the position of the sociologist has focused attention upon this phase of the problem. However, it should be pointed out that while the "caste and class" school has focused attention upon the structural aspects of race relations, they have only documented the concept of caste. They have not provided any new insights concerning the attitudes and behavior of whites and Negroes. Since the concept of caste has been an essentially static concept, it has failed to provide an orientation for the dynamic aspects of race relations. This brings us to another phase of the sociological theories of Park in regard to race relations.

Park's sociological theory was originally a static theory of race relations. His theory not only contained the fatalism inherent in Sumner's concept of the mores. His theory was originally based upon the assumption that the races could not mix or mingle freely. This is apparent even in his concept of the biracial organization. But as Park saw the changes which were occurring in the United States and other parts of the world, he modified his theory to take into account these changes. His latest theory of race relations in the modern world took into account the dynamic elements in the situation. . . .

Current sociological research has not only discarded the older assumptions about racial characteristics but it is approaching the problem of "race relations" from a different standpoint. For the sociologist the problem of "race relations" has become a problem of inter-group relations. This change in viewpoint, it might be pointed out, is evident even in the programs of so-called "intercultural education" which are gradually becoming programs of "inter-group" relations. Sociological theory has had some influence on this new orientation.

In summary, the development of sociological theory in regard to race relations may be stated as follows:

1. The sociological theories of the founders of American sociology as an academic discipline were only implicitly related to the concrete problems of race relations. Their theories concerning race relations were derived from European scholars who were concerned with the universal phenomenon of race contact. Cooley was an exception in that he offered an analysis of race relations in the South based upon his theories of the origin and nature of caste and its relation to class.

2. Sociological theories relating to the concrete problems of race relations in the United States were implicit in the sociological analysis of the Negro problem as a social problem. The analysis of the Negro problem was based upon several fairly clear assumptions: that the Negro is an inferior race because of either biological or social heredity or both; that the Negro because of his physical character cannot be assimilated; and that physical amalgamation is bad and undesirable.

3. The sociological theories implicit in the studies of the Negro problem were developed during the period when the nation held that the attempt to make the Negro a citizen was a mistake and a new accommodation of the races was being achieved in the South under a system of segregation. Therefore, these theories were rationalizations of American public opinion and the dominant attitudes of the American people.

4. Sociological theory in regard to race relations began to assume a more systematic formulation following the first World War. Park was the chief figure in the formulation of this sociological theory which provided the orientation for empirical studies of race relations. These studies were based upon the theory that race was a sociological concept and utilized such social psychological tools as attitudes and social distance and Sumner's concept of the mores. As the relation of the Negro to American life changed and the problems of race relations throughout the world became more insistent Park developed a more dynamic theory of race relations.

5. A so-called new school of thought, utilizing the concept of caste and class, has undertaken new studies of race relations. Whereas this new school has focused attention upon the neglected phase of race relations—the structural aspects —it has documented the concept of caste rather than provided new insights.

6. What is needed is the further development of a dynamic sociological theory of race relations, which will discard all the rationalizations of race prejudice and provide orientation for the study of the constantly changing patterns of race relations in American life.

# 21

# Review of Myrdal's
# An American Dilemma

*E. FRANKLIN FRAZIER*

This study was made possible by the Carnegie Corporation because of "the need of the foundation for fuller light in the formulation and development of its own program" in regard to the Negro. In seeking a director of the study, the foundation felt that, since the "whole question had been for nearly a hundred years so charged with emotion," neither a white nor a colored American scholar would qualify for the position. Moreover, in order not to "lessen the confidence of Negroes" in the complete impartiality of the findings, the foundation did not deem it advisable to select a scholar from a country with a "background or traditions of imperialism." The search for a qualified person resulted in the selection of Dr. Gunnar Myrdal, a professor at the University of Stockholm, who had achieved an international reputation as a social economist.

When the foundation projected the study in 1937, it was probably not foreseen at the time that the work would be published during one of the most serious crises in race relations in the United States. Yet it should be recorded to the credit of Dr. F. P. Keppel and the foundation that they carried through the publication during a critical period of race relations, though the study was written from a point of view and contained conclusions so contrary to traditional ideas concerning race relations. It might be stated, as a matter of fact, that the value and significance of this study are not due so much to its unquestionably intrinsic merits as to its appearance during the present critical stage in race relations. One of the evidences of its timeliness and its widespread reception has been the fact that this bulky and expensive work has quickly gone through four printings.

Abridged from *American Journal of Sociology* 50 (1945): 555–557. Used by permission of The University of Chicago Press. © 1945 by The University of Chicago. All rights reserved.

Following an introduction giving the author's conception or definition of the Negro problem, there are eleven parts. The first part has three chapters dealing with American ideals, the constant concern of whites and Negroes with the problem, and the various facets of the problem. The three chapters in the second part are concerned with the beliefs of Americans about race and the racial background and characteristics of Negroes. In the third part there are two chapters on the Negro population and migration. A fifth of the text is contained in the fourth part, which deals with "Economics." In this section the author goes into every phase of the economic life of the Negro from the days of slavery to the present war boom. The fifth part has four chapters on the Negro in the political life of the nation. The four chapters on "Justice" in the sixth part contain a thorough analysis of the relation of the Negro to the law, the courts and the police, and the problem of violence. In the seventh part the author presents the frankest and most scientific discussion of "social equality" that can be found in the literature on the Negro problem. Social stratification among Negroes in relation to caste and class is the subject of the two chapters in the eighth part. The ninth part contains nine chapters on Negro leadership and protest, Negro personality, and Negro churches, schools, and press. The Negro community is treated in only two chapters comprising the tenth part. In a final chapter—Part XI—the author concludes his study.

In addition to the forty-five chapters of 1,024 pages, there are ten appendixes of over a hundred pages; a bibliography of 37 pages; and over 250 pages of footnotes. The appendixes are extremely important because they contain the author's methodological assumptions not only in regard to the Negro problem but concerning social science in general. . . .

After presenting an analysis of "valuations" or attitudes and their relation to rationalizations, which would be accepted by most sociologists, he offers a critique of the concept "mores." The main point of this criticism is that the concept fails to take into account the dynamic nature of our society. In the second appendix in which he deals with facts and valuations in social science, the author deals with the hidden biases which are implicit in most studies of the Negro problem. According to the author, biases cannot be avoided by "keeping to the facts" or by refusing to arrange results for practical and political utilization. "There is no other device for excluding biases in social sciences," writes the author, "than to face the valuations and to introduce them as explicitly stated, specific, and sufficiently concretized value premises."

This position in regard to value judgments in social science will certainly be opposed by most American sociologists. But when one considers this position in relation to the author's statement that "the value premises should be selected by the criterion of relevance and significance to the culture under study," it would be difficult to challenge the author's position. For example, it is impossible to study discriminations against the Negro unless we assume that the Negro is a human being and an American citizen. Of course, it is conceivable that the sociologist might be concerned *solely* with the general phenomena arising from the association of human beings. If one regards, however, the phenomena in a specific social situation, as, for example, the relation of races in the United States, as inevitable, then there is a fatalistic "valuation," as the author states. This fatalistic "valuation" is traced to the laissez faire bias, which is apparent in Sumner's conception of the mores. Moreover, this fatalistic bias is opposed to all social planning and is not simply characteristic of thought on the Negro problem but may be found in social science generally in the Western world.

Consistent with his position in regard to the role of "valuations" in social science, the author makes clear his viewpoint in this study. He distinguishes between theoretical research which is concerned with causal relations and practical research which is concerned with purposeful relations. In the study of the Negro problem theoretical research is determined by practical purposes. Therefore, the aim of the study is to show precisely "what should be the practical and political opinions and plans for action from the point of view of the various valuations if the holders also had the more correct and comprehensive factual knowledge which science provides." Because of the fact that the Negro problem "cuts so sharply through the body politic," the book is organized around a set of valuations which the author calls the "American Creed," a living reality, by which accomplishments in democracy are judged.

It is in terms of the above "set of valuations" that the Negro problem is defined. The Negro problem is essentially a moral problem, not because of a conflict between valuations held by different persons and groups, but because it is a moral struggle within people themselves. One would certainly agree with the author in the sense that all social problems are moral problems. But it might be questioned whether the problem is on the conscience of white people to the extent implied in his statement of the problem. Although the author is right, in the opinion of the reviewer, when he criticizes the generally held assumption that Negroes are "accommodated" to their inferior status, yet there is sufficient evidence to show that under certain conditions a state of accommodation may be achieved between the races in which conflicts are reduced to a minimum. Under such conditions it is not likely that the Negro problem is on the conscience of the white man. Then, too, for many whites the Negro lives in an entirely different social world or is not a part of the same moral order. It is when the Negro emerges as a human being and a part of the moral order that discrimination against him is on the conscience of the white man.

The unique character and contribution of this study become evident when one considers the manner in which it deals with certain crucial phases of the Negro problem. Without the usual apologies and rationalizations, the author makes clear the fact that in the South the supremacy and impersonality of the law do not exist so far as the Negro is concerned. Negroes are constantly subject to the brutality of white policemen, usually ignorant and poorly paid, who not only maintain caste rules but also protect private whites in their aggressions against Negroes. Consequently, Negroes do not have the feeling of personal security they have in the North. Likewise, the "vicious circle" of discrimination and poverty is analyzed in connection with the rationalizations which the South uses to justify its treatment of Negroes as former slaves.

It is, however, in the treatment of the question of social equality that the author departs from the traditional American treatment of the Negro problem. This is treated under Part VII, entitled "Social Inequality." The author shows clearly that segregation and discrimination are forced upon the Negro and that the policy has its roots in slavery. Moreover, he shows that the theory of "no social equality" is based upon a fear of amalgamation and a magical concept of "blood." This attitude is even shared by the so-called southern liberals. The theory of "no social equality" is designed primarily to keep the Negro on a lower social status, since the "social" cannot be isolated from other spheres of life. The author points out . . . that no responsible Negro leader, no matter what his public professions, ever gave up the demand for full equality.

Something should be said concerning the objectivity of the author. When it was announced that because of his objectivity a foreign scholar was being sought to study the Negro problem, the reviewer was skeptical. But this skepticism was dissipated when he came to know the author and study his methods of research. The author revealed a remarkable facility for getting the feel of the racial situation in the United States. His objectivity was apparent from the beginning in his relations with Negroes. They were simply people to him, and their American characteristics impressed him more than their color or the texture of their hair. Since he saw Negroes primarily as people, then such personal characteristics as their intelligence, temperament, or other personal characteristics could be readily perceived by him. He could size up a Negro for what he was worth because he did not view him either with the pathetic attitude of most friendly white Americans or through the myths that have grown about Negroes in American life. This was the type of objectivity that the Carnegie Foundation evidently had in mind when they sought someone to "approach his task with a fresh mind." But, in bringing to the study a fresh mind, the author did not ignore the work of other scholars. In fact, the success of the project was due to the fact that he could utilize the work of other scholars and secure their co-operation in the present study.

Whether one agrees or disagrees with Dr. Myrdal's theoretical position with reference to social science, one must acknowledge the important contribution which he has made to the scientific study of the Negro problem in the United States. His study is free from the traditional provincialism of most students who have dealt with the problem which he views as a part of American culture and as a part of a world problem. According to the author, the Negro problem is "not only America's greatest failure" but also "America's insurpassably great opportunity for the future," because "America can demonstrate that justice, equality and cooperation are possible between white and colored people." In America, the author believes, there is a desire to conquer color caste. To this task social science can contribute because it is the supreme task of social science "to find the practical formulas" for the "never-ending reconstruction of society."

# 22

# Familial Adjustments of Japanese-Americans to Relocation: First Phase

*LEONARD BLOOM*

There may never have been a problem which captured the attention of American sociologists more promptly, more completely, and more appropriately than the evacuation of the Japanese from the West Coast. . . .

Before proceeding a word must be said on the character of my sources of information. For the most part I have been dependent upon *nisei* trained in Western universities for direct information and for field assistance. My sampling is badly slanted wherever acculturational variables are paramount. The *nisei* who attended our universities were predominantly urban with a good deal of the cultural apparatus which that implies. They were more secure economically than the average Japanese-American. They were committed most thoroughly to the American way of life. . . .

The policy of the Wartime Civil Control Administration of evacuating household groups as units reinforced the group stabilizing tendency, and family members who were not co-residents often returned home. There arose in a few minds the erroneous notion that evacuation by families was mandatory and so groups were re-formed that may have lost their functional character. If this notion seems improbable the reader must recall the flood of rumor in which the

Abridged from *American Sociological Review* 8 (1943): 551–560. Used by permission.

Japanese-Americans struggled at the time of evacuation, and indeed still do. The reëstablishment of family groups was by no means universal, however. Some were restored after evacuation, and some still wait upon administrative action. . . .

With their facility in English the elder children had a large role in making decisions. However, when it became apparent that no distinction was to be made between the *nisei* and their Japanese-born parents and when loyalty tensions arose, the American citizen lost status. The culture conflicts did not resolve. Indeed the marginality of the *nisei* was thrown into high relief, but temporarily the social manifestations of strife were submerged by the necessity for collective action.

Another factor making for group stability was the practice of removing neighborhoods or organized groups together and housing them in the same areas in the assembly centers. Many of these groups had no previous existence but were organized to meet the emergency. Others were loosely integrated community groups which took on the special function and accepted outsiders. . . .

The cumulative and confusing pressures may be appreciated from the following chronology:

January 29, 1942. First Attorney-General's order establishing prohibited restricted zones on West Coast and regulating movement of enemy aliens. Subsequent orders on January 31, February 2, 4, 5, and 7.

February 13. Letter to the President from Pacific Coast Congressional Delegation recommending evacuation from strategic areas of all persons of Japanese ancestry.

February 19. Executive order authorizing designation of military areas from which any person might be excluded. Beginning of voluntary evacuation.

February 21. Tolan Committee begins Pacific Coast hearings on enemy aliens and Japanese-Americans.

March 2. Proclamation by General DeWitt designating Military Areas No. 1 (western half of the coastal states and southern Arizona) and No. 2 (remainder of four states).

March 14. Wartime Civil Control Administration established under Western Defense Command to supervise evacuation.

March 16. Work started on assembly center at Manzanar.

March 18. War Relocation Authority created to relocate evacuated persons.

March 19. Fourteen Western governors oppose settlement of Japanese evacuees in their states.

March 23. One thousand voluntary evacuees from Los Angeles leave to prepare Manzanar center. All persons of Japanese ancestry ordered to evacuate Bainbridge Island near Seattle by March 30.

March 27. Curfew for all persons of Japanese ancestry in Military Area No. 1, requiring them to be at home between 8:00 P.M. and 6:00 A.M., forbidding certain possessions, and restricting travel without permit to five miles from home.

March 29. Further voluntary evacuation from Military Area No. 1 prohibited.

March 30. Three thousand persons of Japanese ancestry ordered to evacuate Terminal Island in Los Angeles Harbor to Santa Anita Assembly Center by April 5.

June 2. Persons of Japanese ancestry forbidden to leave California part of Military Area No. 2 (eastern half of state) anticipatory to evacuation of this area.

June 3. Evacuation of 100,000 persons of Japanese ancestry from Military Area No. 1 completed.

Here are the questions that were being asked: Would there be an evacuation? Would an exception be made of citizens? When would the evacuation come? What areas would be included? How much time would be allowed between notice and evacuation? What property might be taken? What property should be disposed of and how? Should an attempt be made to move inland before the curfew was established? (8,000 did move inland, of which more than half remained outside the centers.) For most of the population the questions were answered in a period in of less than two weeks between the notice of the evacuation date for their area and their actual removal.

Another factor that increased the stress of family adjustment was the detention of more than 4,700 persons. Most of these were *issei* males, the most responsible segment of the community and those most practiced in making overt societal adjustments. Furthermore they comprised a disproportionately large number of family heads. The significance of the figure 4,700 becomes clear upon noting that there were over 23,000 family heads among the Japanese-Americans in the four Western states (Arizona, California, Oregon, and Washington). The capacity to adjust of any family would be damaged by the loss of its responsible head; the effect on the Japanese-American family with its heritage of patriarchal responsibility was often shattering. The statistical support for this statement lies in the fact that 45.6 percent of all *issei* in the four Western states were listed as family heads by the 1940 census, whereas 6.0 percent of *nisei* were so listed.

It is important to note that the condition was not merely a temporary one. By January 1943 about 1,400 detained persons had been placed in relocation centers with their families, 2,000 had been sent to internment camps where aliens defined as disloyal are incarcerated, and the remainder were still in detention camps awaiting hearing.

Although the residence plan in the relocation centers presumed the preservation of the family unit, the limitations of space required compromises with the plan. Detached individuals were housed with small family groups. The average size living quarters for a family of five is a single room 20 by 25 feet; for smaller families less space is allowed. Auditory privacy for individual or family is absent even when housed in separate units, for the necessarily flimsy construction keeps out no noises. The construction provided is known in military parlance as "theatre of operations" type of tar-paper covered barracks and is designed to last for five years. The *nisei* who had not the background of adjustments to the rather alfresco type of native Japanese residence are the most disturbed by living conditions.

The whole problem of the inability of the primary group to isolate itself was and is one of the commonest complaints. To the concern of their elders, children and adolescents became sexually sophisticated and voyeuristically oriented. Lovers became inhibited or defiant or both. The problem is a cultural as well as a personal one when one recalls Japanese conservatism about public demonstrations of affection. . . .

The most important influence on family integration was the loss of function and the absence of need for any kind of collective action. After the intensive collaboration of planning for removal, which knit the group so tightly together for a brief span, there suddenly were no decisions to be made, little work to do, and no household routine. The house-organizing plans were translated into barrack existence with community dining halls, laundries, and toilet facilities. No longer were there any common purposes or activities to provide functional ties and group meanings. The father's authority as head of the household lost much of its functional character, the age-hierarchy was all but destroyed, and group purposes disappeared. Nothing further from the Japanese plan of family organization could have been contrived.

Each member became a free agent, and small children detached themselves from parental supervision, returning to the home barracks perhaps only to sleep. Especially in the assembly centers the age group promptly became the organizing principle, and the clique became a predominant form of organization. Community activities such as religious observances, supervised recreation, education and work were arranged on age lines, thereby reinforcing the tendency. In the relocation centers the system of organized education was the most effective time-filling device.

Almost all observers report that the elders are concerned about the decay in manners of the children. Perhaps the general tensions plus the frictions of barracks existence were responsible for the population becoming verbally less inhibited and more aggressive.

There has been a tendency a priori to interpret the breakup of the Japanese colonies in our cities as assimilative in character. In the very long run this may be true, but the immediate results have been quite the opposite. *Nisei* who never would have acquired any facility in Japanese are learning it. After the first adjustments of relocation the cultural reënforcement that the *issei* received from each other made for reacculturation both of themselves and their children.

Because there are no horizons to the life space, and because there can be none, group-forming decisions are postponed. Having children, for an example, is regarded as extremely undesirable. There is a great deal of doubt as to the wisdom of contracting new marriages. . . .

In retrospect it is difficult to conceive how the population could have met the crisis as well as it did without its strongly integrating primary group forms. Initially at least the emergency yielded a further cohesion. At the end of 1942 two general sets of forces were observable. First a tendency of the *nisei* to withdraw from the familial group with its conservative Japanese cultural attributes, as evidenced by age group formations. The opportunity to move from the centers which has been afforded some persons, mostly *nisei*, reënforces and gives reality to the withdrawal. Second there are those who have tended increasingly to identify themselves with their parents and the parental culture (by no means necessarily with Japan). Partly this may be traced to the frustrations of camp life and the war effort. Partly it is due to their intensive association in small living quarters and their loss of status as a culturally emergent group. If policies and politics permit the tendency to withdraw promises to be ascendant.

# 23

# Ethnic Tolerance: A Function of Social and Personal Control

*BRUNO BETTELHEIM* and *MORRIS JANOWITZ*

In this study of ethnic intolerance we attempt to throw light on the principles of group hostility in general and on ethnic hostility as a special subtype.

The four main hypotheses that the research sought to test were based on sociological theory and dynamic psychology. They were: (1) hostility toward out-groups is a function of the hostile individual's feeling that he has suffered deprivations in the past; (2) such hostility toward out-groups is a function of the hostile individual's anxiety in anticipation of future tasks; (3) the individual blames out-groups for his failure at mastery and projects undesirable characteristics denied in himself upon members of the out-group because of inadequate personal and social controls which favor irrational discharge and evasion rather than rational action; (4) ethnic intolerance can be viewed in terms of the individual's position within the social structure either statically or dynamically. It was assumed that ethnic intolerance was related more to the individual's dynamic movement within the structure of society than to his position at a particular moment. No claim is made that these hypotheses are universally applicable, but they seemed useful in understanding hostility in modern industrialized communities.

A major premise of the study was that persons who believe they have undergone deprivations are disposed to ethnic intolerance. It seemed plausible to

Abridged from *American Journal of Sociology 55* (1949): 137–146. Used by permission of The University of Chicago Press. © 1949 by The University of Chicago. All rights reserved.

study ex-soldiers, since they had suffered deprivations in varying degrees and might be especially responsive to the appeal of intolerance. A random sample of one hundred and fifty male war veterans, all residents of Chicago, was studied. Former officers were eliminated from the study, since their experiences were at variance with those of enlisted men and since most of them came from social and economic backgrounds which differed from those of enlisted men. Hence the sample tended more adequately to represent the economic lower and lower-middle classes. Members of those major ethnic groups toward which hostility is projected were not included. . . .

The data were obtained through intensive interviews in which free associations were always encouraged. The interviewers were psychiatrically trained social workers, experienced in public opinion surveying. The wide range of personal data sought and the special problems of building rapport before gathering data on ethnic attitudes required long interviews which took from four to seven hours and in several cases were carried on in two sessions. The veterans were offered ample opportunity to express personal views on many issues and to recount their wartime experiences before ethnic minorities were mentioned.

On the basis of an exploratory study we found it necessary to distinguish four types of veterans with respect to their ethnic attitudes. For the sake of brevity, only the four types of anti-Semite are mentioned, but a parallel classification as regards anti-Negro attitudes was also developed. . . . (1) The *intensely anti-Semitic* veteran was spontaneously outspoken in expressing a preference for restrictive action against the Jews even before the subject was raised. (2) The *outspoken anti-Semitic* man revealed no spontaneous preference for restrictive action against the Jews. Instead, outspoken hostility toward the Jews emerged only toward the end of the interview when he was directly questioned. As in the case of the intensely anti-Semitic veteran, his thinking contained a wide range of unfavorable stereotypes. (3) The *stereotyped anti-Semitic* man expressed no preference for hostile or restrictive action against the Jews even when questioned directly. Instead, he merely expressed a variety of stereotyped notions about the Jews, including some which were not necessarily unfavorable from his point of view. (4) The *tolerant* veteran revealed no elaborately stereotyped beliefs about the Jews (among the statements of even the most tolerant veterans isolated stereotypes might from time to time be found). Moreover, not even when questioned directly did he advocate restrictive action against the Jews.

The interview situation was so constructed that the responses to questions would permit a clear discrimination between these four types of ethnic intolerance. The first portion of the interview was designed to offer the men an opportunity for spontaneous expression of hostility against minorities without bringing this subject to their attention. In a second portion, especially in connection with Army experiences, ample opportunity was offered to display stereotyped thinking by asking, for example, who the "gold-brickers" or troublemakers had been. Only the last portion contained direct questions on ethnic minorities. There the stimuli "Negro" and "Jew" were introduced to determine which men were consistently tolerant. First it was asked what kinds of soldiers they made, next what the subject thought of social and economic association with them, and then what his views were on possible changes in the current patterns of inter-ethnic relations. Table 1 shows the distribution of degrees of intolerance.

**T A B L E 1.  Distribution of Intolerance**

| | Anti-Semitic | | Anti-Negro | |
|---|---|---|---|---|
| | NO. | PER CENT | NO. | PER CENT |
| Tolerant . . . . . . . . | 61 | 41 | 12 | 8 |
| Stereotyped . . . . . . . | 42 | 28 | 40 | 27 |
| Outspoken . . . . . . . . | 41 | 27 | 74 | 49 |
| Intense . . . . . . . . . | 6 | 4 | 24 | 16 |
| Total . . . . . . . . . | 150 | 100 | 150 | 100 |

We tried to determine whether the men's social and economic history could account for their ethnic intolerance. Among the characteristics studied were age, education, religion, political affiliation, income, and social status. But the data indicate that—subject to certain limitations—these factors of themselves do not seem to account for differences in the degree or nature of intolerance. . . .

[F] or example, . . . no statistically significant relation exists between income and socioeconomic status, on the one hand, and intensity of anti-Semitism, on the other. The same was true for such other categories as education, age, and religious affiliation. Which newspaper, magazine, or radio program the men favored was also unrelated to the intensity of ethnic hostility. The pattern of anti-Negro distribution was similar.

## Social Mobility

The picture changes, however, if a static concept of social status is replaced by the dynamic concept of social mobility. It was possible to gather precise data on the social mobility of one hundred and thirty veterans. They were rated as having experienced downward mobility or upward mobility if they had moved at least one grade up or down on the Alba Edward's socioeconomic scale when compared with their previous civilian employment.

Table 2 shows that ethnic hostility was most highly concentrated in the downwardly mobile group, while the pattern was *significantly* reversed for those who had risen in their social position. Those who had experienced no change presented a picture somewhat in the middle; the relationship between ethnic intolerance and social mobility (as defined in this study) was also present when educational level was held constant.

**TABLE 2. Intolerance and Mobility**

| | Downward Mobility | | No Mobility | | Upward Mobility | | Total | |
| | NO. | PER CENT | NO. | PER CENT | NO. | PER CENT | NO. | PER CENT |
|---|---|---|---|---|---|---|---|---|
| *Anti-Semitic:* | | | | | | | | |
| Tolerant . . . . . . . . . . . . . | 2 | 11 | 25 | 37 | 22 | 50 | 49 | 38 |
| Stereotyped. . . . . . . . . . . | 3 | 17 | 26 | 38 | 8 | 18 | 37 | 28 |
| Outspoken and intense. . . . . | 13 | 72 | 17 | 25 | 14 | 32 | 44 | 34 |
| *Anti-Negro:* | | | | | | | | |
| Tolerant and stereotyped . . . | 5 | 28 | 18 | 26 | 22 | 50 | 45 | 34 |
| Outspoken. . . . . . . . . . . | 5 | 28 | 40 | 59 | 17 | 39 | 62 | 48 |
| Intense . . . . . . . . . . | 8 | 44 | 10 | 15 | 5 | 11 | 23 | 18 |
| Total . . . . . . . | 18 | . . . . . . . . . | 68 | . . . . . . . . . | 44 | . . . . . . . . . | 130 | . . . . . . . . . |

The group which was static showed the highest concentration of stereotyped opinions—that is, they were "middle-of-the-roaders" with regard to anti-Semitism. Over 70 per cent of the stereotyped anti-Semites were found in this middle category. This illuminates the relation between mobility and intolerance. On the other hand, the no-mobility group was most generally in the outspokenly anti-Negro category. . . . In the case of the Jew the social norms were most likely to produce merely stereotyped thinking, while it was correspondingly "normal" to be outspoken in one's hostility toward the Negro.

## Feeling of Deprivation

Whatever their social and economic life-histories had been, all the men interviewed had one common experience—the Army. Reactions to comparable wartime deprivations thus afforded a unique opportunity to examine the hypothesis that the individual who suffers deprivation tries to restore his integration and self-control by the expression of hostility, one form of which may be ethnic hostility. But here a sharp distinction must be introduced between *actual* deprivations experienced and his *feelings* of deprivation. Whether the men reacted favorably to Army life primarily because they experienced relief from the insecurities of civilian life was also pertinent.

Army experiences which involved *objective* deprivations were found not related to differential degrees of ethnic intolerance (combat versis noncombat service, wounds, length of service, etc.). On the other hand, a clear association emerged between the display of *feelings* of deprivation and outspoken or intense anti-Semitic and anti-Negro attitudes.

On the basis of a content analysis it was found that it was possible to make reliable decisions as to whether the veterans (1) accepted it in a matter-of-fact way, (2) were embittered about Army life, or (3) were attached to it or gratified by it. The overwhelming majority of those who were tolerant, regardless of the specific content of their wartime experiences, had an attitude of acceptance toward Army life, while the intolerant veteran presented a completely reversed picture. . . . The latter were overwhelmingly embittered by Army life. In addition, those who declared themselves particularly attached to Army life displayed a high concentration of intolerance.

The judging of one's war experiences as depriving or not is a function of the individual's total personality and of the adequacy of his adjustive mechanisms. The interview records of those who seemed gratified by Army life revealed that they were also the men who described themselves as economically and socially deprived before induction; they seem to have been poorly adjusted to civilian society and to have found gratification and release in the particular adventure and comradeship of Army life.

## Controls for Tolerance

There seems little doubt that frustrating social experiences and the inability to integrate them account to a large degree for those aggressions which are vented in ethnic hostility. While our investigation could not ascertain which particular experiences accounted for the men's frustration, it permitted us to ascertain their readiness to submit in general to the existing controls by society. If, by and large, they accepted social institutions, it seems reasonable to assume that such acceptance implied a willingness to control their own aggressive tendencies for the sake of society. Or, oversimplifying complex emotional tendencies, one might say that those men who felt that society fulfilled its task in protecting them against unavoidable frustrations were also those who, in return, were willing to come to terms with society by controlling their aggressive tendencies as society demands. Hence, the hypothesis correlating the men's acceptance or rejection of society with their ethnic attitudes had to be tested. . . .

Control, technically speaking, is the ability to store tension internally or to discharge it in socially constructive action rather than in unwarranted hostile action. The predominant mechanisms of control which a person uses for dealing with inner tensions are among the most important elements characterizing his personality. Each of these mechanisms of control is more or less adequate for containing a particular type of aggression generated in the individual by anxiety. These controls or restraints remain adequate only if the level of tension does not become overpowering, thereby creating unmasterable anxiety. It will not suffice to investigate the association between control and tolerance in general; it is necessary to discriminate between tolerance as it relates to three types of control over hostile tendencies: (1) external or social control, (2) superego or conscience control, and (3) rational self-control or ego control.

Religion may serve as the prototype of an institution, the acceptance of, or submission to, which was found to be related to tolerance. . . .

The analysis of religious attitudes indicated that veterans who had stable religious convictions tended to be the more tolerant. When the political party system was viewed as another norm-setting institution, a similar relationship of at least partial acceptance or consensus with this basic institution was found to be associated with tolerance. Whether the veteran was Democratic or Republican was in no way indicative of his attitude toward minorities. But the veteran who rejected or condemned both parties ("they are both crooks") tended to be the most hostile toward minorities.

Thus not only greater stability in societal status but the very existence of stable religious and political affiliations as well proved to be correlated with tolerance. These phenomena are indicative of the tolerant individual's relatively greater control over his instinctual tendencies, controls which are strong enough to prevent immediate discharge of tension in asocial action. Such delay in the discharge of tension permits its canalization into socially more acceptable outlets.

To explore more fully this relationship between tolerance and control, the responses to other symbols of societal authority which signify *external* control of the individual were also investigated. Two groups of institutions were analyzed separately. The first group, that of Army control through discipline and officer's authority, is discussed below. The second group was composed of significant representatives of civilian authority to which the men were relatively subject at the time of the interview.

Four institutions were singled out as being most relevant. They were: (1) the administration of veterans' affairs; (2) the political party system; (3) the federal government; and (4) the economic system, as defined by the subjects themselves.

The veterans' views of each of these institutions were quite complex and in some respects ambivalent. Nevertheless, it was possible to analyze attitudes toward them on a continuum of acceptance, rejection, or intermediate. . . .

Controls, it may be said, are not internalized by merely accepting society. On the contrary, general attitudes of accepting existing society and its institutions are the result of previous internalization of societal values as personally transmitted by parents, teachers, and peers. Hence the acceptance of individuals who are representatives of societal values should have been more closely related to internal control than the acceptance of discipline in general, which is more characteristic of external control. Attitudes toward officers seemed suitable guages for the individual's attitudes toward control. . . .

The tolerant veteran appeared able to maintain better relations with his officers; he was more willing to accept the authority and discipline of the Army as represented by them. In general, his attitude was reasonable. When queried as to how the fellows in their outfits got along with the officers, tolerant veterans were significantly more prone to claim they got along well than were the intolerant men.

In the case of the Negro (Table 3), societal controls exercise a restraining influence only on what would be classified as violent, as "intense," intolerance. Violence is generally disapproved of by the controlling institutions, while they approve, if not enforce, stereotyped and outspoken attitudes. The men who were strongly influenced by external controls were, in the majority, stereotyped and outspoken but not intense in their intolerance toward Negroes, as the present data show.

The division between those who rejected and those who accepted external control came between outspoken and intense attitudes toward Negroes. To score "high" on the index of rejection for the four controlling institutions meant that an individual was likely to fall in the intensely anti-Negro category. Thus acceptance of external controls not only was inadequate in conditioning men to be tolerant of the Negroes but was not even enough to prevent them from holding outspoken views in that regard. It served only to restrain demands for violence.

**TABLE 3. Attitudes Toward the Negro and Toward Controlling Institutions**

| | Tolerant | | Stereotyped | | Outspoken | | Intense | | Total | |
|---|---|---|---|---|---|---|---|---|---|---|
| | NO. | PER CENT | NO. | PER CENT | NO. | PER CENT | NO. | PER CENT | NO. | PER CENT |
| Acceptance..... | 9 | 75 | 19 | 48 | 38 | 51 | 6 | 25 | 72 | 48 |
| Intermediate.... | 2 | 17 | 16 | 40 | 23 | 31 | 4 | 17 | 45 | 30 |
| Rejection....... | 1 | 8 | 5 | 12 | 13 | 18 | 14 | 58 | 33 | 22 |
| Total ....... | 12 | ..... | 40 | ..... | 74 | ..... | 24 | ..... | 150 | ..... |

175

## Stereotyped Thinking

Precisely because most of the men in the sample based their restraint of aggressive tendencies on societal controls rather than on inner integration, some aggression remained uncontrolled. This the men needed to explain to themselves —and to others. For an explanation they fell back again on what society, or rather their associates, provided in the way of a justification for minority aggression. It has already been mentioned that most of the men voiced their ethnic attitudes in terms of stereotypes. The use of these stereotypes reveals a further influence—if not control—by society on ethnic attitudes. . . .

One of the hypotheses of this study is that intolerance is a function of anxiety, frustration, and deprivation, while the intolerant person's accusations are ways to justify his aggression. While the rationalizations for this intolerance must permit a minimum of reality testing, they will also condition the ways in which hostile feelings are discharged.

All intolerant veterans avoided reality testing to some degree, and each of them made statements about minorities which showed that they neglected the individual's uniquely personal characteristics—in short, they used stereotypes. As was to be expected, those who were only moderately biased retained more ability to test reality. They were more able to evaluate correctly the individuals whom they met, but they clung to stereotyped thinking about the rest of the discriminated group. In this way it remained possible to retain the stereotyped attitudes which permitted discharge of hostility despite actual experiences to the contrary. Such a limited amount of reality testing did not seem to be available to strongly biased individuals.

Because the intolerant person's rationalizations are closely, although not obviously, connected with his reasons for intolerance, he must take care to protect them. On the other hand, they also reveal the nature of the anxieties which underlie them.

An examination of the five most frequent Negro and five most frequent Jewish stereotypes reveals strikingly different results, each set of which presents a more or less integrated pattern (see Tables 4 and 5). The composite pattern of stereotypes about Jews does not stress personally "obnoxious" characteristics. In the main, they are represented in terms of a powerful, well-organized group which, by inference, threatens the subject.

On the other hand, the stereotypes about the Negro stress the individual, personally "offensive" characteristics of the Negro. As the stereotypes of the group characteristics of Jews implied a threat to the values and well-being of the intolerant white, so, too, those about the Negro were used to describe a conception of the Negro as a threat, particularly because the Negro was "forcing out the whites."

A comparison of the distribution of stereotypes applied to Jews and Negroes, as indicated by this enumeration, with those used by the National Socialists in

**TABLE 4.  Stereotypes Characterizing Jews**

| STEREOTYPE | NO. OF VETERANS MENTIONING STEREOTYPES |
|---|---|
| They are clannish; they help one another . . . . . . . . . . | 37 |
| They have the money. . . . . . . . . . . . . . . . . . . . . . | 26 |
| They control everything (or have an urge to control everything); they are running the country. . . . . . . . . . . . . . . . . | 24 |
| They use underhanded or sharp business methods . . . . . . . . . . . . . . . . . . . . . . . | 24 |
| They do not work; they do not do manual labor . . . . . . . . . . . . . . . . . . . . . . . . . . . . | 19 |

**TABLE 5.  Stereotypes Characterizing Negroes**

| STEREOTYPE | NO. OF VETERANS MENTIONING STEREOTYPES |
|---|---|
| They are sloppy; dirty, filthy. . . . . . . . . . . . . . . . . | 53 |
| They depreciate property . . . . . . . . . . . . . . . . . . . | 33 |
| They are taking over; they are forcing out the whites . . . . . . . . . . . . . . . . . . . . . . . . . | 25 |
| They are lazy; they are slackers in work. . . . . . . . . . . | 22 |
| They are ignorant; have low intelligence. . . . . . . . . . . | 18 |
| They have low character; they are immoral and dishonest. . . . . . . . . . . . . . . . . . . . . | 18 |

Germany permits certain observations. In Germany the whole of the stereotypes, which in the United States were divided between Jews and Negroes, were applied to the Jews. Thus in the United States, where two or more ethnic minorities are available, a tendency emerges to separate the stereotypes into two sets and to assign each of them to one minority group. One of these two sets indicates feelings of being anxious because of one minority's (the Jews') assumed power of overwhelming control. The other set of stereotypes shows feelings of anxiety because of the second minority's (the Negroes') assumed ability to permit itself the enjoyment of primitive, socially unacceptable forms of gratification. Thus, of two minority groups which differ in physical characteristics, such as skin color, the minority showing greater physical difference is used for projecting anxieties associated with dirtiness and sex desires. Conversely, the minority whose physical characteristics are more similar to those of the majority becomes a symbol for anxieties concerning overpowering control. If we apply the frame of reference of dynamic psychology to these observations, then these stereotypes permit further emphasis on the relation between tolerance and control. The individual who has achieved an integration or an inner balance between superego demands and instinctual, asocial strivings does not need to externalize either of them in a vain effort to establish a control that he does not possess. The intolerant man who cannot control his superego demands or instinctual drives projects them upon ethnic minorities as if, by fighting them in this way or by at least discharging excessive tension, he seeks to regain control over unconscious tendencies.

Actual experiences later in life, once the personality has been formed, seem relatively incapable of breaking down this delusional mechanism. Questioning revealed, for example, that, although Army experience threw the men into new and varied contacts with Jews and frequently with Negroes, the stereotypes applied to the service of Jews and Negroes in the Army proved largely an extension of the conceptions of civilian life into Army experiences.

It seems reasonable to assume that, as long as anxiety and insecurity persist as a root of intolerance, the effort to dispel stereotypes by rational propaganda is at best a half-measure. On an individual level only greater personal integration combined with social and economic security seems to offer hope for better inter-ethnic relations. Moreover, those who accept social controls are the more tolerant men, while they are also, relatively speaking, less tolerant of the Negro because Negro discrimination is more obviously condoned, both publicly and privately. This should lead, among other things, to additional efforts to change social practice in ways that will tangibly demonstrate that ethnic discrimination is contrary to the mores of society, a conviction which was very weak even among the more tolerant men.

# Part V

# The Great Promise: 1951-1960

# Introduction

It is a harsh fact of American history that racial minorities have tended to benefit from national involvement in war.[1] The unity and manpower that war requires lead to improved income and opportunities for sectors of the population that are otherwise neglected. The Korean War, which began this fifth decade, was no exception. The rising expectations triggered initially by World War II were now fueled further by the prosperity and tight labor market engendered by this second war.

It was in this context of high minority hopes for the future that America made its great promise to its black citizens. Comparable to the nineteenth century's Emancipation Proclamation ending slavery, the twentieth century's ending of legal racial segregation came on May 17, 1954, in the form of a ruling of the U.S. Supreme Court declaring racially separate public schools inherently unequal and therefore unconstitutional. This historic event has had vast consequences for American life far beyond the Southern public schools originally involved in the court order. Indeed, this Supreme Court decision, Brown *v.* Board of Education, continues to be a major force in racial policies of the United States.

Just before the dramatic decision was handed down, all but the most diehard segregationists were reasonably certain that the High Court would in some form strike down public school segregation by race as a violation of the Fourteenth Amendment of the U.S. Constitution. But that raised question of how the supposedly "Solid South" would react to the ruling. Would there be massive violence? Illegal resistance by the region's public officials? A national rupture caused by the region's defense of its racially segregated society? Many predicted

---

[1] The glaring exception to this statement was the treatment of Japanese-Americans during World War II—as discussed earlier in Part IV. But even here the war set up the conditions for the Japanese-Americans to successfully enter Hawaiian politics in a forceful and effective manner.

bloodshed. Little was ventured publicly by social science on the subject—little, that is, save Selection 24 by Guy Johnson of the University of North Carolina at Chapel Hill. This remarkable paper, wise and accurate in its projections, served as Johnson's 1954 presidential address to the Southern Sociological Society and was presented just a few weeks prior to the Court's handing down its *Brown* opinion on May 17. We can learn a lot from a careful reading of this paper, not just about the South and the desegregation process but also about how social science can be utilized for practical predictions. Projections into the future are always hazardous, especially in a controversial issue such as race relations, which taps the country's deepest values and prejudices. But note the manner in which Johnson modestly but shrewdly constructs his predictions of the region's future desegregation process out of: (1) an estimation of the variance produced by contextual factors (class, racial population percentages, rural-farm differences, and the economy); (2) the most similar phenomenon that had already occurred and been studied (the initial desegregation of higher education); and (3) a complete mastery of the basic situation and the two interacting groups growing out of a lifetime career of studying both the black and white communities of the South. There are few examples, to be sure, of such accurately predictive articles as Selection 24 in the sociological literature.

*Social Problems* began publishing in 1954 as the official journal of the Society for the Study of Social Problems (SSSP). The Society was formed by sociologists who believed that the discipline was beginning to forgo its initial calling as a critical science of society and its problems. This event marks a significant chapter in the continuing history of sociology's tension in being both a critic and a supplicant of society, a tension that was discussed in the Introduction. *Social Problems* immediately reflected the SSSP's stance by concentrating on school desegregation in a series of symposia in its initial volumes. Here the roles of social scientists as expert witnesses and consultants in the original school desegregation cases are candidly described.[2] A financial argument favoring interracial schools in Missouri is advanced.[3] Some of the school conditions that would enhance black achievement in desegregated schools, such as interracial teaching and counseling staffs, are specified.[4] The Supreme Court's complete *Brown* opinion together with the social science addition to the NAACP's brief

[2] Kenneth Clark, "The social scientist as an expert witness in civil rights litigation," *Social Problems 1* (1954): 5–10, and Lewis M. Killian, "The social scientist's role in the preparation of the Florida desegregation brief," *Social Problems 3,* (1956): 211–214.

[3] Vernon Pohlman, Stuart A. Queen, and Mary Faith Pellett Russell, "The cost of segregated schools," *Social Problems 1* (1954): 102–105.

[4] Richard L. Plaut, "Variables affecting the scholastic achievement of Negro children in nonsegregated schools," *Social Problems 2,* (1955): 207–211. This paper and others similar to it published at this point disprove the statement often made currently by a few commentators who favor the continuation of racially separate schools that social scientists of the 1950s actually thought that all desegregated schools would automatically lead to increased black achievement regardless of their circumstances.

are reprinted in full.[5] And two initial descriptions of actual school desegregation in Kansas City, Missouri, and in Delaware are provided.[6]

In its broad coverage, *Social Problems* published articles by nonsociologists who possessed special knowledge of the process (just as the *American Journal of Sociology* and *Social Forces* had in their early years of publication). The most interesting of these articles is Selection 25 by Roy Wilkins, the longtime executive director of the National Association for the Advancement of Colored People (NAACP) and a national black leader. Wilkins's contribution is informative for its view of desegregation through the perspective of the organization that was primarily responsible for the process; the discerning reader will note the consistency of view with the previous article on the NAACP by Seligmann (Selection 11). Just as interesting is Wilkins's list of future concerns—the extension of the process to the North, the tenure rights of black teachers in desegregating school systems, the eventual acceptance of racial change by white Southerners, and the need to link federal monies to the societal inclusion of black citizens. All four of these stated aims were borne out in later years. The last point, for instance, was enacted as Title VI of the 1964 Civil Rights Act. In contrast to Guy Johnson, however, Wilkins was in a position to bring about his predictions. Thus, his NAACP worked hard and long to win Congressional approval of Title VI.

Three years after the Supreme Court's desegregation ruling, the long-awaited confrontation between "states' rights" and federal power occurred over the issue in Little Rock. Arkansas Governor Orval Faubus called out the National Guard to prevent nine black children from following a court order to desegregate the city's all-white Central High School. White mob violence exploded and was reported widely in stories and photographs throughout the world. President Dwight Eisenhower responded by "nationalizing" the Guard (thus taking the federally trained and sponsored Guard out of Faubus's authority) and sending in regular U.S. Army units to restore order and ensure the carrying through of the U.S. District Court's desegregation order. Federal power had not only triumphed, but the executive branch had finally committed itself to supporting when necessary the desegregation orders of the embattled judiciary.

Selection 26 reports on this important episode by studying one segment of the Little Rock community that was placed under particular pressure by the conflict—the white ministry who led major congregations. Most of these men personally believed in the racial desegregation of the public schools, but their congregations generally opposed the process fiercely. Adding to their plight, the denominations they represented typically made pronouncements in favor of racial change yet applied pressures on their clergy that deterred action. Selection

---

[5] Robert L. Carter and Kenneth B. Clark, "Legal background and significance of the May 17th decision: Conclusions; text of the Supreme Court Opinions, May 17, 1954; Appendix to Appellants' Briefs: *Statements by social scientists,*" *Social Problems* 2 (1955) 215–235.

[6] Martin Loeb, "Kansas City does its duty," *Social Problems* 4 (1957): 161–165, and Ralph S. Halloway, "School desegregation in Delaware," *Social Problems* 4 (1957): 166–172.

26 describes this conflict situation and applies a reference group analysis to explain what happened.

The partly structural approach of the Little Rock ministry study was not typical of the sociological literature of this period. Because of the dearth of research funds for work on the subject, little direct work on the unfolding phenomenon was possible. What was conducted was strongly influenced by the popular psychological-reductionist model discussed in Part IV; that is, most of the work centered on racial attitudes and prejudice and largely ignored the more distinctively sociological concerns of social structure. Samples of this work illustrate the point. Various techniques for measuring racial attitudes were published;[7] reductions in group prejudice and social distance brought about by a movie,[8] an intercultural workshop,[9] discussion groups,[10] and school desegregation itself[11] were commonly studied; and the effects of early familial experiences upon prejudice received attention.[12] Prejudice was related to human perception[13] and to the behavior of white policemen in Philadelphia toward black offenders.[14] One of the few major studies of school desegregation during the 1950s merely checked on the attitudes of the residents of Greensboro, North Carolina, toward race and desegregation without any structural analysis whatsoever.[15] Many papers reflected the enormous influence of the psychoanalytically inspired study, *The Authoritarian Personality,* published in 1950. Repeatedly, the authoritarian personality type was shown to be more prejudiced,[16] even among refugee Ukranians;[17] and this phenomenon was held to have significant

[7]*E.g.,* Frank R. Westie, "A technique for the measurement of race attitudes," *American Sociological Review 18* (1953): 73–78.

[8]Russell Middleton, "Ethnic prejudice and susceptibility to persuasion," *American Sociological Review 25* (1960): 679–686.

[9]E. S. Bogardus, "Measuring changes in ethnic reactions," *American Sociological Review 16* (1951): 48–51.

[10]James H. Bossard, "Experiment in intergroup relations: Ten-year summary," *Social Forces 32* (1954): 217–221.

[11]Ernest Q. Campbell, "Some social psychological correlates of direct contact in attitude change," *Social Forces 36* (1958): 335–340.

[12]William McCord, Joan McCord, and A. Howard, "Early familial experiences and bigotry," *American Sociological Review 25* (1960): 717–722.

[13]Alice B. Riddleberger and Annabelle B. Motz, "Prejudice and perception," *American Journal of Sociology 62* (1957): 498–503.

[14]William M. Kephart, "Negro visibility," *American Sociological Review 19* (1954): 462–467, and *idem,* "The Negro offender: An urban research project," *American Journal of Sociology 60* (1954): 46–50.

[15]Melvin Tumin, P. Barton, and B. Burrus, "Education, prejudice, and discrimination: A study in readiness for desegregation," *American Sociological Review 23* (1958): 41–49, and Melvin Tumin, "Readiness and resistance to desegregation: A social portrait of the hard core," *Social Forces 36* (1958): 256–263.

[16]Alan H. Roberts and Milton Rokeach, "Anomie, authoritarianism, and prejudice: A replication," *American Journal of Sociology 61* (1956): 355–358.

[17]Allan Kassof, "The prejudiced personality: A cross-cultural test," *Social Problems 6* (1959): 59–67.

implications for racial change.[18] One interesting paper reinterpreted the authoritarian personality into sociological terms by arguing that it negatively correlated with the number of different social roles that an individual had mastered.[19]

Increasingly, however, sociologists became discontent with this purely psychological model. The dramatic events and consistent patterns of the desegregation process offered forceful reminders of the importance of structural factors. Court orders, not softening white attitudes on race, were recasting American race relations. Indeed, the prejudiced attitudes were beginning to change after the accomplished fact of institutional change rather than the conventional reasoning that "the hearts and minds of men" had to be altered initially.[20] Soon papers began to appear that presented this point of view forcefully. Selections 27 through 31 are representative of this altered direction in sociological thinking about race relations.

First, in Selection 27, Arnold Rose, a founder of the SSSP and long a leader in the study of American race relations at the University of Minnesota, draws a sharp distinction between intergroup relations and prejudice. He concludes that both "are worthy of study in their own right" but that "prejudice has little to do with intergroup relations." Selection 28 presents data that lend support to Rose's contentions. Lewis Killian, a race relations specialist from the University of Massachusetts at Amherst and a native Southerner himself, reports on the shifts in racial behavior of a group of white Southern migrants to the new racial expectations they encounter in Chicago. Their traditional antiblack attitudes do not easily melt away, but their relations with blacks are necessarily altered and these behavioral alterations cause subtle changes of view.

Frank and Margaret Westie, of the University of Indiana, derive in Selection 29 a "social distance pyramid" model from their empirical work on the racial attitudes of both black and white Americans. This influential paper marks an interesting attempt to merge the psychological and sociological approaches by embedding cross-racial attitudes in their social class context. Note how the racial attitudes of both blacks and whites are simultaneously a function of both the social class of the perceiver and the social class of the perceived.

Selection 30 presents an ideal-type dichotomy that is derived from comparative materials of race relations around the globe and has proved highly useful in sociology's thinking about American race relations. Pierre van den Berghe, a race relations specialist at the University of Washington, was born in the former Belgian Congo and has studied race relations in South Africa and Latin America as well as in the United States. This wide comparative experience enables him to distinguish between a paternalistic pattern of race relations, as typified by the

---

[18] Herman Long, "Race, prejudice, and social change," *American Journal of Sociology* 57 (1951): 15-19.

[19] Don Stewart and Thomas Hoult, "A social psychological theory of the authoritarian personality," *American Journal of Sociology* 65 (1960): 274-279.

[20] T. F. Pettigrew, *Racially Separate or Together?* (New York: McGraw-Hill, 1971).

antebellum South, and a competitive pattern that more accurately characterizes late-twentieth-century American race relations.

The final article of Part V emphasizes power as the key concept in race relations. R. A. Schermerhorn, of Case–Western Reserve University, has long been a thoughtful contributor to the evolving sociological theories of race relations. This brief statement, published in 1957, was an early indication of the direction that much of sociological theory would take in the 1960s.

# 24

# A Sociologist Looks at Racial Desegregation in the South

*GUY B. JOHNSON*

## Crisis and Accommodation

. . . I continue to believe, as I did a year ago, that the Supreme Court will hold against compulsory segregation. At least we would do well here in the South to think in terms of that possibility and to be prepared to meet intelligently whatever crisis might be precipitated by the decision of the Court.

. . . The next question, then, is: What is the shape of things to come? Specifically, what is likely to happen during the period of transition? What new accommodations in the relations of white and Negro can we expect? What will the situation be like when it has settled down?

Well, what can a sociologist say that is sound and reasonable about these problems? If he is honest, he will readily admit that while sociology has made great strides in its methodology it is not yet equipped to speak with assurance on a problem as complex as this. However, he should not overdo the modest stance, because if he has profited from his training and from his study of human society, then he of all people is entitled to speak. I would like to think that what I have to say on this subject is shared by practically all other sociologists similarly situated, but *that* remains to be seen; so I must warn you that I am speaking for *one* sociologist, that my analysis is probably a compound of thirty years

Reprinted, abridged, from *Social Forces 33* (October 1954): 1–10. Copyright © The University of North Carolina Press.

of impressions, a pinch of science, and a dash of common sense, garnished somewhat generously with value judgments. Let me add that for reasons of time I shall confine my remarks almost entirely to the public school situation.

There are at least two important things the sociologist can do in order to make an intelligent projection of the course of social change in any given situation. First, he can try to identify the most significant factors in the situation which he is observing and assess their relative weights and their variations. Second, he can find out what has happened in previous instances which are parallel or similar in the hope of gaining better insight into the dynamics of the present situation. Let me discuss these in order....

I submit that first and foremost among the determinants of the future situation in the South is the system of norms and values concerned with white social dominance, social exclusiveness, and the preservation of what is sometimes called the "integrity" of white society and white "racial" types. This value system is not merely southern. It approaches universality in American white society. Its strength varies, of course. It is strongest in the Deep South, it is weaker in areas where there are few Negroes and in the great cosmopolitan centers of the North and West; but it probably represents the overwhelming majority of white people in all sections of the country. The main difference between the South and the rest of the states is that the South has added legal sanctions to its social norms. Being bitter and insecure because of the Emancipation and the Reconstruction, the South wanted to "fix things good." It operated on the principle that 100 percent dominance is a lot better than 95 percent dominance, and that if you gave one little bit of equality to the Negro, the next thing you knew you would be face to face with the problem: Would you want your daughter to marry a Negro?

The second great determinant, which is merely the structural aspect of the first, is the fact of dualism in white and Negro social institutions. Whether it be in the towns and cities where spatial separation accompanies social dualism, or in the rural areas where spatial or ecological separation is not usually definitely patterned, there are two communities, one white and one Negro. In the Negro communities are churches, businesses, private schools, and an amazing range of other voluntary associations and agencies, and throughout the South there are the legally segregated public schools for Negroes. This institutional machinery is the social world of the Negro. It furnishes jobs, status positions, prestige—in short, the satisfaction of most of the basic and derived needs of the Negro.

Now, the southern white people have a serious social, economic, and psychological stake in the structure of white dominance, and they would like to keep it intact. They dread any tampering with the system, and they fear that the removal of one wheel or bolt from the machinery might cause the whole thing to get out of control. Their attitude may be characterized as follows: "We would rather not concede any changes, but if the Supreme Court says we must, then we must. But we will make the changes mean as little as possible in our basic attitudes and values. If the outer wall is weakened, we will strengthen the inner wall around our intimate social relations. Segregation laws may be dead, but long live segregation!"

The Negro also has a stake in the present dual system, and while he resents the imputation of inferiority involved in the compulsory aspect of segregation, this does not mean that he wants, in the foreseeable future, a grand merger with the white community. His attitude may be characterized as follows: "By all means, take away the segregation laws, those accursed symbols of inferiority. I will feel a lot better, but I will know that the millennium has not arrived, so just let me feel my way cautiously in these new contacts with white people."

At the risk of oversimplification, I suggest that these two—the value system of white dominance and the dualistic nature of our social structure—are the basic determining factors in the new adjustments arising from desegregation. There are, however, a number of other factors which are certain to have some weight. Let me cite them briefly.

## CLASS STATUS

Intra-race class differences are obviously less important than inter-race differences, but they will have some influence, and they may become of increasing importance. In urban areas the upper class whites will as a rule have fewer inter-race contacts in the public schools than will the middle and lower class whites, because of the typical ecological patterns in the cities. Insofar as the norms of white race dominance are weakened, race relations will tend to become class relations, and the lower class whites will have a more intense concern with class status.

## POPULATION RATIOS

By and large there is some association between ratio of Negroes to whites and the amount of threat felt by the whites in the removal of legal sanctions, but there are important local variations. In fact, the variations in attitudes, informal controls, and interaction patterns are so great that I would expect some of the "best" and some of the "worst" transition situations to develop in areas where the ratio of Negroes to whites is very high.

## RURAL-URBAN DIFFERENCES

Since the pattern of spatial segregation is relatively weak in rural areas, there would logically be more occasions for having mixed school units than in the cities. But resistance to such changes is likely to be very high in the rural areas, and thus we may expect a high incidence of conflicts, evasive actions, and pressures for compromise arrangements.

## GENERAL ECONOMIC OUTLOOK

The South is on the up industrially and agriculturally, and this is fortunate. It lessens the danger of tensions based on economic insecurity, and it provides a base for the greatly increased expenditures which will have to be made for the public schools. A depression in the next few years would no doubt aggravate the inter-racial situation generally and make the new adjustments all the more difficult.

In addition I want to mention two factors which I surmise will have considerable weight during the fluid initial stage of readjustment, if and when the Supreme Court invalidates legal segregation. The first is the general state of mind of the southern people. It appears to be surprisingly calm, on the whole, in the face of the impending decision of the Court. The very fact that the Court has delayed the process of decision has taken some of the edge off the feeling of crisis and has given the southern people time to become accustomed to the thought of desegregation. Governors, congressmen, editors, and others have counselled calmness and moderation, and the public officials who have threatened to abolish the public schools or to take other drastic measures are very much in the minority. The second factor is the attitudes of persons in positions of leadership and authority who will have to make decisions upon policies and their implementation. I think that there is a real likelihood that there will be a great deal of confusion and variation in the decisions. The public will be wondering what the authorities think, what they are going to do, how firm they will be, etc., while the authorities are likely to be more cautious and vacillating than they need be because they will be hypersensitive to all sorts of pressure groups which claim to represent the prevailing public opinion. . . .

Of interest here is the experience of certain northern and western communities which have decided in the past ten years to "integrate" their schools. Recent studies of several such communities show that when the city officials and the school board adopted a definite policy, put it into effect without delay, and then stood firm, there was very little disturbance during the transition. But when the official policy was uncertain and there was delay in its execution, the opposition had time to crystallize. Pressures were put on the school board, and white students, taking the cue from their parents, caused considerable disorder. In Gary, Indiana, for example, where the integration plan was poorly prepared and timidly proposed, there was a strike led by some of the white high school students as a protest against the admission of Negroes. The tension became so high that the school board was afraid to crack down on the strikers and proceed with its plan. Rioting seemed imminent on several occasions. The strike leader, a boy in his teens, gained much notoriety and became a power to be reckoned with. After two years of intermittent strikes and community turmoil, the school board mobilized enough support and courage to enable it to call the strikers truants and proceed with a firm policy. Relations between the white and Negro students have been considered "good" for the past several years. Negro students participate in most of the school activities, but in the area of social affairs the color line is very much in evidence. This latter statement, incidentally, applies almost universally to the mixed-school situations in the North and West.

At Fort Bragg, North Carolina, and several other military bases in the South there has been some experience with the new Federal policy of nonsegregated schools for the children of military personnel. Observers report that the mixed schools have been accepted as a matter of course, that there are some play contacts between the white and Negro children, but that equal-status social contacts between adults across the color line are quite rare. Admittedly a military base is hardly a "free" situation—the personnel are in what might be called "involuntary servitude"—but the situation does illustrate the importance of authority and uniformity. When one's reference groups are all subject to the same authority and are all expected to observe the same norms, it seems not only futile but somewhat ridiculous to deviate overtly from the expected patterns.

More to the point perhaps is the experience of the southern public institutions of higher learning which have recently admitted Negro students for the first time. Last summer I made a survey of these institutions, and I should like to report on it briefly.

Maryland had admitted Negroes to its university law school about twenty years ago, but little further had happened on the higher education level until a series of test cases in the late 1940's and early 1950's brought decisions favorable to Negro plaintiffs in Oklahoma, Texas, Kentucky, and North Carolina, and Virginia. The result was the admission of Negroes, on the graduate and professional levels only in most instances, to at least twenty institutions in a period of five years, 1948-1952. . . .

The enrollments totalled about 450. Summer school enrollment of Negro students was twice as high as in the regular session. We estimated that 1,000 to 2,000 Negro students had been in contact with white students in the regular sessions alone in the past five years. . . .

Despite numerous predictions of violence, this transition to racial coeducation in southern universities has been accomplished without a single serious incident of friction. There were some rather wild rumors in a few schools at first, but they were soon dispelled. There was also an effort by the administration in several schools to define the privileges of the first Negro students in terms of the state laws and the old social norms; that is, the Negro students were segregated and restricted in various ways. However, this effort was soon abandoned—first, because white students themselves condemned it as unfair, and second, because the Supreme Court made a ruling aginst such treatment. Today there is very little official discrimination against the Negro students. In fact, one can say that there has already emerged a norm in which administration takes pride; namely, that there is equality of campus citizenship.

We found almost universal agreement that the Negro students were handicapped by their inferior educational background, and there was some evidence of a tendency on the part of teachers to "go easy" on grading them, but on the whole they were serious and industrious students who were standing up quite well in the academic race.

White students have expressed relatively little overt rudeness or antagnoism toward these Negro students. Most of them are simply indifferent, but there is a minority who interact with Negro students in a cordial and friendly way. In fact there were several instances of white students taking the initiative in behalf of equal privileges for the Negro student. In the official social affairs of academic organizations—e.g., a law students' dinner or picnic—Negro students have taken part, but in the strictly "social" realm there is almost no Negro participation. All parties seem to understand that new and delicate adjustments are involved, and they have behaved with appropriate restraint. Perhaps the best way to summarize what has happened so far is to say that white and Negro students have already learned new patterns of working, eating, and living in close proximity without serious disturbance to their sense of social privacy.

The differences between this university situation and the public school situation, in terms of numbers, age, sophistication, maturity, etc., are obvious. However, there are probably trends and patterns here which will help in our projections on the public school level.

## Reasonable Projections and Expectations

. . . The fluid initial stage in the transition will be of special importance, and I want to state two propositions with regard to it.

1. *It will be a period of tension, of evasive actions and experiments.* At first there is the possibility that practically nothing happens. The Supreme Court's decision may apply directly only to the instant cases. A few additional communities may begin to fall in line of their own accord, but the normal expectation is that most school district officials will sit tight and wait for legal tests to be directed against them. Prolonged litigation, then, is a distinct possibility, and its total effect will be to make the transition to desegregation a gradual one.

Think of all the evasive measures you can, and you have an idea of the evasions and negations which will be proposed or actually tried out. Among the more obvious petty devices are the gerrymandering of school district lines, complicated transfer regulations, and delay in processing the applications of Negroes who wish to enter a "superior" school. No doubt there will be a heavy increase in enrollment of white students in private schools, because this is one way in which the well-to-do white people can "protect" their children from inter-race contacts. There will be talk of separating high school students along sex lines but I doubt whether such a scheme will win many backers.

But the most startling proposals are the South Carolina plan for turning the schools over completely to private agencies and the Georgia plan for handing out cash subsidies to parents who will then use the money to provide schooling for their children. The theory behind them is that if the state supports no public schools, it is not discriminating against anybody, therefore it is beyond the reach of the Federal Constitution. South Carolina has already had a popular vote on an amendment which, when ratified by the legislature, will erase completely the state's obligation to support a system of public schools. The proponents of this idea imagine that the schools would be taken over, financed, and operated by all sorts of private educational agencies. Some would be white agencies, some would be Negro; thus the state would hope to do by private action what it could no longer do by official action. How the legal act of giving the schools to such agencies can be accomplished I do not know, but assuming that it is done, then what? Simply that the wealthy have good schools, the poor have shabby schools, and a great cry arises for state subsidies. Then, if the state is honest about wanting to see its children get fair opportunities, it grants subsidies to the private agencies. And the minute it does this it is vulnerable under the Federal Constitution. Both the Georgia and the South Carolina plans are unrealistic, but we should not be too surprised if they are given a try. One is reminded of the attempts to evade the Supreme Court's white primary decision of 1944. South Carolina repealed all laws referring to primary elections and allowed the Democratic Party to run its primaries as it saw fit, but the Federal courts lost no time in invalidating this device.

What I am saying here is that the natural reaction of the majority of white people will be to try to define the new situation in terms of the existing norms. At the same time there will be efforts by the liberal or equalitarian minority in the white group to accept the new situation and to modify the social norms to fit, but these will remain *minority* efforts.

2. *The initial period is likely to see an increase in race rumors, an increase of aggression against Negroes, and occasional violence.* Every sensible person would like to believe that the transition can be made without violence. I believe that for the most part it will, but considering the reality of the extreme emotional involvement of certain white groups in the symbols of white dominance, and considering the thousand and one ways in which incidents and rumors, provocations and fears might be combined, it would be a miracle indeed if there were no violence of any sort. In several of our cities there are areas where the Negro population is expanding into formerly white territory, and in some of these there is already a pattern of violence. These are precisely the areas where mixed schools will make sense ecologically, and a certain amount of violence is likely to occur. Minor personal clashes are, of course, likely to happen sporadically almost anywhere.

Perhaps most of us forget that there are still many people who embrace the racial dogmas which we associate with the eighteenth and nineteenth centuries. Also most of us are not aware that there is today a rather active sub-literature of hate—anti-Negro, anti-Jewish, anti-Catholic, and of course all cleverly tied in with anti-communist—which circulates among large segments of the population. . . .

When the most foolish evasive devices are done with, when the initial shock has subsided and the South has settled down to the realization that it is bound to have a certain amount of racial coeducation, what will the situation look like? I suggest some further projections.

3. *There will be no mass mingling of the races in the urban public school.* The mass mingling of the races in the schools is simply not in the cards. Bear in mind that nearly half of the South's ten million Negroes live in urban areas and that almost a fourth live in smaller towns and villages or rural-nonfarm homes. Probably more than three-fourths of these seven million live in Negro residence areas which are spatially separate. In short, they live in distinctly Negro communities. They have no consuming desire to go to school with white pupils just for the sake of associating with them. For the majority of them, the institutions in their community are convenient, accessible, and psychologically comfortable. Their interest will be not to abolish them but to improve them, and they will have little difficulty from here on in getting a share of the public funds which will make their schools as good as any. In the mixed or marginal areas in the cities there may be an occasional mixed school, and there will be a number of the more promising and ambitious Negro scholars who will request and obtain admission to certain "white" schools because certain special courses are available there but not in the Negro schools. But I venture the prediction that not more than ten percent of the total of Negro and white pupils will be attending school together in the cities of the South for a long time to come.

4. *In rural farming areas the proportion of mixed school units will be somewhat higher.* In rural areas there will be delay and resistance at first. Negro leadership will be cautious and willing, if not anxious, to preserve separate schools if they are well financed. As time goes on and the financial burden of trying to buy separation by equalizing every aspect of the school systems becomes quite apparent, the acceptance of mixed schools will become more general. I would estimate that within twenty to twenty-five years as many as half of the rural school units may be composed of student bodies of both races.

5. *The only areas to have complete racial integration in the schools will be those areas which have very low Negro population ratios.* In large parts of the states of West Virginia, Kentucky, Missouri, Oklahoma, and Texas, and in most of the upper piedmont and mountain counties of the South, the ratio of Negroes to whites is very low. Negro education has suffered, because county officials have been loathe to support adequate schools for a few Negro families scattered here and there. Many officials have come to regard compulsory school segregation as a nuisance and a threatened financial drain, and they will not be displeased when the Supreme Court makes it possible for them to absorb their sparse Negro school population.

6. *Official norms of "equal treatment" of all students will soon develop.* The idea of democracy in the classroom is strong in American education, and I believe that white students will on the whole be willing to include their Negro fellow-students in their concept of the "official" equality of school citizenship as such. Thus Negro students will probably participate strongly in athletics,

orchestras, bands, recitals, etc., where competence is important, but less so or not at all in those phases of school life which verge on the "social," such as dramatics, hobby clubs, and social clubs and cliques. Even athletics may present some difficulties at first, because it involves travelling together, but the desire to win, plus the availability of a splendid Negro fullback or pitcher, will soon take care of this situation.

7. *Equal-status social contacts will be very rare.* In those activities which the white group defines as private, initmate, social, the norms of white dominance and out-group exclusion will operate in full force. Violation will bring swift censure and ostracism from one's reference groups. In this realm of the social, there are the makings of many tensions and emotional distrubances.

However, there is a mitigating factor. The Southerner, white and Negro, retains a good deal of the traditional folk pattern of friendliness. He likes to feel that he knows the people with whom he associates. He likes to "personalize" even casual and formal contacts as much as possible. Therefore, we can expect the day-to-day student contacts of white and Negro to partake of this "friendly" and "personal" pattern. I surmise that the routine contacts in the southern schools will have on the whole a warmer quality than they have in non-southern schools.

8. *Negro teachers will probably suffer some loss of jobs, at least temporarily.* Insofar as desegregation permits the actual abandonment of certain schools, it is sure to affect Negro schools and Negro teachers more than white. However, this loss of jobs should not be very extensive, and it should be only temporary. The school population and the numbers in average daily attendance are steadily increasing, and there will be a steady demand for teachers. Negro teachers, who, by the way, have higher indexes of training and experience than white teachers in many southern areas, should gradually find positions in the mixed schools and regain whatever ground they had lost earlier.

9. *The financial cost of the public schools in the South will increase quite heavily.* Anyone who pretends that desegregation will save untold millions of tax dollars is guilty of loose thinking. If the dual school system were composed of two high-quality and absolutely equal parts, then the elimination of unnecessary duplications would effect substantial savings. But we are dealing with a situation in which the Negro school system has until recently been half-starved financially, and equalization of any sort—whether it be in a separate system or in an integrated system—will mean not lower expenditures but higher expenditures. The South is committed to better education, and it is gradually closing the gap between itself and the other regions. It has been spending around one and a half billion dollars a year on its public schools. In order to do a good job of removing the inequalities between white and Negro and between rural and urban schools, and in order to keep up with the expected increase of population, it will have to be spending more than two billion dollars a year by 1960. However, if the favorable income trend continues, it can do this easily enough; in fact it can do it on a smaller percentage of its total income than it is using now.

## Conclusion

You have noticed that in much of my discussion there has been the implication that the change which we face is going to have a gradualistic rather than a revolutionary quality. I realize that there are those who have tried to make "gradualism" a naughty word, but I shall continue to use it. To me it does not suggest a theory or a policy which one must be for or against, but merely a useful and accurate description of the way in which many social changes actually do occur.

I believe that whether the Supreme Court takes a flat stand against legal segregation or reaffirms the separate-but-equal doctrine, the net effect is going to be about the same. The former decision would mean a greater immediate shock, the latter would take a little more time, but both involve consequences which will materialize in a gradual manner.

The net consequences of the abandonment of compulsory segregation may be short of what many people feared they would be, but they may also be short of what many people hoped they would be. I suggest that the greatest positive consequence may be that the South will be rid of the stigma of unfair legal compulsion against the Negro and that the Negro will be rid of a hated symbol of second-class citizenship. And maybe we should be thankful if the Supreme Court does this for us. This sort of thing is hard to abandon voluntarily, and the South might not do it of its own accord for another fifty years.

# 25

# The Role of the National Association for the Advancement of Colored People in the Desegregation Process

*ROY WILKINS*

. . . [P]opular opinion to the contrary, the NAACP would prefer using legal action as a last resort in the many situations which will arise in hundreds of communities. The basic question has been solved: racially segregated schools are unconstitutional. The complexities ahead involve compliance. How shall the Court's opinion be implemented? The approach and program of the NAACP to implementation has already taken shape, influenced in part by the traditional policy of the Association (for first-class citizenship free of discrimination and segregation) and by events immediately before and since May 17.

    1. Pending the handing down of decrees in the specific cases before the highest court, the NAACP has sought to persuade states and school districts to desegregate in compliance with the opinion.

    The first step in this effort was a meeting in Atlanta, Georgia, five days after

Abridged from *Social Problems 2* (1955): 201–204, by permission of *Social Problems* and the Society for the Study of Social Problems.

the decision, of seventeen southern state presidents of the Association where the Atlanta Declaration was formulated. This Declaration asserted:

Having canvassed the situation in each of our states, we approach the future with the utmost confidence . . . We stand ready to work with other law-abiding citizens who are anxious to translate this decision into a program of action to eradicate racial segregation in public education as speedily as possible.

In pursuit of our objectives, we will accelerate our community action program to win public acceptance of the Court's desegregation order from all segments of the population . . . we are confident of the support of teachers, parents, labor, church, civic, fraternal, social, business and professional organizations.

Petitions asking compliance were drawn and local NAACP branches in communities which had had compulsory school segregation presented these to local school boards. Some few boards refused to receive NAACP delegations, the majority received and put aside the petitions, and a goodly number began action at once on desegregation plans.

This NAACP action, plus other factors, including the conviction of responsible public officials that segregation should be eliminated, helped in the Missouri change-over, which must be regarded as the best statewide compliance program so far in the nation. . . .

Two of the five communities which came before the Court have abolished segregation in their schools: Washington, D.C., and Topeka, Kansas. The Delaware district involved already has mixed schools under a lower court decision and the decree can thus only prohibit the state of Delaware (the appellant) from upsetting the present system there. That leaves two school districts, one in Virginia and one in South Carolina, to be directly affected by the decrees.

NAACP local chapters, backed by the national organization, will join other agencies and citizens in these communities in seeking compliance with the terms of the Court order. . . .

2. The NAACP will resist efforts in areas outside the compulsory segregation belt to institute or continue a variety of forms of segregation, using the Court opinion and decrees as added weapons.

It has been popular to charge "the South" with racial discrimination and segregation and to suppose that other areas are guiltless. While the South has been the greatest and most consistent practitioner of racial discrimination, certain Northern communities have also practiced discrimination, even on the school question. Indiana, southern Illinois and southern Ohio until very recently had racially segregated schools, as did Arizona. Less than ten years ago southern New Jersey had separate schools.

Even in the face of the May 17 opinion some Northern towns are persisting in practices which, in effect, enforce segregation in public schools. . . . [S]chool site selection and school construction programs are added to gerrymandering as devices for maintaining segregated patterns. These and other schemes, frequently camouflaged in school board resolutions whose language must be carefully analyzed, will claim the attention of NAACP units throughout the country.

3. The NAACP will seek to safeguard the moral and tenure rights of Negro teachers in the assignment of personnel in desegregated systems. . . .

Thus far, no great problems have arisen with teachers. In Phoenix, Tucson, Washington, Baltimore, St. Louis and smaller cities and towns Negro teachers have been retained in the new system, although, in a very few instances, some have lost their jobs. . . .

4. The NAACP will oppose the allocation of any and all forms of federal aid to education to those states or school districts which refuse to comply with the Supreme Court opinion. . . .

The NAACP position is simply that since racially segregated public school systems have been declared unconstitutional, no federal funds should be allocated to those areas which defy what is now the law of the land. . . .

5. Needless to say, if all other methods fail, the NAACP legal staff will make its services available to any Negro parents in any school district who wish to challenge in court those local school authorities who choose to ignore, evade, or openly defy the ruling of May 17.

The Association believes that the rights of the children to equal education are paramount. The nation's highest court has declared that such equal education cannot be secured in a racially segregated system. While recognizing the existence of certain administrative problems (and certain psychological ones), the NAACP believes all these can be solved in a reasonable time if they are attacked by responsible officials and bodies of citizens—if a beginning is made on a plan to comply. Failing such a beginning, the situations must ultimately be brought before the courts for examination and determination.

The NAACP believes, as was stated at Atlanta, that substantial numbers of white Southerners want to abide by the Constitution and are willing to begin, in their school districts, a program of desegregation. Many of these people have been intimidated by extremely vocal politicians and seekers or holders of public office who, in some places, have crudely cast the school question in a setting where decent people hesitate to become embroiled.

Despite this hysteria and the frantic actions by South Carolina, Georgia and Mississippi legislatures looking to the abolition of the public schools, the NAACP is confident that on a people-to-people, school-district-to-school district level, desegregation will move forward once the Supreme Court has handed down its decrees on procedure. Americans are basicallly law-abiding. Americans are basically fair. There is nothing fair about the Jim Crow school system. Even die-hard opponents of integregation now freely admit (as they scramble for delay and *any* device for non-compliance) that the segregated school was *not* equal. Their unequal and unfair system has been dragged out into the light, spread before the nation's highest court, measured against the guarantees of the United States Constitution and found wanting. At such a stage they will fume and fulminate and call upon tradition and custom; they will deliver political orations, and summon the myths that have served so well in the past. But, unless they should make the extremely unlikely choice of leaving the Federal union, in the end (and sooner than many now think) they will act as Americans have always acted when fair play is demanded. There will be a new order and they will bring it about.

# 26

# Racial and Moral Crisis: The Role of Little Rock Ministers

ERNEST Q. CAMPBELL and THOMAS F. PETTIGREW

This paper analyzes the conduct of the [white] ministers in established denominations in Little Rock, Arkansas, during the crisis over the admission of Negro students to the Central High School in the fall of 1957. How do ministers behave in racial crisis, caught between integrationist and segregationist forces?

One might expect that Little Rock's clergymen would favor school integration. All the major national Protestant bodies have adopted forceful declarations commending the Supreme Court's desegregation decision of 1954 and urging their members to comply with it. And southern pastors have voted in favor of these statements at their church conferences—and sometimes have even issued similar pronouncements to their own congregations. But the southern man of God faces serious congregational opposition if he attempts to express his integrationist beliefs publicly in the local community. The vast majority of southern whites—even those living in the Middle South—are definitely against racial desegregation.

The purpose of this study is to determine how the ministers of established denominations in Little Rock behaved in the conflict. . . .

. . . Little Rock is not a city of the Deep South. Its public transportation had been successfully integrated in 1956, and its voters, as late as March, 1957, had elected two men to the school board who supported the board's plan for token

Abridged from *American Journal of Sociology 64* (1959): 509–516. Used by permission of The University of Chicago Press. © 1959 by The University of Chicago. All rights reserved.

integration of Central High School. And yet Little Rock is a southern city, with southern traditions of race relations. These patterns became of world-wide interest after Governor Faubus called out the National Guard to prevent deseg- regation and thereby set off the most publicized and the most critical chain of events in the integration process to date.

Only two ministers devoted their sermons to the impending change on the Sunday before the fateful opening of school in September, 1957. Both warmly approved of the step and hoped for its success. Other ministers alluded to it in prayer or comment. It was commonly believed that a majority of the leading denominations' clergy favored the school board's "gradual" plan. This impres- sion seemed confirmed when immediately after Governor Faubus had sur- rounded Central High with troops fifteen of the city's most prominent ministers issued a protest in . . . "the strongest language permissible to men of God."

When Negro students appeared at the high school for the first time, they were escorted by four white Protestant ministers and a number of prominent Negro leaders. Two of the four whites are local clergymen, one being the president of the biracial ministerial association, the other, president of the local Human Relations Council. Many of the more influential ministers of the city had been asked the night before to join this escort. Some demurred; others said they would try to come. Only two appeared.

On September 23, the day of the rioting near Central High School, several leaders of the ministerial association personally urged immediate counteraction on the mayor and the chief of police. Later, support was solicited from selected ministers in the state to issue a declaration of Christian principle, but dissension over the statement prevented its publication. Indeed, *no* systematic attempts were made by the clergy to appeal to the conscience of the community. Such statements as individual ministers did express were usually—though not always— appeals for "law and order" rather than a Christian defense of the principle of desegregation.

Several weeks after the rioting, plans for a community-wide prayer service began to develop. Care was taken to present this service in as neutral terms as possible. Compromise and reconciliation were stressed: never was it described as organized prayers for integration. And indorsements came from both sides of the controversy—from President Eisenhower and from Governor Faubus. As one of the sponsors put it: "Good Christians can honestly disagree on the question of segregation or integration. But we can all join together in prayers for guid- ance, that peace may return to our city." The services in the co-operating churches were held on Columbus Day, October 12. All the leading churches participated, with only the working-class sects conspicuously missing. The ser- vices varied widely from informal prayers to elaborate programs, and attend- ances varied widely, too, and totaled perhaps six thousand.

These "prayers for peace" may best be viewed as a ritualistic termination of any attempts by the clergy to direct the course of events in the racial crisis. The prayers had met the national demand for ministerial action and the ministers' own need to act; and they had completed the whole unpleasant business. Despite sporadic efforts by a small number to undertake more effective steps, the ministers lapsed into a general silence that continued throughout the school year.


We began our work in Little Rock in the week after the peace prayers. Following a series of background interviews and a careful analysis of ministerial action as recorded in the press, twenty-nine detailed interviews with ministers were held. Twenty-seven of them are Protestants and two are Jewish; the Roman Catholics did not co-operate.

This sample was not selected randomly; the so-called "snowball technique" was used in order to include the most influential church leaders. This involves asking each interviewee to name the members of the Little Rock clergy that he considers to be "the most influential." The first interview was made with an announced leader of the peace prayers, and interviewing was continued with all the men mentioned as influential until no new names were suggested. We added a number of ministers who were not named but who had taken strongly liberal positions during the crisis. Thus our sample is most heavily weighted with the pastors of the larger churches with the greatest prestige and the pastors of smaller churches who had assumed active roles in the conflict. These two groups, we anticipated, would have to contend with the greatest amount of incompatibility in role. . . .

Information in three broad areas was sought, and to this end a series of open-ended questions was developed. A series of questions was aimed at determining whether the respondent was a segregationist or an integrationist. A segregationist here is defined as one who prefers racial barriers as presently constituted; an integrationist is one to whom the removal of legal and artificial barriers to racial contact is morally preferable to the present system.

Each interviewee was asked to give a complete account of what he had done and said in both his parish and in the community at large regarding the racial crisis. If he had not been active or vocal, we probed him for the reason and to learn if he had felt guilty over his failure to state the moral imperatives.

A final set of questions dealt with the pastor's perception of his congregation's reaction to whatever stand he had taken. If pressure had been applied on him by his parishioners, we probed him to learn exactly what pressure had been used and how.


## The Segregationist

Only five of the twenty-nine clergymen we interviewed were segregationists by our definition. None was avidly so, and, unlike segregationist ministers of the sects, none depended on "chapter-and-verse Scripture" to defend his stand. All men in their late fifties or sixties, they did not think that the crisis was a religious matter. . . . Although all five were affiliated with prominent denominations, they were not among the leaders of the local ministerial body.

These five men have not been publicly active in defending segregation. Each was opposed to violence, and none showed evidence of internal discomfort or conflict. All five co-operated with the neutrally toned prayers for peace. As one of them commented, "You certainly can't go wrong by praying. Praying can't hurt you on anything."

## The Inactive Integrationist

Inactive integrationists had done enough—or believed they had done enough—to acquaint their congregations with their sympathy with racial tolerance and integration, but during the crucial weeks of the crisis they were generally silent. These, representing as they do all major denominations, varied considerably as to age and size of church served. Included among them were virtually all the ministers of high prestige, many of whom had signed the protest against Governor Faubus at the start of the crisis and later were advocates of the peace prayer services. Some had spoken out in favor of "law and order" and in criticism of violence. They had not, however, defended the continued attendance of the Negro students in the high school, and they had not challenged their members to defend educational desegregation as a Christian obligation. They were publicly viewed as integrationists only because they had supported "law and order" and had not defended segregation.

Altogether, the inactive integrationists comprise sixteen out of the twenty-nine of our sample. Because it was not a random sample, we cannot draw inferences regarding the division of the total ministerial community or of ministers of established denominations into integrationist and segregationist camps. However, since the sample underrepresents the uninfluential minister who had not been in the public eye during the crisis, we may conclude that a large majority of Little Rock's men of God did not encourage their members to define the issue as religious, nor did they initiate actions or participate in programs aimed at integration.

## The Active Integrationist

Eight of our respondents can be designated as active integrationists because they continued to defend integration in principle and to insist that support of racial integration is nothing less than a Christian imperative. They were, on the whole, young men who have headed their small churches for only a few years. Most were distrubed that the churches of the city were segregated; some have urged their churches to admit Negroes.

Most of the active integrationists had serious difficulty with their members because of their activities, evidence of which was lowered Sunday-morning attendance, requests for transfer, diminished giving, personal snubs and insults, and rumors of sentiment for their dismissal. One had concluded that his usefulness to his congregation had ended and accordingly had requested to be transferred. By the end of 1958, several others had been removed from their pulpits.

One thing all twenty-nine of the sample had in common was a segregationist congregation.[1] Without exception, they believed that the majority of their members were strong opponents of racial integration. The highest estimate given by any integrationist of the proportion of his congregation which supported his views was 40 per cent; the median estimate for segregation was 75 per cent. Only three interviewees thought that a majority of their members would "accept" a strong public defense of integration by their minister.

Personal integrity, alone, would lead the liberal Little Rock minister to defend integration and condemn those who support segregation. However, the minister is obligated to consider the expectations of his church membership, especially inasmuch as the members' reactions bear upon his own effectiveness.

When an individual is responsible to a public, we distinguish three systems as relevant to his behavior: the self-reference system (SRS), the professional reference system (PRS), and the membership reference system (MRS). The SRS consists of the actor's demands, expectations, and images regarding himself. It may be thought of as what the actor would do in the absence of sanctions from external sources. We have already seen that typically the SRS would support racial integration. The PRS consists of several sources mutually related to his occupational role yet independent of his congregation: national and regional church bodies, the local ecclesiastical hierarchy, if any, the local ministerial association, personal contacts and friendships with fellow ministers, and, probably, an image of "my church." Finally, the MRS consists simply of the minister's congregation. We have already seen that it favored segregation or at least ministerial neutrality.

The net effect of three reference systems seems to favor the cause of integration. Were they equal in strength, and were there no contrary forces internal to any of them, this conclusion is obvious. The minister would then feel committed to support the official national policy of his denomination; his knowledge that fellow ministers were similarly committed would support him, and the local hierarchy would encourage him to make this decision and reassure him should his congregation threaten disaffection. These external influences would reinforce his own values, resulting in forthright action in stating and urging the Christian imperatives. However, internal inconsistencies in the PRS and the SRS restrain what on first examination appears to be an influence toward the defense of integration.

---

[1] Our study of a modest sample of church members bore out the ministers' estimates of predominantly pro-segregation sentiment in their congregations.

## The Professional Reference System

Two overriding characteristics of the PRS minimize its liberalizing influence. First, most of its components cannot or do not impose sanctions for nonconformity to their expectations. Second, those parts of the PRS that can impose sanctions also impose other demands on the minister, inconsistent with the defense of racial integration before members who, in large part, believe in racial separation and whose beliefs are profoundly emotional.

## The Inability to Impose Sanctions

The national and regional associations that serve as the official "voice of the church" are not organized to confer effective rewards or punishments on individual ministers. Especially is this true in the case of failure to espouse national racial policy or to act decisively in the presence of racial tension. This is even more true of the local ministerial association; it does not presume to censure or praise its members. Conversely, the local church hierarchy is an immediate source of sanctions. It has the responsibility of recommending or assigning parishes, and of assisting the pastor in expanding the program of his church.

The probability and the nature of sanctions from fellow ministers among whom one has personal contacts and friends are somewhat more difficult to specify. However, it does not appear likely that he is subject to sanctions if he does not conform to their expectations by liberal behavior on racial matters. Should he indorse and actively support segregationist and violent elements, this would be another matter. If he is silent or guarded, however, it is not likely to subject him to sanction. The active integrationists in Little Rock expressed disappointment at the inaction of their associates while at the same time suggesting possible mitigating circumstances. There is no evidence that personal or professional ties had been damaged.

Among the various components of the PRS, then, only the local ecclesiastica, which does not exist for some, and, to a considerably lesser extent, fellow ministers, are conceivable sources influencing the minister's decision to be silent, restrained, or forthright.

## Conflicting Expectations and Mitigated Pressures

The role of the minister as community reformer is not as institutionalized (i.e., it does not have as significant a built-in system of rewards and punishments) as are certain other roles associated with the ministry. The minister is responsible for the over-all conduct of the affairs of the church and is judged successful or unsuccessful according to how they prosper. He must encourage co-operative endeavor, reconciling differences, and bring people together. Vigor and high morale of the membership are reflected in increased financial support and a growing membership, and his fellow ministers and his church superiors are keenly sensitive to these evidences of his effectiveness. His goal, elusive though it may be, is maximum support from all members of an ever growing congregation.

The church hierarchy keeps records. It hears reports and rumors. It does not like to see divided congregations, alienated ministers, reduced membership, or decreased contributions. Responsible as it is for the destiny of the denomination in a given territory, it compares its changing fortunes with those of rival churches. In assigning ministers to parishes, it rewards some with prominent pulpits and punishes others with posts of low prestige or little promise. However exalted the moral virtue the minister expounds, the hierarchy does not wish him to damn his listeners to hell—unless somehow he gets them back in time to attend service next Sunday. Promotions for him are determined far less by the number of times he defends unpopular causes, however virtuous their merit, than by the state of the physical plant and the state of the coffer.

Now it is especially commendable if the minister can defend the cause and state the imperative with such tact or imprint that cleavages are not opened or loyalties alienated. If, however, the moral imperative and church cohesion are mutually incompatible, there is little doubt that the church superiors favor the latter. One administrator told two of his ministers, "It's o.k. to be liberal, boys; just don't stick your neck out." Indeed, ecclesiastical officials advised younger ministers, systematically, to "go slow," reminding them of the possibility of permanent damage to the church through rash action.

Under these circumstances pressure from the national church to take an advanced position on racial matters loses much· of its force. The minister is rewarded *only* if his efforts do not endanger the membership of the church: "Don't lose your congregation." Similarly, the prospect of an unfavorable response from his congregation protects him from the (possibly liberal) church hierarchy; he need only point to what happened to Pastor X, who did not heed the rumblings in his congregation. The higher officials, themselves keenly aware of local values and customs, will understand. And his fellow ministers, too, are, after all, in the same boat. They give him sympathy, not censure, if he says, "My hands are tied." An informal rationale develops that reassures the pastor: "These things take time," "You can't change people overnight," "You can't talk to people when they won't listen." There is strong sympathy for the forthright pastor who is in real trouble, but he is looked on as an object lesson. Thus the ministers reinforce each other in inaction, despite their common antipathy to segregation.

## The Self-Reference System

. . . It is obvious that the actor has the power of self-sanction, through guilt. A threatening sense of unworthiness, of inadequacy in God's sight, cannot be taken lightly. Similarly, to grant one's self the biblical commendation "Well done" is a significant reward. We have said that the self is an influence favoring action in support of desegregation. Can the inactive integrationist, then, either avoid or control the sense of guilt? . . .

[F]our circumstances—all of which permit of generalization to other cases— appear at least partially to prevent the sense of guilt. These include major characteristics of the ministerial role, several ministerial values and "working propositions," certain techniques for communicating without explicit commitment, and the gratifying reactions of extreme opposition forces.

## The Role Structure

The church, as an institutional structure, sets criteria by which the minister may assess his management of the religious enterprise; it does *not* offer criteria by which to evaluate his stand on controversial issues. This encourages, even compels, the minister to base his self-image, hence his sense of worth or unworth, on his success in managing his church. Thus, if church members do not share his goals, three types of institutionalized responsibilities restrain him in reform.

In the first place, the minister is required to be a cohesive force, to "maintain a fellowship in peace, harmony, and Christian love," rather than to promote dissension. Thus some ministers prayed during the Columbus Day services that members "carry no opinion to the point of disrupting the Christian fellowship."

Second, he is expected to show a progressive increase in the membership of his church. Pro-integration activity, lacking mass support, is likely to drive members to other churches.

Finally, his task is to encourage maximum annual giving and to plan for the improvement and expansion of the plant. It is hardly surprising that several inactive integrationists who were engaged in vital fund-raising campaigns shrank from action that might endanger their success.

## Working Propositions

The minister makes certain assumptions about his work that reduce the likelihood of guilt when he does not defend moral convictions that his members reject. He is, first, a devotee of education, by which he means the gradual growth and development of spiritual assets—in contrast to his counterpart of an earlier period, who was more likely to believe in sudden change through conversion. He also believes that communication with the sinner must be preserved at all costs ("You can't teach those you can't reach") and for long enough to effect gradual change in attitude and behavior. A crisis, when feelings run high, is not the time to risk alienating those one wishes to change. For example, Pastor X acted decisively but, in so doing, damaged or lost his pastorate: "Look at him; he can't do any good now."

## Communication Techniques

The minister may avoid committing himself unequivocally.[2] Some use the "every man a priest" technique, for example, the stating of his own opinion while expressing tolerance for contradictory ones and reminding his listeners that their access to God's truth is equal with his. Others use the "deeper issues" approach; generalities such as the brotherhood of man, brotherly love, humility, and universal justice are discussed without specific reference to the race issue, in the hope that the listener may make the association himself. Still another course is to remind listeners that "God is watching," that the question of race has religious significance and therefore they should "act like Christians." There is also the method of deriding the avowed segregationists without supporting their opposites. The "exaggerated southerner" technique, which may be supplementary to any of the others, involves a heavy southern drawl and, where possible, reference to an aristocratic line of planter descent.

These techniques do not demand belief in integration as a Christian imperative. Further, except for the "every man a priest" technique, they do not commit the speaker to integrationist goals as religious values; the listener may make applications as he chooses. The speaker, on the other hand, can assure himself that the connections are there to be made; he supplies, as it were, a do-it-yourself moral kit.

## Reaction of the Opposition

The ministerial body in Little Rock, except for pastors to dissident fundamentalist sects, is defined by agitated segregationists as a bunch of "race-mixers" and "nigger-lovers." For example, the charge was made that the peace prayers were intended to "further integration under a hypocritical veneer of prayer" and that the sect pastors sponsored prayers for segregation "to show that not all of the city's ministers believe in mixing the races." . . .

[2] For a full description and illustration of such techniques as used in Little Rock see our *Christians in Racial Crisis: A Study of Little Rock's Ministers* (Washington, D.C.: Public Affairs Press, 1959).

The effect of opposition by segregation extremists was to convince certain inactive integrationists that indeed they *had* been courageous and forthright. The minister, having actually appropriated the opposition's evaluation of his behavior, reversing its affective tone found the reassurance he needed that his personal convictions had been adequately and forcefully expressed.

Were the force of the membership reference system not what it is, the professional reference system and the self-reference system would supply support to integration that was not limited to "law and order" appeals and the denunciation of violence. However, since "Don't lose your congregation" is itself a strong professional and personal demand, the force of the PRS is neutralized, and the pressure from the SRS becomes confused and conflicting. Inaction is a typical response to conflicting pressures within both the internal and the external system[s].

It is not surprising, then, that most Little Rock ministers have been far less active and vocal in the racial crisis than the policies of their national church bodies and their sense of identification with them, as well as their own value systems, would lead one to expect. Rather, what is surprising is that a small number continued to express vigorously the moral imperative as they saw it, in the face of congregational disaffection, threatened reprisal, and the lukewarm support or quiet discouragement of their superiors and peers.

# 27

# Intergroup Relations vs. Prejudice: Pertinent Theory for the Study of Social Change

*ARNOLD M. ROSE*

The usual difference between sociologists and social psychologists in the study of race relations has been that the sociologist studies typical behavior patterns—often those of "discrimination" or "accommodation"—whereas the social psychologist studies attitudes and opinions called "prejudice" and "stereotyping," although, of course, there has never been a sharp division of labor. In recent years, there has been a tendency for these two interests to come together; both groups have come to assume that prejudice underlies discriminations, in the sense of the former being a cause of the latter. On the other hand certain authors—Merton (5) and Simpson and Yinger (6), for example—have pointed out that under certain conditions prejudice and discrimination can vary independently. We shall go further and state that it may be desirable to assume that patterns of intergroup relations (including mainly discrimination and segregation) are quite distinct from attitudes of prejudice in that each has a separate and distinct history, cause, and process of change. In other words, from a heuristic standpoint it may be desirable to assume that patterns of intergroup relations, on the one hand, and attitudes of prejudice and stereotyping, on the other hand,

Abridged from *Social Problems* 4 (1957): 173–176, by permission of *Social Problems* and the Society for the Study of Social Problems.

are fairly unrelated phenomena although they have reciprocal influences on each other, as they also have in relation to seemingly extraneous phenomena, such as anxiety levels or class. Perhaps we should have been aware all along that attitudes and behaviors have an independent existence in the same individuals: there is the challenging study by La Piere in 1934 (3) . . . Now there are several public opinion polls showing overwhelming proportions of various local populations against desegregation, and yet in many of the communities sampled, desegregation has proceeded apace without incident.

Let us first define terms. Race relations have to do with behavior patterns that occur in social systems—such as the caste system—which have their own historical development in the culture of a given society. Stereotyping is a universal mental tendency to subsume a large and complex category of phenomena in terms of a relatively few observations generalized to the whole category. Prejudice is a negative or positive attitude, often irrational and emotional in character, toward the stereotyped perception of a category of phenomena. Prejudice seems to take an especially virulent form when its object is an ethnic category of people. . . .

Like all social systems, those affecting race relations are traditional culture patterns which are learned and adopted by new members of the society while they are becoming socialized in it. They define behavior and give it direction. They seem very stable and entirely "natural," but of course they have an origin, are subject to continual change as a result of deliberate or impersonal social forces, and are capable of disappearing entirely. Prejudice can be a mere rationalization of these social systems, but in a more significant psychological sense . . . it is a product of individual experience and development. A whole gamut of studies have established that prejudice is an individual reaction to certain childhood and adult experiences, especially frustrations and restrictions, that are usually unrelated to people of other races. (2) These unpleasant experiences produce a certain kind of personality, which tends to react toward its environment in a certain way, usually a combination of outward conformity and inward hostility. The outward conformity may tend to support with special vigor the established system of race relations, and the inward hostility may provide a special sharpness to a system that requires harsh interpersonal relations between members of two different ethnic groups. But this personality type—the "authoritarian personality" . . . has to manifest itself in this way whether there is another ethnic group around or not. . . . Adelson and Sullivan (1) have shown that persons scoring highest on the California prejudice scale were also found to score the highest on a misanthropy scale. It seems that the "authoritarian personality" hates not only Negroes, Jews, Orientals, and so on, but tends to hate everyone. . . .

There are, of course, alternative theories of prejudice, but they all have reference to individual psychological mechanisms. Because of this feature, I have come gradually to the opinion that race prejudice, as it has been conceptualized and studied by contemporary social psychologists, has little to do with patterns of intergroup relations in our society. The typical Southern system of intergroup relations—although it has some regional variations—is that which sociologists call "caste," or "no social equality." The typical Northern system—again with variations—is that of avoiding and ignoring the existence of Negroes. There is no evidence that the "authoritarian personality" or frustration-aggression or scapegoating, or any known source of "prejudice" in the psychological sense, is any more prevalent in the South than in the North. Yet there is a world of difference in intergroup relations as far as Negroes and whites are concerned.

Since 1940 intergroup relations in the United States have drastically changed. The key values of the systems underlying them have greatly weakened. Many white Southerners are willing to treat Negroes as equals under certain circumstances and many white Northerners have become aware of Negroes in their midst (and find it neither possible nor desirable to exclude them from their group activities). If present trends continue, the two typical systems of Negro-white relationships will disappear within a generation or two (although some of the slower moving effects will remain for centuries, such as tending to marry within the groups, weak traditions of Negroes in business, etc.). But there is little in the American way of life to diminish, at a corresponding rate, frustration and the "authoritarian personality." Prejudice will remain at approximately its present level of virulence, although it seems likely to have to find other objects.

The conditions which led to the development of the caste system in the 19th century are no longer with us. The prosperity and political power of the South are no longer based on a large mass of cheap, unskilled labor engaged in the extremely unpleasant task of cotton growing. New forces have arisen which make the caste system increasingly less desirable and useful to the dominant white group in the South or any other section of the country: these include industrialization and automation, the leadership of the United States in the affairs of the free Western world, rising educational levels among both whites and Negroes, changed patterns of roles between the sexes among whites, and so on. These changes—both negative and positive—have made a mere hollow shell of tradition. The leaders of our nation . . . have become at least vaguely aware of these changes, and have contributed to the dismantling of the elaborate caste system. Prejudice, stereotyping, and other attitudes arising from an authoritarian upbringing, frustration, free-floating anxiety, and so on, are undoubtedly tending to buttress the shell of caste that remains. But the latter attitudes are seemingly not declining as the walls come tumbling down; rather, they are being transferred to new objects and they have new manifestations. Some people, especially in the Deep South, are keeping their authoritarian attitudes and fears focused on changes in race relations, but these seem to be a minority even within the South. In a border city like Kansas City, Martin Loeb tells us, "when the law, either economic or constitutional, is firmly laid down they go along with it almost gratefully." (4) It is important to know what changes of attitudes and other psychological adjustments are accompanying desegregation. This is useful so that anxieties can be reduced, and satisfaction increased. But it does not seem to be important for understanding the broad process of social change, or for engaging in social action to effect change. No study of prejudice, using any definition or any theory, helps us much in understanding or predicting what is going on in the desegregation process today. The explanation is apparently to be looked for in terms of legal, economic, political, and social structural forces.

Thus, prejudice has little to do with intergroup relations. They have to fit into each other at a given period of history, because some of the same people carry them both. But the laws of change—of origin, development and decay— which govern one are independent of those governing the other. One is socio-genic and the other psychogenic, and while they may both inhabit the same individual at a given time, they also may not. The study of their interrelation-ships is interesting, but the study of each one separately is much more important for the understanding and prediction of human behavior. Both are worthy of study in their own right. . . .

# References

1. Adelson, Joseph, and Patrick L. Sullivan, "Ethnocentrism and Misanthropy," *American Psychologist, 7* (July, 1952), 330.
2. Allport, Gordon W., *The Nature of Prejudice* (Cambridge, Mass.: Addison-Wesley, 1954).
3. La Piere, Richard T., "Attitudes versus Actions," *Social Forces, 13* (1934), 230–237. (Selection 16 in this volume.)
4. Loeb, Martin B., "Kansas City Does Its Duty," *Social Problems, 4* (1957): 161–165.
5. Merton, Robert K., "Discrimination and the American Creed," in Robert M. MacIver (ed.), *Discrimination and National Welfare* (New York: Harper, 1949).
6. Simpson, George E., and J. M. Yinger, *Racial and Cultural Minorities* (New York: Harper, 1953).

# 28

# The Adjustment of Southern White Migrants to Northern Urban Norms

*LEWIS M. KILLIAN*

. . . During the lush years of high industrial productivity, which began about 1940, there has been a fairly steady flow of workers from the rural South to the industrial centers of the North, such as Chicago and Detroit. Between 1947 and 1949 the writer studied certain aspects of the adjustment of a group of rural, southern, white laborers to life in the Near West Side of Chicago. The central questions in this research were: 1) Do these native white migrants come to constitute, to any extent, a distinct sub-group in the area of settlement in Chicago? and 2) To what extent, and in what ways, are they able to resolve the conflict between their "southern" attitudes towards Negroes and northern, urban norms and patterns of Negro-white relations?

During the period of field research, 150 southern white migrants were interviewed and the actual behavior of these and many other southern whites was observed. Non-southerners and Negroes who were part of the social world of the migrants, including plant managers, foremen, policemen, teachers, bartenders, and other workers, were also interviewed.

The southern whites were members of many small "clusters" of migrants con-

Reprinted, abridged, from *Social Forces 32* (October 1953): 66–69. Copyright © The University of North Carolina Press.

centrated in an ethnically heterogeneous portion of the Near West Side. The majority of them came from farms and small towns in the South Central States, especially northwestern Tennessee. Although these people were known as "hill-billies" in Chicago, few of them came from mountainous areas and they regarded the name as a misnomer.

The pattern of settlement of the southern whites suggested that they constituted, to some extent, a definite sub-group in the population of the area. Ecological factors partially accounted for their concentration. The Near West Side is an area characterized by the availability of cheap, furnished flats and easy access to industrial plants, and hence is attractive to in-migrants seeking "blue collar" work. In-group ties, carried over from southern communities of origin, also contributed to the development of spatial concentration, however ...

The fact that the somewhat derogatory and often much-resented group label, "hillbilly," was applied to the migrants also pointed to their existence as a distinct group, even as a quasiminority. It was found that a vague, but recognizable, stereotype of the southern white migrant was held by many non-southerners, and that the so-called "hillbillies" were regarded as a distinct, cohesive, ethnic group. While little hostility toward them was discovered, they were generally regarded by non-southern whites as a culturally inferior group. This was especially true in the case of some employers who consciously avoided hiring "hillbillies."

In turn, the southern whites themselves exhibited definite group consciousness. This group consciousness was manifest not only in verbalizations but in the selection of associates. Patronage of the "hillbilly tavern," a gathering place for southern whites during hours of leisure, constituted a form of voluntary segregation.

Of most significance in the context of reference group theory was the "hillbillies'" conception of their own status in the Near West Side. This conception clearly reflected the subjects' comparison of their position in Chicago with the one which they had enjoyed in the South.

Contrary to many stereotyped conceptions of the southern rural migrant, these people were not indigent "po' white trash." They defined themselves, and were regarded in their home communities, as respectable, honest, "working class people." More important, they were members of the dominant ethnic group in a system organized along one axis—white and Negro. Finally, they were established members of small, relatively friendly and intimate communities.

In Chicago, they found themselves only one group in a mosaic of diverse ethnic groups—Old Americans, Irish, Italians, Mexicans, and Negroes. The fact that they were white, native-born, and Protestant lost some of its prestige value in an area dominated culturally and politically by Italian-Americans, most of them Catholic and many of them foreign-born. Negroes, while subject to many subtle forms of discrimination in Chicago, still possessed far more freedom and power than they could enjoy in the rural South. Comparing their position *vis-à-vis* "foreigners" and Negroes in Chicago and in the South, the southern whites felt a relative loss of status which intensified their defensive group consciousness.

The impersonality and anonymity of many types of social relationships in the northern city stood in sharp contrast to the friendly intimacy of the small southern town. As a result, the *laissez-faire* attitude of the city folk was interpreted by the "hillbillies" as evidence of hostility. The term "hillbilly," even when used in jest, was often perceived as a derogatory group label, a slur. Individual altercations between southerners and members of other ethnic groups were frequently perceived as intergroup conflicts. To the feeling that they, as southern whites, were a disadvantaged group was thus added the belief that they were a disliked group. This was true in spite of the fact that only slight hostility to the southern whites as a group was discovered even among the Italians, identified by the "hillbillies" as their worst enemies.

This defensive group consciousness did not, however, result in the development of in-group organization of a formal type. But the "hillbillies," preoccupied with making a living, regarding the South as home, and suspicious of non-southerners, constituted a marginal and unstable element in the institutions and associations of the area. The city church did not perform the social function of community integration for them that the rural church did, and they tended to develop a "vacation attitude" towards church participation. Church leaders who expected these white Protestants to be a source of new strength for their churches were disappointed and bewildered by the failure of the southern whites to continue their church participation after migration. In the schools, the "hillbilly" children constituted an identifiable group but presented no special problems other than that of mobility. The reputation of the "hillbillies" for instability, more than for lack of education or industrial experience, caused them to be regarded by employers as a marginal group of laborers who were conveniently available when there was a shortage of other labor, but who were not as desirable as local workers. On the other hand, the defensive group consciousness of the southerners, and their desire to feel superior to "foreign" workers, combined perhaps with a suspicion that they did not occupy a superior status, led them to create an entirely unrealistic picture of their position in industry. Rather than recognizing their marginal position they conceived of themselves as a highly desirable and superior type of labor, and prided themselves on the very traits of mobility and independence which employers found most objectionable.

Thus it may be said that the southern whites felt themselves to be in, but not of, the Near West Side community. The southern community of origin continued to be home and its norms were still praised as the best, even when they could not be followed. Yet, despite this transient psychology and the persistent loyalty to the home community, few "hillbillies" actually returned to the South to stay; instead, irregular going back and forth, regulated largely by employment opportunities in Chicago, was the pattern. Detached from their native milieu but imperfectly assimilated in their new membership groups, these people were truly marginal.

The relationship of the southern whites to Negroes in Chicago revealed not only the persistence of old group norms but the development of new patterns of behavior in response to new situations. The "hillbillies" constantly praised the southern pattern of racial segregation and deplored the fact that Negroes were "taking over Chicago." In most of their behavior, however, they made a peaceful, if reluctant, accommodation to northern urban patterns.

This is not to imply, however, that this accommodation necessarily involved a reduction of prejudice. It involved, instead, substitution of the private, informal, and indirect techniques of discrimination, characteristic of race relations in the North, for the public, formal and direct manifestations of prejudice found in the South. The southern white who moves to the northern city does not move from a prejudiced society to an unprejudiced society; rather, he moves from one pattern of discrimination into another. Furthermore, in the transition from one milieu to another he becomes a different person. . . .

Because of the existence of informal but effective techniques of segregation in Chicago, the problem of adjusting to the new pattern of race relations was alleviated for the southerners. Yet the great majority of them still felt that the northern pattern was one of the features of living in Chicago which they disliked the most. There were still many situations in which segregation and white supremacy could not be maintained. In such situations the "hillbillies" usually acquiesced, although not without some reluctance. The reasons for this accommodation show clearly the conflict of group norms which confronts the migrant.

A common explanation of the fact that the southern white could not act towards the Negro in Chicago as he did in the South was that different customs prevailed in the North and that they could not be changed by the southern white. This did not mean that the "hillbillies" had come to like the customs, or that they would modify their behavior in the South when they returned. But that they did accept the northern way is shown in statements such as the following one:

One thing I don't like about Chicago is the colored. I don't want to do anything mean to them, but I want to be able to let them alone. But you can't do that up here. When you're in Rome you have to do as the Romans do. I've kind of got used to sitting next to 'em and eating in restaurants with 'em, but I don't like it. I wouldn't expect to do it in the South, but up here you have to.

There was also the feeling that Chicago was not "our city" and that it was not incumbent upon the individual southerner to support and enforce an etiquette of race relations. A woman who had lived in Chicago for twenty years said:

There's nothing you can do about the way the niggers are up here. We're up here in their country and we can't do anything. We have to do what these people up here do, even if we don't like it.

Moreover, the "hillbillies" were quick to perceive the different legal status of the Negro in Chicago and in the South. Many things which they noted were interpreted as evidence that the Negro had equal rights with the white man, or that he even had a preferred status before the law, such as the fact that police protection was sometimes afforded Negroes moving into white neighborhoods. Hence fear of running afoul of the law was the principal deterrent to starting trouble with Negroes.

Another deterrent to forthright adoption of a southern attitude towards Negroes was fear of physical retaliation. The Negro population of Chicago is concentrated in large population aggregates massed in "Black ghettoes." Many Negroes in Chicago will protest assertions of white supremacy, sometimes with violence. As a result, the "hillbillies" not only felt that it was unsafe to assert their ideas of superiority; some felt insecure in the presence of large numbers of Negroes.

Part of the feeling of lack of power to control the Negroes was based on the southerners' perception of the impersonality and heterogeneity of the white population and of the lack of consensus regarding "the Negro's place." These factors are made explicit in the following statement:

> I can't see that you can do anything about the niggers up here. You see, in the South you can count on collaboration. You know that other people feel like you do, and if you start anything you can count on them. But up here you can't be sure that people will back you up, and you might even get hurt if you started something.

While the southern whites protested against the necessary compromises with southern norms, the changes in overt behavior were sometimes accompanied by changes in attitude. These changes were slight, it is true, and did not indicate a general reorientation towards Negroes. But they did occur, as is shown in these somewhat paradoxical remarks:

> There's niggers living in the house with us now—we're the only white family there. The landlady has tried to get us out, but she ain't give us no eviction notice and I ain't fixing to move. She wants to put niggers in my place, but my money is just as good as theirs. I can't find me another place to live. But it ain't so bad. Some of those niggers are better than some of the white people that used to live there. Hell, I got out my knife and started to kill the first one that moved in there, but then I found out he was a nigger I knew. He's a good southern nigger and he stays in his place. You know, in the South we make 'em stay in their place.

It is significant that such changes were, however, almost always specific to a particular situation, or area of contact, and did not lead directly to changes in attitudes concerning contact with Negroes in other situations. 18 southern whites out of the 150 interviewed were actually living in close physical proximity to Negroes—three of them living in the same house with them. Yet 15 of the 18 still tried to avoid contact with Negroes in at least one other type of situation—work, school, or in the "hillbilly taverns." The writer knew many "hillbilly" men who were regular patrons of a "hillbilly tavern" in which a Negro was more likely to be beaten up than served, but who regularly ate lunch in a non-segregated restaurant next door.

In summary: lacking leadership, organization, and consensus in an area where life is highly impersonal and individualistic, the southerners saw no effective way of giving overt expression to their dissatisfaction with the pattern of race relations. The absence of legal sanctions for segregation and other assertions of white supremacy, and an exaggerated conception of Negro strength and unity over against white "weakness" and disunity, constituted powerful deterrents to overt and aggressive action in distasteful situations. While there were some indications of a slight shift of attitudes in the direction of greater friendliness towards Negroes in specific situations, this did not constitute a general reorientation towards Negroes as a group, nor were these new attitudes necessarily carried over into other situations of contact. Necessary, but distasteful, compromises with the cherished reference group norms were usually rationalized with the idea, "Chicago is not our home—when in Rome we must do as the Romans do."

Yet we may suspect that, in spite of themselves, the "hillbillies" were gradually developing new reference groups as they conformed more and more to northern urban patterns of behavior. An unconscious revelation of this process may be seen in the rather amusing comment of a southern woman:

> You know, the last time I was in Tennessee I went to a restaurant. They served colored, but they made 'em go in the back door and eat in the kitchen. I said to my husband, "That sure does look funny after you've lived in Chicago, doesn't it?"

# 29

# The Social-Distance Pyramid: Relationships Between Caste and Class

*FRANK R. WESTIE* and *MARGARET L. WESTIE*

This article presents findings and interpretations of two studies in a larger research program designed to establish empirical relationships between social class and prejudice. Its primary purpose is to narrow the extremely broad range of theoretical propositions concerning class and prejudice.

In the first study, persons in three randomly drawn samples of the Indianapolis population from each of three socioeconomic levels were interviewed regarding the degree of social distance they would maintain between themselves and Negroes [of] varying status in the Negro community. In the second study, Negroes of various socioeconomic status were interviewed regarding the distance they would prefer between themselves and whites in various positions in the white community.

The diagram in Figure 1, a "social-distance pyramid," is reminiscent of diagrams constructed by W. L. Warner, Gunnar Myrdal, and others to illustrate the

Abridged from *American Journal of Sociology 63* (1958): 190–196. Used by permission of The University of Chicago Press. © 1958 by The University of Chicago. All rights reserved.

**FIGURE 1.** Social-Distance Measures Derived Through Analysis of Scale Responses of Whites to Negroes (*left-hand side of diagram*) and Negroes to Whites (*right-hand side of diagram*)*

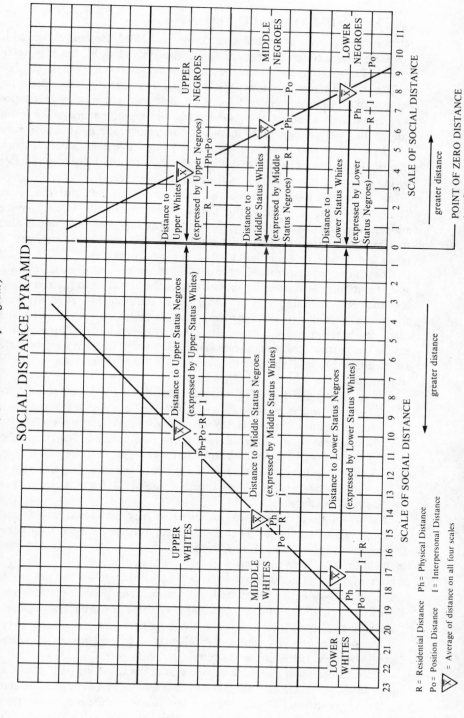

R = Residential Distance   Ph = Physical Distance

Po = Position Distance   I = Interpersonal Distance

⧌X⧍ = Average of distance on all four scales

relationship between caste and class in America. The diagram presented here, however, differs from the previous diagrams of this kind, in that it represents a system of relationships empirically established rather than hypothesized.

The social-distance pyramid depicts the degree of social distance preferred by persons of three socioeconomic levels of their own community in relation to persons on approximately the same level in another community. The left-hand side of the pyramid represents the white community; the right hand represents the Negro community. They are separated by the "caste line," which is an extension of the "point of zero distance" on the scale of social distance represented by the graduated line which forms the base of the pyramid.

As one moves away from the caste line, to right or left, distance increases. The inverted triangles representing the particular classes within each community are placed either closer or farther from the caste line according to the distance that respondents of the particular status preferred to maintain between themselves and persons on equivalent levels in the racial outgroup.

The chart was constructed by analyzing the responses of persons of a given socioeconomic status category on one side of the caste line to persons of equivalent socioeconomic status on the other side of the caste line. Thus, for example, the arrow extending to the right from the high-status whites represents the distance the latter preferred to maintain between themselves and upper-status Negroes. Each arrow represents the distance that persons of a given status preferred to maintain between themselves and those of the same status in the racial outgroup.

The caste line and the point of zero social distance are equated here because it follows that where there is no social distance between Negro and white the caste line ceases to exist. When a Negro is confronted by the caste line, he is in reality up against situations which require the maintenance of certain traditional social distances between Negroes and whites. Perhaps the system is most threatened in the minds of whites when the distance between Negroes and whites approaches the zero point. When a person socially defined as Negro "passes," he "jumps the caste line." . . .

The relationships represented in Figure 1 may be summarized as follows: (1) upper-status whites would maintain least distance between themselves and high-status Negroes, while, reciprocally, high-status Negroes would maintain least distance between themselves and whites of similar position; (2) lower-status whites would maintain greatest distance between themselves and Negroes of low status, while Negroes of lower status would maintain greatest distance between themselves and whites of low status; (3) in all three of the relationships between "equivalent" classes, there is a social distance differential, i.e., at any given level the distance preferred by whites from Negroes is greater than that preferred by Negroes between themselves and whites. . . .

The relationship of each class on one side of the caste line to all classes on the opposite side . . . may be summarized as follows: (1) The higher the status of the Negro as attitude-object, the less the distance preferred by whites of all classes. Similarly, the higher the status of the white as attitude-object, the less the distance preferred by Negroes of all classes. (2) The higher the socioeconomic status of the responding white, the greater the alteration of response with variations in the status of the Negro. Similarly, the higher the status of the responding Negro, the greater the alteration of response with variations in the status of the white as attitude-object. . . .

Possible interpretations, worthy of further research, are grouped under four headings under which the larger portion of them conveniently falls.

## Psychological Insecurity

The upper-class persons feel secure because they are probably less recently mobile and, being at the top, are not likely to strive as hard as those in the intermediary ranks. In their greater security they have less need to use the Negro as a scapegoat to justify their social and economic failures; they do not need a negatively valued Negro group to enhance their own status; and, being less likely to be frustrated in their designs for living (largely status-related in America), they do not need the Negro as an object of aggression. Moreover, whatever their aggressions, if any, they can be vented upon persons of lower status within the majority group.

Ambiguity enters the picture, however, when certain related, though contradictory, interpretations are considered: It may be that the lower-class person, because he is relatively the *least* mobile in the local community, has *greater* security, not less, as to class status than have persons of high status. The lower-class person need have no fear of slipping down the ladder, for, being on the bottom rung, he has no place to fall. Thus it is the lower-class person who should be *least* prejudiced if status insecurity is the explanation. Moreover, the middle class is less prejudiced than the lower class, despite a wealth of evidence that points to the middle class as the most mobile and the most insecure. Furthermore, if prejudice is to be "explained" in terms of psychological insecurity, then there is reason to believe that upper-class Negroes should be *more* prejudiced against whites, not less, than persons on lower levels of the Negro community. It may very well be true, as is often suspected, that persons on the upper level of the Negro community are most frustrated in their designs for living. The upper-class Negro's success in climbing the socioeconomic ladder is compromised and seriously limited by the caste line. The arbitrary and absolute nature of the dictum that "a Negro is a Negro regardless of his individual accomplishments" is probably better and more bitterly known to upper-class Negroes than to any others. Yet these are the people who manifest the least degree of social distance of all groups in the social-distance pyramid. One might argue that their preference for less social distance is simply the next step in their social mobility. It happens, however, that they also manifest less prejudice, as indicated by other measures. Moreover, they allege that they would insist on less distance between themselves and lower-class whites as well as between themselves and more highly placed whites than does any other Negro group.

## Education

According to these interpretations, the upper-class person is better educated than those below him, and education is conducive to a more liberal outlook in general. Moreover, the educated are less likely to indorse the myths that sustain the prevailing system of race relations. In the case of the attitudes of Negroes whose status is high in the Negro community, the argument of education may take the following form: Education is one of the most important criteria of class in the Negro community; thus upper-class Negroes are conspicuously better educated than Negroes below them. Educated Negroes are aware of the Negro's stake in being free of prejudice. . . .

## Conformity

Some sociological theories suggest that the upper class expects greater conformity from its members than does the lower class to certain social norms significant for American race relations. If so, then (a) the middle- or upper-class person is more thoroughly indoctrinated with the value system implied by the term the "American Creed" and has internalized these values to a greater extent than has the lower, and (b) whether or not he has internalized these to an appreciable extent, he at least is more likely than the lower-class person to create that impression, because (c) the upper class has a more rigid system of controls over the individual (one of the most important of which is withdrawal of status) to guarantee conformity.

But the question soon comes to mind: Doesn't the upper class insist on and guarantee conformity to the social norms which require maintenance of social distance between Negroes and whites? Indeed, to fail to maintain distance might be regarded as disreputable, and this in a milieu where respectability is a primary value. Actually, persons on virtually all levels above the very lowest probably feel constrained to conform at least ostensibly to the egalitarian values of the "American Creed" and simultaneously to the discriminatory norms in the relations between whites and Negroes. One project in the present program is designed precisely to test conformity. Our pretest findings suggest that the classes *do* differ in the degree to which the general values subsumed under the "American Creed" are consciously verbalized and also in the degree to which they recognize the conflict between their expressed ideology and their discriminatory attitudes.

Conformity as an interpretation, if valid, would explain why the lower-class person expresses more prejudice than those above him. It does nothing, however, toward accounting for the difference in prejudice between persons of highest status and those of intermediary position. Assuming the middle-class person to be the greatest conformist, it is quite possible that his intermediary opinions result from his unwillingness, on the one hand, to express his prejudices as frankly as does the lower-class person (hence he gets a lower prejudice score than does the lower-class person), while, on the other hand, he is unwilling, also because of his conformism, to deviate from the path of respectability when it comes to indorsing social-distance items that represent extreme departures from the status quo. In the pretest of a study on conflict in values we found many lower-class persons who "don't want to have *anything* to do with 'em" (Negroes), while we often find middle-class persons who would be willing to have a Negro as a "close personal friend" but who, "of course," would not want to have Negroes "live in my neighborhood." It may be this kind of inconsistency that puts the middle-class person "in the middle" as to prejudice.

## Competition

Prejudice may be seen as a function of competition for status-related values, both economic and non-economic, both types of which are defined in the society as unable to be shared. Competition is most intense at the lower levels of both the white and the Negro hierarchy because the scarcity of these values is most acute here and competition between Negroes and whites is most direct. In Indianapolis, for example, Negroes and whites often compete for the same jobs, the same neighborhoods, the same houses, and use of the same public facilities. Face-to-face contacts on the lower level take place under circumstances conducive to definitions of one another as competitors.

If the foregoing interpretations of lower-class attitudes are to any extent correct, it follows that the upper classes of both white and Negro communities are less prejudiced against one another than are those of the lower class because competition is less intense, the scarcity and the objects of competition being less and competition, if it prevails at all, being highly indirect. Actually, white and Negro white-collar workers, businessmen, and professional persons are only rarely in competition with one another. Negroes rarely occupy white-collar positions in white business enterprises, although they do, of course, occupy such positions in larger Negro businesses. White and Negro businessmen typically do not compete for the same customers.

The general empirical relationship . . . that social distance decreases as the status of the attitude-object increases is also consistent with the interpretations based on competition. As the status of the Negro as attitude-object increases, he is further removed from competition with all categories of whites. This is especially true, however, of the relationship between lower-class whites and Negroes.

We are not sure which of these interpretations is correct, nor have we any idea how the ability to explain one compares with that of another. Moreover, we have no idea how particular interpretive variables (if valid) interact with other variables to produce the empirical outcome described by the pyramid. . . . No one of these interpretations or sets of interpretations can adequately explain all the findings.

# 30

# The Dynamics of Racial Prejudice: An Ideal-Type Dichotomy

PIERRE L. VAN DEN BERGHE

This paper presents a conceptualization of racial prejudice within the framework of an ideal-type dichotomy.

For our purposes a "race" is a human grouping which is *culturally* defined in a given society. This grouping is considered different from other groupings similarly defined by virtue of innate and visible physical characteristics. In the extreme case these groupings are considered, rightly or wrongly, as biologically separate subgroups. Thus the same terms, such as "Negro" or "white," cover objectively dissimilar groupings in Brazil, the United States, and the Union of South Africa. It is not the anthropological distinction which is socially important but the cultural definition given in each society. . . .

"Racial prejudice" is a system of reciprocal relations of stereotypy, discrimination and segregation existing between human groupings which are considered as "races." Racial prejudice is a special case of prejudice which may assume many forms (cultural, ethnic, class, religious, etc.). Two or more forms of prejudice may, and often do, operate simultaneously.

Our thesis is that, historically, racial prejudice has polarized around two ideal types which we shall call for taxonomic purposes the "*paternalistic*" and the "*competitive*." Each type is characterized by a cluster of interrelated features.

Reprinted, abridged, from *Social Forces 37* (December 1958): 138-141. Copyright © The University of North Carolina Press.

## The Competitive Type: Its Characteristics

1. The racial majority enjoys the higher status. This majority is itself stratified into classes, and is divided within itself by many conflicts of interest. Only a small portion of that majority constitutes the power élite.

2. This type is found mostly in an urban and industrialized context. Its development is fostered by dynamic conditions with rapid change in technology, migrations, and fluctuations in the business cycle.

3. The interracial competition for jobs is acute since there is no rigid division of labor along racial lines. The educational and economic discrepancy between the racial groups is not clear-cut. The upper strata of the subjugated minority may exceed in education and wealth the lower strata of the dominant minority.

4. Miscegenation is severely disapproved of, or even condemned.

5. Prejudice is laden with sexual frustration and aggression. This aggression expresses itself through stereotypes with sexual content (reproaches of "immorality," lasciviousness, aggressivity, "perversion," etc.), and through overt or covert manifestations of sadism (rape, lynchings with mutilation, torture, castration, etc.). In the majority group, the most prejudiced individuals will exhibit the syndrome of the "Authoritarian Personality." . . . Frustration breeds competitive prejudice and the converse.[1]

6. Ideological conflict will prevail between prejudice values and the rest of the ideology, at least in a "Christian," "liberal," and "democratic" type of Western society. Attempts at solving this conflict will be made by a "schizophrenic" dissociation of the ideology into two discrete spheres of belief and behavior.[2]

7. The majority resorts to the predominant use of extra-legal or illegal sanctions against the minority. If *de facto* racial legislation exists, it will be based *de jure* on nonracial grounds of discrimination (property, literacy, and residential requirements for school attendance, voting, etc.).

8. Mutual antagonism, suspicion, and hatred prevail between the groups concerned. Periodical outbursts of violence such as pogroms, race riots, and lynchings will take place in the more extreme cases.

9. Racial roles are ill-defined and in a constant state of flux. Hence any interracial contact will be laden with constraint, self-consciousness, and emotional involvement.

From this sketchy characterization it can be seen that the competitive type of prejudice is highly maladjusting in any society. The amount of conflict is directly proportional to the intensity of competitive prejudice. Any alleviation of

---

[1] Cf. T. W. Adorno, Else Frenkel-Brunswik, Daniel J. Levinson, R. Newitt Sanford, *The Authoritarian Personality* (New York: Harper and Brothers, 1950), and Selection 23 in this volume.

[2] *Cf.* Gunnar Myrdal, *An American Dilemma: The Negro Problem and Modern Democracy* (New York: Harper and Brothers, 1944), pp. 21, 39, 84–89, 460, 614, 899.

prejudice will increase social cohesion, productivity, etc. The competitive type of prejudice operates at all levels of intensity, although in typical form the intensity is high. The latter increases more easily and rapidly than it diminishes, and it remains rarely constant. This type of prejudice goes through phases of increase and decrease, reaching a rapid climax (characterized by persecutions, pogroms, mass lynchings, etc.) and slowly receding. Aside from these cyclical trends provoked by accidental events such as a sensational murder or rape case, the level of intensity in competitive prejudice is in part a function of the degree of in-groupness or "corporativeness" of the minority. The two factors are directly proportional to one another. A minority cannot organize itself through collective bargaining, militant organizations and the like without increasing at the same time the amount of prejudice against itself. Conversely, with assimilation into the majority by intermixture and acculturation prejudice disappears.

Although this analysis is not limited to the Western World, the competitive type of prejudice is most characteristic of Western societies since the nineteenth century. Typical examples of this type of racial prejudice are the prejudice against Negroes in the United States since the Civil War, against Jews and Gypsies in Europe, against Chinese and Japanese in California, and against Negroes in the great industrial centers of Brazil. There have been prejudice and persecution of a competitive type long before the nineteenth century, but conflicts became more intense with the Industrial Revolution. Competition for jobs became more acute particularly in periods of depression in the business cycle. A highly diversified economy rendered obsolete and impractical a clear-cut division of labor along racial lines. Social mobility increased both vertically and horizontally. All these conditions of rapid change are favorable to a competitive type of prejudice.

## The Paternalistic Type: Its Characteristics

1. The racial minority enjoys the higher status. This minority is a well-integrated ruling class with a minimum of conflict and stratification within this minority. All or practically all adult males of the ruling minority occupy key positions of power in the social system. They all share a common economic interest in the exploitation of the majority.

2. The paternalistic type is found mostly in an agricultural or pastoral economy. The prototype is the servile plantation economy. Stable social conditions favor its development, and, conversely, a paternalistic type of prejudice leads to a static caste system.

3. The division of labor is along strict racial lines with all the menial tasks performed solely by the servile or quasi-servile majority. There is a wide gap between the racial groups in education, occupation, status, and living standards.

4. Miscegenation is widely tolerated for upper-group men with lower-group women. Interracial concubinage is often institutionalized.

5. Sexuality is much more latent than in the competitive type and assumes an altogether different form. . . .

6. Prejudice values are well integrated in the general ideology. Ideological conflicts are absent In the case of Western "liberal" societies, the patterns of prejudice are buttressed by an elaborate and self-consistent set of rationalizations: the "white man's burden," the "civilizing mission of the West," the "backwardness of the natives," the "Christianizing of the heathen," the myth of the "grown-up child," and many other variations on the same theme.

7. This type of prejudice is implemented by legal authority and sanctions. Slaves or "natives" have a special juridical status which discriminates against them but may also protect them against certain arbitrary actions. Their rights and duties are legally defined.

8. The subservient majority accepts its inferior status with relative complacency due to careful indoctrination and curtailment of education. The dominant minority exhibits an attitude of paternalism and "benevolent despotism," trying to maintain the majority in a state of perpetual dependency. Members of the majority are treated as children and expected to behave as such (docility, obedience, respect, irresponsibility). This complementary set of attitudes leads to a relatively peaceful symbiosis. Although unrest may take place, it takes the form of slave revolts, nationalistic movements or religious revivalism where the racial issue is absent or secondary. Pogroms, race riots, lynchings are unknown.

9. Racial roles are sharply defined. Everyone has a place in the system and "knows it."

In general, it may be said that the paternalistic type of prejudice is an adjusting force in the social system. This statement implies of course no value judgment as to the superiority of one type over the other. To the extent that the prejudice ideology is accepted and believed in, a peaceful and stable social order will be maintained. If the patterns of prejudice are undermined, the social structure will collapse. In this respect as in many others, the paternalistic type is the direct opposite of the competitive type.

The historical instances of the paternalistic type have been numerous and by no means confined to the Western World. It is typical of many kingdoms of East Africa where Hamitic peoples such as the Watuzis dominate over Bantu masses. Most colonizing nations, notably Britain, Belgium, France, the Netherlands, and Portugal, have adopted such methods of domination over their subjects in their oversea possessions. The caste system of India probably originated in racial prejudice of the Aryan conquerors against the indigenous Dravidian stock. The feudal systems of Japan and Western Europe show similar traits though we deal here with a class prejudice. The slave economies of the southern United States, the West Indies, and Brazil are typical instances.

The level of intensity at which paternalistic prejudice operates is relatively low; i.e., it does not entail a high level of emotional involvement. It breeds order rather than violence and passion. Furthermore, the level of intensity of prejudice remains constant in contrast to the sharp fluctuations of the competitive type.

If left to themselves without external interference, paternalistic societies show relative stability in contrast to competitive ones. On the other hand the monolithic inflexibility of paternalistic societies makes them highly vulnerable to adverse outside influences. The whole structure then collapses very quickly without the possibility of gradual adjustment which can be worked out in a competitive society. The social revolution brought about by the Civil War in the South of the United States, the present collapse of the European colonial system, and the disintegration of African feudal systems in contact with Western influences are only a few examples of such rapid collapse.

The two types of racial prejudice have certain features in common which justify their treatment as two varieties of the same phenomenon:

1. They both regulate the relationships between two or more corporate groups in which membership is defined on the basis of physically distinguishing characteristics.

2. Both types are based on the dogma of superiority of the dominant group. This alleged superiority may be intellectual, physical, cultural, religious, or "moral."

3. Both types promote the existence of a caste system with concomitant rules of endogamy, avoidance, and etiquette.

4. Both are conservative forces trying to maintain a racial *status-quo.*

5. In both types, the lower the socio-economic status of a member of the dominant group is, the more overt and intense his prejudice will be.

Many problems are left untouched by such a sketchy presentation. (1) The same society may shift from the one type of prejudice to the other as the Southern States of the Union did after the Civil War. (2) The two types of prejudice may coexist within the same country as in South Africa where the competitive type prevails in the large industrial centers (Durban, Johannesburg, Capetown), and the paternalistic type in the rural districts. A similar distinction can be made in Brazil between the traditional rural North and the modern industrial South (São Paulo, Santos, Rio de Janeiro).

In most cases more than two racial groups are present, thereby complicating the problem. Some societies are pyramidically stratified with each caste being more numerous than the next higher up, as in British East Africa (British, Indians, and Africans). . . .

We confined ourselves purposely to *racial* prejudice in order to define the problem more sharply. We believe, however, that our scheme of analysis can *mutatis mutandis* be applied to all kinds of prejudice. As we suggested above, the types apply to class prejudice. In a feudal society class prejudice tends to be paternalistic; in a modern industrial society it is competitive. Religious prejudice can assume both forms, although the militancy and mutual exclusiveness of religious doctrines usually makes religious prejudice competitive. Ethnic, cultural, linguistic prejudices likewise seem to polarize along the two pure types, each basis for prejudice bringing with it its modifications into the scheme.

The weaknesses inherent in the method of pure-type analysis are obvious. We think, however, that the method is scientifically useful if the pure-types conform to four criteria:

1. 'if they are exhaustive, i.e., if they leave no unanalyzable residual category;

2. if the characteristics of each type constitute a functional self-consistent pattern (internal consistency);

3. if the types differ from one another on the same dimensions. They can be direct opposites, "mirror images," or simply differ in relative amount on these dimensions;

4. if empirical systems approximate one of the types, i.e., polarize around these clusters of characteristics.

To the extent that these criteria are met, a pure-type analysis will systematize existing knowledge, point to functional interrelatedness of new variables, and, ideally, provide a base line from which departures can be measured. We believe that the above criteria are met in our dichotomy. . . .

# 31

# Power as a Primary Concept in the Study of Minorities

*R. A. SCHERMERHORN*

Park and Burgess properly insisted upon the reciprocal character of social interaction; from this position it is but a step to the use of sociological analysis so as
to do justice to both sides of an interaction without sufficient inquiry into the
equivalence or lack of equivalence on each side of the relation. The quest for objectivity has been met by focusing equal attention on each aspect of the reciprocal relation, and thus to bias sociological theory in favor of balance, equilibrium,
symmetry, and adjustment. By the very nature of their frame of reference, sociologists in the Park-Burgess tradition have centered attention on the regular,
constant, and equable features of society more than on the dynamic, unstable,
irregular or uneven ones.

This may help to explain why power analysis has been relatively neglected by
American sociologists in the past. There are signs, however, that point to an
increasing awareness of the importance of the power concept, and, more specifically, to a convergence of agreement on its significance for the study of minorities. The searching inquiry of Bierstedt into the theoretical implications of
power realities, and . . . the highly original work of Simon in a . . . more intensive
study of the scientific implications involved in power analysis [are examples] .[1]

[1] H. Simon, "Notes on the observation and measurement of political power," *Journal of
Politics 15* (November 1953): 500–516; R. Bierstedt, "An analysis of social power," *American Sociological Review, 15* (December 1950): 730–738.
Reprinted, abridged, from *Social Forces 35* (October 1956): 53–56. Copyright © The University of North Carolina Press.

Simon's contribution is to show that power, by its very nature is asymmetrical. For example, he points out that absolute dictatorial power is a kind of theoretical limit. In such a dictatorial idealtypical situation, the decision of A would determine that of B without feedback from B to A. Empirically, of course, some feedback is always present. But our insistence on interaction must not blind us to the fact that reciprocity is unequal and uneven. Action on one side of the equation is effective and decisive; on the other side it is resistive, perhaps, but it modifies the outcome very little. At the most it only qualifies the dominant action of the first party. Taking into account these considerations let us define power as *the asymmetrical relationship between two interacting parties in which a perceptible probability of decision resides in one of the two parties, even over the resistance of the other party.*

The terms "party" or "parties" signify either individuals or groups. "Probability" in the definition reminds the research-oriented scientist that potential measurability may be included in the concept of power. . . . Curiously enough, Bierstedt's description of force could serve well to exemplify what we have called "decision" in our definition. He states that it "means the reduction, or limitation, or closure, or even the total elimination of alternatives to the social action of one person or group by another person or group." . . . The expression "even over the resistance of the other party" is one dependent on Max Weber.[2] It simply restates the point above that power, as a constraining pressure, is often sufficient to overcome the countervailing resistance of any feedback.

A major postulate of the theory advanced here is that when contacts between two groups with different cultural lifelines become regular rather than occasional or intermittent, the resulting interaction crystallizes into a social structure reflecting the power differentials and the value congruence of the two social systems in tensional equilibrium. . . .

What is the significance of power relations to the minority situation? It is a twofold one. First, power relations furnish the chief agency through which minorities are differentiated. Second, power relations enable us to set up a typology of minorities in terms of their emergence.

Since power is of many types or dimensions, it may be suggested that the forms of power form a continuum with traditional values or norms at one end of the scale, and coercion at the other. The power of tradition is cultural, while, in a sense, that of coercion is extra-cultural, i.e., involving threat to biological necessities that are subcultural.

Power is regarded as a primary concept because it begins at the beginning. Power relations set the basic frame within which acculturation, discrimination, prejudice, etc. do or do not take place.

In setting forth a theory of this type, it is necessary to proceed through definite stages. At the outset it is important to review the contacts of whole social

---

[2] *From Max Weber,* Essays in Sociology, translated and edited with an introduction by H. H. Gerth and C. Wright Mills (New York: Oxford University Press, 1946), p. 180.

systems or cultures so as to discover the major types of power relations within which the limited forms existing in the United States may be observed as special cases, not as isolated types unrelated to other cultures. In such a review it is crucial to realize that equality of power between two parties is a rare and limiting case. From a purely formal consideration it may therefore be expected that one of the two parties will typically establish forms of superordinance over the other. A further consequence to be predicted is that power will tend toward the coercive end of the scale in these encounters, simply because value controls do not extend to the out-group.

It is hypothesized that the instability of the power situation sets in motion a trend toward equilibrium or resolution of the power clash in one of three forms: (1) extrusion, where the group with greater power eliminates the relatively powerless group from the field either by annihilation or by driving the group from a specified territory; (2) noncontiguous control, where the more powerful group maintains dominance of the other party at a distance (as in colonialism); or (3) incorporative control, where the superordinate group brings the subordinate party within its own geographical boundaries where day-to-day adjustment and a more efficient accommodative system are required. In general, the incorporative mode seems to be the dominant one in the United States, utilizing the techniques of conquest, slavery, or selective admission of immigrants. A testing of these categories with subsequent modification can then be obtained by the use of a research tool like that of the Human Relations Area Files.

A more difficult test of the theory will come in the attempt to outline a set of dominant value-systems in various cultures and to note the modifying effect of congruent values on the power clash. The difficulty is sharpened by the interrelationships between power realities and value systems. In social-psychological terms, value-system here refers to the cultural preferences, selections, and emphases in the social system that serve as the basis of affective identifications for the members of the society. It has already been noted that power at the non-coercive end of the continuum operates through traditional values. In this form, power is more massive, diffuse, and common in a relatively homogeneous society with marked consensus. Consequently it is stable in character. . . .

As yet no adequate typology has been developed for value-systems. . . . Certain relationships between the two variables of power and value factors will appear as in the case of racist ideas which Robin Williams finds embedded in American values.[3] One can note the greater differentials between American and African society, or between the Euro-American culture and that of the American Indian, as compared with the differentials between the "American" society and European society from which the bulk of immigration has come. The interconnections between the value systems and power relations are still obscure, however, constituting a problem for further research. Here again it seems likely that

[3] Robin Williams, Jr., *American Society, A Sociological Interpretation* (New York, A. A. Knopf, 1951), pp. 438–440.

power is the primary concept, since the relation of two social systems is so definitely a function of the power realities involved, with the value variable accounting for variations in acculturative forms within the power framework.

In closing, it is important to note that the present analysis is related to traditional sociological theory organically. The older view regarded the elements of social process subsumed under conflict distributively and reciprocally in balanced fashion after the manner of the Park-Burgess model. In the present frame of reference we treat the same elements *convergently,* i.e., as shaping an outcome or focalizing many items into determinate decisions.[4] There is no contradiction here but simply an alternate set of conceptualizations. One is the obverse of the other. It is simply that power in the present theory emphasizes the asymmetrical, dynamic, or energistic aspects of the social process; in this way it may be possible to deduce more fruitful hypotheses for testing so as to enlarge scientific prediction and control. This in turn will have an increased pertinence for programs of social action.

---

[4] In Grafton's words, "Without power of some sort, there is no struggle, and the strength of the power will determine the effectiveness of the struggle." T. H. Grafton in J. H. S. Bossard et al. (eds.) *Introduction to Sociology* (Harrisburg, Pa.: Stackpole Co., 1952), p. 285. Power is therefore a *sine qua non* of conflict, a necessary, though not necessarily a sufficient, basis of its operation.

# Part VI

# The Civil Rights Movement: 1961–1970

# Introduction

The dramatic opening of the Civil Rights Movement of the 1960s consisted of four black freshmen from North Carolina Agricultural and Technical College "sitting in" at a Woolworth soda fountain in Greensboro, North Carolina, that would not serve them. The students were angry because several of their girl friends had been refused service earlier at the counter. The force of nonviolent resistance had already been demonstrated for them by Dr. Martin Luther King, Jr., in his leadership of the Montgomery, Alabama, city bus boycott. Fueled by mass media attention, the students' refusal to accept racial segregation and second-class treatment any longer set off a spark that ignited a chain reaction through black campuses all over the South. Typically dressed in their best clothes, black students faced abuse, arrest, and even physical harm by challenging racial segregation directly. Their calm, determined courage, their singing of the National Anthem and "We Shall Overcome" on the way to jail—all broadcast by sympathetic mass media—stirred the nation's conscience and proved to be the death knell to the segregation system.

The student sit-ins called further into question the too-simple psychological model of race relations. The four freshmen had not tried first to "change the hearts and minds" of Greensboro's white citizens. Instead they set out directly to alter the institutional practice at issue. In so doing, they released a social movement that was importantly staffed by college students. This phenomenon added to the theoretical ferment that we noted was already developing in the 1950s. The most articulate statement of this influence of the Civil Rights Movement upon sociological theory is Selection 32 by Joseph Himes. For many years a sociologist at North Carolina College and now at the University of North Carolina at Greensboro, Himes drew on his knowledge of both social theory and the black community to point out the many societal functions served by racial conflict. This influential paper is particularly noteworthy for its explicit recognition of social conflict and social consensus as two facets of the same complex reality, a critical point that escaped many writers of this period who advocated "conflict theory" as a complete and separate perspective in opposition to "consensus theory."[1]

This same ferment also led to much discussion of new models of American race relations, new analogies from which fresh insights might be gleaned. The most notable example of a new model was borrowed and refashioned from minority ideologists. Robert Blauner, of the University of California at Berkeley, introduced the ideologically popular colonial model into the formal sociological literature in a 1969 paper that conceptualized the white colonization of blacks as a process rather than as a social system.[2] He argued that this process was necessary for understanding the decade's urban riots, cultural nationalism, and ghetto control politics. But Blauner astutely observed that a literal application of the colonial model did not fit the black–white situation in the United States. On most counts, black Americans actually face more severe problems than most traditionally colonialized peoples. Thus, they are a less autonomous minority who are more thoroughly ghettoized and dispersed. Blauner termed this "internal colonialism" and maintained that the uniqueness of the black American position lay precisely in the ambiguities created by the colonialization process taking place outside of the classical colonial political context.

But if the fit between the colonial model and black-white relations in America is a bit strained, the fit between this new perspective and the varied circumstances of Mexican Americans is nearly complete. Joan Moore, a leading sociological authority on Mexican Americans at the University of Wisconsin at Milwaukee, presents this argument persuasively in Selection 33. She distinguishes among three contrasting types of situations: "classic colonialism," as typified by the unique history of New Mexico; "conflict colonialism," as typified by Texas; and "economic colonialism," as typified by California. In presenting her analysis, Moore provides us with an overview of the vast diversity in the Southwest of Hispanic–Anglo relations.

The next four articles review discrimination against black Americans in four key realms: employment, politics, housing, and education. These papers demonstrate the enhanced sophistication of sociology, both theoretically and empiri-

---

[1] *E.g.,* John Horton, "Order and conflict theories of social problems as competing ideologies," *American Journal of Sociology 71* (1966): 701–713. In fairness to Horton and similar critics, it must be said that it *does* make an enormous difference for any sociological theory whether it assumes conflict and focuses on explaining social order and consensus or whether it assumes order and focuses on explaining conflict. What the discipline needs—and appears to be slowly groping toward—is a broad theoretical base that assumes neither conflict nor order and simultaneously attempts to account for both conditions as part of a single social process.

[2] Robert Blauner, "Internal colonialism and ghetto revolt," *Social Problems 16* (1969): 393–408.

cally, to deal more directly with specific issues of intergroup discrimination.[3] Consider first occupational issues. A large number of empirical studies detailed the dimensions of the problem. It was shown, for example, that blacks had made occupational gains in the 1940s, but these gains were concentrated in rapidly expanding occupations of intermediate or declining desirability to workers.[4] However, gains were not generally attained during the 1950s, with black Southerners actually losing ground.[5] Promotions within a Midwestern meat-packing plant were shown to be given to black workers systematically less often even after age, seniority, and education had been controlled.[6] Moreover, white males appeared to benefit in terms of higher income and occupational status from employment discrimination.[7] And an interesting occupational simulation concluded that the elimination of all racial discrimination in education would not close most of the black-white differences in occupational levels, and even the elimination of all occupational discrimination directly would still require several generations to end these differences.[8]

Within this grim context, the rapid progress of black baseball players was a striking phenomenon of this period. In Selection 34, H. M. Blalock, Jr., considers this intriguing exceptional case and exploits it in order to derive a set of concrete propositions about occupational discrimination. Blalock, a recent president of the American Sociological Association from the University of Washington, is best known for his many important statistical and methodological contributions to sociology. But here he demonstrates how testable theory can be constructed in sociology through a careful structural examination of a well-known societal phenomenon.

Thanks largely to the Voting Rights Act of 1965, black political mobilization increased throughout the last half of the 1960s and into the 1970s. The number of black elected officials throughout the nation, for example, rose steadily from only about 700 in 1967 to more than 4,600 by 1978, though even this 4,600 figure represents less than *one* per cent of all elected officials in the United

---

[3] For a broad representation of this modern work on racial discrimination, see T. F. Pettigrew (ed.), *Racial Discrimination in the United States* (New York: Harper & Row, 1975).

[4] Norval D. Glenn, "Changes in the American occupational gains of Negroes during the 1940s," *Social Forces 41* (1962): 188-195.

[5] Nathan Hare, "Recent trends in the occupational mobility of Negroes," *Social Forces 44* (1965): 166-173.

[6] A. P. Garbin and J. A. Ballweg, "Intra-plant mobility of Negro and white workers," *American Journal of Sociology 71* (1965): 315-319.

[7] Norval D. Glenn, "Occupational benefits to whites from the subordination of Negroes," *American Sociological Review 28* (1963): 443-448, but see also Phillips Cutright's critical comment and Glenn's reply, *American Sociological Review 30* (1965): 110-112 and 416. Robert W. Hodge and Patricia Hodge, "Occupational assimilation as a competitive process," *American Journal of Sociology 71* (1965): 249-264, but see also reinterpretive comment by Alma Taeuber and Karl Taeuber and the reply by the Hodges, *American Journal of Sociology 72* (1966): 273-289.

[8] Stanley Lieberson and Glenn V. Fuguitt, "Negro-white occupational difference in the absence of discrimination," *American Journal of Sociology 73* (1967): 188-200.

States. It should be emphasized that the effectiveness of the Voting Rights Act is due largely to its having been structurally well designed. Instead of attempting to remedy the discrimination against black voters in some global manner in each Southern locality in which it occurred, the act simply judges the degree of each local problem by the past ability of blacks to cast ballots and, when the Attorney General deems it justified, sends in federal examiners to register those illegally disfranchised. Note the two critical structural features: a simple outcome definition of discrimination combined with a remedial end run around the discriminatory agents of local government. No other civil rights act in American history has been so skillfully structured, and no other has been so effective.

Johnnie Daniel, then at Tuskegee Institute, records in Selection 35 the effects of the Voting Rights Act in Alabama just one year after its passage. His findings reveal two clear-cut trends. First, the combination in a county of both federal examiners and black candidates led to the largest increases in black voting. Second, the special effectiveness of the act in hard-core rural counties of black-belt Alabama completely turned around the predictors of the state's black voting, the heaviest black participation now centered in poorer farming areas with high proportions of black population.

Black advances on other fronts began by the 1960s to make the unyielding patterns of housing segregation and discrimination all the more conspicuous. Consequently, twenty-two housing papers centered on this topic alone during this decade in the four journals under review. Detailed attitude studies uncovered sharp inconsistencies in white views toward interracial housing and fair housing legislation.[9] Other research focused on interracial neighborhoods. One study described the difficulties a single black family experienced in entering the suburban housing development of Levittown, Pennsylvania;[10] another showed how negative interracial attitudes often combined with neighborly interracial behavior in changing neighborhoods in Teaneck, New Jersey.[11] An investigation of the South Shore community in Chicago, conducted in the old tradition of the University of Chicago, uncovered restricted interracial interaction but no necessary link between racial transition and such indicators of neighborhood instability as lowered property values.[12] Indeed, research in New Haven, Connecticut, involving small numbers of high-status black families, actually deter-

---

[9] Herbert A. Aurbach, John R. Coleman, and Bernard Mausner, "Restrictive and protective viewpoints of fair housing legislation: A comparative study of attitudes," *Social Problems 8* (1962): 118–125, and Arnold M. Rose, "Inconsistencies in attitudes toward Negro housing," *Social Problems 8* (1962): 286–292.

[10] Marvin Bressler, "The Myers' case: An instance of successful racial invasion," *Social Problems 8* (1962): 126–142.

[11] Joshua A. Fishman, "Some social and psychological determinants of intergroup relations in changing neighborhoods: An introduction to the Bridgeview study," *Social Forces 40* (1961): 42–51.

[12] Harvey Molotch, "Racial integration in a transition community," *American Sociological Review 34* (1969): 878–893, and *idem,* "Racial change in a stable community," *American Journal of Sociology 75* (1969): 226–238.

mined that property values rose as much as or more than average in eight out of nine neighborhoods.[13] And a study of the fair housing law of New York City revealed that black complainants with higher educational and occupational status fared much better under the law and typically went to overwhelmingly white areas.[14]

Much of the housing research looked at the problem in broad demographic and longitudinal terms. Here the work on central city segregation by Karl and Alma Taeuber, summarized in their definitive 1965 volume *Negroes in Cities*, received considerable attention. This important book's major contentions and data are provided in Selection 36 by Karl Taeuber, of the University of Wisconsin at Madison. The fundamental conclusions of this article, conclusions that unfortunately remain true to this day, are that the residential segregation of black Americans is nationally pervasive, qualitatively different from the housing separations between other groups, and not significantly improving. In short, housing discrimination has become the structural linchpin of today's patterns of institutional racism.[15]

Crucial as housing problems are, educational problems have received the most popular attention. The main sociological contribution to this area of race relations is the U.S. Office of Education's *Equal Educational Opportunity Survey* (*EEOS*), published by the U.S. Government Printing Office in 1966. It is popularly known as "the Coleman Report" after the head of the research team, James Coleman, then of Johns Hopkins University and now at the University of Chicago. This study, mandated by the U.S. Congress in the 1964 Civil Rights Act of 1964, is of massive dimensions—more than 600,000 students were tested in schools all over the nation. Though it could provide only a snapshot, a one-point-in-time picture of American education, the *EEOS* proved to be a landmark in research on the schools. Its findings were widely interpreted as supporting racial desegregation efforts, for it suggested that a major educational resource of any school was reflected in the backgrounds of the total student body. Moreover, the *EEOS* indicated that black children in predominantly white schools tended to score somewhat higher on achievement tests than similar black children in predominantly black schools.

Given the official sponsorship of the research and the wide mass media coverage that it eventually received, it is hardly surprising that the *EEOS* came under intense scrutiny and strong criticism.[16] Among the principal criticisms

---

[13] John Howe and Erdman Palmore, "Residential integration and property values," *Social Problems 10* (1964): 52–55.

[14] Florence Cromien and Harold Goldblatt, "The effective social reach of the Fair Housing Practices Law of the City of New York," *Social Problems 9* (1963): 365–370.

[15] For a detailed discussion of this point, see T. F. Pettigrew, "Racial change and social policy," *Annals of the American Academy of Political and Social Science 441* (January 1979): 114–131.

[16] For example, see the following exchange that highlights disciplinary differences in approach to these questions between economics and sociology: Glen G. Cain and Harold W. Watts, "Problems in making policy inferences from the Coleman report," *American Socio-*

was the limitation set by the snapshot, cross-sectional nature of the study. So immediately following the *EEOS* the U.S. Commission on Civil Rights contracted with the National Opinion Research Center (NORC) of the University of Chicago to study the long-term effects of school desegregation on the lives of black Americans. These and other results were contained in another report, *Racial Isolation in the Public Schools,* published in 1967. Robert Crain, then a senior study director at NORC and now at the Rand Corporation, directed this study and, after additional analyses, issued the most significant of the findings in Selection 37. Here Crain focuses upon the importance of interracial schools in enabling blacks to be included in the principal flow of information about job opportunities. By use of an ingenious set of analyses of his largely retrospective data, he suggests that adult blacks who attended interracial schools as children hold better jobs than other comparable blacks less because of better formal training than because of having been "hooked into the network" of informal friendships and information that lead to greater opportunity. This is a critical consideration favoring school integration that is seldom heard in the long-standing public debate about interracial schools.

The years from 1964 to 1968 were also marked by recurrent race riots in the black areas of many major cities, culminating in particularly severe 1967 outbreaks in Newark and Detroit and in general rioting following the assassination of Dr. King on April 4, 1968. These events are among the most intensely studied in the sociological literature of race relations; more than thirty papers relating to them appeared in the four journals under review.[17] They followed one of two general lines of inquiry.[18] The social psychological approach, represented in Selection 38, sought to determine who had and who had not participated and what accounted for this selective participation at the individual level. The structural approach, represented in Selection 39, which opens Part VII, sought to

---

*logical Review 35* (1970): 228–242; James S. Coleman, "Reply to Cain and Watts," *American Sociological Review 35* (1970): 242–249; and Dennis J. Aigner, "A comment on making inferences from the Coleman report," *American Sociological Review 35* (1970): 249–252.

[17]All four journals included in this volume reflected this trend, but *Social Problems* especially devoted its pages to this subject in the late 1960s and early 1970s.

[18]There was in addition a smaller third literature concerned at the social psychological level with the reactions to the race riots of white Americans. One of these investigations tested white reactions to the Detroit riot in nine Detroit suburbs and found that the reactions were conditioned not only by the social status of the respondent but by the climate of white opinion in the particular suburb. See Donald I. Warren, "Suburban isolation and race tension: The Detroit case," *Social Problems 17* (1970): 324–339. Another investigation found that the reactions of middle-class white residents of the Los Angeles area to the Watts riot was conditioned by their prior social contact with black people. Those whites lacking contact were more fearful of blacks, cited more "outside agitator" explanations for the riot, and supported more punitive measures. See Richard T. Morris and Vincent Jeffries, "Violence next door," *Social Forces 46* (1968): 352–358, and Vincent Jeffries and H. Edward Ransford, "Interracial social contact and middle-class white reactions to the Watts riot," *Social Problems 16* (1969): 312–324.

specify the conditions that predicted both the occurrence and the severity of the riots across cities.[19]

H. Edward Ransford, of the University of Southern California, presents in Selection 38 an interesting example of the many social psychological investigations of the riots. Employing survey data gathered after the extensive Watts riot in 1965 in Los Angeles, Ransford checks on the importance of education, isolation, control, and dissatisfaction.[20] He finds that blacks without college educations who have limited contacts with the larger society and who are highly dissatisfied but feel powerless to do anything about it are especially disposed to favor the rioting and probably to have participated in it.

[19] One interesting study of this type compared structural differences across neighborhoods in relation to riot activity in the Detroit race riot of 1967. High activity areas tended to have minimal social interaction among their residents but positive reference orientations; counter-riot areas had extensive informal social interaction and values that were oriented toward the larger society; and areas without riot involvement tended to have the least social organization of all. Donald I. Warren, "Neighborhood structure and riot behavior in Detroit: Some exploratory findings," *Social Problems 16* (1969): 464–484.

[20] For an incisive analysis and description of the Watts riot, see Anthony Oberschall, "The Los Angeles Riot of August, 1965," *Social Problems 15* (1968): 322–341.

# 32

# The Functions of Racial Conflict

## JOSEPH S. HIMES

... [T] here is widespread popular disapproval of social conflict. In some quarters the absence of conflict is thought to signify the existence of social harmony and stability. According to the human relations theme, conflict, aggression, hostility, antagonism and such devisive motives and behaviors are regarded as social heresies and therefore to be avoided. Often the word conflict is associated with images of violence and destruction.

At the same time, in contemporary sociology the problem of social conflict has been largely neglected. As Coser, Dahrendorf and others have pointed out, this tendency issues from preoccupation with models of social structure and theories of equilibrium.[1] Conflicts are treated as strains, tensions or stresses of social structures and regarded as pathological. Little attention is devoted to the investigation of conflict as a functional social process.

However, some of the earlier sociologists employed social conflict as one central element of their conceptual systems. Theory and analysis were cast in terms of a process model. Conflict was viewed as natural and as functioning as an integrative force in society.

To Ludwig Gumplowicz and Gustav Ratzenhofer conflict was the basic social process, while for Lester F. Ward and Albion W. Small it was one of the basic processes. Sumner, Ross, and Cooley envisaged conflict as one of the major forces operating to lace human society together. . . .

[1] Lewis A. Coser, *The Functions of Social Conflict* (Glencoe, Illinois: The Free Press, 1956), p. 20; Ralf Dahrendorf, *Class and Class Conflict in Industrial Society* (Stanford: Stanford University Press, 1959), chap. 5.

Reprinted, abridged, from *Social Forces 45* (September 1966): 1–10. Copyright © The University of North Carolina Press.

At bottom, however, the two analytic models of social organization are really not inconsistent. Dahrendorf argues that consensus-structure and conflict-process are "the two faces of society." That is, social integration results simultaneously from both consensus of values and coercion to compliance. Indeed, in the present study it is observed that the two sources of social integration are complementary and mutually supporting.

Coser has led the revival of sociological attention to the study of social conflict. . . . One latent consequence of this development has been to sensitize some sociologists to conflict as a perspective from which to investigate race relations. Thus race relations have been called "power relations" and it has been proposed that research should be cast in terms of a "conflict model." . . .

In the present discussion the term racial conflict is used in a restricted and specific sense. By racial conflict is meant rational organized overt action by Negroes, initiating demands for specific social goals, and utilizing collective sanctions to enforce these demands. By definition, the following alternative forms of conflict behavior are excluded from the field of analysis.

1. The aggressive or exploitative actions of dominant groups and individuals toward minority groups or individuals.
2. Covert individual antagonisms or affective compensatory or reflexive aggressions, and
3. Spontaneous outbursts or nonrationalized violent behavior.

As here treated, racial conflict involves some rational assessment of both means and ends, and therefore is an instance of what Lewis Coser has called "realistic conflict." Because of the calculating of means and ends, racial conflict is initiating action. It is a deliberate collective enterprise to achieve predetermined social goals. Of necessity, conflict includes a conscious attack upon an overtly defined social abuse.

Merton has pointed out that groups sometimes resort to culturally tabooed means to achieve culturally prescribed ends.[2] Under such circumstances one might assume that if legitimate means were available, they would be employed. But, Vander Zanden has observed, "Non-violent resistance is a tactic well suited to struggles in which a minority lacks access to major sources of power within a society and to the instruments of violent coercion."[3] . . . Three principal manifestations of Negro behavior fit this definition of racial conflict.

1. Legal redress, or the calculated use of court action to achieve and sanction specific group goals. Legal redress has been used most often and successfully in the achievement of voting rights, educational opportunities and public accommodations.

---

[2] Robert K. Merton, *Social Theory and Social Structure* (Glencoe, Illinois: The Free Press, 1957), pp. 123–149.

[3] James W. Vander Zanden, "The Non-Violent Resistance Movement Against Segregation," *American Journal of Sociology, 68* (March 1963), p. 544.

2. Political action, or the use of voting, bloc voting and lobby techniques to achieve legislative and administrative changes and law enforcement.

3. Non-violent mass action, or organized collective participation in overt activity involving pressure and public relations techniques to enforce specific demands.

This paper examines some of the social functions of conflict as here defined. It is asked: Does realistic conflict by Negroes have any system-maintaining and system-enhancing consequences for the larger American society? To this question at least four affirmative answers can be given. Realistic racial conflict (1) alters the social structure, (2) enhances social communication, (3) extends social solidarity and (4) facilitates personal identity. Because of space and time limitations, considerations of societal dysfunctions and goal achievements are omitted.

## Structural Functions

. . . [W]ithin the American social structure race relations are power relations.[4] Thus, realistic social conflict is an enterprise in the calculated mobilization and application of social power to sanction collective demands for specific structural changes. Yet, because of minority status, Negroes have only limited access to the sources of social power. Robert Bierstedt has identified numbers, resources and organization as leading sources of power.[5] Of these categories, resources which Bierstedt specifies as including money, prestige, property and natural and supernatural phenomena, are least accessible to Negroes.

Perforce then, realistic racial conflict specializes in the mobilization of numbers and organization as accessible sources of power. Thus a boycott mobilizes and organizes numbers of individuals to withhold purchasing power. A demonstration organizes and mobilizes numbers of individuals to tap residual moral sentiments and to generate public opinion. Voter registration and bloc voting mobilize and organize numbers of citizens to influence legislative and administrative processes. Legal redress and lobby techniques mobilize organization to activate legal sanctions or the legislative process.

The application of mobilized social power in realistic racial conflict tends to reduce the power differential between actors, to restrict existing status differences, and to alter the directionality of social interaction. First, in conflict situations, race relations are defined unequivocally in power terms. Sentimentality and circumlocution are brushed aside. The power dimension is brought into central position in the structure of interaction. The differential between conflict partners along this dimension is thus reduced. The power advantage of the dominant group is significantly limited. In this connection and perhaps only in

---

[4] See Selection 29 in this volume.

[5] Robert Bierstedt, "An Analysis of Social Power," *American Sociological Review*, 15 (December 1950), pp. 730–738. . . .

this connection, it may be correct to liken embattled Negroes and resisting whites to "armed camps."

Second, alteration of the power dimension of interracial structure tends to modify status arrangements. In the traditional racial structure, discrimination and segregation cast whites and Negroes in rigid and separate orders of superiority and inferiority. The limited and stylized intergroup contacts are confined to a rigid and sterile etiquette. However, in realistic conflict initiating actors assume, for they must, a status coordinate with that of the opposition.[6]

Status coordination is one evident consequence of power equalization. Moreover, it is patently impossible to make demands and to sanction them while acting from the position of a suppliant. That is, the very process of realistic conflict functions to define adversaries in terms of self-conception as status equals. Martin Luther King perceives this function of realistic conflict in the following comment on the use of non-violent action and deliberately induced tension.[7]

Non-violent direct action seeks to create such a crisis and foster such a tension that a community which has constantly refused to negotiate is forced to confront the issue. It seeks so to dramatize the issue that it can no longer be ignored.

That is, social power is used to bring interactors into status relations where issues can be discussed, examined and compromised. There are no suppliants or petitioners and no condescending controllers in a negotiation relationship. By the very nature of the case, interactors occupy equal or approximately equal positions of both status and strength.

Third, power equalization and status coordination affect the interactional dimension of social structure. The up and down flow of interaction between super- and subordinates tends to level out in relations between positional equals. That is, rational demands enforced by calculated sanctions cannot be forced into the molds of supplication and condescension.

The leveling out of social interaction is inherent in such realistic conflict mechanisms as sit-ins, freedom rides, bloc voting, voter registration campaigns and boycotts. Thus, for example, the interruption of social interaction in a boycott implies an assumption of status equality and the leveling of interaction. The relationship that is interrupted is the up and down pattern inherent in the status structure of inequality. No relationship is revealed as preferable to the pattern of supplication and condescension. Whether such structural functions of realistic conflict become institutionalized in the larger social system will depend on the extent of goal achievement of the total Negro revolution. That is, structural consequences of conflict may be institutionalized through the desegregation and nondiscrimination of education, employment, housing,

---

[6] Thomas F. Pettigrew, *A Profile of the Negro American* (Princeton: D. Van Nostrand Co., 1964), p. 167.

[7] Martin Luther King, *Why We Can't Wait* (New York: Harper & Row, 1963), p. 81.

recreation and the like. Changes in these directions will provide system-relevant roles under terms of relatively coordinate status and power not only for the conflict participants, but also for many other individuals. Developments in these directions will also be influenced by many factors and trends apart from the process of realistic racial conflict.

We may now summarize the argument regarding the structural functions of realistic racial conflict in a series of propositions. Realistic conflict postulates race relations as power relations and undertakes to mobilize and apply the social power that is accessible to Negroes as a minority group.

In conflict, the traditional interracial structure is modified along three dimensions. The power differential between interactors is reduced; status differentials are restricted; and social interaction tends to level out in directionality. Whether these structural consequences of realistic conflict become institutionalized in the general social system will depend on the extent and duration of goal achievement in the larger social structure.

## Communicational Functions

It is widely claimed that Negro aggression interrupts or reduces interracial communication. Whites and Negroes are thought to withdraw in suspicion and hostility from established practices of communication. The so-called "normal" agencies and bridges of intergroup contact and communication are believed to become inoperative. Such a view of conflict envisages Negroes and whites as hostile camps eyeing each other across a "no man's land" of antagonism and separation.

It is true that racial conflict tends to interrupt and reduce traditional communication between whites and Negroes. But traditional interracial communication assumes that communicators occupy fixed positions of superiority and inferiority, precludes the consideration of certain significant issues, and confines permitted interchanges to a rigid and sterile etiquette. . . .

It will be evident that intergroup communication under such structural conditions is both restricted in content and asymmetrical in form. However, our analysis indicates that realistic conflict functions to correct these distortions of content and form and to extend the communication process at the secondary mass media level.

First, realistic racial conflict heightens the individual level and extends the social range of attention to racial matters. Individuals who have by long custom learned to see Negroes only incidentally as part of the standard social landscape, are brought up sharply and forced to look at them in a new light. Persons who have been oblivious to Negroes are abruptly and insistently confronted by people and issues which they can neither avoid nor brush aside. Many individuals for the first time perceive Negroes as having problems, characteristics and aspirations that were never before recognized, nor at least so clearly recognized. Racial conflict thus rudely destroys what Gunnar Myrdal aptly called the "convenience of ignorance."[8] . . .

At the same time the "race problem" is brought into the focus of collective attention by realistic conflict. Negroes as well as their problems and claims insist upon having both intensive and extensive considerations. To support this contention one has only to consider the volume of scientific, quasi-scientific and popular literature, the heavy racial loading of the mass media, and the vast number of organizations and meetings that are devoted to the racial issue.

Further, realistic racial conflict tends to modify both the cognitive and affective content of interracial communication. Under terms of conflict whites and Negroes can no longer engage in the exchange of standardized social amenities regarding safe topics within the protection of the status structure and the social etiquette. Communication is made to flow around substantive issues and the calculated demands of Negroes. Communication is about something that has real meaning for the communicators. It makes a difference that they communicate. In fact, under terms of realistic conflict it is no longer possible to avoid communicating. . . .

In conflict the affective character of communication becomes realistic. The communicators infuse their exchanges of cognitive meanings with the feelings that, within the traditional structure, were required to be suppressed and avoided. That Negroes are permitted, indeed often expected to reveal the hurt and humiliation and anger that they formerly were required to bottle up inside. Many white people thus were shocked to discover that the "happy" Negroes whom they "knew" so well were in fact discontented and angry people.

Thus the cognitive-affective distortion of traditional interracial communication is in some measure at least corrected. The flow of understanding and affection that was permitted and encouraged is balanced by normal loading of dissension and hostility. The relationship thus reveals a more symmetrical character of content and form.

Finally, attrition of primary contacts between unequals within the traditional structure and etiquette is succeeded, in part at least, by an inclusive dialogue at the secondary communication level. The drama of conflict and the challenges of leaders tend to elevate the racial issue in the public opinion arena. The mass media respond by reporting and commenting on racial events in great detail. Thus millions of otherwise uninformed or indifferent individuals are drawn into the public opinion process. . . .

[I]t would seem reasonable to conclude that few if any Americans have escaped some degree of involvement in the dialogue over the race issue.

We may now summarize the argument briefly. Realistic racial conflict tends to reduce customary interracial communication between status unequals regarding trivial matters within the established communication etiquette. On the other hand, conflict tends to extend communication regarding significant issues with

[8] Gunnar Myrdal, *An American Dilemma* (New York: Harper & Bros., 1944), pp. 40–42.

genuine feelings and within noncustomary structures and situations. At the secondary level both the volume of communication and the number of communicators are greatly increased by realistic conflict. These observations would seem to warrant the conclusion that communication within the general social system is extended by realistic racial conflict.

## Solidarity Functions

A corollary of the claim that racial conflict interrupts communication is the assertion that conflict also is seriously, perhaps even radically disunifying. Struggles between Negroes and whites are thought to split the society and destroy social solidarity. It is at once evident that such a claim implies the prior existence of a unified or relatively unified biracial system. Notwithstanding difference of status and condition, the racial sectors are envisaged as joined in the consensus and structure of the society.

A judicious examination of the facts suggests that the claim that racial conflict is seriously, perhaps even radically disunifying is not altogether correct. On the one hand, the image of biracial solidarity tends to be exaggerated. On the other, realistic racial conflict serves some important unifying functions within the social system.

As Logan Wilson and William Kolb have observed, the consensus of the society is organized around a core of "ultimate values."[9] "In our own society," they assert, "we have developed such ultimate values as the dignity of the individual, equality of opportunity, the right to life, liberty, and the pursuit of happiness, and the growth of the free personality."

Far from rejecting or challenging these ultimate values, the ideological thrust of realistic racial conflict affirms them.[10] That is, the ultimate values of the society constitute starting points of ideology and action in racial conflict. . . . Negro protest and improvement movements are thoroughly American in assumption and objectives.

This fact creates an interesting strategic dilemma for the White Citizens Councils, the resurgent Ku Klux Klan and similar manifestations of the so-called "white backlash." The ideology of racial conflict has preempted the traditional high ground of the core values and ultimate morality. The reactionary groups are thus left no defensible position within the national ethos from which to mount their attacks.

One consequence of realistic racial conflict, then, is to bring the core values of the society into sharp focus and national attention. People are exhorted, even forced to think about the basic societal tenets and to consider their meaning and

[9] Logan Wilson and William L. Kolb, *Sociological Analysis* (New York: Harcourt, Brace & Co., 1949), p. 513.

[10] Pettigrew, *op. cit.,* p. 193.

applications. A dynamic force is thus joined to latent dedication in support of the unifying values of the society. Thus, . . . far from being altogether disunifying, realistic conflict functions to reaffirm the core and unifying values of the society. . . .

The primacy of core values in realistic racial conflict is revealed in many ways. Martin Luther King places the ultimate values of the society at the center of his theoretic system of non-violent mass action. In his "Letter from Birmingham Jail" he refers to "justice," "freedom," "understanding," "brotherhood," "constitutional rights," "promise of democracy" and "truth." See how he identifies the goal of racial freedom with the basic societal value of freedom. "We will reach the goal of freedom in Birmingham and all over the nation, because the goal of America is freedom."[11]

One impact of realistic racial conflict is upon interpretation of core values and the means of their achievement. Thus, the issue is not whether or not men shall be free and equal, but whether these values are reserved to white men or are applicable to Negroes as well. Or again, the phrases "gradualism" and "direct action" depict an important point of disagreement over means to universally affirmed ends. But, it may be observed that when men agree on the ends of life, their quarrels are not in themselves disunifying.

Further, the very process of realistic racial conflict is intrinsically functional. Participants in the conflict are united by the process of struggle itself. The controversy is a unique and shared social possession. It fills an interactional vacuum maintained in the traditional structure by limited social contacts and alienation.

At the same time . . . a relationship established by conflict may lead in time to other forms of interaction. It is conceivable that Negroes and whites who today struggle over freedom and justice and equality may tomorrow be joined in cooperation in the quest of these values.

Conflict is also unifying because the object of struggle is some social value that both parties to the conflict wish to possess or enjoy. The struggle tends to enhance the value and to reveal its importance to both actors. A new area of consensus is thus defined or a prior area of agreement is enlarged. For example, that Negroes and whites struggle through realistic conflict for justice or freedom or equality tends to clarify these values for both and join them in the consensus regarding their importance.

"Simultaneously," as Vander Zanden observes, "within the larger American society the Negro's tactic of non-violent resistance has gained a considerable degree of legitimacy."[12] That is, conflict itself has been defined as coming within the arena of morally justifiable social action. The means as well as the ends, then, are enveloped within the national ethos and serve to enhance societal solidarity. In this respect realistic racial conflict, like labor-management conflict, tends to enter the "American way of life" and constitutes another point of social integration. . . .

[11] King, *op. cit.*, pp. 77-100.
[12] Vander Zanden, *op. cit.*, p. 544.

[R]ealistic racial conflict is interwoven with political, religious, regional, rural-urban, labor-management, class and the other persistent threads of struggle that characterize the American social fabric. What is decisive is the fact that variously struggling factions are united in the consensus of the ultimate societal values. The conflicts are therefore nonradical, crisscrossing and tend to mitigate each other.

The proposition on the solidarity function of realistic racial conflict can now be formulated briefly. The claims that racial conflict is disruptive of social solidarity, though partially true, tend to obscure other important consequences. Conflict not only projects the combatants into the social consensus; it also acts to reaffirm the ultimate values around which the consensus is organized. Moreover, conflict joins opposing actors in meaningful interaction for ends, whose importance is a matter of further agreement. From this perspective and within a context of multifarious crisscrossing threads of opposition, realistic racial conflict is revealed as helping to "sew" the society together around its underlying societal consensus. . . .

## Identity Functions

The fact is often overlooked that realistic racial conflict permits many Negroes to achieve a substantial measure of identity within the American social system. This function of racial conflict is implied in the foregoing analyses of communication and solidarity. However, the analysis of the identity function of racial conflict begins with a consideration of the alienation of the American Negro people. Huddled into urban and rural slums and concentrated in menial and marginal positions in the work force, Negroes are relegated to inferior and collateral statuses in the social structure. Within this structural situation discrimination prevents their sharing in the valued possessions of the society. Legal and customary norms of segregation exclude them from many meaningful contacts and interactions with members of the dominant group.

Isolated and inferior, Negro people searched for the keys to identity and belonging. The social forces that exclude them from significant participation in the general society also keep them disorganized. Thus identity, the feeling of belonging and the sense of social purpose, could be found neither in membership in the larger society nor in participation in a cohesive racial group. Generation after generation of Negroes live out their lives in fruitless detachment and personal emptiness. . . .

Yet the search for identity goes on. It takes many forms. In the Negro press and voluntary organizations it is reflected in campaigns for race pride and race loyalty. One sector of the Negro intelligentsia invented the "Negro history movement" as a device to create a significant past for a "historyless" people. For the unlettered and unwashed masses the church is the prime agent of group cohesion and identity. The National Association for the Advancement of Colored People and other militant organizations provide an ego-enhancing rallying point for the emancipated and the aggressive. The cult of Negro business, escapist movements like Father Divine's Heaven, and nationalist movements like Marcus Garvey's Universal Negro Improvement Association, and the Black Muslims provide still other arenas for the Negro's search for identity.

Despite this variegated panorama of effort and search, the overriding experience of Negroes remains isolation, inferiority and the ineluctable sense of alienation. Whether involved in the search or not, perhaps just because of such involvement, individuals see themselves as existing outside the basic American social system. . . . Thus self-conception reflects and in turn supports social experience in a repetition of the familar self-fulfilling prophecy.

In this situation, collective conflict had an almost magical although unanticipated effect upon group cohesion and sense of identity among Negroes. Group struggle . . . functions to enhance group solidarity and to clarify group boundaries. The separations among collective units are sharpened and the identity of groups within a social system is established. In the course of conflict collective aims are specified, defined and communicated. Cadres of leaders emerge in a division of labor that grows clearer and more definite. Individuals tend to find niches and become polarized around the collective enterprise. All participants are drawn closer together, both for prosecution of the struggle and for common defense.

As the racial conflict groups become more cohesive and organized, the boundaries with other groups within the American social system become clearer. The distinction between member and nonmember is sharpened. Individuals who stood indecisively between groups or outside the fray are induced or forced to take sides. The zones of intergroup ambiguity diminish. Internally, the conflict groups become more tightly unified and the positions of members are clarified and defined more precisely.

Further, conflict facilitates linkage between the' individual and his local reference group as the agent of conflict. The individual thus achieves both a "commitment" and a "role" as a quasi-official group representative in the collective struggle. Pettigrew writes:[13]

Consider the Student Non-Violent Coordinating Committee (SNICK), . . . The group is cohesive, highly regarded by Negro youth, and dedicated entirely to achieving both personal and societal racial change. Recruits willingly and eagerly devote themselves to the group's goals. And they find themselves systematically rewarded by SNICK for violating the 'Negro' role in every particular. They are expected to evince strong racial pride, to assert their full rights as citizens, to face jail and police brutality unhesitatingly for the cause. . . . Note, . . . that these expected and rewarded actions all publicly commit the member to the group and its aims.

In the general racial conflict system individuals may act as leaders, organizers and specialists. Some others function as sit-inners, picketers, boycotters, demonstrators, voter registration solicitors, etc. Many others, removed from the areas of overt conflict, participate secondarily or vicariously as financial contributors, audience members, mass media respondents, verbal applauders, etc.

In the interactive process of organized group conflict self-involvement is the opposite side of the coin of overt action. Actors become absorbed by ego and emotion into the group and the group is projected through their actions. This linkage of individual and group in ego and action is the substance of identity.

Paradoxically, the personal rewards of participation in conflict groups tend to support and facilitate the larger conflict organization and process. . . . That is, for the individual actor the sense of identity is grounded and sustained by gratification of important personal needs.

In the case of realistic racial conflict, group-based identity functions to facilitate sociopsychic linkage between the individual and the inclusive social system. It was shown above that racial conflict is socially unifying in at least two ways. First, the conflict ideology identifies parties to the conflict with the core values of the social heritage. Thus sit-inners, and demonstrators and boycotters and all the others in the drama of racial conflict conceive themselves as the latter-day warriors for the freedom, justice and equality and the other moral values that are historically and essentially American. For many Negroes the sense of alienation is dispelled by a new sense of significance and purpose. The self-image of these embattled Negroes is consequently significantly enhanced.

Second, the conflict process draws organized Negroes into significant social interaction within the inclusive social system. Some of the crucial issues and part of the principal business of the society engage Negroes of all localities and stations in life. Though often only vicariously and by projection, life acquires a new meaning and quality for even the poorest ghetto dweller and meanest share-cropper. The sense of alienation is diminished and the feeling of membership in the inclusive society is enhanced.

We may now formulate the argument as follows. Intense alienation kept alive the Negro's quest for identity and meaning. Miraculously almost, realistic racial conflict with its ideological apparatus and action system functions to alleviate alienation and to facilitate identity. Conflict enhances group solidarity, clarifies group boundaries and strengthens the individual-group linkage through ego-emotion commitment and overt action. In-group identity is extended to the larger social system through the extension of communication, the enlargement of the network of social interactions and ideological devotion to national core values. It may be said, then, that through realistic racial conflict America gains some new Americans.

# 33

# Colonialism: The Case of the Mexican Americans

*JOAN W. MOORE*

American social scientists should have realized long ago that American minorities are far from being passive objects of study. They are, on the contrary, quite capable of defining themselves. A clear demonstration of this rather embarrassing lag in conceptualization is the current reassessment of sociological thought. It is now plain that the concepts of "acculturation," of "assimilation," and similar paradigms are inappropriate for groups who entered American society not as volunteer immigrants but through some form of involuntary relationship.[1]

The change in thinking has not come because of changes within sociology itself. Quite the contrary. It has come because the minorities have begun to reject certain academic concepts. The new conceptual structure is not given by any academic establishment but comes within a conceptual structure derived from the situation of the African countries. In the colonial situation, rather than either the conquest or the slave situation, the new generation of black intellectuals is finding parallels to their own reactions to American society.

This exploration of colonialism by minority intellectuals has met a varied

---

[1] Oddly enough it now appears that the nature of the introduction into American society matters even more than race, though the two interact. I think this statement can be defended empirically, notwithstanding the emergence of, for example, Japanese-American *sansei* militancy, with its strong race consciousness (see Kitano, 1968).

Abridged from *Social Problems 17* (1970): 463–472, by permission of *Social Problems,* the Society for the Study of Social Problems, and the author.

reaction, to say the least. . . . Blauner's (1969) article in this journal is one of the more ambitious attempts to relate the concept of "colonialism" as developed by Kenneth Clark, Stokely Carmichael and Eldridge Cleaver to sociological analysis. In the process, one kind of blurring is obvious even if not explicit: that is, that "colonialism" was far from uniform in the 19th Century, even in Africa. In addition, Blauner (1969) makes explicit the adaptations he feels are necessary before the concept of colonialism can be meaningfully applied to the American scene. Common to both American internal colonialism of the blacks and European imperial expansion, Blauner argues, were the involuntary nature of the relationship between the two groups, the transformation or destruction of indigenous values, and, finally, racism. But Blauner warns that the situations are really different: "the . . . culture . . . of the (American black) colonized . . . is less developed; it is also less autonomous. In addition, the colonized are a numerical minority, and furthermore, they are ghettoized more totally and are more dispersed than people under classic colonialism."

But such adaptations are not needed in order to apply the concept fruitfully to America's second largest minority—the Mexican Americans. Here the colonial concept need not be analogized. . . . The initial Mexican contact with American society came by conquest, not by choice. Mexican American culture *was* well developed; it *was* autonomous; the colonized *were* a numerical majority. Further, they were—and are—less ghettoized and more dispersed than the American blacks. In fact, their patterns of residence (especially those existing at the turn of the century) are exactly those of "classic colonialism." And they were indigenous to the region and not "imported."[2]

In at least the one state of New Mexico, there was a situation of comparatively "pure" colonialism. Outside of New Mexico, the original conquest colonialism was overlaid, particularly in the 20th century, with a grossly manipulated voluntary immigration. But throughout the American Southwest where the approximately five million Mexican Americans are now concentrated, understanding the Mexican minority requires understanding both conquest colonialism and "voluntary" immigration. It also requires understanding the interaction between colonialism and voluntarism.

In this paper I shall discuss a "culture trait" that is attributed to Mexican Americans both by popular stereotype and by social scientists—that is, a comparatively low degree of formal voluntary organization and hence of organized participation in political life. This is the academic form of the popular question: "What's wrong with the Mexicans? Why can't they organize for political activity?" In fact, as commonly asked, . . . the question begs the question. There is a great deal of variation in three widely different culture areas in the Southwest. And these culture areas differ most importantly in the particular variety of colonialism to which they were subjected. In the "classically" colonial situation, New Mexico, there has been in fact a relatively high order of political participa-

---

[2] "Indigenous" by comparison with the American blacks. Spanish America itself was a colonial system, in which Indians were exploited. . . .

tion, especially by comparison with Texas, which we shall term "conflict colonialism," and California, which we shall term "economic colonialism."[3]

## New Mexico

An area that is now northern New Mexico and parts of southern Colorado was the most successful of the original Spanish colonies. At the beginning of the war between the United States and Mexico, there were more than 50,000 settlers, scattered in villages and cities with a strong upper class as well as a peasantry. There were frontier versions of Spanish colonial institutions that had been developing since 1600. The conquest of New Mexico by the United States was nearly bloodless and thus allowed, as a consequence, an extraordinary continuity between the Mexican period and the United States period. The area became a territory of the United States and statehood was granted in 1912.

Throughout these changes political participation can be followed among the elite and among the masses of people. It can be analyzed in both its traditional manifestations and in contemporary patterns. In all respects it differs greatly in both level and quality from political participation outside this area. The heritage of colonialism helps explain these differences.

On the elite level, Spanish or Mexican leadership remained largely intact through the conquest and was shared with Anglo leadership after the termination of military rule in 1851. The indigenous elite retained considerable strength both in the dominant Republican party and in the state legislature. They were strong enough to ensure a bilingual provision in the 1912 Constitution (the only provision in the region that guarantees Spanish speakers the right to vote and hold office). Sessions of the legislature were—by law—conducted in both languages. Again, this is an extraordinary feature in any part of the continental United States. Just as in many Asian nations controlled by the British in the 19th century, the elite suffered little either economically or politically.

On the lower-class level, in the villages, there was comparatively little articulation of New Mexican villages with the developing urban centers. What there was, however, was usually channeled through a recognized local authority, a *patrón*. Like the class structure, the *patrón* and the network of relations that sustained him were a normal part of the established local social system and not an ad hoc or temporary recognition of an individual's power. Thus political

---

[3] Of course, we are not arguing that colonialist domination—or for that matter the peculiar pattern of voluntary immigration—offers a full explanation of this complex population, or even of the three culture areas which are the focus of this paper. Mexican Americans and the history of the region are far too complexly interwoven to pretend that any analytic thread can unravel the full tapestry. For other theses, see the analyses developed in Grebler *et al.* (1970).

participation on both the elite and the lower-class levels were outgrowths of the existing social system.

Political participation of the elite and the *patrón* system was clearly a colonial phenomenon. An intact society, rather than a structureless mass of individuals, was taken into a territory of the United States with almost no violence. This truly colonial situation involves a totally different process of relationship between subordinate and superordinate from either the voluntary or the forced immigration of the subordinate—that is, totally different from either the "typical" American immigrant on the eastern seaboard or the slave imported from Africa.

A final point remains to be made . . . about proto-political organization in the past. The villages of New Mexico had strong internal organizations not only of the informal, kinship variety but of the formal variety. These were the *penitente* sects and also the cooperative associations, such as those controlling the use of water and the grazing of livestock. That such organizations were mobilized by New Mexican villagers is evidenced by the existence of terrorist groups operating against both Anglo and Spanish landowners. . . .

Let us turn to the present. Political participation of the conventional variety is very high compared to that of Mexican Americans in other states of the Southwest. Presently there is a Spanish American in the United States Senate (Montoya, an "old" name), following the tradition of Dennis Chavez (another "old" name). The state legislature in 1967 was almost one-third Mexican American. (There were no Mexican American legislators in California and no more than six percent in the legislature of any other Southwest state.) This, of course, reflects the fact that it is only in very recent years that Mexican Americans have become a numerical minority in New Mexico, but it also reflects the fact that organized political participation has remained high.

Finally, New Mexico is the locus of the only mass movement among Mexican Americans—the *Alianza Federal de Mercedes,* headed by Rejes Tijerina. In theme, the *Alianza,* which attracted tens of thousands of members, relates specifically to the colonial past, protesting the loss of land and its usurpation by Anglo interests (including, most insultingly, those of the United States Forest Service). It is this loss of land which has ultimately been responsible for the destruction of village (Spanish) culture and the large-scale migration to the cities. In the light of the importance of the traditional village as a base for political mobilization, it is not really surprising that the *Alianza* should have appeared where it did. In content the movement continues local terrorism (haystack-burning) but has now extended beyond the local protest as its members have moved to the cities. Rather than being directed against specific Anglo or Spanish land-grabbers, it has lately been challenging the legality of the Treaty of Guadalupe Hidalgo. . . . It is an ironic feature of the *Alianza* that the generalization of its objectives and of its appeal should be possible only long after most of the alleged land-grabbing had been accomplished.

## Texas

Mexican Americans in Texas had a sharply contrasting historical experience. The Mexican government in Texas was replaced by a revolution of the American settlers. Violence between Anglo-American settlers and Mexican residents continued in south Texas for generations after the annexation of Texas by the United States and the consequent full-scale war. Violence continued in organized fashion well into the 20th Century with armed clashes involving the northern Mexican *guerilleros* and the U.S. Army.

This violence meant a total destruction of Mexican elite political participation by conquest, while such forces as the Texas Rangers were used to suppress Mexican American participation on the lower status or village levels. The ecology of settlement in south Texas remains somewhat reminiscent of that in northern New Mexico: there are many areas that are predominantly Mexican, and even some towns that are still controlled by Mexicans. But there is far more complete Anglo economic and political dominance on the local level. Perhaps most important, Anglo-Americans outnumbered Mexicans by five to one even before the American conquest. By contrast, Mexicans in New Mexico remained the numerical majority for more than 100 years after conquest.

Texas state politics reflect the past just as in New Mexico. Mexican Americans hold some slight representation in the U.S. Congress. There are two Mexican American Congressmen, one from San Antonio and one from Brownsville. . . . A minor representation far below the numerical proportion of Mexican Americans is maintained in the Texas legislature.

It is on the local level that the continued suppression is most apparent. As long ago as 1965 Mexican Americans in the small town of Crystal City won political control in a municipal election that electrified all Mexican Americans in Texas and stirred national attention. But this victory was possible only with statewide help from Mexican American organizations and some powerful union groups. Shortly afterward (after some intimidation from the Texas Rangers) the town returned to Anglo control. Some other small towns (Del Rio, Kingsville, Alice) have recently had demonstrations in protest against local suppressions. Small and insignificant as they were, the demonstrations once again would not have been possible without outside support, primarily from San Antonio. . . .

More general Mexican American political organizations in Texas have a history that is strikingly reminiscent of Negro political organization. . . . Political organization has been middle class, highly oriented toward traditional expressions of "Americanism," and accommodationist. In fact, the first Mexican American political association refused to call itself a political association for fear that it might be too provocative to the Anglo power structure; it was known as a "civic" organization when it was formed in Texas in the late 1920's. Even the name of this group (LULAC or the League of United Latin American Citizens) evokes an atmosphere of middle-class gentility. The second major group, the

American G.I. Forum, was formed in an atmosphere of greater protest, after a Texas town had refused burial to a Mexican American soldier. In recent years, increasing politicization has been manifested by the formation of such a group as PASSO (Political Association of Spanish Speaking Organizations). But in Texas, throughout the modern period the very act of *ethnic* politics has been controversial, even among Mexican Americans.

## California

The California transition between Mexican and American settlement falls midway between the Texas pattern of violence and the relatively smooth change in New Mexico. In northern California the discovery of gold in 1849 almost immediately swamped a sparse Mexican population in a flood of Anglo-American settlers. Prior to this time an orderly transition was in progress. Thus the effect was very much that of violence in Texas: the indigenous Mexican elite was almost totally excluded from political participation. A generation later when the opening of the railroads repeated this demographic discontinuity in southern California the Mexicans suffered the same effect. They again were almost totally excluded from political participation. The New Mexico pattern of social organization on a village level had almost no counterpart in California. Here the Mexican settlements and the economy were built around very large land holdings rather than around villages. This meant, in essence, that even the settlements that survived the American takeover relatively intact tended to lack internal social organization. Villages . . . were more likely to be clusters of ranch employees than an independent, internally coherent community.

In more recent times the peculiar organization of California politics has tended to work against Mexican American participation from the middle and upper status levels. California was quick to adopt the ideas of "direct democracy" of the Progressive era. These tend somewhat to work against ethnic minorities. But this effect is accidental and can hardly be called "internal colonialism," coupled as it was with the anti-establishment ideals of the Progressive era. The concept of "colonialism," in fact, appears most useful with reference to the extreme manipulation of Mexican immigration in the 20th Century. Attracted to the United States by the hundreds of thousands in the 1920's, Mexicans and many of their U.S.-born children were deported ("repatriated") by welfare agencies during the Depression, most notably from California. (Texas had almost no welfare provisions; hence no repatriation.) The economic expansion in World War II required so much labor that Mexican immigration was supplemented by a contract labor arrangement. But, as in the Depression, "too many" were attracted and came to work in the United States without legal status. Again, in 1954, massive sweeps of deportations got rid of Mexicans by the hundreds of thousands in "Operation Wetback." New Mexico was largely spared both waves of deportation; Texas was involved primarily in Operation Wetback rather than in the welfare repatriations. California was deeply involved in both.

This economic manipulation of the nearly bottomless pool of Mexican labor has been quite conscious and enormously useful to the development of California extractive and agricultural enterprises. Only in recent years with increasing—and now overwhelming—porportions of native-born Mexican Americans in the population has the United States been "stuck" with the Mexicans. As one consequence, the naturalization rate of Mexican immigrants has been very low. After all, why relinquish even the partial protection of Mexican citizenship? Furthermore the treatment of Mexicans as economic commodities has greatly reduced both their motivation and their effectiveness as political participants. The motivations that sent Mexican Americans to the United States appear to have been similar to those that sent immigrants from Europe. But the conscious dehumanization of Mexicans in the service of the railroad and citrus industries in California and elsewhere meant an assymmetry in relationship between "host" and immigrant that is less apparent in the European patterns of immigration. Whatever resentment that might have found political voice in the past had no middle class organizational patterns. California was structurally unreceptive and attitudinally hostile.

Thus in California the degree of Mexican political participation remains low. The electoral consequences are even more glaringly below proportional representation than in Texas. There is only one national representative . . . and only one in the state legislature. Los Angeles County (with nearly a million Mexican Americans) has no Supervisor of Mexican descent and the city has no Councilman of Mexican descent. Otherwise, the development of political associations has followed the Texas pattern, although later, with meaningful political organization a post-World War II phenomenon. The G.I. Forum has formed chapters in California. In addition, the Community Service Organization, oriented to local community political mobilization, and the Mexican American Political Association, oriented to state-wide political targets, have repeated the themes of Texas' voluntary association on the level of the growing middle class.

How useful, then, is the concept of colonialism when it is applied to these three culture areas? We argue here that both the nature and extent of political participation in the state of New Mexico can be understood with reference to the "classical" colonial past. We noted that a continuity of elite participation in New Mexico from the period of Mexican rule to the period of American rule paved the way for a high level of conventional political participation. The fact that village social structure remained largely intact is in some measure responsible for the appearance of the only mass movement of Mexicans in the Southwest today—the *Alianza*. But even this movement is an outcome of colonialism; the expropriation of the land by large-scale developers and by federal conservation interests led ultimately to the destruction of the village economic base—and to the movement of the dispossessed in the cities. Once living in the cities in a much closer environment than that of the scattered small villages, they could "get together" and respond to the anti-colonialist protests of a charismatic leader.

Again following this idea, we might categorize the Texas experience as "conflict colonialism." This would reflect the violent discontinuity between the Mexican and the American periods of elite participation and the current struggle for the legitimation of ethnic politics on all levels. In this latter aspect, the "conflict colonialism" of Texas is reminiscent of black politics in the Deep South, although it comes from different origins.

To apply the colonial concept to Mexicans in California, we might usefully use the idea of "economic colonialism." The destruction of elite political strength by massive immigration and the comparative absence of local political organization meant a political vacuum for Mexican Americans. Extreme economic manipulation inhibited any attachment to the reality or the ideals of American society and indirectly allowed as much intimidation as was accomplished by the overt repression of such groups as the Texas Rangers.

To return to Blauner's use of the concept of "internal colonialism:" in the case of the Mexicans in the United States, a major segment of this group who live in New Mexico require no significant conceptual adaptation of the classic analyses of European overseas colonialism. Less adaptation is required in fact than in applying the concepts to such countries as Kenya, Burma, Algeria, and Indonesia. Not only was the relationship between the Mexican and the Anglo-American "involuntary," involving "racism" and the "transformation . . . of indigenous values," but the culture of the Spanish American was well developed, autonomous, a majority numerically, and contained a full social system with an upper and middle as well as lower class. The comparatively non-violent conquest was really almost a postcript to nearly a decade of violence between the United States and Mexico which began in Texas.

The Texas pattern, although markedly different, can still be fitted under a colonialist rubric, with a continuous thread of violence, suppression, and adaptations to both in recent political affairs.

The Mexican experience in California is much more complicated. Mexicans lost nearly all trace of participation in California politics. Hence, there was no political tradition of any kind, even the purely negative experience in Texas. Then, too, the relationship between imported labor and employer was "voluntary," at least on the immigrants' side. The relationships were much more assymmetrical than in the "classic colonial" case.

If any further proof of the applicability of the idea of "colonialism" were needed, we have the developing ideology of the new *chicano* militants themselves. Like the black ideologies, *chicanismo* emphasizes colonialism, but in a manner to transcend the enormous disparities in Mexican American experience. . . .

# References

Blauner, Robert
  1969    "Internal colonialism and ghetto revolt." Social Problems 16 (Spring, 1969): 393–408.
Grebler, Leo *et al.*
  1970    The Mexican American People. New York: Free Press.
Kitano, Harry H. L.
  1968    The Japanese Americans. Englewood Cliffs, N.J.: Prentice-Hall, Inc.

# 34

# Occupational Discrimination: Some Theoretical Propositions

*H. M. BLALOCK, Jr.*

Historically, most American minorities have entered the labor force at or very near the bottom of the occupational ladder. Prior to the restriction of immigration during the first quarter of the 20th Century, each immigrant group was followed by more recent arrivals to take its place at the base of the pyramid. Therefore as the immigrant group became assimilated and developed industrial skills, while simultaneously losing its visibility as a minority, its relative position generally improved in the expanding economy. The Negro has been exposed to a different situation in several important respects. Not only is the economy expanding at a much slower rate, with the major sources of immigration cut off, but the Negro's major handicap—his skin-color—cannot be overcome so readily as language and other cultural characteristics which have given immigrant minorities their visibility. Furthermore, the Northern-born Negro with several generations of urban experience is often more or less automatically classed with more recent Southern migrants of his race. The saliency of skin-color as a characteristic, together with existing prejudices, is sufficiently pronounced to obscure the very real differences between native and migrant Negroes. . . .

Abridged from *Social Problems 9* (1962): 240–247, by permission of *Social Problems*, the Society for the Study of Social Problems, and the author.

Under these circumstances Negroes face the possibility of becoming a more or less permanent lower-class group. With the exception of occupations which service the minority community, it is certainly conceivable that only the least desirable positions will generally be reserved for such a racial minority. On the other hand there are certain types of occupations which, particularly during periods of labor scarcity, have begun to open up to Negroes. The purpose of the present paper is to examine one of these occupations, professional baseball, in some detail and to list a number of theoretical propositions which are immediately suggested by this analysis.

Let us begin with the assumption that a highly visible minority with an initially low occupational status is at a competitive disadvantage as compared with other persons in the labor force. In a competitive situation, therefore, the minority member will be hired only in the least desirable positions unless he possesses some compensatory advantage over his competitors. We can distinguish between two general types of such advantages, positive and negative. From the standpoint of the employer, *positive advantages* can be measured in terms of performance per unit of cost; the minority may possess certain special skills or be willing to work for lower wages. Under *negative advantages* we include those factors which would adversely affect the employer should he fail to hire a certain number of minority members, regardless of performance or cost considerations. For example he may lose minority customers, or he may undergo public censure for failing to comply with fair employment practice laws. Or he may be refused government contracts if his policies are obviously discriminatory.

It is of the nature of most negative advantages possessed by Negroes under present circumstances that these advantages diminish in value once a small token minority labor force has been hired. For example, if an employer can point to one or two Negroes in semi-responsible positions, he can usually clear himself of the charge of discrimination. If such Negroes are highly visible to members of the minority (e.g., the Negro personnel man or the salesman in the Negro community), the employer may actually gain favor with the minority group, given the existing level of discrimination by his competitors. Under these circumstances the strength of the negative advantages diminishes with decreasing discrimination, and occupational opportunities for the minority become stabilized at a point where there are a sufficient number of token representatives to relieve pressure on the employer. Further gains for the minority must come at the expense of increased outside pressure on the employer and increased vigilance in locating and demonstrating discriminatory behavior.

If the minority possesses positive advantages, however, an unstable equilibrium situation is likely to prevail once the initial resistance to employment has been broken unless, of course, more powerful counterforces are brought into operation. Thus if Negroes are willing to work for lower wages than whites, and if the efficiency of operation is not impaired by vehement protests and work stoppages on the part of whites, Negroes will be hired in larger and larger numbers until they have saturated the position concerned, until they demand equal wages, or until the opposition of white workers is aroused to the point where the advantage of hiring Negroes at lower wages is effectively counterbalanced.

Perhaps a more interesting illustration of an unstable equilibrium situation produced by a positive advantage has occurred in . . . major league baseball. Professional baseball has provided Negroes with one of the relatively few avenues for escape from traditional blue-collar occupations. Why should this be the case? In part, the answer can be given in terms of negative advantages: pressure by the growing number of Negro spectators in franchise cities. But such pressure, alone, would not account for the very rapid gains since World War II.

Negro players were completely excluded from both major leagues prior to 1947. As a result, there built up a pool of first-rate Negro athletes whose abilities were superior to those of many whites of major league caliber. Negroes within such a pool actually possessed a positive advantage over a number of white players. Once the racial barrier was broken when Jackie Robinson joined the Brooklyn Dodgers, there was an almost immediate rush to tap this reservoir of skilled manpower. The result has not been a mere effort to hire a token number of Negroes to warm the benches and to ward off the charge of discrimination, but a genuine integration of Negroes into the major leagues. Many are among the highest salaried athletes in the country, having won at least their share of Most Valuable Player awards and other major honors. This is not to say that Negro players do not face some discrimination on the part of their teammates or that they are completely integrated off the job as well as on the field. But we seem to have in professional baseball an occupation which is remarkably free of racial discrimination. And the change occurred almost overnight. . . .

[I]t will be helpful to analyze the case of professional baseball in some detail. We shall then be in a position to state some theoretical propositions which, hopefully, might apply more generally.

## The Case of Professional Baseball

Perhaps the most obvious fact about the baseball profession is its highly competitive nature. Not only is there a high degree of competition among employers for the top athletes, but individual skill is of utmost importance to the productivity of the "work group." Furthermore, skill and performance are easily evaluated. There is a whole series of precise quantitative measures of performance which can be standardized across teams and players—batting averages, slugging averages, home runs, runs batted in, fielding averages, earned run averages, strikeouts, won and lost records, etc. Each player can thus easily be compared with his competitors. There is no question whatsoever as to which batters or pitchers have the best records. In few occupations . . . is individual performance so easily evaluated by all concerned, so variable among persons, and so important to the success of the work group.

It is also the case that a high level of performance clearly works to the advantage of one's teammates, both in terms of prestige and income. Although intra-team rivalries inevitably develop, the fact that teammates share in the rewards of outstanding performance tends to channel such competition into more or less good-natured rivalry. No matter how envious they may be, players must outwardly show respect for the batting or pitching star. His performance yields him high status; the higher the productivity, the higher his prestige. This is in marked contrast to situations in which norms develop which regulate output, thereby equalizing the performances of all members and reducing the importance of individual differences in skill.

Because of the highly competitive nature of the occupation and the fact that when performance slips there are numerous other candidates available to take one's place, it would be highly difficult for the work group to develop effective sanctions restricting performance. Nor does high productivity on the part of some individuals mean fewer jobs for others, as in instances where production is limited by consumer demand. Also, there seems to be little or no systematic hostility directed toward the employer as the superordinate agent forcing performance against the will of the players. The norm of high performance is simply part of the game. . . .

Players on any one team are not in direct competition with most of their teammates. Although there may be perhaps a dozen or so pitchers in competition for starting positions, the more usual case involves competition among only two or three players who are candidates for a given position. Competition is primarily with a host of more or less anonymous players on other teams or in other leagues. A player knows that if his performance slips he will inevitably be replaced, possibly by someone on his own team but equally as likely by someone else. There is no major hierarchy of positions such that if the top man is replaced, every other person moves up one notch. In effect, this means that one gets ahead on the basis of his own performance alone. He cannot generally rely on moving permanently into a position merely if the performance of his nearest rival is lowered. Nor will it help to place barriers or restrictions in the path of his competitors, unless he can simultaneously handicap a large percentage of these persons. . . . His job tenure thus remains inherently insecure. This would seem to be one of the major reasons why the introduction of Negro players did not create an uproar among these professional athletes. Their jobs were threatened, but they had always been threatened, if not by Negroes then by countless others of their own race.

As is true for most other sports, in professional baseball top performance leads to high prestige, income, and acclaim, but it does not imply a corresponding degree of power or control over other players. A team is essentially equalitarian in nature, with persons in authority (coaches, managers) usually being drawn from the ranks of retired rather than active players. There is thus little or no threat of the Negro teammate becoming the white player's boss, and an additional source of resistance to his employment is thereby removed.

In some occupations workers may successfully prevent the hiring of minority group members by threatening to quit work or even to work for a rival employer. The prestige of major league baseball would seem to be too high, however, for such threats to appear realistic. Nor do league rules permit a player to change jobs by joining a competing team if he happens to object to some of his teammates. His freedom of choice is thus very much limited.

In baseball it is also difficult to control the minority's access to the training necessary for high-level performance. Such skill depends to a large extent on innate abilities which vary considerably from individual to individual. Nor does training in baseball require a college education, as in the case of football, or expensive equipment (as with golf), or access to restricted facilities (golf, swimming). Baseball is almost as much a lower-class as a middle-class sport. Although a long period of training or apprenticeship is required, it is difficult for whites to obtain a monopoly on training facilities, as they have in the case of a number of trades and professions. There are few, if any, trade secrets which are not well known to the public.

Another important factor has worked to the advantage of the Negro in organized baseball. In this profession performance depends only to a slight degree on interpersonal relations and manipulative skills. In contrast, a salesman's performance—also easily evaluated—depends to a large extent on his ability to persuade a prospective client. If the client is prejudiced, the Negro salesman is especially handicapped. Although a particular pitcher may be prejudiced against Negroes, there is little he can do to hamper the performance of the Negro slugger, short of an attempt at foul play. Many of baseball's top performers would never win a popularity contest, but for essentially the same reason the Negro athlete's performance is not as directly dependent upon the good-will of whites as would be the case in most managerial-type positions. We might predict, however, that Negroes will find it much more difficult working into coaching and managerial positions in baseball and will have an exceedingly difficult time obtaining positions in the "front office."

Finally, it may be of some significance that although there is a considerable amount of interaction among players both on and off the field, much of this interaction does not involve the wives and other members of the opposite sex. Players must spend a good deal of the season traveling, eating together, living in hotels, and in general recreating away from their home communities. The specter of intermarriage does not so easily arise as would be the case if, for example, a Negro male were hired as a member of an office staff.

## Some Theoretical Propositions

The foregoing analysis of professional baseball suggests some general propositions which might apply to other occupations. In listing these propositions, . . . we shall suppose that the prestige-level of the job and general labor market conditions do not vary. It is especially important that the general prestige-level be considered constant since, because of the positive correlation between the competitive nature of an occupation and its prestige, many of these propositions would otherwise seem obviously false . . . :

1. The greater the importance of high individual performance to the productivity of the work group, the lower the degree of minority discrimination by employers.
2. The greater the competition among employers for persons with high performance levels, the lower the degree of minority discrimination by employers.
3. The easier it is accurately to evaluate an individual's performance level, the lower the degree of minority discrimination by employers.
4. To the degree that high individual performance works to the advantage of other members of the work group who share rewards of high performance, the higher the positive correlation between performance and status within the group, and the lower the degree of minority discrimination by group members.

   NOTE: It is important, here, that there not be disadvantages of high performance which outweigh the advantages (e.g., where total productivity is limited by consumer demand or where there is extensive hostility toward the employer).

5. The fewer the restrictions placed on performance by members of the work group, the lower the degree of minority discrimination. (Restrictions reduce the minority member's advantage with respect to performance.) . . .
6. To the degree that a work group consists of a number of specialists interacting as a team and that there is little or no serious competition among these members, the lower the degree of minority discrimination by group members.
7. To the degree that a group member's position is threatened by anonymous outsiders rather than other members of his own group, the lower the degree of minority discrimination by group members.
8. To the extent that an individual's success depends primarily on his own performance, rather than on limiting or restricting the performance of specific other individuals, the lower the degree of minority discrimination by group members.

   NOTE: Condition 8 is likely whenever there is intense competition and a large number of potential competitors available outside the work group (e.g., a tenure position at an outstanding university).

9. To the degree that high performance does not lead to power over other members of the work group, the lower the degree of minority discrimination by group members.

NOTE: Condition 9 is especially likely when there is no hierarchy of power among group members, but where control is exercised by another category of persons altogether.

10. To the degree that group members find it difficult or disadvantageous to change jobs in order to avoid minority members, the lower the degree of minority discrimination by employers.

11. To the extent that it is difficult to prevent the minority from acquiring the necessary skills for high performance, the lower the degree of discrimination. This is especially likely when:

    (a) skill depends primarily on innate abilities,
    (b) skill can be developed without prolonged or expensive training, or
    (c) it is difficult to maintain a monopoly of skills through secrecy or the control of facilities.

12. To the extent that performance level is relatively independent of skill in interpersonal relations, the lower the degree of discrimination. . . .

NOTE: Proposition 12 is based on the assumption that performance level can be more easily affected by prejudice when such performance depends on interpersonal skills.

13. The lower the degree of purely social interaction on the job (especially interaction involving both sexes), the lower the degree of discrimination.

NOTE: A high degree of social interaction may not only result in the minority member feeling left out and desiring to leave the job, but it may also affect his performance.

## Concluding Remarks

A major question raised by the analysis of professional baseball is that of the typicality of such an occupation. What other occupations have characteristics similar to those of baseball and how many minority group members can be absorbed into these positions? Other entertainment fields immediately come to mind. Competition is intense, box-office appeal is relatively easy to evaluate, and—at least in many types of entertainment—expensive training is less important than talent or native abilities.

Academic and scientific professions also would seem to offer the Negro similar opportunities. Performance is readily evaluated in terms of research contributions or publications and does not depend primarily on interpersonal skills. There is also extensive competition for outstanding personnel, and total productivity is not sharply limited by consumer demand. It is noteworthy that although Negroes have not as yet entered these fields in any numbers, Jews are if anything "overrepresented" in academic and scientific circles. Although there is no question that anti-semitism has proved a handicap, the emphasis within the Jewish subculture given to learning and independent thinking has provided this particular minority with a compensatory positive advantage. Unlike baseball, however, training for academic and scientific careers is both prolonged and expensive. This fact, plus the lack of an intellectual tradition among Negroes, may account for the relatively small number of Negro intellectuals. But with the growing influence of state and national governmental agencies on the hiring of intellectuals, . . . Negroes should obtain additional leverage which, if added to a greater emphasis on intellectual pursuits, should give rise to increasing numbers of Negro academics.

A large number of white-collar occupations are not of this highly competitive nature, however. Especially on the lower rungs of the white-collar ladder, where a low-status minority might be expected to make its greatest initial gains, many positions are either relatively noncompetitive (e.g., stenographer, sales clerk) or highly dependent upon interpersonal skills (e.g., supervisor, realtor, insurance agent). Furthermore, the Negro finds himself in direct competition with another "minority group," women, entering the lower-level white-collar occupations in ever increasing numbers. Not only are women willing to work for lower salaries, but they constitute a relatively docile labor force. Although labor turnover among females may be high, in many instances such a turnover does not constitute a major problem in positions in which personnel are more or less interchangeable and where performance levels are not highly variable. The fact that heterosexual contacts are frequent in these white-collar occupations further militates against the Negro male.

The number of occupations in which Negroes can make use of important positive advantages may thus be quite limited. If this should be the case, perhaps the best strategy would be to encourage Negroes to seek out those white-collar occupations for which the demand is far greater than the supply because of the hesitancy of majority group members to fill these positions. Well-trained and capable Negroes may find it not too difficult to enter such professions as teaching or social work because of the fact that whites with whom they are competing are far less qualified than themselves. Although such a strategy might appear to involve accepting second-best opportunities, it may also help to reduce the Negro's handicaps in entering a wider range of occupations.

# 35

# Negro Political Behavior and Community Political and Socioeconomic Structural Factors

*JOHNNIE DANIEL*

Traditionally Negroes have been isolated from the political systems of the South. As a result, many of them have been unaccustomed to the beliefs, values, and behavior common to political life. However, in the very recent past the southern Negro has begun to surge out of his domain of political impotence. The mid-1960's voter registration drives, the development of political organization by Negro communities, and the 1965 Voting Rights Act have fermented the process of political socialization of the Negro community.

This study focuses on . . . Alabama, and attempts to analyze (a) the changes in Negro political mobilization from 1960 to 1966, and (b) the changes in the relationships between Negro political mobilization and the socioeconomic structure of Alabama communities from 1960 to 1966. . . .

Reprinted, abridged, from *Social Forces 47* (March 1969): 274–280. Copyright © The University of North Carolina Press.

## Hypotheses and Description of Variables

### CHANGE IN NEGRO POLITICAL MOBILIZATION 1960 TO 1966

The measure of Negro political mobilization used in this study is the percent of the Negro voting age population registered to vote. Between 1960 and 1966 this percentage has increased in practically every county in Alabama. There are several possible reasons for these increases: one is the presence of federal voter examiners which gave Negroes the opportunity to register to vote without qualifying tests and discrimination;[1] another is the presence of candidates that gave Negroes an acceptable choice in the forthcoming elections. . . . [T]he following hypothesis was proposed for examination:

*Counties with federal examiners and Negro candidates have higher rates of Negro political mobilization than counties without federal examiners and Negro candidates.*

### SOCIOECONOMIC STRUCTURE AND NEGRO POLITICAL MOBILIZATION

Previous studies have found positive relationships between Negro political mobilization and the following variables: percent of labor force in manufacturing; percent of nonwhite labor force in white-collar occupations; nonwhite median school years completed; and nonwhite median income. These findings are consistent with the generalization that the higher the socioeconomic status the greater the participation in politics.

Other studies have also found negative relationships between Negro political mobilization and the following variables: percent of population urban; percent of labor force in agriculture; percent of farms operated by tenants; and percent of the population that is Negro. Explanations offered for the negative relationship between urbanization and Negro political mobilization stipulate less political interest among urban Negroes than rural Negroes. Explanations for the other negative relationships range from fear of whites of Negro domination, to economic dependence and apathy among Negroes. . . .

It is thought that the registration drives of the mid-1960's disrupted the pat-

---

[1]The 1965 Voting Rights Act permitted adult residents of a state to be registered by federal examiners in those political subdivisions where the attorney general "(1) . . . has received complaints in writing from twenty or more residents of such political subdivision alleging that they have been denied the right to vote . . . and if he believes such complaints to be meritorious, or (2) if in his judgment (considering, among other factors, whether the ratio of nonwhite persons to white persons registered to vote within such subdivisions appears to him to be reasonably attributable to violations of the Fifteenth Amendment or whether substantial evidence exists that bona fide efforts are being made within such subdivision to comply with the Fifteenth Amendment) . . ."

terns cited above and instituted new ones. This expectation led to the following hypothesis:

*The relationship between Negro political mobilization and the socioeconomic structure of Alabama communities changed substantially between 1960 and 1966.*

In order to measure the socioeconomic status of Negroes within a county, an index of nonwhite socioeconomic status was computed. The index that was used is the weighted mean of the following variables: percent of employed nonwhites with white-collar occupations; percent of nonwhite families with incomes of $4,000 or more; and percent of nonwhites 25 years old or over who have completed four years of high school.

## Data

In order to test the hypotheses outlined above, effort was made to acquire political, social, and economic data of temporal comparability from 1960 and 1966. The task of acquiring data for 1960 was not formidable because of the availability of social and economic data from the *Census of Population: 1960*[2] and voter registration data from the *1961 Report of the Commission on Civil Rights.*[3] The census report does not include socioeconomic data on the nonwhite population of counties with less than 1,000 nonwhites; therefore, for some of the analyses only *61* of the *67* counties of Alabama are used.

Nonwhite socioeconomic data for 1966 are not as readily available as such data for 1960, making it necessary to use data of other years and statistical estimates. As a substitute for 1966 data, the 1964 levels of percent of total employment in agriculture and manufacturing were used. For the other socioeconomic data for this year, estimates were computed on the basis of patterns that have been established between 1950 and 1960. The implicit assumption is that the patterns remained constant through 1966. Even though the estimates are not as good as actual figures, they should not deviate very much from them, and should reflect the conditions that existed in 1966.

The voter registration data for 1966 came from a report on the Southern Regional Council of *Voter Registration in the South, Summer, 1966.*[4] Neither these data nor the 1960 voter registration data are error free. . . .

[2] U.S. Department of Commerce, Bureau of the Census, *Census of Population: 1960, Volume 2, General Social and Economic Characteristics* (Washington, D.C.: Government Printing Office, 1961).

[3] U.S. Commission on Civil Rights, *Voting, 1961 Report, Book 1* (Washington, D.C.: Government Printing Office, 1961).

[4] Voter Education Project, *Voter Registration in the South, Summer, 1966* (Atlanta: Southern Regional Council, 1966). The rates of Negro political mobilization for 1966 were computed from the data on the number registered included in this report, and calculations by the researcher of estimates of the voting age population in 1966.

## Findings

### CHANGE IN NEGRO POLITICAL MOBILIZATION 1960 TO 1966

Negro political mobilization increased throughout Alabama between 1960 and 1966. An examination of Table 1 reveals that in more than half of the counties of Alabama, Negro political mobilization increased by *30* percentage points or more. The data presented in Table 1 seem to support the first hypothesis; of the *21* counties that increased in political mobilization by *50* percentage points or more, *11* are counties to which federal examiners were sent, and *5* are counties that are contiguous to these counties.

More support for this hypothesis is given in Table 2 in which mean Negro political mobilization is cross-tabulated by presence and absence of federal examiners and Negro candidates. The counties that have the highest levels of Negro political mobilization are those counties that had both Negro candidates and federal examiners, and the counties that have the lowest levels of Negro political mobilization are those counties that had neither Negro candidates nor federal examiners. . . . The counties that had Negro candidates but no federal examiners and the counties that had federal examiners but no Negro candidates have the same level of Negro political mobilization (*68* percent), indicating that possibly the presence of Negro candidates and the presence of federal voter examiners have similar effects on Negro political mobilization.

**TABLE 1. Number of Counties by Increase in Negro Political Mobilization from 1960 to 1966, and Presence of Federal Voter Examiners, Alabama**

| PERCENT INCREASE IN NEGRO POLITICAL MOBILIZATION | COUNTIES | | NUMBER WITH FEDERAL EXAMINERS |
|---|---|---|---|
| | NUMBER | PERCENT | |
| 0 to 9 . . . . . . . . . | 9 | 13 | 0 |
| 10 to 19 . . . . . . . . | 15 | 22 | 0 |
| 20 to 29 . . . . . . . . | 9 | 13 | 0 |
| 30 to 39 . . . . . . . . | 8 | 12 | 0 |
| 40 to 49 . . . . . . . . | 5 | 7 | 1 |
| 50 to 59 . . . . . . . . | 6 | 9 | 3 |
| 60 to 69 . . . . . . . . | 6 | 9 | 3 |
| 70 to 79 . . . . . . . . | 4 | 6 | 2 |
| 80 to 89 . . . . . . . . | 3 | 4 | 1 |
| 90 to 100. . . . . . . . | 2 | 3 | 2 |

[5] Hubert M. Blalock, Jr., *Toward a Theory of Minority-Group Relations* (New York: John Wiley & Sons, 1967).

**TABLE 2.** Mean Negro Political Mobilization by Presence of Federal Examiners and Negro Candidates by Counties, 1960 and 1966, Alabama

| NEGRO CANDIDATE | FEDERAL EXAMINERS | | |
| --- | --- | --- | --- |
| | IN COUNTY | NOT IN COUNTY | TOTAL |
| In county. . . . . . . . . . | 78 (4) | 68 (4) | 74 (8) |
| Not in county. . . . . . . | 68 (8) | 48 (51) | 51 (59) |
| Total. . . . . . . . . . . . | 70 (12) | 50 (55) | |

These findings indicate that the previously low levels of Negro voter registration cannot be explained simply by Negro apathy; for attention must be given to the prohibitive social system in which they lived. The data seem to support the proposition that given a social system in which Negroes are given the opportunity to register for elections, they perceive their role as meaningful and important, and they will register in large numbers.

## SOCIOECONOMIC STRUCTURE AND NEGRO POLITICAL MOBILIZATION

The political factors outlined above seem to have fostered greater Negro political activity, and it is hypothesized that this activity has changed the structural relationships that have been found to exist between political and socioeconomic variables. To test this hypothesis, correlations were computed between Negro political mobilization and selected socioeconomic characteristics of Alabama counties. The result of this analysis is presented in Table 3, and the difference between the correlations for 1960 and 1966 affirms this hypothesis. . . . [T]he correlations for 1966 are in most cases very different from the 1960 correlations. . . . Whereas survey data might demonstrate a direct relationship between social class and political activity, these findings indicate that one cannot simply predict low rates of political activity among Negroes in ecological areas that have high rates of poverty, agricultural employment, and Negro concentration. . . .

These findings are consistent with some of the propositions proposed by Blalock in his theoretical analysis of minority—dominant group relations.[5] One such proposition states that minority mobilization should be low if there is a low perceived probability of success in reducing discrimination through such mobilization. Negroes have a greater probability of reducing discrimination through politics in counties in which they are a majority than in counties in which they are not. Given the opportunity to register, Negroes became politically mobilized more in counties where they have the greater probability of influencing elec-

**TABLE 3.** Correlation Between Negro Political Mobilization and Socioeconomic Characteristics of Counties, 1960 and 1966, Alabama

| SOCIOECONOMIC CHARACTERISTICS | ZERO-ORDER CORRELATION | |
| --- | --- | --- |
| | 1960 | 1966 |
| Index of nonwhite socioeconomic status[a] .......... | .20 | -.21 |
| Percent of total employment in manufacturing[b] ........................... | .15 | -.20 |
| Incidence of poverty in 1959................... | -.25 | .56 |
| Percent of farms operated by tenants[c]............. | -.50 | .29 |
| Percent nonwhite of total population[a]............. | -.66 | .43 |
| Percent of nonwhites living in urban areas[a]...................................... | -.22 | -.26 |
| Percent of total employment in agriculture[b] ........ | -.01 | .25 |

[a]The 1966 data for these variables are estimates based on the changes between 1950 and 1960. The number of cases of the correlations between the index of nonwhite socioeconomic status and Negro political mobilization is 61 for both 1960 and 1966.

[b]In computing the 1966 correlation, because of the lack of data for 1966 for these variables, data on their 1965 levels were used.

[c]For this variable, because of lack of temporal comparable data, 1959 data were used for the 1960 correlations, and 1964 data for the 1966 correlations.

Computed from: U.S. Department of Commerce, *Census of Population: 1950* and *Census of Population: 1960* (Washington, D.C.: Government Printing Office, 1950 and 1960); *Economic Abstract of Alabama, 1966* (Alabama: Bureau of Business Research, University of Alabama, 1966); U.S. Commission on Civil Rights, *Voting, 1961 Report, Book 1* (Washington, D.C.: Government Printing Office, 1961); and Voter Education Project, *Voter Registration in the South, Summer, 1966* (Atlanta: Southern Regional Council, 1966).

tions, than in counties where this probability is less. A clear conception of the change in the relationship between Negro political mobilization and percent Negro can be obtained from an examination of Figure 1.

Counties with high percent Negro are characterized by poverty, tenant-farming and agricultural employment, and not manufacturing, urbanization, and middle- and upper-class Negroes. It is therefore, not surprising that when one examines the changes in the relationship between Negro political mobilization and these variables, the findings when percent Negro is considered are similar to those when poverty, tenant-farming and agricultural employment are considered; and opposite to those when manufacturing and nonwhite socioeconomic status are considered. . . .

## Conclusions

The aftermath of the mid-1960 voter registration drives left the Negroes in Alabama more politically mobilized than they have been since Reconstruction. Important facets in this change have been the presence of candidates acceptable

**FIGURE 1.**    Negro Political Mobilization by Percent Negro for 1960 and 1966

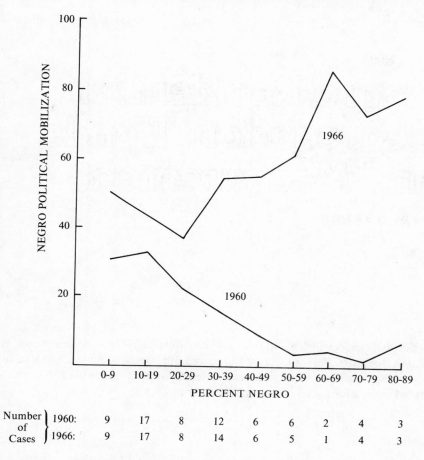

| Number of Cases | | 0-9 | 10-19 | 20-29 | 30-39 | 40-49 | 50-59 | 60-69 | 70-79 | 80-89 |
|---|---|---|---|---|---|---|---|---|---|---|
| | 1960: | 9 | 17 | 8 | 12 | 6 | 6 | 2 | 4 | 3 |
| | 1966: | 9 | 17 | 8 | 14 | 6 | 5 | 1 | 4 | 3 |

to Negroes and the 1965 Voting Rights Act which sent federal examiners to the state giving Negroes a greater incentive and opportunity to register. Concomitant with these increases in Negro political mobilization have been changes in the relationship of this factor with the socioeconomic structure of the community. . . .

Similar patterns of change probably occurred in other southern states where the removal of restrictions of Negro registration was accompanied by encouragement from organized groups to register. This introduction of many Negroes to the political arena in the South undoubtedly increased the political aspirations of the Negroes and the concern of the southern politician for the Negro vote. . . .

# 36

# Negro Residential Segregation: Trends and Measurement

## KARL TAEUBER

Residential segregation of whites and nonwhites effects their separation in schools, hospitals, libraries, parks, stores, and other institutions without legal or direct discrimination. Reviewing these interrelations, Myrdal noted that "residential segregation is basic in a mechanical sense."[1] . . . .

## Method

Comparisons of levels of residential segregation in various cities or at different points in time require a suitable measure. . . .

The history of efforts at formulating numerical measures of the degree of residential segregation is not an inspiring one, and it is fortunately not necessary to review it here in detail.[2] Briefly, several of the proposed indexes, including those most widely cited, have methodologically unsound features, and exag-

---

[1] Gunnar Myrdal, *An American Dilemma,* New York: Harper and Brothers, 1944, Vol. I, p. 618.

[2] Otis Dudley Duncan and Beverly Duncan, "A Methodological Analysis of Segregation Indexes," *American Sociological Review 20* (April, 1955), pp. 210–217.

Abridged from *Social Problems 12* (1964): 42–50, by permission of *Social Problems,* the Society for the Study of Social Problems, and the author.

gerated claims have been made for indexes which, at best, have a relatively narrow research role to play in social investigation.

Methodologically, the most serious fault of several possible indexes is that the city percentage of Negroes is incorporated in their computation. Thus if there were two cities with similar residential patterns, but in one Negroes comprised 10 percent of the population and in the other 50 percent, then some indexes would assign a higher value to the latter city. . . .

The concept of residential segregation is multi-faceted, and no single index can summarize all aspects of a complex spatial distribution. For preliminary research on inter-city differences, I choose to overlook various aspects of the spatial configuration of Negro residential areas such as the number of distinct "ghettos," their shapes, or their specific locations; rather, I prefer to start with a conceptualization of residential segregation as referring to the overall degree of unevenness or dissimilarity in the distributions of white and Negro residences throughout a city. This conceptualization leads directly to the use of the index of dissimilarity, a measure which has become familiar in the sociological literature.[3] Only its particular application to use as a segregation index need be elaborated. . . .

The index can range in value from 0 to 100. If each city block contains only whites, or only nonwhites, and there are no blocks of mixed occupancy, then the distribution is as uneven as possible, and the index will assume a value of 100. On the other hand, if skin color plays no role at all in determining residential location, then any city block chosen at random would be expected to be neither all white nor all nonwhite, but to have each group represented in the same proportion as in the city as a whole. In this case, the segregation index assumes a value of zero, indicating no residential segregation. Specific values of the segregation index between 0 and 100 indicate the minimum percentage of nonwhites who would have to move from blocks containing too high a percentage of nonwhites to blocks containing too low a percentage. This interpretation is obviously for heuristic purposes, and is not intended as a guide for social action.

Computation of such a segregation index requires data showing the numbers of residents of each color in each sub-area of the city. Ordinarily these data come from a decennial census. For sub-areas, the choice is limited to census tracts or city blocks. I prefer to use block data, which means a heavier emphasis on the "fine structure" of the residential distribution, as opposed to the coarser patterns revealed by census tract data. Another advantage of city blocks is their fixed boundaries, which are not subject to the overt gerrymandering with respect to racial enclaves that census tract committees may properly apply to tract boundaries.

---

[3] Duncan and Duncan, "A Methodological Analysis . . . " *op. cit.;* Duncan & Duncan, "Residential Distribution and Occupational Stratification," *American Journal of Sociology* *60* (March, 1955), pp. 493–503.

A few comments on the limitations of the index of dissimilarity (or any other segregation index) may be noted briefly here, and additional comments will be reserved for the discussion. Any segregation index is an average measure, overlooking elements of variation and of detailed patterning in each individual city. The data presented here refer to corporate cities, whereas the use of urbanized areas or metropolitan areas would be preferable. The index has been computed using data for whites and nonwhites because the necessary residential distributions are not available separately for Negroes. Most of the nonwhites in the United States are Negroes and I will use the terms more or less interchangeably, but in considering the findings for western cities with large Oriental populations it is necessary to distinguish between the two categories.

## Findings

Indexes of residential segregation between whites and nonwhites have been computed for 109 cities for which the basic data were available for 1940, 1950, and 1960, and which at the beginning of the period, in 1940, contained more than 1,000 nonwhite occupied dwelling units. One basic fact stands out in examination of the computed index values: There is pronounced residential segregation between whites and nonwhites in all cities with sizable Negro populations. The indexes range in value from 60.1 to 98.0 for all three years. In each year, between one-fourth and one-half of these 109 cities had index values above 90.0, and more than three-fourths had values above 80.0. It can be shown that these values are far higher than could occur by chance under a null hypothesis of no relationship between race and residence. More significantly, indexes for white-nonwhite segregation are far higher than similar indexes for various immigrant groups against native whites, or for various occupational groups against each other.[4] Racial residential segregation is clearly more pronounced than class or ethnic residential segregation, and it is a universal feature of American urban society.

The research strategy for this analysis is comparative, and derives from the focus on racial residential segregation as one aspect of differential urban land use. Two basic questions are posed: What accounts for the variation between cities in the degree of residential segregation at any given point in time? What accounts for the variation between cities in the direction and magnitude of changes over time in the degree of residential segregation?

Average segregation index values for various groupings of cities for 1940 and 1960, along with the average changes in index values during each of the two intercensal periods, are presented in Table 1. The top row of this table sum-

[4]Otis Dudley Duncan and Stanley Lieberson, "Ethnic Segregation and Assimilation," *American Journal of Sociology 64* (January, 1959), pp. 364–374. Duncan and Duncan, *op. cit.,* "Residential Distribution. . . ."

**TABLE 1.** Average Values of Indexes of Residential Segregation for Cities Grouped by Region, Percentage Nonwhite, and City Size, 1940 and 1960, and Changes, 1940–1950 and 1950–1960

| CITY GROUPING | NUMBER OF CITIES | AVERAGE VALUES OF INDEXES | | | |
|---|---|---|---|---|---|
| | | 1940 | CHANGE 1940–50 | CHANGE 1950–60 | 1960 |
| All cities[a] | 109 | 85.2 | +2.0 | −1.2 | 86.1 |
| *Region* | | | | | |
| Northeast | 25 | 83.2 | +0.4 | −4.7 | 78.9 |
| North Central | 29 | 88.4 | +1.5 | −1.5 | 88.4 |
| West | 10 | 82.7 | +0.3 | −6.5 | 76.4 |
| South | 45 | 85.0 | +3.7 | +2.2 | 90.7 |
| S. Atlantic | 22 | 87.0 | +1.9 | +1.9 | 90.6 |
| E. S. Central | 9 | 85.0 | +3.2 | +3.1 | 91.2 |
| W. S. Central | 14 | 81.7 | +6.8 | +2.0 | 90.5 |
| *Percentage nonwhite, 1940* | | | | | |
| 1.2– 4.2 | 22 | 84.8 | +0.4 | −4.4 | 80.8 |
| 4.4– 8.0 | 22 | 84.6 | +1.3 | −3.9 | 81.9 |
| 8.2–12.9 | 22 | 84.8 | +1.9 | −1.9 | 84.8 |
| 14.4–27.5 | 22 | 86.4 | +3.6 | +1.0 | 91.1 |
| 28.5–48.6 | 21 | 85.5 | +3.1 | +3.4 | 92.0 |
| *City size (in thousands), 1940* | | | | | |
| 46– 69 | 22 | 83.8 | +2.5 | +0.6 | 86.8 |
| 71– 111 | 22 | 83.7 | +2.8 | −0.9 | 85.6 |
| 112– 178 | 22 | 86.6 | +1.7 | −2.2 | 86.1 |
| 193– 368 | 22 | 84.9 | +2.7 | −1.1 | 86.5 |
| 385–7,455 | 21 | 87.2 | +0.5 | −2.4 | 85.3 |
| *Interrelationships[b]* | | | | | |

| Region | Size | Percent nonwhite | | | | | |
|---|---|---|---|---|---|---|---|
| North | Small | Low | 20 | 82.9 | +0.6 | −4.6 | 78.9 |
| North | Small | High | 8 | 86.9 | +2.2 | −2.0 | 87.1 |
| North | Large | Low | 29 | 86.3 | +0.8 | −3.6 | 83.4 |
| North | Large | High | 7 | 87.7 | +1.1 | −2.2 | 86.6 |
| South | Small | Low | 3 | 80.8 | +2.6 | +1.7 | 85.2 |
| South | Small | High | 26 | 84.9 | +3.7 | +2.2 | 90.8 |
| South | Large | Low | 2 | 82.0 | +6.5 | +0.2 | 88.6 |
| South | Large | High | 14 | 86.1 | +3.4 | +2.5 | 91.9 |

[a]All cities for which census block data are available for 1940, 1950, and 1960, and which in 1940 contained more than 1,000 nonwhite households.

[b]Size as of 1940; small, less than 150,000; large, above 150,000. Percentage nonwhite as of 1940; low, less than 10.0 percent; high, 10.0 per cent or above.

marizes the average performance for the entire set of cities. At the start of the period, the average value was 85.2, a very high level. During the 1940's the average value increased by 2.0 points; during the 1950's declines wiped out many of the earlier increases, leaving the average in 1960 only a fraction higher than 20 years before.

## REGION

Trends in the size, social status, and composition of Negro urban populations differ between North, South, and West. Regional groupings thus provide a logical starting point for the analysis of inter-city variations in residential segregation. Using the four census regions, in 1940 the North Central cities had, on the average, a greater degree of residential segregation between whites and nonwhites than the other three regions, whose average index values were similar to one another. Within the South, however, there was geographic differentiation, with cities along the Atlantic coast tending to have higher index values than cities farther west, particularly those in Texas.

The changes between 1940 and 1960 altered the rank order and increased the differences between the regions. The average for the western cities declined during each decade, so that by 1960 cities in the West had the lowest average segregation index values. The large numbers of Chinese, Japanese, Filipinos, and Indians in the nonwhite populations of some western cities together with the very rapid rates of growth of Negro population probably contribute to the differentiation of the West from the other regions. Cities in the Northeast had very slight increases during the 1940's, and sizable average declines during the 1950's, so that by 1960 northeastern cities had the second lowest average values. North Central cities, which started out at higher levels, had larger increases during the 1940's and smaller decreases during the 1950's than either the Northeast or the West, and in 1960 the region was only a little below its 1940 position. However, it was no longer the top-ranking region, for the South had larger increases than the other regions during the 1940's, and was the only region to register average increases during the 1950's. By 1960, residential segregation was more pronounced in southern cities than in those of any other region. Within the South, those cities which had been lowest had the largest gains during the 20 year period, so that there was little geographic variation within the South in 1960. . . .

## INTERRELATIONSHIPS

Region, percentage nonwhite, and city size are not independent of each other, but are badly confounded. The bottom panel of Table 1 presents an abbreviated cross-classification of these three variables. Region stands out as the most significant factor with respect to the changes. Percentage nonwhite retains significance: Within most of the region and size groupings, cities with the lower percentages nonwhite have the lower average segregation index values, and the smaller increases or larger decreases over time. Within region and percentage nonwhite groupings, there remains a small positive relationship between city size and segregation index values, but there is no systematic variation in the changes over time.

## Discussion

Substantively, the most interesting finding of this research is the universally high degree of residential segregation between whites and Negroes within the cities of the United States. Whether a city is in the North, South, or West; whether it is a large metropolitan center or a suburb; whether it is a coastal resort town, a rapidly growing industrial center, or a declining mining town; whether nonwhites constitute forty percent of the population or less than one percent; in every case white and Negro residences are highly segregated from each other. . . .

This uniformly high degree of residential segregation between whites and nonwhites has implications for the comparative type of research reported on here. Such inter-city comparisons are necessarily concerned with explaining only the limited range of variation in index values that exists. Cities with high levels of residential segregation cannot be compared with cities with really low levels, because there are no examples of the latter. Thus investigations of the development of patterns of residential segregation require different data and perhaps a different approach. . . .

Even within its own sphere of application—the actual residential intermixture of whites and Negroes—segregation indexes of the type discussed in this analysis have relatively little utility for the analysis of residential segregation within any individual city. To say that the segregation index for Chicago for 1960 was 92.6 can document the obvious fact that Chicago, like every other American city, has a very high degree of residential segregation. This single summary index, however, does not indicate the causes or effects of racial residential segregation in Chicago. Neither does the fact that Chicago has a higher or lower index value than some other city logically support a conclusion that race relations are better or worse in Chicago. The index is but one datum, and he who would misuse it gains a sense of numerical precision at a loss of sociological sensibility.

The same limitations and several others apply to the use of segregation indexes to study change. That the value of an index for a city is higher in 1960 than it was in 1950 does not tell much about the specific pattern of change between 1950 and 1960. . . .

To conclude on a note of affirmation of the value of segregation indexes for comparative studies, a final bit of speculation may be permitted. On the basis of the data presented here, a limited set of data covering a much longer historical period, and a wealth of secondary literature, it seems likely that the degree of residential segregation between whites and nonwhites has been increasing in both northern and southern cities during most of the century since the Civil War. In northern cities, this trend may be partially the result of the rapid increases of Negro population during periods of tight housing supply during the two world wars, along with economic and social practices limiting the ability of Negroes to compete for housing outside of the Negro residential areas. In the South under slavery, residential segregation in urban areas existed, but not in the same forms as today. During the last fifty years, patterns of residential segregation may have been replacing some of the diminishing forms of legal, economic, and social discrimination. To return to the opening theme, perhaps the "mechanical" importance of residential segregation, its powerful impact on extra-legal types of segregation—in schools, parks, etc.,—underlies the continuing rapid increases in southern cities. In the North, the increasingly powerful legal and economic position of urban Negroes combined with the lesser degree of overt social discrimination may finally be overcoming the long-term trend toward increasing residential segregation.

# 37

# School Integration and Occupational Achievement of Negroes

*ROBERT L. CRAIN*

Much has been written about Negro poverty and its roots in the Negro's lack of skills and in racial discrimination. But even if all Negroes had skills and there were no discrimination, the segregation of Negroes, residentially and socially, would lower their incomes, simply because Negroes would continue to be denied access to a valuable resource—information about employment opportunities.

American Negroes live in a society which is largely segregated. In this society, there are whole occupations and industries which have very few Negro workers. Sometimes this is due to historical accident; the industry is located in a region which has few Negroes, for example. In other instances their absence is due to discrimination, sometimes subtle and sometimes not, or it is simply because Negroes do not apply for these jobs. In many cases, they do not apply because they do not know when a job becomes open. It is a common observation that one of the most significant forms of unfair employment practice is the hiring of new employees from referrals made by the present staff; if the staff is all white, the persons who apply will be friends, relatives, and neighbors who are also white. The employer who advertises publicly for help must bear the costs of

Abridged from *American Journal of Sociology* 75 (January 1970): 593–606. Used by permission of the University of Chicago Press. © 1970 by The University of Chicago. All rights reserved.

interviewing large numbers of applicants and must depend only upon the application blank in making a decision. If there is a demand for that type of employment, he is wasting money by advertising when he can staff his plant without doing so. The best jobs are, therefore, not advertised. Even if the employer does advertise publicly, . . . friends, neighbors, and relatives of present employees still have the inside track.

In a segregated community, Negroes must depend upon other Negroes for information about job opportunities. If Negroes are segregated into low-paying employment, they will, of course, have limited knowledge of better-paying opportunities. As Sheppard and Belitsky (1967) observe, for the poor to depend upon friends and relatives is rather like "the blind leading the blind." . . .

Thus we are arguing that occupational opportunities for Negroes will be limited until there is at least partial racial assimilation—until Negroes have sufficient contact with whites to learn about job opportunities and obtain referrals from white employees. There are numerous barriers to this kind of assimilation. The most obvious one is the amount of prejudice of whites toward Negroes and of Negroes toward whites. But even if there were no personal prejudice, the present patterns of racial segregation in social relations and in housing could persist through inertia, and continue to limit sharply the occupational achievement of Negroes for many years.

## School Integration

The public school is an important factor in the process of assimilation. Negroes who have attended integrated schools continue to have a large number of white friends as adults; they are more likely to live in integrated neighborhoods, to favor integrated schooling for their children, and to prefer belonging to integrated voluntary organizations (Crain, 1971). This means they will have greater opportunities to move into a biracial employment market rather than being restricted to the traditional ghetto employers. Hence, Negroes who attended integrated schools should have less-traditional patterns of employment and, as a consequence, higher occupational prestige and income. In order to substantiate this argument, we will present data showing that (a) Negroes from integrated schools are more likely to hold "nontraditional" jobs—jobs which have relatively few Negroes in them, (b) Negroes in nontraditional jobs will earn more money than those in traditional jobs, hence (c) Negroes from integrated schools will have higher incomes, and (d) Negroes with white friendships will have access to information about the labor market which they can use to obtain these nontraditional jobs, hence (e) Negroes from integrated schools will have more knowledge about jobs. We shall present the findings separately for each sex; the pattern is somewhat different for males and females.

Data to establish these five points are drawn from a 1966 survey of Negroes, aged twenty-one to forty-five, living in the metropolitan areas of the North. The sample was weighted to overrepresent Negroes in higher-income neighborhoods and in the smaller metropolitan areas; the tables are hence weighted to reflect the actual population. The true number of cases is approximately 40 percent of the weighted *N*s shown in the tables. Interviewing was conducted by an all-Negro staff.

Block quota sampling was used. . . . The original sample was 1,624 cases and the weighted *N* is 4,153. We will focus largely upon that one-third of the sample which attended northern high schools and who report an occupation; this is 1,231 weighted cases.


## Integration and Nontraditional Employment

Table 1 records the percentage of Negroes for each of the eight major urban occupational groups in the 1960 census and the percentage of alumni of integrated high schools and of segregated high schools in each of these occupations. Negro men tend to be concentrated in the lower blue-collar occupations—operatives, service workers, laborers—and in the lowest of the white-collar occupations—clerical work. Conversely, Negro men tend not to be professionals, managers, salesworkers, or craftsmen, hence, we shall call these four major occupational groups nontraditional. Approximately one-third of the male Negro alumni of integrated high schools are in three nontraditional occupations: crafts, sales, and the professions, while only one-fifth of the Negroes who attended segregated schools are in these three groups. Male Negro managers, owners, and proprietors tend to come from segregated schools, but contact with whites is not necessary to enter these occupations, since almost all Negro managers are in businesses serving largely Negro clientele. (If the data were available, we would hypothesize that Negro businessmen serving white clientele would be more likely to have had integrated schooling.)

Contrary to popular belief, Negroes who attended integrated schools do not come from higher-status or more stable families, and therefore these results do not change when background variables are introduced as controls.

One reason Negro clerks are slightly more likely to be from segregated schools is that Negro clerical positions are available in the largest metropolitan areas where there also is the largest number of segregated schools. When city size is introduced as a control variable, the apparent predominance of men from segregated schools in clerical work becomes smaller.

Negro women from integrated schools are much more likely to enter the professions. But otherwise, our thesis does not hold for women; Negro women from integrated schools are not more likely to have nontraditional jobs.

The eight major occupational groups are broad categories, and we can continue this investigation by looking at differences in the detailed occupational classifications within each major group. In Table 2, we look within each major occupational group and see that Negroes from integrated schools are more likely

TABLE 1. Occupations of Alumni of Segregated and Integrated Northern High Schools, by Sex, and Percentage of Negroes in Each Occupational Group

| | MALES | | | | FEMALES | | | |
| | High School Was | | | | High School Was | | | |
| OCCUPATIONAL GROUP | INTE-GRATED (%) | SEGRE-GATED (%) | DIFFER-ENCE | NEGROES IN GROUP (%) | INTE-GRATED (%) | SEGRE-GATED (%) | DIFFER-ENCE | NEGROES IN GROUP (%) |
|---|---|---|---|---|---|---|---|---|
| Professional | 11 | 8 | +3 | 5.9* | 14 | 4 | +10 | 10.7* |
| Managers, owners, proprietors | 3 | 6 | -3 | 4.2* | 1 | 0 | + 1 | 5.3* |
| Clerical | 11 | 13 | -2 | 11.3 | 22 | 32 | -10 | 6.7* |
| Sales | 3 | 0 | +3 | 4.7* | 2 | 3 | - 1 | 4.7* |
| Craftsmen | 19 | 13 | +6 | 7.5* | 2 | 2 | 0 | 11.4 |
| Operatives | 31 | 40 | -9 | 14.3 | 22 | 21 | + 1 | 13.2 |
| Service | 15 | 10 | +5 | 29.1 | 36 | 38 | - 2 | 38.8 |
| Labor | 6 | 10 | -4 | 27.4 | 0 | 0 | – | 32.7 |
| Total | 99 | 100 | | | 99 | 100 | | |
| N† | (498) | (227) | | | (372) | (134) | | |

Note.—Alumni of southern high schools excluded from this table.
*Indicates nontraditional occupation.
†Weighted; true N is approximately 0.4 times N shown for all tables.

TABLE 2. Percentage of Respondents from Each Major Occupational Group in (Detailed) Occupations Which Are Less Than 3 Percent Negro, by Integration and Region of High School, and by Sex

| MAJOR OCCUPATIONAL GROUP | MALES | | | FEMALES | | |
|---|---|---|---|---|---|---|
| | *High School Was* | | | *High School Was* | | |
| | NORTH, INTEGRATED (%) | NORTH, SEGREGATED (%) | SOUTH, SEGREGATED (%) | NORTH, INTEGRATED (%) | NORTH, SEGREGATED (%) | SOUTH, SEGREGATED (%) |
| Professional | 36 (56) | 33 (18) | 31 (35) | 8 (49) | 0 (6) | 0 (45) |
| Clerical, sales | 19 (67) | 13 (30) | 30 (40) | 58 (89) | 43 (47) | 58 (36) |
| Craftsmen | 56 (93) | 41 (29) | 15 (113) | — | — | — |
| Operatives | 4 (155) | 0 (91) | 0 (179) | — | — | — |
| Service | 8 (76) | 0 (22) | 0 (51) | — | — | — |

Note.—Sign test, differences among northern-educated respondents significant $p < .01$ (one-tailed).

291

to hold those occupations whose work force is less than 3 percent Negro, which we shall define as nontraditional (U.S. Bureau of the Census 1960, Table 3, pp. 21–30). We also see in Table 2 that Negro women from integrated schools are more likely to hold nontraditional occupations in the professions, and in clerical and sales positions. There are no Negro female occupations in the general category of craftsmen, operatives, or service which are not more than 3 percent Negro . . .

These two tables yield convincing evidence (at least for males) of our general point that Negro alumni of integrated schools are in "integrated" jobs. In Table 3, we see that those respondents who hold these nontraditional occupations within each major census classification tend to have higher incomes. In the case of males, those in nontraditional occupations have noticeably higher incomes in all five test groups. However, the pattern for females is completely mixed, and apparently meaningless; for example, the very high correlation for Negro professional women is based almost entirely on the high income of Negro schoolteachers, a traditional occupation.

One might argue that the Negroes in these nontraditional occupations are better qualified, and to some extent this is true. In Table 4, we see that Negroes in nontraditional occupations tend to have higher educational attainment. However, observe that the association between education and nontraditionalism is weaker than the association between income and nontraditionalism; in Table 4, $\gamma$ is generally lower than in Table 3. (Our measures of education and income are distributed through five categories with approximately the same marginals; therefore $\gamma$ in both cases is comparable.)

In Table 4, we again see no pattern for females. Those who have nontraditional occupations are not better educated. This is consistent with the idea that occupational discrimination and inequality is greater for Negro males than for Negro females.

**T A B L E 3.** Association Between Percentage Negro (Detailed Occupational Categories) and Income, Within Major Occupational Categories, by Sex

| OCCUPATIONAL CATEGORIES | Males | | Females | |
|---|---|---|---|---|
| | $\gamma$ | TOTAL $N$ | $\gamma$ | TOTAL $N$ |
| Professional | −.38 | 118 | + .42 | 108 |
| Managers, owners, proprietors | * | 50 | +1.0 | 13 |
| Clerical and sales | −.31 | 173 | − .01 | 193 |
| Craftsmen | −.21 | 303 | +1.0 | 22 |
| Operatives | −.03 | 623 | + .06 | 236 |
| Service | −.65 | 209 | + .18 | 465 |
| Laborers | * | 195 | * | 3 |

*When the data are quartiled, there is no variance in male managerial occupations, which have few Negroes without exception, or in laboring occupations, all of which have many Negroes.

**TABLE 4.** Association Between Negro (Detailed Occupational Categories) and Education, Within Major Census Occupational Categories, by Sex

| MAJOR CATEGORY | Males | | Females | |
|---|---|---|---|---|
| | $\gamma$ | TOTAL $N$ | $\gamma$ | TOTAL $N$ |
| Professional | −.15 | 118 | + .52 | 113 |
| Managers, owners, proprietors | * | 50 | +1.00 | 13 |
| Clerical and sales | −.41 | 177 | − .12 | 204 |
| Craftsmen | −.11 | 307 | + .07 | 28 |
| Operatives | −.03 | 635 | + .01 | 251 |
| Service | −.37 | 209 | − .24 | 511 |
| Labor | * | 197 | * | 3 |

*When the data are quartiled, there is no variance in male managerial occupations, which have few Negroes without exception, or in laboring occupations, all of which have many Negroes.

It seems a reasonable assumption that discrimination against Negroes in employment and the higher salaries in occupations which have few Negroes is a result of competitive efforts on the part of white male employees to protect their economic situations (Hodge and Hodge, 1965). If this is the case, then it seems reasonable that white women, as a class more preoccupied with family and less with occupational roles, would be less likely to press for a similar occupational pattern of discrimination against Negro women.

Even so, Negro women still benefit occupationally from integrated schooling, according to these data. There are too few cases to make a truly firm statement, but Table 1 shows the overwhelming majority of Negro professional women have been educated in integrated schools.

Tables 5 and 6 show that Negroes who attend integrated high schools have higher occupational prestige and higher incomes. (Data on income for women is not presented; since so many women work part-time, the results are difficult to interpret.) The occupational prestige effect is considerably stronger for women than for men. The differences for men do not reach the .05 level of significance, but they are in the predicted direction and are not small. The difference between the median annual income of alumni of integrated and segregated high schools is $344 per year for males. Some of this can be attributed to age (with the increasing number of segregated schools, young Negroes do not have as much opportunity for integration) but more than $200 difference remains after an age control has been introduced in Table 6.

There are only 300 male graduates of northern high schools in the sample, so it is not possible to estimate accurately the real dollar return resulting from an integrated education. The young Negro men from broken homes in this sample are more likely to have gone to integrated schools, and men from stable homes earn approximately $600 more per year when educational attainment, age, and

**T A B L E 5.  Occupational Status of Students from Integrated and Segregated High Schools**

| OCCUPATIONAL STATUS | *Region and Integration of High School* | | |
| | NORTH, INTEGRATED | NORTH, SEGREGATED | SOUTH, SEGREGATED |
| --- | --- | --- | --- |
| Mean occupation prestige, men | 35.7 | 34.0 | 34.6 |
| Standard deviation | 12.3 | 12.6 | 13.8 |
| Total $N$ | (489) | (229) | (494) |
| Mean occupation prestige, women | 36.1 | 31.3 | 31.6 |
| Standard deviation | 13.9 | 12.6 | 16.3 |
| Total $N$ | (372) | (136) | (384) |

Note.–Effect of integration for northern males N.S.; effect for females, $p < .01$ (one-tailed); occupational prestige scores developed at NORC by Robert W. Hodge, Paul M. Siegel, and Peter H. Rossi.

**T A B L E 6.  Income of Alumni of Segregated and Integrated High Schools, for Males, with Background Variables Controlled**

| ADDITIONAL VARIABLES INCLUDED | INCREASE IN ANNUAL INCOME (MEDIANS) DUE TO HIGH SCHOOL INTEGRATION FOR MALES (ROUNDED TO TEN-DOLLAR UNITS) |
| --- | --- |
| None | $ 340 |
| Age | $ 220 |
| Age, stability of family of origin | $ 390 |
| Age, educational attainment | $– 40 |
| Age, educational attainment, and stability of family of origin | $ 210 |

high school integration are controlled. When family stability is introduced as a control, the effect of integration rises sharply, to $390.

Much of the income difference is due to the higher education of alumni of integrated schools. The average high school graduate (including those with college) earns about $800 more per year than the average person who did not finish high school (again, controlling for integration, age, and family stability). Since 20 percent more students from integrated high schools graduate (Crain, 1971), we would expect the increased educational attainment to increase the income of alumni of integrated schools by about $200 per year. We have computed two estimates of the effect of integration independent of education in Table 6. With only age as an additional control, we remove all of the effect of integration; but when we use family stability also, we have $210 remaining independent of education. Clearly, a larger sample is needed to make this estimate; but until one appears we must assume that integration has a net effect on income, independent of other variables including the higher educational attainment which also results from integration, of about $200 per year—not a small difference over the forty- to fifty-year working life of an adult male. Lifetime income of alumni of integrated schools is increased about $10,000; we estimate that only two-thirds of this amount is due to differences in educational attainment. Note that higher educational attainment is not a very parsimonious explanation of the fact that Negroes from integrated schools are more likely to work in nontraditional occupations. In the remainder of this paper we will argue that alumni of integrated schools make more money because they are more likely to associate with whites; they have integrated jobs for the same reason they are more likely to live in integrated neighborhoods.

## The Job-Finding Process

The findings of Tables 5 and 6—that alumni of integrated schools have better jobs and earn more money—is reasonable if one assumes that having informal contacts into the white job market is the crucial factor. Tables 7–11 provide

**T A B L E 7.  Answers to Question on Source of Present Job**

| SOURCE | NATIONAL SAMPLE (%) | NEGRO SAMPLE (%) |
|---|---|---|
| Family | 14 | 13 |
| Friends | 24 | 25 |
| Union | 1 | 3 |
| Want ads | 7 | 10 |
| State employment | 6 | 10 |
| Private employment | 4 | 7 |
| Visiting prospects | 24 | 18 |
| Ask previous employer | 2 | 2 |
| High school | 1 | 0 |
| College | 3 | 1 |
| Other | 16 | 10 |
| Total | 102 | 99 |
| *N* | (566)* | (3,537) |

*Unweighted *N* for national sample aged 21–45, who have worked within the past two years.

some evidence for this point of view. Table 7 gives the responses to the question, "How did you find your present (or last) job?" and compares the responses of the Negroes in our northern metropolitan sample and those of a national sample. The similarities are more striking than the differences, and in general the results point up the importance of informal means of communication in the job hunt. On the whole, the findings are quite consistent with Sheppard and Belitsky's (1967) study on job seeking. Although only a little more than one-third of the respondents say that family or friends referred them to their present job, another one-quarter of the national sample and one-sixth of the Negro sample mentioned "visiting plants" as the way in which they found employment. This presumes that the respondent had some idea of what plants to visit; in a large city, this requires more than a casual knowledge of the labor market. The largest differences between the Negroes and the national sample are in this category. It may well be that Negroes anticipate discrimination and hence are less willing to make the grand tour of possible employers. Negroes use formal means of obtaining job referrals, such as the union, newspaper advertisements, and public or private employment services more than whites do and use family and friends as a referral method less often.

The next question is what kinds of persons are useful sources of information about jobs? In the absence of data, we will make two straightforward assumptions: first, we assume that better-educated persons are more valuable contacts, since they may have more general knowledge, more influence, or may know more precisely what management wants in the way of qualifications. Second, we assume that whites know more about higher-paying jobs than Negroes do. Negroes who attend integrated schools are more likely to associate with whites in later life, and have a double advantage in that their contacts with whites also bring them into contact with persons who are better educated. Respondents were asked whether they could go for advice to a relative or friend who was a college graduate. (They were not asked what race the relative or friend was.) Respondents who attended integrated schools are not more likely to have relatives who are college graduates, but they are considerably more likely to have college educated friends, as shown in Table 8. In this table, there is essentially no difference among northern-educated respondents who had themselves attended college; in all cases, they were likely to have college-educated friends. Southern migrants are at a slight disadvantage here, possibly because they have migrated after completing their education and thus have left their college classmates behind. There is a slight tendency for females with some college education who attended segregated high schools to report more college-educated friends, but the number of such cases is tiny. When we turn to respondents who themselves did not attend college, we find that those who attended integrated high schools have very distinct advantages, while alumni of segregated northern high schools are no more likely to have a college-educated friend available than are migrants who attended southern high schools. Since alumni of integrated high

**TABLE 8.** Percentage of Respondents Who Say They Could Seek Advice from a Friend Who Is a College Graduate, by Integration of High School, Educational Attainment, and Sex

| | Type of High School | | |
|---|---|---|---|
| SEX | NORTHERN, INTEGRATED (%) | NORTHERN, SEGREGATED (%) | SOUTHERN, SEGREGATED (%) |
| *Males:* | | | |
| No college | 62 (354) | 44 (212) | 45 (427) |
| Some college or college graduate | 82 (164) | 85 (48) | 75 (120) |
| *Females:* | | | |
| No college | 47 (536) | 33 (257) | 35 (636) |
| Some college or college graduate | 65 (130) | 78 (56) | 69 (147) |

schools have more white contacts, it seems safe to assume that many of these college graduate friends are white.

From this point, the chain of argument is supported indirectly by the evidence. We hypothesize that better-educated friends are more likely to know of job opportunities. This is supported by Table 9, which shows that those respondents who do have college graduate contacts are considerably more likely to be able to name an employer who would hire them. Notice that the differences are greater for respondents who themselves have some high school or are high school graduates. This is consistent with the possibility that college graduate contacts and other persons that these respondents could use for referrals would be more familiar with occupations requiring at least minimal educational qualifications. Or it may be that respondents with less than eighth-grade educations have access to low-status jobs which are easier to learn about, and which require fewer personal referrals.

Table 10 shows that respondents who have white friends know of more job opportunities than those with fewer white contacts. The results for males, however, are quite weak; the differences for females are considerably stronger. It is possible that Negroes with high levels of white contact are more gregarious in general, and the fact that their friends are white is irrelevant. Table 11 considers this argument by controlling on the response to, "How often do friends and relatives visit your home?" In general, contact with whites is a more important factor than total amount of home visiting.

**TABLE 9.  Knowledge of Another Job Opportunity, by Sex, Education, and Contact with a College Graduate (Percentage)**

|  | *Percentage Knowing of Another Job, by Education* | | | |
| SEX AND CONTACT WITH COLLEGE GRADUATE | EIGHTH GRADE | SOME HIGH SCHOOL | HIGH SCHOOL GRADUATE | ATTENDED COLLEGE |
| --- | --- | --- | --- | --- |
| *Males:* | | | | |
| With college graduate contact | 32 (217) | 37 (414) | 41 (365) | 52 (332) |
| Without college graduate contact | 29 (184) | 17 (185) | 21 (122) | — (30) |
| Difference | + 3 | +20 | +20 | — |
| *Females:* | | | | |
| With college graduate contact | 22 (148) | 29 (459) | 39 (437) | 53 (297) |
| Without college graduate contact | 20 (177) | 19 (372) | 24 (212) | — (58) |
| Difference | + 2 | +10 | +15 | — |

Note.—Net effect of college graduate contact, among those with high school education or less: males, 15%; females, 10%.

**T A B L E 10.** Contacts with Whites and Knowledge of Another Job, by Sex and Education of Respondent (Percentage Knowing of Another Job)

| SEX AND EDUCATION | Contact with Whites | | | |
|---|---|---|---|---|
| | LOW (0) | (1–2) | (3–4) | HIGH (5) |
| Men, high education | – | 55 | 20 | 52 |
| | (30) | (45) | (64) | (215) |
| Men, low education | 24 | 25 | 32 | 29 |
| | (261) | (332) | (359) | (541) |
| Women, high education | – | 34 | 41 | 43 |
| | (30) | (64) | (58) | (203) |
| Women, low education | 12 | 20 | 29 | 30 |
| | (444) | (487) | (386) | (488) |

Note.—For men, net effect of contact with whites, independent of education = +4. For women, net effect of contact with whites, independent of education = +12.

**T A B L E 11.** Percentage Knowing of Another Job by Present Contact with Whites, by Frequency of Friends' Visits, and by Sex (Percentage Naming Another Employer)

| FREQUENCY OF VISITS | Present Contact with Whites | | |
|---|---|---|---|
| | LOW | MEDIUM | HIGH |
| *Males* | | | |
| Few days per week | 34.9 | 33.8 | 38.3 |
| | (189) | (281) | (399) |
| Once per week | 19.6 | 14.2 | 24.1 |
| | (112) | (134) | (170) |
| Less than once per week | 33.0 | 30.5 | 39.6 |
| | (179) | (190) | (182) |
| *Females* | | | |
| Few days per week | 20.3 | 32.6 | 35.8 |
| | (301) | (276) | (338) |
| Once per week | 13.8 | 27.1 | 28.6 |
| | (160) | (207) | (154) |
| Less than once per week | 12.0 | 20.5 | 32.2 |
| | (249) | (273) | (208) |

Note.—Net effects (first col. vs. third col.): For men, net effect of contact with whites, independent of visiting = +3%, net effect of visiting, independent of white contact = +1%. For women, net effect of contact with whites, independent of visiting = +17%, net effect of visiting, independent of white contact = +8%.

**T A B L E  12.  High School Integration and Knowledge of Another Job by Age and Sex of Respondent (Percentage Naming Another Employer)**

| AGE AND SEX | High School Integration | | |
| | NORTH, INTEGRATED | NORTH, SEGREGATED | SOUTH |
|---|---|---|---|
| *Males:* | | | |
| Under 30 | 38 | 38 | 38 |
| | (212) | (169) | (202) |
| 30–39 | 46 | 10 | 30 |
| | (195) | (68) | (189) |
| 40+ | 40 | 15 | 24 |
| | (106) | (27) | (152) |
| *Females:* | | | |
| Under 30 | 35 | 34 | 21 |
| | (306) | (174) | (248) |
| 30–39 | 24 | 18 | 27 |
| | (237) | (78) | (317) |
| 40+ | 30 | 19 | 20 |
| | (106) | (53) | (200) |

Table 12 closes this part of the argument by showing that alumni of integrated schools are more likely to name a prospective employer. This is not the case for respondents under thirty; but the differences among older respondents are quite large for both sexes.

We have presented data showing that part of the effect of school integration on occupational achievement can be attributed to the effect of high contact with whites on job-seeking behavior. There are other effects as well; alumni of integrated schools are more likely to have attended college and score higher on an efficacy scale, which itself is associated with more aggressive job seeking. (Efficacious persons are more likely to know of another job, controlling for sex and educational attainment.) . . .

## Conclusions

There are so many possible ways in which interracial contacts might benefit the Negro job seeker that is is difficult to say what part of the process is most important. Only one-quarter of our sample stated that they obtained their present job through friends, but this did not mean that the other three-quarters did not benefit from informal contact. Even the most casual information about employment can be valuable, and such information tends to filter through the social system in many ways. One irony is that if a single Negro is hired by a large plant, there are more white employees who know that the firm is integrated than there are Negroes; thus we arrive at the curious hypothesis that whites will have more information about jobs which are becoming "open" than will Negroes.

In general, the argument that has been advanced here does not hinge upon actual job discrimination. In the absence of all discrimination and prejudice, American Negroes would still suffer the consequences of racial segregation in housing, voluntary associations, and informal social relations. These consequences are not merely psychic or social in character; they can be measured in crude monetary terms as well. The public school thus becomes a doubly important instrument of social mobility for Negroes; in addition to its obvious educational value, it provides an opportunity to begin building the interracial associations which permit an escape from the ghetto.

## Bibliography

Robert L. Crain, "School Desegregation and the Academic Achievement of Negroes." *The Sociology of Education,* 1971, *44,* 1–26.

Robert W. Hodge and Patricia Hodge, "Occupational Assimilation as a Competitive Process." *American Journal of Sociology,* 1965, *71,* 249–264.

H. L. Sheppard and A. H. Belitsky, *The Job Hunt.* Baltimore: Johns Hopkins University Press, 1967.

U.S. Bureau of the Census, 1960. *Census of the Population. Occupational Characteristics.* Washington, D.C.: GPO, 1960.

# 38

# Isolation, Powerlessness, and Violence: A Study of Attitudes and Participation in the Watts Riot

*H. EDWARD RANSFORD*

. . . [T]here are two related approaches commonly used to explain participation in extreme political behavior. The first deals with the degree to which the individual is structurally isolated or tied to community institutions. The second approach deals with the individual's awareness and evaluation of his isolated condition—for example, his feeling of a lack of control over critical matters or his feeling of discontent due to a marginal postion in society. Following this orientation, this research employs the concepts of racial isolation, perceived powerlessness, and racial dissatisfaction as theoretical tools for explaining the participation of Negroes in violence.

Abridged from *American Journal of Sociology* 73 (1968): 581–591. Used by permission of The University of Chicago Press. © 1968 by The University of Chicago. All rights reserved.

## Study Design and Hypotheses

In the following discussion, the three independent variables of this study (isolation, powerlessness, and dissatisfaction) are discussed separately and jointly, as predictors of violence participation.

### RACIAL ISOLATION

Ralph Ellison has referred to the Negro in this country as the "invisible man."[1] Although this is a descriptive characterization, sociological studies have attempted to conceptualize more precisely the isolation of the American Negro. For example, those studying attitudes of prejudice often view racial isolation as a lack of free and easy contact on an intimate and equal status basis. Though the interracial contact may be frequent, it often involves such wide status differentials that it does not facilitate candid communication, nor is it likely to give the minority person a feeling that he has some stake in the system. In this paper, intimate white contact is viewed as a mediating set of relationships that binds the ethnic individual to majority-group values—essentially conservative values that favor working through democratic channels rather than violently attacking the social system. Accordingly, it is reasoned that Negroes who are more racially isolated (by low degrees of intimate contact with whites) will have fewer channels of communication to air their grievances and will feel little commitment to the leaders and institutions of the community. This group, which is blocked from meaningful white communication, should be more willing to use violent protest than the groups with greater involvement in white society.

### POWERLESSNESS AND RACIAL DISSATISFACTION

In contrast to structural isolation, powerlessness and racial dissatisfaction are the subjective components of our theoretical scheme. A feeling of powerlessness is one form of alienation. It is defined in this research as a low expectancy of control over events. This attitude is seen as an appropriate variable for Negroes living in segregated ghettos; that is, groups which are blocked from full participation in the society are more likely to feel powerless in that society. Powerlessness is also a variable that seems to have a logical relationship to violent protest. Briefly, it is reasoned that Negroes who feel powerless to change their position or to control crucial decisions that affect them will be more willing to use violent means to get their rights than those who feel some control or efficacy within the social system. . . .

Our second attitude measure, racial dissatisfaction, is defined as the degree to which the individual feels that he is being treated badly because of his race. It

[1] Ralph Ellison, *Invisible Man* (New York: Random House, 1952).

is a kind of racial alienation in the sense that the individual perceives his position in society to be illegitimate, due to racial discrimination. The Watts violence represented an extreme expression of frustration and discontent. We would expect those highly dissatisfied with their treatment as Negroes to be the participants in such violence. . . . In comparing our two forms of subjective alienation (powerlessness and racial dissatisfaction), it is important to note that although we expect some correlation between the two attitudes (a certain amount of resentment and dissatisfaction should accompany the feeling of powerlessness), we propose to show that they make an independent contribution to violence.

### UNIFICATION OF PREDICTIVE VARIABLES

We believe that the fullest understanding of violence can be brought to bear by use of a social-psychological design in which the structural variable (racial isolation) is joined with the subjective attitudes of the individual (powerlessness and dissatisfaction). . . .

It is reasoned that racial isolation should be most important for determining participation in violence (a) when individuals feel powerless to shape their destiny under existing conditions or (b) when individuals are highly dissatisfied with their racial treatment. Each of the attitudes is seen as a connecting bridge . . . between racial isolation and violence.

For the first case (that of powerlessness), we are stating that a weak attachment to the majority group and its norms should lead to a radical break from law and order when individuals perceive they cannot effect events important to them; that is, they cannot change their racial position through activity within institutional channels. Violence, in this instance, becomes an alternative pathway of expression and gain. Conversely, racial isolation should have much less effect upon violence when persons feel some control in the system.

For the second case (racial dissatisfaction), we believe isolation should have a far greater effect upon violence when dissatisfaction over racial treatment is intense. Isolation from the society then becomes critical to violence in the sense that the dissatisfied person feels little commitment to the legal order and is more likely to use estreme methods as an outlet for his grievances. Statistically speaking, we expect an interaction effect between isolation and powerlessness, and between isolation and dissatisfaction, in the prediction of violence.

## Methods

. . . The type of social contact to be measured had to be of an intimate and equal status nature, a kind of contact that would facilitate easy communication between the races. First, each Negro respondent was asked if he had current contact with white people in a series of situations: on the job, in his neighborhood, in organizations to which he belongs, and in other situations (such as shopping). After this general survey of white contacts, the respondent was asked, "Have you ever done anything social with these white people, like going to the movies together or visiting in each other's homes?" The responses formed a simple dichotomous variable: "high" contact scores for those who had done something social (61 per cent of the sample) and "low" contact scores for those who had had little or no social contact (39 per cent).

. . . [P]owerlessness is defined as a low expectancy of control over events. Twelve forced-choice items were used to tap this attitude. The majority of items dealt with expectations of control over the political system. The following is an example:

——The world is run by the few people in power, and there is not much the little guy can do about it.

. . . [R]acial dissatisfaction is defined as the degree to which the individual feels he is being treated badly because of his race. A five-item scale was developed to measure this attitude. The questions ask the Negro respondent to compare his treatment (in such areas as housing, work, and general treatment in the community) with various reference groups, such as the southern Negro or the white. Each of the five questions allows a reply on one of three levels: no dissatisfaction, mild dissatisfaction, and intense dissatisfaction. Typical of the items is the following: "If you compare your opportunities and the treatment you get from whites in Los Angeles with Negroes living in the South, would you say you are much better off—a little better off—or treated about the same as the southern Negro—?" After a reliability check of the items, replies to the dissatisfaction measure were dichotomized into high and low groups. The cut was made conceptually, rather than at the median, yielding 99 "highs" and 213 "lows" in dissatisfaction.

The dependent variable of the study is willingness to use violence. Violence is defined in the context of the Watts riot as the willingness to use direct aggression against the groups that are believed to be discriminating, such as the police and white merchants. . . . Would you be willing to "use violence to get Negro rights?" . . . At the time of data collection, buildings were still smoldering; violence in the form of looting, burning, and destruction was not a remote possibility, but a tangible reality. The violence-prone group numbered eighty-three. . . .

## Sample

The sample was composed of three-hundred-twelve Negro males who were heads of the household and between the ages of eighteen and sixty-five. The subjects responded to an interview schedule administered by Negro interviewers. They were chosen by random methods and were interviewed in their own homes or apartments. Both employed and unemployed respondents were included in the sample, although the former were emphasized in the sampling procedure (269 employed in contrast to 43 unemployed). The sample was drawn from three major areas of Los Angeles: a relatively middle-class and integrated area (known as the "Crenshaw" district) and the predominantly lower-class and highly segregated communities of "South Central" and "Watts." . . . [I] t was decided that an approximate fifty-fifty split between middle- and lower-class respondents would be desirable for later analysis. This meant, however, that Crenshaw (middle-class) Negroes were considerably overrepresented. . . .

## Results

We have predicted a greater willingness to use violent methods for three groups: the isolated, the powerless, and the dissatisfied. The data presented in Table 1 confirm these expectations. For all three cases, the percentage differences are statistically significant at better than the .001 level. . . .

It is one thing to establish a relationship based on action willingness and quite another thing to study actual behavior. Unfortunately, only sixteen of the 312 respondents (5 per cent) admitted participation in violent action for Negro rights. This small number did, however, provide some basis for testing our hypotheses. Of the sixteen who participated in violent action, eleven were isolates while only five had social contact. More impressive is the fact that fifteen of the sixteen "violents" scored high in powerlessness, and thirteen of the sixteen felt high

**TABLE 1. Percentage Willing to Use Violence, by Social Contact, Powerlessness, and Racial Dissatisfaction**

| VARIABLES | NOT WILLING (%) | WILLING (%) | TOTAL (%) |
|---|---|---|---|
| Social contact:* | | | |
| High............... | 83 | 17 | 100 ($N$ = 192) |
| Low............... | 56 | 44 | 100 ($N$ = 110) |
| Powerlessness:† | | | |
| High............... | 59 | 41 | 100 ($N$ = 145) |
| Low............... | 84 | 16 | 100 ($N$ = 160) |
| Racial dissatisfaction:‡ | | | |
| High............... | 52 | 48 | 100 ($N$ = 98) |
| Low............... | 83 | 17 | 100 ($N$ = 212) |

*$\chi^2$ = 24.93, $P$ < .001.
†$\chi^2$ = 22.59, $P$ < .001.
‡$\chi^2$ = 30.88, $P$ < .001.
Note.—In this table and the tables that follow, there are often less than 312 cases due to missing data for one or more variables.

degrees of dissatisfaction. Even with a small number, these are definite relationships, encouraging an interpretation that those who are willing to use violence and those who reported actual violent behavior display the same tendency toward powerlessness, racial dissatisfaction, and isolation.

The next task is to explore the interelationships among our predictive variables. For example, we have argued that powerlessness has a specific meaning to violence (a low expectancy of changing conditions within the institutional framework) that should be more than a generalized disaffection; that is, we expected our measures of powerlessness and racial dissatisfaction to have somewhat unique effects upon violence.

The data indicated an interaction effect (interaction $\chi^2 = 7.85$; $P < .01$) between the two attitudes. . . . In sum, the data suggest that the powerless Negro is likely to use violence when his feelings of powerlessness are accompanied by intense dissatisfaction with his position. It can be noted, however, that, even among those who were relatively satisfied with racial conditions, powerlessness had some effect upon violence (a 13 per cent difference, $\chi^2 = 5.41$; $P = .02$). Presumably, a low expectance of exerting control has a somewhat unique effect upon violence.

As a second way of noting an interrelationship between our predictive variables we turn to the more crucial test of the isolation-extremism perspective in which the effect of racial isolation upon violence is controlled by powerlessness and dissatisfaction.[2] It will be recalled that we expected the isolated people . . . to be more violence-prone when [they] perceive they cannot shape their destiny within the institutional framework (high powerlessness) or when they perceive differential treatment as Negroes and, as a result, are dissatisfied. . . . Table 2 . . . shows our hypotheses to be strongly supported in both cases.

**T A B L E 2.   Percentage Willing to Use Violence, by Social Contact Controlling for Powerlessness and Racial Dissatisfaction**

| | *Percentage Willing to Use Violence* | | | |
| | LOW POWER-LESSNESS (%) | HIGH POWER-LESSNESS (%) | LOW DISSATIS-FACTION (%) | HIGH DISSATIS-FACTION (%) |
|---|---|---|---|---|
| Low contact. . | 23 ($N = 31$) | 53 ($N = 78$) | 23 ($N = 47$) | 59 ($N = 63$) |
| High contact. . | 13 ($N = 123$) | 26 ($N = 66$) | 15 ($N = 158$) | 26 ($N = 34$) |
| $\chi^2$ . . . . . . . | $P < .20$ | $P < .01$ | $P < .20$ | $P < .01$ |

Note.—The interaction $\chi^2$ between powerlessness and contact: $P < .05$. The interaction $\chi^2$ between dissatisfaction and contact: $P < .01$.

[2] The independent variables are moderately intercorrelated. For isolation and powerlessness, the $\phi$ correlation is .36, $P < .001$; for isolation and dissatisfaction, the $\phi$ is .40 $P < .001$; for powerlessness and dissatisfaction, the $\phi$ is .33, $P < .001$.

Among the powerless and the dissatisfied, racial isolation has a strong effect upon violence commitment. Conversely, the data show that isolation is much less relevant to violence for those with feelings of control in the system and for the more satisfied. . . .

Apparently, isolation is not only a stronger predictor of violence for the people who feel powerless and dissatisfied, but is *only* a clear and significant determiner of violence for these subjectively alienated persons. For the relatively satisfied and control-oriented groups, the fact of being isolated is not very important in determining violence. This would suggest that a weak normative bond to the majority group (isolation) is not in itself sufficient to explain the participation of the oppressed minority person in violence and that it is the interaction between isolation and feelings of powerlessness (or racial dissatisfaction) that is crucial for predicting violence.

A final attempt at unification involves the cumulative effect of all three of our predictive variables upon violence. Since it was noted that each of the three predictive variables has some effect upon violence (either independently or for specific subgroups), it seemed logical that the combined effect of the three would produce a high violence propensity. Conceptually, a combination of these variables could be seen as ideal types of the alienated and non-alienated Negro. Accordingly, Table 3 arranges the data into these ideal-type combinations.

The group at the top of the table represents the one most detached from society—individuals who are isolated and high in attitudes of powerlessness and dissatisfaction. The group at the bottom of the table is the most involved in the society; these people have intimate white contact, feelings of control, and greater satisfaction with racial conditions. The middle group is made up of those with different combinations of high and low detachment. Note the dramatic difference in willingness to use violence between the "ideal-type" alienated group (65 per cent willing) and the group most bound to society (only 12 per cent willing. . . .

**TABLE 3.** **Percentage Willing to Use Violence, by the Combined Effect of Social Contact, Powerlessness, and Racial Dissatisfaction**

|  | NOT WILLING (%) | WILLING (%) | TOTAL (%) |
|---|---|---|---|
| Ideal-type alienated (low contact, high powerlessness, and high dissatisfaction). . . . . | 35 | 65 | 100 ($N = 51$) |
| Middles in alienation . . . . . . . . | 76 | 24 | 100 ($N = 147$) |
| Ideal-type non-alienated (high contact, low powerlessness, and low dissatisfaction) . . . . . | 88 | 12 | 100 ($N = 107$) |

Note.—$\chi^2 = 49.37; P < .001$ (2 d.f.).

## Spuriousness

It is possible that the relationship between our predictive variables and violence is due to an intercorrelation with other relevant variables. For example, social class should be related both to violence and to our isolation-alienation measures. In addition, we could expect a greater propensity toward violence in geographical areas where an extreme breakdown of legal controls occurred, such as the South Central and Watts areas (in contrast to the Crenshaw area, where no rioting took place). . . . In short, it seems essential to control our isolation-alienation variables by an index of social class and by ghetto area.

. . . Table 4 [see page 310] presents the original relationship between each of the independent variables and violence, controlled by two areas of residence: the South Central–Watts area, at the heart of the curfew zone (where violence occurred), and the Crenshaw area, on the periphery (or outside) of the curfew zone (where violent action was rare). In addition, Table 4 includes a control for education, as a measure of social class.

When the ghetto residence of the respondent is held constant, it appears that our independent variables are important in their own right. Education (social class), however, proved to be a more powerful control variable. Among the college educated, only isolation persists as a predictor of violence; powerlessness and racial dissatisfaction virtually drop out. Yet each variable has a very strong effect upon violence among the high school (lower-class) group. In other words, we do not have an instance of spuriousness, where predictive variables are explained away in both partials, but another set of interaction effects—attitudes of powerlessness and dissatisfaction are predictors of violence only among lower-class respondents. These results may be interpreted in several ways. Persons higher in the class structure may have a considerable amount to lose, in terms of occupational prestige and acceptance in white society, by indorsing extreme methods. The college educated (middle class) may be unwilling to risk their position, regardless of feelings of powerlessness and dissatisfaction. These results may further indicate that middle-class norms favoring diplomacy and the use of democratic channels (as opposed to direct aggression) are overriding any tendency toward violence. An extension of this interpretation is that middle-class Negroes may be activists, but non-violent activists, in the civil rights movement. Thus, class norms may be contouring resentment into more organized forms of protest.

## Conclusions

In an attempt to locate the Negro participant in violence, we find that isolated Negroes and Negroes with intense feelings of powerlessness and dissatisfaction are more prone to violent action than those who are less alienated. In

TABLE 4. Percentage Willing to Use Violence by Contact, Powerlessness, and Racial Dissatisfaction, Controlling for Two Geographical Areas and Education

| INDEPENDENT VARIABLES | Neighborhood | | Education | |
|---|---|---|---|---|
| | SOUTH CENTRAL–WATTS | CRENSHAW | LOW (HIGH SCHOOL OR LESS) | HIGH (SOME COLLEGE) |
| Low contact. . . . . | 53** (N = 62) | 33** (N = 45) | 52** (N = 77) | 24* (N = 33) |
| High contact. . . . . | 27 (N = 83) | 10 (N = 109) | 26 (N = 86) | 10 (N = 105) |
| Low powerlessness. . . . . | 22** (N = 73) | 11* (N = 88) | 19** (N = 67) | 14 (N = 93) |
| High powerlessness . . . . . | 55 (N = 77) | 25 (N = 68) | 51 (N = 100) | 18 (N = 45) |
| Low dissatisfaction . . . . . | 26** (N = 81) | 12** (N = 130) | 22** (N = 96) | 12 (N = 114) |
| High dissatisfaction . . . . . | 53 (N = 68) | 39 (N = 28) | 59 (N = 73) | 17 (N = 24) |

*P < .05.    **P < .01.

Note.—Interaction $\chi^2$ between contact and neighborhood: $P$ is not significant. Interaction $\chi^2$ between powerlessness and neighborhood: $P < .02$. Interaction $\chi^2$ between dissatisfaction and neighborhood: $P$ is not significant. Interaction $\chi^2$ between contact and education: $P$ is not significant. Interaction $\chi^2$ between powerlessness and education: $P < .02$. Interaction $\chi^2$ between dissatisfaction and education: $.05 < P < .10$.

addition, isolation has its strongest effect upon violence when individuals feel powerless to control events in the society or when racial dissatisfaction is intensely felt. For those with higher expectations of control or with greater satisfaction regarding racial treatment, isolation has a much smaller and nonsignificant effect (though in the predicted direction) upon violence. That is, a weak tie with the majority group, per se, appeared insufficient to explain wide-scale participation in extreme action. This study indicates that it is the interaction between a weak bond and a feeling of powerlessness (or dissatisfaction) that is crucial to violent participation. . . .

Ghetto area and education were introduced as controls. Each independent variable (taken separately) retained some significant effect upon violence in two geographical areas (dealing with proximity to the Watts violence) and among the less educated respondents. Powerlessness and dissatisfaction, however, had no effect upon violence among the college educated. . . .

Applying our findings to the context of the Negro revolt of the last fifteen years, we note an important distinction between the non-violent civil rights activists and the violence-prone group introduced in this study. Suggestive (but non-conclusive) evidence indicates that the participants in organized civil rights protests are more likely to be middle class in origin, to hold considerable optimism for equal rights, and to have greater communication with the majority. . . . [T]his study located a very different population—one whose members are intensely dissatisfied, feel powerless to change their position, and have minimum commitment to the larger society. These Negroes have lost faith in the leaders and institutions of the community and presumably have little hope for improvement through organized protest. For them, violence is a means of communicating with white society; anger can be expressed, control exerted—if only for a brief period.

# Part VII

# Consolidation and Retrenchment: 1971–1980

# Introduction

When the original Reconstruction ended in 1876, the United States entered a phase in which racial minorities lost ground. America bound its wounds from the destructive Civil War; but the joining together again of the regional white populations often took place at the expense of racial minorities. The Introduction briefly traced the difficult positions in which the post-Reconstruction phase had placed these minorities by the turn of the century. This historical chapter tempts the comparison of the 1970s with that period of retreat and retrenchment of the last century. Both eras followed idealistic decades that enhanced the rights of the nation's nonwhite citizens. It is to be hoped that the analogy ends there, and this period of retreat will not extend the four decades of the original post-Reconstruction.

Sociological work in the 1970s, as we shall note once again, both reflects and resists this national mood. But sociological activity has not declined in volume, as one might have expected. In fact, race relations articles have increased both in number and quality in recent years, and the editor found the selection of articles for Part VII the most difficult of all. New methods and new theory enriched the field. Structural and historical models have been introduced, with a healthy borrowing of methods from other disciplines, and more ambitious problems tackled. True, the race relations field, like the discipline as a whole, lacked direction and coherence in the 1970s. But the quality and range of the work hold promise of a useful synthesis that must await a later time.

Much of this decade's work has involved a reassessment of the many changes and events of past decades. The first three articles illustrate this reassessment of the past with the new methods and theories. First, Seymour Spilerman offers in Selection 39 a structural analysis of the severity of the race riots of the 1960s. Spilerman, formerly at the University of Wisconsin and the Russell Sage Foundation and now at Columbia University, had earlier attempted to account for the

314

locations of these same riots across cities.[1] Surprisingly, he reaches conclusions concerning the structural correlates of riot severity that he did for riot location: namely, that the patterns of both are *not* related to objective indicators of black well-being, but both the liklihood of a riot and riot severity were reduced in the South and in cities with relatively small black populations. Spilerman regards these complementary results to indicate that the triggering frustrations had nationwide salience and were importantly furthered by intense mass media coverage. These findings may at first seem to be in conflict with those of Ransford in Selection 38, but actually, if anything, the two studies supplement each other across the institutional and individual levels of analysis. Save for each respondent's amount of education and neighborhood, Ransford measured *feelings* of dissatisfaction and not the actual deprivations that are tapped by Spilerman's objective indicators in the aggregate.[2] Spilerman's aggregate findings suggest that the individual conditions that Ransford found to relate to possible riot participation were widely distributed across Western and Northern cities with large numbers of black residents.

While advanced regression methods made possible Spilerman's work, historical methods made possible Selection 40. Edna Bonacich, of the University of California at Riverside, was a prominent contributor to race relations theory throughout the 1970s. In 1972 she introduced her theory of how "the split labor market" leads to particular types of racial exploitation and conflict.[3] Briefly, Bonacich argues that racial minorities often form a labor force that of necessity must undercut the prevailing wages of majority workers in order to secure employment. This two-tier wage system is supported by employers but fiercely resisted by majority workers. And it is in this economic context, she insists, that many race relations patterns in the industrial world are set and must be understood. Often there will be employer and minority alliances, she points out, and the greatest conflict will arise between the minority and the working class of the majority group. Undoubtedly, Bonacich's youth in South Africa, with its sharply split labor force by race, gave her a comparative perspective with which to review American race relations.

---

[1] Seymour Spilerman, "The causes of racial disturbances: A comparison of alternative explanations," *American Sociological Review 35* (1970): 627–649, and *idem,* "The causes of racial disturbances: Tests of an explanation," *American Sociological Review 36* (1971): 427–442.

[2] Moreover, a review of studies of riot participation found that very few of them had uncovered high relationships for a range of deprivation and frustration–aggression measures. Clark McPhail, "Civil disorder participation: A critical examination of recent research," *American Sociological Review 36* (1971): 1058-1073. The power of Ransford's findings came not from his dissatisfaction variables so much as from his multivariate prediction that included social isolation and powerlessness.

[3] Edna Bonacich, "A theory of ethnic antagonism: The split labor market," *American Sociological Review 37* (1972): 547–559. Another interesting contribution by Bonacich during the decade was "A theory of middleman minorities," *American Sociological Review 38* (1973): 583–594.

Bonacich applied her theory specifically to American racial and labor history. First, she applied it to the slaves and free blacks of the 1830-1863 period.[4] She showed how both of these groups were cheaper than white labor and how abolition, in potentially destroying the split labor markets of both the South and the North, threatened intense competition between black and white labor. Selection 40 is her application of split labor market ideas to the past three generations of racial history. Here Bonacich unravels a perplexing puzzle. Why was the recorded black unemployment rate consistently below that of whites into the 1930s, but since the 1950s has remained at roughly twice the white rate? Or, put differently, why has black unemployment steadily worsened as the civil rights of blacks have improved? Her persuasive answer is not encouraging for the future of the least-trained blacks—a prospect that introduces the focus on black income of the next article.

In Selection 41, Wayne Villemez and Alan Rowe of Florida Atlantic University take a careful look at the changes in black income during the 1960s.[5] Though this paper is somewhat technical and requires careful reading, it illustrates an important general lesson that has become increasingly true as sociological methods have advanced: *Basic research answers to policy-relevant questions are often shaped by the indicators adopted.* Villemez and Rowe neatly demonstrate this point by employing a measure of black income gains different from the standard ones used. Instead of the usual ratio measures of median black income divided by median white income, these authors argue for the utility of using income "pie slices" where the proportional size of the black part of total income can be evaluated over time. When this shift is made in what is meant by "black income gain," the results for the 1960s are altered markedly. That which has been widely acclaimed as substantial black progress in median ratio terms suddenly loses its force, and it appears as if only slight black income progress

---

[4] Edna Bonacich, "Abolition, the extension of slavery, and the position of free blacks: A study of split labor markets in the United States, 1830-1863," *American Journal of Sociology 81* (1976): 601-628.

[5] This paper is only one of many interesting articles on black income published in the four journals under review during the 1970s. Recommended examples include one that attempts to demonstrate that racial differences in the quality of schooling are largely irrelevant to within-occupation racial differences in earnings, Ross M. Stolzenberg, "Education, occupation, and wage differences between white and black men," *American Journal of Sociology 81* (1975): 299-323; another that shows industrial unionization is inversely related to black-white income inequality in urban labor markets, Richard C. Hill, "Unionization and racial income inequality in the metropolis," *American Sociological Review 39* (1974): 507-522; two that observe that black Southerners who migrate North in time earn more and have higher labor force participation rates than black Northerners—Larry Long, "Poverty status and receipt of welfare among migrants and nonmigrants in large cities," *American Sociological Review 39* (1974): 46-56, and Larry Long and Lynne Heltman, "Migration and income differences between black and white men in the North," *American Journal of Sociology 80* (1975): 1391-1409—and another that agrees but holds that these differences are due to the selectivity of those who migrate and of those returnees to the South who failed in the North, Stanley Lieberson, "Reconsideration of the income differences found between migrants and northern-born blacks," *American Journal of Sociology 83* (1978): 940-966.

actually occurred during these years. And even these minimal gains went disproportionately to upper-status blacks—just as Bonacich would predict.

Does this mean that researchers can reach any answer that suits their biases by simply manipulating the key indicators? Not completely, of course, for the nature of the data may be such that a variety of indicators will yield essentially the same conclusion. But, yes, this prospect is a danger; thus, it behooves one to check out carefully the basic operations of any study before accepting its conclusions. It also suggests that sociologists should utilize a range of different indicators with the logic behind each spelled out, so that research consumers can easily grasp the significance of this point.

Using more standard indices, Reynolds Farley determines in Selection 42 whether the black gains of the 1960s were maintained in the 1970s. Farley, of the Population Studies Center of the University of Michigan, reaches a mixed conclusion that is consistent with those of the previous two papers. He finds that many of the major black improvements of the 1960s, most of them benefiting the growing middle class, withstood the harsh economic and political climate of the 1970s. Indeed, on some indicators—such as occupational upgrading—these gains continued to mount. Yet Farley also finds that these gains are small when compared to the vast black–white differences that remain. Nor are these trends by any means universal. Indices that tap the poorer black segments of the population even reveal retrogression. For reasons specified in part by Bonacich and by Villemez and Rowe, unemployment and female-headed households increased in the 1970s.

A debate arose within sociology as to the meaning of these counter trends—largely positive for the black middle class, largely negative for the black poor. William Wilson, of the University of Chicago, wrote a controversial volume entitled *The Declining Significance of Race* in which he argues (but does not demonstrate) that class factors are now replacing race factors as explanations for these conditions. Notice that none of the authors of the three previous articles make such an assertion, even though all three sets of results indicate the increasing importance of social class considerations in American race relations. The point is that it is not an either/or situation; the rising significance of class does not necessarrily signal "the declining significance of race." The growing socioeconomic differentiation of black America does mean that the operation of "race" *per se* in black–white relations *is* changing. The greater subtleties of modern racial discrimination operate still for both the prospering and the poor segments of black America, but typically in different ways from how racial discrimination operated in the past. In statistical terms, the increment of the social class main effect is accompanied not by a decrement of the racial main effect but by a stronger interaction between class and race for a wide variety of important dependent variables.

The debate over race and class has its counterpart over the continuing effort to desegregate the nation's public schools racially. White resistance to the process rose as school desegregation extended to the cities of the North and West and both Presidents Richard Nixon and Gerald Ford repeatedly attacked it. Reflecting this changing mood of the country, a few sociologists raised an array of objections to continuing the efforts.[6] First, they maintained that school desegregation simply does not "work," that there are no positive benefits for either black or white children that can justify it. Of course, this argument conveniently ignores the constitutional rights of black children as determined in *Brown*. And in the broad terms of lifetime advantages, we have already seen evidence against this assertion in Robert Crain's article in Part VI. Moreover, even in the narrow terms of black achievement scores to which this objection usually refers, an answer is supplied by a thorough review of seventy-three relevant studies.[7] A majority of these studies conclude that desegregation had a beneficial effect on black achievement; the effect was especially strong when the desegregation was begun in the earliest grades and, surprisingly, was mandatory rather than voluntary. Moreover, the weaker studies in terms of method were less likely to detect positive desegregation effects.[8]

The second and third objections focused on the presumed impossibility of achieving school desegregation in large central cities, objections that sounded embarrassingly similar to ones advanced by Southern politicans soon after the Supreme Court ruled against school segregation by race in 1954. Educational desegregation in big cities causes the "white flight" of students to suburbs and private schools, goes the argument, and therefore the process is "counterproductive." The "white flight" contention assumes that white parents will not tolerate having their children attend thoroughly mixed schools; and this third objection serves to argue further against metropolitan plans for school desegregation that even the critics admit would effectively overcome any problems of "white flight" and resegregation in central cities. Selections 43 and 44 introduce data relevant to both of these objections to interracial schools.

Criticisms of the "white flight" contention were numerous.[9] Most of them centered on the fact that the phenomenon had been stripped out of its historical and demographic context. Large central cities had been losing their white

[6] *E.g.,* D. J. Armor, "The evidence on busing," *The Public Interest,* Summer 1972, No. 28, pp. 90-126, answered by T. F. Pettigrew, E. L. Useem, C. Normand, and M. S. Smith, "Busing: A review of 'the evidence,'" *The Public Interest,* Winter 1973, No. 30, pp. 88-118; and J. S. Coleman, S. D. Kelly, and J. A. Moore, *Trends in School Segregation, 1968-73* (Washington, D.C.: The Urban Institute, 1975).

[7] R. L. Crain and R. E. Mahard, "Desegregation and black achievement," *Law and Contemporary Problems 43* (1979): in press (also a working paper of the Institute of Policy Sciences and Public Affairs, Duke University, October 1977).

[8] Desegregation programs vary widely across schools, of course, so some of them would not be expected to provide achievement increments. For a discussion of the structural features that appear to distinguish merely desegregated schools from genuinely integrated ones, see T. F. Pettigrew, "The case for integrated schools," in T. F. Pettigrew (ed.), *Racial Discrimination in the United States* (New York: Harper & Row, 1975).

[9] Many of these criticisms are contained in T. F. Pettigrew and R. L. Green, "School desegregation in large cities: A critique of the Coleman 'white flight' thesis," *Harvard Educational Review 46* (February 1976): 1-53.

citizens in great numbers for years prior to any school desegregation efforts. Consequently, some critics rename the phenomenon "the hastening up effect" and question the assumption that any loss associated with desegregation consists of white students who would not otherwise have been lost to the city school district. Initial losses of white students in many urban districts that have desegregaged have enhanced resegregation; but over a five- or ten-year period they often constitute merely "fine tuning" around the far more critical factors underlying resegregation of differential birthrates and suburban housing discrimination against black citizens. Thus, Reynolds Farley projects that the Anglo-white proportion of the Los Angeles Unified School District will decrease from 1977 to 1987 from 34 percent to about 13 percent whether or not there were "white flight" as a consequence of school desegregation.[10] Why such a trend is anticipated is explained in Selection 43. David Sly and Louis Pol, both of Florida State University, demonstrate the importance of the underlying demographic dynamics that were largely ignored by proponents of the "white flight" thesis. They discuss the phenomenon in its demographic context and they emphasize both the white mobility patterns since 1955 and the differential birthrates by race across large cities.

Cardell Jacobson, of Central Michigan University, provides in Selection 44 data from one of the few longitudinal opinion studies conducted in this domain. He finds, contrary to the assumptions of those who argue against interracial schooling, that the District Court ruling for desegregation in Milwaukee was actually accompanied by increased support for the process among those most affected. Hence, parents with children in the public schools became more willing to participate, while those without children in school and particularly those with children in parochial schools became considerably less willing.

The final selection pulls together the various theoretical threads of the volume in a balanced and imaginative manner. Ernest Barth, of the University of Washington, and Donald Noel, of the University of Wisconsin at Milwaukee, demonstrate how each of the principal "theories" put forward over the years in the sociology of race relations is best for explaining a different piece of the total puzzle. Thus, they contend that Robert Park's *race cycle* most effectively accounts for intergroup differentiation, *consensus* perspectives for the persistence of intergroup patterns, *interdependence* persepectives for adaptation, and *conflict* perspectives for change. Barth and Noel go further. They fittingly close this volume by suggesting how all four of these theoretical positions might usefully be combined for a more general sociological theory of race relations.

---

[10] Reynolds Farley, *Report to the Honorable Judge Paul Egly,* Pomona, Cal.: Los Angeles County Superior Court, November 1978.

# 39

# Structural Characteristics of Cities and the Severity of Racial Disorders

*SEYMOUR SPILERMAN*

The issue of disorder severity is conceptually a separate matter from accounting for the locations of disturbances. . . .

A plausible argument . . . can be made to the effect that the variation across communities in severity of collective aggression will reflect differences among them in the degree of discontent experienced by their inhabitants. With respect to racial turmoil in the 1960s, it has been reported that the disturbance *locations* were unrelated to a number of objective indicators of Negro social and economic status or to their living conditions in a city (Spilerman 1970b; 1971). This lack of significance of the community characteristics was interpreted as evidence for a thesis that the frustrations which provoked ghetto residents during the period were nationwide in impact and not rooted in circumstances peculiar to the stricken communities. Instead, an explanation was proposed which emphasized the wide availability of television and the role of network news programs in exposing Negroes uniformly to stimuli of a frustrating nature, and in propagating

Abridged from *American Sociological Review 41* (1976): 771–793. Used by permission.

in all cities the same role models regarding how ghetto residents in some communities were responding to the deprivations endemic to Negro life in America.

. . .[S]ince the preceding studies examined only the determinants of disorder location (i.e., outbreak frequency in a city), [i] t still may be the case that the frustrations felt by Negroes which derive from their local situations are salient to other aspects of the disturbance process. In this regard, there is certainly reason to expect community differences to exist in the level of Negro discontent. The conditions under which they live vary enormously among cities, in absolute terms and relative to white circumstance. For instance, in 1960, the range in median Negro income was $1,880 to $9,079; relative to median white income the range was .30 to 1.19.[1] Disparities of such magnitude must mean that an individual's life chances, and a social group's ability to organize and effectively promote its collective interests, are conditioned in dramatically different ways from one community to the next. It is not unreasonable to expect corresponding variations to be present in the degree of frustration that is experienced by Negro residents in these cities.

There is precedent for proposing that the frustrations may come to be expressed in the *intensity* of a release, if not in the frequency of outbreak. Evidence from laboratory studies underscores the importance of the intensity variable. For example, Berkowitz (1965) reports that angered subjects sent shocks of greater frequency *and duration* to stooges. . . . With respect to collective behavior in natural settings, it also has been suggested that "the fury of the destructive reaction will vary with the indignity of the disappointment" (Milgram and Toch, 1969:549 paraphrasing Dollard et al., 1939).

The argument as to why frustration may come to be expressed in severity of aggression, rather than in frequency, can be made in the following way. In our society, acts of collective violence are inhibited by deep-rooted mores as well as by a fear of apprehension and punishment. In fact, despite the large number of racial disturbances during the 1960s, a disorder was actually a rare event in any given community. While some 170 cities (from among the 673 with 1960 populations exceeding 25,000) did experience some racial turmoil during 1961-68, fewer than ten cities witnessed more than five disturbances during that eight-year interval.[2] Viewed from this perspective, even during a decade of great urban unrest the inhibitions which normally deter hostile outbursts appear to have been overcome only infrequently in a particular community.

Breaching the barriers against collective violence may require a precipitant of

---

[1] Figures are from the 1960 Census of Population (U.S. Bureau of the Census, 1963) and pertain to the 413 communities in the contiguous United States with total population exceeding 25,000 and Negro population in excess of 1,000.

[2] Figures in this paper which pertain to the *location* of racial disturbances during the 1960s were computed from the data set used in the author's earlier investigations (Spilerman 1970b; 1971). To be included in that data set, an incident had to involve at least 30 participants, be characterized by primarily Negro aggression, and be "spontaneous" in origin. For additional details on the definition and categorization of the disturbances, see Spilerman (1970b:630).

immense significance. Indeed, 168 of the 341 racial disturbances can be associated with one of two extraordinary events: the massive Newark riot of 1967 (which received extensive television coverage) or the assassination of Martin Luther King. Once the inhibitions against violence have been overcome, however, it is conceivable that the severity of the resulting outburst will be conditioned by the frustrations which have accumulated among Negroes in the community from years of deprivation and powerlessness. As Smelser (1963: 259) has observed, "Once hostile outbursts begin . . . they become a *sign* that a fissure has opened in the social order, and that the situation is now structurally conducive for the expression of hostility." With regard to disturbances during the 1960s, evidence in support of a relation between community-based deprivations and riot severity has been reported by several investigators, principally Downes (1968) and Morgan and Clark (1973). . . .

Two additional factors warrant consideration. First, apart from the relevance of the social and economic organization of a community, there is a possibility that an outbreak of violence will alter the expected intensity of a subsequent disorder in the same city. The most reasonable conjecture is that later disturbances would be less severe since the initial event would have stimulated police preparation and training in crowd control procedures. Second, superimposed upon the foregoing processes, a time trend may exist in disorder severity. For instance, the disturbances, subsequent to the assassination of Martin Luther King may have been unusually destructive and violent because of the intensity of bereavement among Negroes. Or, just as the police in a city which has experienced a disorder may be motivated to routinize their crowd control techniques, these tactics might become more widely diffused as other communities recognize that they may not be immune to racial turmoil. Thus, with the passage of time, the severity of even a *first* racial incident in a city might decline.

The above comments constitute a rationale for investigating the variation in disorder severity, and for doing so with reference to several categories of potential determinants: the social and economic situation of Negroes in a community, the preparation by social control forces, the prior disturbance history of the community, and the location in time of the incident. . . .

## Measurement of Disorder Severity

The measurement of disorder severity raises several conceptual and methodological issues. One matter concerns the question of dimensionality. Wanderer (1968), Downes (1970) and Morgan and Clark (1973) all have treated severity as a unidimensional concept. Indeed, Wanderer reports that the 75 incidents which he analyzed from an eight-category Guttman scale. In our considerably more extensive data set (322 incidents), information on aspects of disorder severity is not systematically available. However, the few inter-correlations which can be computed among the component indicators are large and suggest that a unidimensionality assumption is not unreasonable. We will proceed here under this assumption; additional evidence to support unidimensionality will be presented in a later section.

A second issue concerns specification of the severity scale categories and selection of items appropriate to the construct. . . .

Using data much the same as ours, Downes (1968; 1970) constructed a four-category ordinal scale which incorporates quantitative information on the extent of several kinds of riot activites. We chose to use a somewhat more elaborate version of Downes' scale (Table 1), the main difference being that our instrument specifies numerical bounds at each scale level for crowd size, number of arrests, and number of injuries to supplement the descriptive information pertaining to severity. The bounds were specified to overlap one another because the component aspects of severity are not perfectly correlated. Some disturbances have large crowds but few injuries, while other incidents with relatively few participants may be exceedingly sanguinary and result in a great many injuries. In assessing severity, the coders were instructed to use the bounds as guides, in conjunction with the descriptive materials on a disorder, rather than to code in an inflexible manner.

A final issue concerns measurement properties of the severity scale. Whereas Downes utilized ordinal ranks in his computations, we chose to assign interval scores to the categories, in recognition of the fact that our knowledge about the scale levels exceeds rank order information. . . .

Our primary data sources were Lemberg Center (1968a; 1968b) and the New York Times Index. Newspaper accounts and the Civil Disorder Chronology (Congressional Quarterly, 1967) were consulted in reference to the pre-1967 disturbances, but information concerning those events was too sketchy to permit reliable classification in terms of severity. The incidents analyzed in this study, therefore, are limited to the period 1967-68. Three hundred and twenty-two events satisfied the minimal criteria of violence necessary for consideration as disorders (Spilerman, 1970b:630) and were used in the analysis.

Following the instructions outlined above, two coders, working independently, classified all incidents. Where information on some aspect of severity was missing, they were instructed to assign the incident to a rank category on the

**TABLE 1. Riot Severity Scale**

0. Low intensity—rock and bottle throwing, some fighting, little property damage. Crowd size $< 125$; arrests $< 15$; injuries $< 8$.
1. Rock and bottle throwing, fighting, looting, serious property damage, some arson. Crowd size 75–250; arrests 10–30; injuries 5–15.
2. Substantial violence, looting, arson, and property destruction. Crowd size 200–500; arrests 25–75; injuries 10–40.
3. High intensity—major violence, bloodshed and destruction. Crowd size $> 400$; arrests $> 65$; injuries $> 35$.

basis of available data. Agreement between the coders was obtained in 96 percent of the disorders. In every instance of disagreement, a single rank difference was involved and the matter was resolved by averaging the two values.

To validate the resulting scale as a severity instrument, the component variables (number of arrests, number of injuries, and crowd size), the three-category severity classification employed in the Kerner Report (National Advisory Commission, 1968:65) in conjunction with the 1967 disorders, and the composite indices described in this paper were inter-correlated using a pairwise-present calculation. The results . . . reveal a substantial correspondence between our indices and the other measures of severity. . . .

## Reinforcement Effects and Time Trend

The variables in this study which bear the greatest sociological significance are ones which refer to structural and demographic features of a community. The findings with respect to these factors can inform us about how the severity of hostile outbursts is conditioned by the way our cities are organized and governed and by the pervasiveness of the deprivations to which Negro residents are subjected. Most of the community characteristics that we shall examine change only slowly during a brief time interval, such as the period covered by this study (1967–68); therefore, we will treat them as constant in time and employ cross-sectional procedures. What we shall be investigating, then, is the presence of a severity value that is community specific and relatively stable over time; both properties deriving from its conceptualization as a function of community demography and social organization.

Before addressing this issue, we discuss some *volatile* aspects of a community's severity value. This matter is of importance because we wish to acquire a comprehensive understanding of the determinants of severity and, also, because controls will be necessary for the responsible factors in order to obtain unbiased estimates of the community effects. One possible source of volatility relates to the presence of multiple disturbances in a city during the two-year interval; often they were at different levels of severity. While this may be simply a consequence of random variation about a community's "characteristic value," it also could reflect the influence of systematic factors. In particular, . . . a reinforcement process might operate whereby an outbreak of violence alters the expected severity of a subsequent disorder in the same city. This would happen, for instance, if the police were to increase their preparation in riot control procedures following an initial outburst (thereby lowering the expected severity of later disorders), or if insensitive police actions during the first incident were to leave a residue of bitterness and hostility in the black community (in which case the intensity of subsequent violence might be raised). In either case, the expected severity of a disturbance would be a function of the history of prior racial turmoil in the city. A second potential source of volatility relates to the presence of a time trend. Outbreaks of exceptionally severe disorders following the assassination of Martin Luther King would constitute an example of such temporal variation.

Evidence for both contentions can be found in Table 2. The entries in column (1) report mean severity rank by time period for the first disturbance in a community; in column (2) analogous figures are presented for disturbances subsequent to the first one. These values suggest that disorder severity was a relatively stable phenomenon until the assassination of Martin Luther King. In the weeks following his murder, the severity of a first disorder in a city declined, while communities with a history of racial turmoil incurred a marked increase in intensity of violence. A reversal of this pattern is apparent in the final time periods: first disorders exhibit a severity increase while later outbreaks in a city show a decline.

Although these effects are striking and suggest the operation of both a time trend and different influences upon first and later disorders in a city, the responsible mechanisms are not discernible from an inspection of Table 2. In order to unravel the determinants of the volatility in disorder severity, we resort to a regression formulation in which the processes outlined above are taken into account, and controls are also incorporated for community differences in disorder-*proneness*. Controls for the latter factor are necessary because cities with different characteristic severity values may differ as well in their proneness to incur disturbances, and this feature may be confounded with the aforementioned processes. In particular, communities with high severity potentials might

**TABLE 2.** **Disorder Severity by Ordinal Position of the Disturbance in a City and by Time Period, 1967–68**

| PERIOD | First Disturbance in City[a] | | Subsequent Disturbances in City | |
|---|---|---|---|---|
| | (1) MEAN SEVERITY[b] | NUMBER OF DIS-ORDERS | (2) MEAN SEVERITY[b] | NUMBER OF DIS-ORDERS |
| Jan.–July, 1967 ($t_1$) | .782 | 78 | .913 | 46 |
| Aug., 1967–March, 1968 ($t_2$) | .750 | 16 | .825 | 20 |
| April 1968 ($t_3$)[c] | .510 | 51 | 1.270 | 37 |
| May–July, 1968 ($t_4$) | 1.000 | 13 | .789 | 26 |
| Aug.–Dec. 1968 ($t_5$) | .923 | 13 | .659 | 22 |
| N | | 171 | | 151 |

[a]Includes only cities for which a first disorder occurred in 1967–1968.
[b](Untransformed scale values (0–3) were used to reduce the effect of very high severity scores. The pattern of results is unchanged but the effects more pronounced if transformed severity values (0–12) are used.
[c]Post-Martin Luther King-assassination period.

tend to experience many disorders and therefore would probably undergo a first disturbance in an early time period. This situation would produce a spurious time trend unless the determinants of disorder-proneness are explicitly controlled.

The dependent variable in the regression was disorder severity, while the independent variables were dummy terms for time period, number of prior disorders in the city and South, plus a continuous term for nonwhite population size. The latter two variables were included because they have been cited as major determinants of community disorder-proneness (Spilerman, 1970b). . . .

The results reported in Table 3 [see page 328] provide evidence for each of the preceding contentions regarding the determinants of volatility in disorder severity. With respect to a temporal trend, the entries in column (1) reveal that the post-Martin Luther King-assassination disturbances in April, 1968, were unusually severe, net of the other variables in the equation. On our 12-unit scale, a disturbance at that point in time tended to be approximately one unit more severe than one in the reference interval ($t_1$). This effect appears to have spilled over into the early summer months of 1968; although owing, possibly, to the few incidents in that period, the coefficient for $t_4$ is not statistically significant.

The two community characteristics that were included in the regression because of their known influence on disorder frequency (nonwhite population size and a dummy term for South) have effects on severity which are identical to the ones reported for them in the disorder-proneness study (Spilerman, 1970b:643). Both severity and frequency vary directly with nonwhite population size (a large population provides the human resources for many disturbances and for severe ones). Also, severity and frequency both were substantially lower in the South; according to the specification of equation (1), the average severity of a disturbance in this region was more than one scale unit below that of a non-southern incident, net of the other factors. In the disorder-proneness study, we speculated that the regional difference might reflect lower expectations on the part of southern Negroes regarding the likely rate of improvement in their conditions (and, hence, less frustration from observing the actual rate of progress) and a greater fear of repression and retribution. This same explanation would account for disorders being less severe in the South since the salient point, again, is that there would be fewer potential riot participants in cities in this region.

Perhaps the most intriguing finding concerns the contribution from prior outbreaks. With the occurrence of each incident, the expected severity of a subsequent disorder in the same city declined. It is noteworthy that the contribution from one prior outbreak is not as large as the marginal contribution from two, or from three or more, prior outbreaks. I interpret this to mean that participant exhaustion may have had more to do with the decline in severity than did improved police preparation in response to previous racial turmoil in the city. Under the latter process, a first incident should have had the largest effect, with additional police training and preparation stimulated by subsequent disorders making progressively smaller marginal contributions to the reduction in severity. However, the regression results reveal the reverse pattern, one that is more understandable in terms of an explanation which emphasizes cumulative exhaustion and growing disinterest on the part of potential participants to engaging in yet another disturbance. This interpretation is highly speculative, of course; presumably both processes operated in varying degrees, and a more detailed analysis than we are prepared to undertake here would be necessary to disentangle their separate effects. Nevertheless, irrespective of which interpretation one prefers, the empirical finding is quite clear: severity declined as a function of the number of prior outbreaks in a city. . . .

Because of the tendency of the dummy terms for each higher number of prior disorders to show effects which decrease in an almost linear fashion, we can replace them by a single variable, the number of prior outbreaks in a city. The coefficients for this more concise model are presented in column (2) of Table 3 and differ only in minor ways from the parameters of the preceding equation. These variables will be the controls in our investigation of the impact of community structure and demography on disorder severity. Before undertaking that analysis, we turn to the question of the robustness of the regression results.

### SENSITIVITY ANALYSIS

While we believe that the severity measure accurately depicts the magnitude of violence and destruction that transpired in particular disorders, it is nonetheless true that other researchers, employing alternative methods to assess severity, might have constructed different indices. It behooves us, therefore, to ascertain whether the results we have reported are an artifact of the particular coding scheme that was used or whether they are robust with regard to specification of the severity index. . . .

One potential source of error relates to our assignment of interval scores to the rank differences. In order to ascertain the sensitivity of the findings to the particular values that were selected, the analysis summarized in Table 3 was repeated with alternate specifications of the rank differences. These results are presented in the form of *standardized* regression coefficients in columns (2) through (3) of Table 4.[3] Standardized coefficients are reported because they are more suitable for comparisons which involve different dependent variables than are unstandardized coefficients; the magnitude of the latter will vary with the choice of metric for the dependent variable.

With respect to number of prior disorders, nonwhite population size and South, the results appear *not* to be sensitive to the precise specification of the severity measure. In regard to these variables, our conclusions would not be changed if a moderately different severity index were substituted for ours. The

---

[3] The regression coefficients in column (1) correspond to an assignment of the values 0, 1, 2, 3 to the dependent variable. In column (2), the scale values are the ones which were used in our composite severity index so the entries here are beta coefficients for the second model in Table 3. In column (3), the values 0, 1, 6, 25 were assigned to the severity ranks.

**TABLE 3.** Regressions of Disorder Severity[a] on Time Period, Number of Prior Disturbances, Nonwhite Population Size and Region

| INDEPENDENT VARIABLE | Unstandardized Regression Coefficient[b] | | | |
|---|---|---|---|---|
| | (1) | | (2) | |
| Constant | −6.698** | (−5.09) | −6.772** | (−4.85) |
| $t_2$ | .033 | (0.05) | .019 | (0.03) |
| $t_3$ [c] | .967* | (2.21) | .971* | (2.20) |
| $t_4$ | 1.034 | (1.76) | .928 | (1.60) |
| $t_5$ | .311 | (0.51) | .384 | (0.62) |
| 1 Prior Disorder[d] | −.275 | (−0.60) | | |
| 2 Prior Disorders[d] | −1.668** | (−2.64) | | |
| 3+ Prior Disorders[d] | −2.657** | (−4.05) | | |
| Number of Prior Disorders[d] | | | −.445** | (−3.74) |
| Nonwhite Population Size (log) | .892** | (6.25) | .890** | (6.16) |
| South | −1.146** | (−2.63) | −1.154** | (−2.62) |
| $R^2$ | .149 | | .134 | |
| No. of observations | 300 | | 300 | |

*Significant at $p < .05$.
**Significant at $p < .01$.
[a]Scale values of severity are coded 0, 1, 4, 12.
[b]t-values are in parentheses.
[c]Post-Martin Luther King-assassination period; see Table 2 for exact specification of the time period terms. Deleted term is $t_1$.
[d]During 1961–68.

results for the time period effects, however, do display sensitivity to the values assigned to the rank differences. In particular, if severity were measured on the 0–3 scale we would conclude that the post-Martin Luther King-assassination disorders were not especially violent, while if it were measured on the 0–25 scale we would envision the events of this period as significantly more violent than we have reported with the 0–12 scale. While we believe that our instrument provides a more accurate representation of the severity levels than either of the alternatives, the time period effects should be seen as less well established than the other findings.

A second potential source of error relates to classification of the individual disturbances into severity categories, a task which was performed in accordance with the criteria described in Table 1. For a portion of the incidents we have available quantitative information on facets of severity—crowd size, number of arrests, number of injuries—and were able to replicate the analysis using these components as dependent variables. The results are presented in columns (4) through (6) of Table 4 and are consistent with the findings obtained with our composite index. Number of prior disturbances and the two determinants of disorder-proneness (nonwhite population size and South) show effects that are very similar to the ones already reported for them. With respect to the time

**TABLE 4. Sensitivity of the Regression Results to Alternate Specifications of the Severity Measure**

| INDEPENDENT VARIABLES | STANDARDIZED REGRESSION COEFFICIENT | | | | | |
|---|---|---|---|---|---|---|
| | Dependent Variable | | | | | |
| | (1) SEVERITY 0–3 | (2) SEVERITY 0–12 | (3) SEVERITY 0–25 | (4) CROWD SIZE[a] | (5) LOG ARRESTS | (6) LOG INJURIES |
| $t_2$[b] | .011 | .002 | .001 | .063 | .054 | .071 |
| $t_3$ | .049 | .139** | .161** | .110 | .118* | .156** |
| $t_4$ | .047 | .095 | .107 | −.068 | −.013 | .136* |
| $t_5$ | .047 | .038 | .037 | .024 | −.009 | .107 |
| Number of Prior Disorders[c] | −.293** | −.306** | −.300** | −.177* | −.233** | −.256** |
| Nonwhite Population Size (log) | .459** | .478** | .464** | .615** | .486** | .507** |
| South | −.160** | −.153** | −.145** | −.191** | −.125* | −.157** |
| $R^2$ | .12 | .13 | .13 | .31 | .15 | .17 |
| No. of Observations | 300 | 300 | 300 | 194 | 275 | 241 |

*Significant at $p < .05$.
**Significant at $p < .01$.
†Significance tests not available for individual coefficients in the canonical model.
[a] Alternate assignments of values to crowd size ranks produced comparable results.
[b] Post-Martin Luther King-assassination period.
[c] During 1961–68.

329

period terms, $t_3$ is significant in two of the three equations and $t_4$ is significant in one equation. This provides supporting evidence for the contention that the post-assassination disorders were more severe than incidents in the other time periods. It should also be noted that the fact that these results parallel the ones obtained with the composite index means that the unidimensional conceptualization of severity is not obscuring relationships between components of this construct and the other factors. . . .

We conclude that the results reported in Table 3 are not idiosyncratic of the severity index which was used. Under an assortment of alternative specifications of severity and under different analytic procedures the same substantive assessment would have been reached.

## Community-Based Deprivations and Disorder Severity

In the introductory section, we presented a rationale for investigating the impact of Negro living conditions in a community on the severity of its disorders. We indicated that while the kinds of discontent which derive from community-based deprivations have not been found to be related to the *frequency* of hostile outbursts, there are theoretical considerations and results from other empirical studies (Wanderer, 1968; Downes, 1968; 1970; Morgan and Clark, 1973) which suggest that this may not be the case with disorder severity; that once a disturbance has begun, the frustrations which have accumulated among Negroes as a result of their circumstance in the community may well be expressed in the intensity of the aggression.

To the extent that the frustrations which provoked Negroes to riot during the 1960s were a consequence of local deprivations, we would expect the variation across cities in disorder severity to correspond to the variation in the indicators of the relevant deprivations, once other salient factors have been controlled. This raises the question of which conditions were responsible for the discontent expressed in the rioting. The presence of city differences in important determinants of Negro well-being is not a sufficient reason for concluding that a corresponding variation will exist in the frustration level of inhabitants in different ghettos. Many potential sources of discontent are only that—potential sources—until attention is called to them and they are invested with symbolic import and racial significance. . . . There are other community characteristics whose values in different cities are likely to induce corresponding variations in the level of discontent, irrespective of whether or not they become foci of attention. For instance, there probably is greater discontent where median Negro income is low than where it is high, because of the enormous importance of this factor for access to a variety of institutions and desirable life styles. However, this does not mean that the greater frustration in poor ghettos necessarily will be articulated in severity of rioting; the disorders of the 1960s may have been reactions to entirely different provocations than community conditions.

Because we are not prepared to assert which inequities were especially galling to Negroes or whether they were oriented in this period to a particular reference group, our strategy will be to postulate a number of plausible ways by which frustration may derive from community conditions and then ascertain the relation between measures of the relevant factors and disorder severity. A detailed discussion of this procedure has been presented elsewhere (Spilerman, 1970b: 639-41). . . . In essence, we have selected community characteristics which can serve as indicators for a social disorganization explanation, for reference group explanations and for a thesis which associates the severity of rioting with an unresponsive municipal political structure.

## SOCIAL DISORGANIZATION

According to this perspective on the causes of collective aggression, individuals who are weakly integrated into their community, in the sense of having few associational ties or little personal identification with it, are less encumbered by the constraints which would dissuade others from participating in a destructive outburst. One formulation of this thesis refers to the disorienting effects of rapid population change. A locale which has experienced a substantial influx of new residents would have acquired many persons who are unacquainted with the institutionalized procedures for seeking redress of grievances; at the same time, these individuals would have little investment in solving problems in a manner which avoids rancor and conflict in the community. Frustration is not the animus here; rather, it is the absence of social links which normally permit informal control to be exercised and prevent disputes from polarizing and degenerating into hostility and violence. A second version of the social disorganization thesis stresses the negative association with community that is likely to characterize the attitudes of residents in the worst ghettos because of their continual exposure to crime, filth and dilapidated housing. As indicators of the first formulation, we used the census variables percent change in total population and percent change in nonwhite population. As indicators of the second formulation, we employed the variables percent of nonwhites residing in dwellings constructed before 1950 and percent of nonwhites living in housing with substandard plumbing.

## POLITICAL STRUCTURE

During periods of rapid change in the status of a minority, such as occurred for Negroes during the 1960s, issues frequently arise which require the representation of its views in the municipal government. Also, if bitter disputes involving the group are to be resolved without confrontation and violence, there is a need for city officials to be oriented toward compromise and accommodation. While we lack performance measures on how racial disputes were processed in the many cities which experienced disorders during 1967-68, there is evidence that certain electoral procedures and political structures make for greater responsiveness to the sensitivities of diverse constituents, and we have measures of the presence of these arrangements. In particular, Lieberson and Silverman (1965) . . . have argued that a municipal government will be more representative of community composition when council members are elected from established districts, rather than at large, and when the council districts are small; the rationale being that opportunity is thereby increased for a numerically small but geographically concentrated group to elect its own members. It has also been suggested (Alford and Scoble, 1965) that a mayor-council structure and partisan elections will enhance governmental responsiveness to the diverse and conflicting interests of a socially heterogeneous community. In our analysis we included dummy variables for presence of nonpartisan elections and for mayor-council government and continuous variables for population per councilman and proportion of the city council elected at-large.

### DEPRIVATION EXPLANATIONS

These approaches to explaining frustration may be classified according to whether or not the presence of a reference group is postulated. *Absolute* deprivation explanations attribute the inter-city variation in level of Negro discontent to community differences in social and economic opportunity for ghetto residents. The presumption here is that where many persons earn low incomes or are employed at unsatisfying tasks, discontent will be more widespread. Since it focuses upon the economically most disadvantaged population segment in a community, this is an instance of an underclass explanation of the sources of violence and aggression (Downes, 1968:513-4). As indicators of the level of absolute deprivation of Negroes, the following variables were used: percent of nonwhite males employed in low status occupations (household workers, service workers, laborers); the nonwhite male unemployment rate; nonwhite median family income; and nonwhite median education.

*Relative* deprivation explanations posit the existence of a reference group or an objective standard against which individuals compare their status or their progress. The level of frustration for the underprivileged is usually specified as a function of the size of the gap between the two populations on relevant variables. One possible reference group for Negroes would be whites in the same community. To measure Negro circumstance relative to this group, the absolute deprivation indicators were divided by comparable indices of white living standards. Alternatively, in a highly segregated society such as ours, Negroes may have more familiarity with the stylized version of white family life which is depicted in situation shows on television and may compare their own circumstances to this portrayal. In the disorder-proneness study (Spilerman, 1970b: 640), it was argued that the indicators of *absolute* deprivation provide the appropriate measures for this relative deprivation thesis. Finally, these same community characteristics may be associated with yet additional explanations, which argue an expectational or a competition thesis. . . .

## SIGNIFICANCE OF THE COMMUNITY CHARACTERISTICS

In order to ascertain whether disorders tended to be more severe where the objective measures of Negro circumstance in a community indicate greater disadvantage, it is necessary to include in the analysis other major determinants of severity that are correlated with the community factors of interest (Blalock, 1964:48). Controls were introduced for the variables listed in Table 3 (second model). The importance of adjusting for these effects can be motivated in the following way: because of the Negro revolt character of the disturbances in the 1960s, the term for Negro population size measures the availability of participants for large (and severe) disorders; holding this variable constant allows us to compare communities having different sized pools of potential participants. The term for South permits an additive regional adjustment in the relationship between the community variables and disorder severity; it is introduced in recognition of the very different cultural traditions of the geographic regions in race relations. (We already have seen that the regional effect is to depress severity in the South.) In an analogous fashion, the controls for number of previous disturbances and for time period adjust for any obscuring effects arising from these volatile determinants of disorder severity.

In Table 5 we report zero-order correlations between each of the community characteristics and disorder severity (column 1) and partial correlations (column 2) controlling for the variables in Table 3. (The latter entries derive from 21 regressions, each containing the controls and a single deprivation indicator.) We see that while there are several significant zero-order effects, none remains significant once the control variables are entered into the equation. Again, these results are not an artifact of the particular interval values that were assigned to the severity ranks or of the manner in which the disturbances were categorized. The analysis was replicated taking as dependent variables the two alternate interval assignments (see Table 4) and the three quantitative components of severity (crowd size, number of arrests, number of injuries). This exercise produced results that are virtually identical with the ones reported here.

Another approach to evaluating the importance of the explanations which associate disorder severity with Negro deprivation in a community is to assess the joint contribution from each cluster of variables toward accounting for the unexplained variation in the dependent variable. The terms in each cluster listed in Table 5 were therefore entered into a regression equation containing the controls. These results are reported in Table 6. In no instance does a cluster add as much as two percentage points of explained variation to the 13.4 percent accounted for by the control variables (column 3); also, in every case, the added $R^2$ is insiginifcant at the .10 level, as judged by a conventional F-test.

**T A B L E 5.** Correlations Between Disorder Severity and Aspects of Community Structure[a]

| COMMUNITY ATTRIBUTE | (1) ZERO-ORDER CORRELATION WITH DISORDER SEVERITY[b] | (2) PARTIAL CORRELATION, CONTROLLING FOR REGION, NONWHITE POPULATION, TEMPORAL EFFECTS AND NUMBER OF PREVIOUS DISTURBANCES[c] |
|---|---|---|
| Region and Nonwhite Population Size[d] | | |
| South (Dummy) | −.062 | −.151**[g] |
| Nonwhite Population (log x) | .270** | .339**[g] |
| Indicators of Social Disorganization[d] | | |
| Percent Change in Total Population, 1950–60 | −.093 | −.016 |
| Percent Change in Total Population, 1960–70 | −.053 | .008 |
| Percent Change in Nonwhite Population, 1950–60 | .048 | .099 |
| Percent Change in Nonwhite Population, 1960–70 | .001 | .035 |
| Percent of Nonwhites Living in Housing Built before 1950 | .083 | −.014 |
| Percent of Nonwhites Living in Housing with Substandard Plumbing | .130* | .018 |
| Indicators of Absolute Deprivation[d] | | |
| Percent of Nonwhite Males Employed in Traditionally Negro Occupations[f] | −.139* | −.084 |
| Nonwhite Male Unemployment Rate, 1960 | .068 | .044 |
| Nonwhite Male Unemployment Rate, 1970 | .047 | .027 |
| Nonwhite Median Family Income | .060 | .034 |
| Nonwhite Median Education | .021 | −.065 |
| Indicators of Relative Deprivation[d] | | |
| Percent of Nonwhite Males Employed in Traditionally Negro Occupations Divided by White Figure | −.105 | −.049 |
| Nonwhite Median Family Income Divided by White Income | .074 | .063 |

**TABLE 5.** Continued

| COMMUNITY ATTRIBUTE | (1) ZERO-ORDER CORRELATION WITH DISORDER SEVERITY[b] | (2) PARTIAL CORRELATION, CONTROLLING FOR REGION, NONWHITE POPULATION, TEMPORAL EFFECTS AND NUMBER OF PREVIOUS DISTURBANCES[c] |
|---|---|---|
| Nonwhite Unemployment Rate Divided by White Rate, 1960 | .028 | .031 |
| Nonwhite Unemployment Rate Divided by White Rate, 1970 | −.016 | .012 |
| Nonwhite Median Education Divided by White Education | .019* | .005 |
| Percent Nonwhite ($\sqrt{x}$ ) | .148** | .033 |
| Indicators of Political Structure[e] | | |
| Population per Councilman | .175** | −.019 |
| Percent of City Council Elected At-Large | −.089 | −.040 |
| Presence of Nonpartisan Elections | −.066 | −.022 |
| Presence of Mayor-Council Gov't. | .110* | .018 |

*Significant at $p < .05$.
**Significant at $p < .01$.
[a]Number of observations equals 300.
[b]Disorder Severity coded (0–12).
[c]Control variables specified by equation (2) of Table 3. A separate regression was run for each community characteristic, containing it and the controls.
[d]Source: U.S. Census of Population (1963; 1973).
[e]Source: Municipal Yearbook (1965).
[f]Service workers + household workers + laborers.
[g]Controls are for other variables in equation (2) of Table 3.

We stress that this result is not a consequence of the deprivation indicators and nonwhite population size sharing the same variation. In no case does the significance of the population term in a regression fail to reach the .01 level in the presence of either a single deprivation measure or a variable cluster. Indeed, while none of the clusters, entered after the controls increased the $R^2$ by as much as two percentage points (over the initial 13.4 points), the nonwhite population term alone, entered after the other controls and any cluster of deprivation indicators, adds a minimum of 7.2 percentage points to the explained variation (column 2).

TABLE 6. Percent of Variance in Disorder Severity Accounted for by Different Variable Clusters

| VARIABLE CLUSTER[a] | (1) PERCENT OF TOTAL VARIANCE EXPLAINED BY CLUSTER AND CONTROLS[b] | (2) PERCENT OF TOTAL VARIANCE EXPLAINED BY NONWHITE POPULATION WHEN ENTERED AFTER CLUSTER AND CONTROLS[b] | (3) PERCENT OF TOTAL VARIANCE EXPLAINED BY CLUSTER WHEN ENTERED AFTER NONWHITE POPULATION AND OTHER CONTROLS[b] |
|---|---|---|---|
| Nonwhite Population[c] | 13.4 | — | — |
| Social Disorganization | 6.0 | 9.5 | 1.8 |
| Absolute Deprivation | 4.2 | 10.6 | 1.4 |
| Relative Deprivation | 6.7 | 7.5 | .8 |
| Political Structure | 6.4 | 7.2 | .2 |

[a]See Table 5 for a description of the variables included in each cluster.
[b]In this table "controls" refer to all variables in Table 3, column 2, except nonwhite population.
[c]This cluster refers to the equation of Table 3, column 2.

336

Our analysis therefore indicates that in the period of the 1960s, the severity of a disturbance had little basis in community organization or economic structure. Holding constant a measure of the size of the pool of potential participants and several determinants of the volatility in severity it is *not* the case that an outbreak of racial violence tended to be more severe where Negro status is low (in absolute terms or relative to one of several reference groups), where community disorganization is extensive, or where the structure of the municipal government suggests it would be unresponsive to the interests of Negro constituents. Instead, as we have reported with respect to the determinants of disorder-proneness (Spilerman, 1970b; 1971), the only stable community characteristics that are related to severity are nonwhite population size and a contextual term for South.

These results are at variance with the findings by Morgan and Clark (1973) who argue that disorder severity in the mid-1960s was a function of the grievance level of Negroes in a community. In particular, they report that severity was raised by racial inequality in housing conditions but depressed by inequality in occupational status. We find their analysis less than persuasive for the following reasons. (1) Their assertions are based on only 23 observations. . . . (2) They confounded disturbances of very different types. Although their explanatory variables were justified as indicators of Negro grievances in a community, the disorders they analyzed include incidents in which the aggression was perpetrated by whites, as well as instances of Negro aggression. . . . (3) Morgan and Clark failed to include proper controls for the size of the potential participant pool, which is necessary to ascertain the contribution from the grievance indicators net of city differences in available manpower for mounting a severe disturbance. They did incorporate a term for city size but this is not the correct control for potential participants. Where rioting is principally by Negroes, adjustments should be made for the size of this population group (or its relevant age cohort). . . .

## Conclusions

We have sought in this investigation to ascertain whether certain structural arrangements or demographic features of a community were responsible for especially severe disturbances during the 1960s. In previous studies (Spilerman, 1970b; 1971), we reported that the disturbance *locations* were unrelated to a number of objective indicators of Negro well-being in a locale. As a result, it was suggested that explanations of the causes of the riots must be sought in frustrations which carried nationwide salience, and the areal distribution of the incidents should be understood in terms of mechanisms which promoted geographic diffuseness in the impact of provocations. Our findings with respect to the determinants of disorder severity underscore that assessment. The severity of a disturbance, as well as its location, appears not to have been contingent upon Negro living conditions or their social or economic status in a community. Nor surprising, it is also the case that the effects of the control variables—nonwhite population size and South—were much the same in the two studies: large ghetto populations provided the participants for frequent and for severe disturbances; also, net of this factor, a southern city tended to have fewer and less violent outbursts, possibly because Negroes in that region held lower expectations regarding improvements in their circumstances and were more fearful of retribution from participating in racial protest.

Taken together, these studies suggest that despite considerable differences in Negro circumstance from one city to the next, this consideration did not find expression in the two aspects of the disturbance process that we have examined. Although we would not claim that local conditions never influenced disorder-proneness or disorder severity, we do assert the absence of a systematic tendency for either of these facets of the racial turmoil to be associated with the extent of Negro deprivation in a community. This assessment is neither unreasonable nor counter-intuitive when viewed against other characteristics of the disturbances and against trends which were operative during the period. In particular, the incidents tended to cluster in time following a few dramatic events such as the massive Newark disorder in July, 1967, and the assassination of Martin Luther King in April, 1968. Also, the entire time interval during which disorders occurred in large numbers was itself concentrated within a few years in the mid-1960s. It is difficult to conceive of the kinds of developments in individual communities which could account for this sudden and practically simultaneous occurrence of hundreds of outbursts.

We also can enumerate trends which functioned to produce a geographically uniform pattern of behavior by Negroes. For one, black consciousness and black solidarity were very real phenomena during the 1960s, having been stimulated by the imaginative and appealing tactics of civil rights activists in desegregating retail establishments in the South and placing Negroes on the voter rolls. For another, various civil rights bills were before Congress during much of the decade; these were salient to Negroes in all communities and would have served to heighten their racial awareness and racial identification. Yet, the factor I would stress as being responsible in a most essential way for the outbreaks having occurred in great numbers and for community conditions having been irrelevant to the disorder process is the wide availability of television and its network news structure.

By bringing scenes of civil rights marches, demonstrations and sit-ins into every ghetto, television contributed in a fundamental way to the creation of a black solidarity that would transcend the boundaries of community. Of more immediate relevance to the outbursts, the extensive media coverage accorded to many of the incidents, with the actions of participants depicted in full relief, served to familiarize Negroes elsewhere with the details of rioting and with the motivations of rioters. Observing the behavior of persons who face similar deprivations and must contend with the same discriminatory institutions as oneself—in short, individuals with whom the viewer could identify—provided a model of how he, too, might protest the indignities of his circumstance. By conveying the intensity and emotion of a confrontation, television provided an essential mechanism for riot contagion; also, as a result of its national network structure, the provocations which arose in diverse settings were made visible in the ghettos of every city.

The importance of television as a vehicle for the propagation of violent acts is not restricted to racial disorders. There is considerable evidence that skyjackings, prison riots, bomb threats and aggressive crimes of other sorts have been spread by television and the other mass media. Indeed, a question which eventually will have to concern this nation is the determination of a policy to guide the reporting of destructive and potentially contagious events....

# References

Alford, Robert R. and Harry M. Scoble
1965 "Political and socioeconomic characteristics of American cities." Pp. 82–97 in Municipal Yearbook. Chicago: International City Manager's Association.
Berkowitz, Leonard
1965 "Some aspects of observed aggression." Journal of Personality and Social Psychology 1: 359–69.
Blalock, Hubert
1957 "Percent non-white and discrimination in the South." American Sociological Review 22: 677–82.
1964 Causal Inferences in Nonexperimental Research, Chapel Hill: University of North Carolina.
Congressional Quarterly Service
1967 Urban Problems and Civil Disorder. Special Report No. 36: 3–6.
Dollard, J., L. Doob, N. Miller, O. Mowrer and R. Sears
1939 Frustration and Aggression. New Haven: Yale University Press.
Downes, Bryan T.
1968 "The social characteristics of riot cities: a comparative study." Social Science Quarterly 49: 504–20.
1970 "A critical reexamination of the social and political characteristics of riot cities." Social Science Quarterly 51: 349–60.
Lemberg Center for the Study of Violence
1968a Compilation of the 1967 Disorders. Brandeis University. Unpublished.
1968b Riot Data Review. Numbers 1–3. Brandeis University. Mimeographed.
Lieberson, Stanley and Arnold R. Silverman
1965 "The precipitants and underlying conditions of race riots." American Sociological Review 30: 887–98.
Milgram, Stanley and Hans Toch
1969 "Collective behavior: crowds and social movements." Pp. 507–610 in Gardner Lindzey and Elliott Aronson (eds.), Handbook of Social Psychology, 2nd edition. Reading, Ma: Addison-Wesley.

Morgan, William R. and Terry N. Clark
  1973   "The causes of racial disorders: a grievance-level explanation." American Sociological Review 38: 611–24.
Municipal Yearbook
  1965   Chicago: International City Manager's Association.
  1966   Chicago: International City Manager's Association.
National Advisory Commission on Civil Disorders
  1968   A Report [by the Kerner Commission]. Washington, D.C.: U.S. Government Printing Office.
Smelser, Neil J.
  1963   Theory of Collective Behavior. New York: Free Press.
Spilerman, Seymour
  1970b   "The causes of racial disturbances: a comparison of alternative explanations." American Sociological Review 35: 627–49.
  1971   "The causes of racial disturbances: tests of an explanation." American Sociological Review 36:427–42.
U.S. Bureau of the Census
  1963   1960 Census of Population: Volume 1. Characteristics of the Population. Washington, D.C.: U.S. Government Printing Office.
  1973   1970 Census of Population: Volume 1. Characteristics of the Population. Washington, D.C.: U.S. Government Printing Office.
Wanderer, Jules J.
  1968   "1967 riots: a test of the congruity of events." Social Problems 16: 193–8.

# 40

# Advanced Capitalism and Black/White Race Relations in the United States: A Split Labor Market Interpretation

*EDNA BONACICH*

Currently one of the most noteworthy features of the position of black people in the United States is a high degree of unemployment running at roughly twice the white rate and aggravated by higher black than white hidden unemployment (Ross, 1967). This has not always been the case. According to Killingsworth (1968:2):

> The roughly two-to-one ratio between white and Negro unemployment rates has been widely publicized, and some otherwise well-informed persons have formed the impression that this relationship has "always" existed—at least as far back as the figures go. That is not so. The two-to-one ratio first appeared in 1954, and it has persisted through good years and bad since then. But the ratio was only about 160 in the 1947–49 period; the 1940 Census reported a ratio of 118, and the 1930 Census showed a ratio of 92.

Abridged from *American Sociological Review 41* (1976): 34–51. Used by permission.

Unemployment statistics as currently defined were not collected prior to 1940; however, earlier censuses computed the proportion of the population which was gainfully employed. The complement of this figure gives us not only the proportion unemployed (defined as persons in the labor force who are out of work) but also those who have not entered the labor force. As a measure of unemployment, it has the advantage of not omitting hidden unemployment, and disadvantage of including those who would genuinely not be part of the labor force (such as students and the independently wealthy). Table 1 presents the census findings on black versus white proportion not gainfully employed for males ten years and older. It is evident that black rates were lower than white and that lower black "unemployment" was not a regionally restricted phenomenon. In a word, there appears to have been a reversal in the relative rate of unemployment for blacks and whites. From 1940, black unemployment exceeds white and climbs rapidly to the current two-to-one ratio. The reversal took place some time during the 1930s.

The rise in relative unemployment among blacks raises a question regarding the role of race in advanced capitalism. While black slavery and share-cropping were of unambiguous benefit to the owners of land and capital, the gains from high unemployment in one segment of the population are less evident. Two approaches to this question can be distinguished in the literature. One sees a continued advantage to the employer in keeping blacks as a marginal workforce, useful for dealing with economic fluctuations and helping to divide and weaken the working class (e.g., Baron, 1971:34; Gordon, 1972:53–81; Reich, 1972; Tabb, 1970:26–7). The other, exemplified by Willhelm (1971), asserts that the technology of advanced capitalism has lessened the need for unskilled labor, which was the primary role played by blacks in the past. Blacks have become

**TABLE 1. Proportion of Males Ten Years Old or Over Not Gainfully Employed, 1910–1930, by Region.***

|      |       | BLACK | WHITE** | BLACK WHITE |
|------|-------|-------|---------|-------------|
| 1910 |       | 12.6  | 20.6    | .61         |
| 1920 |       | 18.9  | 22.2    | .85         |
| 1930 |       | 19.8  | 24.2    | .82         |
| 1920 | North | 13.5  | 21.6    | .62         |
|      | West  | 10.5  | 21.3    | .49         |
|      | South | 20.0  | 23.7    | .84         |
| 1930 | North | 17.5  | 24.1    | .73         |
|      | West  | 18.2  | 23.4    | .78         |
|      | South | 20.4  | 24.9    | .82         |

*Source: U.S. Department of Commerce, Bureau of Census. Negroes in the United States, 1920–32. Washington, D.C.: 1935:28.
**White rates are based on combining native-born and foreign-born whites.

useless to the economy and to the capitalist class and, combining this fact with persistent racism, may even face genocide. . . .

Each of these approaches has problems. It takes some convoluted reasoning to find the interests of the employer served by unemployment, and one could argue with equal cogency that his interests are hurt by reduction in "surplus value" to be expropriated (Harris, 1972), by the decline of a market and by the creation of a dangerously dissatisfied element in the population. In addition, it is difficult to see why black unemployment would be more beneficial to the capitalist class now than it was before 1940.

Interpreting black disadvantage as a product of technological advances, rather than a planned strategy of capitalists, makes more sense on the surface; but this approach errs in the opposite direction in treating technology as an impersonal force which imposes itself on society without human choice. Technology should be seen as a resource which parties can use in a variety of ways to further their interests, or which they may choose not to use if their interests are harmed by its introduction. Thus, despite the availability of labor-saving technology, the South African economy tends to be under-mechanized in large measure because African labor is so cheap that mechanization does not pay (van den Berghe, 1967:185). In addition, there is no reason to assume that technological advances inevitably displace the unskilled. During the 1920s and 1930s there was considerable technological innovation in certain industries in the United States. For example, the meat-packing industry rationalized its production process through the introduction of some machinery and an assembly line (disassembly in this case). The craft of meat-cutting was divided into fairly simple activities enabling unskilled and semi-skilled labor to be used in place of skilled labor. This mechanization may be seen, in part, as an attack on craft unions and the power they wielded by controlling access to training in complex skills (Tuttle, 1970a:89–90).

In order to understand the shift to high unemployment of blacks in advanced capitalism we need to look behind the process of automation in the post-World War II era. Who would profit by automation of industries? Why did technological advances during this period hurt unskilled (and disproportionately black) labor? The answers lie in the historical evolution of class conflict in this country. The period between World War I and the New Deal was characterized by a racially split labor market, encouraging the employment of black "cheap labor" but also generating considerable conflict. New Deal labor legislation temporarily helped to resolve the conflicts but created pressure to mechanize unskilled work, as well as other forces, which threw blacks out of work. This paper attempts to trace the dominant forces at work during this evolution.

## The Split Labor Market: World War I to the New Deal

A split labor market refers to a difference in the price of labor between two or more groups of workers, holding constant their efficiency and productivity

(Bonacich, 1972). The price differential includes not only wages but any costs incurred by the employer connected with his labor supply, such as housing, recruitment, training and discipline. A racially (black/white) split labor market began with slavery (Bonacich, 1975) and persisted well into the twentieth century in industrial America. During the period under investigation the price difference showed most clearly in wage rates and degree of unionization.

*Wages*

Northern and southern states differ in the degree to which racial wage differentials were openly drawn but both regions show various more covert means of maintaining a difference. In the South blacks sometimes received lower wages than whites for the same work. Table 2 illustrates this difference in the Virginia building trades using data (described as "the most complete data on variations between the wages of white and Negro workers") from the reports of the Commissioner of Labor of Virginia (Reid, 1969:17). Alternatively, blacks and whites had different job titles and were paid at different wage rates (Table 3), yet it is not clear that the "value" of the work in the production process was any less for black workers than for white workers.

The northern picture is more complicated. Blacks and whites doing the same work in the same plant rarely were paid different wages. But a wage differential appears in two more disguised forms. First, as in the South, one finds racial segregation by job title, with "black" jobs generally paying less. For example, a steel foundry in Chicago employing 135 people in 1927, 35 of whom were black, paid white workers an average wage of $37 a week and black workers an average of $29 (Spero and Harris, 1966:175). . . .

Such discrepancies are typical and generally accounted for by the fact that

**T A B L E  2.  Average Daily Pay Rate for White and Black Workers in the Building Trades in Virginia, 1927***

| OCCUPATIONS | WHITE RATE | BLACK RATE |
|-------------|------------|------------|
| Apprentices | $ 3.35 | $3.00 |
| Bricklayers | 11.00 | 9.60 |
| Carpenters | 6.24 | 4.22 |
| Cement Workers | 6.33 | 4.42 |
| Helpers | 3.37 | 3.08 |
| Laborers | 3.25 | 3.06 |
| Lathers | 6.08 | 5.40 |
| Painters & Decorators | 4.00 | 5.81 |
| Plasterers | 9.26 | 9.12 |
| Plumbers & Gas Fitters | 4.04 | 4.49 |
| Sheet Metal Workers | 4.75 | 6.16 |
| Miscellaneous | 4.29 | 2.75 |

*Source: Reid (1969:17).

**TABLE 3.** Average Daily Pay Rate for White and Black Workers in the Foundry Industry, Birmingham, Alabama, 1926*

| White | | Black | |
|---|---|---|---|
| CRAFT | RATE | CRAFT | RATE |
| Machinists | $6.16 | Molder's Helpers | $3.60 |
| Molders | 6.32 | Clippers | 3.60 |
| Pattern Makers | 6.48 | Crane Operators | 5.00 |
| Blacksmiths | 6.48 | Cupola Tenders | 3.85 |
| Electricians | 6.32 | Rammers | 4.00 |
| Carpenters | 6.00 | Pit Foremen | 4.50 |
| Core Makers | 6.32 | Core Foremen | 5.00 |
| Core Foremen | 5.75 | | |

*Adapted from Spero and Harris (1966:170).

blacks were concentrated in unskilled and semi-skilled jobs; but job classifications are sometimes arbitrary and a "skill" may require very little training. For example, Bailer (1943:421) points out that before World War II only 10 percent of jobs in the automobile industry required more than one year of training or experience.

The second indirect form of wage differential appears in segregation by firm, i.e., black workers are employed by firms which pay a lower wage rate than firms employing white workers even though they may be engaged in the same work. According to Hill (cited in Reid, 1969:16), "working as the only wage earners of a business such as building tradesmen, laundresses, garment workers, the rule is to force upon [black workers] smaller compensation than white would get."

Some may argue that, despite apparent similarities in job title, black workers were less efficient to employ and that wages reflect "productivity." Black and white labor would be equal in price to the employer, the higher wages of whites being balanced by their greater efficiency. By and large the evidence goes against this supposition. For example, the Chicago Commission of Race Relations (1922:373-8) sent questionnaires to 137 firms and interviewed 93 employers concerning their experience with black workers. Their conclusion was that "despite occasional statements that the Negro is slow or shiftless, the volume of evidence before the Commission shows that Negroes are satisfactory employees and compare favorably with other racial groups" (Chicago Commission, 1922: 378). It seems reasonable to conclude that the causes of the wage differential lie elsewhere.

*Unions*

More important than wage differences, in the period under investigation, was a difference in labor militance. White workers were more likely than blacks to form unions, to make demands for improved conditions (including wages) and to engage in costly strikes. This militance threatened to raise the price of labor substantially. If black labor was less militant, it would be cheaper to employ.

The picture of black union activity is complicated by the fact that a number of "white" unions openly excluded blacks while many others discriminated more covertly (Wesley, 1927:254–81). It may be that this discrimination entirely accounts for black underrepresentation in the unions. However, each group entered the situation with a different historical experience which, I would argue, shaped their initial orientation towards unions. And as we shall see, union discrimination was partly a product as well as a cause of black anti-unionism.

Greater white worker recognition of class conflict with the capitalist class was partly a product of longer experience in the industrial labor market. When they were raw immigrants, Europeans had also played a "cheap labor" role. But the wartime decline in immigration, coupled with the Immigration Act of 1924, meant that the white work force was becoming increasingly seasoned. Not-so-new immigrants began to join or form labor organizations and make demands for higher wages and improved work conditions. For example, in the organizing campaign of 1918 in the steel industry, white immigrants were the first to respond (Brody, 1960:223–4). In addition, unlike the blacks, some white immigrants came from countries where the concept of a politically active working class was well developed. These elements were feared by capital and denounced as un-American and communist. The exclusion of European immigrants in 1924 was, perhaps, not only a reaction by "native" labor to the threat of undercutting, but also a response by capital to the dangers of a "corrupting" element in the work force.

Some blacks had been members of the industrial proletariat for years and were at least as class conscious as white workers. But with the coming of World War I a large, impoverished peasantry entered both northern and southern industrial labor markets for the first time. This class was vulnerable to exploitation as cheap labor.

At least three factors were at work making blacks more "exploitable." First, they tended to be desperately poor; jobs and wage levels which were distasteful to some seemed attractive to them. . . . Wages for farm labor in the South were around 75 cents a day compared to 40 cents to $1.00 an hour for unskilled labor in Chicago (Spear, 1967: 156). What looked undesirable to many white workers looked like a "golden opportunity" to black migrants from the South (Spero and Harris, 1966: 114). At least at the outset, their discontent would be lower.

A second factor was a tradition of paternalism in the South, begun under slavery but extending well beyond it. Mixed with a hearty dose of intimidation by southern land-owners there was, nonetheless, a personal relationship between employer and employee which sometimes bound the worker to his employer. Black workers were not accustomed to intervening organizations, like unions, which expressed an explicitly antagonistic relationship to the employer. They had not had much exposure to the ideals and goals of organized labor. "The attachment which the Negro had been taught to feel for his employer in the South was quickly sensed and exploited by northern industrialists" (Cayton and Mitchell, 1970:61).

Third, a long history of discrimination and hostility by white labor led black workers to be chary of joining their organizations. It was in part the product of a split labor market begun under slavery (Bonacich, 1975) which led white workers to erect defensive barriers against the threat of being undermined, and this history created considerable black suspicion against the unions.

Precise figures on union membership are difficult to obtain, but scraps of information have come down to us from past studies. . . . In 1930, according to Wolters (1970a:138-9), the NAACP calculated that a maximum of three percent of the 1,500,000 nonagricultural black workers were in unions and almost half of these were in the Brotherhood of Sleeping Car Porters. The country-wide rate of union membership in non-agricultural work in 1930 was around ten percent.

In New York, a 1919 survey found that less than .003 percent of black women working in 217 industrial establishments were union members. "Even in the shops where the white women were well organized, Negro women working there seldom held union membership" (Franklin, 1936:96). A 1928 survey, also conducted in New York and this time not restricted to women, found that 3.8 percent of union members were black while the 1930 census revealed the black proportion of gainful workers in the city was 14.1 percent. "This leaves no doubt that on the whole Negro workers were far less organized than others" (Franklin, 1936:114).

There are important exceptions to this picture. Some black workers were active union members and even leaders in the "white" labor movement. Black workers sometimes organized their own unions either under the umbrella of the American Federation of Labor or independently. The former arrangement was not very satisfactory (Spero and Harris, 1966:95-101). Black locals were chartered directly by the AFL, an organization which could not negotiate wage rates itself. They were dependent on agreements arrived at by the white unions and did little to improve black bargaining power. Independent black unionism was not much more successful (Spero and Harris, 1966:116-27). Many of these unions failed after brief histories. The most successful, the Brotherhood of Sleeping Car Porters, was unable to bring off a threatened strike and eventually requested affiliation with the AFL (Marshall, 1965:26).

Lack of unionization among blacks affected their bargaining position which in turn affected wage levels. . . . The Shipbuilding Labor Adjustment Board, created during World War I, accepted the southern system of dividing work into black and white, unequally paid, occupations. "Since most Negroes in the industry were unorganized, they had no representation on the Board, and hence no opposition to such plans was voiced" (Rubin, 1970:38).

In sum, a lesser degree of involvement in labor unions meant that black workers could be used by employers to cut costs. This was achieved both by avoiding demands for improved wages and work conditions, and by avoiding the costs of labor conflict itself.

## DYNAMICS

Split labor markets develop dynamics which can perpetuate or increase the original price differential. The chief parties to the interaction are capital, higher priced labor and cheap labor. A schematic representation of the interactions for the post-World War I period is presented in Figure 1.

Figure 1 begins with the class conflict between capital and white labor (1). Efforts by white workers to improve their position, especially through militant trade unionism, threatened to drive up the price of labor. Capital, in an effort to keep costs down, sought an alternative labor supply which would be cheaper (2). Blacks were facing economic displacement in the South while European sources were drying up. Besides, for reasons suggested above, blacks seemed an ideal group with whom to fight the aspirations of white labor (3). That they were so used is demonstrated by three types of evidence: the use of black strike-breakers, the displacement of white workers with black and efforts to gain the loyalty of the black community.

### Strike-Breaking

The use of blacks as strike-breakers was not uncommon during this period. According to Jacobson (1968:5), "In strikebound plants employers found it easier to recruit strikebreakers among Negroes who never developed a trade

**FIGURE 1.    Interactions in the Split Labor Market, World War I to the New Deal**

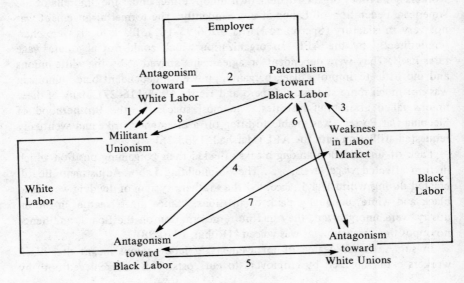

union consciousness and could see no reason why they should forsake a much needed day's pay for a white man's union." . . .

Perhaps the most important use of black strike-breaking occurred in the great steel strike of 1919. Foster (1920:206) reports that blacks already working in the steel mills were less likely to participate in the strike (e.g., in the Homestead Steel Works 1,737 of the 14,687 employees were black but only eight joined the unions and one struck; among white unskilled workers in the same plant at least 75 percent joined the unions and 90 percent struck). In addition, 30,000 to 40,000 blacks were brought into the mills from outside as strike-breakers, some fron northern cities, and most from the South. Black strike-breakers "were used in all the large districts and were a big factor in breaking the strike" (Foster, 1920:207).

## Displacement

Strike-breaking sometimes proves to be a short-term relationship in that strikers may return to their position once the conflict is resolved. A more stable relationship with black labor also emerged in the form of substituting black for white in non-strike situations. . . .

[E]xamples are found in a variety of industries. For instance, in the metal industry during the fall of 1916 the Aluminum Ore Company of East St. Louis "embarked upon a policy of increasing the Negro labor force in order to limit the future demands of white workers" (Rudwick, 1964:16-7). In November, 1916 they increased the number of black employees from 10-12 to 280; in December, to 410; in February, 1917, to 470. In the bituminous coal industry, there was an increase in the use of black labor, in part because of "the ease with which Negro labor, because of limited industrial opportunity and low economic standards, can be used in labor difficulties" (Spero and Harris, 1966:208). . . . In general, "employers came to refer to their Negro help as 'strike insurance'" (Cayton and Mitchell, 1970:x).

The great migration of blacks northwards during and after World War I must be understood in this context. Not only were economic conditions bad in the rural South, but positive inducements were being offered by industrial employers. Labor recruiters were sent South to encourage migration (Brody, 1960:184-5; Spear, 1967:133). While recruitment was partly a product of labor shortage caused by the war and the decline in European immigration, it is also evident that employers saw in this black "industrial reserve" a population which could be used to keep out unions and displace troublesome and increasingly expensive white labor.

## Loyalty

Displacement was sometimes accompanied by efforts to gain the loyalty of the black work force, thereby forestalling the development of unions among them and maintaining the "cheap labor" status. . . . On a larger scale, employers would make overtures to black workers and community leaders, giving money and urging workers to come to the employer for aid. Leaders in the black community would, in turn, urge black workers to be a docile and loyal work-force, keeping faith with the employer.

In the Chicago meat-packing industry, for example, packers "made financial efforts to obtain good relationships with institutions in the black community such as the YMCA and the churches" (Fogel, 1970:32). Their efforts bore fruit. When faced with a strike in 1921, the packers had black ministers read messages to their congregants urging them not to join the strike. The Urban League supplied the packers with 450 strike-breakers. "The dependence of the League upon wealthy whites for financial support . . . may have influenced its actions" (Fogel, 1970:35).

One of the most outstanding cases of paternalism occurred in the automobile industry. The Ford Company, especially at its Rouge plant, "followed a definite policy of employing Negroes in all capacities" (Bailer, 1943:422). As a result, "Negroes have traditionally shown greater loyalty to Ford than to any other automobile manufacturer" (Bailer, 1944:554), and this loyalty enabled Ford to resist unionization of his plants. . . .

Another facet of paternalism was the development of "industrial representation plans" or company unions. "Migrant Negroes from the South proved peculiarly susceptible to this form of organization" (Cayton and Mitchell, 1970: 61), and they received support from some black community leadership. . . .

Needless to say, not all black leadership responded to paternalistic overtures by capital, but a significant element did. According to Foster (1920:210), "It is a lamentable fact, well known to all organizers who have worked in industries employing considerable numbers of negroes, that there is a large and influential black leadership, including ministers, politicians, editors, doctors, lawyers, social workers, etc., who as a matter of race tactics are violently opposed to their people going into the trade unions." Even black nationalist Marcus Garvey took an anti-union, pro-employer, stance. He saw the white capitalist as a friend of black workers because of the latter's relative cheapness and advocated a strategy of continued undercutting. "If the Negro takes my advice he will organize by himself and keep his scale of wage a little lower than the whites . . . By doing so he will keep the good will of the white employer" (Spero and Harris, 1966: 136).

The substitution of black labor for white was, in part, accompanied by the process, described earlier, of division of skills into simpler, assembly line tasks. Black migrants were largely unskilled while the union movement's strength lay in controlling access to training in complex skills. A way of cracking the unions' power was to break down the skills and substitute unskilled labor. Black labor was not the only source of substitution, but it was an important and growing element.

Returning to Figure 1, the efforts to develop the black labor force aroused the ire of white labor (4) which felt a threat to their efforts to improve their lot. The antagonism towards black workers was not simply race prejudice but a fear that blacks, because of their weakness in the labor market, could be used by capital as a tool to weaken or destroy their organizations or take away their jobs. As Spero and Harris (1966:128) state: "The use of Negroes for strike breaking has . . . led the white trade unionist to regard the black workers as an enemy of the labor movement." White workers reacted by trying to exclude black workers or to keep them restricted to certain jobs. (See Bonacich, 1972, for a more thorough discussion of the reasoning behind these reactions.)

Black workers came on the industrial scene unfamiliar, for the most part, with the aspirations of organized labor. They were not an easy element to organize to start out with, but whatever potential for organization was present was discouraged by white union antipathy and exclusion (5). Union policies frequently meant that black workers had no alternative but to turn to strike-breaking as the only means of entering white-dominated lines of work. Sometimes even strike-breaking did not secure long-term employment as white workers roared back, anxious to see them dismissed.

Interaction 5 was mutually reinforcing. Blacks distrusted the unions because they discriminated, and the unions discriminated because blacks didn't support them. The circle of antagonism was difficult to break out of. Even if the unions opened their doors, as was not uncommon, black workers were apt to view the action as self-serving, to protect the unions from scabbing by blacks. It would take more than non-discrimination to end the distrust, and many white unionists were not willing even to take the first step of lowering the barriers to membership.

The policies of the employer fed the division between black and white workers (6). Employer paternalism led black workers to feel they had more to gain by allying with capital than with white labor. Besides, behind it lay a veiled threat: blacks would be hired and given preference over white workers so long as they remained out of the unions. . . .

The antagonism of the labor movement to black workers weakened still further the latter's position in the labor market (7). White labor severely restricted the alternatives of black labor by maintaining control over important lines of work. The perpetuation of the black labor force in a weak position kept them as a target group for capital's efforts to undermine the union movement. Finally, to close the "system," the efforts by capital to utilize black labor to their detriment added to the militance of white workers (8). Strikes were sometimes called over this very issue, which could unite white workers in a common grievance (Tuttle, 1970a:107-8).

This interpretation of the division between black and white workers differs from one which sees it as created by the capitalist class to "divide and rule." If employers create a price differential, they must be paying one group of workers more than they have to, which would only be rational if paying more to one group enabled them to pay another substantially less. Capital would have to be "bribing" white labor to help keep black labor cheap. Such a convoluted strategy may indeed be in operation, but a number of facts argue against it.

First, as we have seen, workers do not enter the labor market with a clean slate upon which the employer arbitrarily marks his price; there are forces which differentiate the labor force before he touches it. Second, a strategy of bribery is hard to combine with the facts of displacement and strike-breaking. If capital wanted to keep white labor loyal why undermine them? Third, the evidence suggests that bribery and the exacting of loyalty were strategies directed more toward cheap labor than higher priced labor. As a means of maintaining labor costs as low as possible, this makes more sense.

What fits the evidence better is a picture of a capitalist class faced with (rather than creating) a labor market differentiated in terms of bargaining power (or price). Capital turns toward the cheaper labor pool as a more desirable work force, a choice consistent with the simple pursuit of higher profits. Higher priced labor resists being displaced, and the racist structures they erect to protect themselves are antagonistic to the interests of capital.

### EFFECTS OF THE SPLIT LABOR MARKET

The "system" described above had implications for black labor force participation. Blacks were more desirable employees than whites which helps to explain their higher employment rates in 1920 and 1930. However considerable conflict was generated in the process and some of the nation's worst race riots occurred during this period. East St. Louis erupted in 1917 (Rudwick, 1964). Twenty-six riots broke out in 1919 (Lee and Humphrey, 1968:ix), the most destructive in Chicago (Chicago Commission, 1922; Tuttle, 1970b). Detroit and Harlem blew up in 1925 and 1935, respectively. The importance of labor conflict in these riots is subject to some dispute. Undoubtedly, they were complex affairs with more than a single cause. However, the East St. Louis riot was directly precipitated by the introduction of blacks to break a strike at the Aluminum Ore Company (Marshall, 1965:22), and Tuttle (1970a; 1970b:108-56) argues convincingly that the Chicago riot of 1919 was intimately tied to labor conflict, especially in the stockyards.

Another negative effect was the precipitous decline of the trade union movement. Union membership reached a peak of 5,047,800 in 1920. It dropped sharply to 3,622,000 by 1923 and continued falling to 3,442,600 in 1929 and 2,973,000 in 1933 (Bernstein 1950:2; 1960:84). "By 1930 union membership constituted a bare 10.2 percent of the more than 30 million nonagricultural employees counted in the census, a marked drop from 19.4 percent in 1920" (Bernstein, 1960:84).

I am not suggesting that the decline was entirely a product of the black/white split labor market. This was an era of virtually unrestrained union-busting and the use by employers of every device imaginable to keep independent labor organizations out of their plants (Bernstein, 1950:7-14). However, the split labor market played a part in the decline.

Industrial unions suffered most. Craft unions which were able to maintain control over access to training, in the building trades, printing trades and railways, held their membership or increased it (Bernstein, 1960:86). The unions which survived the open-shop drives of the corporations were those which discriminated most severely against blacks (Jacobson, 1968:4; Marshall, 1965: 22-3), suggesting that discrimination by the unions was not a totally irrational short-term reaction.

## Protection as a Resolution

White labor had dealt with this problem in a variety of ways in the past. Two prominent strategies were exclusion (keeping blacks out of the territory) and caste (dividing "white work" from "black work," so that cheaper blacks were not substitutable). By the 1930s, the former strategy had failed totally, and a caste arrangement was holding only in its strongest bastions. These resolutions could too easily be attacked by capital. A new solution was called for.

The New Deal provided such a solution in the form of protection by the Federal Government. Section 7a of the National Industrial Recovery Act (1933) reads as follows:

(1) That employees shall have the right to organize and bargain collectively through representatives of their own choosing, and shall be free from the interference, restraint, or coercion of employers of labor, or their agents, in the designation of such representatives or in self-organization or in other concerted activities for the purpose of collective bargaining or mutual aid or protection; (2) that no employee and no one seeking employment shall be required as a condition of employment to join any company union or to refrain from joining, organizing, or assisting a labor organization of his choosing; and (3) that employers shall comply with the maximum hours of labor, minimum rates of pay, and other conditions of employment approved or prescribed by the President.

Thus, it protected unions from employer efforts to undermine them, ensured the right of independent unions to organize and bargain collectively and outlawed sweatshops and cheap labor. Although the NIRA was shot down by the Supreme Court in 1935, these principles were kept alive in other legislation such as the National Labor Relations (Wagner) Act of 1935 and the Fair Labor Standards Act of 1938.

The racially split labor market was not the only precipitant of these laws, but it was one of their major beneficiaries. In effect, they legislated it out of existence, making it illegal for employers to use blacks as strike-breakers or "strike insurance," denying the legitimacy, of the company union and taking away the advantage to be had in paying blacks lower wages for longer hours. Protective legislation ideally made the price of labor equal regardless of race.

This ideal was not totally realized in practice. The process of establishing protective barriers took time and was never complete. Powerful capitalists were often able to by-pass the laws or find loopholes in them. One important stand-out was Henry Ford, and a split labor market pattern continued into the early 1940s in the automobile industry (Bailer, 1944). . . . Despite loopholes and evasions, protection for the unions gradually came to be enforced in most of the major industries in the nation.

### SHORT-TERM EFFECTS (1935-1945)

In the short run, protective legislation dramatically altered the split labor market. The New Deal brought black and white labor closer together than ever before, enabling them to form a "radical coalition" (Bonacich, 1975).

The labor movement received a tremendous spurt from protective legislation. The American Federation of Labor took advantage of the new laws and began organizing campaigns. During two months in 1933, for example, they moved from a membership of 2,126,798 to 3,926,796 (Cayton and Mitchell, 1970: 123), but most of the new vigor was associated with the emergence of a new organization, the Congress of Industrial Organizations. Denouncing craft union-ism and advocating broad-based industrial unions, the CIO successfully pene-trated the automobile, steel, rubber, electrical goods and meat-packing industries by 1940. The AFL responded by moving more toward industrial unionism. Be-tween them total union membership rose from 2,805,000 in 1933 to 8,410,000 in 1941. The latter figure represents 23 percent of non-agricultural workers (Dubofsky, 1970:12-4).

Black workers were not excluded from this new development. A shift in orientation was evident in both camps. White labor became more active in recruiting black support, and the black community became more supportive of organized labor. [See Selection 12.]

The shift in white labor was especially noticeable in the CIO. This organiza-tion adopted many programs to attract blacks including "financial contributions to organizations like the NAACP and Negro churches and newspapers, the adop-tion of equalitarian racial resolutions, the use of Negroes to organize in Negro communities, the creation of the Committee to Abolish Racial Discrimination, and interlocking officials between unions and such organizations as the NAACP and the National Urban League" (Marshall, 1965:38-9). . . .

At first the black community feared protective legislation, believing it would strengthen the AFL without stopping it from discriminating against blacks. Efforts were made to introduce an amendment to the Wagner Act outlawing racial discrimination, but to no avail (Wolters, 1970a). These early suspicions gradually disappeared especially with the emergence of the CIO. . . . While exact figures are not available, one estimate gives black union membership in 1930 as around 56,000. By 1940, it had risen to 600,000 and during World War II reached 1,250,000 (Marshall, 1965:49).

The short-term emergence of a radical coalition provides support for our previous analysis. The fact that blacks could be used as cheap labor contributed to white union antagonism towards them. When the cheap labor status was made illegal and "management . . . ended its conspicuous relations with the black community and no longer demanded or commanded loyalty" (Olson, 1970: 163), unions could accept black workers much more warmly, with ramifications for how black workers responded. In addition, when the option of siding with the employer was removed, black workers had every reason to join forces enthusiastically with organized labor. Franklin's description (1936:266) of the effect of the New Deal and its immediate aftermath in New York applies to the nation as a whole: "The role of the Negro worker as a strike-breaker has about come to an end." In terms of Figure 1, the split labor market interactions had been short-circuited at arrow 2.

## LONG-TERM EFFECTS: FIGHTING THE HIGH COST OF LABOR

Protective legislation swung the balance of power in the class struggle between capital and labor towards the labor side, but it could not be expected that the capitalist class would accept such a state of affairs lying down. Protective legislation drove up the price of labor, threatening the very existence of firms throughout the economic spectrum.

Wolters (1970b:119) describes the impact of the New Deal on a small cotton textile mill in Greensboro, Georgia:

> Before the NRA, the daily wage of workers in this mill was about seventy-five cents for a ten-hour day; afterward, wages ranged from $2 to $2.40 for an eight-hour day. The machinery in this mill was obsolete, and the firm had been able to compete with more modernized mills only because labor costs were so low. With the coming of the NRA the mill at Greensboro had three choices: to maintain employment, pay code wages, and operate at a loss; to ignore the NRA stipulation; or to install more productive machinery and pay code wages to fewer workers.

Oppenheimer (1974:11) makes a similar point for the garment industry. Sweatshops in the Northeast, which became organized and had safety features introduced, then faced competition from sweatshops in the Far East. . . .

At least three options were open to the capitalist class. (Of course, not every capitalist had all three alternatives available.) First, they could relocate part of the industrial process overseas to make use of cheaper foreign labor. Second, they could relocate internally to those sectors of the economy where organized labor and/or protection had not yet penetrated. And third, they could mechanize, displacing jobs which had previously been performed by "cheap labor." These processes all had a negative impact on black employment.

### Relocation Overseas

Treating the late 1960s, Jaleé (1973:80) points out that roughly 20 percent of American investment in manufacturing industry went abroad. At that time a high proportion went to Europe which "has the use of cheaper labor than in the United States" (Jaleé 1973:82). Today the "runaway shop" is found wherever cheap labor is available. "Smith-Corona makes typewriters in Italy. U.S. Plywood makes veneers in Peru, South Korea, and Nigeria. National Cash Register has plants in Taiwan and Japan. Sears Roebuck manufactures shoes in Spain . . . Heinz makes tomato paste in Portugal and cans pineapples in Mexico" (Zimmerman et al., 1973:6), and so forth.

The runaway shop has hurt black unskilled and semi-skilled labor disproportionately, partly because white labor is more concentrated in the production of goods with high technological content, which are more likely to be produced here. For example, in moving a radio plant to Taiwan at the cost of 7,000 American jobs, Zenith reported that 38 percent of those laid off would be blacks (Zimmerman et al., 1973:8). Black workers in the United States are in competition with overseas labor at the same level of skill but overseas labor is considerably cheaper to employ.

### Internal Relocation

There remains gaps and loopholes in the present protective structure, and capital has moved internally to avail itself of these. An illustration is provided by the meat-packing industry, the major industrial employer of blacks before the New Deal. Since the late 1940s and early 1950s, the big meat-packing cities of Chicago, Kansas City, East St. Louis and Omaha, have lost meat-packing plants—particularly to the South where hourly wages are $1.86 compared to $3.08 in the Midwest. By 1947 the large midwestern packers were all unionized and could not themselves take advantage of cheaper labor elsewhere. But small, low-cost operators could open without unions to serve local and regional markets. Between 1946 and 1965, the four largest packers were forced to close a net 250 plants, and the industry became decentralized. Black workers were adversely affected by this shift. In 1950 the big mid-western cities employed 16,960 blacks in meat-packing. By 1960 the number had declined to 10,350. While black workers did not lose a disproportionate number of jobs, their overrepresentation in the industry meant a greater impact on group unemployment (Fogel, 1970:58-65). In this particular case internal relocation took advantage of another segment of black workers: non-union, southern women (Fogel, 1970:65-6). Other minorities, such as Mexican illegal aliens and poor immigrants from other countries, have played a part in this type of displacemnt (e.g., Lan, 1971, on the use of Chinese "sweatshop" labor in the San Francisco garment industry). Regardless of where new sources of cheap labor came from, the losers have been black industrial workers who had made important gains under the New Deal.

Given that cheap labor jobs are still scattered through the economy, why do the black urban unemployed not flock to them? The answer, I believe, lies in two inter-related factors. First, black industrial workers, unlike new immigrants, had come, during the late 1930s and early 1940s, to develop a working class consciousness. They rejected the sweatshop as had white workers before them.

Employers have long justified the use of cheap minority labor on the grounds that "whites will not do the work." The same can be said of blacks today. Both groups are unwilling to work under rough conditions for low wages. If the job were "decent," they would willingly do it. The availability of a "cheap labor" alternative enables the employer to avoid improving the job and raising wages (Abrams and Abrams, 1975:24–6).

The second factor is "welfare." This institution may, in part, be seen as a mechanism which keeps people from having no alternative but the sweatshop. It is part of the apparatus which protects organized labor from being undercut. Protective legislation would be totally ineffective if large segments of the population were close to starvation. Employers would by-pass the laws and the starving people would gladly avail themselves of the jobs, however dreadful and low-paying. Of course, this phenomenon does occur in the United States, e.g., among many Mexican illegal immigrants (Samora, 1971). But a significant difference between black and immigrant poor lies in legal status. Blacks are unambiguously eligible for various forms of welfare and unemployment compensation which many new immigrants, particularly illegals, are not. Blacks have an "alternative" to the sweatshop.

Internal relocation helps to perpetuate a "dual labor market," i.e., a division of the economy into central and peripheral industries, the former offering higher wage, union jobs, and the latter relying on cheap, nonunion labor. If they try to escape the welfare trap, black workers tend to get locked into the peripheral economy with a ceiling on opportunities for advancement. (There is an extensive and growing literature on this topic partially reviewed by Gordon, 1972:43–52.)

The persistence of peripheral or marginal firms operating on cheap labor means that a split labor market is not dead in this country. Protective legislation has changed its shape somewhat, increasing the segregation, by industry and plant, of higher priced from cheap labor. And the ethnic composition of cheap labor has shifted away from blacks to some extent (Oppenheimer, 1974:16) to other nonwhite immigrants. But the New Deal did not, in the long run, successfully eradicate the problem.

## Automation

The move to automate does not arise simply as a response to technological innovation. Rather it is, at least in part, a response to rising labor costs. In the steel industry for instance, rising wages have led to an increase in capital relative to labor. "The United Steelworkers are resigned to continued long-term shrinkage of its core membership in basic steel" (Averitt, 1968:147). . . .

A number of authors trace a link between automation and black unemployment (e.g., Ferman et al., 1968:276–7; Willhelm, 1971:188–224). Northrup (1965:87) sums up the situation well:

An important factor in the Negro unemployment problem was industry's substitution of machinery for unskilled labor. Ever higher minimum wages, the rapid rise under union pressure of unskilled labor rates, and the competition from West European and Japanese industry (with the much lower labor rates paid in these countries) all spurred this labor-replacement program. Negroes laid off as a result of these developments and young Negroes who found that industry was no longer hiring the unskilled became significant proportions of the hardcore, long-term unemployed.

To the three processes must be added certain "rigidities" in the system which make blacks suffer disproportionately from displacement. For example, poor ghetto schools make it more difficult for blacks to move out of the unskilled ranks. Union seniority rules, which may be "universalistic" and protect against the employer's natural desire to lay off his oldest, most expensive workers, may in practice have racist consequences because of the trend towards later entrance to industrial work among blacks. Similarly, discrimination in apprenticeship programs hurts black acquisition of skills while unions perceive efforts to change their rules as "union busting" (Strauss and Ingerman, 1968). And residential restrictions make it difficult for black workers to follow decentralizing industries as they flee highly taxed central cities.

## CONCLUSION

Let us return to the two approaches to the question of high black unemployment in advanced capitalism presented at the beginning of the paper. The first suggested that significant elements in the white community, especially the corporate capitalist class, benefited from black unemployment. While there may be indirect sources of gain, the conclusion to be drawn from this paper would be that large capitalists are unable to take advantage of ghetto labor and abandon it to marginal enterprises. The second argument, that technological advance has left blacks useless to the economy, gained some support, but I hope to have shown that it was not the product of impersonal economic forces. Rather, it was one effect of a complex history of class struggle.

This history is summarized in Figure 2. The "displacement" phase was one in which blacks were desirable employees relative to whites but threatened the gains of the latter. Protective legislation equalized the two groups in terms of labor price but also drove up the price of labor, leading capital to seek cheaper alternatives. As a result, black labor has been by-passed for machines and other cheap labor groups, here and abroad, creating a class of hard-core unemployed in the ghettos. This reality took a while to emerge after the New Deal and only became full-blown in the mid-1950s when black unemployment reached its current two-to-one ratio. The timing helps to explain the rising despair of the 1960s.

Our conclusion is not cause for optimism over solving the problems of split labor markets. Immediately after the New Deal, it appeared they could be eradicated by government intervention, but the passing years have shown this to be a false hope. As long as there is "cheap labor" anywhere in the world, there may not be a solution within capitalism.

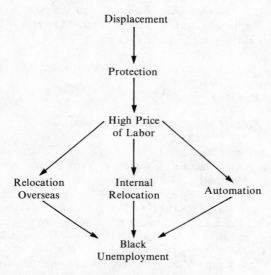

**FIGURE 2.   The Historical Development of Black Unemployment**

# References

Abrams, Elliott and Franklin S. Abrams
  1975   "Immigration policy—who gets in." Public Interest 38: 3–29.
Averitt, Robert T.
  1968   The Dual Economy: The Dynamics of American Industry Structure. New York: Norton.
Bailer, Lloyd H.
  1943   "The Negro automobile worker." Journal of Political Economy 51: 415–28.
  1944   "The automobile unions and Negro labor." Political Science Quarterly 59: 548–77.
Baron, Harold M.
  1972   "The demand for black labor: historical notes on the political economy of racism." Radical America 5: 1–46.
Bernstein, Irving
  1950   The New Deal Collective Bargaining Policy. Berkeley: University of California Press.
  1960   The Lean Years: A History of the American Worker 1920–1933. Cambridge, Ma.: Riverside Press.
Bonacich, Edna
  1972   "A theory of ethnic antagonism: the split labor market." American Sociological Review 37: 547–59.

1976    "Abolition, the extension of slavery, and the position of free blacks: a study of split labor markets in the United States, 1830–1863." American Journal of Sociology 81: 601–628.

Brody, David
1960    Steelworkers in America: The Nonunion Era. Cambridge: Harvard University Press.

Cayton, Horace R. and George S. Mitchell
[1939]
1970    Black Workers and the New Unions. Westport, Ct.: Negro Universities Press.

Chicago Commission of Race Relations
1922    The Negro in Chicago: A Study of Race Relations and a Race Riot. Chicago: University of Chicago Press.

Dubofsky, Melvyn
1970    American Labor since the New Deal. Chicago: Quadrangle.

Ferman, Louis A., Joyce L. Kornbluh and J. A. Miller (eds.)
1968    Negroes and Jobs. Ann Arbor: University of Michigan Press.

Fogel, Walter A.
1970    The Negro in the Meat Industry. Philadelphia: University of Pennsylvania Press.

Foster, William Z.
1920    The Great Steel Strike and Its Lessons. New York: Huebsch.

Franklin, Charles L.
1936    The Negro Labor Unionist of New York: Problems and Conditions among Negroes in the Labor Unions in Manhattan with Special Reference to the N.R.A. and Post-N.R.A. Situations. New York: Columbia University Press.

Gordon, David M.
1972    Theories of Poverty and Underemployment. Lexington, Ma.: Heath.

Harris, Donald J.
1972    "The black ghetto as colony: a theoretical critique and alternative formulation." Review of Black Political Economy 2: 3–33.

Jacobson, Julius (ed.)
1968    The Negro and the American Labor Movement. Garden City. N.Y.: Doubleday Anchor.

Jaleé, Pierre
1973    Imperialism in the Seventies. New York: Third Press.

Killingsworth, Charles C.
1968    Jobs and Income for Negroes. Ann Arbor: University of Michigan Press.

Lan, Dean
1971    "The Chinatown sweatshops." Amerasia Journal 1: 40–57.

Lee, Alfred McClung and Norman D. Humphrey
1968    Race Riot (Detroit, 1943). New York: Octagon.

Marshall, Ray
1965    The Negro and Organized Labor. New York: Wiley.

Northrup, Herbert R.
1965    "Equal opportunity and equal pay." Pp. 85–107 in H. R. Northrup and

Richard L. Rowan (eds.), The Negro and Equal Opportunity. Ann Arbor: Bureau of Industrial Relations.

Olson, James S.
1970    "Race, class, and progress: black leadership and industrial unionism, 1936–1945." Pp. 153–64 in Milton Cantor (ed.), Black Labor in America. Westport, Ct.: Negro Universities Press.

Oppenheimer, Martin
1974    "The sub-proletariat: dark skins and dirty work." Insurgent Sociologist 4: 7–20.

Reich, Michael
1972    "Economic theories of racism." Pp. 67–79 in Martin Carnoy (ed.), Schooling in a Corporate Society. New York: David McKay.

Reid, Ira De A.
[1930]
1969    Negro Membership in American Labor Unions. New York: Negro Universities Press.

Ross, Arthur M.
1967    "The Negro in the American economy." Pp. 3–48 in Arthur M. Ross and Herbert Hill (eds.), Employment, Race, and Poverty. New York: Harcourt, Brace and World.

Rowan, Richard L.
1968    The Negro in the Steel Industry. Philadelphia: University of Pennsylvania Press.

Rubin, Lester
1970    The Negro in the Shipbuilding Industry. Philadelphia: University of Pennsylvania Press.

Rudwick, Elliott M.
1964    Race Riot at East St. Louis, July 2, 1917. Carbondale, Il.: Southern Illinois University Press.

Samora, Julian
1971    Los Mojados: The Wetback Story. Notre Dame: University of Notre Dame Press.

Saxton, Alexander
1971    The Indispensible Enemy: Labor and the Anti-Chinese Movement in California. Berkeley: University of California Press.

Spear, Allan H.
1967    Black Chicago: The Making of a Negro Ghetto, 1890–1920. Chicago: University of Chicago Press.

Spero, Sterling D. and Abram L. Harris
[1931]
1966    The Black Worker: The Negro and the Labor Movement. Port Washington: Kennikat.

Strauss, George and Sidney Ingerman
1968    "Public policy and discrimination in apprenticeship." Pp. 198–322 in Louis Ferman, Joyce Kornbluh and J. A. Miller (eds.), Negroes and Jobs. Ann Arbor: University of Michigan Press.

Tabb, William K.
   1970    The Political Economy of the Black Ghetto. New York: Norton.
Tuttle, William M., Jr.
   1970a   "Labor conflict and racial violence: the black worker in Chicago, 1897-1904." Pp. 53-85 in Milton Cantor (ed.), Black Labor in America. Westport, Ct.: Negro Universities Press.
   1970b   Race Riot: Chicago in the Red Summer of 1919. New York: Atheneum.
U.S. Department of Labor
   1974    Manpower Report of the President. Washington, D.C.: U.S. Government Printing Office.
van den Berghe, Pierre L.
   1967    South Africa: A Study in Conflict. Berkeley: University of California Press.
Wesley, Charles H.
   1927    Negro Labor in the United States, 1850-1925. New York: Vanguard.
Willhelm, Sidney M.
   1971    Who Needs the Negro? Garden City: Doubleday Anchor.
Wolters, Raymond
   1970a   "Closed shop and white shop: the Negro response to collective bargaining, 1933-1935." Pp. 137-52 in Milton Cantor (ed.), Black Labor in America. Westport, Ct.: Negro Universities Press.
   1970b   Negroes and the Great Depression: The Problem of Economic Recovery. Westport, Ct.: Greenwood.
Worthman, Paul
   1970    "Black workers and labor unions in Birmingham, Alabama, 1897-1904." Pp. 53-85 in Milton Cantor (ed.), Black Labor in America. Westport, Ct.: Negro Universities Press.
Zimmerman, Mitch and The United Front Press Staff
   1973    International Runaway Shop. San Francisco: United Front Press.

# 41

# Black Economic Gains in the Sixties: A Methodological Critique and Reassessment

*WAYNE J. VILLEMEZ* and *ALAN R. ROWE*

Since the recent publication of the 1970 census data on income distribution, a number of researchers have attempted to assess the magnitude of black economic gains in the previous decade. Most have concluded that these gains have been substantial. In the most well-publicized of these attempts, Wattenberg and Scammon (1973) called the gains since 1960 a "massive achievement." Others (e.g., Farley and Hermalin, 1972; Freeman, 1973) have been somewhat less euphoric, but have nonetheless pointed to large and meaningful black gains. All have failed to focus on distributional changes and instead have based their analyses in large degree upon comparisons of the ratios of black to white median income over time, which shows a steady increase; and upon comparisons within each group of median income at $T_1$ to median income at $T_2$, which invariably shows a greater percentage gain for blacks.

Yet there are other data which make these findings suspect. For example, nonwhites made up 26.9 percent of those below the poverty level in 1959, and

Reprinted, abridged, from *Social Forces 54* (September 1975): 181–193. Copyright © The University of North Carolina Press.

31.1 percent in 1970 (Bureau of the Census, 1973a). . . . And for a more subtle indicator, the ratio of black to white infant mortality rates remained virtually constant from 1959-70, with the black 1970 rate (30.2/1000) still higher than the white 1950 rate (26.8/1000) (Bureau of the Census, 1973a). These, and a great many other statistics from related areas, seem at variance with the notion of substantial black economic gains. . . . Those insisting on substantial gains point to the undeniably larger ratio of black to white median income, while those denying "massive success" point to similar black-white absolute gains in median family income and discount ratio gains. In a recent article on the subject, *Newsweek* (July 16, 1973) likens this debate to "the ancient argument over whether a glass is half full or half empty." The real problem, of course, is a lack of definitive knowledge, a problem not resolvable by simplistic opposition of optimists vs. pessimists.

These findings of significant gains are also at variance with the earlier predictions of many scholars. In 1965, for example, Broom and Glenn (1967:115) noted: "The Negro-white occupational gap obviously is still very wide and it is closing so slowly that it will not disappear within the next century unless the rate of Negro gains sharply accelerates." Later, they added: ". . . the relative economic status of Negroes may drop far below its present level within the next few years. Only unforeseen developments could bring about a rapid increase in the near future" (122). . . . In this paper we contend that no "unforeseen developments" have occurred and that the recently reported "substantial black gains" are an artifact of both the researchers' method and their focus on gaps rather than distributions.

Because of the skewness of income distributions, meaningful direct comparisons usually involve the median rather than the mean. . . . Unfortunately, such a positional measure creates problems. For one, almost all distributional information, save the midpoints, must be discarded, resulting in very crude comparisons. Also, the comparison of the relative positions of the midpoints of two distributions when both midpoints are rising can easily lead to misinterpretations. For example, in such a situation the black-to-white ratio could increase at the same time the absolute gap was increasing, making interpretation of the larger ratio ambiguous. Further, to note that the midpoint of a given distribution has increased by X percent—a common procedure—is to say nothing very meaningful, for in the same time period the entire distribution could theoretically have collapsed about the higher midpoint. This type of comparison is also problematic for a simpler reason. For example, Farley and Hermalin (1972:354) note: "Median family income among whites rose about 25 percent while that of blacks went up 40 percent, and as an outcome, the ratio of nonwhite to white income rose." The fact that these two percentages are for different bases is ignored. When the medians in question are examined, it is seen that in absolute dollars the white gain of 25 percent is slightly larger than the black gain of 40 percent (specifically, $2,688 vs. $2,530). In the light of previous economic discrimination it may seem reasonable that such a small black loss be termed a gain, but no amount of juggling of percentages and ratios can change an absolute loss into anything but, perhaps, a moral gain. As Templeton (1973:18) aptly noted: ". . . people don't buy meat with percentages or pay rent with ratios." Even if we accept the comparison of medians as valid, all that can be concluded is that blacks at last have ceased to lose—their gain in the previous decade almost matched that of whites. But to say that blacks managed to hold their position vis-à-vis whites is quite different from saying that they gained on whites. Naturally, given almost equal absolute increments, the black-to-white ratio would increase a constant added to numerator and denominator of any fraction will increase the value of that fraction, but will not affect the difference between numerator and denominator. This is more clearly seen if we extend an actual case. The ratio of black-to-white family income in 1969 was 0.63 (Farley and Hermalin, 1972:355). If we gave every family in the country—black and white— an additional $10,000, this ratio would increase to 0.82. . . . We could note further that it would take a gain in median of $20,000 to reach 0.88, a gain of $30,000 to reach 0.93, a gain of $40,000 to reach 0.95—and it gets worse. The curve of ratio gain naturally flattens considerably at the upper reaches: the early "dramatic" gains were caused by low starting points, nothing more. The idea of thirty- and forty-thousand-dollar gains in median income is absurd, of course. But these figures are merely the logical extension of what has been cited as evidence of "black success." If the upper range of a statistic is meaningless, we should view its middle range with extreme suspicion. The argument here, however, is not that looking at absolute gains in median income is more meaningful than looking at percentage gains (or that the absolute difference between white and black medians is any more meaningful than the ratio of the former to the latter). For one thing, the absolute difference is affected too much, in the long run, by inflation. Further, we would hardly wish to argue that a difference between $19,000 and $20,000 is of the same importance as a difference between $5,000 and $6,000. To do so would be to ignore the principle of the diminishing marginal utility of income. Our intention is simply to point out the limitations of the ratio of black to white median income as a measure of inequality.

Another type of evidence of black gains that has been presented is based on two distributional measures of income inequality, Delta (the index of dissimilarity) and the Gini index. Farley and Hermalin (1972), for example, use both of these measures to demonstrate a decrease in inequality between 1959 and 1969. Delta is based on the sum of differences between black and white percentages in various income categories. The Gini index is based on the ratio of the area between a line of equal income distribution and a Lorenz curve representing actual distribution to the total area under the line of equality. Delta and the Gini index share a common flaw; both express only gross changes and give no indication of where these changes occurred. For example, a black attainment of parity in the low-income categories would have roughly the same effect on both indices as the attainment of parity in the high-income categories. Yet obviously, in terms of the attainment of equality, these two cases are not the same. And there are further problems with the Gini index. Bowman (1951) demonstrated clearly that the index is not an adequate measure of changes in inequality when applied to the entire income range; it is more appropriate for assessing changes in the upper range of income alone. . . .

Clearly, despite the seeming acceptance by many of the "fact" of substantial black gains in the 1960s, neither the magnitude nor even the existence of such gains has been unequivocally demonstrated. This paper represents an attempt to cut through the methodological underbrush and reveal whether there have been black gains, and if so to what degree and in which sectors of the population. To accomplish this, a different method of assessing changes in income inequality was devised.

## Methods

. . . The more complete information contained in the mean can be used, and the inherent bias avoided, if the reported mean income of the population and of various subgroups is employed only indirectly. It is possible to reconstitute the total aggregate earned income of the population and of any subpopulation by simply multiplying the appropriate mean by the size of the population. Proportional shares of the total aggregate held by various subgroups can then be assessed, and changes in the size of these shares can be compared over time. This measure, unlike median ratios, would not be confounded by general rises in income (since the comparison would be strictly of shares of whatever the total income is), would employ all available information, and would allow direct assessment of black gains relative to white gains. Further, the mean is less susceptible to sampling error and thus more reliable than the median (Blalock, 1972). Crudely put, this method involves reconstructing the income "pie" and examining the proportional size of the black slice. If blacks have gained on whites, the relative size of their slice should have increased. This type of comparison also allows the reconstruction of the "slices" of various black and white occupational and educational groupings, and thus a determination of exactly where gains and losses have occurred. Further, if we regard a group's proportion of the total earned income as their actual share, and the proportion of the total earning population that that group represents as their "expected" share, then the actual minus expected proportion for each group will provide a clear indicator of their relative economic standing. A comparison of economic standing, thus defined, will then provide an unequivocal picture of income distributional changes over time. However, interpretation of a simple measure of actual minus expected proportional shares could be confounded by, among other things, the interaction between shifting labor demand and a changing economy (i.e., by mutual changes in actual and expected). This difficulty can be alleviated by standardizing for the proportional size of the category population over which this actual minus expected figure must be distributed. The resulting measure would be (Ai-Ei)/Ei, where A=actual, E=expected. But, while adequate, this measure results in both positive and negative numbers (since zero represents absolute proportional equality), and direct comparisons among categories are thus somewhat cumbersome. This inelegance can be removed and the measure made more intuitively meaningful by simply adding one to the figure above, thus making 1.0 represent absolute proportional equality. The measure becomes, then, 1 + (Ai-Ei)/Ei, hereafter referred to as the Distributional Fairness Index, or DFI. If we divided total earned income at time one by the total earning population at that time, the resulting figure, X, would represent the number of dollars that would be earned by each individual if there were absolute income equality—a "fair share." But fair share $X_1$ would not equal fair share $X_2$, because of changes in total income earned, changes in the size of the earning population, and changes in the value of the dollar. However, since the interest is only in changes in i-equality, it is entirely appropriate to set $X_1 = X_2 = 1$, and deal only in "shares" *per se*. The computation $(A_i - E_i)/E_i$ indicates the proportion over (or under) a fair share received by category $i$. The DFI, 1 + (Ai-Ei)/Ei, is thus directly interpretable as the share received by members of category $i$.[1] For example, in the North and West in 1959, white professionals received 0.165 of the total income earned and represented 0.115 of the earning population, in 1969 they received 0.206 of the total income and represented 0.152 of the population. The DFI for this group in 1959 and 1969 (computed with six significant figures), respectively, is 1.435 and 1.353. We can thus note that white professionals received 1.435 shares per man in 1959, and only 1.353 shares per man in 1969—a net loss. In terms of actual dollars, of course, they gained (since the total income earned in 1969, and thus each share, was larger), but this is irrelevant to the assessment of changes in inequality. We can make a valid comparison, then, with black professionals in terms of gain or loss in shares per man during the same decade. This is an extremely liberal measure of gains in that the expected figure

---

[1] It should be noted that the formula, $1 + (A_i - E_i)/E_i$, is conceptual in nature, representing the "fair share" concept. Since, obviously, $1 + (x - y)/y = \frac{x}{y}$, a more efficient computing formula for the DFI would be simply: $\frac{A_i}{E_i}$. For another alternative, simple algebra will show that $1 + (A_i - E_i)/E_i$ is also equal to the ratio of the mean income of the group to the total population mean. For, since any $A_g = \frac{N_g X_g}{N_p X_p}$ and $E_g = \frac{N_g}{N_p}$, by definition, it follows that $\frac{X_g}{X_p} = \frac{N_g X_g \times N_p}{N_p X_p \times N_g}$. The conceptual formula is important, however, for it allows the DFI to be interpreted in terms of "group share of aggregate income." Obviously the DFI for any race-occupation group could change because of a change in the mean income of that group, because of changes in overall mean income, or because of changes in both. In this context it doesn't matter at all what has occasioned the change in shares—the change itself is the only relevant datum in assessing trends in inequality. The intracategory dynamics of those trends might also be of interest, but could hardly be revealed by the same index.

represents only the earning population.[2] Thus, unchanging or even increasing black unemployment would not have any direct effect on the DFI since it would influence both the actual and expected figures. Changes in total income due to increased GNP, inflation, etc., would also not be problematic since, in effect, the "size of the pie" is being controlled for by the nature of the DFI. Finally, only wage, salary and net self-employment income is considered, which adds to the liberality of the measure. Black gains in this sector, if any, will be greater than their gains in other forms of personal income.

## ANALYSIS AND FINDINGS

In order to make more direct comparisons, only males with income, 25–64, in 1959 and 1969 will be considered. The same figures will be calculated for males with income, 25–34, since some have contended that black gains were primarily among the young. Our analysis is of large units (regions); so reliability is not a problem. . . .

Table 1 presents the DFI for black and white census occupational and educational groups in the North and West and South, 1959 and 1969. It will be noticed that in most occupational groupings earnings represent less than one share per man. This is to be expected. The "fair share" upon which the DFI is based is simply an heuristic device. We expect that some occupational groupings will be more highly rewarded than others: the appropriate comparison is between similar occupations differentiated only by race (which allows us to ignore population distributional inequalities in the occupational structure as a whole).

From Table 1 it is immediately apparent that black gains in the decade have not been substantial. The largest white loss was only two-tenths of a share per man in the South and less than that per man in the North and West. Losses of this magnitude could have resulted in large black gains, but did not. For example, if one-tenth of a share was taken from every white professional, technical and kindred worker in 1969 and redistributed to black PTK workers, the blacks would gain over 3.60 shares per man. Owing to the population differential a very small per-man loss for whites, if given directly to blacks, can result in a very large per-man gain. Given this, the fact that the largest black gain is small

---

[2] Family income is eschewed and "persons of income" used instead for a number of reasons. Primary among these is the desire to assess changes in income equality without incorporating unemployment directly into the measures. It is well known that a greater percentage of black than white adult males have no income (see, among others, Broom and Glenn, 1965) and the use of family income would build in the effect of this difference. Another consideration is the need for a one-to-one comparison—family income can be misleading as a strict determiner of equality since comparisons necessarily are among differing numbers of wage-earners per family and different numbers who must share the wage. Terrell (1971) notes that in 1968 the mean family size for nonfarm whites was 3.58 members, as compared to 4.31 for nonfarm black families. Terrell details a number of basic differences between black and white families and concludes: "Black income supports more people, is not augmented to the same degree by nonrecorded returns to housing, is spent on consumer goods which cost more, and is earned by the efforts of more people . . ." (390).

**TABLE 1. Distributional Fairness Index (shares per man) for Occupation and Education by Region for Whites and Blacks in 1959 and 1969**

| | NORTH AND WEST | | | | SOUTH | | | |
|---|---|---|---|---|---|---|---|---|
| | Whites | | Blacks* | | Whites | | Blacks* | |
| | 1959 | 1969 | 1959 | 1969 | 1959 | 1969 | 1959 | 1969 |
| *Occupation* | | | | | | | | |
| Prof., tech., & kindred | 1.453 | 1.353 | 1.000 | 1.002 | 1.736 | 1.546 | 0.833 | 0.997 |
| Managers, off., proprietors, & kindred | 1.581 | 1.434 | 1.000 | 0.931 | 1.700 | 1.500 | 0.667 | 0.904 |
| Sales | 1.169 | 1.186 | 1.000 | 0.746 | 1.246 | 1.239 | 1.000 | 0.666 |
| Clerical | 0.881 | 0.875 | 0.600 | 0.706 | 1.057 | 0.981 | 0.667 | 0.746 |
| Crafts | 0.950 | 0.932 | 0.750 | 0.738 | 1.000 | 0.932 | 0.556 | 0.622 |
| Operatives | 0.816 | 0.801 | 0.647 | 0.685 | 0.836 | 0.800 | 0.524 | 0.581 |
| Laborers | 0.667 | 0.690 | 0.545 | 0.619 | 0.600 | 0.625 | 0.465 | 0.486 |
| Service | 0.700 | 0.721 | 0.500 | 0.584 | 0.758 | 0.734 | 0.500 | 0.505 |
| Farmers & farm man. | 0.609 | 0.731 | † | 0.372 | 0.632 | 0.700 | 0.182 | 0.286 |
| Farm laborers | 0.385 | 0.470 | † | 0.326 | 0.333 | 0.451 | 0.200 | 0.270 |
| *Education* | | | | | | | | |
| 4+ yrs. college | 1.672 | 1.534 | 1.004 | 1.120 | 1.992 | 1.740 | 0.997 | 1.057 |
| 1–3 yrs. college | 1.230 | 1.118 | 0.767 | 0.794 | 1.482 | 1.245 | 0.702 | 0.750 |
| 12 yrs. | 1.022 | 0.962 | 0.721 | 0.721 | 1.201 | 1.049 | 0.624 | 0.667 |
| 0–11 yrs. | 0.832 | 0.806 | 0.613 | 0.636 | 0.833 | 0.808 | 0.493 | 0.509 |

*Although the figures for 1959 are based on nonwhite, 94 percent of the nonwhite populations identified themselves as blacks (Bureau of the Census, 1961:table 44).

†Share less than .0005.

Sources: Bureau of the Census (1963: tables 2 & 3; 1973b: tables 3 & 4).

indicates that the white losses in the higher occupational categories were, for the most part, redistributed among whites. . . . In the North and West, the general pattern revealed by Table 1 is small white losses in the higher occupations matched by very small black gains in the lower occupations. In the South, there are small white losses in every nonfarm category save laborers, and black gains in every category except sales. This supports the common contention that black gains in the South have exceeded black gains in the North and West. Yet it should be noted that except in one category (clerical) the 1969 black-white gap in the South still exceeded the 1959 gap in the North and West. The black gains in the South, in other words, are largely a function of how much there was to be gained. . . .

A somewhat different pattern emerges for the North and West when we examine gains and losses by educational categories. Between 1959 and 1969 whites lost slightly in every category and blacks gained slightly in all but one (12 years). The pattern in the South is similar, except that there blacks gained in all categories.

The exact extent of black gains is detailed in three different ways in Table 2: "gain," which details actual improvement in black shares per man: "gain on whites," which incorporates white losses; and "1969 gap as a percentage of 1959 gap," which demonstrates the distance yet to be travelled toward equality. As can be seen in column 1, all gains in the North and West are negligible, and there were losses in the managerial, sales and crafts categories. The gains in the South were larger (column 4) but still not substantial and there was a loss among sales workers. Even if we consider gain on whites rather than just gains (column 2), the North and West exhibit little change. In the South there was some substantial gain (column 5). For example, the managerial workers gained almost half a share per man on whites. Columns 3 and 6 of Table 2 show the 1969 "share gap" as a percentage of the 1959 share-gap in each category. This demonstrates progress made in terms of the initial extent of inequality. The most striking figures here are the three-digit percentages for sales workers in the North and West and sales and laborers in the South. These figures further corroborate the point mentioned above that in the North and West, what progress there was is most noticeable at the bottom, while in the South the top gained slightly more.

In terms of educational categories, there was a gain per man on whites of over a quarter-share per man in the 4+ years of college category in both the North and West and South, and in the 1-3 years of college category in the South. Other gains were smaller, but again larger in the South. The figures in columns 3 and 6 indicate that highly educated blacks in the North and West closed the share-gap to a slightly greater extent than those in the South, while the high school and some college groups fared better in the South. In general, these findings are in accord with the Broom and Glenn (1967) prediction that discrimination-caused differences in status at the higher educational levels would soon disappear, but the disappearance is proving to be a slow one. In addition, one must recall that in the most educated black sector (those 25-34 years old),

TABLE 2. Black Gain and Black Gain on Whites in Shares per Man 1959–1969 (including 1969 gap as percent of 1959) for Occupation and Education by Region

| | North and West | | | South | | |
|---|---|---|---|---|---|---|
| | BLACK GAIN | BLACK GAIN ON WHITES | 1969 GAP AS % OF 1959 | BLACK GAIN | BLACK GAIN ON WHITES | 1969 GAP AS % OF 1959 |
| *Occupation* | | | | | | |
| Prof., tech., & kindred | 0.002 | 0.084 | 80.7 | 0.164 | 0.354 | 60.8 |
| Managers, off., proprietors, & kindred | -0.069 | 0.078 | 86.6 | 0.237 | 0.437 | 57.7 |
| Sales | -0.254 | -0.271 | 260.4 | -0.334 | -0.327 | 232.9 |
| Clerical | 0.106 | 0.112 | 60.1 | 0.079 | 0.155 | 60.3 |
| Crafts | -0.012 | 0.006 | 97.0 | 0.066 | 0.134 | 69.8 |
| Operatives | 0.038 | 0.053 | 68.6 | 0.057 | 0.093 | 70.2 |
| Laborers | 0.074 | 0.051 | 58.2 | 0.021 | -0.004 | 103.0 |
| Service | 0.084 | 0.063 | 68.5 | 0.005 | 0.029 | 88.8 |
| Farmers & farm man. | * | * | * | 0.104 | 0.036 | 92.0 |
| Farm laborers | * | * | * | 0.070 | -0.048 | 136.1 |
| *Education* | | | | | | |
| 4+ yrs. college | 0.116 | 0.254 | 62.0 | 0.060 | 0.312 | 68.6 |
| 1–3 yrs. college | 0.027 | 0.139 | 70.0 | 0.048 | 0.285 | 63.5 |
| 12 yrs. | 0.000 | 0.060 | 80.1 | 0.043 | 0.195 | 66.2 |
| 0–11 yrs. | 0.023 | 0.049 | 77.6 | 0.016 | 0.041 | 87.9 |

*Data not available.
Source: Derived from Table 1.

371

only 7.9 percent of the black population in 1972 had completed four or more years of college (Bureau of the Census, 1973a). Equality for this cream at the top cannot significantly affect the economic status of the black population as a whole.[3]

To determine if significant gains among younger blacks were being masked by a concentration on the total population, DFIs were computed separately for 25-34 year-old males. A comparison of the last column in Table 3 with columns 3 and 6 in Table 2 shows that this age group—especially the more educated among them—did close the gap to a somewhat greater extent than did older groups. The difference, however, is not large enough to evoke enthusiasm about future trends, despite the fact that these data concern only changes in results, not opportunities.

Finally, it is theoretically possible that in the preceding decade many black workers could have shifted from occupations in which their incomes were far below those of whites to occupations in which their incomes were only slightly below, and done this in such a way as to effect a gap-narrowing in the aggregate with little change within each occupation. As a check on this, DFIs for the total aggregate population were computed. The figures in Table 4 show that aggregate gains for both the total population and the younger population are not more impressive than category gains. Both point to the same conclusion: there have been no substantial gains.

TABLE 3. Distributional Fairness Index (shares per man) 1959-1969 and 1969 Gap as Percent of 1959 for Young Males (25-34) by Education Categories by Region

|  | White | | Black | | 1969 GAP AS % OF |
|---|---|---|---|---|---|
|  | 1959 | 1969 | 1959 | 1969 | 1959 |
| *North and West* |  |  |  |  |  |
| 4+ yrs. college | 1.311 | 1.248 | 0.949 | 1.082 | 45.9 |
| 1–3 yrs. college | 1.103 | 1.048 | 0.809 | 0.854 | 66.0 |
| 12 yrs. | 1.019 | 0.984 | 0.763 | 0.789 | 72.2 |
| 0–11 yrs. | 0.874 | 0.849 | 0.656 | 0.682 | 76.6 |
| *South* |  |  |  |  |  |
| 4+ yrs. college | 1.573 | 1.424 | 0.881 | 1.004 | 60.7 |
| 1–3 yrs. college | 1.278 | 1.136 | 0.738 | 0.804 | 61.5 |
| 12 yrs. | 1.147 | 1.040 | 0.636 | 0.719 | 62.8 |
| 0–11 yrs. | 0.868 | 0.832 | 0.493 | 0.559 | 72.8 |

Sources: Bureau of the Census (1963: tables 2 & 3; 1973b; tables 3 & 4).

[3] This creaming off the top of a small proportion of blacks has undoubtedly exacerbated whatever intraracial income inequities existed a decade ago. (For an excellent discussion of this point see Thurow, 1969.)

**TABLE 4.** Distributional Fairness Index for All Males with Earnings 25-64, and All Males with Earnings 25-34, 1959 and 1969, by Region, Including Black Gain, Black Gain on Whites, and 1969 Gap as Percent of 1959

| | 1959 | | 1969 | | BLACK GAIN | BLACK GAIN ON WHITES | 1969 GAP AS % OF 1959 |
|---|---|---|---|---|---|---|---|
| | WHITE | BLACK | WHITE | BLACK | | | |
| *North and West* | | | | | | | |
| All Males | 1.023 | 0.663 | 1.022 | 0.702 | 0.039 | 0.040 | 88.8 |
| Young Males | 1.022 | 0.720 | 1.019 | 0.755 | 0.055 | 0.058 | 80.1 |
| *South* | | | | | | | |
| All Males | 1.102 | 0.495 | 1.074 | 0.575 | 0.080 | 0.108 | 82.2 |
| Young Males | 1.095 | 0.540 | 1.061 | 0.652 | 0.112 | 0.146 | 73.7 |

Sources: Bureau of the Census (1963: tables 2 & 3; 1973b: tables 3 & 4).

## Conclusions and Implications

These findings indicate that the magnitude of black economic gains in the decade of the sixties has been slight. To be sure, gains have been made in some areas, but they are neither dramatic nor compelling. That the walls of economic discrimination have so successfully weathered the trumpeting of "affirmative action" lends verification to the predictions of many pessimistic scholars who saw the attainment of black economic equality as a far-distant goal. In 196[7] (194), Broom and Glenn wrote: "These ends will be achieved at great cost, a far greater cost than has yet been offered, and they lie at a greater distance than most have been willing to admit." Our more recent findings do not contradict this statement.

The pattern of gains and losses is also significant. There have been white losses, but they have not been matched by black gains: these losses, by and large, have been redistributed among other whites. This fact creates a potential two-pronged problem. On the one hand, despite ever-rising expectations, most blacks are gaining very little on whites. On the other, higher whites are losing, and their losses—ostensibly to blacks—are matched by increasing black dissatisfaction. . . . In short, there has been a redistribution of income, and the *zeitgeist* of the sixties would convince all but the blacks that if others lost, they must have gained substantially. And popularizations as well as scholarly works employing comparisons of median ratios add to this conviction. Reissman (1973:6) has noted: ". . . the majority of white Americans who had accepted the efforts to reduce racial discrimination may well reach a limit after which they retreat to earlier prejudices and practices because their own favored status is threatened." The same thought was expressed much earlier and more cynically by Machiavelli: ". . . men forget more readily the death of their father than the loss of their patrimony." This becomes doubly true if the supposed recipients of the lost patrimony seem ungrateful. And to point to median ratio gains, which signal absolute but not relative advancement, as an alleviating factor is to deny the import of relative deprivation. As Reissman (1973:26) succinctly noted: "It makes little sense for those who continue to suffer from inequality to be content with general progress as long as their situation remains unaltered." These findings demonstrate clearly that black "progress" has, in most cases, only matched white progress—leaving the situation only slightly altered.

Finally, the recent spate of publication, scholarly and governmental, heralding the significant achievements of the decade would make an interesting case study—not only in political sociology, but more appropriately in the sociology of knowledge. Those prior researchers who have used the ratio of black to white median income were clearly objective scholars, influenced only by customary practice in the field. The influence of *Weltanschauung,* it would seem, is subtle, indeed.

# References

Blalock, Hubert M. 1972. *Social Statistics.* New York: McGraw-Hill.

Bowman, M. J. 1951. "A Graphical Analysis of Personal Income Distribution in the U.S." In *Readings in the Theory of Income Distribution III.* Homewood, Illinois: Irwin.

Broom, Leonard, and Norval D. Glenn. 1967. *Transformation of the Negro American.* New York: Harper.

Bureau of the Census. 1961. *United States Census of Population, 1960: Final Report.* Washington: Government Printing Office.

——. 1963. *United States Census of Population, 1960: Occupation by Earnings and Education.* Washington: Government Printing Office.

——. 1970. *1970 Census Users' Guide.* Washington: Government Printing Office.

——. 1973a. *Current Population Reports: The Social and Economic Status of the Black Population in the United States, 1972.* Washington: Government Printing Office.

Farley, R., and A. Hermalin. 1972. "The 1960s: A Decade of Progress for Blacks?" *Demography* 9(August):353-70.

Freeman, R. B. 1973. "Changes in the Labor Market for Black Americans, 1948-72." In *Brookings Papers on Economic Activity I.* Washington: Brookings Institution.

Reissman, Leonard. 1973. *Inequality in American Society.* Glenview, Ill.: Scott, Foresman.

Templeton, I.. 1973. "To the Editor of Commentary." *Commentary* 56(August)18-9.

Terrell, H. S. 1971. "The Data on Relative White-Nonwhite Income and Earnings Reexamined: A Comment on the Papers by Guthrie and Ashenfelter." *Journal of Human Resources* 6(Summer):384-91.

Thurow, Lester C. 1969, *Poverty and Discrimination.* Washington: Brookings Institution.

Wattenberg, Ben J., and Richard M. Scammon. 1973. "Black Progress and Liberal Rhetoric." *Commentary* 55(April):35-44.

# 42

# Trends in Racial Inequalities: Have the Gains of the 1960s Disappeared in the 1970s?

*REYNOLDS FARLEY*

. . . This analysis investigates whether the black gains of the 1960s disappeared in the 1970s. Data concerning educational attainment, employment, occupational prestige, income and earnings will be examined.

## Trends in Educational Attainment

Throughout this century there has been a secular trend toward greater educational attainment. Although this involved both races, the years of schooling completed by blacks have always been fewer than those completed by whites (Folger and Nam, 1967: Table V-6; Hauser and Featherman, 1976: Table 8). Figure 1 indicates the educational attainment of the population age 25 and over. These data, and those analyzed in later sections, were gathered in decennial censuses or in the Census Bureau's monthly Current Population Survey. Wherever

Abridged from *American Sociological Review 42* (1977): 189–208. Used by permission.

possible, data for the white and black population have been used. Prior to 1968, many tabulations were made for nonwhites rather than for blacks and, when necessary, these have been analyzed.

Figure 1 shows the first and third quartiles of educational attainment and a time series of indexes of educational dissimilarity calculated from educational distributions of eight categories. This measure of the overlap of the black and white distributions takes on its minimum value of zero when the distributions are identical. If, on the other hand, all whites had attainments greater than any blacks, the index would equal 100—meaning no overlap of the distributions and maximum dissimilarity.

Racial differences in attainment gradually diminished after the Depression. In 1940, the difference at the first quartile point was about four and one-half years of schooling but, by the late 1960s, the difference was under three years. At the other extreme, the racial gap at the third quartile point—which was about four years in 1940—decreased to less than one year in the late 1960s for both sexes. The trend toward smaller racial differences in attainment persisted into the 1970s. The indexes of dissimilarity continued their decline and, at present, educational distributions overlap more than at previous dates.

Changes in the attainment of adults occur primarily because older individuals with few years of schooling are replaced by younger people who have greater attainment. Education trends can be studied further by analyzing the attainment of the birth cohorts recently completing schooling. Table 1 indicates attainment at ages 25 to 29 using the same measures as Figure 1.

Over time, racial differences as assessed by the index of dissimilarity declined, and the first quartile points of the black and white educational distributions are closer now than they were in the 1960s and very much closer than thirty years ago. This occurred primarily because of a racial convergence in secondary school completion. Shortly after World War II, approximately two-thirds of the whites compared to one-third of the nonwhites finished twelve years of education (B. Duncan, 1968: Table 26). Blacks have pretty much "caught up" with whites at this level and, among those in their early twenties today, 85 percent of the whites and 72 percent of the blacks completed high school (U.S. Bureau of the Census, 1976a: Table 1).

The racial gap at the third quartile point has grown larger among both sexes. This occurred because, throughout most of the post-World War II span, increases in college enrollment were greater among whites than among blacks. In 1969, 36 percent of white men 18 to 24 were enrolled in college compared to 16 percent of black men—a difference of twenty percentage points which was twice the difference recorded in the Census of 1950 (U.S. Bureau of the Census 1953: Tables 104 and 112; 1970a: Table 1). As a consequence, the racial difference among those completing college widened.

Future trends in educational attainment depend largely upon college enrollment rates. If black enrollment rates approach those of whites, the long-term trend toward educational convergence will continue. Between 1969 and 1975,

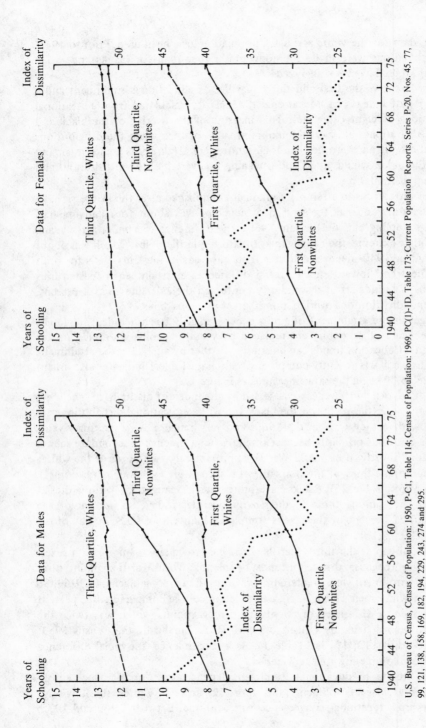

U.S. Bureau of Census, Census of Population: 1950, P-C1, Table 114; Census of Population: 1969, PC(1)-1D, Table 173; Current Population Reports, Series P-20, Nos. 45, 77, 99, 121, 138, 158, 169, 182, 194, 229, 243, 274 and 295.

**FIGURE 1. First and Third Quartiles of Educational Attainment and Indexes of Educational Dissimilarity, 1940 to 1975, Population Age 25 and Over**

**TABLE 1.** First and Third Quartiles of Educational Attainment for Cohorts at Age 25 to 29 and Indexes of Dissimilarity

| YEARS OF BIRTH OF COHORTS | YEAR REACHING AGES 25–29 | First Quartile | | | Third Quartile | | | INDEX OF DISSIMILARITY |
|---|---|---|---|---|---|---|---|---|
| | | WHITE | BLACK OR NONWHITE | RACIAL DIFF. | WHITE | BLACK OR NONWHITE | RACIAL DIFF. | |
| Males | | | | | | | | |
| 1910–14 | 1940 | 8.3 | 3.7 | 4.6 | 12.5 | 8.8 | 3.7 | 48 |
| 1920–24 | 1950 | 9.0 | 5.6 | 3.4 | 12.8 | 11.5 | 1.3 | 38 |
| 1930–34 | 1960 | 10.0 | 7.8 | 2.2 | 13.8 | 12.4 | 1.4 | 26 |
| 1935–39 | 1965 | 11.4 | 9.4 | 2.0 | 14.1 | 12.6 | 1.5 | 23 |
| 1940–44 | 1970 | 11.9 | 9.8 | 2.1 | 15.2 | 12.7 | 2.5 | 20 |
| 1945–49 | 1975 | 12.2 | 11.5 | .7 | 16.0 | 13.7 | 2.3 | 20 |
| Females | | | | | | | | |
| 1910–14 | 1940 | 8.5 | 5.2 | 3.3 | 12.5 | 9.9 | 2.6 | 43 |
| 1920–24 | 1950 | 9.6 | 6.4 | 3.2 | 12.6 | 12.0 | .6 | 33 |
| 1930–34 | 1960 | 10.5 | 8.6 | 1.9 | 12.8 | 12.5 | .3 | 24 |
| 1935–39 | 1965 | 11.5 | 9.5 | 2.0 | 12.8 | 12.6 | .2 | 23 |
| 1940–44 | 1970 | 11.9 | 10.0 | 1.9 | 13.7 | 12.7 | 1.0 | 20 |
| 1945–49 | 1975 | 12.1 | 11.3 | .8 | 14.9 | 13.1 | 1.8 | 13 |

Sources: U.S. Bureau of the Census, Census of Population: 1950, P–C1, Table 115; Census of Population: 1960, PC(1)–1D, Table 173; Census of Population: 1970, PC(1)–D1, Table 199; Current Population Reports, Series P–20, No. 158, Table 4; No. 295, Table 1.

college enrollment rates of blacks increased more than those of whites, suggesting that racial difference in attainment may attenuate (U.S. Bureau of the Census, 1970a: Table 1; 1976b: Table 6). The social and economic processes which brought about a convergence of attainment at the secondary school level in the 1950s and 1960s may have similar effects on college attendance in the 1970s (Hauser and Featherman, 1976:110–6).

## Trends in Unemployment and Employment

If blacks occupy a marginal position in the nation's economy, they would be the last hired and the first fired. In a period of economic contraction such as the 1970s, we would expect unemployment to rise more rapidly among blacks than among whites.

### TRENDS IN UNEMPLOYMENT

Unemployment rates are calculated for those who are in the labor force. If a person 16 or over worked for pay or was temporarily absent from a job because of illness, a vacation or a strike, that person was classified by the Census Bureau as employed. The unemployed population includes those persons who did not work but made specific efforts to find jobs, those waiting to be recalled from lay-offs and those awaiting the start of new jobs. . . .

Data concerning unemployment are available from 1948 to the present. The nation's unemployment rates declined during the Korean and Vietnamese wars but rose in other periods. . . . This rate climbed rapidly in 1974, and in 1975 it was at the highest level since the nation mobilized for World War II (U.S. Bureau of Labor Statistics, 1976: Table 1).

Descriptions of the employment status of nonwhites frequently focus upon high unemployment rates. Throughout much of the post-World War II era, the unemployment rate for nonwhite men has been twice as great as that for white men. . . .

From the mid-1950s to the late 1960s, the ratio of unemployment rates among men persisted at about two to one. At the end of the 1960s, the economy expanded and the ratio of unemployment rates decreased to the levels observed during the Korean War. During the 1970s, unemployment increased more rapidly among nonwhites than among whites. The proportion unemployed went up from 5 to 13 percent among nonwhite men between 1969 and 1975 while it increased from 3 to 7 percent among whites (U.S. Bureau of Labor Statistics, 1976: Table 1; 1960: Table A-1). The ratio of unemployment rates rose and much of the improvement registered in the late 1960s was negated. Nevertheless, this ratio in the mid-1970s is lower than it was around 1960 when the national unemployment rate was much smaller.

Racial differences in unemployment have been smaller among women than among men. The ratio of nonwhite to white unemployment rates has been less than two to one for most of the post-World War II period and, even during the recession of the 1970s, the rise in unemployment was no greater among non-white women than among white women. Apparently, black women have maintained their employment position *vis-à-vis* whites and, on this measure, the gains of the 1960s have not diminished.

## TRENDS IN EMPLOYMENT

Unemployment rates may inaccurately reflect labor force conditions since numerous unemployed individuals may become discouraged, give up the battle to find work and drop out of the labor force. Nonparticipation in the labor force also may indicate the relative position of blacks. To analyze these trends, we studied changes in the proportion of population who held a job, that is, employed persons as a proportion of the total adult population. If one is interested in the generation of income and the elimination of poverty, it may be more meaningful to consider employment trends rather than unemployment trends (Shiskin, 1976). . . . No distinction has been made between workers who held part- or full-time jobs.

The data for men show modest decreases in the proportion of white men at work. This occurred, in part, because of a sharp reduction in the proportion employed among men over 55—a change undoubtedly brought about by expansion of Social Security benefits and private pension plans. At younger ages there have been small declines in labor force participation rates and substantial year-to-year fluctuations in unemployment.

At all dates, the proportion employed has been lower among nonwhite than among white men and the proportion at work has declined since the early 1950s. Among nonwhites, labor force participation rates have decreased not only among men over 55 but among those at younger ages. For instance, in 1953, about 96 percent of the nonwhite men 25 to 55 were labor force participants, but this figure dropped to 89 percent in 1975. (U.S. Department of Labor, 1975; Table A-4; U.S. Bureau of Labor Statistics, 1976: Table 1). At ages 16 to 24, labor force participation rates once were approximately equal for white and nonwhite men but this too changed, and the proportion of young men in the labor force is now substantially lower among nonwhites than among whites.

In the mid-1970s, the trend toward lower labor force participation combined with high unemployment rates to produce sharp decreases in the proportion of nonwhite men with jobs. . . . [I]n 1975 and early 1976 about three-quarters of adult white men, but less than two-thirds of nonwhite men were employed, and racial differences on this indicator are now larger than before.

Decreases in employment adversely affect the income of nonwhite families. However, it is necessary to know more about the activities of men who are not in the labor force. If fewer men work because they attend school or are retired, we would draw different conclusions than if they do not work because jobs are unavailable.

Since 1967, the Bureau of Labor Statistics has tabulated the activities of persons not [i]n the labor force. They are classified as keeping a home, going to school, unable to work or not working for "other reasons." If the lack of economic opportunities accounts for the decreasing proportion of nonwhite men at work, we would anticipate that a growing proportion of nonwhite men would not be in the labor force because of "other reasons" but the data are not consistent with this speculation. In the 1970s, there has not been a sharp increase in the proportion who are not in the labor force because of "other reasons." Rather, there has been a modest rise in the proportion in this category, as well as increases in the proportion unable to work or going to school (U.S. Bureau of Labor Statistics 1976: Table 1; 1970: Table A-1).

Employment trends among men cannot be readily summarized. The pattern of nonwhite unemployment rates being twice those of white rates emerged in the mid-1950s (Killingsworth, 1968:20-2). This ratio temporarily fell below two to one in the later 1960s, but climbed back to about two to one in the present decade. This, however, is only one facet. Since the 1950s, labor force participation has decreased among nonwhite men and, thus, the racial differences in the proportion of men who have jobs has increased. On this indicator, black men appear to fall behind white men in both prosperous and lean times.

. . . The fraction of nonwhite women holding jobs has changed little in the last two decades, and at all dates just over 40 percent were employed. The recession of the mid-1970s reduced employment by a modest amount. A different trend characterizes white women, for the proportion at work has risen about one-half a percentage point each year since the 1950s. Traditionally, a higher proportion of black than white women have worked (Bowen and Finegan, 1969:91). This difference has disappeared and, in 1975, the proportion at work was slightly higher for white than for nonwhite women.

## Occupational Change

Since the 1950s there has been a modest upgrading of the occupations pursued by white workers, but among nonwhites there has been a more dramatic shift into higher status jobs and thus racial differences in occupational prestige have declined.

. . . The decennial censuses and monthly labor force reports classify workers into eleven major categories. Persons in each category have been assigned a prestige score using the system developed by O. D. Duncan (1961, ch. 6; Hauser et al., 1975: Table 1). At the lower end, laborers were assigned a score of 7 while professionals, at the other extreme, were scored 75. . . . [T]he first and third quartiles of the . . . prestige distribution [are then compared] . To assess the similarity of the white and nonwhite distributions, indexes of occupational dissimilarity also are [inspected].

Between 1950 and 1970, the first and third quartiles of the white distribution changed very little, but among nonwhites the first and third quartiles rose. Particularly sharp jumps at the first quartile point occurred in the 1960s as nonwhites moved out of low prestige jobs as farm laborers or factory workers. As a result, the occupational distributions of white and nonwhite men became increasingly alike (Hauser and Featherman, 1974a:259-61). The dissimilarity index for men fell from 43 in 1940 . . . to 37 in 1960 to 31 at the end of that decade and to 26 in 1975. The relative improvements in the occupational status of nonwhite women were even greater than those for nonwhite men. In 1940, three-quarters of employed black women worked as domestic servants or as farm laborers. This changed as black women moved into service jobs, clerical and sales positions. By 1975, only 10 percent worked as domestic servants or on farms (U.S. Bureau of Labor Statistics, 1976: Table 19).

The occupations of nonwhite workers were upgraded during the 1960s and 1970s. We examined annual changes in the numbers of whites and nonwhites employed in each of the major occupational categories and found that the number of nonwhites working at non-manual jobs or as craftsmen grew much more rapidly than the number of white workers in those occupations. Presumably, barriers to black employment in these prestigious jobs fell during the 1960s and 1970s. . . . Two of the white-collar occupations—managers and sales—involve supervising other employees or meeting the public as a representative of the employer—jobs which were once reserved to whites. Gains in nonwhite employment in these classifications during the 1970s appear to exceed the gains of the 1960s (Garfinkle, 1975).

Throughout the period after the Depression, the occupational distribution of nonwhites improved as nonwhites moved away from jobs on farms or in domestic service. Substantial gains were registered by blacks after 1960 and were not negated in the 1970s. Nevertheless, these changes have not eliminated the very large gap between the occupations pursued by whites and by nonwhites. Despite three and one-half decades of improvements, the average prestige score for nonwhite workers in 1975 was inferior to that of white workers in 1940 (U.S. Bureau of the Census, 1943b: Table 62; U.S. Bureau of Labor Statistics, 1976: Table 19).

## Family Income Trends

The most widely used statistics concerning the economic status of blacks are those showing median family incomes. The Census Bureau has tabulated such data since 1947; a summary is presented in Table 2.

Shortly after World War II, the median income of whites was approximately double that of nonwhites (see Table 2). Gains were made by blacks, especially in

**TABLE 2.  Trends in the Income of White and Black Families: 1947 to 1975**

| YEAR | Median Family Income in Constant Dollars[a] | | BLACK MEDIAN INCOME AS PERCENT OF WHITE | INDEX OF DISSIMI- LARITY[b] |
|------|--------|--------|--------|--------|
|      | BLACKS | WHITES |        |        |
| 1947 | $3,888 | $ 7,608 | 51% | 38.3 |
| 1950 | 4,178 | 7,702 | 54 | 36.8 |
| 1955 | 5,113 | 9,271 | 55 | 34.7 |
| 1960 | 5,871 | 10,604 | 55 | 31.7 |
| 1965 | 6,812 | 12,370 | 55 | 32.8 |
| 1967 | 7,859 | 13,273 | 59 | 31.0 |
| 1968 | 8,292 | 13,826 | 60 | 29.1 |
| 1969 | 8,807 | 14,379 | 61 | 28.9 |
| 1970 | 8,703 | 14,188 | 61 | 27.3 |
| 1971 | 8,558 | 14,182 | 60 | 28.2 |
| 1972 | 8,831 | 14,858 | 59 | 28.0 |
| 1973 | 8,804 | 15,254 | 58 | 29.3 |
| 1974[c] | 8,737 | 14,633 | 60 | 27.8 |
| 1975 | 8,779 | 14,268 | 62 | 26.3 |

[a]Amounts shown in constant 1975 dollars. Data for 1947 to 1965 refer to whites and nonwhites.

[b]Indexes of dissimilarity computed from seven-category constant dollar income distributions.

[c]Revised 1974 income figures. For details see Current Population Survey, Series P–60, No. 103.

Sources: U.S. Bureau of the Census, Current Population Reports, Series P–60 No. 103, Table 4.

the late 1960s, and an income peak was reached around 1970 when black families had a median income 64 percent as great as whites (Wohlstetter and Coleman, 1972:19-29: Thurow, 1969: Figure 2-2).

Ratios of medians offer one assessment, but a more complete view may be obtained by measuring the overlap of the two income distributions. Indexes of income dissimilarity are shown on the right in Table 2. Between 1947 and 1960 this index declined from 38 to 32, indicating a growing overlap. During the 1960s, further gains were made by nonwhites and, at the the end of that decade, the income distributions of the races overlapped more than at previous dates.

Family income trends in the most recent six-year span differ greatly from those of the preceding period. Rather than growing, family income, as measured in constant dollars, stagnated in the 1970s and, in 1975, the median incomes of families of both races were slightly lower than they were in 1969. The trend toward higher ratios of black to white medians ceased and the indexes of dissimilarity which measure the overlap of the income distributions of black and white families declined more slowly in the 1970s than in the 1960s. If family income is the criterion of status, there is no evidence that the pattern of improvement which was seen in the 1960s continued into the 1970s. On the other hand, blacks have not fallen further behind whites.

## CHANGES IN FAMILY COMPOSITION

Trends in family income are influenced by changes in living arrangements of children and parents. Since 1960, four major shifts in American family structure are evident. First, a growing proportion of marriages end in divorce. The divorce rate—as indexed by the ratio of divorces to married women—began to increase in the 1950s (Glick and Norton, 1973: Table 1) and continues to rise (U.S. National Center for Health Statistics, 1976a: Table 2; Preston, 1975). Approximately one out of five first marriages of women who reached marriagable age in the 1940s ended in divorce. If present rates persist, about one in three of the first marriages of women who reached the same ages in the 1960s will be terminated by divorce (Glick and Norton, 1973; Table 2; U.S. Bureau of the Census, 1972: Table F).

Second, an increasing proportion of women are heads of families. In 1960, about five percent of white and 15 percent of nonwhite women ages 25 to 44 were family heads. By 1975, these proportions grew to nine percent among white women and 32 percent among black women (U.S. Bureau of the Census, 1964: Table 2; 1975c: Table 2).

Third, the percentage of births out of wedlock ha[s] risen sharply. The proportion of births which were illegitimate was two percent among whites in 1960 and 22 percent for nonwhites (U.S. National Center for Health Statistics, 1969: Table 1-24). The fertility rates of married women have fallen more rapidly than those of single women (Cutright and Galle, 1973) and the proportion of births illegitimate in 1974 was seven percent among whites and 47 percent among blacks (U.S. National Center for Health Statistics, 1976b: Table 11).

Finally, the proportion of children who live with both parents—real or adoptive—has declined. In 1960, 90 percent of white children under 18 and 66 percent of nonwhite children lived with both parents. Fifteen years later, these proportions fell to 85 percent for whites and 49 percent for blacks (U.S. Bureau of the Census, 1964: Tables 1, 2, 19; 1975c: Table 4).

Families headed by women traditionally have had incomes about one-half as great as families headed by men, and children in families headed by a woman are much more likely to be impoverished than children in families headed by a man (U.S. Bureau of the Census, 1963a: Table 224; 1975b: Table 2; 1976c: Table 17). If we analyzed trends in family income or welfare without controlling for changes in living arrangements, we would underestimate the improvements which may have occurred. . . .

During the 1960s, black families of both types—husband-wife and female-headed—experienced greater gains in income than comparable white families. The 1969 to 1975 interval was much less prosperous than the preceding decade, and the growth rate of the median income of families was actually negative.

Nevertheless, the median income of husband-wife black families rose and the rate of increase was greater than for similar white families, that is, 1.2 percent annually for husband-wife blacks versus 0.1 percent for whites. The median income of families headed by black women did not change but that of similar white families fell by 0.9 percent annually.

There appears to be a puzzle. The median income of total black families declined in this span and the racial difference in purchasing power remained essentially constant at about $5,500. However, the median income of the most common types of black families—husband-wife and female-headed—rose or remained unchanged and, for families of these types, the racial difference in purchasing power decreased substantially. This is explained by the shifting distributions of families by type. Female-headed families—the lowest income families—became a larger component of total black families, increasing from 28 percent in 1969 to 36 percent in 1975 while husband-wife families fell from 68 to 60 percent (U.S. Bureau of the Census, 1970b: Table 17; 1976c: Table 1). This suggests that the analysis of family income trends must take into account the changing living arrangements of children and adults.

## TRENDS IN PERSONAL EARNINGS

Since changes in family composition confound trends in family income, it is important to examine the earnings of individuals. If blacks improved in economic status in the 1960s and maintained these gains into the 1970s, we would expect that the earnings of blacks would rise faster than those of whites and that blacks and whites would begin to receive similar pay for such characteristics as educational attainment and occupational achievement. In this section we analyze, first, whether the earnings of blacks rose faster than those of whites and, second, whether blacks and whites receive similar pay for ostensibly similar characteristics.

Data describing the earnings of individuals are obtained in the decennial censuses, and tape files of the one-in-one-thousand samples of the censuses of 1960 and 1970 were used. Every March the Census Bureau's Current Population Survey gathers information about earnings from the occupants of 50,000 households. Tape files of the March survey may be used to analyze the earnings process on an annual basis. Data from the March, 1975, survey were studied in this investigation.

The earnings an individual obtains are influenced by his or her education and occupation. Additionally, wage levels traditionally have been lower in the South than elsewhere and, other things being equal, we anticipate that earnings are positively related to the number of hours worked. Finally, experience in the labor market should affect earnings independent of other factors. The model used in this paper specifies that an individual's earnings are a linear function of region of residence, education, occupation, time worked and experience.

To ascertain parameters for this model, each individual in the 1960, 1970 and

1975 samples was classified by sex and race. Each received a score for region—one for the South and zero for other regions. The education score equaled the number of school years completed. The occupational prestige scores were based upon the detailed—not the broad—occupational categories (Featherman et al., 1975; O. D. Duncan, 1961). An estimate of hours worked was derived from weeks worked in the year for which earnings were reported and the hours worked in the year for which earnings were reported and the hours worked during the week prior to the census or survey. This variable is identified as Time in the tables. Experience was estimated by taking the respondent's current age, subtracting years of schooling and the constant, six. For most men, this represents years of labor force experience. For many currently employed women, however, this is an imperfect indicator of work experience since they may have been out of the labor force for long periods. Human capital may deteriorate with age and, to represent this effect, the experience variable was squared. This is identified as Decay in the tables (see Mincer, 1974:ch. 5). Earnings, the dependent variable, refers to the year prior to the census or survey, that is, to earnings obtained in 1959, 1969 or 1974.

This analysis is restricted to black and white persons 25 to 54 who reported earnings and who indicated the number of hours they worked. Thus, it excludes the long-term unemployed, those who took their first jobs during the year of the census or survey, and those who worked in 1959, 1969 or 1974 but were not working at the time of the census or survey.

A variety of models have described racial differences in earnings and the returns to human capital. Because census data are analyzed, the model presented in this paper omits several variables which may influence earnings such as intelligence, timing of labor force experience or characteristics of the family of origin. If these or other relevant variables were included, they might provide additional information about racial discrimination.

Means and standard deviations of the variables are shown in Table 3. Figures in the first row reveal that the earnings of blacks have risen faster than those of whites. Between 1959 and 1969, the mean earnings of white men rose 27 percent; those of black men rose 51 percent. Among women, the increases were 24 percent for whites and 69 percent for blacks. From 1969 to 1974, the earnings of whites—in constant dollars—actually declined but blacks reported gains. Data in Table 3 refer to a select subgroup of the population. However, when all persons who reported earnings or all persons with income are considered, a similar conclusion is reached. The earnings of black men and women rose faster than those of whites during the early 1970s. On this measure, the gains of the 1960s were not negated and the racial difference in earnings declined in the 1970s (U.S. Bureau of the Census, 1970b: Tables 45 and 54; 1976c: Tables 11 and 12).

Table 3 indicates that a decreasing fraction of blacks live in the South and that the educational attainment of black workers has risen more than that of whites. Occupational upgrading has been somewhat greater for blacks than for

**TABLE 3.  Means and Standard Deviation of Variables Used in the Analysis of Earnings: Employed Persons 25 to 54**

| | | MALES | | | | | | FEMALES | | | | | |
|---|---|---|---|---|---|---|---|---|---|---|---|---|---|
| | | 1959 | | 1969 | | 1974 | | 1959 | | 1969 | | 1974 | |
| VARIABLES | | WHITE | BLACK | WHITE | BLACK | WHITE | BLACK | WHITE | BLACK | WHITE | BLACK | WHITE | BLACK |
| Earnings[a] | $\bar{X}$ | $10,638 | 5,473 | 13,522 | 8,260 | 13,432 | 9,137 | 4,762 | 2,954 | 5,901 | 4,995 | 5,760 | 5,652 |
| | $\sigma$ | $10,375 | 2,303 | 9,410 | 5,541 | 9,630 | 4,995 | 3,531 | 2,440 | 4,459 | 3,625 | 4,153 | 4,181 |
| Region | $\bar{X}$ | .26 | .57 | .28 | .50 | .29 | .49 | .27 | .57 | .29 | .52 | .31 | .53 |
| | $\sigma$ | .44 | .49 | .45 | .50 | .46 | .50 | .44 | .50 | .45 | .50 | .46 | .50 |
| Education | $\bar{X}$ | 11.2 | 8.5 | 12.1 | 10.1 | 12.9 | 11.2 | 11.4 | 9.5 | 12.0 | 10.8 | 12.6 | 11.9 |
| | $\sigma$ | 3.3 | 3.8 | 3.3 | 3.5 | 3.1 | 3.3 | 2.8 | 3.6 | 2.7 | 3.2 | 2.7 | 2.8 |
| Occupation | $\bar{X}$ | 37.2 | 18.9 | 42.3 | 24.9 | 44.3 | 27.7 | 38.1 | 20.1 | 42.6 | 28.6 | 44.8 | 33.3 |
| | $\sigma$ | 22.6 | 15.4 | 24.0 | 18.8 | 24.2 | 20.4 | 19.6 | 18.1 | 20.9 | 22.1 | 21.1 | 22.8 |
| Time | $\bar{X}$ | 2,145 | 1,852 | 2,157 | 1,950 | 2,184 | 1,910 | 1,614 | 1,453 | 1,585 | 1,620 | 1,617 | 1,651 |
| | $\sigma$ | 579 | 654 | 526 | 533 | 695 | 621 | 709 | 752 | 684 | 621 | 734 | 641 |
| Experience | $\bar{X}$ | 22 | 24 | 21 | 23 | 20 | 21 | 23 | 24 | 22 | 22 | 20 | 20 |
| | $\sigma$ | 10 | 10 | 10 | 10 | 10 | 10 | 9 | 10 | 10 | 10 | 10 | 10 |
| Decay | $\bar{X}$ | 577 | 692 | 538 | 608 | 485 | 538 | 606 | 648 | 577 | 577 | 507 | 495 |
| | $\sigma$ | 437 | 507 | 425 | 485 | 414 | 478 | 415 | 478 | 417 | 455 | 412 | 418 |

[a]Shown in 1974 dollars.

Sources: U.S. Bureau of the Census: Censuses of Population and Housing, 1960 and 1970 tape files of one in 1,000 samples; Current Population Survey, March, 1975, tape file.

whites. Among men, there is a persistent racial difference in the number of hours worked per year. The racial difference in years of experience has been small at all dates.

Next, we considered whether the earnings blacks and whites receive, as determined by their characteristics, have changed over time. The upper panel of Table 4 shows the regression models for males and the lower panel refers to females. The first line of the upper panel indicates that, in 1959, residing in the South had the net effect of reducing a white man's earnings by $1,002. Each year of schooling was associated with a net increase in earnings of $676, each occupational prestige point was worth $95 and every additional hour worked netted a white man $1.93. The returns for an additional year of experience were $603. These returns to characteristics are expressed in constant 1974 dollars.

The regression coefficients show that black men are paid less for their attributes than are whites. At all dates, the earnings penalty associated with living in the South was about twice as great for blacks as for whites. For both races, returns to schooling increased in the 1960s and fell back in the 1970s, but a large racial difference was maintained. In 1974, an additional year of schooling—independent of other variables—was worth about $600 to a white but only $200 to a black. The returns to occupational prestige have not changed greatly and, at all dates, an increment of one point on the occupational prestige scale was worth about half as much for blacks as for whites. Apparently, the racial difference in returns to hours worked has been mitigated. The earnings returns for labor force experience are much greater for whites than for blacks and there is no indication of a diminution in the fifteen-year span covered by these data. These models suggest that black men are paid less than whites for ostensively identical characteristics and that there have been few changes in this pattern.

Among women, there have been alterations in the rates of return and the earnings of black women are approaching those of white women. In 1959, black women benefited considerably less than white women for each year of education, but the difference attenuated and there is now almost no racial difference in returns to education among women. By 1974, the increment in earnings associated with occupational prestige was also similar for whites and blacks. The racial difference in returns for hours worked also has diminished.

For white women, the earnings returns associated with experience, as measured in this paper, were essentially nil. That is, each of the regression coefficients was smaller than its standard error. Among black women, earnings were related to experience and, over time, the returns for experience increased sharply. Black women have a different pattern of labor force participation by age than white women, and it may be that black women typically have greater on-the-job seniority than do white women of comparable age. This may account for the advantages black women obtain on this determinant of earnings.

The figures in Table 3 reveal that blacks earn less than whites. One reason is that blacks have different characteristics than whites. For example, more blacks

**TABLE 4.** Determinants of Earnings for Males and Females 25 to 54 by Race, Constant 1974 Dollars: 1959, 1969 and 1974

| DATA FOR MALES | Independent Variables | | | | | | a | $R^2$ | ERROR OF ESTIMATE | N |
|---|---|---|---|---|---|---|---|---|---|---|
| | REGION | EDUC. | OCC. | TIME | EXPER. | DECAY | | | | |
| | Metric Coefficients[a] | | | | | | | | | |
| **White Males** | | | | | | | | | | |
| 1959 | $-1,002.06 (135.79) | 675.70 (25.15) | 94.61 (3.25) | 1.93 (.10) | 602.54 (28.70) | -10.22 (.62) | -11,713 | .154 | 9,541 | 26,066 |
| 1969 | -1,438.70 (112.64) | 699.74 (21.63) | 103.32 (2.64) | 2.62 (.09) | 622.38 (23.25) | -10.79 (.53) | -11,855 | .235 | 8,232 | 26,684 |
| 1974 | -862.44 (146.68) | 586.52 (30.85) | 94.96 (3.52) | 1.76 (.10) | 702.92 (29.97) | -12.79 (.71) | -9,535 | .188 | 8,680 | 17,008 |
| **Black Males** | | | | | | | | | | |
| 1959 | -2,095.53 (142.39) | 195.98 (25.20) | 51.54 (5.01) | 1.16 (.11) | 155.07 (34.45) | -2.58 (.67) | -100 | .250 | 3,415 | 2,446 |
| 1969 | -2,370.78 (202.33) | 285.00 (38.78) | 59.37 (5.99) | 1.86 (.19) | 183.65 (45.71) | -3.00 (.96) | -838 | .218 | 4,709 | 2,506 |
| 1974 | -1,999.55 (235.52) | 203.38 (52.44) | 43.01 (6.86) | 2.12 (.19) | 188.16 (48.98) | -3.56 (1.09) | 631 | .247 | 4,332 | 1,459 |
| | Standardized Coefficients | | | | | | | | | |
| **White Males** | | | | | | | | | | |
| 1959 | -.043 | .217 | .206 | .108 | .552 | -.429 | | | | |
| 1969 | -.069 | .243 | .263 | .146 | .643 | -.487 | | | | |
| 1974 | -.041 | .188 | .239 | .126 | .721 | -.550 | | | | |
| **Black Males** | | | | | | | | | | |
| 1959 | -.266 | .190 | .204 | .195 | .398 | -.336 | | | | |
| 1969 | -.214 | .181 | .201 | .179 | .334 | -.263 | | | | |
| 1974 | -.200 | .134 | .175 | .264 | .394 | -.341 | | | | |

Data for Females

**Metric Coefficients[a]**

| | | | | | | | | | | |
|---|---|---|---|---|---|---|---|---|---|---|
| White Females | | | | | | | | | | |
| 1959 | $ −603.71 (66.24) | 229.86 (13.87) | 28.02 (1.83) | 1.97 (.04) | 11.80 (15.29) | .19 (.34) | −2,330 | .253 | 3,053 | 10,863 |
| 1969 | −575.08 (70.77) | 317.04 (15.32) | 39.80 (1.84) | 2.86 (.05) | −14.90 (15.31) | .84 (.35) | −4,133 | .302 | 3,726 | 13,615 |
| 1974 | −599.37 (74.15) | 279.20 (17.24) | 40.84 (1.95) | 2.57 (.05) | .92 (15.61) | .48 (.37) | −3,832 | .358 | 3,329 | 9,607 |
| Black Females | | | | | | | | | | |
| 1959 | −1,109.01 (91.64) | 97.73 (18.45) | 54.74 (3.14) | 1.00 (.06) | 35.65 (22.13) | −.52 (.44) | −388 | .462 | 1,790 | 1,613 |
| 1969 | −1,046.32 (128.97) | 248.26 (27.88) | 52.03 (3.54) | 1.76 (.10) | 49.82 (30.75) | −.74 (.67) | −2,156 | .378 | 2,859 | 2,033 |
| 1974 | −929.78 (197.19) | 277.73 (48.96) | 44.98 (5.76) | 1.94 (.16) | 115.91 (45.13) | −2.12 (1.04) | −3,134 | .312 | 3,458 | 1,293 |

**Standardized Coefficients**

| | | | | | | |
|---|---|---|---|---|---|---|
| White Females | | | | | | |
| 1959 | −.076 | .185 | .156 | .395 | .030 | .022 |
| 1969 | −.059 | .192 | .186 | .439 | −.032 | .078 |
| 1974 | −.066 | .173 | .207 | .455 | .002 | .048 |
| Black Females | | | | | | |
| 1959 | −.225 | .143 | .405 | .307 | .143 | −.102 |
| 1969 | −.144 | .219 | .317 | .301 | .133 | −.093 |
| 1974 | −.111 | .185 | .245 | .298 | .268 | −.212 |

[a]Standard errors in parentheses.
Sources: See Table 3.

than whites live in the South where wages are low. Blacks also complete fewer years of schooling than whites and work at less prestigious jobs. Another reason is that blacks generally are paid less for a given characteristic than are whites. From both analytic and policy viewpoints, we would like to know whether the racial differences in earnings result primarily from racial differences in characteristics or from racial differences in the earnings returns which are associated with the characteristics we have considered.

The racial difference in earnings may be decomposed in many different fashions. . . . One method is illustrated in Table 5. In the equation which regressed the earnings of blacks upon the characteristics of blacks, it was assumed that blacks had the average characteristics of whites rather than their own characteristics. What effect this change would have upon the average earnings of blacks was ascertained. In 1959, if black men had the regional distribution of whites but retained their own returns for region, their average earnings would have been $650 greater, if they had the educational attainment of whites but retained their own rates of return, their average earnings would have risen $542. . . .

Racial differences in characteristics do not account for the entire racial difference in earnings. There is a residual, reflecting the difference in the returns blacks and whites receive for their characteristics. In Table 5, this is labeled "the difference not associated with the independent variables." . . . We note that this decomposition is not unique, and that different models of the earnings process might give different estimates of discrimination.

The top rows of Table 5 indicate that the racial difference in the earnings of men changed very little during the 1960s but decreased by about $1,000 in the early 1970s. At each date, racial differences in characteristics accounted for a substantial fraction of the difference in earnings. If black men had the characteristics of whites in 1959 and 1969, they would have earned an average of $2,500 more and, in 1974, an additional $2,000. Nevertheless, this did not account for the entire racial difference. A black man with the average characteristics of a white man and paid at the return rates blacks received for their characteristics would have earned much less than the typical white man because of racial differences in pay rates. In 1959 and 1969, this difference, which reflects discrimination, was $2,800 and, in 1974, $2,300. At each date, about 53 percent of the racial difference in earnings was attributable to discrimination as estimated by this model. . . .

## Conclusion

During the prosperous 1960s, racial differences in education, occupation and income generally declined. We investigated whether this trend continued into the 1970s and concluded that the gains of the 1960s apparently were not solely attributable to the prosperity of that decade, since racial differences in status

TABLE 5. Decomposition of Racial Difference in Earnings in Constant 1974 Dollars: 1959, 1969 and 1974

| | Males | | | Females | | |
|---|---|---|---|---|---|---|
| | 1959 | 1969 | 1974 | 1959 | 1969 | 1974 |
| Earnings of Whites | $10,638 | 13,522 | 13,432 | $4,762 | 5,901 | 5,760 |
| Earnings of Blacks | 5,473 | 8,260 | 9,137 | 2,954 | 4,995 | 5,652 |
| Racial Difference | +5,165 | +5,262 | +4,295 | +1,808 | +906 | +108 |
| Components of Earnings Difference Associated with Racial Difference in Independent Variables:[a] | | | | | | |
| Region | +650 | +512 | +401 | +331 | +243 | +212 |
| Education | +542 | +574 | +329 | +191 | +294 | +202 |
| Occupation | +941 | +1,034 | +715 | +989 | +725 | +520 |
| Time | +340 | +383 | +584 | +160 | −61 | −65 |
| Experience[b] | −57 | −55 | −5 | 0 | +4 | −1 |
| Total | +2,416 | +2,448 | +2,024 | +1,671 | +1,205 | +868 |
| Component of Earnings Difference Not Associated with Racial Differences in Independent Variables | +2,749 | +2,814 | +2,271 | +137 | −299 | −760 |

[a]Change in earnings which would occur if blacks retained their own rates of return but had the characteristics of whites.
[b]Includes the effects of the Experience and Decay variables.

narrowed in the 1970s as they did in the previous decade. Blacks and whites, especially the young, are more alike in years of school completed than ever before. Racial differences in the occupations of employed workers continue to decline. The income gap separating black and white families has remained constant, but this is largely a consequence of the sharp rise of female-headed families among blacks. Indexes describing the income of specific types of families or the earnings of individuals generally reveal that racial differences moderated during the early years of the 1970s.

In some areas, the gains are impressive. Black women, for instance, obtain earnings comparable to those of white women with similar characteristics. However, not all indicators show improvement. Employment opportunities are apparently severely limited for many black men. The very high rates of unemployment and nonparticipation in the labor force suggest that numerous young blacks experience great difficulty in launching careers.

The four processes . . . —the urbanization of blacks, the growing demand by blacks for civil rights, more liberal court rulings and laws, and reductions in the prejudicial attitudes of whites—have provided blacks with greater opportunities to compete for economic rewards. The occupational upgrading of blacks and their growing representation in politics imply that they are more represented in American decision making than they were at the start of World War II. These changes mean that, even during a pervasive recession, blacks did not lose the gains they previously experienced.

On the other hand, reductions in inequality are small when compared to the remaining racial differences on many indicators. A continuation of the trends of the 1960s and 1970s offers no hope that racial differences will be eliminated soon. For instance, a higher proportion of white men in 1940 than black men in 1976 held white-collar jobs. The purchasing power of the typical black family in 1974 was equivalent to that of a white family twenty years earlier, and the earnings of black men lag far behind those of white men (Table 3).

# References

Bowen, W. S. and A. T. Finegan
  1969   The Economics of Labor Force Participation. Princeton: Princeton University Press.
Cutright, P. and O. Galle
  1973   "The effect of illegitimacy on U.S. general fertility rates and population growth." Population Studies 27:515-26.
Duncan, B.
  1968   "Trends in output and distribution of schooling." Pp. 601-72 in E. Sheldon and W. Moore (eds.), Indicators of Social Change. New York: Russell Sage.
Duncan, O. D.
  1961   "A socioeconomic index for all occupations." Ch. 6 in A. Reiss, Jr.

(ed.), Occupations and Social Status. New York: Free Press.

Duncan, O. D., D. Featherman and B. Duncan
1972 Socioeconomic Background and Achievement. New York: Seminar.

Featherman, D., M. Sobel and D. Dickens
1975 A Manual for Coding Occupations and Industries into Detailed 1970 Categories and a Listing of 1970-Basis Duncan-Socioeconomic and NORC Prestige Scores. Madison: University of Wisconsin, Center for Demography and Ecology.

Folger, J. and C. Nam
1967 Education of the American Population. Washington, D.C.: U.S. Government Printing Office.

Garfinkle, S.
1975 "Occupations of women and black workers, 1962–74." Monthly Labor Review 98:25–35.

Glick, P. and A. Norton
1973 "Perspectives on the recent upturn in divorce and remarriage." Demography 10: 301–14.

Hauser, R. and D. Featherman
1974a "White-nonwhite differentials in occupational mobility among men in the United States, 1962–1972." Demography 11: 247–66.
1976 "Equality of schooling: trends and prospects." Sociology of Education 49:99–120.

Hauser, R., J. Koffel, H. Travis and P. Dickinson
1975 "Temporal change in occupational mobility: evidence for men in the United States." American Sociological Review 40: 279–97.

Killingsworth, C.
1968 Jobs and Income for Negroes. Ann Arbor: University of Michigan, Institute for Labor and Industrial Relations.

Mincer, J.
1974 Schooling, Experience and Earnings. New York: National Bureau of Economic Research.

Preston, S.
1975 "Estimating the proportion of American marriages that end in divorce." Sociological Methods and Research 3:435–60.

Shiskin, J.
1976 "Employment and unemployment: the doughnut or the hole." Monthly Labor Review 99:3–10.

Thurow, L.
1969 Poverty and Discrimination. Washington: Brookings Institution.

U.S. Bureau of the Census
1943a Sixteenth Census of the United States: 1940. Population Characteristics of the Nonwhite Population by Race.
1943b Sixteenth Census of the United States: 1940. Population, Vol. III, Part I.
1953 Census of Population: 1950, P-C1.
1963 Census of Population: 1960, PC(1)-1C.
1964 Census of Population: 1960, PC(2)-4B.
1970a Current Population Reports, Series P-20, No. 206.

1970b   Current Population Reports, Series P-60. No. 75.

1972    Current Population Reports, Series P-20, No. 239.

1975a   Current Population Reports, Series P-23. No. 54.

1975b   Current Population Reports, Series P-60, No. 98.

1975c   Current Population Reports, Series P-20, No. 287.

1976a   Current Population reports, Series P-20. 295.

1976b   Current Population Reports, Series P-20, No. 294.

1976c   Current Population Reports, Series P-60, No. 103.

U.S. Department of Labor

1975    Manpower Report of the President.

U.S. National Center for Health Statistics

1969    Vital Statistics of the United States, 1967, Vol. I.

1976a   Monthly Vital Statistics Report, Vol. 25, No. 1 (supplement).

1976b   Monthly Vital Statistics Report, Vol. 24, No. 11 (supplement 2).

Wohlstetter, A. and S. Coleman

1972    "Race differences in income." Pp. 3–82 in A. Pascal (ed.), Racial Dis-
        crimination in Economic Life. Lexington, Ma.: Heath.

# 43

# The Demographic Context of School Segregation and Desegregation

*DAVID F. SLY* and *LOUIS G. POL*

Policy analysts and other social scientists have shown concern over the extent to which school desegregation has caused white-flight (Clotfelter; Coleman et al.; Farley; Giles et al.; Rossell). Although various methods and different data sets have been employed to investigate this question, no one has specifically looked at the extent to which the migration of whites from central cities to suburbs is a product of school desegregation. Because the percent of white, central city students has declined dramatically in recent years as desegregation efforts have increased, it has become common to assume that this is the result of whites fleeing desegregation or its threat. This is evident in one recent discussion (Coleman et al., 2) when, after indicating that government policy does not always achieve desired effects, the authors claim, "The most obvious such individual action, of course, is a move of residence to flee integration." Similarly, at later points the authors (Coleman et al., 76,78) imply the effect of school desegregation when they assert, "Desegregation in central cities hastens this process of residential segregation (between cities & suburbs) . . . ;" and again when they conclude, "In the large cities (among the largest 22 central city school districts) there is a sizeable loss of whites when desegregation takes place."

Reprinted, abridged, from *Social Forces* 56 (June 1978); 1072–1086. Copyright © The University of North Carolina Press.

In this paper two tests of the hypothesis that school desegregation leads to white flight are offered. In the first test data are presented which allow an examination of the volume of white central city-to-ring mobility within metropolitan areas for the two periods 1955–60 and 1965–70. If white-flight is a generalized response to desegregation and/or the threat of desegregation, the rate of city-to-ring white mobility can be expected to rise between these two periods in most of the areas examined. The second test of the hypothesis merely attempts to establish a cross-sectional association between the two variables. In this test, rates of central city-to-ring white migration are correlated with school segregation indices to test the assumption that areas having higher levels of segregation also have lower rates of migration.

The data to be analyzed do not allow a perfect test of the hypothesis, nor is it the purpose of this paper to argue that white-flight to escape school desegregation does not exist. Our objectives are far more modest; they are to present data which at a minimum imply that white migration from cities to rings may be less of a response to school desegregation than is normally thought, and to begin to place the whole question of segregation and desegregation in the context of the historical development of central city populations.

Twenty-two standard metropolitan statistical areas are analyzed. These areas were selected because of their size, "These 22 largest central city school districts are classified according to 1972 enrollment and an Office of Education metropolitan status classification. They represent 22 of the 23 largest central city districts; Albuquerque is excluded (the 22nd largest) because it is not among the largest 50 cities in total population" (Coleman et al., 23).

## School Desegregation and White-Flight

Proponents of the school desegregation–white-flight hypothesis argue that school desegregation, and the threat of school desegregation, lead to the mass exodus of whites from the central cities of metropolitan areas to their rings. These investigators have not measured white-flight with data on the migration of whites from central cities to rings of metropolitan areas, but rather with the changing proportions of whites in central city schools—most often central city *public* schools. If this hypothesis is to be supported, they argue, one would expect substantial reductions in the percent of white central city public school students in recent years.

. . . [T]here have been substantial declines in both the relative and absolute number of white students in central city public schools. From 1968 through 1972 the absolute number of white central city public school students declined in all but two of the cities studied. . . . Among the 20 cities where reductions did occur, declines were substantial and dramatic; in nine they exceeded 20 percent, and in only four were they less than 10 percent.

Data . . . also document the marked tendency during this period for the relative number of white central city public school students to decline. . . . [T]hese data clearly document a sharp decline in the percent of white students in central city public schools; however, it is equally important to note that they do not document the existence of white-flight; nor do they measure its magnitude.

Direct data measuring white city-to-suburban migration for corresponding periods are not available; nor are data on the reasons for migration from central cities to suburbs. The latter data would be particularly important even if the former were available since a measure of volume at a single point in time tells us nothing about why whites are fleeing cities. Lacking data which would allow a direct test of the white-flight hypothesis, we decided to make a more indirect test of the hypothesis by comparing the absolute and relative flows of white migration from central cities to suburbs during two time periods. The periods selected were determined by the availability of census data, but there is sufficient overlap with the 1968–72 period to justify their use. Table 1 contains data showing white migration from central cities-to-rings during the periods 1955–60 and 1965–70. If school desegregation leads to white-flight, white migration from central cities-to-rings should increase during the later period. This assumption is predicated on the fact that during the earlier period, despite the 1954 court ruling, there was little effort to desegregate schools. But by the later period additional court rulings dictated desegregation and indicated that " . . . delays in desegregating school systems are no longer tolerable." Although there have been substantial differences in the timing of desegregation in these cities (in some, efforts have still been minimal) it is clear that by the later period the threat of desegregation was present (U.S. Civil Rights Commission). In short, even though this is not an ideal test of the white-flight hypothesis, it comes closer (through the nature of the data employed) to testing the hypothesis than do data on changing proportions of students.[1]

Data in Table 1 cast doubt on the white-flight hypothesis. In 16 of the 22 cities examined, the absolute number of white central city-to-ring migrants declined from the earlier to the later period. Moreover, with the exception of Columbus (a college town) each of the remaining cities (Houston, Dallas, Tampa, New Orleans, and Atlanta) which had an increase in the absolute number of migrants was located in a southern metropolitan area. The expansion and development of these metropolitan areas is generally recognized to be behind the development of older metropolitan areas in the rest of the country (Kasarda). Changes in the absolute number of central city-to-ring migrants, however, might merely reflect diminution of the white central city population size while the continually increasing number of white migrants from the central cities to the

---

[1] None of the data presented here has been corrected for the potential confounding influences of annexation. Most of the cities included in the analysis, however, underwent very little, if any, annexation with the exception of 3: Columbus, Memphis, and Indianapolis. Similarly, the Coleman et al. data have not been adjusted for any boundary changes.

rings in the South could merely reflect a different stage of the metropolitaniza-
tion process.

We can speculate as to whether this is the case by examining data presented in
columns five and eleven of Table 1. It is important to note that these figures
are not rates in the strict sense of the "at risk" notion of a rate, but they do
represent the proportion of the estimated 1955 and 1965 central city populations which moved to the rings during the periods 1955-60 and 1965-70. Thus,
before the rates will decline from one period to the next, the number of central
city-to-ring migrants will have to decrease at a more rapid rate than the total
central city population. (As the white central city population declines in size, it
will take fewer central city-to-ring white migrants to produce a rate of the same
magnitude.) The rates, however, may also be influenced in the opposite direction
owing to the fact that heavy out-migration of whites during the earlier periods
may reduce the number of potential central city-to-ring migrants during the
last period.

With these precautions in mind, we may note that in 16 of the 22 metropolitan areas examined, the rate of white migration from central cities-to-rings was
lower during the period 1965-70 than during the period 1955-60. Each of the
cities which had an absolute increase in the number of white central city-to-ring
migrants also had a rate which increased from the first to the second period; in 4
of the metropolitan areas (Houston, Columbus, Tampa, and New Orleans) these
increases were substantial. Among the 16 metropolitan areas which had lower
rates during the later than the earlier period there was wide variation in the
amount of decline in the rate. In Detroit, for example, the rate hardly declined
(a 1.8 percent difference), but in Memphis and Indianapolis the rates declined
by 44 and 51 percent, respectively. . . .

Data in Table 1 also show the volume and rate of within central city mobility
among whites during each period. In only 2 cities (Houston and Indianapolis)
did the absolute volume of this type of white mobility increase from 1955-60 to
1965-70; there was no city which had a higher rate of within-city mobility
during the later than the earlier period. As in the case of city-to-ring mobility,
there were substantial differences in the pace of decline of both the absolute
volume and the rate of mobility between the different areas. In short, these data
not only cast doubt on the school desegregation-white-flight hypothesis, but
they might also indicate that school desegregation and/or the threat of school
desegregation has lent a degree of stability to metropolitan and central city
residential mobility.

Finally, if school desegregation causes white-flight we should expect to find
that as the level of segregation increases the rate of white migration from central
cities-to-rings decreases. (Those cities with the highest levels of school segregation would have the lowest rates of white city-to-ring migration.) The measure
of segregation with which we have correlated the white city-to-ring rates of
migration reported in Table 1 has been taken from Coleman et al. and represents the proportion of white students in the same school with the average black

**T A B L E  1.**  Mobility of the White Population Within and From Central Cities of Metropolitan Areas: 1955–60 and 1965–70 (in thousands)*

| METROPOLITAN AREA‡ | 1955–1960 | | | | | | 1965–1970 | | | | | |
|---|---|---|---|---|---|---|---|---|---|---|---|---|
| | CENTRAL CITY TOTAL POPULATION | MOVER FROM CENTRAL CITY TO RING | MOVER WITHIN CENTRAL CITY | NON-MOVER IN CENTRAL CITY | CENTRAL CITY TO RING RATE | WITHIN CENTRAL CITY RATE | CENTRAL CITY TOTAL POPULATION | MOVER FROM CENTRAL CITY TO RING | MOVER WITHIN CENTRAL CITY | NON-MOVER IN CENTRAL CITY | CENTRAL CITY TO RING RATE | WITHIN CENTRAL CITY RATE |
| New York | 6,096 | 411 | 1,940 | 3,608 | .065 | .306 | 5,790 | 329 | 1,528 | 3,489 | .055 | .257 |
| Los Angeles | 2,172 | 349 | 665 | 866 | .173 | .330 | 2,456 | 279 | 618 | 1,103 | .120 | .267 |
| Chicago | 2,463 | 356 | 910 | 1,253 | .134 | .343 | 2,102 | 290 | 589 | 1,159 | .127 | .258 |
| Philadelphia | 1,338 | 167 | 376 | 852 | .116 | .261 | 1,202 | 126 | 258 | 784 | .099 | .203 |
| Detroit | 1,079 | 260 | 305 | 665 | .210 | .246 | 790 | 193 | 167 | 557 | .206 | .178 |
| Houston | 633 | 32 | 207 | 266 | .062 | .393 | 880 | 96 | 220 | 364 | .127 | .290 |
| Baltimore | 556 | 106 | 165 | 329 | .175 | .273 | 453 | 85 | 97 | 274 | .167 | .192 |
| Dallas | 509 | 39 | 177 | 194 | .093 | .418 | 583 | 58 | 146 | 241 | .106 | .286 |
| Cleveland | 559 | 143 | 174 | 294 | .229 | .279 | 423 | 95 | 101 | 239 | .194 | .205 |
| Washington | 324 | 88 | 86 | 135 | .219 | .215 | 211 | 48 | 30 | 92 | .180 | .111 |
| Memphis | 280 | 17 | 91 | 126 | .070 | .365 | 353 | 12 | 89 | 169 | .039 | .280 |
| Milwaukee | 601 | 72 | 208 | 215 | .125 | .359 | 564 | 66 | 143 | 297 | .112 | .245 |
| San Diego | 472 | 47 | 126 | 130 | .125 | .334 | 592 | 42 | 114 | 212 | .079 | .215 |
| Columbus | 346 | 34 | 124 | 133 | .108 | .393 | 401 | 49 | 100 | 176 | .132 | .269 |
| Tampa | 355 | 24 | 79 | 145 | .068 | .221 | 385 | 38 | 67 | 192 | .103 | .182 |
| St. Louis | 485 | 130 | 177 | 239 | .232 | .316 | 345 | 73 | 83 | 74 | .176 | .200 |
| New Orleans | 356 | 33 | 117 | 180 | .094 | .332 | 304 | 46 | 70 | 163 | .139 | .213 |
| Indianapolis | 334 | 44 | 112 | 155 | .132 | .338 | 557 | 29 | 136 | 273 | .064 | .306 |
| Boston | 573 | 81 | 179 | 301 | .127 | .283 | 500 | 59 | 109 | 263 | .110 | .203 |
| Atlanta | 274 | 51 | 80 | 119 | .221 | .347 | 226 | 64 | 50 | 99 | .255 | .199 |
| Denver | 411 | 56 | 125 | 175 | .144 | .324 | 430 | 53 | 104 | 191 | .126 | .247 |
| San Francisco | 814 | 124 | 238 | 381 | .139 | .265 | 809 | 97 | 175 | 392 | .119 | .216 |

*U.S. Bureau of the Census (b, Table 4); (e, Table 15).

‡This table does not include data on persons moving from metropolitan areas, but it is highly unlikely that moves of this distance are made to escape desegregation and/or the threat of desegregation.

student. The correlation between the 1968 levels of central city school segregation and the 1955–60 white city-to-ring rate of migration was only –.095 while the 1968 levels of segregation were only correlated at .038 with the 1965–70 rates of white central city-to-ring migration. Surprisingly, however, the 1955–60 and 1965–70 rates of white city-to-ring migration are more closely associated with 1973 levels of segregation (.308 and .265, respectively), but these correlations are in the opposite direction of what the school desegregation–white-flight hypothesis would lead us to expect. Moreover, when compared to the correlations mentioned above they tend to suggest that white city-to-ring migration has a greater impact on segregation than vice-versa, and that the association between these two variables becomes stronger when a time-lag is allowed to operate.

While these data do not suggest that school desegregation and the threat of desegregation lead to white-flight, it is important to note that a far more rigorous test of the hypothesis is needed. For instance, as noted earlier we have not identified the reasons for moving, we have only documented the extent of movement during two periods of time. Similarly, it is possible that the decline in central city-to-ring mobility is related to changes in the deconcentration of the metropolitan population and the centrifugal movement of manufacturing and business activity. Yet, these general processes of metropolitan development have continued, and it seems reasonable, therefore, to conclude that there is not much evidence to support the desegregation–white-flight hypothesis.

## Demographic Influences on Public School Segregation

Absolute changes in the number of central city public school students can result from a number of different sources. Increases in this population may result from (1) the migration of school-aged children into central cities, (2) the movement of larger birth cohorts into school attendance age than birth cohorts leaving school attendance age, (3) the addition of population through the annexation of territory, and (4) the transfer of students from private to public schools. Decreases in the number of central city public school students, on the other hand, can result from (1) the migration of school age population from cities, (2) the advance of smaller birth cohorts into school attendance age than birth cohorts leaving school attendance age, (3) the transfer of public school students to private schools, and (4) the attrition of students from such sources as deaths and dropping out. When interest is in changes in the proportional representation of whites and blacks, it is important to consider the relative contribution from each of the above sources within each population separately; each source may differentially contribute to the total change in each population. In short, changes in proportional number result from changes in the absolute numbers of both blacks and whites; thus, to explain the former it is necessary to consider all of the sources of change in the latter in each population separately.

While direct data are not readily available to estimate the contribution of each component to the absolute change in the central city public school population of each racial group, some data are available to indicate that factors other than recent migration influence the relative number of whites in central cities. For instance, in the first panel of Table 2 the median ages of the black and white female central city populations are shown from 1950, 1960, and 1970. In most cities the general pattern is a marked aging of the white female population and a sharp decline in the median age of the black female population. Moreover, even in those cities where the white female population did not age, the black female population became younger so that in all cities, relative to the white, the black population became younger. Changes such as these result not only from migration, but also from other factors such as annexation and reproductive change; in turn, such changes in the relative age composition of the black and white population influence their respective reproductive potentials. In general, young populations can be expected to produce more children than older populations (Coale). Thus, the combined influences of the historical pattern of white migration from cities and black migration to cities, coupled with difference in rates of natural change produced by the 1960s central city black populations whose reproductive potential was higher than the white central city populations has led to a decline in the proportion of the population that is white.

The fact that these two segments of central city populations aged in opposite directions is important. Equally important is the variation in the magnitude of the changes which did occur. In 7 cities (Houston, Dallas, Memphis, San Diego, Columbus, Indianapolis, and Denver) the median age of the white female population declined over the 20-year period, but only in Columbus and Indianapolis did this decline exceed 3.4 years. In these cities, however, there was a pronounced decline in the black female median age; the decline was at least six years in all except Houston where it was 5.2. Among cities where the white female population did age, the median increased by at least 7 years in 7 of the cities (New York, Philadelphia, Detroit, Baltimore, Washington, St. Louis, and San Francisco), and with the exception of the first two and last one, each exhibited a decline in the black female median of at least four years. In all of the remaining cities, the white female median age increased by less than 7 years but more than 4 years except in Milwaukee and Atlanta while the declines in the black median ranged from 3.7 in Cleveland to nearly 13 in Boston. In short, although the black female populations in all cities became younger relative to the white populations, there was a considerable variation in the extent to which this resulted from changes in the white and black female populations and the magnitudes of the changes in each.

These data are significant because they indicate the extent of variation in the combined influence of all the components of population change on the composition of the white and black central city populations. However, they are also important because of the strong influence age composition has on the birth rate.

**TABLE 2.** Median Age of the White and Black Central City Female Populations and Crude Birth Rates of the White and Black Central City Populations: 1950, 1960, 1970*

| CENTRAL CITY | MEDIAN AGE | | | | | | CRUDE BIRTH RATE | | | | | |
| | White | | | Black | | | White | | | Black | | |
| | 1950 | 1960 | 1970 | 1950 | 1960 | 1970 | 1950 | 1960 | 1970 | 1950 | 1960 | 1970 |
|---|---|---|---|---|---|---|---|---|---|---|---|---|
| New York | 28.9 | 31.3 | 37.6 | 30.1 | 27.9 | 26.8 | 18.0 | 18.6 | 16.3 | 28.9 | 30.7 | 24.6 |
| Los Angeles | 33.2 | 33.1 | 33.4 | 31.1 | 27.7 | 25.6 | 19.8 | 20.1 | 17.6 | 27.1 | 33.1 | 23.9 |
| Chicago | 30.4 | 32.5 | 36.6 | 29.5 | 25.6 | 23.7 | 20.1 | 21.3 | 16.8 | 31.1 | 36.9 | 27.9 |
| Philadelphia | 30.6 | 33.9 | 37.9 | 29.3 | 28.2 | 26.5 | 18.7 | 19.5 | 15.2 | 28.2 | 29.9 | 23.1 |
| Detroit | 27.8 | 31.8 | 39.7 | 28.8 | 26.3 | 24.3 | 23.3 | 19.0 | 16.9 | 31.7 | 27.8 | 26.4 |
| Houston | 28.8 | 28.1 | 27.8 | 28.2 | 24.8 | 23.0 | 28.9 | 18.5 | 20.8 | 34.6 | 30.1 | 26.4 |
| Baltimore | 31.5 | 35.0 | 39.4 | 28.2 | 24.9 | 23.7 | 19.0 | 19.8 | 14.3 | 30.4 | 34.3 | 22.1 |
| Dallas | 31.2 | 31.1 | 30.4 | 30.2 | 25.2 | 22.3 | 25.9 | 24.0 | 20.0 | 28.1 | 38.5 | 28.4 |
| Cleveland | 28.9 | 29.8 | 33.7 | 28.8 | 26.6 | 25.1 | 22.3 | 23.0 | 19.0 | 30.1 | 30.3 | 24.2 |
| Washington | 34.7 | 42.4 | 45.7 | 29.8 | 27.6 | 25.6 | 21.4 | 17.9 | 9.8 | 30.7 | 32.7 | 24.1 |
| Memphis | 30.2 | 30.7 | 29.3 | 29.2 | 25.5 | 22.7 | 21.6 | 21.8 | 17.3 | 30.6 | 34.0 | 26.9 |
| Milwaukee | 30.6 | 29.9 | 32.0 | 26.8 | 20.6 | 19.7 | 17.4 | 25.3 | 17.7 | 38.0 | 43.3 | 29.8 |
| San Diego | 31.1 | 29.4 | 29.4 | 28.8 | 22.5 | 21.6 | 25.3 | 24.4 | 36.0 | 36.4 | 40.2 | 33.9 |
| Columbus | 31.8 | 29.0 | 26.9 | 30.7 | 26.2 | 24.2 | 23.2 | 26.7 | 21.9 | 26.2 | 32.4 | 26.2 |
| Tampa | 31.7 | 32.7 | 36.0 | 31.0 | 26.4 | 24.2 | 29.9 | 35.4 | 21.1 | 35.4 | 29.7 | 32.7 |
| St. Louis | 34.1 | 37.6 | 44.0 | 30.6 | 37.0 | 24.6 | 22.0 | 22.3 | 16.7 | 30.1 | 34.9 | 25.3 |
| New Orleans | 32.5 | 34.6 | 37.9 | 28.5 | 25.5 | 23.5 | 22.3 | 21.4 | 15.1 | 33.6 | 33.7 | 24.4 |
| Indianapolis | 32.6 | 32.0 | 29.1 | 30.7 | 27.3 | 24.2 | 23.8 | 27.8 | 16.1 | 28.4 | 35.4 | 24.8 |
| Boston | 28.2 | 30.1 | 32.2 | 29.1 | 25.7 | 19.6 | 19.9 | 21.1 | 16.1 | 28.3 | 36.2 | 24.7 |
| Atlanta | 32.3 | 33.8 | 35.4 | 30.1 | 26.7 | 24.4 | 18.7 | 21.1 | 17.4 | 51.4 | 31.2 | 25.5 |
| Denver | 31.8 | 31.8 | 30.5 | 29.7 | 25.4 | 23.7 | — | 23.4 | 18.7 | — | 32.9 | 25.6 |
| San Francisco | 34.4 | 38.5 | 41.4 | 28.2 | 24.9 | 25.3 | 18.4 | 17.3 | 12.7 | 35.7 | 31.4 | 22.7 |

*U.S. Bureau of the Census (a, Table 53; c, Table 20; d, Table 24); U.S. National Center of Health Statistics (a, Table 13; b, Table 3-1; c, Table 2-1).

Yet, it is important to examine actual birth rates since these are affected by a number of factors in addition to age composition. The crude birth rates for the white and black central city populations in the second panel of Table 2 clearly indicate the extent to which the black population has had a strong propensity to produce more potential students than the white population. Moreover, the general trend in these rates suggests that this gap was the widest in many of these cities around 1960 when much of the later school age population was being born. In the cities where this was the case, it resulted from a tendency for white birth rates to be about equal in 1950 and 1960 before declining by 1970 while black birth rates increased during the early period before declining by the latter. The important point, however, is that there has been a history of substantial differences in the relative number of black and white births, and this has favored a decline in the percent of students white.

One method which can be employed to obtain a general idea of the potential of differences such as those in the Table is to assume a closed population and let these rates operate for a number of years. For example, if we apply the 1950 birth rates of New York's white and black populations to populations numbering 1,000 in the first year and allow them to grow through time, in 10 years the total number of births from both populations would be 524, but nearly 63 percent of the births would be black. In reality, of course, a number of additional factors such as differences in infant mortality and migration influence the outcome of such birth rate differentials. But the magnitude of these differentials makes it less surprising that Coleman et al. (79) should find that white flight (the proportion of white students in the central city public schools) is greatest at the elementary level.

Finally, if reproductive differentials significantly affect levels of public school segregation, we should expect that they are inversely related to the Coleman et al. (38) measure of the proportion of white schoolmates for the average black. That is, the higher the crude birth rate differential (where black birth rates are higher than white) the lower the proportion white schoolmates for the average black. The latter measure, however, represents the effects of the birth rate differentials which were operating during each of the years when all the children in school were born while the birth rates we have are only for a single year, and must therefore be viewed merely as an indicator of the reproductive factor.

With this shortcoming in mind, we correlated the difference between the black and white birth rates in 1960 with the proportion white schoolmates for the average black in 1973 expecting that if the former does influence the latter the two variables should be inversely related. The resulting coefficient (-.433) indicates that the two variables are related in the predicted direction. Similarly, when the differences in the proportion white schoolmates to average black between 1968 and 1973 (Coleman et al., 38) were correlated with the 1960 birth rate differentials (a plus one was added to each of the former to eliminate negative signs), the obtained coefficient (-.431) strongly suggests that where black fertility is higher than white, increasing segregation can be expected.

## Conclusions

While there can be little doubt that the recent migration of whites from central cities is contributing to the patterns of school segregation in many cities, these data indicate that recent migration patterns are probably contributing much less to this phenomenon than has been suggested by many previous investigators. Our analysis indicates that the levels of school segregation in cities and changes in these, as well as differences in levels between cities, are influenced by the reproductive differentials of blacks and whites. Indeed, the simple correlation coefficients presented suggest that differences in segregation between cities are more closely related to birth rate differentials than they are to white-flight, and the comparison of the volume and rate of white city-to-ring migration during two periods of time indicates that in many of the cities examined there has actually been a decline in white-flight.

Unfortunately our analysis, like that of all previous researchers, lacks data on the reasons for white moves. It is possible that even though there has been a decline in the volume and rate of white city-to-ring migration, more whites are leaving cities to escape desegregation. If this is the case, it is important to note that (1) it has not yet been established, and (2) city-to-ring migration is usually done not for one, but for various reasons. The migration data presented in this paper, however, do suggest that if there is white-flight, its volume is not making whites flee cities any faster than they have in the past. Finally, our analysis does show that to try to infer white-flight from declining proportions of white public school students can grossly overstate the volume of this factor not just because it assumes that all whites move to escape school desegregation, but also because it fails to take account of the substantial birth rate differential between whites and blacks in all cities. This differential has been strongly influenced by migration but not merely by white-flight. In this sense, it is important to take account of the historical patterns of white migration from central cities and black migration to central cities, and the effects which these counter movements have had in the composition of the respective central city populations. Our analysis indicates a substantial aging of the white population in many cities and a concomitant decline in the age of all black central city populations. These changes are likely to insure a decreasing proportion of white students in central cities.

## References

Coale, A. J. 1964. "How a Population Ages or Grows Younger." In Ronald Freedman (ed.), *Population: The Vital Revolution.* New York: Anchor Books.
Clotfelter, Charles T. 1974. "The Detroit Decision and 'White Flight.'" Unpublished Ph.D. dissertation, Harvard University.

Coleman, James S., Sara D. Kelly, and John A. Moore. 1975. *Trends in School Segregation, 1968–73*. Washington: The Urban Institute.

Farley, R. 1975. "Racial Integration in the Public Schools, 1967 to 1972: Assessing the Effects of Governmental Policies." *Sociological Focus 8* (January):1–26.

Giles, M. W., E. F. Cataldo, and D. S. Gatlen. 1975. "White Flight and Percent Black: The Tipping Point Re-examined." *Social Science Quarterly 56*(June): 85–92.

Kasarda, J. D. 1976. "The Changing Occupational Structure of the American Metropolis: Apropos the Urban Problem," in an issue sponsored by the *American Journal of Sociology* entitled *The Changing Faces of the Suburbs*, ed. by Barry Schwartz. Chicago: University of Chicago Press.

Rossell, C. H. 1975. "The Political and Social Impact of School Desegregation Policy: A Preliminary Report." Presented at annual meeting of the American Political Science Association.

U.S. Bureau of the Census. a:1952. *U.S. Census of Population: 1950. Vol. II, Characteristics of the Population*. Washington: Government Printing Office.

——. b:1963. *U.S. Census of Population: 1960. Subject Reports. Mobility for Metropolitan Areas*. Final Report PC(2)–2c. Washington: Government Printing Office.

——. c:1963. *U.S. Census of Population: 1960. Vol. I, Characteristics of the Population*. Washington: Government Printing Office.

——. d:1971. *U.S. Census of Population: 1970. Final Report PC(1), Characteristics of the Population*. Washington: Government Printing Office.

——. e:1973. *U.S. Census of Population: 1970. Subject Reports. Mobility for Metropolitan Areas*. Final Report PC(2), 2c. Washington: Government Printing Office.

U.S. Civil Rights Commission. 1975. *Twenty Years After Brown: Equality of Educational Opportunity*. Washington: Government Printing Office.

U.S. National Center of Health Statistics. a:1953. *Vital Statistics of the United States, 1950. Vol. II*. Washington: Government Printing Office.

——. b:1963. *Vital Statistics of the United States, 1960. Vol. I*. Washington: Government Printing Office.

——. c:1975. *Vital Statistics of the United States, 1970. Vol. I*. Washington: Government Printing Office.

# 44

# Desegregation Rulings and Public Attitude Changes: White Resistance or Resignation?

## CARDELL K. JACOBSON

What effect does a court ruling which orders a city to desegregate its schools have on the attitudes and feelings of residents of the city? Are attitudes about racial issues hardened or eased? Is there increased resistance or resigned acceptance?

Two alternative reactions to a court desegregation order might be predicted from social theory and research. On the one hand, considerable research shows that greater prejudice and resistance to integration emerge as situations become increasingly specific, concrete, intimate, and proximate (Westie 1965). Moreover, many who "favor" integration as an abstract principle are nevertheless opposed to busing as a means of achieving it. These studies suggest that whites will become more resistant to integration after an important desegregation decision because imminent racial contact has become significantly more likely. According to this view, one would also expect whites to resist and change more on specific items such as the desirability of busing as a means to achieve racial balance than on more general items such as the desirability of integration. This

Abridged from *American Journal of Sociology 84* (1978): 698–705. Used by permission of The University of Chicago Press. ©1978 by The University of Chicago. All rights reserved.

argument also predicts that parents with children in the public schools are more likely to change than either those who do not have children in the schools or those who have children in parochial schools, since parents of public school children are the only ones directly affected by the court order. We shall call this theoretical orientation the proximity-resistance argument.

At the same time another body of research literature suggests that at least some people will respond positively or show resigned acceptance of a desegregation order. Numerous studies suggest that attitudes conform to an accomplished fact. (For a more thorough review of this literature, see Pettigrew [1971, chap. 11].) Hyman and Sheatsley (1964) have shown that public acceptance of integration accompanied integration of the public schools in the South. The continuance of this trend is indicated as late as February 1976, with the Gallup Poll reporting that only 15% of white southern parents objected to sending their children to a school where a few of the children were black, a decrease from 61% in 1963 (Gallup Opinion Index 1976, p. 9).

In more specific research on the law and attitude changes, Colombotos (1969) found that the percentage of physicians in New York State who favored the Medicare hospitalization program for the elderly jumped from 38 before the law was passed to 70 in the 10 months after it was passed (but still before it had been implemented). Muir (1967) also found that the Supreme Court decision banning prayer in public classrooms resulted in general attitudinal compliance by officials and teachers in one public school system, though the changes were facilitated or impeded by various other groups to which they belonged. Thus it is clear that at least some legal rulings can affect attitudes before the law is actually implemented. We shall refer to this attitude-conformity literature and its theoretical orientation as the social-adjustment argument.

The social-adjustment argument also predicts a "negative" reaction to integration on the part of parents whose children attend parochial schools. Whether intentionally or not, these parents have made a decision that has exempted their children from the integration order and guaranteed their attendance in predominantly white schools. Thus negative reactions to an integration order would help justify their children's attendance at a parochial school.

## Method

The data reported here are from two telephone surveys conducted by the *Milwaukee Journal* research staff for a series of articles on a desegregation case against the Milwaukee Public Schools. The first survey was conducted in May and early June of 1975. The case had been heard by the federal court more than a year earlier. On January 19, 1976, the judge ruled that the school system was illegally segregated and appointed a special master to oversee the formation and implementation of a desegregation plan. Busing was not mentioned in the decision though it was not ruled out. The ruling involved only the City of Milwaukee; the suburbs were not affected. The second survey was begun one week after the ruling (and some eight months after the earlier survey) and, though shorter than the first, included several items from the earlier survey.

The samples were obtained through random digit dialing. This procedure eliminates most of the biases usually present in telephone surveys, including unlisted numbers (8% in Milwaukee), unpublished numbers (an additional 4%), and out-of-date directory numbers. Professional interviewers conducted the interviews. The refusal rate was a low 7%, and complete data were obtained for almost all respondents. . . .

The first survey elicited complete response data from 563 white and 122 black city residents. The second, smaller survey obtained complete data from 317 whites and 65 blacks. Owing to the small number of blacks in the samples the analysis focuses only on the changes in white attitudes. . . . The characteristics of the sample matched closely those found in the special city census taken in 1975.

The substantive items from the surveys included both general race relations questions and specific items about integration and busing (see table 1). Answers allowed for items 1, 2, and 5 were: yes, don't know, and no. Item 3 could be answered: a lot, a little, or not at all. Item 4 was scored on a four-point scale: objection to some, half, or more than half minority students, or no objection. The last two specific items on busing were scored on a five-point scale from strongly approve to strongly disapprove.

It should be noted that the predictions are not concerned with differences between the three groups per se but rather with the direction and differences in the amount of change in each of the three groups: To assess these differences the interaction component of an analysis of variance using an unweighted means solution was examined. A separate analysis of variance was conducted for each item using the full range of responses. (The table reports grouped data for clarity.) Since the analysis of variance does not tell which groups changed, a further test, Duncan's multiple-range test—an a posteriori test from the analysis of variance—was conducted for the appropriate comparisons. . . Note, however, that the test of the two theoretical orientations is based on the direction of the results as well as the statistical significance of the comparisons.

# Results

The direction of the results for the general item of desirability of integration as a goal (1) provides weak support for the social-adjustment argument (see Table 1). The interaction between time and groups was not statistically significant, however, nor were the individual tests for the two groups of primary interest, parents with children in public schools and parents with children in parochial schools. On the somewhat peripheral items of perceived discrimination (2) and neighborhood integration (3) the results were mixed. The smaller percentage of parents with children in the public schools who say there is discrimination supports the proximity-resistance argument, but the even larger negative reaction by parents of children in parochial schools lends support to the social-adjustment theory. The interaction effect was also significant. The fact that all three groups became more negative may reflect changed attitudes about affirmative action programs more than changes in attitudes about discrimination. Likewise, the decrease in item 3 may reflect larger attitudinal changes in society. Neither item 2 nor 3 provides strong support for either theoretical argument.

The results on the specific school issues are more clear-cut (items 4 through 7). The interaction is significant on three of the four items. Furthermore, on each of the four items the changes for the parents of students in the public schools are all in the direction that supports the social-adjustment argument. Fewer parents of public school children object to their children attending school with minority students, more approve of busing from other neighborhoods into their own, and slightly more approve of busing from their neighborhood to other neighborhoods. The changes on some items are quite small, but the differences in the direction of attitudinal change by the three different groups as well as the magnitude of the changes are of theoretical interest. Thus it is important that parents with children in the public schools, on each item, became more supportive of integration and busing, while the others either showed no change or became less supportive.

The results from parents of the parochial school students on three of the four items also support the social-adjustment theory. There was no change on item 5, but on the other three specific school items these parents exhibited strong negative change.[1] A much larger percentage of these parents would object to their child being in a school where some or half of the students were minority students, and fewer said they would approve of busing either into or from their neighborhood. The change on these last two items was even more dramatic among the parents of the parochial students who strongly disapproved. The percentage of parents who strongly disapproved of busing into their neighborhood increased from 45.8 to 75.8, while on the bus-out question the percentage rose from 52.5 to 81.8.

We had predicted that there would be more change on the specific items than on the more general items. A close examination of the changes reported in table 1 reveals that this did not occur, except for parents of parochial school students. There is, however, much more consistency on the specific items than on the

[1] Alternatively, these changes may reflect changes in the enrollment patterns of public and parochial schools. However, two factors argue against such an interpretation of the results. First, the second survey was completed soon after the ruling (within two weeks). Thus parents did not have time to withdraw their students from the public schools and enroll them in parochial schools before they were interviewed. Second, the enrollment patterns in the Milwaukee Public School system show no dramatic change in the years preceding the decision. Like most urban public school systems, Milwaukee had experienced declining enrollments for a number of years, but the patterns show no change that can be attributed to the ruling. In fact, the decline from 1974–1975 to 1975–76 (the year the case was heard) appeared to be levelling off from the previous declines (. . . 1972–73–128,488; 1973–74–123,452; 1974–75–118,584; and 1975–76–115,708). [See Selection 43.]

**TABLE 1.** Attitudinal Changes of White Parents (by Presence or Absence of Children) to Desegregation Ruling

| SURVEY ITEMS | MAY 1975 | JANUARY 1976 | CHANGE | THEORETICAL ORIENTATION SUPPORTED |
|---|---|---|---|---|
| | | *Percentages* | | |
| | | *General Racial Issues* | | |
| 1. In general, do you believe that racial integration of the schools is a desirable goal? (Yes): | | | | |
| Children in public schools[a] | 43.3 | 46.4 | +3.1 | Social adjustment (weak) |
| Without children in schools[b] | 49.6 | 40.1 | −9.5** | — |
| Children in parochial schools[c] | 48.3 | 40.6 | −7.7 | Social adjustment (weak) |
| Total | 47.9 | 41.5 | −6.4 | — |
| 2. In general, do you think that minorities are discriminated against in obtaining jobs? (Yes):* | | | | |
| Children in public schools | 31.9 | 20.3 | −11.6** | Proximity-resistance |
| Without children in schools | 28.3 | 25.1 | −3.2 | — |
| Children in parochial schools | 39.3 | 9.1 | −30.2** | Social adjustment |
| Total | 30.4 | 22.4 | −8.0 | — |
| 3. If a family of another race with about the same income and education as you moved next door, would you mind it a lot, a little or not at all? (A little or a lot): | | | | |
| Children in public schools | 24.4 | 11.5 | −13.1** | Social adjustment |
| Without children in schools | 21.2 | 15.8 | −5.4 | — |
| Children in parochial schools | 26.7 | 18.2 | −8.5 | Neither |
| Total | 22.6 | 15.1 | −7.5 | — |
| | | *Specific School Issues* | | |
| 4. Do you or would you object to your children attending a school where *some (half, more than half)* of the students are of another race? (Some of half):* | | | | |
| Children in public schools | 34.6 | 26.5 | −8.1 | Social adjustment |
| Without children in schools | Not asked of parents without children in school | | | |

412

| | First survey | Second survey | Change | Theory |
|---|---|---|---|---|
| Children in parochial schools | 28.3 | 45.5 | +17.2** | — |
| Total | 32.7 | 32.6 | -0.1 | Social adjustment |

5. Would you approve or disapprove of busing children to a school outside their neighborhood to achieve racial integration in schools? (Approve):

| | First survey | Second survey | Change | Theory |
|---|---|---|---|---|
| Children in public schools | 22.0 | 29.0 | +7.0 | Social adjustment |
| Without children in schools | 22.8 | 23.0 | +0.2 | — |
| Children in parochial schools | 16.9 | 18.2 | +1.3 | Neither |
| Total | 22.0 | 23.8 | +1.8 | — |

6. How do you feel about busing of children *from other neighborhoods into your neighborhood* so that schools will be racially integrated? (strongly approve to strongly disapprove). (Approve or strongly approve):*

| | First survey | Second survey | Change | Theory |
|---|---|---|---|---|
| Children in public schools | 21.9 | 27.5 | +5.6 | Social adjustment |
| Without children in schools | 20.8 | 18.6 | -2.2 | — |
| Children in parochial schools | 22.0 | 9.1 | -12.9** | Social adjustment |
| Total | 21.2 | 19.6 | -1.6 | — |

7. How do you feel about busing children *from your neighborhood to schools in other neighborhoods* to achieve racial integration? (Approve or strongly approve):*

| | First survey | Second survey | Change | Theory |
|---|---|---|---|---|
| Children in public schools | 12.0 | 14.4 | +2.4 | Social adjustment |
| Without children in schools | 18.3 | 16.3 | -2.0 | — |
| Children in parochial schools | 14.8 | 3.0 | -11.8** | Social adjustment |
| Total | 16.3 | 14.5 | -1.8 | — |

[a] $N = 142$ in the first survey, 69 in the second survey.

[b] $N = 360$ in the first survey, 215 in the second survey.

[c] $N = 61$ in the first survey, 33 in the second survey.

*$P < .05$ for interaction of group and time (analysis of variance).

**$P < .05$ based on Duncan's multiple-range test, an a posteriori contrast test from the analysis of variance. Note, however, that the test of the theories is based on direction of the results, as well as the statistical significance of these individual tests. Further, as one reviewer rightfully noted, the analysis of variance tests were not completely independent and thus the "experiment-wide" level of significance is something higher than the .05 reported for each individual test.

general ones. In fact, if one considers only items 1, 4, 5, 6, and 7, which deal specifically with school issues, there is strong support for the social-adjustment theoretical orientation. The expected differences in direction appear in all five cases for the parents of students in the public schools and are present in four of the five cases for the parochial school students (the binomial probability of obtaining results supportive of one theory nine times out of 10 is .02).

It is important to note that the positive changes among parents with students in the public schools occurred during a time when some national leaders and social scientists questioned whether busing, at least in large cities, is an appropriate means of achieving integration. Furthermore, these changes occurred despite negative attitudinal changes in the total community (see totals for the items in Table 1).

## Implications

The results have important implications. A sizable literature has emphasized negative reactions to court-ordered integration and busing. However, in this case the judge's ruling resulted in favorable attitude changes among those most affected, parents of the students in the public schools. Furthermore, though busing was not mentioned by the judge, the favorable attitude changes included attitudes toward busing, not just integration.

The history of integration in the United States certainly shows that most Americans will accept integration—although the stance taken by the community leaders is a critical variable affecting community response to integration. In Milwaukee most leaders, including the mayor and city council, were generally supportive of the desegregation ruling. The majority of the school board members, the defendants, were not. Under these conditions we have found some acceptance of the desegragation ruling. The positive changes by the parents of the public school children are perhaps small, but they loom large considering what caused them (and considering how deeply entrenched racial prejudice is in American society). There were no increased intergroup contacts, no changes in school feeder patterns, no increased neighborhood integration. There was only the ruling. Like several earlier investigators of law and attitudes we have found that the law can change public opinion. . . .

## References

Colombotos, John. 1969. "Physicians and Medicare: A Before-After Study of the Effects of Legislation on Attitudes." *American Sociological Review 34* (June): 318–34.

Gallup Opinion Index. 1976. Report no. 127 (February). Princeton, N.J.: American Institute of Public Opinion.

Hyman, Herbert H., and Paul B. Sheatsley. 1964. "Attitudes toward Desegregation." *Scientific American 211* (July): 16–23.

Muir, William K., Jr. 1967. *Prayer in the Public Schools: Law and Attitude Change*. Chicago: University of Chicago Press.

Pettigrew, Thomas F. 1971. *Racially Separate or Together?* New York: McGraw-Hill.

Westie, Frank R. 1965. "The American Dilemma: An Empirical Test." *American Sociological Review 30* (August): 527–38.

# 45

# Conceptual Frameworks for the Analysis of Race Relations: An Evaluation

*ERNEST A. T. BARTH* and *DONALD L. NOEL*

This paper presents a general frame of reference designed to classify and focus the major theoretical perspectives which have relevance for the sociology of race and ethnic relations. Societies and their subsystems of racial and ethnic differentiation constitute the units of analysis and the central concern is to analyze race and ethnic relations within the context of general sociological theory. The central theoretical task confronting sociology is that of explaining how order is achieved, maintained, and altered in social systems. Accordingly, a sociological analysis of race and ethnic relations must explain the observed variations in the dependent variables specified by this task. More precisely, this involves explanation of the emergence, persistence, adaptation, and change of systems of ethnic differentiation. The empirical problems posed by this set of dependent variables may be stated as follows:

1. What structural conditions and processes account for the *emergence and initial stabilization* of various types of ethnic differentiation?

Reprinted, abridged, from *Social Forces 50* (March 1972): 333–348. Copyright © The University of North Carolina Press.

2. What structural conditions and processes account for the long-range *stability* of systems of ethnic differentiation?

3. What structural conditions and processes account for *adaptation* in systems of ethnic differentiation through time?

4. What structural conditions and processes account for *change* of systems of ethnic differentiation through time?

The major objective of any scientific theory is to explain the observed variation in the significant dependent variables. Once these variables have been identified, various theoretical frameworks may be evaluated in terms of the power and efficiency of their explanations. The independent variables which are combined to constitute the propositional base of a general theory are selected so as to provide maximum explanatory power relative to the dependent variables. The search for efficient independent variables is facilitated by classifying the potentially relevant variables, both dependent and independent, in terms of their rates of variation over the different time periods. Some variables manifest relatively high rates of variation over short periods of time while others vary little in the short run, their variations being observable only over fairly long periods of time. For example, the relative economic power of black Americans changes little from year to year whereas the behavior of individual whites towards blacks fluctuates rapidly as a function of the situation. Variables which manifest very little variation in the short run can, for all practical purposes, be considered as constants for studies limited to such time periods. On the other hand, a trend curve fitted to short-run variables frequently reveals little long-run variation. Such variables may be considered constants for purposes of long-run analysis. Hence, given the fundamental premise that a constant cannot explain a variable, nor a variable a constant, it may be concluded that the independent variables selected to explain the variation in a dependent variable should vary at roughly the same rate as the dependent variable.

Selecting the relevant variables is the first step toward theory; but a theory, conceived as a set of logically interrelated propositions which explain observed phenomena, never emerges full blown. Conceptual tinkering and experimentation are vital to the emergence of a theory, and a conceptual frame of reference is the usual forerunner of a theory. The frame of reference includes a set of assumptions and postulates regarding the nature of reality, one or more empirical problems to be explained, and a cluster of interrelated concepts which define what is to be observed in order to construct a meaningful explanation. Theory exists only with the emergence of explanatory propositions, but the frame of reference significantly affects the theory which is constructed because, as Newcomb (1950:94) says, it "functions as a preceptual context which exercises a selective influence upon the way in which something is perceived."

Sociologists have elaborated a number of frames of reference for analyzing behavior. The race-cycle framework constitutes a special case of an evolutionary model of society and was developed with race relations specifically in mind. The consensus, interdependence, and conflict frameworks are derived from the three

|  | Conceptual Framework | | | |
| SOCIOLOGICAL PROBLEM | RACE CYCLE | CON-SENSUS | INTER-DEPEN-DENCE | CONFLICT |
| --- | --- | --- | --- | --- |
| Emergency | 1 | | | 2 |
| Persistence | | 1 | 2 | 2 |
| Adaptation | | 2 | 1 | 2 |
| Change | 2 | 2 | 2 | 1 |

Key: 1 denotes area of primary contribution.
     2 denotes area of secondary contribution.

**FIGURE 1.   Major Conceptual Frameworks Related to the Key Problems in the Sociology of Race and Ethnic Relations**

major models utilized in contemporary sociology—structural functionalism, symbolic interactionism, and conflict—and are applicable to a wide range of behavior. While each framework ostensibly provides a conceptual base for constructing a general theory of race and ethnic relations, the frameworks vary in their utility dependent upon the specific empirical problem to be explained (see Figure 1). Hence, a combination of frameworks must be utilized if we are to construct an adequate general theory. Accordingly, the present objective is to review each conceptual framework in order to delineate the implied propositions and make explicit the relevance of each framework for the explanation of the major empirical problems in the field.

## The Race-Cycle Framework

The race relations cycle framework is uniquely suited to the task of explaining variations in the structural patterns of emerging systems of ethnic differentiation. In essence it proposes that variations in the precontact characteristics of the groups coming into contact combine with variations in patterns of initial contact to produce predictable variations in the initial structure of ethnic differentiation. This natural history approach entails both a major strength and a major weakness as regards the analysis of race relations. On the one hand the emphasis upon process, which derives from the inherently evolutionary nature of a cycle approach, is a valuable reminder that race relations are dynamic and continuously marked by change. On the other hand, the cycle approach as initially formulated by Robert E. Park (1950) posits a unilinear evolution of race relations which is quite inconsistent with their development in many societies. This defect has largely been remedied by subsequent modifications of Park's original cycle.

Unfortunately, race-cycle theorists have not capitalized on the framework's inherent emphasis on process. Rather they have analyzed discrete stages in the cycle without carefully specifying the key variables or structural conditions associated with movement from one stage to another. In addition, there has been a tendency to overextend the application of the framework. Rather than restricting it to the analysis of the emergence and initial stabilization of a particular interethnic system, proponents of the race cycle have tried to use it to explain stability, adaptation, and change also. While the race cycle may have some relevance for these problems, other frameworks have greater power to explain the evolution of the system from an initially stabilized position. Moreover, the explanatory utility of the race cycle is largely limited to the emergence of the initial pattern of ethnic differentiation involving any two ethnic groups. While the breakdown of the initial pattern of ethnic differentiation might be viewed as signaling the start of a new race cycle, subsequent patterns are much more crucially influenced by the intimate relationships and institutionalized power differentials characteristic of the prior pattern than they are by conditions of precontact and initial contact. In short, the cycle approach is most adequate to explain the emergency of the pattern of ethnic differentiation which follows initial contact.

In presenting his pioneer formulation of a race-cycle framework, Park (1950: 150) observed that:

> In the relations of races there is a cycle of events which tends everywhere to repeat itself . . . The race relations cycle which takes the form, to state it abstractly, of contact, competition, accommodation and eventual assimilation, is apparently progressive and irreversible. Customs regulations, immigration restrictions and racial barriers may slacken the tempo of the movement; may perhaps halt it altogether for a time; but cannot change its direction; cannot at any rate reverse it. . . .

This is clearly a unilinear evolutionary model as it implies that there is a probability of 1.00 that each stage of the cycle will lead to and culminate in the next with assimilation—amalgamation ultimately assured. A cursory inspection of cross-cultural data, or even a careful analysis of data on American ethnic relations, reveals the weakness of this position. In cases where initial contact has led to either annihilation or mass expulsion, the cycle is obviously terminated short of assimilation—amalgamation. In other cases, a temporary accommodation has reverted back to competition and resulted in a new form of accommodation. This is exemplified by the history of blacks in the colonies. They were reduced to the status of slaves after initially being accorded the status of bondsmen (Palmer, 1966). Thus, the initial (temporary and unstable) accommodation between any two groups may revert back to competition before generating a new accommodation and relations between groups may at any point in the cycle lead to stable outcomes other than assimilation. Indeed, there are at least five theoretically possible stable outcomes of interethnic contact:

1. Exclusion, encompassing expulsion and annihilation;
2. Symbiosis, a stable relation of more or less equally beneficial exchange between members of distinct sociopolitical systems;

3. Ethnic stratification, involving supersubordination within a single political system;

4. Pluralism, the equalitarian integration of distinct ethnic groups within a common political and economic system; and

5. Assimilation, the biological, cultural, social, and psychological fusion of distinct groups to create a new ethnically undifferentiated society.

It might be argued that exclusion, which terminates interethnic contact, is the only viable long-run alternative to assimilation inasmuch as the middle three outcomes are inherently unstable. This is perhaps true if one takes a very long-run time perspective, but from this perspective all structures (including assimilation) are inherently unstable. Moreover, it is both dubious and unfalsifiable (Lyman, 1968:18) to argue that groups which have not assimilated are nevertheless definitely going to assimilate—ultimately. The centuries-long separatism of the Jews, which may be duplicated by the French-Canadians and some American-Indian groups, suggests that it is more realistic to think in terms of a variety of relatively stable outcomes.

These inadequacies in Park's cycle have been largely resolved by elaborating the basic cycle. Brown (1934), for example, expanded the number of stages in the race cycle and estimated the probability of a variety of alternative succeeding steps (including three stable outcomes) at each of several stages in the cycle. More recently Lieberson (1961) has further refined the basic cycle by considering the relative power of the groups involved as a means of specifying the probability of conflict (introduced as an invariant second stage by Brown) and the predominant direction of assimilation (i.e., after the model provided by the host population or that provided by the migrants). A number of modifications of the original cycle, including hypothetical probabilities for each stage, are incorporated in Figure 2.

Given five possible stable outcomes of intergroup contact, the immediate task is to specify the conditions under which any given outcome is most likely. Three major classes of variables determine the *initial* outcome. These are the cultural and social-structural characteristics of the groups prior to contact, the characteristics of the migration—and the migrants, and the nature and context of the initial contacts. While it is highly desirable to assign relative weights to these variables, this is beyond the present level of development of the field. Hence, we must be satisfied to . . . illustrate the significance of several variables.

Among the significant precontact variables affecting the pattern of ethnic differentiation, the degree of cultural complementarity has probably been most frequently discussed. Lindgren (1938) stresses that cultural complementarity greatly facilitated the formation of stable symbiotic relations between the Tungus and Cossacks in Northwest Manchuria. Similarly, M. W. Smith (1940) indicates that the complementarity of economic interests and of marital attitudes between the Puyallup Indians and the early white migrants facilitated a quick and peaceful pluralistic outcome. However, when whites looking for land and timber migrated with their families, contacts became strained and the under-

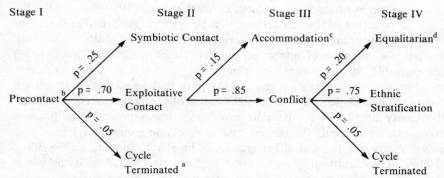

Stage I          Stage II          Stage III          Stage IV

a This schematization is a provisional one primarily intended to illustrate the logic of the race cycle. The indicated probabilities are necessarily hypothetical until an adequate sample of comparative studies is compiled.
b The most significant precontact variables include cultural complementarity, the patterns of migration (rate, composition, etc.), relative power, and the motives and goals of the migrants.
c Accommodation refers to all of the possible stable outcomes of interethnic contact, equalitarian or inequalitarian, *except* exclusion. The exclusion outcome, which includes both annihilation and mass expulsion, effectively terminates the cycle. The cycle may also be terminated by *total* assimilation but this outcome can only occur as the *culmination* of a *process* of assimilation which begins with initial contact.
d Equalitarian outcomes include assimilation, pluralism and symmetrical symbiosis.

**FIGURE 2.    The Race Cycle: A Specification of Stages and Outcomes**

mining of the Puyallup social structure commenced. Similarly, the contradictory patterns of belief concerning land ownership which characterized the Kikuyu peoples of Kenya and the European settlers led to a long period of struggle (Leakey, 1954) which even today has not been fully resolved. Recently Mason (1970:153-154) has emphasized the relative sociocultural complexity, or stage of development, of the contacting groups as another critical determinant of the emergent pattern of ethnic differentiation.

At least three distinct aspects of the pattern of migration have been linked to variations in the initial pattern of ethnic differentiation. These are the type of migration, the causes of migration, and the characteristics of the migrants. At present, the independent effects of different aspects of migration have not been adequately isolated from their combined effects but a variety of propositions have been advanced relating the emergence of a given pattern of ethnic differentiation to such variables as the unit of migration, the goals of the migrants, the rapidity of their influx, and their specific motives for migrating (e.g., see Degler, 1971:228-232; Mason, 1970:148-152). Significant advances in this area wait further development and synthesis of typologies of migration primarily focused upon the analysis of racial and ethnic relations (e.g., see Lieberson, 1961; Price, 1969:190-213, 228-232; Schermerhorn, 1970:96-102).

The influence of the precontact variables and of the pattern of migration is focused and mediated by the structure of the initial contacts. The significance of structural influences for the subsequent development of race relations is revealed by van den Berghe's (1970:68-78) comparative analysis of acculturation and

miscegenation in Africa and the Americas. Schermerhorn (1970) has also emphasized the structure of the contact situation by specifying different sequences or
"recurrent historical patterns" of emergence as contexts which significantly
mediate the outcome of intergroup contacts. More specifically, Noel (1968)
has suggested that ethnocentrism, competition, and relative power decisively
structure the contact situation and thereby provide the basis for constructing a
theory of the emergence and initial stabilization of ethnic stratification. In brief,
the theory holds that competition provides the motivation for stratification,
ethnocentrism channels the competition along ethnic group lines, and relative
power determines whether either group will be able to subordinate the other.
If either ethnocentrism or competition is moderate to mild or if the power
differential is small an equalitarian outcome is likely, whereas a marked degree
of all three will give rise to an inequalitarian outcome. These variables affect
not only the initial pattern of ethnic differentiation but all subsequent patterns.

Once a system of ethnic differentiation is established, attention shifts to the
problem of maintenance of that system. All structures are eventually eroded or
revamped, abandoned or overhauled; but when they have just been established
the immediate concern is to forestall change. This characteristically involves an
attempt to legitimate the new structure inasmuch as continued reliance upon
sheer power is highly inefficient. As Park (1950:150) observed, "The struggle
for existence terminates in a struggle for status, for recognition, for position and
prestige within an existing political and moral order." Hence, we need to evaluate the consensus framework as a solution to the problem of persistence.

## The Consensus Framework

Although the consensus framework has relevance for the origin, adaptation,
and change of systems of ethnic stratification, its primary value inheres in the
explanation it provides for the persistence of an established system. From the
consensus perspective "it is a condition of the stability of social systems that
there should be an integration of the component units to constitute a 'common
value system'" (Parsons, 1954:388). In short, the consensus framework posits
a high degree of value consensus within and between all segments of society as
the crucial factor in the persistence of social structure. This explanation is
rooted in both the symbolic—interactionist and the structural-functional models
of society.

The structural-functional roots are revealed by the basic assumptions about
the nature of man and society which underlie the framework's explanation of
structural persistence. Consensus-oriented sociologists are inclined to stress that
the various structural units or elements (whether concrete groups or functional
subsystems) of societies are mutually dependent and therefore the well-being of
the whole requires the cooperation of the parts and promotes the welfare, or
interests, of the parts. This postulated identity of interests between the parts

and the whole permits the assumption that stratification, which the function-alists view as a requirement of societies as social systems, is compatible with the needs of all or most of the society's component units. From the Parsonian point of view, stratification reflects the extent to which various social units adhere to the values derived from the society's basic needs or requirements. Consensus theorists argue that without common values the stratification structure would be highly unstable inasmuch as the inequitable distribution of rewards would not be perceived as legitimate. Finally, these theorists postulate that societies and their component structures tend to persist. Once established, a stratification structure may survive for generations simply because it is unchallenged. The postulate that man is a creature of habit and custom reinforces the postulate of structural persistence by affirming, as Lenski (1966:32) states, that men "accept and take for granted even those distributive arrangements which work to their disadvantage and are not essential."

The symbolic-interactionist model of society provides an additional basis for the consensus explanation of structural persistence. For interactionists, individ-uals interacting in a bounded situation constitute the basic unit of society. Social behavior is assumed to be organized and purposive (i.e., goal oriented); *and* stable, cooperative, goal-directed behavior requires *shared* symbols. The essence of symbolic interactionism is that men do not interact by reacting to one another's actions *per se* but rather they interpret or define each other's actions (Blumer, 1962:180). The meaning of an act is not inherent in or intrinsic to the act; hence, cooperative interaction requires that any given action (includ-ing vocal) has the same meaning for the various participants. In short, "the definition of the situation provides the frame of reference of social interaction, and . . . organized social relations presuppose the existence of a body of common definitions among the groups members" (Miyamoto, 1959:51). As men acquire shared meanings and values regarding a host of actions, objects, and persons, they acquire a culture which allows them "to predict each other's behavior most of the time and gauge their own behavior to the predicted behavior of others" (Rose, 1962:11-12; also see Blumer, 1962:183-184, 187-190). Shared defini-tions, rooted in shared meanings and values, are conceived as basic to stability in social relations.

The role of shared definitions is crucial in the realm of interethnic relations. Ethnicity is by no means an entirely subjective phenomenon but the social definitions of ethnicity and of appropriate intergroup behavior are highly significant. Numerous physical traits are highly visible, but in any given society few are associated with institutionalized discrimination. An individual is not assigned to a specific ethnic group because he shares certain observable charac-teristics with other members of the group. He is assigned because there is general agreement (consensus) that he belongs to the group regardless of whether there are actually any physical or cultural similarities. Only by acknowledging the ultimate importance of the shared social definition can we explain the fact that a physically white, obviously Caucasoid person can be classified as a Negro in the United States while a dark-skinned, obviously Negroid person may be classified as "white" (i.e., *branco*) in Brazil. When men define themselves as fundamentally alike or different, they act in accordance with this definition regardless of its veracity. As Shibutani and Kwan (1965:38) state, "What is of decisive importance is that human beings interact not so much in terms of what they actually are but in terms of the conceptions that they form of themselves and of one another."

Insofar as ethnicity is considered important, consensus regarding the ethnic identity of participants in an intergroup situation is a necessary but not a sufficient condition for stable interaction. Unless the minority and dominant participants embrace common conceptions regarding appropriate or proper behavior vis-à-vis each other, stain and/or conflict will characterize the relationship. These shared conceptions must be complementary. That is, where a white defines a black as subordinate, the black must define the white as superordinate if stress is to be minimized. Moreover, the means (form and content) of expressing deference and superiority must be agreed upon. Where this degree of consensus is achieved, stability is built into the pattern of interethnic relations and the stratification system in general. Normative consensus indicates that dominant and subordinate alike view the system as just and proper (i.e., moral) and therefore neither will seek to alter the system (Shibutani and Kwan, 1965:280). Indeed, given value consensus and the absence of incompatible structural elements, changes in interethnic or any other action patterns might well be "viewed as deriving from 'external' sources, and thus in some sense accidental" (Moore, 1960:811).

The perfect integration attendant upon complete value-consensus and structural compatibility is only approximated in any society. The postulate of perfect integration stems from the systemic theory of society. The concept of societies as social systems is a very useful heuristic device, but we must bear in mind that concrete societies are not "perfect" systems. The various structural elements are asymmetrically interdependent and thus almost inevitably unevenly integrated into the whole. Modern urban societies in particular are characterized by structural variations in dependence upon the whole. This differential autonomy generates diverse interests which are then justified by diverse (and sometimes conflicting) values. Unequal dependence and the associated diversity of interests and values is rooted in the increasing social differentiation and functional specialization of urban societies. The structural ambiguity (i.e., uncertainty in role behavior due to absent, ambiguous, or conflicting norms and values) characteristic of urban-mass societies necessarily impairs the efficiency and effectiveness of value consensus as a stabilizing mechanism. Conflicting principles of social control and social organization not only persist in urban societies, they may well be inherent in such societies in that they reflect contradictory functional requirements of social systems (Sjoberg, 1960; also see Moore, 1960:815; van den Berghe, 1963; Wagley and Harris, 1958:241–242).

This, of course, does not deny that consensus is a highly significant *factor* in the stabilization and integration of many, if not most, urban societies to say nothing of less highly differentiated societies. Value-consensus generally tends to be achieved through deliberate, rational processes and there are many such attempts in contemporary urban societies. For example, legal processes tend to create and maintain a consistent set of legal norms and the dialogue between theologians, philosophers and social critics serves the same function in the realm of moral and ethical norms. As societies urbanize, however, their stability does becomes increasingly based on interdependence with the result that the need for consensus *between* social units is greatly reduced. Thus, by stressing values to the exclusion of interdependence and coercive power, the consensus framework provides only a partial explanation of stability. Recent analyses of "plural societies" (e.g., M. G. Smith, 1965; van den Berghe, 1965) clearly demonstrate that a high degree of consensus is not an essential basis of societal integration and persistence.

The plural society is one characterized by fundamental differences, even incompatibilities, in the institutional systems (i.e., beliefs, values, and interaction patterns) adhered to by different segments of the society. In making value-consensus prerequisite to the existence of a stable social system, the reality of plural societies is ignored. M. G. Smith (1965:88, 86, xi) notes that "the monopoly of power by one cultural section is the essential precondition for the maintenance of the plural society" and "in order that the consensual theory may apply to the plural society, we are required to interpret all modes of subordination as willing submission, and thus as *prima facie* evidence of shared moral sentiments between the subordinate and dominant group." Clearly communication symbols must be shared between groups and there must be widespread conviction regarding the morality of the system among members of the dominant group if the plural society is to be stable. However, the critical issue is the presence or absence of consensus *between* groups on other than communication symbols. The absence of such consensus in plural societies such as South Africa and the British West Indian societies necessitates reliance upon coercion and interdependence as sources of unity and stability.

Theoretically, both interdependence (especially symmetrical) and coercion may generate consensus over time. Blumer (1966), in challenging the necessity of common values as the basis for joint action, notes that compromise, duress, mutual advantage, and sheer necessity may all motivate stable cooperation and he adds: "in very large measure, society becomes the formation of workable relations." These workable relations, even if highly inequalitarian, may eventually be redefined as traditional and accepted as right and proper by all concerned. Nevertheless ethnically stratified societies characterized by dissensus, tension, and internal contradictions have persisted for long periods. Leaving aside the moot issue of whether consensus or conflict is more basic in social systems (for diverse viewpoints on this issue, see Adams, 1966; Horton, 1966; Williams, 1966), we conclude that:

1. The consensus framework makes its primary contribution to a compre-

hensive theory of intergroup relations via the explanation which it provides for the problem of stability of established patterns of ethnic relations; and

2. In general, consensus is probably the single most important and most efficient basis of maintaining ethnic patterns although it is never the only basis and in some societies it is of very little importance.

It is undoubtedly true that patterns of ethnic relations as well as total societies are invariably maintained by some combination of consensus, interdependence, sociability, and coercion (Williams, 1966; also see Blumer, 1966:538–539; van den Berghe, 1970:82–84).

## The Interdependence Framework

In all societies the various component social units are interrelated and dependent upon each other to some degree. As role differentiation and specialization increase—i.e., as the society urbanizes—these interdependencies become increasingly extensive and vital to the survival of the society (Hammond, 1966). In the urban society, interdependence forces social groups or subsystems to cooperate with each other, regardless of value-consensus or dissensus, in order that each may achieve a variety of goals which they cannot achieve alone. Individuals of diverse value orientations must take each other's desires and values into account because each needs the other in order to maximize their own outcomes. As Heilbroner (1962:4) states, "We are rich, not as individuals, but as members of a rich society, and our easy assumption of material sufficiency is actually only as reliable as the bonds which forge us into a social whole."

In the rapidly changing urban environment this prevasive interdependence is highly relevant to the maintenance of order.[7] The explanation of order, defined as an arrangement of parts into a whole characterized by the capacity to function as a unit in its environment, constitutes sociology's theoretical focus because order subsumes the more heralded stability and change. The problem of adaptation, the maintenance of order, is unique precisely because it overlaps both stability and change. This unique nature must be clarified before the relevance of interdependence is analyzed.

Adaptation is an empirical problem distinct from both stability and change. As opposed to stability, adaptation requires that social systems be receptive to modifications to assure that they will not be destroyed by their own rigidity in the face of internal contradictions and environmental changes (Coser, 1956: 155–157). In short, the maintenance of order is not identical to the maintenance of the status quo. Conversely, as opposed to change, adaptation envisions that only a few structures (preferably the less essential ones) be permitted to vary at any given time and these at rates not exceeding rather severely restricted limits (e.g., see Olsen, 1968:150–151). However, it is not minimal change but the minimization of change which defines adaptation. Only that degree of change which is essential to the maintenance of order is adaptive. At the limit, fundmental change of one or more system elements may constitute the only possible adaptive response, but generally order is maintained via the incorporation of minor modifications within a basically unchanged system. Hence, adaptation ceases to be a distinct sociological problem only in the limiting cases. In general the difference between adaptation and stability inheres in the fact of system modification; that between adaptation and change inheres in function—the former maintains an existent order while the latter creates a new order.

From the perspective of any specific group or subsystem the adaptive problem is one of maximizing the group's outcomes. Thus we may describe a group's adaptive capacity as its ability to enhance its status relative to the other groups in a society. From the perspective of the society as a whole, however, adaptive capacity is the ability to maintain sufficient distributive justice between groups and sufficient efficiency in transactions with the environment to assure order. This requires adjustment to internal strains and external stresses without disintegration (i.e., disappearance as a distinct boundary-maintaining system). In essence, adaptation is the ability to respond to these stresses and strains with the degree of change necessary to assure the maintenance of an integrated system. This adaptive process may be a nonconscious, nondeliberative adjustment via traditional mechanisms, but in urban societies it is typically a conscious process involving contention between distinct interest groups. In either event, adaptation implies a moving equilibrium—an ordered process of change which does not disrupt ongoing social processes (see Angell, 1965:151; Parsons and Shils, 1954: 107).

The relevance of interdependence for adaptation inheres in two inescapable consequences of the fact of interdependence:

1. It creates awareness throughout the system of pressures for change affecting any part of the system; and

2. It provides sanctions to curtail or eliminate these pressures.

Interdependence necessarily requires a concern with pressures for change for it implies that any "disturbance"—be it an internal strain or an external force—occurring in or impinging upon any part of the system will ramify throughout and have significant consequences for numerous parts of the system. From such a perspective, change is hardly likely to be defined as a rare and inconsequential phenomenon. Rather the interdependence perspective envisions change as a pervasive phenomenon which may be initiated at any structural point. The potential disruptiveness of change necessitates that pressures toward change be carefully observed and taken into account if order is to be maintained. If the pressures for change are internal, interdependence leads to the imposition of sanctions which must be heeded because the element seeking change is dependent upon the other elements (Olsen, 1968:151). If the pressures are external, the entire system makes an adjustive response because all of the elements are directly or indirectly affected due to their interrelatedness. In either event, the change instituted is the minimal change perceived to be consistent with the maintenance of order in the system as a whole.

Adaptive processes—pressures for change and responses to them—occur continually. This is necessarily so, short of a society which is completely insulated from the environment and characterized by perfect consensus and perfect structural compatibility. Structural imperfections—e.g., marked life-chance differentials unsupported by perfect consensus—generate many or few adaptations primarily as a function of the scope and degree of interdependence. Scope refers to the range and number of ties between elements in a system. Scope is universal (extensive) when each pair of system elements interconnect, and intensive when the interconnections between each pair of elements are multiple. The degree of interdependence refers to the variations in mutuality in the ties between any pairs of elements. Symmetry represents the ultimate degree of interdependence while highly asymmetrical interconnections represent minimal interdependence.

The crucial effects of the scope and degree of interdependence upon the adaptive process are summarized in the following two propositions. First, the greater the intensive and extensive scope of interdependence between system elements (e.g., ethnic groups), the greater the number and effectiveness—other things being equal—of social change attempts initiated by the element(s) having greater functional autonomy. Second, the closer the approach to symmetrical interdependence between elements, the greater the number and effectiveness—other things being equal—of social change attempts initiated by the element(s) having lesser autonomy. In short, symmetry is positively related to "progressive" adaptations (i.e., those conducive to greater equality) while scope is negatively related. As applied to race relations this means that, with symmetry held constant, increases in the scope of interdependence work to the dominant group's advantage while decreases (e.g., via increasing separatism) work to the subordinate group's advantage. Conversely, with scope held constant, an increase in symmetry benefits the subordinate group while a decrease facilitates further imposition of inequality by the dominant group. As regards scope, the primary source of leverage is the number of opportunities to exert control; as regards symmetry, the primary mechanism is that of relative resources.

Our analysis here is compatible with van den Berghe's (1970:84) assertion that "The more economic interdependence there is, the less feasible apartheid becomes." Unfortunately, South African reality is one of highly asymmetrical interdependence: "Although it is true that the *prosperity* of the whites depends entirely on the nonwhites, the sheer day-to-day *survival* of the nonwhites depends directly on the industrial complex now controlled by the whites" (van den Berghe, 1967:139). . . .

In addition to technological changes, demographic and a variety of other changes in life conditions may alter the pattern (i.e., scope and degree) of interdependence and set the adaptive process in motion (Shibutani and Kwan, 1965: 341-371). As a result of changing conditions which affect a slight change in the power balance (in either direction), new sociocultural forms which do not materially affect the existing system of ethnic stratification are institutionalized.

For example, due to the now acknowledged ability of blacks to disrupt the social order, token changes have occurred in the policies and practices of many organizations including unions, political parties, and boards of education. Thus, transfer of some black students to previously all-white high schools is not intended to promote integration so much as to prevent continued disruption of the local educational system. Similarly, the removal of discriminatory clauses from union constitutions may have little effect on actual racial practices. Such changes are adaptive insofar as they represent concessions which function to maintain order and forestall more sweeping changes. Of course, order may also be maintained by introducing adaptive changes which are repressive or inequalitarian in nature. Thus, South Africa has consistently "improved" its repressive techniques while steadfastly resisting significant alteration of key elements of its social structure (Kuper, 1965:29, 68-70; van den Berghe, 1965:216, 1970: 210-223).

If successful, adaptive modifications of the existing sociocultural pattern prevent basic structural changes in the short run. They do this by repression or by partially satisfying the interests of the subordinate groups, thereby simultaneously reducing pressure upon and reinforcing the legitimacy of the established system (Dahrendorf, 1959:224-225, 233-234). Nevertheless, adaptations may be the precursors of extensive change in the long run (Coser, 1957:202). Those who benefit from the adaptive concessions may sooner or later use their new resources as a basis for launching a more sweeping protest. . . . [T]he better educational facilities provided for black Americans in the period 1940-52 in an effort to ward off the 1954 Brown Decision have undoubtedly been a factor in the abundance of effective leadership and organizational talent in the civil rights movement of the 1960s. The cumulative impact of negative adaptations—i.e., concessions to groups seeking to institutionalize or strengthen a pattern of inequality—may also generate significant structural change. Where positive adaptive mechanisms (e.g., mobility, political participation) are denied or severely constrained, revolt is possible. Thus, the increasingly repressive steps being taken by the Nationalist party to institutionalize apartheid in South Africa may result in violent rebellion by the black Africans and their allies (van den Berghe, 1965). . . .

Adaptation thus stands between stability and change. It preserves the status quo essentially unchanged in the short run via timely concessions, but these concessions often foreshadow basic change via the gradual accretion of resources. Interdependence, as a derivative of its general unifying function, provides a crucial basis for mediating and mitigating stresses and strains that threaten social order. It generalizes sensitivity to the need for system modifications and facilitates their introduction by providing the necessary sanctions. In spite of this adaptability, however, radical structural changes ultimately occur in all aspects of social systems. Thus, an adequate theory of ethnic differentiation must account for major changes in a given pattern of ethnic relations as well as for the pattern's origin, persistence and adaptation. To this we now turn.

## The Conflict Framework

The analysis of social change inevitably engenders consideration of conflict. A conflict relationship is one in which the interacting social units are oriented toward the attainment of incompatible or mutually exclusive goals (Dahrendorf, 1959:135, 209). The goals being sought by the parties to the conflict may be the same or different. The crucial factor is simply that the participants perceive the situation as one where goal attainment by their group is inversely related to goal attainment by the other group. Conflict so conceived has relevance for each of the major theoretical problems posed in this article. It is frequently a factor in the emergence of a system of ethnic relations and it may also promote stability, once the system is established, via an uneasy equilibrium between more or less equal contenders. Conflict may also promote either adaptation or basic system change. These varied consequences indicate that conflict by itself does not automatically generate change. Nevertheless, the conflict framework has traditionally been focused upon the explanation of change and the present contention is that conflict is more useful than alternative perspectives in understanding change in established structures of ethnic relations.

With its central assumption that change is inherent in social systems the conflict perspective is necessarily oriented toward change. Social change is viewed as inherent because it is rooted in certain inevitable structural conditions. These include the fact of a changing environment but also the inevitable existence of structural incompatibilities, the inherent dysfunctional aspects of fundamental social structures (e.g., authority structures), and the existence of inequalities in power, material comforts, and other desirable rewards. Schermerhorn (1961:54–55) notes that: "the various subunits of any society—and particularly the more complex ones—are marked by disparities in numbers, cohesive organization, and resources. . . . This basic asymmetry is an essential human condition, a circumstance that sets the currents of social change in motion." These structural incompatibilities, power differentials, and other structural "flaws" inevitably generate conflict oriented toward improving the status of one's own group, be it ethnic, economic or political.

The nature of conflict—i.e., the pursuit of incompatible goals—necessarily means that to the extent that one group obtains its goals the opposing group must fail to obtain its goals. This leaves a continuing interest in change which, although it may remain latent for a time following the resolution of any specific conflict, will reemerge under certain conditions to stimulate active conflict anew. This continuing interest in change and reemergence of conflict does not guarantee change in any given instance. Nevertheless, the persistent interest of some segment of the population in change is consistent with the assumption that change is ubiquitous. The assumption is not unique to the conflict framework, nor would it constitute an explanation of change if it were, but its centrality facilitates the selection of concepts which are relevant to the analysis and explanation of change. Thus, the conflict framework stresses the concepts (i.e., variables) whose precise measurement enables social scientists to specify both the arena of conflict and the probability of change.

These concepts—e.g., vested interests, power, coercion—facilitate the derivation of two key propositions implicit in the conflict framework. First, conflict centers around vested interests—i.e., the crucial, shared values or objects in which some groups have an established claim which operates to the disadvantage of other groups. Differential vested interests assure that pressures for change will be opposed and thereby generate a continuous struggle for power and advantage. Second, changes in the relative coercive power of the contending groups largely determine the direction and extent of social structural change. Unless the power balance has been altered no change should be expected to result from conflict.[1] The perpetuation of a traditional power balance contributes to the stability of the established system. By contrast, when the power balance is modified, fundamental change awaits only the perception of this redistribution of power and its subsequent translation into organized action (Blalock, 1967: 109–112, 126–131). Dominant groups no less than subordinate groups characteristically seek to expand and take advantage of increases in their power in order to reinforce or advance their interests (Schermerhorn, 1961:55).

While the conflict view has ancient roots its modern impetus was provided by the Marxian emphasis upon the inevitability of the clash of groups with divergent interests. While Marx emphasized social classes as the primary units of conflict, American conflict has been equally or more often structured along ethnic group lines. A few scholars (particularly Cox, 1959) have interpreted American race relations in essentially Marxian terms, but the general emphasis has been upon race *per se* as the basis of group identification, loyalty and cleavage. Until World War II the race-caste system in the United States was relatively stable precisely because the power differential between blacks and whites was so vast and stable. In the absence of major external pressure upon American society, Negroes had to be "content" with minor improvements in their status.

Since World War II the situation has changed markedly. The general international situation, the emergence of the African nations and changes in the black community have resulted in a genuine shift in the power balance underlying the American race-caste system (e.g., see Isaacs, 1963). The adaptive changes of previous decades were cumulative and by the late 1940s a Negro middle class had emerged with sufficient strength to act as the decisive catalylst necessary to effectively challenge the race-caste system (Kronus, 1971:12–15). The organizational skills and leadership initially provided by the middle class generated triumphs which stimulated group pride, solidarity, and collective self-awareness

---

[1] La Piere (1965:479–480) ignores this point and thus unwisely dismisses the conflict framework as a means of explaining change on the grounds that conflict can occur without consequent change. In truth, it is not conflict *per se* but the power balance which crucially affects the persistence and change of social patterns. Thus, the power framework (Blalock, 1967:109) or the power-conflict framework (Schermerhorn, 1970) is a more appropriate name.

which in turn stimulated mass participation in the civil rights movement. At this point there was a shift in strategy; away from litigation with its achievement of concessions—albeit increasingly significant concessions—to organized mass protest with the objective of achieving complete freedom and equality for blacks *now*. The movement is divided with respect to how extensively the fabric of American society as a whole must be changed to achieve this objective, but there is virtual unanimity as regards the primary significance of organized power as the instrument for achieving whatever basic changes are necessary. This power may be expressed via guerrilla warfare, peaceful (but disruptive) demonstrations, or via negotiation as a powerful (and therefore respected and accepted) pressure group participating as an equal in the traditional American political process.

Ethnicity has always been a significant factor in American politics. The enduring importance of ethnic interest groups has been masked by the cultural myth that civil rights are the rights of individuals. Now, however, the mask has been removed for, as Danzig (1964:41) says, ". . . the Negro has made us forcefully aware that the rights and privileges of an individual rest upon the status attained by the group to which he belongs—that is to say, by the power it controls and can use." Blacks are simply the most recent American minority to organize and effectively marshal their rights and advance their interests. The conflict and struggle so characteristic of the racial arena in contemporary America is typically a correlate of significant change in systems of ethnic stratification. Basic change is rarely smooth, automatic, and continuous. Rather it tends to be convulsive, episodic, and discontinuous for: ". . . rigidities in social structures may require opposition forces to gather momentum before they can effect adjustments [and hence] the dynamics of social structure is (sic) characterized not so much by continuously adjusted equilibrium states as by intermittent reorganizations in a dialectical pattern" (Blau, 1964:11).

The clash of opposing interests (economic, political, or otherwise) is central to basic change in the group structure of society, but this does not deny that other frameworks contribute to a comprehensive understanding of change. For example, interdependence may be interwoven with conflict in such a way that they jointly produce basic change. That is, interdependent groups may react against one another as well as in concert, and when they (Olsen, 1968: 151–152; van den Berghe, 1963: 702–703) do clash basic change is usually generated. Our analysis has emphasized the primary utility of each perspective with no intent of implying a unicausal explanation of a given problem.

## Conclusions

Race relations are social relations and hence they pose the same kinds of analytic problems for the sociologist as are posed by other types of social relations. Thus, in the sociological study of race and ethnic relations, the objective is to explain how patterns of ethnic differentiation emerge, how they are stabilized and maintained through time, and how they ultimately disintegrate or are transformed. Since the analytic problems or issues are the same, the sociological models which guide and inform the analysis of other aspects of the social structure should also facilitate the analysis of race and ethnic relations. In short, we contend that understanding of race and ethnic relations is most likely to be advanced by focusing on general sociological issues.

Unfortunately, sociologists have rarely dealt with the problem of the emergence of complex social patterns and this has certainly been true in regard to patterns of stratification, as Lenski (1966:ix) has reminded us. Thus our effort to understand the origin of ethnic patterns has focused upon specification and refinement of Park's pioneer race-cycle framework. (Perhaps the analysis of various contact cycles—and particularly those initiated by internal differentiation rather than migration—will provide clues useful in the development of a theory of the origin of social structures generally.) The initial contacts between peoples who differ in ways that are defined as socially significant can lead to a variety of outcomes, and the cycle framework calls attention to a number of variables which affect the outcome. In particular, we suggest that ethnocentrism, competition, and the relative power of the groups involved constitute a set of variables which are necessary and sufficient to explain the emergence of ethnic stratification, which is perhaps the most common outcome of initial contact.

Given the establishment of any system, the problem of persistence becomes crucial. Drawing from the consensus and conflict frameworks, it is clear that both common values and differential power are commonly relied upon means of assuring the continuance of a given system. Consensus makes its primary contribution in the solution of this problem but this does not necessarily mean that it is always the most important stabilizing factor. Indeed, consensus is of relatively minor importance in the stability of the "plural" societies. Nevertheless, it seems justified to conclude that while consensus may or may not be the most important or the most effective stabilizing factor, it is clearly the most efficient way to maintain a system of ethnic differentiation.

The stability of a given system is also crucially affected by the flexibility or adaptability of its various structural components. The fact of structural interdependence both necessitates adaptability and increases the probability that it will be forthcoming. Interdependence enhances the sensitivity of the parts to the forces affecting the system as a whole and the resulting "knowledge" of the state of the whole moderates both the demands for and the resistance to change exhibited by various parts. Interdependence constitutes a major basis of societal integration and as van den Berghe (1963:697) has stated, "Relatively integrated societies can change faster than societies in a state of strain and conflict." Such adaptability promotes survival inasmuch as minor changes or concessions to structural subgroups (or the environment) constitute a safety valve capable of significantly prolonging the basic features of the status quo.

Ultimately, of course, systems do change in fundamental respects, and the cumulative impact of adaptive concessions may be a significant factor in basic structural change. However, whether such cumulation is a factor or not, radical change is generally rooted in the clash of vested interests and alterations in the power balance. Appeals to basic values (e.g., the Supreme Court's 1954 decision on school segregation) play a role in generating change but the changes resulting from such appeals are usually adaptive, not radical. If the emergence of a powerful, organized group willing to use its power (procedurally if possible, violently if necessary) against the entrenched establishment is not a prerequisite of radical change, it at least seems accurate to say that the use of such power is more effective than the appeal to legitimacy. It is also more efficient in terms of rapidity but not necessarily in terms of the human costs involved.

In assigning coercion the primary role in securing change, and consensus a major role in structural stability, we are in no sense equating consensus with stability and conflict with change. Rather we have repeatedly stressed that multiple perspectives are essential to a comprehensive explanation of each of the major empirical problems posed. This explanation is not advanced, however, by ignoring the apparent primacy of a given variable or perspective vis-à-vis a given problem. In short, we are advocating a strategy of allocation (Schermerhorn, 1970:52, 234) by applying a specific framework primarily, but not exclusively, to the explanation of a specific empirical problem. If our application of general sociological perspectives to race relations is on the right track, the next step is to engage in comparative analyses oriented toward measuring the explanatory contribution of the various frameworks, singly and in combination, much more precisely. The present general framework constitutes a schema which hopefully will facilitate the collection and organization of the comparative data necessary to achieve this increased precision.

# References

Adams, B. N.
  1966   "Coercion and Consensus Theories: Some Unresolved Issues." *American Journal of Sociology 71* (May): 714–717.
Angell, Robert C.
  1965   *Free Society and Moral Crisis.* Ann Arbor: University of Michigan Press.
Blalock, Hubert M.
  1967   *Toward a Theory of Minority-Group Relations.* New York: Wiley.
Blau, Peter M.
  1964   *Exchange and Power in Social Life.* New York: Wiley.
Blumer, H.
  1962   "Society as Symbolic Interaction." Pp. 179–192 in Arnold M. Rose (ed.), *Human Behavior and Social Processes.* Boston: Houghton-Mifflin.
  1966   "Sociological Implications of the Thought of George Herbert Mead." *American Journal of Sociology 71* (March): 535–544.
Brown, W. O.
  1934   "Culture Contact and Race Conflict." Pp. 34–47 in Edward B. Reuter

(ed.). *Race and Culture Contacts*. New York: McGraw-Hill.

Coser, Lewis
1956    *The Functions of Social Conflict*. Glencoe: Free Press.
1957    "Social Conflict and the Theory of Social Change." *British Journal of Sociology 8* (September): 197–207.

Cox, Oliver C.
1959    *Caste, Class and Race*. New York: Monthly Review Press.

Dahrendorf, Ralf
1959    *Class and Class Conflict in Industrial Society*. Stanford: Stanford University Press.

Danzig, D.
1964    "The Meaning of Negro Strategy." *Commentary 37* (February): 41–46.

Degler, Carl N.
1971    *Neither Black Nor White*. New York: Macmillan.

Hammond, P. E.
1966    "Secularization, Incorporaton and Social Relations." *American Journal of Sociology 72* (September): 188–194.

Heilbroner, Robert L.
1962    *The Making of Economic Society*. Englewood Cliffs: Prentice-Hall.

Horton, J.
1966    "Order and Conflict Theories of Social Problems as Competing Ideologies." *American Journal of Sociology 71* (May): 701–713.

Isaacs, Harold R.
1963    *The New World of Negro Americans*. New York: Viking.

Kronus, Sidney
1971    *The Black Middle Class*. Columbus: Merrill.

Kuper, Leo
1965    *An African Bourgeoisie*. New Haven: Yale University Press.

La Piere, Richard T.
1965    *Social Change*. New York: McGraw-Hill.

Leakey, Louis S. B.
1954    *Mau Mau and Kikuyu*. New York: Day.

Lenski, Gerhard E.
1966    *Power and Privilege*. New York: McGraw-Hill.

Lieberson, S.
1961    "A Societal Theory of Race and Ethnic Relations." *American Sociological Review 26* (December): 902–910.

Lindgren, E. J.
1938    "An Example of Culture Contact Without Conflict: Reindeer Tungus and Cossacks of Northwest Manchuria." *American Anthropologist 40* (October–December): 605–621.

Lyman, S. M.
1968    "The Race Relations Cycle of Robert E. Park." *Pacific Sociological Review 22* (Spring): 16–22.

Mason, Philip
1970    *Race Relations*. London: Oxford University Press.

Miyamoto, S. F.
1959    "The Social Act: Re-Examination of a Concept." *Pacific Sociological Review 2* (Fall): 51–55.
Moore, W. E.
1960    "A Reconsideration of Theories of Social Change." *American Sociological Review 25* (December): 810–818.
Newcomb, Theodore
1950    *Social Psychology*. New York: Dryden.
Noel, D. L.
1968    "A Theory of the Origin of Ethnic Stratification." *Social Problems 16* (Fall): 157–172.
Olsen, Marvin E.
1968    *The Process of Social Organization*. New York: Holt, Rinehart & Winston.
Palmer, P. C.
1966    "Servant into Slave: The Evolution of the Legal Status of the Negro Laborer in Colonial Virginia." *South Atlantic Quarterly 65* (Summer): 355–370.
Park, Robert E.
1950    *Race and Culture*. Glencoe: Free Press.
Parsons, Talcott
1954    *Essays in Sociological Theory*. Glencoe: Free Press.
Parsons, Talcott, and Edward A. Shils
1954    *Toward A General Theory of Action*. Cambridge: Harvard University Press.
Price, C.
1969    "The Study of Assimilation." Pp. 181–237 in John A. Jackson (ed.), *Migration*. London: Cambridge University Press.
Rose, A. M.
1962    "A Systematic Summary of Symbolic Interaction Theory." Pp. 3–19 in Arnold M. Rose (ed.), *Human Behavior and Social Processes*. Boston: Houghton-Mifflin.
Schermerhorn, Richard A.
1961    *Society and Power*. New York: Random House.
1970    *Comparative Ethnic Relations*. New York: Random House.
Shibutani, Tamotsu, and Kian M. Kwan
1965    *Ethnic Stratification*. New York: Macmillan.
Sjoberg, G.
1960    "Contradictory Functional Requirements and Social Systems." *Journal of Conflict Resolution 4* (June): 198–208.
Smith, Michael G.
1965    *The Plural Society in the British West Indies*. Berkeley and Los Angeles: University of California Press.
Smith, M. W.
1940    "The Puyallup of Washington." Pp. 3–36 in Ralph Linton (ed.), *Acculturation in Seven American Indian Tribes*. New York: Appleton-Century.

van den Berghe, Pierre
  1963   "Dialectic and Functionalism: Toward a Theoretical Synthesis." *American Sociological Review 28* (October): 695–705.
  1965   *South Africa, A Study in Conflict.* Middletown: Wesleyan University Press.
  1967   *Race and Racism.* New York: Wiley.
  1970   *Race and Ethnicity.* New York: Basic Books.
Wagley, Charles, and Marvin Harris
  1958   *Minorities in the New World.* New York: Columbia University Press.
Williams, R. M., Jr.
  1966   "Some Further Comments on Chronic Controversies." *American Journal of Sociology 71* (May): 717–721.

# Index

Abrams, Elliott, 357, 359
Abrams, Franklin S., 357, 359
Adam, Barry D., xxxii*n.*
Adams, Bert N., 425, 434
Adams, Charles Francis, 36
Adelson, Joseph, 211, 213
Adorno, T. W., 133, 183*n.*, 228*n.*
Aigner, Dennis J., 243*n.*
Ainsfield Award, 90
Alabama Bureau of Business Research, 278*t.*
Alexander, Will, 48
Alford, Robert R., 332, 339
Alianza Federal de Mercedes, 259
Allport, Gordon W., 133
Aluminum Ore Company, 349
American Bar Association, 83
American Federation of Labor (AFL), 347, 354
American G.I. Forum, 261–62
*American Journal of Sociology (AJS)*, xxi, xxvii, 2–4, 6–7, 10, 15, 28, 33, 46, 48–50, 81, 91, 113, 122, 154–59, 168, 182, 200, 220, 287, 302, 408
American Sociological Association (ASA), xxi–xxiii, xxviii–xxix, 3, 5, 28, 46, 48–49, 89, 92, 130, 240
*American Sociological Review (ASR)*, xxvii–xxix, xxxii, 92, 131, 151, 163, 320, 341, 376
Angell, James R., 50
Angell, Robert C., 427, 434
Armor, D. J., 318*n.*
Aronson, Elliott, 339
Aurbach, Herbert A., 241*n.*
Averitt, Robert T., 357, 359

Back, Kurt W., xxviii*n.*, xxxii
Bahr, Howard M., 91*n.*, 92*n.*, 130*n.*, 133*n.*
Bailer, Lloyd H., 345, 350, 354, 359

Ballweg, John A., 240*n.*
Banks, W. S. M., 131*n.*
Baron, Harold M., 342, 359
Barth, Ernest A., xxx, 319
Barton, P., 183*n.*
Becker, Ernest, xxi–xxiii
Becker, Howard, xxv*n.*
Beecher, John, 89*n.*
Belin, H. E. A., 4*n.*
Belitsky, A. H., 288, 296
Berkowitz, Leonard, 321, 339
Bernstein, Irving, 352–53, 359
Berreman, Gerald D., 129*n.*
Bettelheim, Bruno, xxvi, 133
Beynon, E. D., 90*n.*
Bierstedt, Robert, 233–34, 247
Blackburn, Frank W., 3*n.*
Black Muslims, 254
Blackwell, James E., 5*n.*, 24*n.*, 30*n.*, 90*n.*, 128*n.*
Blalock, Hubert M., 240, 276*n.*, 333, 339, 366, 375, 431, 434
Blau, Peter M., 432, 434
Blauner, Robert, 239, 257, 263–64
Bloom, Leonard, xv, 132
Blumer, H., 423, 425–26, 434
Boas, F., 50
Boaz, Professor, 30
Bogardus, Emory S., xv, xvi, 91–92, 183*n.*
Bohn, Frank, 49*n.*
Bonacich, Edna, xxxi, xxxiii, 89, 315–17, 344, 347, 351, 354, 359
Bonapart, Napoleon, 42
Bossard, James H. S., 183*n.*, 236*n.*
Bowen, W. S., 382, 394
Bowman, M. J., 366, 375
Bracey, John, 128*n.*
Bressler, Marvin, 241*n.*
Brinton, Hugh, 93*n.*
Brody, David, 346, 349, 360

Brooks, Maxwell R., 130n.
Broom, Leonard, 364, 368n., 370, 374-75
Brotherhood Award, 133
Brotherhood of Sleeping Car Porters, 347
Brotherhood Week, 133
Brown, W. O., 420, 434
Brown v. Board of Education, xxviii,
  xxxiii, 49, 180-81, 196-99, 318, 429, 434
Bryan, William J., 73
Bryce, James, 35
Buchanan v. Varley, 83
Buckley, Edmund, 4n.
Burgess, Ernest W., 103n., 155, 233, 236
Burrus, B., 183n.

Cain, Glen G., 242n.
Campbell, Ernest Q., xxx, 183n., 208n.
Cantor, Milton, 361-62
Carmichael, Stokely, 257
Carnegie Corporation, 159
Carnoy, Martin, 361
Carter, Robert L., 182n.
Cataldo, E. F., 397, 407
Cayton, Horace R., 128, 347, 349-50, 354,
  360
Chavez, Dennis, 259
Chicago, 214-19
Chicago Commission of Race Relations,
  345, 352
Chicago Tribune, 83
Chinese Exclusion Act, xv
Civil Rights Act, 182, 240-42
Civil Rights Movement, xvii, xxxviii, 238
Clark, Kenneth B., 181n., 182n., 257
Clark, Terry N., 322, 330, 337, 339
Cleaver, Eldridge, 257
Clossen, Carlos C., 3
Clotfelter, Charles T., 397, 406
Coale, A. J., 403, 406
Cole, William E., 133n.
Coleman, James S., 242-43, 318n., 397-98,
  399n., 400, 405, 407
Coleman, John R., 241n.
Coleman, S., 384, 396
Collier, James, 3
Colombotos, John, 409, 414
Commission on Inter-Racial Cooperation:
  see Southern Regional Council
Committee to Abolish Racial Discrimina-
  tion, 354
Community Service Organization, 262
Comte, Auguste, xvii
Congressional Quarterly, 323, 339
Congress of Industrial Organizations (CIO),
  89, 354
Cook, S. W., xxviiin.
Cooley, Charles Horton, xxi, 5, 33, 151-53,
  157, 245
Coser, Lewis A., 245-46, 426, 429

Cox, Oliver Cromwell, xxiv, 128-30, 431,
  435
Crain, Robert L., xxx, 243, 288, 294,
  301, 318
Crisis, 5
Cromien, Florence, 242n.
Cullen, Countee, 139
Cutler, Stephen J., 93n.
Cutright, Phillips, 240n., 385, 394

Dahrendorf, Ralf, 245-46, 429-30, 435
Daniel, Johnnie, xxiv, xxx, 241
Daniel, V. E., 129n.
Danzig, D., 432, 435
Darwin, Charles, 12
Davis, Kingsley, 135, 138
Davis, W. Allison, 93, 136n., 141n.
Degler, Carl N., 421, 435
de Lapouge, Georges V., 3
Denver Opinion Research Center, 147
de Tocqueville, Alexis, xvii, 23-24
Dewey, John, 50
Dickens, D., 387, 395
Dickinson, P., 382, 395
Dillehay, Ronald C., 93n.
Divine, Father, 254
Dollard, John, 321, 339
Doob, Leonard, 321, 339
Dow, Grove S., 154
Downes, Bryan T., 322-23, 330, 332, 339
Drake, St. Clair, 128
Dubofsky, Melvin, 354, 360
DuBois, W. E. B., xiii, xxiv-xxv, 5, 26-28,
  49, 83, 91, 99n., 100, 101n., 109n.,
  128, 139
DuBois-Johnson-Frazier Award, 49, 130
Dugsdale, E. T. S., 140
Dunbar, Paul Lawrence, 41
Duncan, Beverly, 280n.-82n., 377, 382,
  394
Duncan, Otis Dudley, 280n.-82n., 382,
  397, 394-95
Durkheim, Emile, xvii

Edward, Alba, 170
Edwards, G. Franklin, 90n.
Eisenhower, President Dwight D., xxxiii,
  182
Ellison, Ralph, 303
Ellwood, Charles A., 154
Embree, E. R., 109n.
Equal Educational Opportunity Survey
  (EEOS), 242-43
Eutsler, Ronald B., 89n.

Fair Labor Standards Act, 353
Faris, Ellsworth, 48
Farley, Reynolds, xxxi, 317, 319, 363-65,
  375, 397, 407

Faubus, Governor Orval, 182
Featherman, David, 376, 380, 383, 387, 395
Federal Council of Churches, 133
Federal Emergency Relief Administration, 95
Ferman, Louis A., 357–58, 360
Fifteenth Amendment, 153, 274n.
Finegan, A. T., 382, 394
Fishman, Joshua A., 241n.
Fitzhugh, George, 151–52
Fogel, Walter A., 350, 356, 360
Folger, John K., 376, 395
*Footnotes,* xxiii
Ford, Henry, 353
Ford, President Gerald, 318
Forsyth, J. M., xxixn.
Foster, William Z., 348, 350, 360
Fourteenth Amendment, xiv, 4, 58, 180
Francis, Robert C., 89n.
Franklin, Charles L., 347, 354, 360
Franklin, John Hope, xviin.
Frazier, E. Franklin, xxiv, xxvi, xxxii–xxxiii, 89–92, 106n., 128, 129n., 130n.
Frederick the Great, 42
Freeman, R. B., 363, 375
Frenkel-Brunswik, Else, 183n., 228n.
Fuguitt, Glenn V., 240n.

Galle, Omer R., 385, 394
Gallup Poll, 409, 414
Galton, Francis, 3, 92, 152
Garbin, Albeno P., 240n.
Gardner, Burleigh B., 93, 136n., 141n.
Gardner, Mary R., 93, 136n., 141n.
Garfinkle, Stuart, 383, 395
Garrison, William Lloyd, 15
Garvey, Marcus, 254, 350
Garvey Movement, 61
Gaston, Jerry, xxxn.
Gatlen, D. S., 397, 407
General Allotment Act (Dawes Act), xiv
Gerth, Hans, 234n.
Giddings, Franklin H., xxi, xxii, 46, 151–53
Giles, M. W., 397, 407
Gilman, Charlotte P., 4n.
Gist, Noel P., 93n.
Glenn, Norval D., 240, 364, 368n., 370, 374–75
Glick, Paul, 385, 395
Goldblatt, Harold, 242n.
Gomillion, Charles C., 129
Gordon, David M., 342, 357, 360
Grafton, Thomas H., 236n.
Grandfather Clause, xiv, 83
Grebler, Leo, 258n., 264
Gumplowicz, Ludwig, 151, 245

Halloway, Ralph S., 182n.
Hammond, Phillip E., 426, 435
Handman, Max S., 91
Hare, Nathan, 240n.
Harlem, 49, 63–69, 130
Harris, Abram L., 344, 345t., 346–47, 349–51, 361
Harris, Donald J., 343, 360
Harris, Marvin, 424, 437
Harvey, O. L., 88n.
Hauser, Robert, 376, 380–83, 395
Hayes, President Rutherford B., xxn.
Hayner, Norman S., 92n.
Haynes, George F., 133
Heilbroner, Robert L., 426, 435
Heltman, Lynne, 316n.
Hermalin, A., 363–65, 375
Herskovits, Melville, 89–91
Hill, Herbert, 345, 361
Hill, Mozell C., 128–29
Hill, Richard C., 316n.
Himes, Joseph, xxiv, xxx, 238
Hitler, Adolf, 133, 140
Hodge, Patricia, 240n., 293, 301
Hodge, Robert W., 240n., 293, 294t., 301
Horton, John, 239n., 425, 435
Hoult, Thomas, 184n.
Howard, A., 183n.
Howard, George E., 46n.
Howe, John, 242n.
Hughes, Henry, 151
Human Relations Area Files, 235
Humphrey, Norman D., 352, 360
Hurston, Zora, 111n.
Hyman, Herbert H., 409, 415

Immigration Act, xv, xxxii, 47, 346
Ingerman, Sidney, 358, 361
Inkeles, Alex, 93n.
Isaacs, Harold R., 431, 435

Jackson, John A., 436
Jacobson, Cardell, 319
Jacobson, Julius, 348, 353, 360
Jalee, Pierre, 355–56, 360
James, William, 5, 142
Janowitz, Morris, xxiv, xxvi, xxxn., 5n., 90n., 128n., 133
Jefferson, Thomas, 23–24
Jeffries, Vincent, 243n.
Johnson, Charles S., xxiv–xxvi, xxx, 89, 90n., 103n., 128, 130–31, 141
Johnson, Guy B., xxv, xxx–xxxi, 49, 89n., 181–82
Johnson, Michael P., 93n.
Johnson, T. J., 91n.–92n., 130n., 133n.
Jones, Butler, xxxn., 128n.
Jones, Reverend M. Ashby, 48, 49n.

Jones Act, xvi
Jordan, Winthrop D., xx*n.*

Kasarda, John D., 399, 409
Kassof, Allan, 183*n.*
Kelley, Mrs. Florence, 82
Kelly, Sara D., 318*n.,* 397–98, 399*n.,* 400,
    405, 407
Kelman, Herbert C., 93*n.*
Kephart, William M., 183*n.*
Keppel, F. P., 159
Kerner Report, xx*n.,* 324
Killian, Lewis M., xxx, 5, 181*n.,* 184
Killingsworth, Charles C., 341, 360, 382,
    395
Kimball, Solon T., 132*n.*
King, Charles E., 129*n.*
King, Martin Luther, Jr., xx*n.,* 238, 248,
    252, 322, 325–26, 328*t.*–29*t.,* 338
Kitano, Harry H. L., 256*n.,* 264
Koffel, J., 382, 395
Kolb, William, 251
Kornbluh, Joyce L., 357–58, 360
Kroeber, A. L., 136
Kronus, Sidney, 431, 435
Ku Klux Klan, xxiii, xxv–xxvi, xxxii, 70–
    75, 79, 251
Kuper, Leo, 429, 435
Kwan, Kian M., 424, 436

Lam, Margaret M., 92*n.*
Lan, Dean, 357, 360
LaPiere, Richard T., xv, 93, 211, 213,
    431, 435
Lavender, A. D., xxix*n.*
Lazarsfeld, Paul F., xxviii*n.*
League of United Latin American Citizens,
    260
Leakey, Louis S. B., 421, 435
Lee, Alfred McClung, 352, 360
Lemberg Center for the Study of Violence,
    323, 339
Lengerman, Patricia M., 92*n.*
Lenski, Gerhard, 423, 433, 435
LePlay, Frédéric, xvii
Levinson, Daniel J., 183*n.,* 228*n.*
Lieberson, Stanley, 240*n.,* 282*n.,* 316*n.,*
    332, 339, 420–21, 435
Lincoln, Abraham, xx*n.,* 24
Lindgren, E. J., 420, 435
Lindzey, Gardner, 339
Linton, Ralph, 436
Livingstone, David, 7
Llano, Antonio, 4*n.*
Loeb, Martin, 182*n.,* 212–13
Logan, Rayford, 2
Lone Wolf *v.* Hitchcock, xiv
Long, Herman, 184*n.*

Long, Larry, 316*n.*
Los Braceros Program, xvii
Lubbock, Sir John, 11
Lundborg, Herman, 92*n.*
Lyman, S. M., 420, 435

MacIver, Robert M., 213
Mahard, R. E., 318*n.*
Manning, Seaton, 89*n.*
Marcson, Simon, 133*n.*
Marshall, Ray, 347, 352–54, 360
Marx, Karl, xvii, 431
Mason, Philip, 421, 435
Masuoka, Jitsuichi, 92*n.*
Maus, Heinz, 3*n.*
Mausner, Bernard, 241*n.*
McCarthy, J. D., xxxii*n.*
McCord, Joan, 183*n.*
McCord, William, 183*n.*
McDougall, William, 142
McKenzie, Fayette A., 6*n.*
McPhail, Clark, 315*n.*
Mecklin, John M., 4*n.,* 154
Medicare, 409
Meier, August, 128*n.*
Merton, Robert K., 210, 213, 246
Mexican American Political Association,
    262
Middleton, Russell, 183*n.*
Milgram, Stanley, 321, 339
Miller, J. A., 357–58, 360
Miller, Kelly, 23
Miller, Neal, 321, 339
Mills, C. Wright, 234*n.*
Milwaukee, 409–14
*Milwaukee Journal,* 409
Mincer, J., 387, 395
Mitchell, George S., 347, 349–50, 354,
    360
Mitchell, Mayor, 82
Miyamoto, S. Frank, 423, 436
Molotch, Harvey, 241*n.*
Montagu, M. F. Ashley, 129*n.*
Montoya, Senator Joseph M., 259
Moore, Joan, xvi, 239
Moore, John A., 318*n.,* 397–98, 399*n.,*
    400, 405, 407
Moore, Wilbert E., 394, 424, 436
Morgan, Lloyd, 142
Morgan, William R., 322, 330, 337, 339
Morris, Richard T., 243*n.*
Moskowitz, Henry, 82
Most Valuable Player Award, 267
Motz, Annabelle B., 183*n.*
Mowrer, O., 321, 339
Muir, William K., Jr., 409, 415
Murchison, John, xxiv, 88, 89*n.*
Myrdal, Gunnar, xxiv–xxv, 5, 91, 130–31,
    152, 159, 162, 220, 228*n.,* 250, 280

Nam, Charles B., 376, 395
National Association for the Advancement of Colored People (NAACP), 5, 49, 82–84, 181–82, 196–99, 253, 347, 354
National Industrial Recovery Act (NIRA), 97, 353
National Labor Relations (Wagner) Act, 353
National Opinion Research Center (NORC), 243
National Urban League, 49, 130, 350, 354
*Negro Yearbook,* 49
Nell, William C., 15–16, 29
Newcomb, Theodore, 417, 436
New Deal, 353–58
*Newsweek,* 364
*New York Evening Post,* 82
Niagara Conference, xiii, 83
Nisbet, Robert A., xvii
Nixon, President Richard M., xx*n.,* 318
Noel, Donald L., xxx, 319, 422, 436
Normand, C., 318*n.*
Norris-LaGuardia Anti-Injunction Law, 97
Northrup, Herbert R., 357, 360
Norton, A., 385, 395

Oberschall, Anthony, 244*n.*
Odum, Howard W., 48, 153
Ogburn, William, xxii–xxiv
Olsen, Marvin, 426, 432, 436
Operation Wetback, xvii, 261–62
Oppenheimer, Martin, 355, 357, 361
*Opportunity,* 130
*Outlook,* 36
Ovington, Miss Mary White, 82

Palmer, Edward N., 129*n.*
Palmer, P. C., 419, 436
Palmore, Erdman, 242*n.*
Pan-African Movement, 61
Park, Robert E., xxviii, 5–6, 48, 90–92, 99*n.,* 130, 140, 142, 150, 155–56, 158, 233, 236, 319, 418–20, 422, 433, 436
Parsons, Talcott, 422, 426, 436
Pascal, A., 396
Pennington, James C., 100
Pettigrew, Thomas H., xxviii*n.,* xxx, xxxii*n.,* 184*n.,* 208*n.,* 240*n.,* 242*n.,* 248*n.,* 251*n.,* 254, 318*n.,* 409*n.,* 415
Phillips, Wendell, 15
Plaut, Richard L., 181*n.*
Pohlman, Vernon, 181*n.*
Pol, Louis, 319
Polaris Scientific Institute, 52
Political Association of Spanish Speaking Organizations, 261
Preston, S., 395
Price, C., 421, 436

Provinse, John H., 132*n.*
Puckett, Newbell N., 110*n.*

Queen, Stuart A., 181*n.*

Rademaker, John A., 92*n.*
Ransford, H. Edward, xxxiii, 243*n.,* 244, 315
Raper, Arthur, 49
Ratzenhofer, Gustav, 151, 246
Redfield, Robert, 91
Reece, Ernest J., 48*n.*
Reich, Michael, 342, 361
Reid, Ira D., xxiv, xxxi, 49, 344, 345, 361
Reiss, Albert J., 394
Reissman, Leonard, 374–75
Reuter, Edward B., 3, 46*n.,* 141, 435
Reynolds, Charles N., 92*n.*
Riddleberger, Alice B., 183*n.*
Risley, Sir Herbert, 141
Roberts, Alan H., 183*n.*
Roberts, Harry W., 129*n.*
Robinson, Jackie, 267
Rockefeller, John D., Jr., 69
Rokeach, Milton, 183*n.*
Rose, Arnold M., 184, 241*n.,* 423, 434, 436
Ross, Arthur M., 89*n.,* 341, 361
Ross, Edward A., xxi, 29, 151, 153, 245
Rossell, C. H., 397, 407
Rossi, Peter H., 294*t.*
Rowan, Richard L., 360
Rowe, Alan, xxxi, 316
Rubin, Lester, 347, 361
Rudwick, Elliott M., 128*n.,* 348, 352, 361
Russell, Charles Edward, 82
Russell, Mary Faith Pellett, 181*n.*

Samora, Julian, 357, 361
Sanford, R. Nevitt, 183*n.,* 228*n.*
Saxton, Alexander, 361
Scammon, Richard M., 363, 375
Schermerhorn, R. A., 185, 421–22, 430–31, 434, 436
Schuman, Howard, 93*n.*
Scoble, Harry M., 332, 339
Sears, Louis M., 47
Sears, R., 321, 339
Seitz, M. R., 91*n.*–92*n.,* 130*n.,* 133*n.*
Seligmann, Herbert J., 49, 182
Sellin, Thorstein, 93*n.*
Senart, Emile, 136
Sewell, William H., xxviii*n.*
Shaler, Professor, 19
Sheatsley, Paul B., 409, 415
Sheldon, Eleanor B., 394
Sheppard, Harold L., 288, 296
Sherohman, James, xxx*n.*
Shibutani, Tamotsu, 424, 436
Shils, Edward A., 426, 436

Shipbuilding Labor Adjustment Board, 347
Shiskin, J., 381, 395
Siegel, Paul M., 294*t.*
Silverman, Arnold R., 332, 339
Simmel, Georg, xvii
Simmons, Roberta G., xxxii*n.*
Simon, Herbert, 233–34
Simons, Sarah E., 6*n.*
Simpson, George E., 210, 213
Simpson, Richard L., xxviii
Singleton, Royce, Jr., xvii, xx*n.*
Sjoberg, Gideon, 424, 436
Sly, David, 319
Small, Albion, xxi–xxiii, xxv, xxix, xxxii, 2–4, 48, 151, 153, 245
Smelser, Neil J., 322, 340
Smith, Charles U., 5
Smith, M. G., 425, 436
Smith, M. S., 318*n.*
Smith, M. W., 420, 436
Smith, William C., 48*n.*
Sobel, Michael, 387, 395
*Social Forces*, xxvii–xxx, 48–49, 54, 63, 70, 76, 82, 94, 99, 109, 117, 133–34, 143, 182, 186, 214, 227, 233, 245, 273, 363, 397, 416
*Social Problems*, xxvii–xxix, xxx*n.*, 196, 210, 256, 265, 280
Society for the Study of Social Problems (SSSP), 181, 184, 196, 210, 256, 265, 280
Southern Regional Council, 48, 61, 84, 133, 149, 275, 278*t.*
Southern Sociological Society (SSS), 181
Spear, Allan H., 346, 349, 361
Spencer, Herbert, 4, 11, 48, 50
Spero, Sterling D., 344, 345*t.*, 346–47, 349–51, 361
Spicer, Edward, xiv
Spilerman, Seymour, xxx, 314–15, 320, 321*n.*, 323, 326, 331–32, 337, 340
Spingarn Medal, 84
Standing, T. G., 90*n.*
Stewart, Don, 184*n.*
Stolzenberg, Ross M., 316*n.*
Stone, Alfred H., xxv, 5, 28, 29, 31–32
Storey, Moorfield, 83
Stouffer, Samuel, xxiii
Strauss, George, 358, 361
Student Non-Violent Coordinating Committee (SNICC), 254
Sullivan, Patrick L., 211, 213
Sumner, Honorable Charles, 141
Sumner, William G., xxi–xxii, 35, 151–52, 157–58, 161, 245

Tabb, William K., 342, 361
Taeuber, Alma, 240*n.*, 242
Taeuber, Karl, 240*n.*, 242

Taylor, Griffin, 93*n.*
Taylor, Paul S., 91, 92*n*
Templeton, I., 365, 375
Terrell, H. S., 368*n.*, 375
Texas Rangers, 260
Texas White Primary Case, 84
*Thirty Years of Lynching*, 83
Thomas, W. I., xxii–xxiii, xxx–xxxi, xxxiv*n.*, 4–5, 48, 50, 155
Thompson, Edgar T., 135*n.*–36*n.*, 156
Thurow, Lester C., 372*n.*, 375, 384, 395
Tijerina, Rejes, 259
Toch, Hans, 321, 339
Tönnies, Ferdinand, xvii
Travis, Harry, 382, 395
Treaty of Guadalupe Hidalgo, xvi, 259
Treaty of Paris, xvi
Truman, President Harry S., xx*n.*
Tumin, Melvin, 183*n.*
Turner, Jonathan H., xvii, xx*n.*
Tuttle, William N., Jr., 343, 351–52, 362

U.S. Bureau of the Census, xv–xvi, 54–57, 94–96, 101–102, 106–107, 275*n.*, 278*t.*, 282, 283*t.*, 292, 301, 321*n.*, 335*t.*, 341–42, 364, 369*t.*, 371*t.*, 372, 373*t.*, 375–77, 379*t.*, 380, 383, 384*t.*, 385–87, 388*t.*, 391*t.*, 395–96, 401*t.*, 404*t.*, 407
U.S. Civil Rights Commission, xx*t.*, 275*n.*, 278*t.*, 399, 407
U.S. Communist party, 89
U.S. Department of Labor, 380–83, 396
U.S. Forest Service, 259
U.S. National Center of Health Statistics, 385, 396, 407
Useem, E. L., 318*n.*

Valentine, Charles A., 91*n.*
van den Berghe, Pierre L., 184, 343, 362, 421, 424–26, 428–29, 432–33, 436
Vander Zanden, James W., xxxi, 246, 252
Vesey, Denmark, 101
Villard, Oswald Garrison, 82
Villemez, Wayne J., xxi, 316
Vincent, George, xxi–xxii
Voter Education Project, 275*n.*, 278*t.*

Wagley, Charles, 424, 437
Wagner-Connery Law, 97
Wald, Miss Lillian D., 82
Walling, William English, 82–83
Walters, Bishop Alexander, 82
Wanderer, Jules J., 322, 330, 340
Ward, Lester, xxi, 151–52, 245
Warner, W. Lloyd, 89*n.*, 93, 129, 134–38, 220
Warren, Donald I., 243*n.*–44*n.*
Warren, Governor Earl, 131
Wartime Civil Control Administration, 163

Washington, Booker T., 5, 38, 42, 101*n.*, 154
Wattenberg, Ben J., 363, 375
Watts, 244, 304–11
Watts, Harold W., 242*n.*
Weatherly, Ulysses G., 3, 154
Weber, Max, xvii, 234
Wesley, Charles H., 346, 362
West, Max, 4*n.*
Westie, Frank R., 183*n.*, 184, 408, 415
Westie, Margaret, 184
White Citizens Council, 251
*Who's Who in Colored America,* 102–103
Wilensky, Harold L., xxviii*n.*
Wilkins, Roy, xxiv, 182

Willhelm, Sidney M., 342, 357, 362
Williams, Robin M., Jr., xxiv–xxvi, xxix, xxxii, 91, 235*n.*, 425–26, 437
Wilson, Logan, 251
Wilson, William, 317
Wohlstetter, A., 384, 396
Wolters, Raymond, 347, 354–55, 362
Woolston, Howard B., 46–47
Work, Monroe, xxiv, xxxi, 4, 49
Worthman, Paul, 362

Yancey, William L., xxxii*n.*
Yinger, J. Milton, 93*n.*, 210, 213
Y.M.C.A., 40, 350
Young, Kimball, 131